# *Measurement Theory*
# *for the Behavioral Sciences*

A Series of Books in Psychology

*Editors:*
Richard C. Atkinson
Jonathan Freedman
Gardner Lindzey
Richard F. Thompson

# Measurement Theory
# for the Behavioral Sciences

### Edwin E. Ghiselli
*Late of University of California, Berkeley*

### John P. Campbell
*University of Minnesota*

### Sheldon Zedeck
*University of California, Berkeley*

*W. H. Freeman and Company, San Francisco*

*Project Editor:* Pearl C. Vapnek
*Designer:* Sharon Helen Smith
*Production Coordination:* Ron Newcomer & Associates
*Illustration Coordinator:* Audre Loverde
*Compositor:* Bi-Comp, Inc.
*Printer and Binder:* The Maple-Vail Book Manufacturing Group


**Library of Congress Cataloging in Publication Data**

Ghiselli, Edwin Ernest, 1907–
    Measurement theory for the behavioral sciences.

    (A Series of books in psychology)
    Includes bibliographies and index.
    1. Psychometrics. I. Campbell, John Paul,
1937–    joint author. II. Zedeck, Sheldon, joint
author. III. Title.
BF39.G49    150'.72        80-27069
ISBN 0-7167-1048-X
ISBN 0-7167-1252-0 (pbk.)

Printed in the United States of America

9  8  7  6  5  4  3  2  1

# Contents

# *Preface*

In his preface to *Theory of Psychological Measurement*, Edwin E. Ghiselli described the text as having certain characteristics, which we hope are also incorporated in this text. This text is meant to be an introductory rather than an intermediate or advanced text, and the basic prerequisites for a course that used this book would be introductory psychology and an introductory course in descriptive statistics. Perhaps only the latter is really necessary since these basic principles of measurement are applicable to many fields besides psychology. This increased applicability is signified by the title, *Measurement Theory for the Behavioral Sciences*. However, the introductory psychology course does acquaint one with the kinds of variables for which the measurement principles discussed here are appropriate and would therefore, we think, be valuable.

The development of each topic begins at the elementary level and proceeds in fairly painstaking detail to the more complex. The basic formulas that represent the central elements of a reliability, validity, or scaling model are developed from start to finish using only simple algebra and incorporating where possible a full discussion of the assumptions and/or value judgments that they incorporate. The things that a theory of measurement tells a researcher or practitioner to do (for example, to test students reliably or to avoid discrimination in hiring) are partly a function of the technical features of the theory and partly a function of the value judgments on which it is based. We firmly believe that if the student will take the time to understand how these basic formulas came to be, he or she will then have a much firmer grasp of what a particular datum (for example, the standard error of measurement) really means, the value judgments on which it is based, and the ways it may be used to make decisions about individuals. Presenting a set of definitions or a set of rules for when to apply formulas is *not* our objective here. We want readers to understand the basic components of the psychological measurement problem well enough to formulate their own rules and to understand how their own value judgments must be integrated with the technology of assessing the psychological characteristics of individuals. Because of varying backgrounds, many readers will move through the basic formulas and development of models with ease, while others will struggle. However, if we did not believe the outcome was worth the struggle, the book would have been written differently. It has been our collective experience that almost all students who have progressed this far in their education can master these ideas if they try; and while hard work may not be the magic elixer of life that some people claim, it does have its rewards.

Having said this, we also want to point out that we have tried to make this text applicable to a broader range of students by including a Technical Section to some chapters. Some of the longer and more detailed algebraic development is reserved for these technical sections and can be skipped by those students who don't wish to go quite as far as others.

The emphasis of much of the material is on shades of gray and not black and white. The world is not dichromatic, and we have tried to remain as unopinionated as possible in areas where others might announce that there is one true way. Readers can make up their own minds later in life, but now is not the time for chest-thumping about the virtues of a particular point of view.

All the basic topics covered in *Theory of Psychological Measurement* have been retained. Each of the original chapters was revised to make it easier for a wider range of students to use and to incorporate recent thinking in each area. Chapter revision involved presentation of new material, reorganization, and integration of parts of some chapters with parts of others. In addition, we have added introductory chapters on psychological scaling and test construction and have expanded considerably the chapter on validity of measurement to reflect recent developments in these areas. A number of important topics have not been included because their basic development requires a greater familiarity with statistical models than we wish to demand of students. For example, Cronbach's generalizability model of the reliability problem is a useful integration of a number of ideas. However, a discussion of Cronbach's model must necessarily begin with a discussion of the analysis of variance strategy, and that is beyond the scope of this book.

It was our intent to present the basics of measurement theory in as thorough and understandable a manner as possible for the junior, senior, or first-year graduate student who has not been previously exposed to this material in any great quantity. We take full responsibility for the degree to which we have failed in this regard. However, any success we might have must be shared with many people. Considerable thanks go to the students who have used mimeographed portions of the revised chapters as class material. Special thanks is reserved for Professor William Meredith, who critiqued the entire manuscript. He has been a valuable friend to each one of us. Also, special thanks to Rick Jacobs, who prepared most of the Glossary.

A final word must be directed at the first author by the second and third authors. It is difficult to assess the impact that Professor Ghiselli has had on each of us. Let us only say that to have such a colleague during one's formative years is incredibly lucky, and we thank him for it. His stature as an applied psychologist is exceeded only by his stature as a human being—which, until better methods are developed, is beyond measurement. The things that Ghiselli said about Robert Tryon in his preface to *Theory of Psychological Measurement* are also true of him. To have experienced both these men is indeed fortunate.

*April 1980*

*E. E. Ghiselli*
*J. P. Campbell*
*S. Zedeck*

## Postscript

Edwin E. Ghiselli died on June 26, 1980, while touring Italy. One of Ed's last involvements with this book was to comment on the above preface. Under protest, he agreed to retain the last paragraph, which we inserted to recognize him as a scholar and, most importantly, as a person. Yet he wasn't finished. In a discussion regarding whether this book was to be dedicated to anyone, it was suggested that the dedication be to Elizabeth Laurie Zedeck, a profoundly retarded child who died before her third birthday. The dedication Ed wrote was as follows:

> To Elizabeth. In dedicating this book to Elizabeth, we wish to remember a sweet and gentle child whose short, innocent life touched all of us—and one very deeply indeed.

Only such an individual as Ed could have written the above for someone who never had the opportunity to experience life. He was a rare human being, and we will miss him. We can only conclude with Ed's perspective: *Così è se vi pare* (So it is if it seems that way to you).

*September 1980*

*John P. Campbell*
*Sheldon Zedeck*

# Measurement Theory
## for the Behavioral Sciences

# 1

## *Introduction*

When we compare the locomotive characteristics of amoebas, cats, and human beings, we see vast differences. The oozing motion of the amoeba, the easy pace of the cat, and the jerky walk of the human being are clearly dissimilar. Indeed, so vast are the differences between the various kinds of organisms that the differences among individuals of any one kind may seem small and insignificant.

Yet if we direct our attention toward any one kind of creature, we see large and significant differences. One amoeba flows along an undeviating path, whereas another wanders aimlessly. One cat boldly pursues a direct course, whereas another darts from one protective shelter to another. One man walks "ten feet tall" with shoulders back, whereas another shuffles along with a slouch.

The differences among individuals of any one kind are very real, and substantial in magnitude. The task of the psychologist is to understand the behavior of individuals and the differences among them. He or she is therefore interested in the sources of the differences and in the factors that cause one individual to behave in one way and another to behave quite differently. The psychologist is also interested in the factors that cause changes in the individual—improvements in performance, reductions in ability, or fluctuations in social adjustment.

Consider an example that has been relevant for a long time and, unfortunately, will most likely continue to be. People exhibit varying amounts of racial prejudice. This characteristic of people has caused nothing but trouble for the United States. One important task for psychologists and other behavioral scientists is to understand this characteristic and the conditions that relate to it and to find ways of changing it.

## Purposes of Psychological Measurement

Before the factors determining the psychological characteristics of individuals can be systematically examined, those very characteristics must be described. This is the purpose of psychological measurement. Measurement essentially is concerned with the methods used to provide quantitative descriptions of the extent to which individuals manifest or possess specified characteristics. Therefore it is important that we understand something of the theoretical and applied problems of psychological measurement and how to use the quantitative descriptions produced by the methods, or operations, of measurement.

Many varied operations have been devised for measuring the numerous characteristics that living creatures manifest or possess. There are tests of knowledge and of problem solving, questionnaires wherein the individual reports self-perceptions, and rating procedures that require one individual to judge the traits of others. In one way or another, all these devices yield descriptions of the extent to which individuals manifest or possess specified traits. These quantitative descriptions, or scores, given by the various operations of measurement differ widely in their utility and meaningfulness. Some are valuable as they stand, whereas others must be subjected to further operations, usually of a mathematical nature, so that they can be transformed to other values or scores that are more meaningful and useful.

Determining criteria for evaluating the usefulness of these quantitative descriptions, or scores, is the primary mission of psychological measurement theory. You will soon see that without a measurement theory of some kind, trying to explain or change the psychological characteristics of individuals is an impossible task.

## Topics in Psychological Measurement

Psychological measurement is a broad field, replete with both methodological and theoretical problems. In this book we do not cover all the basic problems, nor do we even present a complete discussion of those we do consider. Our principal concern is with providing an introduction to some of the fundamental aspects of measurement and a description of the differences among individuals.

We begin with a general consideration of some of the basic problems in the psychological description of individuals, discussing such matters as the definition of psychological characteristics, the development of operations designed to measure those characteristics, and the ways in which individuals differ from one another. This leads us to a consideration of the use of distributions of scores, or norms, as a basis for giving some meaning to scores and for making scores on different characteristics comparable. Therefore we discuss ways and means for describing and dealing with *distributions* of scores and for *standardizing* and comparing scores within distributions.

For many practical and theoretical problems, indices of the degree of co-relationship between two or more characteristics are necessary. Such indices tell us about the similarity of individuals on different traits, something of the factors that determine differences among individuals, and the accuracy with which we can predict one trait from another. Consequently we delve a bit into the topic of *correlation* and examine ways for describing the degree of association between human characteristics. Next, we discuss the concept of *regression,* or prediction.

Many of the tests and other operations we use in measuring individuals are complex, being composed of a series of items, subtests, or other kinds of parts or components that are added together. Consequently we must examine the implications of combining diverse components into *composites*.

The instruments used to describe individuals quantitatively in terms of various psychological characteristics never measure those characteristics with perfect precision. Some are highly reliable, and others have a lesser degree of reliability. The *reliability* of measurement is a problem of fundamental importance. We consider the various approaches that have been made to the problem of reliability and discuss ways and means for estimating the degree to which various measurement methods give reliable measurements.

We discuss the problem of the *validity* of measurement. Validity has to do with prediction and with the determination of the characteristics actually measured by a given method. As is the case with the reliability of measurement, we see that there are differing views about the nature of measurement. We examine these various approaches to validity in order to gain some insight into the problem.

We return to the problem of composite variables and consider ways in which the components forming a composite can be differentially weighted, along with the effects of such weighting. The *differential weighting* of variables has considerable importance with respect to the problem of prediction of an individual's standing on one trait from a composite of his or her scores on a series of other traits. In addition, we briefly discuss nonlinear prediction to explain more complex situations.

The last two chapters briefly identify the various concepts and procedures for collecting data and making quantitative assessments, followed by a consideration of item analyses. These two chapters are on
scaling and test construction, respectively. The former chapter concerns itself with the meaningful interpretation that we can attribute to
differences between responses and respondents. The latter chapter
concerns itself with test construction, the effect of item properties on
reliability and validity, and finally, a brief discussion of the use of
individual items rather than whole, conventional tests for measuring
traits.

## Theories and Models for Psychological Measurement

It has so often been said that the world is complex that the import of
this statement is frequently forgotten. Indeed, sometimes it seems that
the complexity is so great that no one individual, or group, will ever be
able to understand it completely. Often the facts available are not sufficient to make a total, integrated picture. Furthermore, that which at
one time appears to be fact seems pure fantasy at another time. Once it
was "obvious" that the sun revolved around the earth. Now we know
that the reverse is true. Even if we do have a goodly number of facts,
and they are facts that "stand still" and remain facts, the complexities
of their relationships are usually so great that we are unable to grasp
them.

Yet we must deal with the world and its inhabitants, and we must
take action. Therefore *some* understanding is necessary. To integrate
the fragments of knowledge we do have and to bring some comprehensible order to the chaos of ignorance and some understanding to the
complexity, we often do a peculiar thing: we create an abstract world in
our minds and pretend it is the real world. When as scientists we create
a substitute world, we term it a theoretical model.

A theoretical model, therefore, "stands in" for some phenomenon;
that is, it is a representation of the phenomenon. In order to provide an
integration of the partial knowledge we have about the phenomenon
and to make it meaningful, the model must necessarily go beyond the
known facts. Consequently the model describes features of the phenomenon that are not given directly by the facts. If the model is a good
representation, the inferred features will be like those of the phenomenon; if it is a poor one, they will not. Without models, we could make
virtually no predictions.

Consider the ancients' view of the shape of the world. They noted,
for example, that unless a surface is flat, objects placed on it slide off.
Since people and objects maintain their position on the surface of the

earth and do not slide off, it seemed to the ancients that the surface of the earth necessarily must be flat. To be sure, there appeared to be some inconsistencies, such as the fact that ships approaching from the distance appeared to rise out of the sea. But this could be explained away as being due to valleys and hills on the sea similar in nature to the valleys and hills on the land, irregular fluctuations from the basic plane of the earth.

In many instances where we are dealing with phenomena about which we have only fragments of information, we develop a theory or model into which the bits fit so as to organize them into a meaningful whole. Many of the features of our model are not given by the available facts, and we develop them by interpolations and extrapolations from those facts we do have—by inference, by plain "horseback" guess, and by nothing more nor less than our imaginations. Thus the ancients' model of the flat earth had an edge, a top, and a bottom (even though no one had ever seen the edge and the bottom) because they observed that all flat things like tabletops and coins have edges, tops, and bottoms. Since objects have to be supported by something or else they fall, the ancients decided that a giant must be holding up the earth.

Today it is obvious to us that the ancients' model of the world is incorrect. Yet in spite of their completely false notions, they were able to accomplish some remarkable feats of navigation. In the time of the pharaohs the Egyptians were able to sail from the Red Sea to the far southern regions of Africa, and the Phoenicians were able to sail from their home ports in the Middle East to the distant land now called Spain.

Thus a model may be manifestly incorrect and still be useful as a description of a set of phenomena and useful for making predictions about them. Being more sophisticated and wiser than our ancestors, we realize that the world is round. If we wish to sail or fly from San Francisco to Singapore, we plot our course as an arc on a sphere. Nevertheless, if we are planning a short voyage or flight—say, from San Francisco to Los Angeles—we would probably not bother to use the more complicated, spherical model but would be satisfied with the simpler, flat model of the ancients. We would plot our course as a straight line on a plane as given by a Mercator projection rather than as an arc on a globe. For the relatively short distance involved, the error resulting from the use of the incorrect flat model rather than the more correct spherical model is, for all practical purposes, negligible. Practicality, then, may lead us to adopt a model that we know is incorrect or partially correct, but that nonetheless in restricted areas is useful for description and prediction.

Superior though our spherical model of the world may be compared with the flat model of the ancients, we must recognize that it, too, is not correct. Common observation indicates that the surface of the earth, pocked as it is with valleys and knobbed with mountains, is certainly not like the surface of a smooth sphere. If we use a sphere as a model, it is only an approximate representation of the surface of the earth. The exterior of the earth obviously is a very complex surface, not a simple and smooth one like the surface of a true sphere. Nevertheless, we might say that it is not unreasonable to take a sphere as a representation of the earth. The differences between the surface of a sphere and the true surface of the earth are not great, and for practical purposes of planning a journey we do not introduce much error by pretending the world is spherical. As a matter of fact, recent evidence suggests that the earth is somewhat pear-shaped. The surface of a pear-shaped object is far more complex than that of a sphere and consequently more difficult to deal with. But if the "peardness" of the earth is not too great, a spherical model may still serve with reasonable accuracy. If we believe the error is not too great, we should be willing to tolerate it for the sake of greater ease of comprehending and describing movements along the surface. Indeed, we do not know precisely what the shape of the world is. We do know that it is very complicated and that, while certainly not precisely spherical, it is nevertheless something like a sphere. Furthermore, the shape of the earth is not constant, but changes over time. Various celestial and terrestrial forces are at work, and even puny man changes the surface of the earth. The moral of the story is that a model may be adopted to simplify a complex situation, to make it understandable and consequently "livable," even though the model is contrary to fact.

If we decide that we are going to consider the world as a sphere, then we can represent it by a physical model, perhaps by means of a ball. But the mathematical properties of a sphere are well known, so instead of a ball we could use as our model the various mathematical formulas that describe a sphere. There are formulas that permit us to calculate the total surface of a sphere or the various portions of it, the lengths of arcs on its surface, and the like. All these formulas are related to one another and provide ways for describing spheres. Knowing the characteristics of certain parts of a sphere, we can calculate the characteristics of other parts. In some instances, then, it is not necessary to have a physical model as a representation of a set of phenomena; instead, we can use a mathematical model, which gives us very precise descriptions and is more convenient.

A more recent example concerns the efforts of the National Aeronautics and Space Administration (NASA) to explore the moon. The initial flight plans for a manned orbit of the moon were based on the model that the moon's crust was of fairly uniform density, and thus its gravitational field was uniform. However, this turned out not to be the case.

The moon has some regions that are much denser than others, and this caused the orbits of the spacecraft to change over time. Incorporating some of these density variations in the model, even though they still aren't a perfect representation of reality, yielded flight-path predictions of acceptable accuracy. Keep in mind that without a model of the moon's structure the Apollo flights could never have been made. The task for the NASA scientists was to use a model that yielded useful predictions, even though the model itself (in this case a mathematical representation of the moon's structure) was not a perfect representation of reality. The task is the same for behavioral scientists when they try to explain and make predictions about human behavior.

As we consider the various problems of psychological measurement, we find it helpful from time to time to talk about models. We find models useful not only for purposes of description and prediction but also for simplification of complex phenomena so that they become comprehensible. The models in many instances may be manifestly incorrect representations; nevertheless, they are useful when we are beset with incomplete facts and rendered helpless by a complexity beyond our understanding. Again, keep in mind that models are representations of conditions and that they are not perfect. This is especially true in the area of psychological measurement where we are dealing with constructs that are not directly observable, but only inferred.

Suppose that, in order to describe the way in which intelligence is distributed among children, we administer an intelligence test to 50 children. We shall undoubtedly find that the distribution of scores is quite irregular and that scores vary. For instance, the number of children who have an IQ of 99 or 101 may be greater than the number who have an IQ of 100. Since our facts are few, there being only 50 children, we are likely to ascribe the irregularity in the distribution to an insufficient number of cases. We would say that if we had a larger number of children, the distribution would be quite smooth. We would therefore disregard certain of our facts and adopt as a model of the distribution of intelligence one that is smooth but has the same average and variability as our actual distribution.

When we give the same test many times to the same individuals, we often find that the score of each person changes from time to time. The variations in an individual's score are random, showing no systematic improvement or reduction. To understand these results, we say that each person possesses a given true amount of the ability measured by the test but the score varies from time to time because of the effects of unsystematic and variable factors in the situation. On one occasion a person's score may be a little lower because of a cold, and on another it may be a little higher because the lighting is extra bright and thus the individual can see better the questions and responses. We do not know that this actually occurs, but it is a reasonable explanation of the variation. So we can set up a simple mathematical model to explain and to understand test performance in a reasonable fashion by saying that the score an individual obtains on a given administration of a test is true ability plus an error.

So we see that it is sometimes helpful to use theoretical models to represent distributions of scores, rather than the actual distribution itself, and to represent the factors that determine an individual's performance on a test. In this same way models are useful for dealing with other problems in psychological measurement when our facts are incomplete, when we have doubts about the adequacy of our measuring devices, and when the phenomena with which we deal are complex.

---

## Suggested Readings

Dubin, R. 1969. *Theory building*. New York: Free Press.

Kaplan, A. 1964. *The conduct of inquiry*. Scranton, Pa.: Chandler.

Kuhn, T. 1970. *The structure of scientific revolutions*. 2nd ed. Chicago: University of Chicago Press.

McCain, G., and M. Segal. 1973. *The game of science*. 2nd ed. Monterey, Ca.: Brooks/Cole.

# 2

## Describing
## Individual Differences

Sometimes the variation among individuals is qualitative, being in terms of kind; and in other instances it is quantitative, being in terms of frequency, amount, or degree. When we propose to study individual differences, we must specify or define the property with which we are concerned. From this definition we can develop a series of operations, or measurement methods, that will permit us to describe individuals in terms of that property. Qualitative description is termed *classification,* and quantitative description is termed *measurement*. Measurement involves the use of numbers, that is, values that provide quantitative descriptions of individuals and that can be manipulated to give us further information about those individuals.

### Describing Variables

The properties that individuals manifest may be such tangible characteristics as smoothness or size, or such intangible qualities as attitude toward war or the trait of sociability. Some properties may be manifested by all members of a particular population. Thus all living creatures possess the property of life, all books the property of pages, and all fish the property of being water dwellers. On the other hand, the members of a given population may differ with respect to a particular property. A property in which individuals differ among themselves is termed a *variable*. Thus shape is a property in which stones vary, weight a property in which people vary, and foreign policy a property in which political parties vary. There are various ways in which individuals may differ with respect to a property. They may differ qualitatively, as in kind, or quantitatively, as in amount. College students vary not only in kind in terms of major subject but also in degree in terms of academic performance. Furthermore, there are different types of quantitative variations. In some cases quantitative variables are discontinuous and show breaks or steps, such as the variable "number of boxcars in a freight train," where a fractional boxcar is a meaningless concept. In other cases quantitative variables are continuous, such as length, where the differences between individuals may be infinitesimally small or very great, and the variable is a continuum.

### Variables as Constructs

We have defined variables as characteristics or qualities in which individuals differ among themselves. In some cases this characteristic or quality is quite concrete and tangible. Thus if we are interested in the number of children per family, we can see, touch, and otherwise observe this characteristic of families. But in other cases, particularly with psychological variables, this is not true. There is nothing tangible or concrete about the characteristic labeled human intelligence, although the individuals being studied are quite concrete. In such cases we can term the variable an intellectual *construct*.

What is length? It certainly is not the ruler by means of which we measure it. It is not a line drawn by a pencil. Rather, it is the distance along an imaginary line between two points. It is a concept—an intellectual construct. What is initiative? It is the capacity to develop under one's own power new modes of attack on a problem. It is not the number of new modes of attack that the individual writes down on a piece of paper, such as "things to try." It is not the dollar volume of new business the salesperson brings in. Rather it is a concept, an intellectual construct; but it is a characteristic of individuals that many people have deemed important—important enough to define and measure. This illustrates one of the prime dilemmas concerning the study of human behavior. Many extremely important characteristics of people are intangible and require indirect means of measurement and successive approximations to the variable we have in mind. In fact it almost seems that the more important the variable, the more difficult it is to measure. Consider such crucial variables as scholastic aptitude, motivation to work, ability to cope with stress, and creativity.

By comparison, the measurement task in physics and chemistry is relatively simpler. One objective of this book is to explore the problems of measuring intangible constructs. The physical sciences employ standards with respect to the variables of interest. There is a National Bureau of Standards regarding weights and measures. These concepts are thus easily measured and are also concepts for which there is perfect agreement. This is not the case for psychological measurement. It is doubtful that we could find any psychological variable of interest for which there would be total acceptance with respect to its measurement or definition.

### Variable and Constant Properties

A given characteristic or quality is a variable when individuals manifest different kinds or amounts of it. However, for those individuals who manifest any one kind or amount, the property is *constant*. Taking all human beings as a whole, sex is a variable. However, for men alone and for women alone, it is a constant. Inasmuch as different individuals earn different scores on an arithmetic test, arithmetic ability as reflected in the score is a variable. However, for individuals who earn a score of 42 on the test, arithmetic test score is a constant; for those who earn a score of 43, it is a constant; and for those who earn any other given score, it is also a constant.

### Qualitative Versus Quantitative Variables

All variables can be classified into one or the other of two general types: those that are *qualitative variables* and those that are *quantitative variables*. When the variable is qualitative, individuals differ in kind; and when it is quantitative, they differ in frequency, degree, or amount. With qualitative variables the categories into which individuals are placed are not ordered, whereas with quantitative variables the categories are ordered.

Occupation is an example of a qualitative variable. We can classify workers as managerial, sales, clerical, service, or industrial. In this system of categorization there is no natural ordering in the system itself. Any ordering either is purely arbitrary, such as alphabetical, or is accomplished on the basis of some characteristic other than that involved in the variable under consideration, such as the number of individuals in each category. Other examples of qualitative variables are major in college, psychiatric diagnosis, and type of hallucinatory drug.

With quantitative variables, on the other hand, there is a natural ordering of categories since the different categories represent different degrees, amounts, or frequencies of the property in question. The categories are ordered in terms of "moreness" of the property. Consider the variable "number of children in the family." With this variable we have a series of categories—0, 1, 2, 3, and so on—that naturally arrange themselves in order as determined by the frequency of the characteristic under consideration. Order is inherent in the categories themselves. Similarly, suppose we have height as a variable and have measured the heights of individuals to the nearest tenth of a foot. We have the categories 5.0, 5.1, and 5.2 feet, which arrange themselves in order naturally, with the categories having successively larger and greater amounts of the trait under consideration. Other examples of quantitative variables are "strength of pull," "scholastic aptitude," and "emotional stability."

### Types of Quantitative Variables

Quantitative variables can be subdivided into two types: *ranked variables* and *scalar variables*. Ranked variables merely provide an ordering of individuals, whereas scalar variables provide a description of the frequency, degree, or amount of the characteristic. Position of the child in a family as first born, second born, etc., and final status in a race as first, second, etc., are examples of ranked variables. The weight of people such as 162, 167, and 198 pounds for John, Jim, and James, respectively, and the number of dollars each earns per year, for example, $12,500, $14,000 and $22,000, respectively, are examples of scalar variables. These latter variables indicate rank and amount as well as differences between the individuals.

### Types of Ranked Variables

Like qualitative variables, ranked variables provide a series of categories that are discrete and separate. However, unlike the categories of qualitative variables, those of ranked variables are ordered. These successive categories do not necessarily represent equal increments of the particular characteristic or quality, but merely more of it, with the amount unspecified. When a person says she prefers vanilla ice cream to chocolate, and chocolate to strawberry, this does not mean that in terms of desirability she would place chocolate halfway between vanilla and strawberry. All it means is that if she cannot have vanilla, she will take chocolate, and barring chocolate she will take strawberry.

The ranked variables just described are rankings of individuals because at each rank, that is, in each category, there is a single individual. It is also possible to have a ranking of groups. With this type of ranking we may have more than one individual at each rank or in each category. The food preferences of a person might be given by this type of variable. The first preference might be turkey, veal cutlets, or pot roast, and it does not matter which is provided. If these are not available, lamb chops or chicken are considered, and again it does not matter which. If these also are ruled out, the person will take ham, meatballs, or pork chops. Similarly, the members of a particular society may regard themselves as being first-class citizens, second-class citizens, and third-class citizens. The differences between classes are in terms of properties such as rights, privileges, and the like, but the amounts of differences between the groups are not specified. Finally, a teacher may find it convenient to divide students according to those who have a high interest in mathematics, those who are indifferent to mathematics, and those who dislike mathematics. The teacher has then placed the pupils into three groups that are ranked in terms of the variable "interest in mathematics."

### Types of Scalar Variables

*Discontinuous versus continuous scales*     Scalar variables can be further subdivided into *discontinuous scales* and *continuous scales*. With discontinuous scales the categories are ordered but are discrete or separate from each other. An individual clearly falls into one category or another. Family size is an example. In this respect, discontinuous variables are similar to qualitative and ranked variables, which also provide separate and distinct categories. With continuous scales there are not categories as such; rather, there is a continuum that represents gradually greater and greater amounts of the characteristic or quality. On such scales individuals can differ among themselves by very large amounts or by infinitely small degrees. Height is an example.

*Ratio versus interval scales*     Scalar variables can be classified another way into what have been termed *ratio scales* and *interval scales*. Ratio scales are those where the absolute zero is known, and interval scales are those in which the absolute zero is not known.

In order to compare two or more individuals in terms of the amount of some property they possess or manifest, we must measure that property on a scale in which the absolute zero is known. If we do not know the point on the scale that represents a complete absence of the property, then we cannot make statements about the ratio of one individual to another in terms of the amount of the property or about the proportion that one individual is to the other.

We can say that an individual who is 50 inches tall is two-thirds as tall as one who is 75 inches tall and that the latter is 50 percent taller than the former, because the ruler by means of which we measure height has an absolute zero point on the scale that indicates the complete absence of the property. Similarly, we can say that an individual who taps a finger 500 times in 2 minutes taps only two-thirds as fast as one who taps 750 times in 2 minutes and that the latter taps at a rate 50 percent faster than the former, because on the scale of tapping, zero means no taps at all.

But suppose we are measuring arithmetic ability and use a test composed entirely of problems involving multiplication and division of three-digit numbers. We are not willing to say that an individual who fails to solve a single problem correctly has zero arithmetic ability, because we know it is possible that if simpler problems were presented—say, the addition of 2 and 2—the person might be able to solve them. The zero on our test, then, does not represent an absolute zero or a complete absence of arithmetic ability; rather it is an arbitrary designation. Consequently we cannot say that an individual who solves 50 multiplication problems correctly has two-thirds the arithmetic ability of one who solves 75 problems correctly and that the latter is 50 percent superior to the former in arithmetic ability.

The ratios and proportions in situations such as this are meaningless because the magnitudes of the property are measured not in terms of "distance" from an absolute zero but only in terms of "distance" from an arbitrary zero. The zero is like the zero on a Fahrenheit or Centigrade thermometer, which is arbitrarily established and has no particular reference to the absolute zero of temperature. It is as if we had a ratio scale and to all values on it some constant value of *unknown magnitude* had been added.

For many if not most psychological variables, the scales are interval rather than ratio scales. The zero points on the scales are arbitrary points, not absolute zero representing a complete absence of the traits being measured. Consequently we are seldom able to say that as compared with one individual another manifests a certain proportion of a psychological trait or that one individual manifests a certain greater percentage of a trait than does another individual.

It may seem impossible for a scale to have any practical value if it does not have an absolute zero. However, we can easily show that it is possible. Suppose there are two towers on the same level field. By placing a ruler alongside each tower, or by using some comparable but less clumsy procedure, we can determine their heights. If we are interested in getting as far above sea level as possible, we merely climb to the top of the taller tower. We do not know how far above sea level the tops of the towers are, but we can say that the one is higher above it than the other. Similarly, though we cannot say that the individual who earns a score of 75 on an arithmetic test is 50 per cent better in arithmetic ability than the individual who earns a score of 50, we do know that the former is superior to the latter.

## Determining Individual Differences on a Variable

When we set about studying individual differences, the first step is to define the variable in which we are interested. From among the multitude of characteristics and qualities manifested by the individuals with whom we are concerned, we abstract one particular property that we describe, specify, and differentiate from other properties. Our definition should indicate the type of variable it is, whether qualitative or quantitative, and, if quantitative, which specific type. Having defined our variable, we then devise a series of operations or measurement methods that permit us to observe similarities and differences among individuals. These operations involve a series of rules to be followed, stipulate the procedures and instruments to be used, and provide a categorization of individuals so that we have a description of them in terms of the variable.

For example, we may have defined a construct labeled "anxiety." Suppose the type of anxiety we have in mind is a very severe and debilitating kind that is known to afflict only a small segment of the population. Suppose our definition also implies that we should use a paper-and-pencil test as the operation to measure it. However, when we give our test to a random sample from the general population, we find that almost half the sample scores at the high end and would appear to be suffering from severe anxiety. Obviously, something is wrong with either our definition or our measurement operation. The task for the researcher is to find out which.

The process of defining our variable and devising operations that we can use in the description of individual differences is a never-ending one. Not only is there an interaction between the definition and the devising of operations, but also the results obtained from our operations give us new insights into the nature of our variable so that we redefine it and modify our operations. The development of ways for describing individuals, then, is a dynamic process.

## Defining Variables

We define the variable in which we are interested to help understand the nature of the property with which we are concerning ourselves and as a basis for developing the operations we shall use to obtain descriptions of individual differences in that property. Definition is never an easy task, so let us consider some matters that bear directly upon the definition of variables.

### Importance of Precise Definitions

The clearer and more specific the definition of a variable, the more useful it is. Not only does it describe the nature of the property, but it also differentiates the property from other properties. It directly suggests the kinds of operations that should be employed in obtaining a categorization of individuals in terms of that property. A definition that is vague conveys only in a general way information about the nature of the variable and is of little value in providing guides for the development of appropriate operations.

Let us consider the variable "adjustment," so often used in psychodynamics. We speak of people as making good or poor adjustments; hence we are saying that there is some type of behavior in which individuals differ. By good adjustment do we mean the capacity to adjust leg length when walking on a hillside? Do we mean giving socially approved versus socially disapproved responses to frustrating situations? Do we mean tolerance of the action of others? Do we mean ability to learn from experience? Do we mean all of these things or any of them? The term "adjustment" is so vague that we do not really know what is implied, and we do not know how it may be measured.

If we title the variable "emotional adjustment," we have some notion of the limits of the property. We could specify it perhaps by saying that the property is "the reaction to problem situations." We could specify the problem situations as those in which the individual is confronted by a conflict, and the reaction as the extent to which the behavior does not meet with the approval of other members of society. This definition is a considerable improvement. It more adequately circumscribes the property, and it suggests operations by means of which individual differences can be described; for example, by statements on the part of the individual's peers. Even so, our definition is not so precise as we might like, but at least it is a workable one. Further considerations of the problem, the results of studies of emotional adjustment, and greater refinement in theory will help us to further specify our definition.

### Trait Names and Variable Definitions

We name variables in order to identify them, the name of a variable providing a summary of the definition. Thus we may have a variable that we define as "the capacity of a member of a group to influence the other members with respect to the setting and achievement of group goals." Rather than identify the variable by means of this long and involved definition, we simply label it "leadership." The *trait name* "leadership," then, stands for the definition and is a more convenient label for the variable.

We choose a trait name that is appropriate, a name that gives a reasonable representation of the definition. But because it is short and concise, the trait name in and of itself does not represent all the details and facets of the definition. Consequently one trait name may equally well represent several different definitions. The trait name "sociability" may be used to represent a trait defined as "the tendency to seek the company of others and to associate and interact with them" just as well as a trait defined as "the capacity to get along with others and to be understanding of and sensitive to the feelings, opinions, and motives of others."

The trait name comes from the definition, not vice versa. Therefore it would not be proper to say that either the one or the other is a better or more valid definition of "sociability." In these two definitions we have specified two different though perhaps related traits. The label "sociability" is attached to both because it appears appropriate to both. This does, of course, lead to confusion, and in the interests of clarity it would be better to attach different labels to the two variables. However, in a field such as psychology, in which basic ideas and concepts are so rapidly developing and changing, it is perhaps understandable that the same trait name is used with different connotations. One person may use a given trait name to identify a trait defined one way, and another to identify a trait defined differently. Indeed, one investigator may change the definition of a trait as it becomes better understood and still retain the same trait name. As a consequence we must be exceedingly careful in comparing the results of different investigators or the findings of different psychological tests in which nominally the same trait is involved.

## Variables and Kinds of Individuals

The kind of individual with whom we are concerned sometimes dictates the way in which we must consider the property as varying. For example, the variable "accuracy in aerial navigation" would seem obviously to be a continuous quantitative variable, with individuals differing in the degree of accuracy with which they determine the location of their aircraft. However, while it may be true that some aerial navigators locate their aircraft with more accuracy than others, even the poorest navigator is considerably superior in aerial navigation to a person who has had no training whatsoever in that technology. Indeed, the latter would not even know how to begin the process of determining location, and the instruments would be completely unfamiliar to him. Therefore if we restrict ourselves to aerial navigators, we shall certainly consider our variable to be a quantitative continuous one. On the other hand, if we take as our individuals everybody, we may prefer to think of it as a discontinuous quantitative variable, with the two steps of "none" and "some" proficiency in aerial navigation.

## Factors in Defining Variables

The way in which we define a variable is a function of the theories and knowledge we have about the property and the individuals for whom it is a variable. As conceptualizations and theoretical formulations change and become more refined, and as our knowledge increases, our definitions of variables change so that what we once defined as a simple variable we now see as a complex variable, and what we had taken as five different variables we now see as one variable. Variables are not static, unchanging, universal truisms.

It was once generally held that people possessed a single, general, all-important ability. This property, termed "intelligence," was simultaneously defined as quickness and accuracy of sensation and perception, ability to learn, and capacity to reason. Since intelligence was thought of as being a general capacity, the operations by which individual differences in intelligence were to be indicated were obvious. Income, social status, rank, and position were taken as indices of intelligence. As more and more knowledge about individual differences and abilities was amassed, it seemed that people possessed not just one all-important ability that determined the degree of success achievable in such different activities as school performance and proficiency with a pick and shovel, but rather several different and perhaps independent abilities. The property that had been termed "intelligence" came to be viewed as an aggregation of different properties. So the definition of intelligence was modified to include only those abilities involving judgment, reasoning, and the like, as exercised in abstract form and as manifested in verbal behavior and in response to verbal stimuli. Intelligence, then, was measured by tests involving questions requiring powers of analysis and synthesis, comparisons of similarities and differences, and the like. Today even this notion of intelligence is not uniformly held, and many would separate the property into smaller bits, defining each differently. As a consequence, today when we are concerned with ability, we try to define the ability very specifically, seeking to differentiate it from other types of abilities.

It is possible that the future will show that there are 20 or 30 basic abilities possessed in different degrees by different individuals, or that there are thousands of them, or that *ability is a completely erroneous concept*. At the present time, however, we can define abilities in ways that at least currently are meaningful to us, and from our definitions we set up operations by means of which these abilities can be measured. We can employ the results of these operations in many useful ways for both theoretical and practical purposes, just as it was possible for traders in the Middle Ages to sail a ship from Venice to London by using navigational procedures based on the incorrect notion that the world was flat.

## Operations and Determining Individual Differences

After defining our variable, we are in a position to develop operations that permit us to observe individual differences in the property. These operations are set forth in rules that stipulate the procedures, instruments, and devices to be used. In psychological measurement the quantitative description of an individual given by the operations is termed the *raw score*. If the instrument we use for measuring the proficiency of salespeople is the amount of their annual commissions, a salesperson may have a raw score of $11,000. If we measure aggression in preschool children by counting the number of times a child strikes another during a 3-hour period, a child who strikes another twice has a raw score of 2. An individual who is rated 4 on a 5-point scale of leadership has a raw score of 4. An individual who answers correctly 30 out of 50 questions on an arithmetic test has a raw score on arithmetic ability of 30.

In certain circumstances the numerical values given directly by the measuring instruments (that is, the raw scores) are changed in one way or another to a different set of numerical values. The rules for the operations may specify that the raw scores be divided by some constant or changed in some other way. These new values are termed *transformed scores*. Scores are transformed to make the numerical values more convenient for recording or for arithmetic manipulation, or to provide more meaningful quantitative descriptions of individuals. More about transformation later.

### Developing Operations from Definition of Variable

The particular operations developed and the rules that govern them stem directly from the definition of the variable. For example, we may define height of people as "the linear distance between the soles of the feet and the top of the head." From this definition we can develop a series of rules to govern the operations appropriate for use in the measurement of height. The phrase "linear distance" indicates that we wish to obtain the shortest line between two points. One point falls at the soles of the feet, and therefore we stipulate that both feet must be on the same plane. Linear distance implies a quantitative continuous variable, so our rules stipulate a standard ruler marked either in inches or in centimeters. Height implies the upright body rather than some other posture such as sitting, so the rules also stipulate that the individual be standing as erect as possible and perpendicular to the plane passing under the soles of the feet. The rules go on to say that one end of the ruler, the end marked zero, be placed exactly on the plane on which the individual's feet rest. The ruler must be perpendicular to this plane, and parallel to this plane another plane must be established that just touches the top of the head. The point of intersection between this plane and the scale on the ruler will be taken as the individual's height. The ruler is to be read to the nearest sixteenth of an inch or to the nearest millimeter; the decision as to which marker is nearest to the plane depends entirely on the judgment of whoever is doing the measuring.

This example demonstrates how the operating rules stem from the definition of the variable and illustrates all the major elements that must be contained in the rules. They indicate procedures, instruments or devices, and the nature of the descriptions of individuals that result from the operations.

Simple as the process of measuring height might seem, these rules are rather lengthy. Even so, they are not sufficiently detailed and do not deal with many important problems. What is meant by a standard ruler? How does one determine whether the individual being measured is in fact standing completely erect? What does one do with people who have great masses of hair? These matters, too, could be dealt with by rules, but still further questions not covered by them would arise. Operating rules, then, are never complete; they are changed and improved as more and more experience is gained with them.

Let us take as another example the variable "arithmetic ability," which we may define as "proficiency in solving arithmetic problems quickly and accurately." This definition seems quite adequate as a basis for developing appropriate operations. It seems reasonable to conceive of the operations as involving a paper-and-pencil test on which appear a number of arithmetic problems, a quarter of which involve addition, a quarter subtraction, a quarter multiplication, and a quarter division. We have instructions to the subjects telling them what they are to do, how they are to record their answers, and so on. There are additional instructions to the examiner delineating such matters as how these instructions are to be given to the subjects, the timing of the test, and the scoring procedure.

Helpful as this definition might seem as a basis for developing appropriate operations, it is not clear in certain important aspects. Why use a paper-and-pencil test? This type of device is not prescribed by the definition of the variable or even implied by it. We might just as well use the oral examination method. Why should the problems be 25 percent each of addition, subtraction, multiplication, and division? Why not some other proportions? Should the problems be simple or complex? Should they be presented in their barest form such as "2 + 2 = ____," or in some context such as "Two apples and two apples are how many apples?" How many problems should there be, and how much time should be allowed to solve them? Instead of counting the number of correct answers the individual gets in a specified time, why not measure the amount of time it takes to solve a given number of problems correctly?

### Practical Considerations in Determining Operations

While the definition of the variable provides the basis for the development of the necessary operations, it is by no means a precise blueprint. The details of the operations and many of their major aspects are dictated by very practical considerations. Knowledge about the psychological processes, experience with operations previously used in obtaining descriptions of individuals on similar variables, and a substantial measure of wisdom, common sense, and indeed sheer intuition play a great part in the selection of specific rules, procedures, and instruments.

For example, the experienced test constructor knows that reliable descriptions are not obtained by short tests; and yet if the test is too long, people become tired or bored. In general, objective scoring of people's responses gives more reliable descriptions than those that involve others' judgments of them. Yet with certain kinds of responses, such as "appropriateness of behavior in a social situation," and with certain traits, such as "cooperativeness," only subjective evaluation may be possible.

Even though the definition may clearly indicate that the variable is a particular type, it may not be possible to utilize operations directly appropriate to that type. If we wish to measure attitudes of people toward many social issues, the time and effort to construct continuous scales measuring each of these attitudes may be prohibitive. Perhaps we may have to utilize some simple operations involving two-category discontinuous scales such as "approve" and "disapprove." Supervisors may be unwilling to devote the time to evaluating each of their subordinates on 10 different rating scales measuring different aspects of job performance, but may be willing to rank their people in terms of their overall success. When faced with such realities of life, we are forced to make compromises in developing our operations, and by making certain assumptions about them, we seek to bring the final operations closer in nature to what we would like them to be. The operations we develop, then, while coming from the definition of the variable, are at least one stage removed from it. Hence they may or may not perfectly reflect that which is explicit or even implicit in the definition.

### Operations and Definition of Variable

It therefore follows that in developing a specific set of operations, we are in a very real sense redefining our variable, or at least further specifying its definition. We might say that the variable is nothing more or less than the result of the particular set of operations that we prescribed beforehand. Thus we would be forced to make such statements as "Emotional stability in these particular preschool children is what Smithers, the nursery school teacher, says it is" and "Intelligence is that which is measured by test $X$." In a sense this is true. However, if we are content with saying "Intelligence is what this test measures," then we are limited in the generalizations we can make. It is possible that a set of somewhat dissimilar operations will also be labeled "intelligence." The relationship, if any, between the two operations is an empirical question. To examine this relationship, we can use one or more validation strategies (discussed at length in a later chapter). The results of the validation indicate the amount of confidence we can place in our definition.

## Use of Numbers in Classification, Ranking, and Measurement

We have said that the end result of the operations we employ in differentiating among individuals in terms of a given property is some sort of description of those individuals in terms of how they manifest that property. These descriptions may be in verbal form, but—particularly with quantitative variables—they are also given by numbers. Therefore we need to examine something of the nature of numbers and their use as descriptions of individuals.

### Numerical Descriptions Assigned by Operations

Numbers have two important characteristics for measurement. First, they provide a means by which individuals can be classified or arranged in a systematic way in terms of the degree to which they possess some particular characteristic. All people who earn a score of 42 on an arithmetic test are placed in the same category; those who earn a score of 43, in another category; and those who earn a score of 44, in still another category. From these numbers we know that those in the first category possess less arithmetic ability than those in the second, and those in the second less than those in the third. We also can infer that all the people with the same score have the same amount of the property as measured by the particular test on a particular occasion. (However, it is the nature of psychological tests to be influenced by various sources of error; these sources will be discussed in Chapters 8 and 9 on reliability.)

A second characteristic of numbers is that they can be manipulated and combined by arithmetic processes to give more precise descriptions or other meanings. By averaging the numerical values given by repeated measurements on the same individual with the same measuring device, we obtain a quantitative description that is more precise in the sense that it is more reproducible if additional measurements of the same kind are taken. That is, we obtain a more reliable estimate of the individual's ability. By averaging the ratings of aggressiveness assigned to a child by four nursery school teachers, we are more likely to have a value that will occur if additional ratings of the same trait are made by other teachers. By combining numbers indicative of the classes to which an individual belongs in terms of different variables, or by manipulating them in other ways, we may obtain somewhat different or new descriptions of the individual.

### Qualitative Variables

When we are dealing with a qualitative variable, the operations we use assign individuals to one or another of two or more different categories or classes. Ordinarily we designate or "name" the classes in verbal terms so as to indicate the manner in which the members of each class manifest the particular property. For the variable "sex" we have the two designations "male" and "female," and for the variable "major in college" we have such designations as "economics," "history," "physiology," and "chemistry."

Sometimes, however, we may use letters or numbers as designations rather than words. When we use numbers in this fashion, we use them because their symbols, the numerals, are simple, convenient, familiar, and unambiguous. We use them merely to identify or "name" classes or individuals so that they can be distinguished from one another. Hence when numbers are used in this classificatory fashion, they are termed a *nominal scale*. Football and basketball players carry numbers on their uniforms so that the spectators can tell one player from another. Numerals are used merely because they are more convenient than names.

However, when we use numbers in this nominal fashion, we remove from them their ability to signify order and therefore their arithmetical properties of combinability and manipulability. The numbers are assigned to individuals by operations that are quite different from those employed with quantitative variables. With nominal numbers the operations may be just random assignment or first come, first numbered.

### Ranked Variables

When we are dealing with ranked variables, the operations we employ *order* individuals or groups in terms of the frequency, amount, or degree to which they manifest some property. The individual or group that manifests the property to the greatest extent is assigned the number 1, the individual or group that manifests it to the next greatest degree is assigned number 2, and so on. Numbers used in this fashion are termed an *ordinal scale*. With ranking we avail ourselves only of the property of order in numbers, and not of the properties of combinability and manipulability. The difference between individuals or groups ranked first and second is not 1 of the property, but merely a difference in frequency, amount, or degree that is not specified. Consequently the difference, whatever it may be, is not necessarily the same as the difference between individuals or groups ranked second and third. If we are told that someone finished first and someone else finished second in the race, we only know position and nothing about the difference between the two runners in terms of time, distance finished ahead, and the like.

### Discontinuous Quantitative Variables

Discontinuous quantitative variables provide a series of categories that are ordered. The individuals in successive categories differ in the frequency, amount, or degree of some property by equal increments of that property. Consider the scale "right-handedness" where the operations of measurement involve building a tower with 10 blocks and counting the number of blocks placed on the tower with the right hand. The lowest category in this scale contains individuals who never use their right hands but only their left, the next category those who placed one block with the right and the rest with their left, the next those who place two blocks with their right, and so on. The difference between the individuals in any two neighboring categories is the same, being 1 of the property. Let us take another variable, "number of cents in paper money carried at the moment by the individual." Here the lowest category contains individuals who have no paper money, the next those who have 100 cents, the next those who have 200 cents, and so on. In this case the difference between individuals in any two neighboring categories is the same, but in this instance it is 100 of the property.

Numbers ordinarily are assigned to the different categories in such a way as to indicate the frequency, amount, or degree of the property manifested by the individuals in them. For the scale of "handedness" just described, the successive categories would be labeled 0, 1, 2, and so on; and for the scale of "cents" 0, 100, 200, and the like.

### Continuous Quantitative Variables

With a continuous quantitative variable we have a continuum rather than a series of discrete categories. To provide descriptions of individuals, we arbitrarily "mark off" intervals along the scale, the intervals representing equal amounts or degrees of the property. We mark off linear distance in inches, feet, and miles or in millimeters, centimeters, meters, and kilometers. We mark off weight in ounces, pounds, and tons or in milligrams, grams, and kilograms. Time we mark off in seconds, minutes, hours, days, weeks, and so forth.

Numbers are assigned to these markers, and they are assigned in order to indicate equal increments of the property. Thus on a ruler the difference between the first-inch mark and the second-inch mark is 1 inch, and this is also the difference between the twenty-fifth-inch mark and the twenty-sixth-inch mark. The positions of the individual on the scale relative to these markers is taken as his or her quantitative description. An individual whose height falls at the sixty-seventh-inch mark on a scale of height is assigned the number 67, and one whose height falls halfway between the sixty-seventh-inch and the sixty-eighth-inch mark is assigned the number 67.5.

### Operations and Continuous Scales

We have said that with continuous quantitative scales, there is a continuum on which individuals can be placed in terms of the amount of some property they manifest. The difference between two individuals may be great or it may be small. Theoretically the difference may become smaller and smaller until it vanishes and both individuals are located at exactly the very same point on the continuum.

In actual practice our operations never provide us with a continuous scale. What they give us in fact are measurements to some nearest imaginary marker. We might measure height to the nearest quarter of an inch, and reaction time to the nearest hundredth of a second. In reading to the nearest marker, we assign the same numerical description to all these individuals in a given range or class interval.

Therefore when a scale is continuous, the quantitative description assigned to an individual never is precise but rather is an approximation. If the measuring device is crude, the intervals may be few and broad, giving quite imprecise quantitative descriptions of individuals. If the measuring device is more refined, it may divide the continuum into a large number of narrow intervals, thereby providing much more precise descriptions. As the categories increase in number and become narrower and narrower, we approach a true continuum.

The particular operations we use may divide the continuum into equal intervals, or unfortunately they may divide it into intervals of unequal size. Indeed, we may have no direct information at all as to whether the intervals are or are not equally spaced along the continuum. Perhaps all we can do is to infer that they are or are not. If we have reason to suppose that they are not equally spaced, that is, if we believe the units along the scale are not equal, then we can apply further operations in an attempt to equalize them. We can transform the numerical values assigned to the individuals as quantitative descriptions to other numerical values that are equally spaced along the continuum. We consider such procedures later. Suffice it to say now that these procedures ordinarily involve assumptions, perhaps about the nature of the variable, the distribution of individuals in the variable, or the characteristics of the operations—assumptions that many are unwilling to make.

If the intervals between the numbers on the scale are equal or otherwise known, our operations are said to have produced an *interval scale*. An interval scale implies that we can give meaning to the distances between points and that arithmetic operations can be carried out on the intervals. For example, the Fahrenheit temperature scale is an interval scale. It takes 10 calories of heat to raise the temperature of a cubic centimeter of water from 40° to 50°. Likewise it takes 10 calories to raise it from 70° to 80°. Also, it takes twice as much heat to raise the temperature of a substance from 40° to 50° as it does from 35° to 40°. Notice, however, that the numbers on the scale are completely arbitrary. We could add or subtract a constant from each temperature and not change the meaning of the intervals.

An all-important question for psychological measurement theory is how we can provide meaning for the intervals between scores when our objective is to develop a quantitative measure of a psychological variable. For example, can we say that an interval of 105–120 on an intelligence test represents a greater increment in intelligence than an interval 100–105? This problem is examined more closely in the next chapter.

For certain variables it is possible to devise operations that will yield a so-called *ratio scale*. In this instance the raw scores themselves directly indicate how much of the variable is present. There is nothing arbitrary about them. Age is such a variable. Saying that an individual is 35 years old has a very precise meaning. Ratio scales have a natural and meaningful zero point, and this makes it possible to perform arithmetic operations directly on the numbers themselves. For example, we can say that an individual who is 60 is three times as old as someone who is 20. However, if two individuals have ability interval-scale scores of 60 and 20, respectively, the former does not have three times as much ability as the latter. The reason is that a score of zero is not a meaningful point on an ability scale. Ratio scales occur very rarely in psychology and are really not very crucial to the enterprise. What is crucial is being able to interpret the intervals between raw scores.

## Dichotomous Variables

With qualitative variables the operations of classification may separate individuals into only two categories. When we classify people according to sex, we divide them into men and women. Forced-choice items dealing with occupational interest (for example, "prefer the job of bookkeeper to that of salesclerk") also result in a dichotomous classification of individuals, as does the self-perception item "Which best describes you, intelligent or sociable?" These are examples of *dichotomous variables*.

Usually we think of the operations of measurement as providing a range of scores so that individuals are distributed among a wide variety of quantitative descriptions or categories that are ordered along a scale. However, quite often in psychological measurement we deal with tests that separate people into only two categories. The items in an objective test usually are of this kind, the responses being classified as "correct" or "incorrect." On opinion and personality inventories the responses may be limited to two alternatives such as "like" or "dislike" and "yes" or "no." With certain rating devices only two steps of responses are permitted. Thus with adjective checklists the individual is checked as being or not being "cheerful," "shy," and the like.

## Types of Dichotomous Scales

We can distinguish two types of dichotomous scales: those based on variables that are truly dichotomous and those based on variables that are truly continuous or multistep discontinuous quantitative variables. In the *discontinuous dichotomous scales* the two categories are clearly different, even though they may form an order of more or less of some property. Male versus female is one example. Winning versus losing a race is another. On the other hand, with the *dichotomous scales based on continuous or multistep variables,* we have variables along which individuals differ from one another perhaps by very small amounts, but the scale is artificially divided into two portions or zones. There is some critical point on the scale, and all individuals who fall above it are placed in one category, the higher one, and those who fall below it are placed in the other category, the lower one. "Pass" or "fail" interpretation of test scores is an example. Those scoring below 60 fail, and those scoring 60 or better pass.

## Combining Dichotomous Variables into Multistep Scales

Many tests used in psychological measurement consist of a series of items or questions each of which is scored in a dichotomous fashion. An individual's response to each item is classified as being "correct" or "incorrect," and on each item is given a score of 1 or 0. A total test score is computed by adding together the scores obtained on the individual items; that is, by counting up the number of responses that are classified as correct or of a particular kind.

But now the question arises as to the nature of this variable. Obviously it is a quantitative variable, but is it discontinuous or continuous? The answer to this question depends on how we regard the individual items. If we think of the items as being discontinuous scales, then the total scores form a discontinuous scale involving the frequency with which the individual manifests a particular property. On the other hand, if we conceive of each item as being a continuous scale with the scores dichotomized because the items are crude measuring devices, then we say that the total scores represent points on a continuous scale.

---

## Summary

Individuals differ among themselves in a variety of ways. In some properties, such as sex and occupation, individuals differ in kind or in sort; in other properties, such as height and intelligence, they differ in amount, degree, or frequency. We can therefore distinguish between those variables that are qualitative and those that are quantitative. Quantitative variables can be further classified into ranked variables and scalar variables. Ranked variables place individuals in order in terms of the amount, degree, or frequency with which they possess some property, and scalar variables place them into one or another point on a continuum.

When we wish to examine the differences among individuals on a variable, the first step is to define that variable, describing and specifying it, and differentiating it from other variables. The way in which we define a variable is determined by the particular theories and concepts we have about it, together with whatever pertinent information there may be.

From the definition of the variable we develop operations by means of which we describe individuals on that variable. Operations are a series of rules to be followed in applying specified procedures and instruments that provide a categorization, and therefore a description, of individuals in terms of that variable. The operations are termed classification when the variable is qualitative, ranking when the variable is ranked, and measurement when the variable is scalar. Our concern is with operations of measurement.

Even though the operations stem from the definition of the variable, many of the features of the actual operations we finally develop are dictated by practical considerations. In developing a test, we are influenced by such factors as convenience in administration and scoring. Therefore, while the operations are based on the definition, they are at least one stage removed from it and in a very real sense redefine the variable.

The end result of the application of a set of operations is the assignment of individuals to categories or their placement along a continuum. Sometimes verbal labels are used to designate categories or points along a scale; but in measurement, numerals are ordinarily employed. Numbers are useful because they provide a way for the arrangement of individuals in terms of the degree, amount, or frequency with which they possess some property, and because numbers can be manipulated arithmetically to give more precise descriptions and new meanings.

In psychological measurement we frequently utilize operations that yield only a twofold classification of individuals. For example, the responses to the items of an objective test are scored as being "correct" or "incorrect." When the operations yield a twofold classification of individuals, depending on our theoretical notions about the trait we may consider the two steps to represent either a truly discontinuous dichotomous variable or the two portions of a multistep or continuous scale arbitrarily dichotomized by crude operations of measurement. So our theoretical notions about the variable dictate the interpretation we put on the results obtained from the operations of measurement.

---

## Suggested Readings

Anastasi, A. 1958. *Differential psychology.* 3rd ed. New York: Macmillan.

Anastasi, A. (Ed.). 1965. *Individual differences.* New York: Wiley.

Coombs, C. H. 1960. A theory of data. *Psychological Review,* 67:143–159.

Guilford, J. P. 1954. *Psychometric methods.* 2nd ed. New York: McGraw-Hill. Chap. 1.

Nunnally, J. C. 1978. *Psychometric theory.* 2nd ed. New York: McGraw-Hill. Chap. 1.

Stevens, S. S. Measurement. 1959. In C. W. Churchman (Ed.), *Measurement: Definitions and theories.* New York: Wiley. Pp. 18–36.

Stevens, S. S. 1961. Ratio scales, partition scales and confusion scales. In H. Gulliksen and S. Messick (Eds.), *Psychological scaling: Theory and applications.* New York: Wiley. Pp. 49–66.

Torgerson, W. 1958. *Theory and methods of scaling.* New York: Wiley. Chaps. 1 and 2.

Tyler, L. E. 1965. *The psychology of human differences.* 3rd ed. Englewood Cliffs, N.J.: Prentice-Hall.

# 3

## Basic Aspects of
## Psychological Measurement

In Chapter 2 we examined the nature of variables, separating them into qualitative and quantitative variables. The latter we further subdivided into ranked and scalar variables. The operations by means of which we obtain quantitative descriptions of individuals in terms of scalar variables we termed measurement. Since our primary interest is in the measurement of psychological traits, we must now direct our attention to some fundamental aspects of measurement, namely, the equality of units of measurement, the meaningfulness of scores, and the equivalence of measurements on different scales. Our logic, together with the circumstances we find with psychological variables, leads us to the position that in many cases the raw scores yielded by the operations of measurement are meaningful and useful only when they are referenced to the distributions of scores earned by a number of other individuals.

### Equality of Units in Scalar Variables

To be useful for measuring individuals, the successive categories of a discontinuous quantitative scale and the successive markers on a continuous quantitative scale must represent equal increments in the amount, frequency, or degree of the property being measured. If the difference in amount, frequency, or degree of the property between any two neighboring categories or markers is not the same as the difference between all other pairs of categories or markers, then we have a scale of unequal units and our measurements have very little precision. In this section we examine the necessity for equal units. We also inquire into the determination of equality of units and see whether there are any circumstances where the inequality of units is not too serious.

### Determining Equality of Units

With most devices that measure some physical property it is possible to ascertain through appropriate operations whether or not the units along a scale are equal. These operations are termed appropriate because they pertain to the variable under consideration and stem from certain conceptions we have about the property.

As an example let us say we wish to develop a scale of weight. The theory of gravitation tells us that two objects of equal weight will exert downward force. We take a beam that we support exactly in the center and say that when two objects placed at the extremities of the beam exactly balance the beam, they are equal in weight; and when they do not balance it, they differ in weight. Now we take any object such as a stone, and arbitrarily call it one unit of weight. We then find another stone that exactly balances the first stone. Operationally we say that the two stones are equal in weight; that is, are equal units representing equal amounts of the property of weight. In this fashion we can collect a number of stones of the same weight, each being considered a unit of weight. Now we wish to weigh a box. We place it at one extreme of the beam and place at the other extreme as many stones (units of weight) as are necessary to balance the beam. This number of units we term "the weight of the box." It makes no difference on which arm of the beam we place the box or the stones, nor does it matter which particular stones in our collection we use. Thus operationally we say the weight of the box is so many units (that is, equal-weight stones).

In psychological measurement also, the operations we employ to determine whether the units on a scale do or do not represent equal amounts of the property must follow from some theoretical notions we have about the property and from assumptions about it we are willing to make. As an illustration of the problem of the equality of psychological units, let us take a case where we wish to measure sales ability. We might measure the sales ability of people selling a given product by counting the number of dollars' worth of merchandise each person sells. If we do this, we are in effect saying that one dollar of merchandise sold is exactly equivalent to any other dollar of merchandise sold.

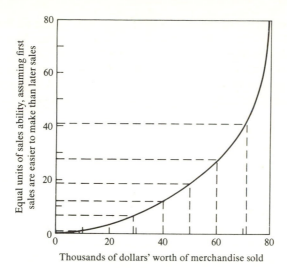

**Figure 3-1**   Hypothetical relationship between dollars' worth of merchandise sold and sales ability.

That is, the difference in dollars of sales between a person who sells $10,000 worth of merchandise and one who sells $20,000 worth reflects the same amount of sales ability as the difference between a person who sells $60,000 and one who sells $70,000.

Let us say that each salesperson has his or her own area and that all areas are equivalent in the nature and number of potential customers. We might argue that people differ in their willingness to buy. The first sales would probably be to those people who are quite ready to buy and therefore such sales could be accomplished with little effort. However, later sales would be considerably more difficult to make. In other words, the increment reflected by increasing sales from zero to $1 is less than the increment reflected by increasing sales from $1 to $2, and so on. The situation would be like that shown in Figure 3-1. If we take the curve in this figure as representing the relationship between "true" sales ability and dollars' worth of merchandise sold, then it is clear that the difference in sales ability reflected by the difference between $60,000 and $70,000 is about five times greater than the difference in sales ability represented by the difference between $10,000 and $20,000. Consequently if we adopt this point of view, we have to conclude that dollars' worth of merchandise sold is not a scale of sales ability on which the units are equal.

### When Inequality Is of Little Importance

Even though the operations we use to ascertain whether or not the units on a scale are equal may indicate that they are not, in some circumstances their inequality is of little importance. The situation in which the scale is applied may be such that for all practical purposes equal differences between scores can be taken as reflecting equal amounts of the property, or just about equal amounts.

Let us consider the case of a ruler in which the inch marks are not all the same distance apart. Suppose we have a ruler on which some pairs of markers are only ½ inch apart, some are 1 inch apart, and some are 1½ inches apart. Let us further suppose that these "units" of different sizes are distributed randomly along the ruler. Under these conditions the average size of the units between, say, the zeroth and the fifteenth marker is likely to be the same as the average size of the units between the fifteenth and the thirtieth marker. Now it is true that, for example, the difference between 5 and 6 on this scale is not equal in the amount of the property to the difference between 6 and 7, and the difference between 19 and 20 is not the same as the difference between 20 and 21. However, over long distances these inequalities tend to average out. Suppose the size of the smallest object being measured was 200 units on the "true" scale, and the size of the largest was 20,000 units. It is very likely that on the scale with unequal units any two objects measured as being, say, 400 units different in length would differ almost exactly by that amount on the "true" scale. Discrepancies between the two scales would be so small as to be insignificant, because differences in the sizes of the units would tend to average out.

Similarly, with a mental test we might be able to ignore the fact that the items do not represent equal units of the trait being measured. Suppose we have a test comprised of a number of items, and the individual's score is the number answered correctly within a specified time limit. Let us further suppose that items of all levels of difficulty are distributed randomly throughout the test. If the average difficulty of the items answered correctly by all individuals is the same, then we can say that the difference in ability reflected by the difference between scores of 50 and 100 is the same or very nearly the same as the difference in ability reflected by the difference between scores of 200 and 250.

There are many circumstances in psychological measurement where this situation occurs and the discrepancies in the size of the units would be expected to average out. Mental tests, personality and interest inventories, attitude questionnaires, and similar devices are comprised of a number of items arranged in such a fashion that inequalities in units are overcome by the sheer number of them. However, this is by no means always the case, and it would be incorrect to assume that the averaging-out process invariably occurs. Sometimes, for example, in aptitude or ability tests, items are deliberately arranged in increasing order of difficulty so that the average difficulty of the items answered by one individual, who earns a low score, may be quite different from the average difficulty of those answered by another, who earns a high score.

## Meaningfulness of Scores

As a result of the operations of measurement, an individual is assigned a number as a quantitative description, the number representing the frequency, amount, or degree to which the person manifests some property. An important question is how to give meaning to the specific numbers used as raw scores.

### Referring Scores to Scale

The numbers assigned as a result of the operations of measurement are sometimes given in reference to the scale and sometimes not. In the first case, scores are given as so many or so much "something-or-anothers." The height of a tree is described as being 25 feet, the weight of a child as 67 pounds, and the speed of response of a subject to a stimulus light as 0.28 seconds. In the second case, scores are given merely as numbers with no direct reference at all to the scale. Indeed, the only reference is to the measuring instrument used. Thus it is said that a patient received a score of 23 on the ABC Neurotic Inventory, a child attained a score of 247 on the XYZ Intelligence Test, and a worker was assigned a rating of 74 on the company's Employee Evaluation Form.

In general, scores that are given in terms that refer to the scale itself convey more information than those that are not. Yet merely stating scores as so many "something-or-anothers" does not in and of itself ensure greater meaning. Unless the units in which the scale is expressed are familiar, the advantage is lost. Quantitative descriptions expressed in inches, dollars, hours, quarts, pounds, centimeters, or kilograms have considerable significance because we have frequently used them and have compared many different individuals in the properties they indicate. But scores expressed in cythi, cafiz, dha, lev, and koruny convey little or no information. Indeed, to say that a city is 3 farskh distant or that an individual's wages are 20 abbasi tells us no more than a rating of 4 assigned to a nursery school child in "need for security" or a score of 59 earned by a child on the Smithers Test for Mechanical Aptitude.

In our earlier discussion we saw that the markers on a scale are established arbitrarily. The facts of the matter are that we can establish a unit as any amount of the property we want and can utilize as many different systems of units as we wish for the same continuum. We could say that an individual earns $42.50 per day or, equally well, that his earnings are 5,000 eyrir. The height of a woman could be given as 65.5 inches or as 2.5 alen. The time required by a student to solve a problem could be said to be 40 minutes or 1 candle. In cases such as these the units of the two systems pertain to the same scale and are merely different arbitrary systems of markers. Therefore one system of units can be readily changed into the other system. By additional operations, then, it is possible to transform scores that are expressed in unfamiliar terms to values that are familiar and therefore meaningful. Transformations of this sort are common. In the United States we historically expressed distances in terms of miles, whereas distances given in kilometers meant little to us. However, miles and kilometers are merely two different sets of arbitrary markers on the same continuous scale of distance, and one resolves simply and directly into the other, which we are now in the process of doing. Similarly we can transmute kilograms to pounds and liters to quarts.

It is unfortunate but true that with most psychological measuring devices, such as tests, inventories, rating scales, and questionnaires, the raw scores given directly by the operations of measurement seldom have a reference to a scale, and when they do the scale is very likely to be expressed in quite unfamiliar units. Scores on objective measuring devices are likely to be expressed only as so many "points" if they are given any reference at all. The information that a person made a score of 41 on an arithmetic test, a score of 215 on a sales-interest inventory, a score of 3 on a rating scale of initiative, or a score of 84 on a sociability inventory tells us little or nothing about the individual in terms of how much of those particular properties he or she possesses. However, in some circumstances it is possible to transmute the values of the raw scores to values that do have more meaning; this we discuss later.

### Referring Scores to Others of Same Kind

Suppose that instead of describing the individual's wages as $42.50 or 5,000 eyrir per day, we said that they are equal to those of the lowest-paid individual. Suppose we reported the woman as being average in height instead of as being 65.5 inches or 2.5 alen. Suppose we said of the student that he took a little less than average time to solve the problem rather than saying he took 40 minutes or 1 candle. In no case would we know the absolute amounts of the properties the individuals manifested, but nevertheless we would have descriptions of them that were indeed quite meaningful and useful.

In many cases, then, if we know how the individual stands in the property *relative* to other individuals of his or her kind, we have a quantitative description that is quite meaningful. If Fertaldig Ulderput, a man from Mars, is described to us as being 312 xlath (Martian units of height) tall, we really know nothing about him. But if we were told that Mr. Ulderput is 10 feet tall, unquestionably we should have some meaningful information. The description 10 feet is in terms that are quite familiar to us. Yet this quantitative description may not be sufficient. If Fertaldig were an earth man, he would be a "whopper," but perhaps he is a runt among Martians. In addition to expressing the value of his height in units that are familiar to us, if that value also gives us some indication of how he compares in height with other Martians, we have a quantitative description that is exceedingly meaningful.

It is meaningful to know that an object is 8 inches long. We can conceptualize it and get a "feel" of it. If in addition we know that the object is a mouse, our concept of the object is considerably richer. We now think of the object as "very large" because most mice are only 2 or 3 inches long. However, if the object is a snake, we think of it as "tiny" because most snakes are several feet long. These additional meanings come not from the scores themselves of the mouse and the snake, but rather from the general knowledge we have of how mice and snakes run in length. "Very large" and "tiny" are not meanings we get directly from the quantitative description "8 inches." In effect we recall the information we have gathered from various sources concerning the lengths of mice and snakes, and we reference the score of our individual to the scores of others of his or her kind. If a score tells us not only the amount of the property the individual possesses as measured on the scale but also where the score falls relative to the scores of others who are alike in kind, it does indeed provide a most valuable quantitative description. Later we see the extent to which this can be accomplished.

## Comparability of Scales

Sometimes we need to compare the similarities and differences among the traits of a given individual. For example, we might wish to ascertain whether an individual manifests greater clerical aptitude, mechanical aptitude, or sales aptitude. Or we may wish to determine whether a social group is most deficient in leadership, morale, cohesiveness, or internal structure. Only if the scores on the different scales are comparable can we say that an individual possesses more of one property than he or she does of another.

## Equivalence of Units

When we make comparisons within the individual on different scales, we are asking whether that individual manifests more of one property than of another and, if so, what the magnitude of the difference is. If we are to make comparisons of this sort, then the scores on the different scales must be comparable. For example, we can say that an automobile is wider than it is tall, because both scores are expressed in the same units, namely, units of length. We can say that a nursery school child evidences more acts of friendship than of aggressiveness, because both scores are expressed in terms of number of acts. We can say that a business establishment has more salespeople than clerks, because both quantitative descriptions are in terms of numbers of employees. In each of these cases the units in which the two variables are expressed are comparable.

However, on the same basis we cannot say that an automobile is wider than it is heavy, nor a child friendlier than tall, nor a student better in English than in sociability; nor can we say that a business establishment has more salespeople than it has support from the public. We cannot make these comparisons because the amounts of the two properties in each case are expressed in quite different terms. We could say for an automobile that the number of inches of width is greater than the number of pounds of weight. And for the same automobile we could say that the number of inches of width is less than the number of grams of weight. Comparisons of this sort are meaningless because the markers on the scales are arbitrary, and we can make as few or as many of them on the scales as we wish.

It is only when scores on the different scales are expressed precisely in the same terms that we can say they are comparable. We have to conclude, then, that it is impossible to make comparisons within the individual on most psychological traits because they are expressed in such quite different terms as number of seconds, number of items, number of units on a rating scale, and number of attempts. Only if by a series of further operations we can transmute the raw scores to values that are equivalent will it be possible to make comparisons within the individual.

## Referring Scores to Others of Same Kind

Let us pursue further the matter of comparisons within the individual, that is, comparisons of the individual's scores on two or more different variables. We have seen that in order to make this type of comparison, it is necessary for all scales to be expressed in the same type of units. Suppose that students' academic performance is evaluated on a scale of $0 = F$ to $4 = A$. A student whose grade-point average is 3.6 in literature courses and 3.2 in history courses apparently achieves greater superiority in the former subject than in the latter. But let us suppose that when we examine the grades earned by the thousands of students who have attended this particular university, we find that the highest grade average attained by any student in literature courses is 4.0, whereas the highest average attained by any student in history courses is 3.2. While it is theoretically possible for students to earn grades as high as 4.0 in both literature and history, the facts of the matter are that no student has ever done so in history. Therefore our particular student is not equal to the best in literature, but he is equal to the best in history.

We might say, then, that two scores, each assessed independently of each other and on a different variable, are comparable if they represent the same standing in the same population on those scales. If we are told that a man is 5 feet tall and weighs 250 pounds, we immediately say of him that he is heavier than he is tall. We know that the average height of men is somewhere between 5 and 6 feet and the average weight somewhere between 100 and 200 pounds. The man in question clearly is below the average of other men in height and above the average of other men in weight.

An alternative to the above is to measure different characteristics on the same scale where there is a direct comparison of the characteristics. For example, we could ask "Is John taller than he is heavy?" The response, "yes" or "no," is based on the respondent's comparison of one trait to another. The choice of "taller" indicates that "heavy" cannot be indicated. In other words, questions and responses are dependent on each other such that the choice of one eliminates the choice of the other. Another example will demonstrate this more appropriately. If the respondent is asked to *rank order* (without permitting ties) his or her preference for certain values—for example, security, money, achievement, opportunity to benefit society, opportunity for personal growth—then we are forcing a within-person comparison. If the characteristic "personal growth" is ranked 1, then *none* of the other values can be ranked 1. The information we obtain is the *relative preference for an individual and not between individuals.*

For situations in which we are concerned with comparisons between persons, suppose that we know that the range of scores of fifth-grade children on a particular spelling test is 75–150 points and on a particular arithmetic test 10–40 points. A fifth-grade child who earns a score of 145 on the spelling test and 11 on the arithmetic test would be characterized as being better in spelling than in arithmetic. Essentially what we are doing is comparing the child's scores with those earned on the two tests by others of his or her kind, namely, fifth-grade children. We ignore the descriptions of ability given by the raw scores in and of themselves and take as descriptions of ability the positions of his or her scores relative to those of other children. Comparability is attained not through rendering the units on the various scales equal, but rather through comparing the individual's scores on different variables with the distributions of scores earned by a population of individuals in his or her same general class. We discuss these problems again in the next section.

## Describing and Establishing Norms

Various types of populations are used as a basis for establishing *norms*. In actual practice, of course, we ordinarily do not have all members of a population but only a sample. The selection of groups is a function of the purpose for which the measurements are being made. Thus the norms for a typing achievement test might be based on the scores earned by "trained typists in general" or by "tenth-graders who have completed a one-semester course in typing," depending on the type of person in whom we are interested.

One special group that is both useful and meaningful in the establishment of norms is the adult population. When norms based on scores earned by this group are used, they are typically reported separately for subgroups for whom differences in scores are apparent, such as for men and women. The samples of individuals utilized in the preparation of these norms can be examined in order to ascertain how representative they are by comparing their characteristics with those given for the population by the census figures.

### Adequacy of Groups

The adequacy of a group used in the establishment of norms obviously is a function of the number of cases involved and their representativeness. If the number of cases is small, we cannot put much dependence on the norms since another group consisting of the same number of persons might give quite different results. The larger the number of cases, the more stable will be the norms and the more confidence we can have in them.

Large numbers alone are not sufficient to ensure adequate norms. We must be sure that the individuals used in the sample are fully representative of the total group the norms are to represent. For example, college seniors would not be representative of college students in general, nor would bank managers be representative of the population of "business and industrial managers." In some instances where very special groups are involved, such as those in rare occupations such as sailmakers, or those with special characteristics, such as blindness, numbers of cases might have to be sacrificed in order to achieve representativeness. We should not add seamstresses to sailmakers nor partially blind individuals to the totally blind merely to increase the number of cases.

## Describing Distributions of Scores

When we make assessments of a group of people on a characteristic, we obtain a set of scores that can be put into the form of a frequency distribution. The *frequency distribution* is a listing of the obtained scores and the number of people obtaining each score. If we are going to use the frequency distributions of scores earned by a particular group of individuals as frames of reference for giving meaning to scores, then we must be able to describe the nature of those distributions. Such descriptions are necessary so that we can ascertain the extent to which the scores earned by different groups on the same test provide the same frames of reference. There are a number of ways, mathematically and otherwise, for making such comparisons. However, we deal here only with certain ones, statistical devices that are particularly pertinent to our present discussion and for our later developments.

### Ways Frequency Distributions Differ

Let us compare the graphic form of two distributions of scores given in Figure 3-2. First, we see that by and large the scores in distribution *A* are lower than those in distribution *B*. Therefore we want some way of indicating the general level of a set of scores, that is, where they fall on the *average,* or the central tendency of the distribution. Second, it is apparent that the scores in the two distributions vary among themselves in different degrees. The scores in distribution *A* tend to cluster together rather closely, whereas those in distribution *B* tend to scatter or spread out more. Hence we need an index of the degree to which scores exhibit *variation* among themselves. Third, we can see that the distribution of scores in *B* is symmetrical (that is, the distribution can be evenly divided about a single score), whereas the scores in *A* are distributed in an asymmetrical, lopsided, or skewed fashion. Therefore an index of *skewness* is necessary. Fourth, it is obvious that distribution

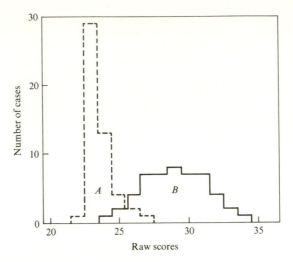

**Figure 3-2**  Two distributions of scores with different characteristics.

*A* is sharply peaked or *leptokurtic,* while distribution *B* tends to be flat or *platykurtic*. This property of peakness or flatness is referred to as *kurtosis*.

### Measures of Central Tendency

For our purposes, the most useful index of the average level of scores, or measure of *central tendency,* in a distribution is their *arithmetic mean*. The mean of a set of scores is defined as the sum of the scores divided by the number of scores. Therefore the formula for the arithmetic mean is

$$\bar{X} = \frac{X_a + \cdots + X_n}{n} = \frac{\Sigma X}{n} \tag{3-1}$$

where $\bar{X}$ is the mean and $X$ represents the raw scores earned by the $a$ to $n$ individuals so that $\Sigma X$ represents the sum of all the raw scores. In computing the mean, we simply add together or sum ($\Sigma$) the scores of all individuals and divide by the number of individuals ($n$).

The mean has the interesting property of being a point of balance in the distribution of scores. First, if we take the difference between each score in the distribution and the mean of the distribution, the sum of the differences is zero. In other words, the sum of the positive differences from the mean is exactly equal to the sum of the negative differences. Raw scores are symbolized by $X$, and the difference between the raw score and the mean, called a *deviation score,* is symbolized by $x$. The deviation score for any one individual is

$$x = X - \bar{X} \qquad (3\text{-}2)$$

Let us now sum the deviation scores for all individuals:

$$\Sigma x = \Sigma(X - \bar{X})$$

If there are a total of $n$ individuals, that is, $a$ to $n$ individuals, we can write the above equation as

$$\Sigma x = (X_a - \bar{X}) + (X_b - \bar{X}) + \cdots + (X_{n-1} - \bar{X}) + (X_n - \bar{X})$$

Rearranging terms gives

$$\begin{aligned}
\Sigma x &= X_a + X_b + \cdots + X_{n-1} + X_n - \bar{X} - \cdots - \bar{X} \\
&= \Sigma X - \Sigma \bar{X}
\end{aligned}$$

The term $\Sigma \bar{X}$ involves adding the mean (a constant) to itself $n$ times (the number of cases there are). Summing a constant, an unvarying value, to itself a given number of times is the same as multiplying that constant by the number. In other words,

$$\Sigma \bar{X} = n\bar{X}$$

Hence

$$\Sigma x = \Sigma X - n\bar{X}$$

Substituting for the mean $\bar{X}$ from Equation 3-1 gives

$$\begin{aligned}
\Sigma x &= \Sigma X - n\,\frac{\Sigma X}{n} \\
&= \Sigma X - \Sigma X \\
&= 0 \qquad (3\text{-}3)
\end{aligned}$$

If we divide both sides of Equation 3-3 by $n$, we can see that the mean of the deviation scores also equals zero:

$$\bar{x} = \frac{\Sigma x}{n} = \frac{0}{n} = 0 \qquad (3\text{-}4)$$

As an example, suppose we had the following distribution: 2, 7, 9, 12, and 20, $\Sigma X = 50$, $n = 5$, and thus $\bar{X} = 10$. Subtracting 10 from each score (see Equation 3-2) yields $-8$, $-3$, $-1$, $+2$, and $+10$ or $\Sigma x = 0$, and therefore $\bar{x} = 0$.

Furthermore, the sum of the squares of the differences between the raw scores and the mean, $\Sigma x^2$, *is smaller than the sum of the squares of the differences between the raw scores and any other point on the scale.* Hence it is said that the mean is the *point of least squares*. The value $\Sigma x^2$ is a minimum value and is always smaller than the sum of the squared deviations about any other value. Using the same distribution on which we determined the $\Sigma x$, we find that the $\Sigma x^2$ is $(-8)^2 + (-3)^2 + (-1)^2 + (+2)^2 + (+10)^2 = 64 + 9 + 1 + 4 + 100 = 178$. If we had determined the deviation score $(x)$ by subtracting a value other than the mean, for example 11, then the following would result: $\Sigma x = (2 - 11) + (7 - 11) + (9 - 11) + (12 - 11) + (20 - 11) = (-9) + (-4) + (-2) + (+1) + (+9) = -5$ and $\Sigma x^2 = (-9)^2 + (-4)^2 + (-2)^2 + (+1)^2 + (+9)^2 = 183$. This latter value is higher than the $\Sigma x^2$ determined when the mean was used. Keep in mind this operation and the fact that the mean is the point of least squares, because when we discuss regression analysis, we do so in terms of the method of least squares.

If we wish, we could compute the mean of the squares of the deviation scores by dividing $\Sigma x^2$ by $n$ and

$$\frac{\Sigma x^2}{n} = \text{the average squared deviation about the mean}$$

The mean of the squared deviations from the mean of the distribution also is a minimum value. Therefore the mean of a set of scores is that point on the scale that is a center point in a least-squares sense.

Briefly, there are two other measures of central tendency. One is the *mode,* or the score that is most frequently obtained. To obtain the mode, we examine a frequency distribution, and the value that is associated with the greatest $n$ is the mode. For example, in the following distribution, the mode is 4.

| $X$ | $n$ |
| --- | --- |
| 1 | 6 |
| 2 | 9 |
| 3 | 12 |
| 4 | 14 |
| 5 | 4 |

The second measure is the *median,* or the value above which and below which 50 percent of the scores fall. There are methods for determining the precise value of the median that can be found in standard psychological statistics texts (see the Suggested Readings at the end of this chapter). For our purposes, one can see that the approximate value of the median for the above distribution is 3. These measures, in addition to the mean, all provide *indices* of the most representative or descriptive value of the distribution.

### Standard Deviation and Variance

The mean of the squares of the deviation scores, the value we just discussed, has the property of varying with the extent to which the scores in a distribution cluster together or spread out. That is, it is an indication of the range of scores in the distribution. Two distributions can have the same mean, yet the range of scores in each distribution can differ. For example, the mean of one distribution may be 40 with a wide range of 5 to 75, while a second distribution with the same mean of 40 has a narrow range of 35 to 45. To distinguish the fact that these two distributions differ, and therefore have different implications, we need a measure of the range or variability of the distributions. Hence the mean of the squares of the deviation scores, or its square root, is commonly used as an index of the variability of scores. The square root of the mean of the squares of the deviations scores is termed the *standard deviation:*

$$\sigma_x = \sqrt{\frac{\Sigma x^2}{n}} \tag{3-5}$$

The square of the standard deviation, that is, the mean of the squared deviations itself, is termed the *variance:*

$$\sigma_x^2 = \frac{\Sigma x^2}{n} \tag{3-6}$$

To compute the standard deviation by Equation 3-5, we need the values of the scores in deviation form, $x$.

Simple though Equations 3-5 and 3-6 appear, they are not very convenient for computation since they require that the raw scores first be transformed into deviation scores. Let us therefore derive a formula that is more practical for computational purposes because it uses the raw scores directly. (We apologize for burdening you now and then with these derivations. However, if you take a few extra moments to plow through them you will be rewarded with a much firmer grasp of the concepts themselves.)

$$\sigma_x^2 = \frac{\Sigma x^2}{n}$$

But $x = X - \bar{X}$. Therefore

$$\sigma_x^2 = \frac{\Sigma(X - \bar{X})^2}{n}$$
$$= \frac{\Sigma(X^2 - 2X\bar{X} + \bar{X}^2)}{n}$$
$$= \frac{\Sigma X^2 - \Sigma 2X\bar{X} + \Sigma\bar{X}^2}{n}$$

Remembering that 2 and $\bar{X}$ are constants, we get

$$\sigma_x^2 = \frac{\Sigma X^2 - 2\bar{X}\Sigma X + n\bar{X}^2}{n}$$
$$= \frac{\Sigma X^2}{n} - 2\bar{X}\,\frac{\Sigma X}{n} + \frac{n\bar{X}^2}{n}$$
$$= \frac{\Sigma X^2}{n} - 2\bar{X}\bar{X} + \bar{X}^2$$
$$= \frac{\Sigma X^2}{n} - 2\bar{X}^2 + \bar{X}^2$$

$$\sigma_x^2 = \frac{\Sigma X^2}{n} - \bar{X}^2 \tag{3-7}$$

$$\sigma_x = \sqrt{\frac{\Sigma X^2}{n} - \bar{X}^2} \tag{3-8}$$

The standard deviation of scores is precisely the same in raw-score form as it is in deviation-score form. We can see this in Equation 3-7. If we used deviation scores rather than raw scores, then the term $\bar{X}^2$ would be zero because the mean of deviation scores is zero, and the term $\Sigma X^2/n$ would be written as $\Sigma x^2/n$ (see Equation 3-6) without changing the value of $\sigma$. When we use deviation scores, obviously all we are doing is subtracting a constant $\bar{X}$ from all scores (Equation 3-2) and therefore we do not change the nature of the distribution or its shape, nor do we affect the range of scores. Hence for the standard deviation of a set of scores, we can write either $\sigma_X$ or $\sigma_x$.

In this section, as elsewhere is this book, we are developing the algebraic definitions of important quantities in the most straightforward manner possible. We are not generally concerned with the *statistical* problem of estimating *population* characteristics from *sample* data. That is a matter for books on *statistics* (for example, Hays, 1973), not psy-

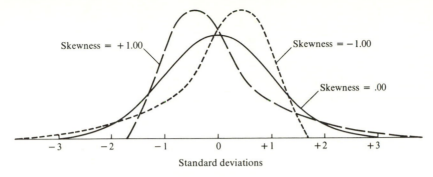

*Figure 3-3* Frequency distributions differing in skewness.

chological measurement. To illustrate the difference, the best *sample estimate* of the *population variance* is

$$s_x^2 = \frac{\Sigma x^2}{n - 1}$$

The symbol $s_x^2$ is typically used to designate the sample estimate of the population variance, while $\sigma_x^2$ describes the variance of whatever set of scores we actually have. On the average the variance of scores obtained from samples drawn randomly from a larger population are a bit too small. The mathematical statistician tells us that $n - 1$ should be used instead of $n$ to correct this slight *bias*. Again however, our task in this book is to develop appropriate descriptions and not worry about appropriate statistical inferences. Thus we will use $\sigma_x^2$ or $s_x^2$, whichever is more convenient and appropriate.

## Skewness

A distribution of scores can be symmetrical, as with distribution *B* in Figure 3-2, or skewed, as with distribution *A*. As may be seen in Figure 3-3, distributions can vary both in the direction and in the degree of skewness. It just so happens that the mean of the cubes of deviation scores ($\Sigma x^3/n$) is related to both the direction and the degree of skewness. When the distribution of scores is symmetrical, the mean of the cubes of the deviation scores is zero. When the distribution of scores is positively skewed (the long "tail" of the distribution pointing toward the higher score values as with distribution *A* in Figure 3-2), the mean of the cubes of the deviation scores is positive. Thus there are more low

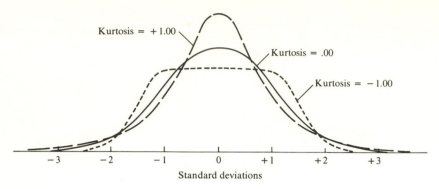

Kurtosis = + 1.00

Kurtosis = .00

Kurtosis = − 1.00

Standard deviations

***Figure 3-4***    Frequency distributions differing in kurtosis.

scorers. When the distribution of scores is negatively skewed (the long "tail" of the distribution pointing toward the smaller score values), the mean of the cubes of the deviation scores is negative. Thus there are more high scorers. Furthermore, the larger the mean of the cubes of the deviation scores, the greater the degree of skewness.

To compare the skewness of the two distributions of scores, we should be sure the variation among the scores is the same in both cases. Therefore, rather than using the mean of the cubes of the deviation scores as an index of skewness, we refer it to the standard deviation of the distribution or in the computation, to the cube of the standard deviation. The index of skewness ($Sk$), then, is

$$Sk = \frac{\Sigma x^3/n}{\sigma_x^3} \tag{3-9}$$

### Kurtosis

In some distributions that are called leptokurtic, there is a heavy piling up of scores in one region of the scale; whereas in others that are called platykurtic, the scores tend to distribute more or less evenly throughout. Figure 3-4 shows some examples of distributions that differ in degree of kurtosis. Just as the mean of the cubes of the deviation scores is related to skewness, so the mean of the deviation scores to the fourth power ($\Sigma x^4/n$) is related to kurtosis. Again for an index we wish to hold the variation of scores constant and therefore reference the mean of the deviation scores to the fourth power of the standard deviation. The ratio of the mean of the deviation scores to the fourth power, to the fourth power of the standard deviation, is quite a satisfactory index of

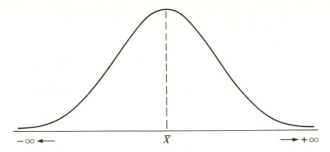

*Figure 3-5*   Normal frequency distribution.

kurtosis. However, by convention we subtract 3 from this ratio for reasons that will be clear when we discuss the normal frequency distribution. Our index of kurtosis (*Ku*), then, is

$$Ku = \frac{\Sigma x^4 / n}{\sigma_x^4} - 3 \tag{3-10}$$

When this value is positive, the distribution of scores is leptokurtic; and when it is negative, the distribution is platykurtic.

### Characteristics of Normal Frequency Distribution

It is apparent that distributions of scores vary widely in their shape, manifesting different degrees and combinations of skewness and kurtosis. It therefore would be well to establish one particular distribution as a frame of reference for comparison purposes. If possible, this distribution should be so commonly found as to be characteristic, or nearly so, of the distributions of scores on a wide variety of qualities. Such a distribution does exist, and it is termed the *normal frequency distribution* (see Figure 3-5).

The normal frequency distribution is symmetrical and bell-shaped. It is found for a variety of both physical and psychological traits. This is not to say that the frequency distributions of these traits always, or indeed ever, have precisely the characteristics of a normal frequency distribution, but rather that very often they quite closely approximate it in shape. The normal frequency distribution also has been termed the curve of error because it is closely approximated in those situations where a "score" is determined by a large number of factors that operate under conditions of equal likelihood of having an effect. For example, if one tossed a thousand coins a million times, or for that matter,

**Table 3-1**  Expansion of binomial $(p + q)^N$, where $p = q = 0.5$ and $N = 8$, to illustrate the normal frequency distribution

| | | |
|---|---|---|
| $p^8$ | 1(0.00390625) | 0.00390625 |
| $8p^7q$ | 8(0.0078125)(0.5) | 0.03125000 |
| $28p^6q^2$ | 28(0.015625)(0.25) | 0.10937500 |
| $56p^5q^3$ | 56(0.03125)(0.125) | 0.21875000 |
| $70p^4q^4$ | 70(0.0625)(0.0625) | 0.27343750 |
| $56p^3q^5$ | 56(0.125)(0.03125) | 0.21875000 |
| $28p^2q^6$ | 28(0.25)(0.015625) | 0.10937500 |
| $8pq^7$ | 8(0.5)(0.0078125) | 0.03125000 |
| $q^8$ | 1(0.00390625) | 0.00390625 |
| $\Sigma$ | | 1.00000000 |

thirty coins a thousand times, counted up the number of heads occurring on each toss, and made a frequency distribution of these "scores," the distribution would be very similar in shape to that of a normal distribution.

The normal frequency distribution can be precisely stated mathematically (see Hays, 1973). One statement is that it is the expansion of the binomial $(p + q)^N$, where $p = q = 0.5$ and $N$ is an infinitely large number. By way of illustration, this binomial is expanded to the eighth power in Table 3-1. This particular expansion gives us a frequency distribution of nine steps or score values and is plotted as a frequency polygon in Figure 3-6. If $N$ is an infinitely large number, then the number of steps along the scale is infinitely large and the curve becomes smooth and does not have the "corners" we see in the distribution in Figure 3-6. A normal frequency distribution has a skewness of zero (Figure 3-3) and a kurtosis of zero (Figure 3-4).

The normal frequency distribution is defined by a particular formula and is a *theoretical curve*. Its tails (see Figure 3-5) never reach the base line; rather, they approach it asymptotically so that in a true normal frequency distribution, there can never be a score value with a frequency of zero. Consequently it is never correct to say of any distribution of actual scores that the distribution is normal, even if both its skewness and its kurtosis are zero. Distributions of actual scores may have characteristics that closely approximate those of a normal frequency distribution, but they never have all of them. When we say that a distribution of scores is normal, we really mean that its characteristics are very similar to those of a normal distribution. A normal frequency distribution, then, is purely a theoretical frequency distribution.

We can see from Table 3-1 that it would be possible to calculate the proportion of cases falling between any two points in such a distribu-

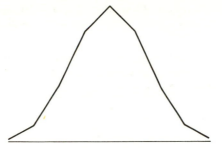

*Figure 3-6*   Expansion of binomial $(p + q)^N$, where $p = q = 0.5$ and $N = 8$, to illustrate normal frequency distribution.

tion. This has been done mathematically so that the properties of the distribution are well known. The proportions of cases falling below various score values in a normal frequency distribution are given in Appendix A.

### Normal Frequency Distribution as a Model

For one reason or another we may believe that the particular distribution of scores given by the operations of measurement does not reflect the true distribution of the trait being measured. In some instances the individuals being measured may be drawn not from one but from two or more different populations; for example, men and women or apprentices and masters of a trade. But in many instances, even though the group does constitute a representative sample of the population with which we are concerned, we may be led to reject the distribution of their scores as being descriptive of the way in which the trait is distributed in the population.

It may be that we suspect there is some artifact in the measuring device or in the measuring situation. For example, suppose we find that on a particular test most people make low scores and relatively few people earn high scores. We might argue that this particular positively skewed distribution of scores resulted from the fact that the items in the test were too difficult for the group. Had we happened to develop somewhat easier items, the distribution of scores would have been different. Similarly, if we have parents rate their children on some trait such as intelligence, probably most children will be assigned high ratings and relatively few will be assigned low ones. This negatively skewed distribution might be expected, because in general parents are likely to be lenient in judging their offspring. The distribution of scores as it stands would be rejected because it represents a mutilation of the true distribution of the trait due to an error of leniency on the part of the raters.

Furthermore, if we do not believe that the units along our scale are equal, we do not expect the distribution of scores as given by our operations of measurement to mirror the way in which the trait actually is distributed among individuals. For example, we might have a situation such as that in Figure 3-1 where successive units along the scale represent greater and greater amounts of the trait. A "unit" at the lower end of the scale represents a smaller amount of the trait than one at the higher end. Under such circumstances it would not be surprising to find that the upper end of the distribution is "pushed" down and a negatively skewed distribution of scores results.

Now it may be that we are perfectly happy with the distribution of scores given by our operations of measurement. We believe that the distribution is not affected by artifacts in the measuring instrument or measurement situation, or if there are any such effects, they are of such a minor nature that they can be ignored. On the other hand, if we have reason to believe that the distribution of scores gives a distorted picture of the distribution of the trait, we are faced with some decisions.

Perhaps the most common decision is to admit that the distribution of scores given by our operations of measurement does not correctly reflect the distribution of the trait. We are unable to state the extent to which the distribution of scores gives a distorted picture of the distribution of the trait, because we have no idea of what the correct distribution is like. In effect we throw up our hands and admit defeat but go ahead and use the scores anyway.

From theoretical considerations of one sort or another, we might have an idea of the way in which the trait is distributed. Thus from our notions about hemispherical dominance in the brain, we might decide that measures of preference for use of the right and left hands should be bimodal. That is, we should be saying that on a scale of hand preference there should be a large proportion of individuals toward one end of the scale (those who prefer to use the right hand), another substantial proportion at the other end of the scale (those who prefer to use the left hand), and few falling in the middle of the scale (those who have no hand preference). We develop, then, a model of the distribution of the trait from our theory. Clearly the adequacy of our model is a direct function of the adequacy of our theoretical considerations. If the theory is faulty, so will be our model.

Once we make up our minds about the model of the distribution of the trait, that is, the shape of the frequency distribution of scores, we must make a further decision. First, we can attempt to design operations of measurement yielding scores that distribute in the same manner as our model. If the scores do not distribute in the way desired, the operations will be modified or discarded and new ones developed. Second, we can transmute our raw scores to other values of such a nature that the new transmuted scores do distribute in accordance with the model. Finally, we can say that the distribution of scores of the particular sample of individuals we have does possess the characteristics of the model even though it does not.

There are, of course, a wide variety of differently shaped distributions that could be adopted as the theoretical model of the distribution of psychological traits. Of all the possible distributions there appears to be more basis for choosing the normal frequency distribution. We have seen that if we measure the properties of large and representative populations of living things with a wide variety of measuring devices, particularly devices that measure physical properties, the distributions of scores tend to be shaped more like a normal distribution than any other type of distribution. This is not to say that the empirically obtained distributions of scores ever precisely fit a normal distribution, but rather that in many instances there is a very close approximation. Indeed, to many it seems that the bulk of the distributions of scores are simply chance variations from a normal distribution.

Frequently as we increase the numbers of cases, the shape of the distribution of scores more and more closely approaches that of the normal frequency distribution. By way of example, Figure 3-7a gives the distribution of scores earned on a test by 50 individuals. For comparison purposes a theoretical normal curve is superimposed on the empirical distribution. Clearly, the shape of the distribution of scores of this small sample of individuals is quite different from that of a normal distribution. Figure 3-7b shows the distribution when the number of cases is increased to 100, and in Figure 3-7c the distribution includes the scores of 1,000 individuals. It is apparent that in this instance, as in many others, as we increase the number of cases, the shape of the distribution of scores comes closer and closer to that of a normal frequency distribution. Thus if we had just the 50 cases, we might be willing to say that the distribution of the trait is normal even though the scores of our sample clearly are not normally distributed. We would use the mean and standard deviation of our normally distributed trait and attribute to our empirical distribution the characteristics of a normal distribution.

The fact that the shapes of so many frequency distributions of scores approach that of a normal frequency distribution has been sufficient justification for some psychologists to hold that the normal frequency distribution of traits is the rule. Their position is strengthened by the ease of "explaining away" frequency distributions that are not normal as resulting from the use of poorly devised measuring instruments or

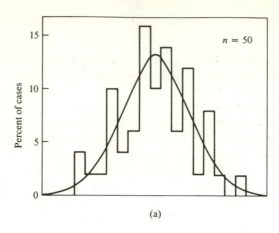

(a)

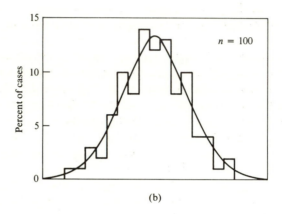

(b)

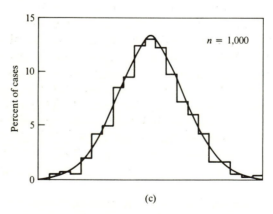

(c)

*Figure 3-7*   Illustration of how increasing the number of cases results, in some instances, in a distribution of scores that more and more closely approximates a normal frequency distribution.

small or nonrepresentative samples of individuals. For other psychologists the normal frequency distribution appears to be a reasonable hypothesis to be adhered to in "appropriate" circumstances. Finally there are those who completely reject the normal frequency distribution as a "law." They prefer to hold to whatever shape of distribution of scores the measuring device happens to yield. Apparently they have more faith in their capacity for devising satisfactory operations of measurement than in their capacity for theorizing.

The decision of whether or not to adopt a normal distribution as a model seems to depend largely on one's particular biases and inclinations. Often the decision appears to be reached on intuitive rather than explicit grounds, and certainly the entire matter is discussed with more heat than light. The position most often taken is that characteristics are normally distributed. If the empirical data do not support this, then we have two alternatives, provided the sample is large. Either we normalize our distribution (see the next chapter) or we use the raw-score distribution's properties as they are, but still apply statistical tests and analyses to it that are based on a normal distribution. This latter alternative is feasible because many analyses are *robust;* that is, they yield equivalent results regardless of whether the assumptions of normality are violated or not.

---

## Technical Section

### Mean and Standard Deviation of Dichotomous Variables

As we saw in Chapter 2, many of the variables with which we deal in psychological measurement are dichotomous. That is, the operations of measurement sometimes merely give us an assignment of individuals to one or the other of two categories. In an attitude survey, people respond to a question by saying they are either favorably or unfavorably inclined, and in a spelling test a word is spelled either correctly or incorrectly. With dichotomous variables that are discontinuous, persons who fall in one category typically are assigned the convenient score of 1, and those in the other a score of 0 (though the two numerical values assigned to the categories are irrelevant because of the effects of linear transformations, which are discussed in Chapter 4).

Let us now consider the mean and standard deviation of scores on dichotomous variables. For a dichotomous variable we can write

$$p = \frac{f_1}{n} \quad \text{and} \quad q = \frac{f_0}{n} \tag{3-11}$$

where $p$ is the proportion and $f_1$ the number of cases that earn a score of 1, $q$ is the proportion and $f_0$ the number of cases that earn a score of 0, and $n$ is the total number of cases. Therefore

$$p + q = 1 \qquad p = 1 - q \qquad q = 1 - p$$

Since with a discontinuous dichotomous variable, we have only two possible scores, 0 and 1, we can write the formula for the mean as

$$\bar{X} = \frac{f_0 X_0 + f_1 X_1}{n}$$

But $X_0 = 0$ and therefore the first term in the numerator is zero and drops out. Furthermore $X_1 = 1$ and therefore the second term in the numerator is $f_1 1$ or simply $f_1$. Hence

$$\bar{X} = \frac{f_1}{n} = p \tag{3-12}$$

That is, with a discontinuous dichotomous variable, the mean is simply the proportion of persons falling in the upper category. Thus if 48 out of 200 cases fall in the upper category, the mean is $^{48}/_{200}$ or 0.24. From Equation 3-6 we know that the variance of a set of scores is

$$\sigma_x^2 = \frac{\Sigma x^2}{n}$$

Remembering that a deviation score is the raw score minus the mean, we have for a dichotomous variable

| Raw Scores | Deviation Scores |
|------------|------------------|
| $X_1 = 1$ | $x_1 = 1 - p = q$ |
| $X_0 = 0$ | $x_0 = 0 - p = -p$ |

For a dichotomous variable, therefore, the variance is

$$\sigma_x^2 = \frac{f_0 x_0{}^2 + f_1 x_1{}^2}{n}$$

$$= \frac{f_0 (-p)^2 + f_1 q^2}{n}$$

$$= \frac{f_0 p^2}{n} + \frac{f_1 q^2}{n}$$

$$= \frac{f_0}{n} p^2 + \frac{f_1}{n} q^2$$

$$= qp^2 + pq^2$$
$$= pq(p + q)$$
$$= pq(1)$$
$$\sigma_x^2 = pq \qquad (3\text{-}13)$$
$$\sigma_x = \sqrt{pq} \qquad (3\text{-}14)$$

Even if you don't bother with the above derivation, the important thing is that the standard deviation of scores on a dichotomous variable is equal to the square root of the product of the proportions of individuals who fall in the two categories. Thus the proportion of cases falling in the upper category is 0.24, the proportion falling in the lower category is 0.76, and the standard deviation is $\sqrt{(0.24)(0.76)} = \sqrt{0.1824}$ or 0.43. These are exactly the same values we would get if we used the raw-score formula for the mean and variance. The only reason for deriving them here is that they are easier to use with dichotomous data.

## Summary

It is desirable but not essential for the successive categories of a discontinuous multistep scale, and the successive "markers" on a continuous scale, to represent equal increments in the amount, frequency, or degree of the property being measured. That is, the units along a scale should be equal. With many measuring devices it is possible through appropriate operations to determine whether in fact the units are equal. The operations are termed appropriate because they pertain to the variable under consideration and follow logically from the particular theoretical conceptions we have about the nature of the variable.

In certain situations, even though we may be certain that the units of measurement are not equal, such inequality is of little practical importance and can be ignored. If the units are unequal but the various sizes are distributed randomly throughout the scale, their differences will tend to average out, particularly when a large number of them is involved.

To be useful, a quantitative description or a score must be meaningful. A meaningful score is given in terms that directly convey some notion of the amount, degree, or frequency of the property that the individual possesses. Most scores on psychological traits are expressed merely in terms of "points," without any reference to the trait being measured or to a frame of reference such as an absolute zero. Relating an individual's scores to the distribution of scores by other individuals does provide something of a frame of reference, and therefore does give more meaning to scores.

Sometimes we wish to make comparisons within the individual so that we can know in which traits the person is strong and in which the person is weak. Comparisons of this sort can be made only if the scores on the different variables are expressed in the same terms. That is, only when scores on different variables are comparable, can we say an individual possesses more of one property than of another. Referencing an individual's score on each variable to distributions of scores on those variables does provide a kind of comparability among variables. At least it permits us to say that relative to other individuals this person is higher on certain traits than he or she is on others.

A distribution of scores used as a frame of reference to make scores meaningful and comparable is termed a set of norms. Since distributions of scores are so useful, it is necessary to describe them. Distributions differ from one another in many ways, but when they are used as norms, the most useful descriptions of them are the mean and variation of the scores, and the shape of the distribution as given by the skewness and kurtosis.

Inasmuch as there are substantial variations in the shapes of distributions of scores, it would be useful to have one particular distribution as a frame of reference. The shape of this distribution should be characteristic, or nearly so, of the shapes of the distributions of a wide variety of properties. Such a distribution does exist and is termed the normal frequency distribution. This distribution is symmetrical and is shaped like a bell. The distributions of scores closely approximate the normal distribution in so many instances that it is useful as a theoretical model of distributions of scores.

---

## Suggested Readings

American Psychological Association. 1974. *Standards for educational and psychological tests*. Washington, D.C.: American Psychological Association. Pp. 19–24 (section on norms).

Anastasi, A. 1976. *Psychological testing*. 4th ed. New York: Macmillan. Chap. 4.

Hays, W. L. 1973. *Statistics for the social sciences*. 2nd ed. New York: Holt, Rinehart and Winston. Chap. 6.

Lorge, I., and R. L. Thorndike. 1967. Procedures for establishing norms. In D. N. Jackson and S. Messick (Eds.), *Problems in human assessment*. New York: McGraw-Hill. Pp. 791–793.

McNemar, Q. 1969. *Psychological statistics*. 4th ed. New York: Wiley. Chaps. 3 and 4.

# 4

## *Transforming Scores*

In Chapter 3 we saw that under many circumstances measurements of human characteristics cannot utilize an absolute zero as a reference point. Furthermore, we saw that the units in scales of psychological traits are not likely to be expressed in meaningful ways in the sense that they immediately convey a notion of the amount of some property that the individual possesses or manifests. Finally, we saw that the comparability of scores on different scales poses a number of problems. We also saw that if we use the distribution of scores earned by a representative group of individuals on the variables in which we are interested, most of these problems are given some resolution. Using distributions of scores as frames of reference, or norms, provides a basis for giving scores meaning and for making statements about the comparability of scores on different variables.

In this chapter we consider percentile ranks and various kinds of standard scores as ways of referencing scores directly to a distribution. Since the members of some desired population may not be available in establishing norms, we present a procedure for estimating the distribution of scores on a given test for that population. Finally, we deal with the problem of combining scores from different samples.

### *Percentile Ranks*

In everyday communication one of the common ways of describing both people and things is to state the proportion of other individuals that a particular individual exceeds in the characteristic or quality under consideration. While we may not state the proportion with any degree of exactness, it nevertheless is implicit in our statement. We say, "There are few desserts I like better than strawberry shortcake." That is, we are saying that if we had available a random sample of all sorts of desserts, we would reject the very large bulk of them, perhaps 95 percent, in favor of strawberry shortcake. Similarly we say, "One-round Smith is about as poor a welterweight fighter as they come." We mean that if a representative sample of welterweight prizefighters were matched with Mr. Smith, in our opinion he could beat very few of them, perhaps only 3 or 4 percent. Hence if a person is described as exceeding 99 percent of other people in height, we immediately know that he or she is tall; if an individual is described as exceeding 50 percent in leadership, we know that the person is average in this trait; and if he or she is described as exceeding only 3 percent in knowledge of chemistry, we know that the individual really doesn't know very much chemistry. Statements of the percentages of persons exceeded, then, are a familiar means of quantitative description and are immediately meaningful.

### Describing Percentile Ranks and Percentiles

The *percentile rank* of a score is the percentage of persons in the reference group who earn lower scores. Therefore if an individual earns a raw score of 217 on a given test and his or her score is superior to the scores earned by 70 percent of the persons in the norming group, it is said that his or her percentile rank is 70. The raw score of 217, then, is the 70th percentile.

Recall that when we are dealing with a continuous scale (percentile ranks are most useful with continuous scales or multistep scales with several steps), a score represents a region or an interval of the scale rather than a point on it. Consequently, by convention we say that the score of 217 occupies the interval of 216.5 to 217.5 and we assume that individuals who obtain the score of 217 are distributed equally throughout this interval. More correctly, then, we should say that the raw score of 216.5 is the 70th percentile.

### Computing Percentile Ranks

In developing percentile ranks, we simply determine the percentage of cases falling below the lower limit of each raw-score interval. Table 4-1 illustrates the computational process. One person or 0.7 percent of the

*Table 4-1*   Computation of percentiles and percentile ranks
(total number of cases = 150)

| Raw Score | Lower Limit of Raw-Score Interval | Frequency | Number of Cases Earning Lower Scores | Percentile Rank |
|---|---|---|---|---|
| 71 | 70.5 | 0 | 150 | 100.0 |
| 70 | 69.5 | 1 | 149 | 99.3 |
| 69 | 68.5 | 3 | 146 | 97.3 |
| 68 | 67.5 | 10 | 136 | 90.7 |
| 67 | 66.5 | 14 | 122 | 81.3 |
| 66 | 65.5 | 10 | 112 | 74.7 |
| 65 | 64.5 | 20 | 92 | 61.3 |
| 64 | 63.5 | 15 | 77 | 51.3 |
| 63 | 62.5 | 25 | 52 | 34.7 |
| 62 | 61.5 | 23 | 29 | 19.3 |
| 61 | 60.5 | 6 | 23 | 15.3 |
| 60 | 59.5 | 12 | 11 | 7.3 |
| 59 | 58.5 | 6 | 5 | 3.3 |
| 58 | 57.5 | 4 | 1 | 0.7 |
| 57 | 56.5 | 1 | 0 | 0.0 |
| 56 | 55.5 | 0 | 0 | 0.0 |

cases (1/150 = 0.007 or 0.7 percent) earns scores less than 57.5, five
people or 3.3 percent of the cases (5/150 = 0.033 or 3.3 percent) earn
scores less than 58.5, and so on. To obtain the percentile rank of an
actual score, we have to interpolate between the percentile ranks of its
lower and upper limits. For example, the percentile ranks of the lower
and upper limits of a raw score of 60 (59.5 and 60.5) are 7.3 and 15.3.
Now assuming as we have that individuals who earn a score of 60 are
actually distributed equally throughout this interval and recalling that
the score is taken to be in the middle of the interval, half the distance
above the lower limit, we can calculate the percentile rank of the score
of 60 as follows:

$$7.3 + 0.5(15.3 - 7.3) = 11.3$$

We should therefore say that 11.3 percent of the cases fall below a raw
score of 60 and that an individual who earns a score of 60 has the
percentile rank of 11.3.

A similar interpolation must be made to obtain the percentiles corresponding to the midpoints of all the other score intervals. For example,
a score of 70 is at the midpoint of the interval 69.5 to 70.5, and the
percentile corresponding to this midpoint is halfway between 100.0 and

99.3, or 99.65. The percentiles for all the scores (that is, the midpoints) are given in the last column of Table 4-1. The important thing to re-member is that we are after the percentile score corresponding to a specific raw score, which is in turn viewed as the midpoint of a particu-lar score interval. The percentage of cases falling below an interval boundary (that is, the last column of Table 4-1) is not a percentile score itself; it is a necessary computation on the road to computing the actual percentiles.

### Finding Scores for Specific Percentiles

It is also important that we not confuse the task of finding the percentile corresponding to a specific score with the converse. That is, we might want to go the other way and find the score corresponding to a specific percentile. For example, a frequent question is: What point on the score continuum corresponds to the 50th percentile on the percentile continuum? Keep in mind that in the previous section we went from scores to percentiles. Now we want to go from percentiles to scores.

Suppose we try to find the score at the 50th percentile for the data shown in Table 4-1. In the last column we see that 34.7 percent of the cases fall below a score of 62.5. Also we note that 51.3 percent of the cases fall below a score of 63.5. This says that a score corresponding to the 50th percentile is somewhere between 62.5 and 63.5 and it's a lot closer to 63.5 than to 62.5. How close? Again we have to interpolate. This particular score interval contains 51.3 to 34.7 percent or 16.6 percent of the cases (51.3 minus 34.7 equals 16.6). However, to reach the 50th percentile, we need 50.0 to 34.7 percent or 15.3 percent of the cases in that interval (50.0 minus 34.7 equals 15.3). Thus we must travel 15.3 ÷ 16.6 or .92 of the way up the interval. Since the score interval itself is 63.5 to 62.5 or 1.0 units wide, the score corresponding to the 50th percentile is equal to 62.5 + .92 × 1.0 or 63.42. Thus the 50th percentile in this distribution is a score of 63.42. A similar procedure would be followed to find the score corresponding to any other percen-tile.

### Describing Units in Percentile Ranks

When raw scores are transmuted into percentile ranks, the units within a test and between tests are made comparable—at least after a fashion. The units are expressed not in terms of equal amounts of some psycho-logical trait but rather in terms of numbers of people. We are dealing with frequencies rather than with a scale of measurement. As a consequence, it cannot be said that differences between percentile ranks can be used to indicate amounts or degrees of differences in traits.

Suppose the percentile ranks of three individuals *A, B,* and *C* on a particular test are 70, 60, and 50, respectively. While it is apparent that *A* is superior to *B* and *B* is superior to *C,* we cannot say that the difference between *A* and *B* in the property being measured is the same in magnitude as the difference between *B* and *C.* What we can say is that the number of persons by which *A* exceeds *B* is the same as the number by which *B* exceeds *C.*

As another example, suppose that the percentile ranks of one person on three different tests *X, Y,* and *Z* are 70, 60, and 50, respectively. We can say that compared with other people this person is better on *X* than on *Y* and better on *Y* than on *Z.* But we cannot say that the difference between this person's abilities as measured by tests *X* and *Y* is the same as the difference between his or her abilities as measured by tests *Y* and *Z.* Again what we must talk about are the differences in numbers of persons exceeded.

### *Characteristics of Percentile-Rank Distribution*

The frequency distribution of percentile ranks earned by the group on which they are determined necessarily is rectangular in shape. That is, 10 percent of the cases fall below the percentile rank of 10, another 10 percent fall between that rank and the percentile rank of 20, and so on. Therefore all distributions of percentile ranks have the same shape and hence the same averages and variabilities. The use of percentile ranks forces scores into a particular shape of distribution—rectangular (see Figure 4-1); hence implicitly the shape of the distribution of raw scores is discarded and is considered to be unimportant.

## *Standard Scores*

In Chapter 3 we saw that it is possible to describe mathematically certain characteristics of a frequency distribution in terms of the average of and variation among the scores. Since we wish to reference an individual's raw score to the total distribution of scores, we should be able to accomplish this mathematically by taking into account the mean and standard deviation of the total distribution. This is in fact accomplished by means of *standard scores.*

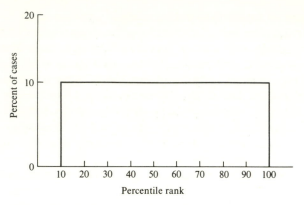

**Figure 4-1**    Rectangular distribution.

### Describing Standard Scores

We can obtain some notion about an individual's standing on a given test if we know whether his or her score exceeds or falls below the mean score of his or her particular group and the magnitude of the difference. However, the information given by this difference alone is limited. If the scores of other individuals in general do not differ much from the mean, then a given difference might be considered quite large; whereas if the scores of others in general differ greatly from the mean, then that difference would be considered to be relatively small.

The standard deviation provides a quantitative description of the extent to which the scores earned by a group of individuals cluster around the mean value or depart from it. Therefore we can use it as an index of the extent of variation among scores. Knowing the difference between an individual's score and the mean, together with the direction of the difference, we can make statements about the relative value of the score by comparing the difference, which is the deviation score, with the standard deviation. We can then say that relative to other scores this particular score tends to be high or low, and we can at the same time give some information about where in the distribution the score falls.

A *standard score,* symbolized by z, is computed by the formula

$$z = \frac{X - \bar{X}}{\sigma_x} = \frac{x}{\sigma_x} \qquad (4\text{-}1)$$

From this formula we can see that a standard score expresses an individual's score in units that are given as standard deviations of the distribution of scores of his or her group.

### Characteristics of Standard-Score Distribution

When each of the raw scores in a distribution is transformed to a standard score, the mean of the distribution of standard scores, $\bar{z}$, necessarily is zero, and the variance, $\sigma_z^2$, and the standard deviation are 1.00. These propositions are easily demonstrated as follows:

$$\bar{z} = \frac{\Sigma z}{n} = \frac{\Sigma(x/\sigma_x)}{n} = \frac{(1/\sigma_x)\Sigma x}{n} = \frac{1}{\sigma_x}\frac{\Sigma x}{n}$$

Since the deviation scores in a distribution always sum to zero, we know that $\Sigma x/n = 0$. Therefore

$$\bar{z} = \frac{1}{\sigma_x} 0 = 0 \tag{4-2}$$

The variance of standard scores is

$$\sigma_z^2 = \frac{\Sigma z^2}{n}$$
$$= \frac{\Sigma(x/\sigma_x)^2}{n} = \frac{\Sigma(x^2/\sigma_x^2)}{n} = \frac{(1/\sigma_x^2)\Sigma x^2}{n} = \frac{1}{\sigma_x^2}\frac{\Sigma x^2}{n}$$

Since $\Sigma x^2/n = \sigma_x^2$, we can write

$$\sigma_z^2 = \frac{1}{\sigma_x^2} \sigma_x^2 = 1 \tag{4-3}$$

Since the standard deviation is the square root of the variance and the variance of standard scores is 1, the standard deviation of standard scores also is 1. In view of the fact that the mean of standard scores is zero, they are, of course, deviation scores. Indeed, we can think of standard scores as being deviation scores that have a standard deviation of 1.

The transformation of raw scores into standard scores does not change the shape of the distribution of scores. This is obvious from the formula for standard scores, Equation 4-1, which clearly indicates that all is done is to subtract one constant (the mean) and divide by another constant (the standard deviation). Every score is treated in exactly the same manner, and therefore the relationship between raw and standard scores is linear and, of course, perfect. This is readily observable in Figure 4-2, which shows both raw and standard scores for three distributions.

If we use standard scores, we are presuming that the particular shape

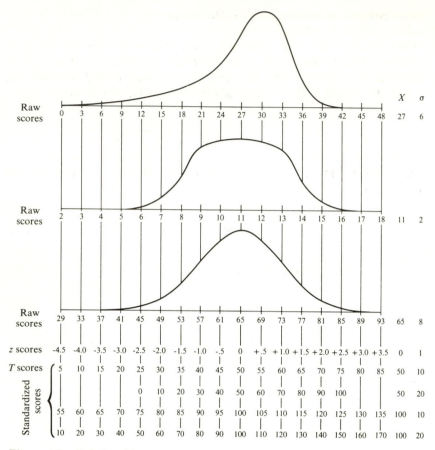

*Figure 4-2*   Relationships among raw, standard, and standardized scores for three frequency distributions.

of the distribution of raw scores given by the test is important inasmuch as it is retained. With some tests the distribution of scores may be positively skewed, and with others it may be negatively skewed; and with some the kurtosis may be positive, and with others it may be negative. This means that we should be forced to conclude that in some traits there are many persons who stand high while in others there are few. While this might not be an unreasonable state of affairs to expect, nevertheless the situation is confusing since tests that apparently measure the same abilities or traits sometimes show quite different-shaped distributions of scores even when administered to the same group of subjects. Furthermore, removing or adding easy or difficult items in a test will result in a significant shift in the shape of the distribution of scores earned by one group of individuals.

The transformation of raw scores into standard scores necessarily assumes that the units of measurement as given by the raw scores are all equal. This is obvious since all that is done, as we indicated above, is to subtract one constant from each score and to divide by another.

### Standardizing Scores with Specified Means and Standard Deviations

A difficulty with standard scores, though perhaps a minor one, lies in the fact that they are given in both positive and negative values, and as fractional numbers. These characteristics make them somewhat difficult to deal with arithmetically and lead to computational errors.

To overcome the arithmetical difficulties involved in standard scores, sometimes transformations are made using values other than zero for the mean and 1.00 for the standard deviation. The mean can be set at any convenient value such as 50 or 100, and the standard deviation at 10 or 20. One form of *standardized score* is symbolized as $T$, and has a mean of 50 and a standard deviation of 10. In Figure 4-2, $T$ scores are shown as the first row of standardized scores. The three remaining rows have transformations with different means and standard deviations. One type of standardized score, not represented in Figure 4-2, is based on a mean of 500 and a standard deviation of 100. This form of standardized score is usually used in tests for admission to undergraduate or graduate schools (for example, the Graduate Record Exam). The essential point is that we can transform any set of distributions to be comparable; we do this by transforming the obtained raw-score distribution to a distribution with a specified mean and standard deviation.

The formula for the frequently used standardized $T$ score is

$$T = \frac{10}{\sigma} X + \left( 50 - \frac{10\bar{X}}{\sigma} \right) \qquad (4\text{-}4)$$

Essentially, what we are doing is multiplying the $z$ score by 10 and then adding 50. For example, as shown in Figure 4-2, a raw score of 57 (in the distribution whose $\bar{X} = 65$ and $\sigma = 8$) has a standard $z$ score of $-1.0$. Multiplying the $z$ score by 10 yields $-10$; adding 50 results in a standardized $T$ score of 40. Again, standardized scores retain the same shape as their raw-score distribution. Whatever presuppositions are made with respect to standard $z$ scores also hold for the standardized $T$ scores.

### Uses for Standard or Standardized Scores

Suppose we learn that Jason received the raw scores of 45 on an arithmetic test and 72 on a history test. On the other hand, Cindy, who is in another class, received a 39 on arithmetic and an 80 on history. What kinds of between- or within-person comparisons can be made? Not many, unless we convert to $z$ or $T$ scores. We obtain the $\bar{X}$'s and $\sigma$'s for Jason's two classes and also for Cindy's two classes, and conversions to $T$ scores provide the following: Jason has $T$ scores of 40 and 64 on arithmetic and history, respectively, whereas Cindy has 50 and 51, respectively. The comparisons we can make are as follows: First, Jason is doing better in history than in arithmetic relative to the other students' performance in each of those classes. He is below average in arithmetic but above average in history. Likewise, Cindy is above average, and equal, in her performance in history and arithmetic. Second, compared to other students in Cindy's arithmetic class, she is better in arithmetic than is Jason. The reverse is true for history. None of these comparisons can be made if we *only* have raw scores.

## Normalizing Scores

If for some reason we wish to adopt the normal frequency distribution as a model but find that the operations of measurement yield scores that are distributed in another fashion, then it is necessary to transmute the raw scores to other values that are normally distributed. Remember that a standard score won't do it because that preserves the shape of the original distribution of raw scores, and percentile scores create a rectangular distribution. A number of techniques have been developed for normalizing a set of scores, but we discuss only the most popular one and the one easiest to use.

### Converting Percentiles to Normalized Standard Scores

We have said that the normal distribution is a theoretical distribution that has been defined to be a certain shape. By definition its properties are precisely known. One important characteristic that is known is the area under the curve between any two points on the horizontal score continuum. It has been most convenient to define the total area under the curve as being equal to 1.0 and to represent the score continuum in standard-score terms with the mean zero and a standard deviation of 1. Thus the area under the curve between any two standard scores is in the form of a two-decimal number; that is, a proportion. It is also true that the area between any two points (or above one point or below one point) corresponds to the number of people falling between those two points. Equating the total area under the curve to 1.0 makes the area between any two points equal to the proportion of people scoring between those two points. Likewise the area of the curve that is below a particular point on the score continuum corresponds to the proportion of people falling below that point.

Now, if we know an individual's percentile score, we know the percentage of the group that falls below his or her raw score. It should be a simple matter to then use the normal curve to find the normalized standard score below which the same number of observations fall. By definition, in a normal distribution a certain percentile score must correspond to a specific normalized standard score. Therefore, if we first transform raw scores to percentile scores, and then use the normal curve to transform the percentile scores to standard-deviation units along the base line of the normal curve, the resulting standard scores should be distributed normally.

The table in Appendix A makes it easy. For example, if an individual scores at the 63rd percentile, we find this value in the first column (a) of the table. It says that this percentile corresponds to a normalized standard score (column b) of $+.33$, which means the individual is approximately one-third of a standard deviation above the mean of a normal distribution. To normalize all the scores in the distribution, we would make the same transformation for each person.

### Sampling and Normalizing

Obviously the normalizing of scores is done on a sample of individuals. Usually we wish to apply the transmuted scores to other individuals not in the particular sample. Thus we apply our measuring device to a sample of individuals, and on the basis of their raw scores set up the function that normalizes the scores. This establishes our norms, and we proceed to apply these norms to individuals tested on other occasions or in other situations.

The adequacy of such normalized and standardized scores clearly is a direct function of the representativeness of the sample and of the number of cases in it. This dependence on sampling is, of course, not peculiar to this particular type of norm. It is more likely to be forgotten, however, because we have used a theoretical model as a basis for transmuting scores, which suggests quite incorrectly that the raw scores have now somehow been made absolute and true.

## Combining Scores from Different Samples

Occasionally a measuring device has been administered to a number of different samples all drawn from the same population, and it is desired to combine the scores of all cases into a single distribution. When this situation arises, either of two conditions may hold:

1. All groups are measured under the same conditions with exactly the same measuring device.
2. Different groups are measured under different conditions and/or with different forms of the measuring device.

### Measuring Under Same Conditions

When a number of groups of individuals are measured separately but under the same conditions and with the same measuring device, we are likely to find that the means and standard deviations of the scores of the various groups differ. If there is reason to suppose that the various samples were drawn in a truly random fashion, then it can be held that differences in the distributions of scores are merely chance variations. Therefore we should be justified in throwing all scores into a common distribution.

For example, we might administer a particular reading test to the sixth-grade children in each of 10 different schools. The same test is administered to all groups, and the same instructions and testing conditions are used throughout. Nevertheless, we may find differences among the groups in the means and standard deviations of their scores and in the shapes of the distributions of their scores. If the schools are representative of the schools in the particular area, then we should expect the total group of sixth-grade children whom we have tested to be representative of the population of sixth-grade children in that area. Differences among groups in terms of their scores, then, would be ignored, and all scores would be combined into the same distribution.

### Measuring Under Different Conditions

Under these circumstances we are likely to find differences among the means and standard deviations of the scores of the various groups and differences in the shapes of the distributions of scores. However, in this case we do not think we can account for the differences on the basis of sampling error. Rather, it appears to us that these differences arise out of differences in conditions or in measuring devices.

Some examples will clarify the problem. Suppose we administer a typing test to 50 typists who use brand *A* typewriter and the same test to 50 other typists who use brand *B* typewriter. Any differences in scores that occur between these groups might well be the result of using different types of machines, that is, being tested under different conditions. If for each group we transform the scores to standard or standardized scores, we equalize their means and standard deviations and hence differences in measured performance due to differences in testing conditions. Similarly, suppose two elementary school teachers rate the students in their classes in emotional adjustment. Differences between ratings assigned the two groups may occur not because the groups differ in degree of emotional adjustment but because one rater is more lenient in assigning ratings than is the other. By transmuting each set of ratings separately to standard scores, we eliminate the differences due to using different forms of the same measuring device, that is, two different raters.

The combination of scores of groups tested under different conditions or with different forms of the same measuring device is illustrated in Table 4-2. If the distributions of scores of the different groups vary in shape, they too may be made the same by normalizing the scores within each group.

In essence, what is being suggested is that differences in means and standard deviations of the scores of the various groups be eliminated through the use of standard or standardized scores, and differences in the shapes of the distributions of scores eliminated through normalizing procedures. The following assumptions therefore are being made:

1. There are no differences among the scores of the various groups that can be accounted for on the basis of sampling error, and the true distribution of the trait being measured is exactly the same in all groups. That is, if the same measuring device were administered to all groups and under exactly the same conditions, the distributions of scores of all groups would be exactly the same.

2. There is a perfect correlation between measurements taken under different conditions or with different forms of the measuring device. That is, if there were several groups tested under different conditions or with different forms of the measuring device, an individual would have the same standing in any group with which he or she was tested, regardless of the group.

Neither of these assumptions is ever completely valid. Different forms of a test never do measure quite the same properties, different conditions of testing introduce different factors that affect performance,

**Table 4-2** Method of combining scores of groups tested under different conditions or with different forms of same test by transmuting scores of each group to standard scores

### Transmutation of Scores

| X | Group A | | Group B | | Group C | |
|---|---|---|---|---|---|---|
| | $f$ | $z$ | $f$ | $z$ | $f$ | $z$ |
| 27 | 1 | +1.90 | 1 | +1.91 | 1 | +2.29 |
| 26 | 2 | +1.26 | 1 | +1.48 | 0 | +1.98 |
| 25 | 3 | +0.63 | 2 | +1.06 | 1 | +1.68 |
| 24 | 4 | 0.00 | 2 | +0.64 | 1 | +1.37 |
| 23 | 3 | −0.63 | 3 | +0.21 | 2 | +1.37 |
| 22 | 2 | −1.26 | 3 | −0.21 | 3 | +1.07 |
| 21 | 1 | −1.90 | 2 | −0.64 | 3 | +0.70 |
| 20 | | | 2 | −1.06 | 4 | +0.46 |
| 19 | | | 1 | −1.48 | 4 | +0.15 |
| 18 | | | 1 | −1.91 | 3 | −0.15 |
| 17 | | | | | 3 | −0.46 |
| 16 | | | | | 3 | −0.70 |
| 15 | | | | | 2 | −1.07 |
| 14 | | | | | 1 | −1.37 |
| 13 | | | | | 1 | −1.68 |
| 12 | | | | | 0 | −1.98 |
| 11 | | | | | 1 | −2.29 |
| $n$ | 16 | | 18 | | 30 | |
| $\bar{X}$ | 24.00 | | 21.50 | | 18.50 | |
| $\sigma_X$ | 1.58 | | 2.36 | | 3.28 | |

### Distribution of Standard Scores

| $z$ | Group A | Group B | Group C | Total |
|---|---|---|---|---|
| +2.25 to +2.74 | 0 | 0 | 1 | 1 |
| +1.75 to +2.24 | 1 | 1 | 0 | 2 |
| +1.25 to +1.74 | 2 | 1 | 2 | 5 |
| +0.75 to +1.24 | 0 | 2 | 2 | 4 |
| +0.25 to +0.74 | 3 | 2 | 6 | 11 |
| −0.24 to +0.24 | 4 | 6 | 8 | 18 |
| −0.25 to −0.74 | 3 | 2 | 6 | 11 |
| −0.75 to −1.24 | 0 | 2 | 2 | 4 |
| −1.25 to −1.74 | 2 | 1 | 2 | 5 |
| −1.75 to −2.24 | 1 | 1 | 0 | 2 |
| −2.25 to −2.74 | 0 | 0 | 1 | 1 |
| $n$ | 16 | 18 | 30 | 64 |
| $\bar{z}$ | 0.00 | 0.00 | 0.00 | 0.00 |
| $\sigma_z$ | 1.00 | 1.00 | 1.00 | 1.00 |

and variations in sampling are always with us. Therefore transmuting the scores of all groups to standard or standardized scores actually introduces an error. However, as we have seen, in some cases it also reduces error. Consequently it is a matter of judgment, or perhaps faith, whether the errors introduced by this procedure are greater or lesser than those that are eliminated.

### Combining Scores When Groups Differ

Sometimes it may be the case that we have obtained data from several groups that really differ in terms of the mean and/or standard deviation of the characteristic being measured. Suppose we are measuring heights of school children and we take a random sample from each school in the city. For various reasons it may very well be that the average height of students from the various schools is actually different. The observed differences among the means of our sample are not due to sampling error and are not due to the fact that some schools measure height with a ruler that has 11 inches per foot and some do not. They are real; each school is drawing students from genuinely different subgroups.

Under these conditions it would *not* be proper to standardize scores within each sample and then combine the standard scores from each group. This kind of transformation would wipe out real differences. However, suppose we still wanted to get a total distribution for city school children in general. *If* the combined groups could be considered a representative sample of city school children, as it would be if the sample sizes were proportional to the total school size, then we would do the following. The *raw scores* of all the samples would be combined, and the standard-score transformation would be carried out on the total group. The differences among subgroups would then still be represented in the total distribution.

To sum up, if we believe that the differences between groups is due to some kind of systematic difference in the measuring instrument (not in the people), then scores should be standardized within each subgroup and the standard scores combined into one distribution. If the differences between groups are due to sampling error or to real differences in the characteristic being measured, then the raw scores should be combined first and the standard scores computed on the total sample. Keep in mind that if we go the latter route and one of the schools did use a ruler with one less inch per foot, the differences due to the bogus ruler would be ground in as real differences in height.

## *Summary*

In this chapter we considered ways for standardizing scores, that is, referencing them to a distribution of scores. Standardizing scores involves transmuting raw scores to other values that are more meaningful and that, at least after a fashion, make scores on different variables comparable.

One way of referencing a score to a distribution of scores is to determine the percentage of individuals who have lower scores than that one. Such a percentage, termed a percentile rank, is meaningful because it immediately tells how an individual stands relative to other individuals. Percentile ranks on different variables are comparable in the sense that they indicate those traits in which the individual stands high relative to other individuals, and those in which the individual stands low.

A second way of referencing an individual's score to a distribution of scores is to divide that person's deviation score by the standard deviation of the distribution. These transmuted values, termed standard scores, have a mean of 0 and a standard deviation of 1. Consequently, when standard scores are used, all distributions have the same mean and standard deviation. Since standard scores are expressed in terms of the mean and standard deviation of the distribution, they tell where an individual falls in it. In this sense they are meaningful and are comparable from one variable to another.

Standard scores are difficult to deal with arithmetically because they are given in positive and negative values, and as fractional numbers. For convenience, sometimes raw scores are transmuted to values that have a mean other than 0 and a standard deviation other than 1. For example, standardizing scores with a mean of 50 or 100 and a standard deviation of 10 or 20 gives scores all of which are positive and whole numbers.

If the normal frequency distribution is adopted as a model, then scores that are distributed in a different fashion may be transmuted to other values that are distributed normally. One way of accomplishing this is to find some function of the raw scores, such as their square root or logarithm, that does give a normal distribution. In most instances this is not a useful method because it is difficult to find the exact function. A more direct and popular way is to first transform raw scores to percentile ranks. The table of the normal distributions can then be used to transform the percentile ranks to normalized standard scores.

Occasionally we wish to establish norms on a test when different groups have been tested under somewhat different conditions or with different forms of the test. If it is assumed that there are no differences among the groups in the trait being measured, and that there is a perfect correlation between measurements taken under the different conditions or with different forms of the test, then standard scores can be determined for each group separately and all scores can be combined in the same distribution.

---

## Suggested Readings

Anastasi, A. 1976. *Psychological testing.* 4th ed. New York, Macmillan. Chap. 4.

McNemar, Q. 1969. *Psychological statistics.* 4th ed. New York: Wiley. Chap. 4.

# 5

# *Concept of Correlation*

In the previous chapters, especially Chapters 3 and 4, we briefly discussed basic principles, concepts, and approaches for analyzing and describing univariate data. Specifically, we discussed measures of central tendency and measures of variability, all of which can be used to describe and summarize data applicable to a single variable. In this chapter, we are concerned with correlation, which is a statistical concept used to describe the relationship between two variables. Just as there were alternative measures of central tendency and variability, each with its own advantages and disadvantages, there are alternative measures of correlations. Here, too, the various indices of correlation have their distinct advantages and disadvantages. Since we are concerned with the relationship between *two* variables, problems arise because the variables may not be measured in the same units or along the same scale; or the variability in one variable may be more or less than the variability in the second variable; or the relationship may not be simple, such as a linear one, but may be curvilinear. As a consequence of these problems, we have developed several indices of correlation. For example, a measure that takes into account the *proportion of accountable variation* in one variable by another is an index of correlation. However, we may obtain a different value of the correlation if we look at how much of $X$ variability is accounted for or explained by $Y$ variability than if we were concerned with how much of $Y$ variability was accounted for by $X$ variability. Or we can use the *trend of a line* passing through the points of a scatterplot depicting all pairs of data as an index of correlation. However, if one variable is measured in terms of pounds, the index of association between this variable and a second variable resulting from examining the trend will differ from the index assessing the same data, but in this case the first variable is measured in terms of ounces. As you will see, however, there is a generalized measure of linear association, the *Pearsonian correlation coefficient*. An essential point in this chapter, though, is that an understanding and appreciation of correlational concepts and statistics requires nothing more complex than an understanding of the basic statistics of means and variations.

Inasmuch as many of the problems in psychological measurement involve the degree to which scores on different variables are related, correlation is a concept of utmost importance. When we speak of correlation, we are referring to the extent to which scores on one variable go hand in hand with scores on another. In other words, we are referring to the extent to which the order of individuals on one variable is similar to the order on another variable, or the extent to which an individual has the same standing on two variables. By *order,* we generally mean the way the same individuals are ranked on two variables. If the rank order for one variable (for example, from highest to lowest scores) is similar to the rank order for a second variable, then there is good correlation between those two variables for that specific group of persons.

Essentially there are two general types of problems for which we need a quantitative description of the relationship that exists between scores on two variables. One is the accuracy with which scores on one variable can be predicted from scores on another. The second is the extent to which individual differences in two variables can be attributed to the same determining factors. In the first case we are concerned with *predicting* or forecasting one kind of behavior from another. In the second case we are seeking some *understanding* of the factors that determine the differences among individuals in their behavior. This permits us the opportunity to better understand the concepts, constructs, or variables with which psychologists are concerned.

Ordinarily the first of these problems arises from practical considerations. For example, we might be interested in knowing the accuracy with which we can predict or forecast the success of individuals on the job of machinist, knowing the scores they earn on a test of spatial visualization. If scores on the test are highly related to measures of success on the job of machinist, then knowing the score an individual earns on the test enables us to predict with reasonable accuracy how good a machinist he or she will turn out to be. We might also wish to know whether our predictions from scores on the test of spatial visualization are better or poorer than those we might make from scores on a test of finger dexterity. If scores on the test of spatial visualization are more highly related to measures of job success than are scores on the test of finger dexterity, then it is clear that if we use the first rather than the second test, our predictions will be more accurate.

The second problem usually arises from theoretical considerations. For example, we might ask whether it is reasonable to postulate a general trait of manual dexterity. To answer this question, we could administer to a group of individuals several different tests that by their very nature would seem to measure this trait. That is, all sets of operations seem to follow equally well from the definition of the trait. We might use tests that involve quickly and accurately placing small pegs into holes, twisting knobs to designated positions, packing blocks into a box, and twisting nuts onto bolts. If scores on all these tests are highly related so that the order of individuals on any one is very similar to the order on all the others, then it would appear that very nearly the same abilities and traits account for individual differences on all of them. We might label these hypothetical common abilities and traits "manual dexterity." Suppose in addition we find that scores on these tests are completely unrelated to scores on other tests that by their very nature seem to measure quite different traits, such as tests of reasoning, spatial visualization, and mechanical information. We would feel more certain about the nature of our hypothesized trait of manual dexterity because it is clear that our tests are measuring a restricted domain of abilities and not some set of completely dissimilar abilities.

Both of these types of problems require knowledge about the extent of relationships among abilities. In the first case, descriptions of the degree of relationships among variables indicate the accuracy with which we can predict scores on one from scores on another. In the second case, descriptions of the degree of relationships among variables give us some notion of the extent to which scores on them are determined by the same factors, thus permitting us to draw inferences about the nature of the psychological traits that underlie individual differences.

It is therefore apparent that we need some way to describe the degree of relationship between variables. In this chapter we consider the theoretical and practical foundations for measuring degrees of relationship, as well as developing the commonly used index of relationship, a statistic known as the Pearsonian correlation coefficient. Chapter 6 is specifically concerned with how the index of relationship is used in problems of predicting one variable from another. Parts of this chapter, as well as parts of Chapter 10 pertaining to validity, deal with correlation as a means for understanding variables.

On first consideration of the problem it might seem to be a fairly simple matter to develop an index or coefficient that gives a quantitative description of the degree of relationship between two variables, and in a certain sense this is true. Nevertheless, for such an index to give us the precision of description we frequently need, and especially to be of such a character as to permit us to draw the inferences we wish to draw, we find it necessary to take one or another of certain theoretical positions. These theoretical positions give more meaning to the coefficient of correlation but require the use of hypothetical models that some may be unwilling to accept, holding that these models do not coincide sufficiently with the characteristics of relationships as they actually exist in the real world.

## Types of Relationships Between Variables

To examine the nature of the relationships between two variables, we can plot the scores of each person on those two variables in a chart called a *scatter diagram*. The scatter diagram is used to represent a bivariate or joint frequency distribution. It is the graph for the two-variable case and gives the distribution of scores on two variables simultaneously. Examples of scatter diagrams are given in Figures 5-1 and 5-5. In these figures each point represents the two scores of an individual, one on variable $X$ and the other on variable $Y$. For illustrative purposes, assume that no individual has the same pair of scores as any other individual.

When we examine the ways in which the points arrange themselves in the diagrams shown in Figures 5-1 and 5-5, we can see that there is a variety of different types of relationships that can hold between scores on two variables. The relationship may be linear or nonlinear; it may be high or low or some intermediate degree; and it may be positive or negative.

### Linear and Nonlinear Correlation

In a linear relationship the points in the scatter diagram tend to swarm around a straight line, whereas in a nonlinear relationship they tend to swarm around a curved line. By inspection it appears that a straight line best fits through the points in Figures 5-1a and b. On the other hand, it is obvious that the best-fitting lines through the points in Figures 5-1c and d are curved.

By and large the representations of most relationships found between scores yielded by measures of ability, personality, and performance are

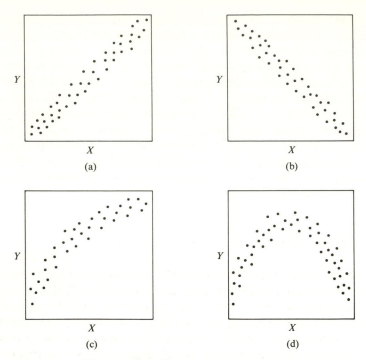

***Figure 5-1***    Linear and nonlinear correlation. (a) Positive linear correlation. (b) Negative linear correlation. (c) Nonlinear correlation. (d) Nonlinear correlation.

linear. Curvilinear relationships, while rarely representing the data better than linear relationships, are worth studying. For example, sometimes the relationship between measures of motivation and performance, such as in problem solving, is curvilinear, as is represented in Figure 5-1c. Those individuals with low levels of motivation ($X$) tend to perform poorly ($Y$). As we move up to persons having higher and higher levels of motivation, we find a tendency for their performance to be better and better. However, the increase in performance is not proportional to the increase in motivation. The difference in performance for high motivation levels is less than the difference in performance for low motivation levels. The curvilinear relationship shown in Figure 5-1d is even less frequently encountered. Such a curvilinear relationship is sometimes found with certain groups of employees when the scores they earn on an intelligence test ($X$) are plotted against the length of time they remain on the job ($Y$). Those who earn either low or high scores on the test tend to stay on the job a shorter time than those who earn average scores.

Because linear correlation is a good representation of the relationship between scores yielded by the very large proportion of devices used in psychological measurement, we consider it in detail. While it cannot be denied that the relationships between some psychological variables are nonlinear, nevertheless with the tests commonly used in the measurement of psychological traits, the relationships among their scores ordinarily are linear or very close to being linear. This does not mean that we should ignore curvilinear relationships. On the contrary, we should determine at the outset of our investigations the form of the relationship. This can be done by plotting all or a sample of data points and then, by "eyeball" analysis, assess whether linear or nonlinear fits are more appropriate.

### Degrees of Correlation

Some human characteristics are associated with each other to a very high degree, others to intermediate degrees, and still others are completely unrelated. If we measured the length of the right and left arms of normal people, we should find a very high degree of relationship between the two sets of measurements. The person with the longest right arm probably would have the longest left arm, the person with the second-longest right arm would have the second-longest left arm, and so on. The height and weight of people obviously are related, but the relationship between these two properties is far from perfect. By and large those people who are tall weigh more than those who are short, and conversely those who are heavy tend to be taller than those who are light in weight. But there are many exceptions to the general tendency so that we are not surprised by the appearance either of Mr. Stringbean, who is very tall but weighs little, or of Mr. Five-by-Five, who is short but weighs a great deal. Finally, if we examined the relationship between grades and the length of the left foot of students in college, we would probably find that on the average those who earn high grades have just the same size foot as those who earn poor grades, and conversely those with large feet earn just the same grades as those with small feet. There is, then, no relationship at all between these two variables.

When the relationship between scores on two tests is high, it means that individual differences in the two traits being measured are determined by very nearly the same factors. That is, whatever factor or construct is given to explain why persons differ on scores of one test can also be used to explain differences in scores on the second test. When the relationship is low, then it means that individual differences in the two traits are determined by quite different factors. Thus, the degree of correlation is one way of beginning our understanding of the variables.

### Positive and Negative Correlation

The direction of the relationship between scores on two variables may be either positive or negative. When a positive relationship exists between two variables, then high scores on one tend to be associated with high scores on the other, and low scores on one with low scores on the other, as shown in Figure 5-1a. With a negative relationship the reverse is true; high scores on one variable are associated with low scores on the other, and low scores on one with high scores on the other, as in Figure 5-1b. The two relationships can be of the same degree but differ in their direction, as do the relationships shown in Figures 5-1a and b. The relationships in Figures 5-1a and 5-1b may be identical, for example, .75, but 5-1a is +.75 and 5-1b is −.75.

## Association Between Variables in Terms of Common Variation

The scores we obtain from the application of a set of operations are the quantitative descriptions we have of the extent to which individuals possess or manifest some trait. When the scores yielded by two different sets of operations are related, it means that the two variables they measure have something in common. That is, differences among individuals in one variable are due to some extent to the same factors that determine differences among them in the other variable. Since, as we pointed out in Chapter 3, measures of variability are used to describe and summarize individuals, we can first approach correlation in terms of common variation. As you will see, correlation can be explained by utilizing the statistics for variation, except now we are concerned with the variation common to two sets of data, or two variables.

Figure 5-2 is a *bivariate distribution,* the joint frequency distribution of scores on two variables. This scatter diagram is represented with a series of columns for the various values of the $X$ variable and a series of rows for the various values of the $Y$ variable. At the bottom of the diagram is given the frequency distribution of scores on $X(fX)$, and to the left the frequency distribution of scores on $Y(fY)$. On variable $X$ three individuals earn a score of 12, five a score of 13, and twelve a score of 14; and on variable $Y$ three earn a score of 84, five a score of 85, and twelve a score of 86. In a scatter diagram these distributions are termed the *marginal distributions*. In each of the cells in the scatter

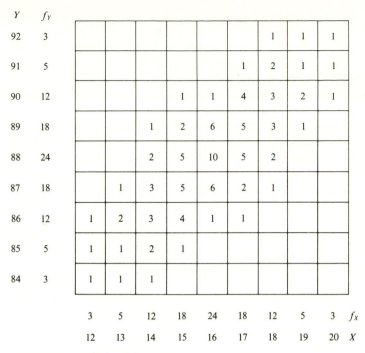

| Y | $f_Y$ | 12 | 13 | 14 | 15 | 16 | 17 | 18 | 19 | 20 |
|---|---|---|---|---|---|---|---|---|---|---|
| 92 | 3 | | | | | | | 1 | 1 | 1 |
| 91 | 5 | | | | | | 1 | 2 | 1 | 1 |
| 90 | 12 | | | | 1 | 1 | 4 | 3 | 2 | 1 |
| 89 | 18 | | | 1 | 2 | 6 | 5 | 3 | 1 | |
| 88 | 24 | | | 2 | 5 | 10 | 5 | 2 | | |
| 87 | 18 | | 1 | 3 | 5 | 6 | 2 | 1 | | |
| 86 | 12 | 1 | 2 | 3 | 4 | 1 | 1 | | | |
| 85 | 5 | 1 | 1 | 2 | 1 | | | | | |
| 84 | 3 | 1 | 1 | 1 | | | | | | |
| $f_X$ | | 3 | 5 | 12 | 18 | 24 | 18 | 12 | 5 | 3 |
| X | | 12 | 13 | 14 | 15 | 16 | 17 | 18 | 19 | 20 |

*Figure 5-2*  Relationship between two variables.

diagram is given the number of individuals earning a particular pair of scores. Thus two individuals earn a score of 14 on $X$ and 85 on $Y$, and five individuals earn a score of 17 on $X$ and 88 on $Y$.

If we take the cases that fall in any given column, that is, those individuals who have the same particular score on $X$, we see that they differ among themselves in their $Y$ scores. Similarly, we find that the cases falling in any given row, that is, those individuals who have the same particular score on $Y$, differ among themselves in their $X$ scores. As we have said, the scores yielded by a set of operations are the quantitative descriptions we have of the extent to which individuals possess or manifest some trait. Therefore we can say of the three cases with the same $X$ score of 20 that for them $X$ is a constant and $Y$ is a variable since they have different $Y$ scores (90, 91, and 92). All three individuals are the same in the degree to which they possess or manifest trait $X$, but differ among themselves in the degree to which they possess or manifest trait $Y$. Similarly, we can say of the twelve cases with $Y$ scores of 86 that for them $Y$ is a constant and $X$ is a variable. All twelve individuals are the same in the degree to which they possess or manifest trait $Y$, but differ among themselves in the degree to which they possess or manifest trait $X$. By sorting individuals according to their $X$ scores into columns, for those in any given column we are holding $X$ constant and are permitting $Y$ to vary; and by sorting them according to their $Y$ scores into rows, for those in any given row we are holding $Y$ constant and are permitting $X$ to vary. Consequently, in each of the columns we have a distribution of scores on the $Y$ variable with the effects of the $X$ variable eliminated, and in each of the rows we have a distribution of the scores on the $X$ variable with the effects of the $Y$ variable eliminated. Eliminating the effects of a variable means that the factors that are influencing differences in one variable, for example, the $X$ variable, are not influencing differences on $Y$ in a specific column, since all individuals in the column have the same $X$ score. The factors influencing differences in $Y$ columns are *other* than those influencing the $X$ variable.

### Effects of Holding Variation Constant in One Variable

We have just seen that when we consider the individuals whose scores fall in any given column or row in a scatter diagram, we have a group of individuals for whom one property is a variable and the other is a constant. That is, in one property the individuals differ among themselves, and in the other they are all the same. Let us now examine the extent of variation in one variable when variation in the other is held constant, in relation to the association between the two variables.

Figure 5-3 gives a scatter diagram that represents the association between the scores of 50 individuals on two variables, $X$ and $Y$. In this figure each pair of scores is represented by solid dots. For simplicity let us just consider variation in $Y$ as a consequence of the relationship between $X$ and $Y$. We shall therefore be dealing with the columns in the scatter diagram, though we could just as well deal with the rows, thereby examining the variation in $X$ as a consequence of the relationship between $X$ and $Y$.

The purpose of examining the scatter diagram in Figure 5-3 is to provide several bits of information. First, we can see that scores on the two variables can be described by a linear representation. Second, we can see that scores on the two variables are positively related. Low scores on the one tend to be associated with low scores on the other, and high scores on the one tend to be associated with high scores on the other. The distribution of $Y$ scores earned by the entire 50 cases is given in the marginal distribution to the right in column $y$. The mean of the raw scores on $Y$ for the entire 50 cases is 20.0. The means of the $Y$ scores of the individuals in each column are given at the foot of the figure in row $\bar{Y}$ and are represented in the scatter diagram by open circles.

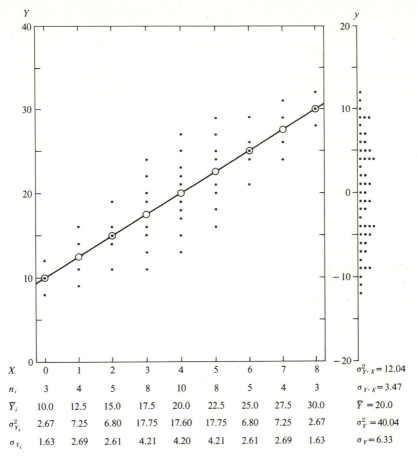

| X | 0 | 1 | 2 | 3 | 4 | 5 | 6 | 7 | 8 | |
|---|---|---|---|---|---|---|---|---|---|---|
| $n_i$ | 3 | 4 | 5 | 8 | 10 | 8 | 5 | 4 | 3 | $\sigma^2_{Y \cdot X} = 12.04$ |
| $\overline{Y}_i$ | 10.0 | 12.5 | 15.0 | 17.5 | 20.0 | 22.5 | 25.0 | 27.5 | 30.0 | $\sigma_{Y \cdot X} = 3.47$ |
| $\sigma^2_{Y_i}$ | 2.67 | 7.25 | 6.80 | 17.75 | 17.60 | 17.75 | 6.80 | 7.25 | 2.67 | $\overline{Y} = 20.0$ |
| $\sigma_{Y_i}$ | 1.63 | 2.69 | 2.61 | 4.21 | 4.20 | 4.21 | 2.61 | 2.69 | 1.63 | $\sigma^2_Y = 40.04$ |
| | | | | | | | | | | $\sigma_Y = 6.33$ |

*Figure 5-3*   Linear correlation wherein means of scores in columns all fall precisely on same straight line.

If we take the cases in any column, we have a distribution of $Y$ scores when $X$ is constant. The variance in the columns can be compared to the total variance of $Y$, which is determined by Equation 3-8 and which is without regard to any $X$ information. The total distribution of $Y$ scores for all individuals regardless of their $X$ scores is represented to the right of the chart in column $y$. This comparison would tell us whether holding $X$ constant has any effect on the range of individual differences in $Y$. In other words, do those individuals who have similar $X$ scores have similar $Y$ scores? If those individuals who have the same $X$ score differ very slightly in $Y$, then we can conclude that there is a relationship. In Figure 5-3, those individuals who have low scores on $X$ also have low scores on $Y$, and those who have high scores on $X$ have high scores on $Y$.

At the foot of Figure 5-3 in row $\sigma_{Y_i}$ are given the standard deviations of the $Y$ scores of the individuals in each column. These values range from 1.63 to 4.21, which may be compared with the standard deviation of the total distribution of $Y$ scores, which is 6.33. Hence we can say that in the case given in Figure 5-3, when we hold $X$ constant by dealing only with individuals all of whom have the same $X$ score, the variation in column $Y$ scores becomes smaller than the total variation in $Y$ scores as a consequence of the relationship between $X$ and $Y$.

If $X$ and $Y$ were completely unrelated, then the extent of variation of $Y$ scores in each of the columns would be the same as the extent of the total variation of $Y$ scores. That is, the $\sigma$ of each column would be equal to 6.33. On the other hand, if $X$ and $Y$ were perfectly correlated, then there would be no variation of $Y$ scores in any of the columns since all individuals in any given column would have precisely the same $Y$ score. That is, the $\sigma$ of each column would be equal to 0.00.

A comparison of the standard deviation of the $Y$ scores in any given column with the standard deviation of the total distribution of scores would tell us directly how much the variation in $Y$ scores is reduced when $X$ is held constant. We are concerned with the reduced variation in $Y$ because a reduction in variation of $Y$ implies a higher percentage of common causal factors and thus more similarity between $X$ and $Y$. Thus, if knowing $X$ means that there is less variation for corresponding $Y$'s, then we have increased our understanding of both $X$ and $Y$. In any event, in row $\sigma_{Y_i}$ of Figure 5-3 we can see that the standard deviations of the $Y$ scores in the various columns differ among themselves and therefore, depending on which column we choose, we would say that holding $X$ constant has a great effect or a small effect. For example, when we consider those individuals who have an $X$ score of 8, we find that the standard deviation of their $Y$ scores is only 1.63; whereas when we consider those cases who have an $X$ score of 5, we find the standard deviation of their $Y$ scores to be 4.21—nearly three times as large.

We should therefore like some way of obtaining a general description of the extent of variation in $Y$ scores when $X$ is held constant, one that describes all columns. When one property, such as $Y$, is variable and another, such as $X$, is held constant in relation to it, the scores are sometimes symbolized as $Y \cdot X$. Hence we symbolize the standard deviation of the total distribution of $Y_i$ scores gathered from all the columns as $\sigma_{Y \cdot X}$. This is termed the *partial standard deviation* since it describes the extent of variation in one variable with the effects of the other held constant or eliminated. Similarly, we should symbolize the standard deviation of the total distribution of $X_i$ or $X \cdot Y$ scores, the variation in the $X$ scores of the rows with $Y$ held constant, as $\sigma_{X \cdot Y}$.

The variance of the total distribution of $Y_i$ or $Y \cdot X$ scores, $\sigma_{Y \cdot X}^2$, is nothing more nor less than the weighted mean of the variances $\sigma_i^2$ of the columns. Recall from Chapter 3 that the mean is the statistic that is used to summarize a distribution. In the present case, we have a distribution of column variances, and because the sample size of each column varies, we calculate the weighted mean of the variances of the columns. If we have $k$ columns, the *partial variance* or weighted mean of the variances is

$$\sigma^2_{Y \cdot X} = \frac{n_i \sigma^2_{Y_i} + \cdots + n_k \sigma^2_{Y_k}}{n} \tag{5-1}$$

For the relationship illustrated in Figure 5-3 the partial variance is 12.04, computed as the weighted mean of the variances of the columns from Equation 5-1 as follows:

$$\sigma^2_{Y \cdot X} = \frac{\begin{array}{c} 3(2.67) + 4(7.25) + 5(6.80) + 8(17.75) + 10(17.60) \\ + \; 8(17.75) + 5(6.80) + 4(7.25) + 3(2.67) \end{array}}{50}$$

$$= \frac{602.02}{50} = 12.04$$

The partial standard deviation is the square root of 12.04, which is 3.47.

Let us now look at another relationship, that between the pairs of scores of another 50 individuals, depicted in Figure 5-4. Again we have a positive relationship between the two variables, since low scores on the one tend to be associated with low scores on the other and high scores on the one with high scores on the other. But whereas the points in the first scatter diagram tended to swarm around a straight line, in this case they tend to swarm around a curved line.

The distribution of the $Y$ scores earned by the entire 50 cases represented in Figure 5-4, given in the marginal distribution to the right in column $y$, has a mean of 17.0. The means of the $Y$ scores of the individuals in each column are given at the foot of the figure in row $\bar{Y}_i$ and are represented in the scatter diagram by open circles.

A comparison of the variation of the $Y$ scores in any column with the total variation in $Y$ again tells us the effects of holding $X$ constant on the variation in $Y$. The standard deviations of the $Y$ scores in each of the columns are given in row $\sigma_{Y_i}$ at the foot of Figure 5-4, and range from 1.63 to 3.57. They are all smaller than the standard deviation of the total distribution of $Y$ scores, which is 9.60. Again we have a case wherein by holding $X$ constant by dealing only with individuals all of whom have the same $X$ score, the variation in $Y$ scores becomes smaller than the total variation in $Y$ scores as a consequence of the relationship between $X$ and $Y$. The partial standard deviation $\sigma_{Y \cdot X}$, computed from Equation 5-1, which gives a summary description for the whole scatter diagram

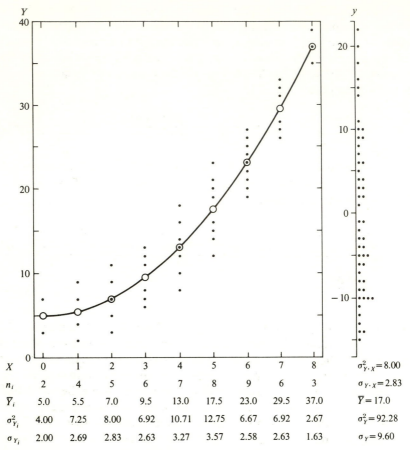

| $X$ | 0 | 1 | 2 | 3 | 4 | 5 | 6 | 7 | 8 | $\sigma^2_{Y \cdot X} = 8.00$ |
|---|---|---|---|---|---|---|---|---|---|---|
| $n_i$ | 2 | 4 | 5 | 6 | 7 | 8 | 9 | 6 | 3 | $\sigma_{Y \cdot X} = 2.83$ |
| $\overline{Y}_i$ | 5.0 | 5.5 | 7.0 | 9.5 | 13.0 | 17.5 | 23.0 | 29.5 | 37.0 | $\overline{Y} = 17.0$ |
| $\sigma^2_{Y_i}$ | 4.00 | 7.25 | 8.00 | 6.92 | 10.71 | 12.75 | 6.67 | 6.92 | 2.67 | $\sigma^2_Y = 92.28$ |
| $\sigma_{Y_i}$ | 2.00 | 2.69 | 2.83 | 2.63 | 3.27 | 3.57 | 2.58 | 2.63 | 1.63 | $\sigma_Y = 9.60$ |

*Figure 5-4*   Nonlinear correlation wherein means of scores in columns all fall precisely on same curved line.

of the variation in the columns, is 2.83, which is substantially smaller than the standard deviation of the total distribution of $Y$ scores, which is 9.60.

In Figure 5-5 are four scatter diagrams illustrating different degrees of relationship. Figure 5-5a shows two variables that are completely unrelated, Figure 5-5d two variables that are highly related, and Figures 5-5b and c pairs of variables related to degrees intermediate between these two extremes. We can see in Figure 5-5a that when there is no relationship at all between $X$ and $Y$, $Y$ scores for individuals all of whom have the same $X$ score are the same as the total variation in $Y$ scores. That is, column variances would be equal to total variance. To more easily grasp this concept as illustrated in Figure 5-5, consider that a crude

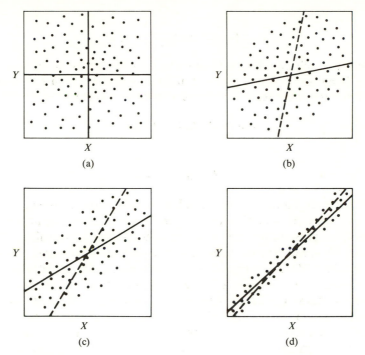

***Figure 5-5***   Various degrees of relationship between two variables.

estimate of variation is the range, or highest score minus the lowest score. Notice that the range of the marginal distribution in Figure 5-5a is about equal to the range of scores for any point on $X$. But as we go to higher and higher degrees of relationship, as in Figures 5-5b to d, relative to the total variation or range in $Y$ scores the variation in $Y$ scores for individuals all of whom have the same $X$ score becomes smaller and smaller. The same state of affairs also holds if we consider the variation in the $X$ scores of those individuals all of whom have the same $Y$ score in comparison with the total variation in $X$ scores.

Hence it is apparent that the higher the degree of relationship between two variables, the less the variation among the scores in the columns and in the rows. When there is no relationship at all between two variables, then the variation among the scores in any column or in any row is equal to the total variation. That is, when there is no relationship between the two variables,

$$\sigma_{Y \cdot X} = \sigma_Y \quad \text{and} \quad \sigma_{X \cdot Y} = \sigma_X$$

or

$$\sigma^2_{Y \cdot X} = \sigma^2_Y \quad \text{and} \quad \sigma^2_{X \cdot Y} = \sigma^2_X$$

When the relationship between the two variables is perfect and linear, then there is no variation at all among the scores in any column or in any row. That is, when the relationship is perfect,

$$\sigma_{Y \cdot X} = 0 \quad \text{and} \quad \sigma_{X \cdot Y} = 0$$

or

$$\sigma^2_{Y \cdot X} = 0 \quad \text{and} \quad \sigma^2_{X \cdot Y} = 0$$

Whatever the factors are that produce the differences among individuals in a variable—be the factors innate or learned characteristics, abilities, or personality traits—we can hold their observable effects constant by selecting individuals all of whom have the same score on that variable. When we eliminate the differences among individuals in their scores on a variable, then, we presume that the effects of the factors that cause the differences also are eliminated. If people were all the same in variable $X$, then the variation among them in variable $Y$ would be described by $\sigma_{Y \cdot X}$ rather than by $\sigma_Y$. Similarly, if people were all the same in variable $Y$, then the variation among them in variable $X$ would be described by $\sigma_{X \cdot Y}$ rather than by $\sigma_X$.

Suppose that, having eliminated the differences among individuals in variable $X$, we also found that we had eliminated all the differences among them in variable $Y$. That is, all those who have the same $X$ score have the same $Y$ score. This would mean that the factors that produce differences among individuals in variable $X$ are precisely and entirely the same factors that produce differences among them in variable $Y$. In this case, of course, the two variables would be perfectly correlated. On the other hand, suppose that, having eliminated all the differences among individuals in variable $X$, we found that the extent of the differences among them in variable $Y$ was not changed at all. This would mean that the factors that produce differences among them in variable $X$ are completely different from the factors that produce differences among them in variable $Y$. In this case the two variables would be completely uncorrelated.

The total variation in a variable, that is, the extent to which individuals differ among themselves in that variable, can be measured either by the variance or by the standard deviation of the total distribution of scores on that variable. The extent of variation, or the extent to which individuals differ among themselves in a variable when the factors that produce the differences among them in a second variable are held constant, is measured by the *partial variance* or the *partial standard deviation* of the first variable.

To summarize:

$\sigma_Y^2$ = extent of total variation among individuals in $Y$

$\sigma_{Y \cdot X}^2$ = extent of variation among individuals in $Y$ remaining after variation among them in $X$ has been eliminated, and factors that produce individual differences in $X$ have been held constant; that is, $\sigma_{Y \cdot X}^2$ is the variation in $Y$ due to factors *other* than those that produce differences among individuals in $X$

Therefore we can say

$\sigma_Y^2 - \sigma_{Y \cdot X}^2$ = extent of variation among individuals in $Y$ due to the *same* factors that produce differences among them in $X$

Let us symbolize this variation as $\sigma_{Y'}^2$ so that

$$\sigma_{Y'}^2 = \sigma_Y^2 - \sigma_{Y \cdot X}^2 \qquad (5\text{-}2)$$

Consequently,

$\dfrac{\sigma_{Y'}^2}{\sigma_Y^2}$ = proportion of total variation among individuals on variable $Y$ that can be accounted for by the same factors that produce differences among them in $X$ when the extent of variation is measured by the variance of scores $\qquad$ (5-3)

If we prefer to measure the variation among individuals by means of the standard deviation of their scores rather than by the variance, as is the common practice, we write Equation 5-3 as

$\dfrac{\sigma_{Y'}}{\sigma_Y}$ = proportion of total variation among individuals on variable $Y$ that can be accounted for by the same factors that produce differences among them in $X$ when the extent of variation is measured by the standard deviation of scores $\quad$ (5-4)

Substituting for $\sigma_{Y'}$ from Equation 5-2 in Equation 5-4 gives

$$\begin{aligned}
\frac{\sigma_{Y'}}{\sigma_Y} &= \frac{\sqrt{\sigma_Y^2 - \sigma_{Y \cdot X}^2}}{\sigma_Y} \\[2mm]
&= \sqrt{\frac{\sigma_Y^2 - \sigma_{Y \cdot X}^2}{\sigma_Y^2}} \\[2mm]
&= \sqrt{\frac{\sigma_Y^2}{\sigma_Y^2} - \frac{\sigma_{Y \cdot X}^2}{\sigma_Y^2}} \\[2mm]
&= \sqrt{1 - \frac{\sigma_{Y \cdot X}^2}{\sigma_Y^2}} \qquad (5\text{-}5)
\end{aligned}$$

By a similar development for variable $X$, we could show

$$\frac{\sigma_{X'}}{\sigma_X} = \sqrt{1 - \frac{\sigma_{X \cdot Y}^2}{\sigma_X^2}} \qquad (5\text{-}6)$$

### Proportion of Accountable Variation as Index of Relationship

We have seen that the magnitudes of $\sigma_{Y \cdot X}^2$ and of $\sigma_{X \cdot Y}^2$ vary with the degree of relationship between $X$ and $Y$. The higher the relationship between the two variables, the smaller are $\sigma_{Y \cdot X}^2$ and $\sigma_{X \cdot Y}^2$. We have also seen that when there is no relationship between $X$ and $Y$,

$$\sigma_{Y \cdot X}^2 = \sigma_Y^2 \quad \text{and} \quad \sigma_{X \cdot Y}^2 = \sigma_X^2$$

and when the relationship between $X$ and $Y$ is perfect and linear,

$$\sigma_{Y \cdot X}^2 = 0 \quad \text{and} \quad \sigma_{X \cdot Y}^2 = 0$$

When there is no relationship between the two variables, then the numerator of the second term in Equations 5-5 and 5-6 equals the denominator, so that the term becomes 1 and the entire formula equals 0.00. When the relationship between the two variables is perfect, then the numerator of the second term in Equations 5-5 and 5-6 is zero, so that the term becomes 0 and the entire formula equals 1.00. For degrees of relationship between these two extremes the formulas would give intermediate values. Therefore the *proportion of accountable variation,* $\sigma_{Y'}/\sigma_Y$ and $\sigma_{X'}/\sigma_X$, provides an index or coefficient indicative of the degree of relationship between two variables.

As an illustration, we can apply Equation 5-5 to the data in Figure 5-3:

$$\frac{\sigma_{Y'}}{\sigma_Y} = \sqrt{1 - \frac{12.04}{40.04}} = \sqrt{1 - 0.30} = \sqrt{0.70} = 0.84$$

We cannot compute the relationship between the two variables from Equation 5-6 because we did not go through the process of computing $\sigma_{X \cdot Y}^2$ and $\sigma_X^2$. Had we computed these values, then we also could have a statement of the relationship between $X$ and $Y$ by comparing the variation in $X$ when $Y$ is constant with the total variation in $X$.

### *Proportion of Accountable Variation as Index of Linear and Nonlinear Relationships*

We developed Equations 5-5 and 5-6 from accountable variation taking the variation in the columns or in the rows as the variation in the scores on one variable when variation in the scores on the other is held constant. In developing Equations 5-5 and 5-6, we imposed no conditions with respect to the nature of the relationship, and therefore they can be used regardless of whether the relationship is linear or nonlinear. Hence they are generalized formulas indicative of the degree of relationship between two variables. The name given to both these parallel formulas is the *correlation ratio*. The correlation ratio is symbolized as $\eta$ (eta), and thus also referred to as the *eta coefficient*. This coefficient is

$$\eta_{Y \cdot X} = \sqrt{1 - \frac{\sigma_{Y \cdot X}^2}{\sigma_Y^2}} \tag{5-7}$$

$$\eta_{X \cdot Y} = \sqrt{1 - \frac{\sigma_{X \cdot Y}^2}{\sigma_X^2}} \tag{5-8}$$

If we apply Equation 5-7 to the data in Figure 5-4, we find for these data, which are related in a curvilinear fashion, that

$$\frac{\sigma_{Y'}}{\sigma_Y} = \eta_{Y \cdot X} = \sqrt{1 - \frac{8.00}{92.28}} = \sqrt{1 - 0.08} = \sqrt{0.92} = 0.96$$

In summary, the correlation ratio is one index of association. It provides an index of the relationship in terms of the variation in one variable accounted for by another variable. The correlation ratio is equally appropriate for linear or nonlinear relationships. This can be viewed as an advantage in that it is a general index of association, or it can be viewed as a disadvantage in that it provides no indication of the extent or lack of linearity. The index also does not indicate whether the relationship, linear or curvilinear, is positive or negative. Finally, $\eta_{Y \cdot X}$ and $\eta_{X \cdot Y}$ will provide two different values for the same data if $\sigma_Y^2 \neq \sigma_X^2$ and/or $\sigma_{Y \cdot X}^2 \neq \sigma_{X \cdot Y}^2$. Because of these "disadvantages" it is necessary to develop alternative indices of association. Keep in mind, though, that the correlation ratio as a general index of association provides useful information, often in a preliminary sense, since it indicates whether it is even worth pursuing the extent of linearity and also direction. However, before proceeding to alternative measures of association, it is necessary to review the concept of homoscedasticity.

### Homoscedasticity as a Model

Common observation indicates that height and weight in human beings are positively correlated, though we recognize that the relationship is by no means perfect. Consequently, if we take people of any given height, we expect, and indeed we find, that the variation among them in weight is smaller than the variation in weight among all individuals regardless of height. By taking people all of whom are the same height we have eliminated the effects of whatever specific combinations of factors that produced differences among them in height at that particular point in time. Equations 5-5 and 5-6 permit us to calculate the extent to which variation among individuals in weight is reduced as a result of holding height constant.

We expect the degree to which the variation among individuals in weight is reduced to be the same regardless of whether we hold height constant by considering only individuals who are 5.5 feet tall or only individuals who are 5.9 feet tall. That is, by taking individuals of any given height, regardless of what that particular height may be, we presume we are holding the same set of factors constant. But suppose we find that for those individuals whose height is 5.5 feet the variation among them in weight is substantially smaller than it is for those individuals whose height is 5.9 feet. Then clearly a very complex situation holds with respect to the factors that determine height and weight. Indeed, these factors would seem to be related in a most intricate fashion. With people who are shorter, there would seem to be a more intimate relationship between height and weight than there is with people who are taller. Whatever the factors that produce differences among individuals in height may be, these factors are of such a nature that when they produce individuals who are short, they also produce individuals who are homogeneous in weight; and when they produce individuals who are tall, they also produce individuals who are quite heterogeneous in weight.

Let us look again at the examples of the relationships given in Figures 5-3 and 5-4. In both these cases we can see that the extent of variation among individuals is not equal. Indeed, there appears to be a systematic relationship between the extent of variation among individuals in their $Y$ scores and their $X$ scores. Those individuals with either low or high $X$ scores tend to differ less among themselves in their $Y$ scores than those whose $X$ scores have an intermediate value.

Complicated relationships such as these are very difficult to understand. If the extent of variation in the $Y$ scores in all columns were precisely the same and the extent of variation in the $X$ scores in all rows were precisely the same, then the situation would be far more comprehensible and interpretable. We can conceive of a set of factors—

nutritional, genetic, or whatever—that determine height. To some extent these factors also determine weight. But when the effects of these factors that produce differences among individuals in height are held constant, then we expect the differences in weight among all individuals—regardless of their particular weight—to be reduced to the same extent.

When the standard deviations of the scores in all the columns are equal to each other and the standard deviations of the scores in all rows also are equal to each other, we say that the relationship is homoscedastic. *Homoscedasticity* is a state of affairs that is much more easily understood and explained than is *heteroscedasticity* (unequal column and row variances) and therefore a state of affairs we wish actually held. The facts of the matter are that in many cases the relationships between scores on psychological variables are very nearly homoscedastic. In many instances the variation among the standard deviations of the scores in the columns and the variation among the standard deviations of the scores in the rows appear to vary from one another in a completely unsystematic fashion and are very similar in magnitude. Because the number of cases in any given column or row ordinarily is small, it seems reasonable to explain the differences as being due to the random effects of sampling error. In the examples of relationships given in Figures 5-3 and 5-4, it will be observed that there are very few cases having either high or low scores on variable $X$ so that we cannot put very much dependence on the extent of their variation in $Y$ scores. Frequently as we increase the number of individuals whose scores enter into the relationship, the condition of homoscedasticity is more and more closely approximated, thus giving support to the notion that the differences among the columns and among the rows in their standard deviations are the result of sampling error.

Finally, with the exception of very rare circumstances, when the scores on the two variables being related are normally distributed, homoscedasticity holds. In this case the distributions of the scores in the columns and in the rows also are very likely to be normally distributed. Hence if we can justify the normalizing of scores, we are very likely to have a relationship that is homoscedastic.

As a consequence we might take homoscedasticity as a model. We should then be saying that the relationships between our variables are homoscedastic—or so nearly homoscedastic that the difference is quite unimportant. Now we can more easily comprehend formulas such as Equations 5-5 and 5-6, and in effect we are saying that the determinants of behavior are simple. Furthermore, we do not have to regard the partial standard deviation as a summary statement or average description of the entire scatter diagram, but rather as a description of the extent of variation among individuals in one variable after the effects of the factors that produce individual differences in another are held constant and eliminated. Homoscedasticity implies a simplicity in the interpretation of behavior, and even though it may not be precisely correct, many are willing to accept it because it does seem to have some justification and at least is comprehensible.

Nevertheless, homoscedasticity does not hold for all relationships. Indeed, there are striking departures from it that cannot easily be explained away as resulting from sampling error or from scales with inadequate or unequal units. If we do not have a homoscedastic relationship or cannot justify acceptance of homoscedasticity as a model, then the partial standard deviation is merely a summary statement of the distributions of scores in the columns and rows and Equations 5-5 and 5-6 also are summary statements. We can draw very few implications from the partial standard deviation and formulas related to it, and we are admitting that the factors determining the relationship between two variables operate in a most complex manner. One attempt to deal with heteroscedastic conditions is to use nonlinear, or configural, or moderated regression analyses (see Chapter 11).

## Indices Describing Nature of Relationship Between Variables

In describing the nature of the relationships that hold between variables, we said of some that the scores tend to swarm around a straight line and of others that they tend to swarm around a curved line. Basic to the theory of correlation and to the development of an index of the degree of relationship is the matter of the nature of the association. In this section we discuss the problem of describing a relationship in terms of a line running through the swarm of points. The basic statistical concept employed in this section will be the mean.

### Describing Relationships

If the relationship between two variables is positive, then low scores on the one tend to be associated with low scores on the other and high scores on the one tend to be associated with high scores on the other. If the relationship is negative, then the trend is in the other direction, with low scores on one variable tending to be associated with high scores on the other. With positive relationships, then, as we proceed from low to high scores on one variable, we find higher and higher scores on the other, and with negative relationships we find just the reverse.

Let us now examine the trend in the relationship shown in Figure 5-3.

For simplicity we shall again deal only with the columns, though we could just as well deal with the rows. In this figure each pair of scores is represented by a solid dot. We can see that scores on the two variables are positively related. As we consider individuals who have higher and higher $X$ scores, we find that on the average they have higher and higher $Y$ scores. To show this, we can calculate the mean of the $Y$ scores for the individuals in each column. The means are given at the foot of the scatter diagram and are represented in the chart by open circles. To show the trend graphically, a line has been drawn through the means of the columns. A line drawn through a scatter diagram to represent the trend of the association is termed a *regression line*. The purpose of discussing a regression line in this chapter is to develop a measure of association and not to discuss the means for predicting one variable from another (which is in Chapter 6).

If we look at the regression line in Figure 5-3, we can see that the trend or the relationship between $X$ and $Y$ is quite regular. Indeed, the regression line is a straight line, and therefore we call the relationship a linear relationship. Linear relationships indicate that similar differences on one variable, for example, the difference between 3 and 4 and the difference between 7 and 8, are associated with equal differences on the second variable. By looking at the $\bar{Y}$ row, we see that the difference between each value is 2.5 units.

A line can be described by an equation. In the case of a straight line when the two variables are $X$ and $Y$, the equation is

$$Y = a_Y + b_{Y \cdot X} X$$

where $a_Y$ and $b_{Y \cdot X}$ are constants; $a_Y$ being the intercept, that value of $Y$ when $X$ is zero, and $b_{Y \cdot X}$ the slope of the line relative to the $X$ axis of the chart, the number of units change in $Y$ for each unit change in $X$. Knowing $a_Y$ and $b_{Y \cdot X}$, if we enter any given value of $X$ in the formula, we can calculate a value of $Y$ such that the pair of values $X$ and $Y$ describe a point falling on the line.

We can also write the equation for a straight line as

$$X = a_X + b_{X \cdot Y} Y$$

where $a_X$, the intercept, is the value of $X$ when $Y$ is zero, and $b_{X \cdot Y}$ is the slope of the line relative to the $Y$ axis. Knowing $a_X$ and $b_{X \cdot Y}$, if we enter any given value of $Y$ in the formula, we can calculate a value of $X$ such that the pair of values $X$ and $Y$ describe a point falling on the line.

Let us look at the relationship represented in Figure 5-3. It is apparent that this is a linear relationship since the points all swarm around a straight line. Furthermore, it can be seen that the means of the $Y$ scores in the columns (represented by circles) all fall precisely on the same straight line. From the equation for this straight line, we can calculate the mean of the $Y$ scores, $\bar{Y}_i$, falling in any given column $X_i$. We write the equation for this straight line as

$$\bar{Y}_i = a_Y + b_{Y \cdot X} X_i \qquad (5\text{-}9)$$

If we were concerned with the regression line drawn through the means of the $X$ scores in the rows, these means also falling precisely on a straight line, the regression equation would be

$$\bar{X}_i = a_X + b_{X \cdot Y} Y_i \qquad (5\text{-}10)$$

When the equation for a line is used to describe the trend of the relationship in a scatter diagram, it is termed a *regression equation,* and in the case of a linear relationship the slope of the line, *b,* is termed a *regression coefficient.* In this chapter, we are mainly concerned with the regression coefficient as an *index of correlation;* in Chapter 6 we will be concerned with the use of the regression equation for prediction.

A comparison of Equations 5-9 and 5-10 indicates that these two equations describe different lines since their intercepts $a_Y$ and $a_X$ and their slopes $b_{Y \cdot X}$ and $b_{X \cdot Y}$ are not necessarily the same. Consequently in every scatter diagram we have two regression lines, one that cuts through the columns and around which the $Y$ scores in the columns cluster and one that cuts through the rows and around which the $X$ scores in the rows cluster.

When a positive relationship exists between two variables, as in Figure 5-1a, then the regression coefficient $b$ is positive, indicating for every unit increase in $X$ the number of units of increase in $Y$. When the relationship is negative, as in Figure 5-1b, then the regression coefficient is negative, indicating for every unit increase in $X$ the number of units of decrease in $Y$.

Now let us look at the relationship shown in Figure 5-4. Again we can see by inspection that the relationship is positive. On the average, low $X$ scores are associated with low $Y$ scores, and high $X$ scores are associated with high $Y$ scores. Furthermore, if we examine the regression line that is drawn through the means of the columns, we see that, as in the previous example, the trend of the association is quite regular. However, in this case the trend does not follow a straight line but rather a curved one, and therefore we call the relationship a curvilinear or nonlinear relationship. This time we can see that for a difference on the $X$ variable of one unit (for example, between 3 and 4), there is a *different* amount of change on $Y$ than there is for another difference on the $X$ variable (for example, between 7 and 8). The first difference on $Y$ is 3.5

units, whereas the second difference on $Y$ is 7.5. Note that the differences in $\bar{Y}_i$ range from 0.5 to 7.5.

As in the previous example, we can set up an equation that describes the regression line and therefore the nature of the relationship between scores on the two variables. There are, of course, a wide variety of different curved lines and an equal number of equations to describe them. The equation for the particular curve shown in Figure 5-4 is

$$\bar{Y}_i = a_Y + b_{Y \cdot X} X_i^2$$

The regression line in this example is a very simple curve, and consequently the regression equation also is very simple. With other curvilinear relationships the regression equation may involve more than just two constants and more functions than just a single square, and the function may be of a more complex nature. Whether the regression line is straight or curved, the nature of the relationship can be described by an equation.

With cases such as the two we have just described, not only is the nature of the relationship simple but also we can give some reasonable explanation of the relationship. For example, in the first case, which is a linear relationship, suppose that scores on an intelligence test are the $X$ variable and grades earned in school are the $Y$ variable. We recognize that school grades depend on the operation of a number of factors, such as reading ability and interest in academic work, and that intelligence is only one of them. Therefore we do not expect a perfect relationship between intelligence and school grades. Nevertheless, as we consider individuals of greater and greater degrees of intelligence, we do expect them to earn better and better grades, with equal increases in intelligence on the average to be associated with equal increases in grades.

In the second case, which is a curvilinear relationship, suppose that athletic prowess of high school students is the $X$ variable and the number of other children in school knowing a student is the $Y$ variable. Again we have a reasonable explanation of the basis of the relationship. We do, of course, recognize the fact that the number of students who know a given student is a function of a variety of factors and that athletic prowess is only one of them. Yet we expect that on the average the more a student participates in school athletics and the more proficiency he or she displays in school sports, the larger is the number of other students who know him or her. Furthermore, we might also expect the student who manifests a very high level of athletic proficiency to be known by a disproportionately greater number of students because he or she has a disproportionately greater opportunity to be seen in action. Therefore, a curvilinear relationship might well be anticipated.

### Regression Coefficient as Index of Linear Relationship

As we have seen, linear correlation is of great importance for problems in psychological measurement. We wish therefore to have some index or coefficient that indicates the degree of relationship between scores on two variables when the relationship between those variables is linear. In Equations 5-7 and 5-8 we developed indices in terms of variation that permit us to describe quantitatively the degree of relationship between two variables. However, these formulas are general ones, and we wish now to consider the quantitative description of relationships that are of a linear sort.

Figure 5-5 shows four different degrees of relationship between variables, with each of the variables having equal variance. In Figure 5-5a the two variables are completely unrelated, and in Figure 5-5d they are very closely related. Figures 5-5b and c represent intermediate degrees of relationship. In each of the four diagrams in Figure 5-5 the two regression lines have been drawn. The solid lines represent the straight lines drawn through the means of the $Y$ scores in the columns, and the dotted lines the straight lines drawn through the $X$ scores of the rows. By inspection we can see that as we proceed from Figure 5-5a through b and c to d, we have higher and higher degrees of relationship between pairs of variables. In our earlier discussion we saw from these diagrams that the higher the degree of relationship between two variables, the smaller the variation among the scores in the columns and in the rows. Now we can also see from these diagrams that the higher the degree of relationship between two variables, the steeper the regression line. The solid lines that are drawn through the means of the columns are referred to their base line $X$, the abscissa; and the dotted lines that are drawn through the means of the rows are referred to their base line $Y$, the ordinate.

The *slope* of the regression line, then, reflects the degree of relationship that holds between two variables; that is, the steeper the line, the higher the degree of relationship. In our presentation of Equations 5-9 and 5-10, the regression equations, we saw that the regression coefficient $b$ describes the degree of slope of the regression line, the trend of the association between the two variables. The regression coefficient, then, gives a measure of the degree to which two variables are related. The larger the magnitude of the regression coefficient, the higher the degree of relationship. When the relationship is positive, the regression coefficient is positive; and when the relationship is negative, the regression coefficient is negative. In view of the value of the regression coefficient as a measure of relationship, we must develop a formula that will permit easy calculation of this constant. Note that the value of the regression coefficient, as compared to that of the correlation ratio, is that the index provides information for linear relationships and also indicates directionality.

### Developing the Regression Coefficient

Again, the reason for developing the slope of a line is to indicate its use as a measure of association between two variables. To develop the formula for the regression coefficient, it is simpler to deal with deviation scores (see Chapter 3). If we deal with deviation scores, we write the regression equation from Equation 5-9 as

$$\bar{y}_i = a_y + b_{y \cdot x} x_i$$

These deviation scores are the deviations from the means of the entire distributions. Consequently, $\bar{y}_i$ refers to those scores, expressed as deviations from the mean of the entire $Y$ distribution, that fall in column $i$.

It will be demonstrated in the Technical Section of Chapter 6 that the regression lines cross at the point representing the means of the distribution. Since with deviation scores the means are zero (Equation 3-5), the intercept $a$ necessarily is zero. Thus, when $x_i$ is zero, $\bar{y}_i$ is zero, and when $\bar{y}_i$ is zero, $\bar{x}_i$ is zero. We can therefore write the two regression equations in deviation-score form as

$$\bar{y}_i = b_{y \cdot x} x_i \qquad (5\text{-}11)$$

$$\bar{x}_i = b_{x \cdot y} y_i \qquad (5\text{-}12)$$

and thus focus our attention in this section on the $b$'s.

Let us now derive a formula that will permit us to compute the regression coefficients from deviation scores. For any value of $x$, that is, for any column $x_i$,

$$\bar{y}_i = \frac{\Sigma y_i}{n_i} \quad \text{or} \quad n_i \bar{y}_i = \Sigma y_i$$

Substituting for $\bar{y}_i$ from Equation 5-11, we have

$$n_i b_{y \cdot x} x_i = \Sigma y_i$$

Let us now multiply both sides of the equation by $x_i$, remembering that $x$ is a constant for this column since all individuals falling in it have the same $x$ score:

$$n_i b_{y \cdot x} x_i^2 = x_i \Sigma y_i$$

But a constant times the sum of a variable is equal to the sum of the constant times the variable. In other words, $x_i \Sigma y_i = \Sigma x_i y_i$. Therefore

$$n_i b_{y \cdot x} x_i^2 = \Sigma x_i y_i$$

Now let us sum these equations for the entire scatter diagram, letting there be 1 to $k$ columns or values of $x$:

$$n_1 b_{y \cdot x} x_1^2 + \cdots + n_k b_{y \cdot x} x_k^2 = \Sigma x_1 y_1 + \cdots + \Sigma x_k y_k$$

The sum of the sums of the columns equals the sum of the entire scatter diagram. Hence

$$\Sigma x_1 y_1 + \cdots + \Sigma x_k y_k = \Sigma xy$$

Therefore

$$n_1 b_{y \cdot x} x_1^2 + \cdots + n_k b_{y \cdot x} x_k^2 = \Sigma xy$$

$$b_{y \cdot x}(n_1 x_1^2 + \cdots + n_k x_k^2) = \Sigma xy$$

In the above equation, $n_1$ to $n_k$ are the frequencies with which each of the various values of $x$ occurs. Therefore the terms in the parentheses represent a frequency distribution with each value of $x$ squared. So we could write

$$n_1 x_1^2 + \cdots + n_k x_k^2 = f_1 x_1^2 + \cdots + f_k x_k^2 = \Sigma fx^2 = \Sigma x^2$$

Hence

$$b_{y \cdot x} \Sigma x^2 = \Sigma xy$$

Dividing both sides of the equation by the total number of cases, $n$, we have

$$b_{y \cdot x} \frac{\Sigma x^2}{n} = \frac{\Sigma xy}{n}$$

$$b_{y \cdot x} \sigma_x^2 = \frac{\Sigma xy}{n}$$

$$b_{y \cdot x} = \frac{\Sigma xy}{n \sigma_x^2} \tag{5-13}$$

By a similar derivation, it can be shown that

$$b_{x \cdot y} = \frac{\Sigma xy}{n \sigma_y^2} \tag{5-14}$$

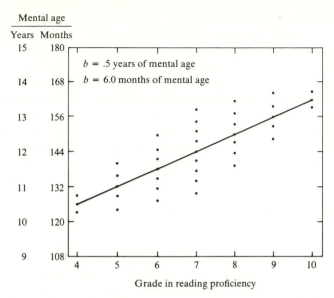

Mental age

Years Months

*b* = .5 years of mental age

*b* = 6.0 months of mental age

Grade in reading proficiency

*Figure 5-6*   Effects of the nature of units on magnitude of regression coefficient.

The only difference between Equation 5-13 and Equation 5-14 is in the variance term in the denominator. Therefore unless the variances of the scores on the two variables are equal, that is, $\sigma_x^2 = \sigma_y^2$, the two regression coefficients necessarily differ in magnitude. In most instances where either raw or deviation scores are used, the variances of the two distributions will not be equal. If, however standard scores ($z$ scores) are used, then the two regression coefficients will necessarily be equal since the variances of both distributions will have the value of 1.00.

In summary, $b_{y \cdot x}$ is an index of the association between two variables. The better the relationship, the higher the value so long as the units and the variance of $x$ and $y$ stay the same. In addition, it is possible for the numerator of the equations to be negative, which occurs when a low deviation value (below the mean) is multiplied by a high deviation value (above the mean) on the second variable. Thus, $b_{y \cdot x}$ indicates direction. However, there are still two problems. First, as already indicated, if $\sigma_y^2 \neq \sigma_x^2$, we will obtain two different values of the relationship for the same set of data. Second, the value provided by this index is, in part, a function of the units of measurement. Let us look at the scatter diagram shown in Figure 5-6. Here we see illustrated a hypothetical relationship between intelligence as measured by mental age and reading proficiency as measured by grade level achieved. If we express mental age in units of years, then the regression coefficient is +.5; and if we express it in units of months, then it is +6.0. For one and the same relationship, then, we can have different values of $b$ depending on the nature of the units in which we happen to express our variables. In the case just given, it really makes no difference whether we express mental age in years or in months, since all we wish to know is the relationship between intelligence and reading ability. Thus, it would be nice to develop a measure of association that is not prone to these two problems. Before doing so, how does the regression coefficient relate to the proportion of accountable variation?

## Relationship Between Accountable Variation and Regression Coefficient

In Equation 5-5 we developed a formula that indicates the proportion of variation among individuals in one variable that is accounted for by variation among them in another variable. We also saw that the proportion of accountable variation provides an index of the extent to which two variables are correlated. The greater the proportion of variation in one variable that can be accounted for by the same factors that produce variation in the other, the higher the two variables are related. In Equations 5-13 and 5-14 we developed formulas for the regression coefficient, which describes the slope of the regression line. We also saw that the regression coefficient provides an index of the extent to which two variables are correlated. Let us now consider the relationship between the proportion of accountable variation and the regression coefficient.

### Relationship Between Proportion of Accountable Variation and Regression Coefficient

The accountable variance, in deviation-score form, is

$$\sigma_{y'}^2 = \sigma_y^2 - \sigma_{y \cdot x}^2 \tag{5-15}$$

Solving for $\sigma_{y \cdot x}^2$, we have

$$\sigma_{y \cdot x}^2 = \sigma_y^2 - \sigma_{y'}^2 \tag{5-16}$$

Now, recall the condition under which we first developed the regression formulas (Equations 5-9 and 5-10), namely, the condition that the regression line is a straight line passing directly through the means of the columns. The deviations from the regression line, symbolized as $v$, then are in fact the deviations from the means of the columns and therefore $v = y_i$. Since the partial variance is the mean of the squares of the deviations from the means of the columns, we can write for the case where the regression line passes through the means of the columns

$$\frac{\Sigma v^2}{n} = \frac{\Sigma (y_i - \bar{y}_i)^2}{n} = \sigma_{y \cdot x}^2$$

As you will see in the Technical Section of Chapter 6,

$$\frac{\Sigma v^2}{n} = \sigma_y^2 - b_{y \cdot x}^2 \sigma_x^2$$

Thus

$$\frac{\Sigma v^2}{n} = \sigma_{y \cdot x}^2 = \sigma_y^2 - b_{y \cdot x}^2 \sigma_x^2$$

Substituting for $\sigma_{y \cdot x}^2$ from the above in Equation 5-16, we have

$$\sigma_y^2 - b_{y \cdot x}^2 \sigma_x^2 = \sigma_y^2 - \sigma_{y'}^2$$

$$\sigma_{y'}^2 = b_{y \cdot x}^2 \sigma_x^2$$

$$\sigma_{y'} = b_{y \cdot x} \sigma_x \qquad (5\text{-}17)$$

Similarly, we could show

$$\sigma_{x'} = b_{x \cdot y} \sigma_y \qquad (5\text{-}18)$$

Hence, given the condition that the regression lines pass directly through the means of the columns and rows, we could calculate from the regression coefficient the extent of variation in one variable that is due to the same factors that produce differences among them in another.

We also said that both the proportion of accountable variation ($\sigma_{y'}/\sigma_y$ and $\sigma_{x'}/\sigma_x$) and the regression coefficient ($b_{y \cdot x}$ and $b_{x \cdot y}$) are indices of the degree of correlation between variables. If we divide Equation 5-17 by $\sigma_y$ and Equation 5-18 by $\sigma_x$, we can see the relationship between these two indices:

$$\frac{\sigma_{y'}}{\sigma_y} = b_{y \cdot x} \frac{\sigma_x}{\sigma_y} \qquad (5\text{-}19)$$

$$\frac{\sigma_{x'}}{\sigma_x} = b_{x \cdot y} \frac{\sigma_y}{\sigma_x} \qquad (5\text{-}20)$$

With given values of $\sigma_x$ and $\sigma_y$, then, as the proportion of accountable variation increases, so does the magnitude of the regression coefficient. However, it is also apparent that $\sigma_{y'}/\sigma_y$ does not equal $b_{y \cdot x}$, nor does $\sigma_{x'}/\sigma_x$ equal $b_{x \cdot y}$. Hence when we calculate these two values for a given set of data, they give us different quantitative descriptions of the degree of relationship. Only when $\sigma_x = \sigma_y$ will the proportion of accountable variation, with variation being measured by the standard deviation, equal the regression coefficient.

Our task now is to develop an index or coefficient that describes the degree of relationship existing between two variables when the relationship is taken to be linear. The index should be of such a nature that when there is little or no relationship between the two variables, its value is small; and when the relationship is high, its value is large. When the relationship is positive, the sign of the index should be positive; and when the relationship is negative, the sign of the index should be negative. Finally, an index of relationship for a given set of data should be given as a single number summarizing and describing *all* aspects of the relationship.

In previous sections we saw how both the proportion of accountable variation and the regression coefficient provide indices of the degree of relationship between two variables. Now we shall review the adequacy of these two values as indices of relationship. As already indicated, they are deficient in certain respects, but we shall be able to develop from them another index, the Pearsonian correlation coefficient, which is much more satisfactory. We shall critically evaluate this coefficient, and then consider it in relation to models of correlation.

### Review of Accountable Variation and Regression Coefficient

For simplicity we will discuss the indices in terms of deviation scores. The accountable variation among individuals is measured by $\sigma_{y'}/\sigma_y$ and $\sigma_{x'}/\sigma_x$ and varies with the degree of relationship existing between two variables. The higher the degree of relationship, the higher are the values $\sigma_{y'}/\sigma_y$ and $\sigma_{x'}/\sigma_x$. The regression coefficient $b$ measuring the slope of the regression line also varies with the degree of relationship between two variables. The higher the degree of relationship, the higher is the value of $b$ (again, so long as the variances of the two variables remain the same), indicating steeper and steeper regression lines. Let us now see how well $\sigma_{y'}/\sigma_y$, $\sigma_{x'}/\sigma_x$, and $b$ serve as indices of relationship.

**Proportion of accountable variation as index of relationship**    We have seen that when the relationship between two variables is low, the value of the proportion of accountable variation, $\sigma_{y'}/\sigma_y$ and $\sigma_{x'}/\sigma_x$, is low; and when the relationship is high, the value of the proportion of accountable variation is high. When there is no relationship at all between two variables, the variation among individuals in the columns and rows of a scatter diagram is equal to the total variation. That is, the partial variance is equal to the total variance:

$$\sigma_{y \cdot x}^2 = \sigma_y^2 \quad \text{and} \quad \sigma_{x \cdot y}^2 = \sigma_x^2$$

Equations 5-5 and 5-6 give the proportion of accountable variation in terms of the partial and total variances. (The following formulas are in deviation-score form, whereas the earlier presentation of Equations 5-5 and 5-6 were in raw-score form. The result of the formulas is the same whether raw or deviation scores are used.)

$$\frac{\sigma_{y'}}{\sigma_y} = \sqrt{1 - \frac{\sigma_{y \cdot x}^2}{\sigma_y^2}} \tag{5-5}$$

$$\frac{\sigma_{x'}}{\sigma_x} = \sqrt{1 - \frac{\sigma_{x \cdot y}^2}{\sigma_x^2}} \tag{5-6}$$

When the partial variation equals the total variation, then the numerator of the second term to the right in the equations equals the denominator so that it becomes equal to zero. Hence the lowest value that $\sigma_{y'}/\sigma_y$ and $\sigma_{x'}/\sigma_x$ can take is zero, and this occurs when there is no relationship at all between the two variables.

When the two variables are perfectly and linearly correlated, then there is no variation at all among the individuals either in the columns or in the rows. In this case the partial variance is zero so that the fraction becomes zero and the entire expression under the square-root sign becomes 1. Hence the highest value that $\sigma_{y'}/\sigma_y$ and $\sigma_{x'}/\sigma_x$ can take is unity, and this occurs when the relationship between the two variables is perfect. This is a most desirable characteristic for an index of relationship to have. It permits easy comparisons among relationships in terms of their degrees.

However, as an index of relationship, the proportion of accountable variation has the undesirable feature of not indicating the direction of the relationship. From Equations 5-5 and 5-6, it can be seen that $\sigma_{y'}/\sigma_y$ and $\sigma_{x'}/\sigma_x$ are always positive. Furthermore, for any given set of data in which $\sigma_y$ does not equal $\sigma_x$, there may be two different values of accountable variation, one for $\sigma_{y'}/\sigma_y$ and the other for $\sigma_{x'}/\sigma_x$.

*Regression coefficient as index of relationship*    In our earlier discussion of linear correlation, we saw that the closer the association between two variables, the steeper the slope of the regression line. Since the slope of the regression line is described by the regression coefficient, we can say that the higher the degree of relationship between scores on two variables, the higher the value of the regression coefficient. The regression coefficient, therefore, can be used as an index of the degree of relationship between two variables.

When two variables are completely unrelated, the means of the scores in all the columns are equal to each other and so are the means of the rows. Consequently the regression lines are parallel to the base lines and, having no slope, the regression coefficients that describe them are zero. Hence when $b = 0$, the two variables are uncorrelated. In this way $b$ has a most desirable feature as an index of relationship. However, when $b$ is determined from raw or deviation scores, it does not have a single maximum value, and in this way it is deficient. It will be recalled that $b$ describes the number of units of change in one variable that is associated with one unit of increase in the other. This number may be very small or it may be very large, but it has no absolute ceiling for all bivariate distributions. The largest value it could have for any given set of data would be the difference between the lowest and the highest scores earned, and this range, of course, differs with different sets of data. Thus the comparability of $b$ coefficients from two different sets of data is diminished.

A second desirable feature of the regression coefficient as an index of linear correlation is that it indicates the direction of the relationship. When the relationship is positive, then $b$ is positive, indicating that an increase in one variable is associated with an increase in the other. When the relationship is negative, then $b$ is negative, indicating that an increase in one variable is associated with a decrease in the other.

However, again, the regression coefficient has two important shortcomings. First, as we have seen in Equations 5-13 and 5-14, for any bivariate distribution of raw or deviation scores, there are two regression coefficients, and ordinarily they are different in magnitude. Hence the regression coefficient does not give a single, unique description of the relationship. But more important, the magnitude of the regression coefficient is a function of the nature of the units in which the scale is expressed.

## Coefficient of Linear Correlation

We have seen the need in psychological measurement for an index that describes the degree of relationship between variables that are associated in a linear fashion. We have also set forth the characteristics that such an index should possess if it is to be useful. Finally, we have considered two possible indices, the proportion of accountable variation and the regression coefficient, and we have seen that they are not altogether satisfactory. We now develop the commonly used index of linear relationship, the *Pearsonian correlation coefficient,* named after Karl Pearson, the famous English biometrician who first developed it. Depending on how we view this coefficient, it may or may not possess the features we wish in an index of relationship. We can best begin our development of the Pearsonian coefficient from the regression coefficient, and then we shall be able to relate it to accountable variation.

## Pearsonian Coefficient

We saw that one important shortcoming of the regression coefficient lies in the fact that while its magnitude does vary with the degree of relationship that exists between the two variables, it also varies with the nature of the units in which those variables are expressed. Consequently we might have two relationships that are of precisely the same degree, yet the regression coefficient of one might be quite different in magnitude from the regression coefficient of the other.

If scores on all variables were expressed in terms of the same units, this problem would be resolved. In Chapters 3 and 4 we dealt with the problem of making scores on different variables comparable. We said that if scores are referenced to the total distribution in which they occur, then in one sense scores in one variable can be considered comparable to scores in another. One way of doing this is by means of standard scores. A given standard score in two variables has the same meaning in the sense that it refers to an individual who stands the same distance from the mean in terms of standard-score units. If we are willing to accept standard scores on different variables as being expressed in the same units, then the problem of units in connection with the regression coefficient is solved. If we transmute scores on all variables to standard scores when we speak of a change in one variable being associated with a certain number of units of change in another variable, as we do with the regression coefficient, then we are doing so in terms of standard-deviation units.

Let us therefore specify the use of standard scores when we compute our index of correlation, the regression coefficient. To differentiate the circumstance when standard scores are used in the computation of the regression coefficient, rather than raw or deviation scores, the symbol $r$ is used instead of $b$. Since $r$ is so commonly used as an index of relationship, it is termed a coefficient of correlation, the Pearsonian correlation coefficient.

Let us begin our derivation of $r$ with the formula for the regression coefficient given as Equation 5-13:

$$b_{y \cdot x} = \frac{\Sigma xy}{n \sigma_x^2} \qquad (5\text{-}13)$$

In standard scores this formula is

$$b_{z_y \cdot z_x} = r_{y \cdot x} = \frac{\Sigma z_x z_y}{n \sigma_{z_x}}$$

Recall that $z = (X - \bar{X})/\sigma$; we are not changing the shape of the distribution or affecting the interpretation. We are merely taking each person's score and determining its deviation from the mean relative to the amount of deviation in the entire distribution. This process allows us to make direct comparisons of individual scores from distributions that have different units, means, standard deviations, and the like.

To continue, since the variance of standard scores, $\sigma_{z_x}^2$, is 1.00,

$$r_{y \cdot x} = \frac{\Sigma z_x z_y}{n} \qquad (5\text{-}21)$$

The formula for the other regression coefficient is

$$b_{x \cdot y} = \frac{\Sigma xy}{n \sigma_y^2}$$

In standard scores this would be

$$r_{x \cdot y} = \frac{\Sigma z_x z_y}{n} \qquad (5\text{-}22)$$

The terms to the right in Equations 5-21 and 5-22 are precisely the same. Hence we can say that $r_{y \cdot x} = r_{x \cdot y}$. Since the Pearsonian correlation coefficient is the regression coefficient when scores on both variables are expressed as standard scores, we can say that when the bivariate distribution of two sets of standard scores is examined, the two regression lines have exactly the same slope. Hence with standard scores the two regression coefficients have precisely the same value and are commonly symbolized as $r_{xy}$. We can also see from Equations 5-21 and 5-22 that the Pearsonian correlation coefficient also is a mean, being the mean of the cross products of standard scores.

Ordinarily the formula for the Pearsonian coefficient is given in terms of deviation rather than standard scores. Since $z_x = x/\sigma_x$ and $z_y = y/\sigma_y$,

$$r_{xy} = \frac{\Sigma(x/\sigma_x)(y/\sigma_y)}{n}$$

$$= \frac{(1/\sigma_x\sigma_y)\Sigma xy}{n}$$

$$= \frac{\Sigma xy}{n\sigma_x\sigma_y} \qquad (5\text{-}23)$$

### Maximum and Minimum Values of Pearsonian Coefficient

Let us now see what the minimum and maximum values of the Pearsonian correlation coefficient are. That is, when we apply Equation 5-23 or its equivalents to a set of data and perform the indicated computations, what are the smallest and largest values we could possibly obtain?

When there is no relationship at all between two variables, the two regression lines are parallel to their base lines. The lines, then, have the slope of .00; hence the value of the coefficient of correlation $r$ is .00. This, of course, is a minimum value. If we are dealing with the special case where the means of the scores in the columns and rows fall exactly on straight lines, then when the two variables are completely uncorrelated, the means of the scores in all the columns are equal to each other and are equal to the mean of the total distribution of $Y$ scores. Similarly, the means of the scores in all the rows are equal to each other and are equal to the mean of the $X$ scores.

When the correlation between two variables is perfect, then by definition each person's standard score on one variable is exactly equal to his or her standard score on the other variable. That is, $z_x = z_y$. Therefore, from Equation 5-21,

$$r_{xy} = \frac{\Sigma z_x z_y}{n} = \frac{\Sigma z^2}{n}$$

But this is the variance of standard scores, which is 1.00 (Equation 4-3). Therefore the highest value that $r$ can attain is 1.00, which represents a perfect correlation.

### Effects of Shapes of Distributions on Maximum Value of Pearsonian Coefficient

Up to now in our development of the Pearsonian correlation coefficient, we have not mentioned the shapes of the distributions of scores in the two variables, and we have imposed no conditions whatsoever concern-

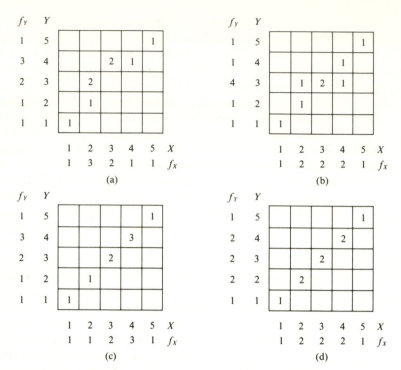

*Figure 5-7*   Effects of the nature of distributions of scores on maximum value of *r*. (a) Two distributions skewed in opposite directions, *r* = .91. (b) One platykurtic and one leptokurtic distribution, *r* = .92. (c) Two distributions skewed in same direction, *r* = 1.00. (d) Two distributions with same degree of kurtosis, *r* = 1.00.

ing their nature. But let us see what effects they might have on the maximum value that *r* can take.

In Figure 5-7a we have two distributions of scores, both of which are skewed in opposite directions. Suppose we deliberately try to place the scores of the eight individuals in the scatter diagram so that the highest possible relationship holds. If we are completely successful, we have all individuals placed in the cells in the diagonal running from the upper right-hand corner of the diagram to the lower left-hand corner. But because of the nature of the two distributions of scores this is impossible. The best we can do is represented in Figure 5-7a. This is the highest possible relationship that can exist between scores on these two particular variables for these particular eight cases. When we compute the Pearsonian coefficient by means of Equation 5-23, we find it to be only .91.

Similarly, in Figure 5-7b we have two variables whose distributions of scores differ in degree of kurtosis. In this diagram also the cases are placed as nearly as possible to fall in the diagonal of cells running from the upper right-hand to the lower left-hand corner. The highest possible value for the Pearsonian coefficient in this instance is only .92.

Therefore we can see from these examples that when the distributions of scores on the two variables differ in shape, the maximum value for *r* is less than 1.00. The maximum value varies with the nature of the two distributions and is lower the more the two distributions differ in skewness and kurtosis. However, we can see in Figures 5-7c and d that it is not the shapes of the distributions of scores as such that limit the maximum value of *r*, but only the differences in shape. In these two diagrams we have distributions that in one case are highly skewed and in the other are highly platykurtic; yet because in both variables the distributions are of the same shape, all individuals can be placed in the diagonal cells, resulting in maximum coefficients of 1.00.

### Solving the Problem of Maximum Value of Pearsonian Coefficient

We have just seen that unless the distributions of scores on both variables being related have exactly the same skewness and kurtosis (that is, the same shape), it is impossible for the Pearsonian coefficient computed from their scores ever to have a value as high as 1.00. Therefore if we wish to define the Pearsonian coefficient as always having a maximum possible value of 1.00, we have to specify that it is to be applied only in those instances where the shapes of the distributions of scores on both variables being related are precisely the same shape. Hence this specification would so limit the instances where the Pearsonian coefficient could be used that it would be valueless.

We might solve this problem of the maximum value of *r* by taking the normal frequency distribution as a model. We adopt the position that the large proportion of frequency distributions are so nearly similar to a normal distribution that a normal distribution gives quite a good representation of them. This point of view is something like the one we adopt with respect to the shape of the world. We say that the world is spherical in shape even though the obvious irregularities on its surface, the mountains and valleys, prove it is not. Nevertheless, for most practical purposes we can ignore the differences between the true shape of the world and that of our model. So while actual distributions of scores are not precisely normal, we might say that we consider them as being so without any great loss or without introducing any great degree of inaccuracy of description. Indeed, in most instances if we compute the Pearsonian coefficient between raw scores and then transmute the scores to other values that do distribute in a normal fashion, we find that the Pearsonian coefficient for the normalized scores ordinarily will be greater, but not more than about .02 to .05. Furthermore, even with distributions of scores such as those in Figures 5-7a and b, which differ markedly from a normal distribution, the maximum value of $r$ is not greatly below 1.00. Finally, since only in very rare instances are relationships between psychological variables anywhere near perfect, the fact that the maximum value of 1.00 cannot be attained might be considered purely an academic problem. Yet, as with all imperfect models, the instances of great deviation from them are troublesome. It is of little help to assure the mountain climber that conceptually he is walking along a plain. Nor does it help when one is seeking to relate ratings highly negatively skewed through the leniency error with positively skewed scores on a test that is too difficult for the individuals being tested.

### Pearsonian Coefficient and Accountable Variation

The following relationships are developed in the Technical Section at the end of this chapter:

$$\sigma_{y \cdot x}^2 = \sigma_y^2 (1 - r_{xy}^2) \tag{5-24}$$

$$r_{xy} = \frac{\sigma_{y'}}{\sigma_y} \tag{5-25}$$

Similarly,

$$r_{xy} = \frac{\sigma_{x'}}{\sigma_x} \tag{5-26}$$

Therefore we can say that the Pearsonian coefficient directly gives us the proportion of accountable variation. Since the terms to the left in Equations 5-25 and 5-26 are the same, obviously both equations have the same value. Clearly, these formulas are most meaningful with normal linear correlation. In particular, as the means of the columns and rows depart from the regression lines and as the distributions of scores in the columns and rows depart from homoscedasticity, Equations 5-25 and 5-26 become less and less adequate as descriptions of a linear relationship.

### Computing Pearsonian Coefficient

It is not very convenient to compute the Pearsonian coefficient either from Equation 5-21 or from Equation 5-23 since they involve standard and deviation scores. Thus we use the following formula (developed in the Technical Section) for the computation of the Pearsonian correlation coefficient directly from raw scores:

$$r_{XY} = \frac{\Sigma XY/n - \bar{X}\bar{Y}}{\sigma_X \sigma_Y} \tag{5-27}$$

Equations 5-21, 5-23, and 5-27 are all mathematically equivalent and hence yield the same value for $r$ when computed from the same set of data.

Thus, in summary, this last measure of association is the one with the least problems. It indicates the strength of a linear relationship; it takes into account the direction of the relationship; it provides one value regardless of the units of measurement for $X$ and/or $Y$; and it has a direct relationship to the proportion of accountable variation. Now we will discuss measures of association that are necessary when the $X$ and/or $Y$ variables are other than continuous. Keep in mind, though, that these additional measures are approximations of the Pearsonian coefficient and retain all the benefits mentioned above.

## Correlation with Dichotomous Variables

Usually we think of psychological tests as providing a range of scores so that individuals are distributed along a wide variety of quantitative descriptions that are ordered along a continuous scale. However, quite often in psychological measurement we deal with measuring instruments that separate people into categories that are only two in number. The items in an objective test usually are of this kind, the individual's responses being classified as being "correct" or "incorrect." With opinion and personality inventories the responses may be limited to two alternatives such as "yes" or "no," "like" or "dislike." With certain rating devices only two steps of response are permitted. Thus with adjective checklists the individual is either checked or not checked as being "cheerful," "shy," and so on. Finally we may have items involving the choice between two qualitatively different alternatives. Thus in an interest inventory the individual may be asked questions such as whether the occupation of "clerk" or of "mechanic" interests him or her more, and in a personality inventory the person may be asked questions such as whether the trait of "cheerfulness" or "industriousness" better describes him or her.

### Correlation with Truly Dichotomous Variables

Let us now turn to the problem of correlation involving truly dichotomous variables. With these variables there are only two possible scores,

0 and 1. In developing the Pearsonian coefficient, we did not stipulate that the variables being related were multistep variables, but only that the quantitative descriptions vary from low amounts of the traits being measured to higher amounts. Dichotomous scales are only a special case of multistep scales, and therefore there is no reason why we cannot directly apply the Pearsonian coefficient to them. However, since we are dealing with individual differences in only two stages rather than in many, there are formulas that are mathematically equivalent to the Pearsonian coefficient but easier to calculate for this special case. When we are dealing with dichotomous variables that are qualitative in nature, we can arbitrarily assign the values of 0 and 1 to the two categories.

There are two types of correlation we need to consider. In one we are concerned with the relationship between a discontinuous dichotomous variable (for example, sex) and a continuous or multistep one (for example, intelligence), and in the other we consider the correlation between two dichotomous variables (for example, sex and right- or left-handedness). The coefficient for the first type of relationship is termed the *point biserial coefficient* and is symbolized as $r_{\mathrm{pbis}}$. The coefficient of correlation for the second type of relationship is termed the *phi coefficient* and is symbolized as $\phi$.

Let us say that $X$ is the dichotomous variable and $Y$ is the continuous variable. Thus $X$ can be either 0 or 1. The formula for the point biserial coefficient is

$$r_{\mathrm{pbis}} = \frac{\bar{Y}_1 - \bar{Y}}{\sigma_y} \sqrt{\frac{p_x}{q_x}} \tag{5-28}$$

where $\bar{Y}_1$ is the average of the $Y$ scores for those whose $X$ score is 1, $\bar{Y}$ is the average $Y$ score for all subjects, $\sigma_y$ is the standard deviation of the $Y$ scores, $p_x$ is the mean of the $X$ scores (see Equation 3-12), and $q_x = 1 - p_x$.

Equation 5-28 is quite simple and easy to compute. But since sometimes we are dealing with a large number of dichotomous variables—for example, the many items of a test—the computations become laborious. Hence Equation 5-28 has been plotted in Figure 5-8, which permits the quick estimation of the point biserial coefficient when $(\bar{Y}_1 - \bar{Y})/\sigma_y$ and $p_x$ are known. For example, if the difference between the means divided by the standard deviation is .35 and $p$ is .25, the biserial coefficient is .20; and if the first value is .50 and the second is .45, the coefficient is .45.

Now let us turn to the relationship between two discontinuous dichotomous variables. In this case there are only two degrees of $X$ and $Y$, namely, 0 and 1. The phi coefficient is

$$\phi = \frac{p_c - p_x p_y}{\sqrt{p_x q_x p_y q_y}} \qquad (5\text{-}29)$$

where $p_c$ is the number of people who score in the higher category of *both* variables, and $p_x$, $p_y$, $q_x$, and $q_y$ are derived from operations involving Equation 3-12.

Suppose that the proportion of individuals falling in the top category of $X$, $p_x$, is .30; the proportion in the top category of $Y$, $p_y$, is .60; and the proportion who score in the top category on both variables, $p_c$, is .25. Then the relationship between the two variables as measured by the phi coefficient is

$$= \frac{.25 - (.30)(.60)}{\sqrt{(.30)(.70)(.60)(.40)}} = \frac{.25 - .18}{\sqrt{.0504}} = \frac{.07}{.2245} = .31$$

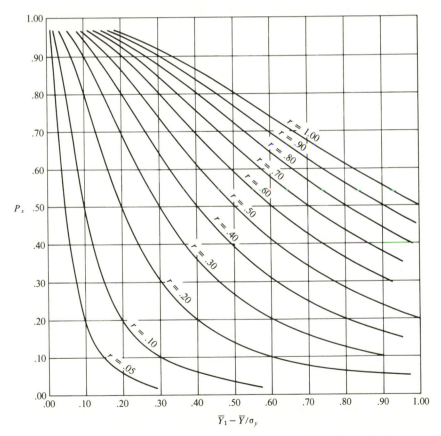

*Figure 5-8*    Chart for estimating point biserial coefficient of correlation.

### Upper Limits of Coefficients from Truly Dichotomous Variables

As is the case with the Pearsonian coefficient, the highest value that the point biserial and the phi coefficients can reach is a function of the distribution of cases in the two variables being related. For the phi coefficient, only if the proportions falling in the top categories on both variables are precisely the same is it possible to obtain a coefficient of $+1.00$. However, under such circumstances it would be impossible to obtain a perfect negative coefficient of $-1.00$. If $p_x$ is precisely equal to $q_y$, then it is possible to obtain a perfect negative coefficient, but not a perfect positive coefficient. Only when

$$p_x = q_x = p_y = q_y = .50$$

is it possible to obtain a perfect positive and a perfect negative coefficient. The greater the dissimilarity between $p_x$ and $p_y$, the lower is the upper limit of phi. By a similar effect there are upper limits to the point biserial coefficient of correlation.

### Correlation with Continuous Dichotomous Variables

When we have a dichotomous variable that is formed from a continuous variable arbitrarily divided into two parts, or is assumed to be so, we must make some assumption about the nature of the distribution of scores on the continuous variable in order to compute a coefficient of correlation. Since we know nothing about the distribution of scores on the continuous variable that is dichotomized—otherwise we would have the multistep scores on the continuous variable—the most convenient assumption is that it is normal. Again formulas for the correlation of such variables can be derived that are the mathematical equivalents of the Pearsonian coefficient. However, these formulas involve the characteristics of the normal frequency distribution and are too complex to develop here.

It is to be noted that because of the assumption of normality, and indeed because of the prior assumption that the variable is a continuous one, these formulas are largely used only in connection with theoretical problems. For the practical problems of psychological measurement the formulas for correlation involving discontinuous dichotomous variables are more pertinent.

Again we have two types of correlation, one involving a dichotomous ("pass" or "fail" a test, where passing means obtaining or surpassing a minimum number of points) and a continuous variable and the other involving two dichotomous variables ("pass" or "fail" a test and "graduate" or "not graduate," where graduation depends on a grade-point average of 2.00 or greater). For the first type of correlation the coefficient is termed the *biserial coefficient,* and for the second it is termed the *tetrachoric coefficient.*

The formula for the biserial coefficient of correlation is

$$r_{bis} = \left( \frac{\bar{Y}_1 - \bar{Y}}{\sigma_y} \right) \frac{p_x}{o} \qquad (5\text{-}30)$$

where $p_x$ is the proportion of individuals falling in the upper category of variable $X$, the dichotomized variable, $\bar{Y}_1$ is their mean score on the continuous variable $Y$, $\bar{Y}$ and $\sigma_y$ are the mean and standard deviation of the scores of all cases on $Y$, and $o$ is the ordinate of the normal distribution curve at the point above which $p_x$ cases fall.

Equation 5-30 can readily be plotted in the form of a chart that permits the estimation of the biserial coefficient. Such a chart is presented in Figure 5-9. The values we need to estimate the biserial coefficient are $p_x$ and $(\bar{Y}_1 - \bar{Y})/\sigma_y$. Reading from Figure 5-9, we can see that if the first value is .35 and the latter is .10, the biserial coefficient is .10; and if the first value is .15 and the second is .70, then the biserial coefficient is about .45.

The formula for the tetrachoric coefficient of correlation is a very complex one and will not be given here. A convenient table that permits reasonably accurate estimates of the tetrachoric coefficient is given as Table 5-1. To estimate the coefficient, we need merely to know (*a*) the number of cases who are in the high category on both variables, (*b*) the number who are high on variable $Y$ and low on variable $X$, (*c*) the number who are low on $Y$ and high on $X$, and (*d*) the number who are low on both variables. We then compute the ratio *ad/bc*, enter Table 5-1 with the resulting value, and find our estimate of the tetrachoric coefficient. Suppose we have the following bivariate distribution of scores on two dichotomous variables:

|  |  | X |  |
|---|---|---|---|
| $Y$ |  | Low | High |
| High |  | 21 | 13 |
| Low |  | 35 | 5 |

Then $a = 13, b = 21, c = 5$, and $d = 35$. To estimate the tetrachoric coefficient, we calculate

$$\frac{(13)(35)}{(21)(5)} = \frac{455}{105} = 4.31$$

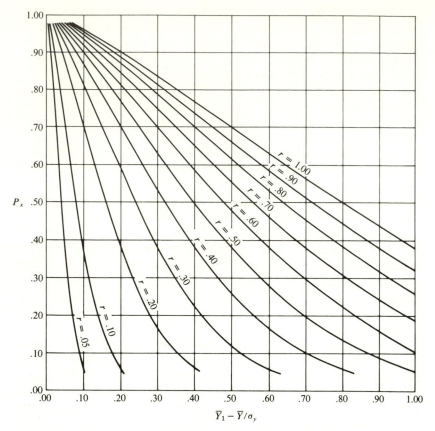

*Figure 5-9*   Chart for estimating biserial coefficient of correlation.

Entering Table 5-1 with the value 4.31, we find that our estimate of the tetrachoric coefficient $r_{tet}$ is .52. In the event that the numerator ($ad$) is smaller than the denominator ($bc$), the two are interchanged and the value $bc/ad$ is computed. This is a negative correlation. We again enter the table with our number and find the estimate of the tetrachoric coefficient, but we place a minus sign before it to indicate that the relationship is negative.

When the marginal distributions of both variables are 0.5 and 0.5, that is, when 0.5 of the cases fall in one category of each dichotomous variable and 0.5 fall in the other, the estimates of the tetrachoric coefficient from Table 5-1 are accurate to two decimal places. As the marginal distributions differ from the proportions 0.5 and 0.5, the estimates of the tetrachoric coefficient are less and less accurate. But even with marginal distributions of 0.3 and 0.7 on both variables, the error is no

*Table 5-1*  Estimating tetrachoric coefficient of correlation

| $r_{tet}$ | ad/bc | $r_{tet}$ | ad/bc | $r_{tet}$ | ad/bc |
|------|---------|------|-----------|------|---------------|
| .00 | 0–1.00 | .34 | 2.42–2.48 | .68 | 7.76–8.11 |
| .01 | 1.01–1.03 | .35 | 2.49–2.55 | .69 | 8.12–8.49 |
| .02 | 1.04–1.06 | .36 | 2.56–2.63 | .70 | 8.50–8.90 |
| .03 | 1.07–1.08 | .37 | 2.64–2.71 | .71 | 8.91–9.35 |
| .04 | 1.09–1.11 | .38 | 2.72–2.79 | .72 | 9.36–9.82 |
| .05 | 1.12–1.14 | .39 | 2.80–2.87 | .73 | 9.83–10.33 |
| .06 | 1.15–1.17 | .40 | 2.88–2.96 | .74 | 10.34–10.90 |
| .07 | 1.18–1.20 | .41 | 2.97–3.05 | .75 | 10.91–11.51 |
| .08 | 1.21–1.23 | .42 | 3.06–3.14 | .76 | 11.52–12.16 |
| .09 | 1.24–1.27 | .43 | 3.15–3.24 | .77 | 12.17–12.89 |
| .10 | 1.28–1.30 | .44 | 3.25–3.34 | .78 | 12.90–13.70 |
| .11 | 1.31–1.33 | .45 | 3.35–3.45 | .79 | 13.71–14.58 |
| .12 | 1.34–1.37 | .46 | 3.46–3.56 | .80 | 14.59–15.57 |
| .13 | 1.38–1.40 | .47 | 3.57–3.68 | .81 | 15.58–16.65 |
| .14 | 1.41–1.44 | .48 | 3.69–3.80 | .82 | 16.66–17.88 |
| .15 | 1.45–1.48 | .49 | 3.81–3.92 | .83 | 17.89–19.28 |
| .16 | 1.49–1.52 | .50 | 3.93–4.06 | .84 | 19.29–20.65 |
| .17 | 1.53–1.56 | .51 | 4.07–4.20 | .85 | 20.66–22.68 |
| .18 | 1.57–1.60 | .52 | 4.21–4.34 | .86 | 22.69–24.76 |
| .19 | 1.61–1.64 | .53 | 4.35–4.49 | .87 | 24.77–27.22 |
| .20 | 1.65–1.69 | .54 | 4.50–4.66 | .88 | 27.23–30.09 |
| .21 | 1.70–1.73 | .55 | 4.67–4.82 | .89 | 30.10–33.60 |
| .22 | 1.74–1.78 | .56 | 4.83–4.99 | .90 | 33.61–37.79 |
| .23 | 1.79–1.83 | .57 | 5.00–5.18 | .91 | 37.80–43.06 |
| .24 | 1.84–1.88 | .58 | 5.19–5.38 | .92 | 43.07–49.83 |
| .25 | 1.89–1.93 | .59 | 5.39–5.59 | .93 | 49.84–58.79 |
| .26 | 1.94–1.98 | .60 | 5.60–5.80 | .94 | 58.80–70.95 |
| .27 | 1.99–2.04 | .61 | 5.81–6.03 | .95 | 70.96–89.01 |
| .28 | 2.05–2.10 | .62 | 6.04–6.28 | .96 | 89.02–117.54 |
| .29 | 2.11–2.15 | .63 | 6.29–6.54 | .97 | 117.55–169.67 |
| .30 | 2.16–2.22 | .64 | 6.55–6.81 | .98 | 169.68–293.12 |
| .31 | 2.23–2.28 | .65 | 6.82–7.10 | .99 | 293.13–923.97 |
| .32 | 2.29–2.34 | .66 | 7.11–7.42 | 1.00 | 923.98 |
| .33 | 2.35–2.41 | .67 | 7.43–7.75 | | |

$a$ = number of cases high on both variables
$b$ = number of cases high on $y$ and low on $x$
$c$ = number of cases low on $y$ and high on $x$
$d$ = number of cases low on both variables

SOURCE: M. D. Davidoff and H. W. Goheen, A table for the rapid determination of the tetrachoric correlation coefficient, *Psychometrika*, 18:115–121, 1953.

larger than about 0.02; and with greater departures in the marginal distributions from 0.5 and 0.5, the error seldom is greater than about 0.05. Consequently the estimates of the tetrachoric coefficient given by Table 5-1 are sufficiently accurate for almost all practical purposes. When the proportions of cases in the two categories of the dichotomous variables are quite different, as with 0.05 of the cases falling in one category and 0.95 in the other, the tetrachoric coefficient is quite undependable as an index and should not be used.

When we use the tetrachoric coefficient of correlation, we are in effect normalizing the scores on both variables being related; that is, we are taking both distributions to have the same shape. As a consequence the maximum value of the tetrachoric coefficient is always unity, a circumstance that is seldom true with the phi coefficient. When two dichotomous variables are being related, the value of the phi coefficient is always equal to or lower than the value of the tetrachoric coefficient.

---

## Technical Section

### Pearsonian Coefficient and Accountable Variation

From Equation 5-13 we saw that

$$b_{y \cdot x} = \frac{\Sigma xy}{n \sigma_x^2}$$

Substituting for $b_{y \cdot x}$ from Equation 5-13 into $\Sigma v^2 / n = \sigma_y^2 - b_{y \cdot x}^2 \sigma_x^2$ (see page 105), we have

$$\frac{\Sigma v^2}{n} = \sigma_y^2 - \left( \frac{\Sigma xy}{n} \right)^2 \frac{\sigma_x^2}{\sigma_x^4}$$

From Equation 5-23 we know that $\Sigma xy / n = \sigma_x \sigma_y r_{xy}$. Also we have shown that $\Sigma v^2 / n = \sigma_{y \cdot x}^2$. Hence

$$\sigma_{y \cdot x}^2 = \sigma_y^2 - \frac{\sigma_x^2 \sigma_y^2 r_{xy}^2 \sigma_x^2}{\sigma_x^4}$$

$$= \sigma_y^2 - \sigma_y^2 r_{xy}^2$$

$$\sigma_{y \cdot x}^2 = \sigma_y^2 (1 - r_{xy}^2) \qquad (5\text{-}24)$$

Rearranging terms, we get

$$r_{x \cdot y}^2 = \frac{\sigma_y^2 - \sigma_{y \cdot x}^2}{\sigma_y^2}$$

From Equation 5-2 we know that $\sigma_y^2 - \sigma_{y \cdot x}^2$, which we have symbolized as $\sigma_{y'}^2$, is an accountable variance. Therefore

$$r_{xy}^2 = \frac{\sigma_{y'}^2}{\sigma_y^2}$$

$$r_{xy} = \frac{\sigma_{y'}}{\sigma_y} \qquad (5\text{-}25)$$

and similarly

$$r_{xy} = \frac{\sigma_{x'}}{\sigma_x} \qquad (5\text{-}26)$$

### Computing Pearsonian Coefficient from Raw Scores

Since $x = X - \bar{X}$ and $y = Y - \bar{Y}$, we can write Equation 5-23, $r_{xy} = \Sigma xy/n\sigma_x\sigma_y$, as

$$= \frac{\Sigma(X - \bar{X})(Y - \bar{Y})}{n\sigma_x\sigma_y}$$

$$= \frac{\Sigma(XY - \bar{Y}X - \bar{X}Y + \bar{X}\bar{Y})}{n\sigma_x\sigma_y}$$

$$= \frac{\Sigma XY/n - \bar{Y}(\Sigma X/n) - \bar{X}(\Sigma Y/n) + \Sigma\bar{X}\bar{Y}/n}{\sigma_x\sigma_y}$$

$$= \frac{\Sigma XY/n - \bar{Y}\bar{X} - \bar{X}\bar{Y} + \bar{X}\bar{Y}}{\sigma_x\sigma_y}$$

$$= \frac{\Sigma XY/n - \bar{X}\bar{Y}}{\sigma_x\sigma_y} \qquad (5\text{-}27)$$

## Summary

When the scores on two variables are related, it means that differences among individuals on one are to some degree due to the same factors that produce differences among them on the other. Furthermore, it means that scores on one can be predicted on a better-than-chance basis from scores on the other. Since the relationships between variables have these important implications, it is desirable to have some index or coefficient that describes the degree of relationship between two variables. Inasmuch as linear relationships are so characteristically found between scores on psychological traits, we wish to develop a coefficient of linear correlation.

The bivariate distribution, or scatter diagram, of the scores on two variables places individuals in columns in terms of their scores on variable $X$, and in rows in terms of their scores on variable $Y$. Therefore, for individuals in any column, $X$ is a constant and $Y$ a variable; and for individuals in any row, $Y$ is a constant and $X$ a variable. If one property is held constant, a comparison of the extent of variation among individuals in the other with the total variation among individuals permits an estimation of the degree to which the same factors produce differences among individuals in both. This value, the proportion of accountable variation, varies with the degree of relationship between the two variables and hence can be used as an index of relationship.

If the extent of variation in $Y$ scores with $X$ constant differs from column to column, or the variation in $X$ scores with $Y$ constant varies from row to row, the interpretation of the effects of common factors is difficult. With this heteroscedasticity the proportion of accountable variation is only an average statement. Therefore it may be desirable to adopt homoscedasticity (equal variation in all columns and equal variation in all rows) as a model. In such a case, the average variation in the columns is used as a description of the variation in all columns, and the average variation in the rows as a description of the variation in all rows. Homoscedasticity holds when scores on both variables are normally distributed.

Linear relationship also can be defined as that situation wherein the means of the $Y$ scores in the columns all fall on a straight line, and the means of the $X$ scores in the rows also fall on a straight line. These two lines are termed regression lines, and each is described by the regression equation. The slope of a regression line is described by the regression coefficient, one of the terms in the regression equation. Inasmuch as the magnitude of the regression coefficient varies with the degree of relationship between two variables, it too can be used as an index of association. It has the desirable feature of indicating whether the relationship is positive or negative.

Although the proportion of accountable variation and the regression coefficient can be used as indices of the degree of relationship between two variables, they both have serious shortcomings when used in this way. For any given relationship, both of them have two values and hence give two different descriptions of the degree of relationship. The proportion of accountable variation does not tell whether the relationship is positive or negative, and the regression coefficient is dependent on the nature of the units of measurement.

This last shortcoming of the regression coefficient can be overcome if scores on all variables are expressed as standard scores. When the regression coefficient is computed by using standard scores, its two values for any given relationship are equal, and so it gives a single description of the degree of relationship. The regression coefficient in this form is termed the Pearsonian coefficient and is the sum of the cross products of the standard scores on the two variables divided by the number of cases.

When the relationship between two variables is perfect, the Pearsonian coefficient has its maximum value of 1.00; and when no relationship at all exists between two variables, the coefficient has its minimum value of .00. However, the coefficient can only achieve the value of 1.00 when scores on both variables being related have precisely the same shape. But even with frequency distributions quite different in shape, the maximum value of the Pearsonian coefficient is quite high. This and other problems are resolved if the model of normal linear correlation is adopted. When scores are normally distributed, it can be expected that the means of the columns and rows will fall precisely on the regression lines, and the relationship will be homoscedastic, with the distributions of scores in each column and row also being normal.

While the Pearsonian coefficient was derived in terms of multistep or continuous variables, it can also be applied to dichotomous variables. Dichotomous variables are of two sorts, those that are two-step discontinuous variables and those that are multistep or continuous variables that have been dichotomized.

With discontinuous dichotomous variables the Pearsonian coefficient can be directly applied. However, for convenience in computation, formulas somewhat different from, though mathematically equal to, the basic formula for the Pearsonian coefficient are used. When scores on two discontinuous dichotomous variables are being related, the coefficient is termed phi; and when scores on a discontinuous dichotomous variable are being related to those on either a multistep or a continuous variable, the coefficient is termed the point biserial.

With multistep or continuous variables that are dichotomized, it must be assumed that the dichotomized variables are normally distributed. The coefficient of correlation between two such dichotomized variables is termed the tetrachoric, and the coefficient of correlation between such a dichotomized variable and a multistep or continuous variable is termed the biserial. The biserial coefficient is readily computed from a formula, but the formula for the tetrachoric coefficient is too complex and so the value is estimated from a table. Because the tetrachoric and biserial coefficients are based upon normal distributions of scores, their values ordinarily are higher than those of the phi and point biserial coefficients.

## Suggested Readings

Binder, A. 1959. Considerations of the place of assumptions in correlational analysis. *American Psychologist*. 14:504–510.

Cheshire, L., M. Saffir, and L. L. Thurstone. 1933. *Computing diagrams for the tetrachoric correlation coefficient*. Chicago: University of Chicago Bookstore.

Cohen, J., and P. Cohen. 1975. *Applied multiple regression/correlation analysis for the behavioral sciences*. Hillsdale, N.J.: Lawrence Erlbaum Associates. Chap. 2.

Davidoff, M. D. 1954. Note on "A table for the rapid determination of the tetrachoric correlation." *Psychometrika*. 19:163–164.

Hays, W. L. 1973. *Statistics for the social sciences*. 2nd ed. New York: Holt, Rinehart and Winston. Chaps. 16 and 17.

Kerlinger, F. N., and E. J. Pedhazur. 1973. *Multiple regression in behavioral research*. New York: Holt, Rinehart and Winston. Chap. 2.

McNemar, Q. 1969. *Psychological statistics*. 4th ed. New York: Wiley. Chaps. 8, 9, and 12.

# 6

## *Concept of Regression*

As indicated in Chapter 5, we are interested in correlation because it provides a means for *predicting* scores on one variable from scores on another variable, and also it contributes to the *understanding* of the factors that determine the behavioral differences among individuals. Now that we have developed measures of association (in Chapter 5), particularly in light of their values as indices of common accountable variation, we are ready to discuss regression or prediction. Again, if we demonstrate that there is a correlation between two variables, then in effect we are indicating that knowledge of one variable provides information about a second variable. The main problem with which we are concerned is the accuracy of this prediction.

Also, as indicated, we are especially interested in prediction problems because of practical considerations. Keep in mind, though, that measurement is used for *prediction* and *assessment*. Measurement for prediction purposes is direct; that is, we are interested in predicting behavior on one variable from knowledge of another variable. However, measurement for assessment also involves prediction, though in an indirect fashion.

Recall that measurement is the assignment of a quantitative or qualitative label (nominal, ordinal, interval, or ratio) to behavior. If someone is measured and assessed to be "psychopathic," then indirectly we are assessing or predicting that this person will exhibit certain behaviors. Essentially, this person has an antisocial personality that is marked by a lack of ethical or moral development, and is unable to follow approved modes of behavior. If no effective treatment is applied, then we *predict* that this person may exhibit impulsive, emotionally immature, irresponsible, and unethical behavior. Another individual is measured and assessed to be "paranoid," that is, possessing delusions of persecution. Given certain information and patterns of behavior, a *prediction* that the person may inflict harm on another may be made.

The above examples of the relationship between assessment and implied prediction are taken from the behavior domain of clinicians. They are intentionally drawn from this discipline because in our experience many students of clinical or abnormal psychology believe that measurement and measurement theory are relatively unimportant. To the extent that it exists, this assumption is naive. Any personality characterization obtained through clinical assessment is measurement and consequently implies prediction. Thus clinical students ought to be concerned with, aware of, and appreciative of measurement problems involved in prediction (this chapter), reliability (Chapters 8 and 9), validity (Chapter 10), differential weighting (Chapter 11), and so on.

Let us return to the more direct prediction problems. We have all been involved in situations when predictions were made about us. We took aptitude tests in high school to determine our potential for success in college. Some of us took aptitude tests to predict the likelihood of success in graduate school, medical school, law school, and the like. Then most of us have taken employment tests, been interviewed, or provided biographical or background information prior to being hired for work in organizations. These latter bits of information are used to predict performance on the job. The conceptual underpinning of predictions is discussed in Chapter 10, on validity. The purpose of this chapter is to present the fundamental measurement and statistical notions behind prediction.

The material in this chapter is especially relevant because we no longer really have a choice as to whether we should be serious about prediction or not. There currently exist federal guidelines and orders with respect to employment-selection decisions. No longer can we assume that a high school diploma is a necessary prerequisite for a job. We must now demonstrate that there is a relationship between graduation from high school and success on the job. Not only is this required by law but it also makes good sense! So let us proceed to the discussion and development of the appropriate statistics for prediction problems.

## Regression Equation

As indicated in Chapter 5 and illustrated in Figure 5-3, a line drawn through the means in a scatter diagram provides a representation of the association and is referred to as the *regression line*. All lines can be described by an equation. The equation for the straight line drawn through the column means is

$$\bar{Y}_i = a_Y + b_{Y \cdot X} X_i \tag{6-1}$$

where $a_Y$ is the $Y$ intercept or value of $Y$ when $X$ is zero and $b_{Y \cdot X}$ is the regression coefficient. The equation for the line drawn through the row means is

$$\bar{X}_i = a_X + b_{X \cdot Y} Y_i \tag{6-2}$$

where $a_X$ is the value of $X$ when $Y$ is zero and $b_{X \cdot Y}$ is the regression coefficient. Thus, for each scatter diagram we have two equations.

In the example of a linear relationship given in Figure 5-3, it can be seen by inspection that

$$a_Y = 10 \quad \text{and} \quad b_{Y \cdot X} = 2.5$$

Therefore, the regression equation in this instance is

$$\bar{Y}_i = 10 + 2.5 X_i$$

Recall, that in every scatterplot, we have two regression equations. Equation 6-1 is used when we are "regressing $Y$ on $X$" or trying to predict $Y$ from information on $X$. Equation 6-2 is used when we are "regressing $X$ on $Y$" or trying to predict $X$ from $Y$. The former is obtained by drawing the trend line through the column means, and the latter by drawing the trend line through the row means.

### Equivalence of Means

Two regression lines for the same set of data are not a problem as was the potential problem for two values of association or correlation. Two regression lines are necessary since we use these regression lines to predict $Y$ from $X$ and/or $X$ from $Y$. There is an interesting property associated with these two regression lines that we will now develop.

Let us determine the value of $\bar{Y}_i$, the mean of the $Y$ scores in a column, when $X$ in the regression equation is taken as the mean of all of the $X$ scores, $\bar{X}$. Let there be $k$ values of $X$, that is, $k$ columns in the scatter diagram. There are, then, $k$ different values of $X$ that can be placed in the regression equation, Equation 6-1, and $k$ values of $\bar{Y}_i$ will be obtained. The regression equation is

$$\bar{Y}_i = a_Y + b_{Y \cdot X} X_i$$

This is the equation for the mean of the $Y$ scores in any single column $i$. Now let us multiply both sides of the equation by $n_i$, the number of cases in that column:

$$n_i \bar{Y}_i = n_i a_Y + n_i b_{Y \cdot X} X_i$$

But $\bar{Y}_i = \Sigma Y_i / n_i$, or $n_i \bar{Y}_i = \Sigma Y_i$. Furthermore, since the number of times a constant is summed to itself is equal to that number times the constant, we can write $\Sigma X_i = n_i X_i$. Hence

$$\Sigma Y_i = n_i a_Y + b_{Y \cdot X} \Sigma X_i$$

This is the equation for any one column. The other columns in the scatter diagram have similar equations. Let us now add together the equations for all columns, that is, column 1 plus column 2, and so on, to column $k$. The result is

$$\Sigma Y_1 + \cdots \Sigma Y_k = n_1 a_Y + \cdots + n_k a_Y + b_{Y \cdot X} \Sigma X_1 \cdots + b_{Y \cdot X} \Sigma X_k$$

But the sum of the $Y$ scores in the entire scatter diagram, $\Sigma Y$, is equal to the sum of the sums of the $Y$ scores in all the columns; that is,

$$\Sigma Y = \Sigma Y_1 + \cdots + \Sigma Y_k$$

Therefore

$$\begin{aligned} \Sigma Y &= n_1 a_Y + \cdots + n_k a_Y + b_{Y \cdot X} \Sigma X_1 + \cdots + b_{Y \cdot X} \Sigma X_k \\ &= a_Y(n_1 + \cdots + n_k) + b_{Y \cdot X}(\Sigma X_1 + \cdots + \Sigma X_k) \end{aligned}$$

The total number of cases in the entire scatter diagram is equal to the sum of the numbers of cases in all the columns; that is,

$$n = n_1 + \cdots + n_k$$

and the sum of all the $X$ scores in the entire scatter diagram, $\Sigma X$, is equal to the sum of the sums of the $X$ scores in all the columns; that is,

$$\Sigma X = \Sigma X_1 + \cdots + \Sigma X_k$$

Therefore

$$\Sigma Y = a_Y n + b_{Y \cdot X} \Sigma X$$

Dividing both sides of the equation by $n$, the total number of cases, we have

$$\frac{\Sigma Y}{n} = \frac{a_Y n}{n} + b_{Y \cdot X} \frac{\Sigma X}{n}$$

$$\bar{Y} = a_Y + b_{Y \cdot X} \bar{X} \qquad (6\text{-}3)$$

$\bar{Y}$, of course, is the mean of all the $Y$ scores in the scatter diagram, and $\bar{X}$ is the mean of all the $X$ scores. By a similar derivation, we could show

$$\bar{X} = a_X + b_{X \cdot Y} \bar{Y} \qquad (6\text{-}4)$$

Therefore if we place $\bar{X}$, the mean of $X$, in the one regression equation and solve it, the result will be $\bar{Y}$, the mean value of $Y$. If we place $\bar{Y}$, the mean value of $Y$, in the other regression equation and solve it, the result will be $\bar{X}$, the mean value of $X$. Thus if in our scatter diagram we plot a point for $\bar{Y}_i$ for that value of $X$ that equals the mean of all the $X$ scores and also plot another point for $\bar{X}_i$ for that value of $Y$ that equals the mean of the $Y$ scores, the two points will fall exactly at the same place. Since one of these is a point on one regression line, and the other a point on the other regression line, we can see that the regression lines have the property that they intersect or cross each other at the means of the two distributions, $\bar{X}$ and $\bar{Y}$.

### Deviation-Score Form

So far we mainly have been considering only raw scores. If now we deal with deviation scores, we write the regression equation from Equation 5-9 as

$$\bar{y}_i = a_y + b_{y \cdot x} x_i$$

These deviation scores are the deviations from the means of the entire distributions. Consequently $\bar{y}_i$ refers to those scores, expressed as deviations from the mean of the entire $Y$ distribution, that fall in column $i$.

From Equations 6-3 and 6-4 we know that the regression lines cross at the point representing the means of the distributions. Since with deviation scores the means are zero (Equation 3-5), the intercept $a$

necessarily is zero. That is, when $x_i$ is zero, $\bar{y}_i$ is zero; and when $y_i$ is zero, $\bar{x}_i$ is zero. We can therefore write the two regression equations in deviation-score form as

$$\bar{y}_i = b_{y \cdot x} x_i \tag{6-5}$$

$$\bar{x}_i = b_{x \cdot y} y_i \tag{6-6}$$

### Determining the Intercept

In Chapter 5 we developed the formula for the regression coefficient, $b$. The other statistic in the regression equation, the *intercept,* tells us the value of one variable when the other variable is zero. Since the intercept is of little concern in subsequent discussion, we simply present the raw-score formula for computing the value. The intercept value of $Y$ is found by

$$a_Y = \frac{\Sigma Y_i - b_{Y \cdot X} \Sigma X_i}{n} \tag{6-7}$$

and the formula for the $X$ intercept is

$$a_X = \frac{\Sigma X_i - b_{X \cdot Y} \Sigma Y_i}{n} \tag{6-8}$$

## Models of Correlation Based on Regression Lines

Let us look at the scatter diagram in Figure 6-1. When we connect the means of the $Y$ scores in the successive columns with a line (the solid line), it is quite a jagged affair and constitutes a very complex curve indeed. The equation for this curve would be extremely complicated. Yet as we look at the means of the columns, it appears that they fluctuate in a random fashion around a straight line (the dotted line), and therefore we might be inclined to term the relationship linear.

What would be our reaction to the statement that the dots in Figure 6-1 do not "swarm around" a straight line? Undoubtedly we would first point out that altogether there are only 34 cases and that with such a small total number we would not feel secure in making any definite statements about the means of the columns, each of which is based on very few cases. Furthermore, we would say that if the nature of the relationship between the two variables is as complicated a curve as is actually represented by the line drawn through the means of the columns, we would be positing a most complex association between the

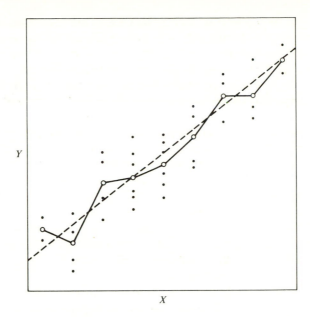

***Figure 6-1*** Relationship termed *linear* even though means of scores in columns do not all fall precisely on same straight line.

two variables. We would be saying, from left to right in Figure 6-1, that as $X$ increases, $Y$ first decreases, then markedly increases, and then decreases more gradually. Suppose that variable $X$ is an intelligence test and variable $Y$ is grades earned in school. Then we would be maintaining that children with very low intelligence do poorly in school but that those who are a little brighter do even less well, those still brighter do considerably better, and so on. This description of the relationship makes neither good common sense nor good psychological sense.

A much simpler hypothesis, and undoubtedly a more reasonable one, is that the relationship between $X$ and $Y$ is linear, but because there are so few cases in our particular group, the means of the columns depart from a straight line just because of sampling error. In effect we are saying that if we did not have just 34 cases but perhaps 34,000 cases, the means of the columns would fall on a straight line. In actual practice, with a situation such as that in Figure 6-1—where the means of the columns (and of the rows) appear to fluctuate in a random fashion around a straight line—as we increase the number of cases, the means of the columns are very likely to come closer and closer to a straight line. But the fact remains that with the limited number of cases ordinarily available to us, seldom do all the means fall exactly on the same straight line. As a matter of fact, even with as many as 34 million cases the means of the columns probably would not fall on the same straight line, though the discrepancies would likely be ever so small and per-haps discernible only in the fourth or fifth decimal place.

Let us now consider the example given in Figure 6-2. Again we see that a line drawn through the means of the columns (the solid line) is a jagged thing and forms an extremely complicated curve. Such a com-plex relationship would be difficult to represent by an equation and almost impossible to explain in terms of a functional relationship. If variable $X$ is the athletic prowess of high school students and $Y$ the number of other students knowing each student, taking a line running through the means of the columns in Figure 6-2 as the relationship between these two variables would lead to very curious conclusions. We would have to say that very unathletic students are not well known, those a bit more athletically inclined are even less well known, those still more athletic are known considerably better, and those still more athletic are again less well known.

But as in the example shown in Figure 6-1, we see that the means of the columns appear to fluctuate around a regular line, in this case a smoother and simpler curve than that drawn through the means of the columns. Again we are likely to find that as we increase the numbers of cases, the means of the columns will more and more closely approach a smooth and simple curve. Therefore undoubtedly we should be willing to hypothesize that the simple curve as represented by the dotted line in Figure 6-2 or one very similar to it, would hold if we increased the number of cases.

Only rarely is it found that the means of the columns and the means of the rows fall precisely on the same straight lines or on smooth and simple curves. Yet ordinarily, as we have just seen, we are unwilling to accept as a description of the relationship between the two variables the complex curve that in fact passes through these means. We look for simplicity and regularity in nature partly because it seems more rea-sonable to us to conceive of a world that is simple and regular, and partly because as yet we do not have the mental power or the intellec-tual tools to deal with complexity and irregularity.

Consequently when we deal with the relationship between scores on two variables, we adopt a straight line or some simple curve as a model and use it to describe the nature of the relationship. The equations for the regression lines that we adopt for a particular set of data, then, do not in fact perfectly describe the association between the two variables as we observe it from the scores earned by a particular sample of individuals. The lines do describe the general trend, and it is our hy-pothesis that they give a better description. We hypothesize that the straight lines or simple curves we adopt are the best approximations we

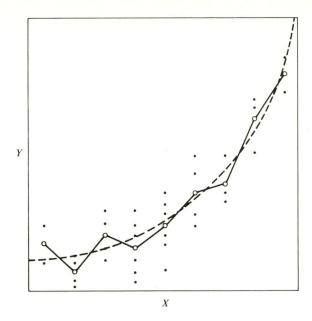

*Figure 6-2*    Relationship termed *curvilinear* with a simple curved relationship even though means of scores in columns do not all fall precisely on same simple curve.

can get to the regression lines that would characterize the relationship between two variables if, instead of our limited sample of individuals, we had an infinitely large number who were of the same general sort as those in our particular sample.

### Best-Fitting Straight Line in Least-Squares Sense

Let us now see whether we can derive the regression coefficient without reference to the means of the columns and rows. That is, let us see whether we can derive it on the basis of straight lines (the regression lines) that give the best fit to all the points in the scatter diagram. We shall be considering all the individual points in the scatter diagram, each of which represents a pair of scores, and not just the means as we did in the previous derivation in Chapter 5.

Figure 6-3 shows the scatter diagram of the relationship between two variables for nine cases (*a-i*). Obviously we can run an infinite number of different straight lines through this set of points, but which of these lines should we consider to give the best fit? In common parlance we

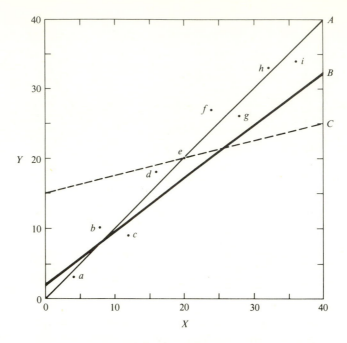

***Figure 6-3*** Three different straight lines drawn through a
set of points.

say that the best-fitting straight line runs through the "middle" of the
points. However, this is a bit vague and we need a more precise statement of what constitutes the best-fitting straight line. We might say that
the straight line that best fits the points is one where the differences
between the points and the line are at a minimum. That is, if we calculated the difference between each point in a column (or row) and the
point where the straight line passes through it, the mean of these deviations would be smaller than the mean of the deviations from any other
line.

By inspection it is apparent that line *A* in Figure 6-3 gives the best fit
to the nine points, line *B* the second-best fit, and line *C* the poorest fit.
Indeed, line *C* hardly represents the points at all. Table 6-1 gives the
deviations of the nine points from the three lines. In the table we see
that the means of the deviations from lines *A* and *C* are equal, both
being zero, and are smaller than the mean of the deviations from line *B*,
which is 2.33. It is therefore clear that the mean of the absolute deviations does not distinguish between straight lines in terms of the adequacy with which they fit a set of points.

However, the mean of the squares of the deviations does give an

*Table 6-1*   Deviations from three straight lines and squares of their deviations

| Point | Deviations from Line: | | | Square of the Deviations from Line: | | |
|---|---|---|---|---|---|---|
| | *A* | *B* | *C* | *A* | *B* | *C* |
| *a* | −1 | −2 | −13 | 1 | 4 | 169 |
| *b* | +2 | +2 | − 6 | 4 | 4 | 36 |
| *c* | −3 | −2 | − 9 | 9 | 4 | 81 |
| *d* | +2 | +4 | − 1 | 4 | 16 | 1 |
| *e* | 0 | −3 | 0 | 0 | 9 | 0 |
| *f* | +3 | +7 | + 6 | 9 | 49 | 36 |
| *g* | −2 | +3 | + 4 | 4 | 9 | 16 |
| *h* | +1 | +7 | + 9 | 1 | 49 | 81 |
| *i* | −2 | +5 | +10 | 4 | 25 | 100 |
| Sum | 0 | 21 | 0 | 36 | 169 | 520 |
| Mean | 0.00 | 2.33 | 0.00 | 4.00 | 18.77 | 57.78 |

index of fit that is more descriptive of the degree to which the different lines fit a set of points. It will be observed in Table 6-1 that the mean of the squares of the deviations is least for line *A*, the best-fitting line, and is greatest for line *C*, the poorest-fitting line. For this reason, and for other mathematical considerations, the best-fitting line is taken as that line from which the mean of the squared deviations is at a minimum; the best-fitting line is a *least-squares solution*. This is consistent with our previous discussion, in that understanding the basic statistical properties of the *mean* facilitates understanding of correlation and regression. That is, recall from Chapter 3 that we demonstrated that the *mean is the point of least squares*. The equation for the straight line that in a least-squares sense gives us the best fit through the points in a scatter diagram is developed in the Technical Section at the end of this chapter.

The regression line as given by Equation 6-1 and its equivalents is that straight line that in a scatter diagram is the line of best fit in a least-squares sense. The mean of the squares of the deviations from it is less than the mean of the squares of the deviations from any other straight line that might be drawn through the columns in the scatter diagram. The same reasoning, of course, would hold for the line drawn through the rows.

We can therefore take the regression coefficient either way we may wish. We can, as in our original derivation, impose the condition that the means of the rows and of the columns fall precisely on straight lines; or we can impose no conditions at all except that we are fitting a straight line in a least-squares sense. With the first derivation we define the regression coefficient as the slope of the regression line when the means of the scores in both the columns and the rows fall precisely on straight lines. With the second development we define the regression coefficient as the slope of the regression line when the regression lines are the best-fitting straight lines in a least-squares sense. It should be obvious that the regression lines obtained by our first development also are best-fitting straight lines since we saw that the mean of a distribution—for example, the mean of the distribution of scores in a column or in a row of a scatter diagram—is the point of least squares.

The value of the regression equation lies not only in its ability to describe a bivariate distribution, but also in its utility as a tool for predictions. That is, once we derive the equation for a set of data from one sample, we can use that equation to make predictions for subjects from a *similar* sample. If the equation is $\bar{Y} = 2 + 3X$ and a subject obtains an $X$ score of 4, we would predict that the $Y$ score would be 14. This type of prediction, from one variable to another, is especially important for educational and employment situations. The ability to predict and especially the error in prediction are discussed in subsequent sections of this chapter.

### Example of Regression Equation for Prediction

Suppose we obtain the following relationship and equation for the situation in which we are trying to predict success ($Y$) on a job (evaluated by the supervisor on a 7-point scale ranging from poor to excellent performance) from scores on a preemployment test, $X$ (whose scores range from a low of 0 to a high of 100):

$$r_{XY} = .45$$
$$Y = .2 + .07X$$

This information is based on a sample of 100 and the $r_{XY}$ is statistically significant (not a chance or random result). If an individual comes along and scores 55 on the test, the predicted performance level for that individual is 4.05 (= .2 + .07(55)). A test score of 33 results in a predicted performance level of 2.51 (= .2 + .07(33)). Similar predictions are made likewise.

### Regression Equation and Pearsonian Coefficient

We have shown in Equation 6-5 that

$$\bar{y}_i = b_{y \cdot x} x_i$$

This is the regression equation in deviation-score form. When standard scores are used, this equation is written as

$$\bar{z}_{y_i} = r_{xy} z_{x_i} \qquad (6\text{-}9)$$

and similarly

$$\bar{z}_{x_i} = r_{xy} z_{y_i} \qquad (6\text{-}10)$$

Very seldom are two variables perfectly related. Consequently the coefficient of correlation between two variables ordinarily is less than 1.00. If we examine Equations 6-9 and 6-10, we can see the origin of the term "regression," which we have used so often in our discussion of correlation and in this chapter. If we take any value for $r_{xy}$ that is less than 1.00 and insert any value for $z_{x_i}$ in Equation 6-9, we find that $\bar{z}_{y_i}$ will be smaller than $z_{x_i}$, that is, closer to the mean. Hence we have a "regression" toward the mean. The same situation, of course, would hold for $\bar{z}_{x_i}$ and $z_{y_i}$ in Equation 6-10. To illustrate the "regression toward the mean" phenomenon, consider the following data, where $r_{xy} = .60$ and $z_{x_i} = 1.00$. Thus an individual is 1 standard deviation above the mean of his or her group on the $X$ variable. If there was a zero correlation, we would predict this person's $Y$ score to be the mean of the $Y$ distribution (the reason for this prediction is discussed more fully in the next section), or $\bar{z}_{y_i} = 0.00$. However, since there is a correlation, applying Equation 6-9 indicates a predicted $\bar{z}_{y_i}$ score of .60. Thus we are predicting that this individual will be .6 of a standard deviation above the mean on the $Y$ variable. We are regressing toward the mean in that the predicted $Y$ score is closer to its mean than is the obtained $X$ score to its mean. In this way we are "hedging" our bet when we are asked to predict or guess one score from another. Regression is a conservative strategy. The less you know, the more you regress toward the mean.

Since $z = x/\sigma$, we can write Equation 6-9 as

$$\frac{\bar{y}_i}{\sigma_y} = r_{xy} \frac{x_i}{\sigma_x}$$

Therefore

$$\bar{y}_i = r_{xy} \frac{\sigma_y}{\sigma_x} x_i \qquad (6\text{-}11)$$

and

$$\bar{x}_i = r_{xy} \frac{\sigma_x}{\sigma_y} y_i \qquad (6\text{-}12)$$

Equations 6-11 and 6-12 are the regression equations in deviation-score form utilizing $r$ instead of $b$.

Since $y = Y - \bar{Y}$ and $x = X - \bar{X}$, we can write Equation 6-11 as

$$\bar{Y}_i - \bar{Y} = r_{xy} \frac{\sigma_y}{\sigma_x} (X_i - \bar{X})$$

Rearranging terms gives

$$\bar{Y}_i = r_{xy} \frac{\sigma_y}{\sigma_x} (X_i - \bar{X}) + \bar{Y} \qquad (6\text{-}13)$$

Similarly,

$$\bar{X}_i = r_{xy} \frac{\sigma_x}{\sigma_y} (Y_i - \bar{Y}) + \bar{X} \qquad (6\text{-}14)$$

Equations 6-13 and 6-14 are raw-score forms of the regression equations. Thus Equations 6-4, 6-10, 6-11, 6-12, 6-13, and 6-14 are all equivalent ways of expressing the regression equation and incorporating the Pearson correlation coefficient.

### Pearsonian Coefficient as Describing Regression Line

There are two reasons that the regression line is important to us. First, as already briefly indicated, it is useful when we wish to predict scores on one variable from scores on another. Second, it contains information that provides a description of the nature of the functional relationship between two variables. In Chapter 5 we saw that with linear relationships the slope of the regression line is given by the regression coefficient. Since the Pearsonian coefficient is derived from the regression coefficient, and indeed is no more nor less than one form of it, it too describes the regression line. Let us therefore examine specifically the kinds of descriptions this coefficient can be interpreted as giving of the regression line.

Suppose we know nothing about a person except that he or she took a particular test, test $Y$. Let us say that we wish to know this person's score on it. What would be our best guess or prediction? Since the person's score might be anywhere in the total distribution of $Y$ scores, we might say that any $Y$ score picked at random is just as good a guess as any other $Y$ score. However, this is not true because obviously we would like to select a score that is least likely to be in error, that is, a score of such a value that the difference between it and the $Y$ score the individual actually earned is at a minimum. It will be recalled that in Chapter 3 we saw that the mean of a distribution of scores is that score in the distribution from which the squared deviations or differences are at a minimum. Therefore if we choose the mean of the $Y$ scores as our best prediction of the $Y$ score of our individual, the predicted score is that score that in the long run is least likely to be in error. The mean of the distribution is our best guess of the score for any individual.

But suppose we know something else about the individual, say his or her score on text $X$. Now what would be our best prediction of this person's $Y$ score? Let us presume that scores on the two tests are positively related in a linear fashion. Again our best guess would be the mean, though in this case it would be the mean of the $Y$ scores of those individuals who earned the same score as this person did on test $X$. That is, if there is a correlation between $X$ and $Y$, then in effect, for given $X$ scores, we have reduced variation in $Y$. This should be recalled from our discussion and development of eta. Thus without a correlation, we "guess" the mean of the total distribution that has a certain variance. If there is a correlation, we "guess" the mean of the $Y$ distribution for the particular $X$ score; in this case the variance of $Y$ is less than that of the total variance.

Therefore if the regression line goes through the means of the columns or the means of the rows if we are predicting $X$ from $Y$, we can use the regression equation to obtain the best prediction of the individual's $Y$ score from the only other information we have about this person, his or her score on test $X$. Consequently the regression equation is of utmost importance for predicting an individual's score on one variable from the score on another. The reason for two equations for the same set of data is simple. Sometimes we want to predict $Y$ from $X$ (referred to as the regression of $Y$ on $X$) and thus Equation 6-1 is used; and sometimes we want to predict $X$ from $Y$ (referred to as the regression of $X$ on $Y$) and then Equation 6-2 is used.

As another example of prediction, suppose we have the following data on two tests:

$$\bar{X} = 10 \qquad \sigma_x = 2 \qquad \bar{Y} = 100 \qquad \sigma_y = 20 \qquad r_{xy} = .50$$

Let us now predict the score on test $Y$ of an individual whose $X$ score is 12, and therefore whose $x$ score is $+2$ and whose $z_x$ score is $+1$. We apply Equations 6-13, 6-11, and 6-9 as follows:

$$\bar{Y}_i = (.50)20/2(12 - 10) + 100 = 110 \qquad (6\text{-}13)$$

$$\bar{y}_i = (.50)20/2(2) = 10 \qquad (6\text{-}11)$$

$$\bar{z}_{y_i} = (.50)(1) = .5 \qquad (6\text{-}9)$$

Thus the predicted raw score is 110, or 10 points above the mean, or .5 standard deviations above the mean.

In Equations 6-9 and 6-10 we saw that the Pearsonian coefficient describes the regression line when scores on both variables are expressed in standard-score form. Now let us see how this coefficient can be interpreted.

When we first developed the regression equation, we dealt only with that circumstance wherein the means of the columns and of the rows fall precisely on straight lines. If we accept this circumstance, then the Pearsonian coefficient is very valuable in terms of the interpretations that can be made directly from it. It precisely describes the functional relationship between two variables, and from it we can directly obtain the best possible prediction of scores in one variable from scores in the other. However, as we saw, seldom if ever do we actually find the means of the columns or of the rows falling precisely on the same straight line. Therefore, valuable as this would make the Pearsonian coefficient in terms of the information it gives us directly, the circumstances in which it could be applied would be so limited that it would be useless.

Taking linear correlation to refer to the general tendency of the points in the bivariate distribution to "swarm" around a straight line, we show in the Technical Section at the end of this chapter that in a least-squares sense the regression equation describes the straight line that best fits the "swarm" of points. We might, then, define the Pearsonian coefficient as the slope of the regression line when scores on both variables are expressed as standard scores and the regression line is the best-fitting line in a least-squares sense. Now of what conceivable value would such a line in and of itself be to us? To be sure, it does describe the general tendency of the "swarm" of points, but that is all it does for us. It does not tell us about the characteristics of the functional relationship, nor does it permit us to make the type of prediction we want from scores on one variable to scores on the other.

Finally, we might adopt linear correlation as a model, taking the best-fitting straight line in a least-squares sense as defining our model. With standard scores this is given, of course, by the Pearsonian coefficient. As a representation of the functional relationship between the two variables, the regression equation then represents our *theory* of how the two variables are related. In prediction we use the regression equation to obtain estimates of the means of the scores in the columns and in the rows. Therefore we use estimates in making our predictions. These estimates have some value, since an estimate is better than no information at all. In a somewhat similar fashion, for practical purposes of navigation we may adopt the theory that the world is flat. If we are concerned only with a small portion of the earth's surface, say the eastern Mediterranean Sea, we pass a plane through the earth's surface, projecting the features on the surface of the sphere to the plane.

By using a theoretical model whose characteristics are quite similar to, but perhaps not precisely the same as, those of the facts of the matter, we have a good representation of those facts and we can make good predictions about them. Obviously our model is better the more congruent its characteristics are with the facts. Hence the model of a flat world is quite satisfactory if we are concerned only with the eastern Mediterranean Sea but is of considerably less value if we are concerned with the entire Pacific Ocean. Similarly, our model of linear correlation is quite good if the means of the columns and of the rows fluctuate in a random fashion around a straight line and their deviations from it are small. Such a model is of substantially less value if the fluctuations of the means from the regression line are great or if, instead of swarming around a straight line, the points tend to swarm around a line with substantial curvature.

Indeed, we may have more faith in the model of linear correlation than in the characteristics of a particular set of data. Let us say that in the bivariate distribution of the scores of a particular sample of individuals, the means of the columns and of the rows do not fall on straight lines but rather fluctuate randomly around straight lines. We would probably hypothesize that with other samples we would have the same state of affairs but with the particular fluctuations of the means of the columns and of the rows varying from sample to sample. Hence we would conclude that if we had the entire population rather than just a sample, the means of the columns and of the rows would fall precisely on straight lines. We take the best-fitting straight lines in a least-squares sense in our original sample as the best estimate of the regression line in the population. Consequently we would believe that with other samples prediction from the straight line of best fit will be more accurate than predictions from the means of the columns or of the rows of our original sample.

### Variation from Regression Line

We have seen that when we restrict linear correlation to those situations where the means of the columns and of the rows fall on straight lines, the regression equation gives us the best prediction of an individual's score on one variable from his or her score on the other. That is, the best prediction of an individual's $y$ score from the $x$ score is $\bar{y}_i$, and the best prediction of the $x$ score from the $y$ score is $\bar{x}_i$. We would also like to know the magnitude of the error of our prediction. The error of prediction for any given individual is

$$y - \bar{y}_i$$

That is, the difference between an individual's actual $y$ score and the score we predict for this person, $\bar{y}_i$, is our error. A distribution of these errors for all individuals would give a good index of how far off we are in predicting $y$ from $x$. The wider the distribution, the larger our error; and the smaller the distribution, the smaller our error. Recall from Chapter 3 that the standard deviation, one measure of variation, provides an index of how spread out a distribution is, and thus we can use it as an index of the extent of our errors of prediction. This value, $\sigma_{y-\bar{y}}$, is symbolized as $\sigma_{y \cdot x}$. This is the partial standard deviation and refers to the variation in $y$ when $x$ is constant. Similarly, $\sigma_{x \cdot y}$ would describe the distribution of our errors in predicting $x$ scores from $y$ scores. Recall from Chapter 5 that the value represents the extent in variation in one variable due to factors *other* than those causing variation in a second variable.

The formula for the standard deviation of these errors in prediction is developed in the Technical Section at the end of this chapter. Essentially we symbolize these differences as

$$v = y - \bar{y}_i$$

and the variance or the square of the standard deviation when we are dealing with deviations from the regression line is

$$\frac{\Sigma v^2}{n} = \sigma_y^2 - b_{y \cdot x}^2 \sigma_x^2 \qquad (6\text{-}15)$$

This in turn equals

$$\frac{\Sigma v^2}{n} = \sigma_y^2 (1 - r_{xy}^2) \qquad (6\text{-}16)$$

This formula is also developed in the Technical Section.

This, then, is the variance of the distribution of errors in predicting $y$ from $x$ that we symbolized as $\sigma_{y \cdot x}$. Therefore we can write Equation 6-16 as

$$\sigma_{y \cdot x}^2 = \sigma_y^2 (1 - r_{xy}^2) \qquad (6\text{-}17)$$

and

$$\sigma^2_{x \cdot y} = \sigma^2_x (1 - r^2_{xy}) \tag{6-18}$$

From these two equations we can write

$$\sigma_{y \cdot x} = \sigma_y \sqrt{1 - r^2_{xy}} \tag{6-19}$$

$$\sigma_{x \cdot y} = \sigma_x \sqrt{1 - r^2_{xy}} \tag{6-20}$$

Equations 6-19 and 6-20 are called the *standard error of estimate* or the *standard error of prediction* because they describe the extent of error in predicting scores on one variable from scores on the other. Since we are dealing with deviations from values that fall on the regression lines, the means of the columns and of the rows or our estimates of them (Equations 6-19 and 6-20) also describe the extent to which individual points in the scatter diagram vary from the regression line.

If we are dealing with standard scores, then $\sigma_y = \sigma_x = 1$; hence Equations 6-19 and 6-20 become

$$\sigma_{z_y \cdot z_x} = \sqrt{1 - r^2_{xy}} \tag{6-21}$$

and

$$\sigma_{z_x \cdot z_y} = \sqrt{1 - r^2_{xy}} \tag{6-22}$$

It will be observed that the terms to the right in Equations 6-21 and 6-22 are the same. Therefore $\sigma_{z_y \cdot z_x} = \sigma_{z_x \cdot z_y}$. Consequently when individual differences in the two variables being related are given in standard-score form, the extent of variation in the columns is exactly the same as the extent of variation in the rows. The relationship between the standard error of estimate and the Pearsonian correlation coefficient is shown in Figure 6-4. The higher the relationship between the two variables, the more accurately scores on one are predicted from scores on the other. Furthermore, equal increases in the magnitude of the coefficient are associated with disproportionately greater and greater decreases in the error of prediction.

Essentially what we are saying is that if there is perfect correlation between $X$ and $Y$, then $r_{xy} = 1.00$ and $\sigma_{z_y \cdot z_x} = 0.00$. That is, there is no variability in the columns; all points fall on the regression line and there is no error. If on the other hand $r_{xy} = 0.00$, then $\sigma_{z_y \cdot z_x} = 1.00$, which is equivalent to $\sigma_{z_y}$ (the standard deviation of a distribution of $z$ scores is 1.00). Thus the extent of error knowing the $x$ score is the same as the extent of error without knowing the $x$ score. Or suppose $r_{xy} = .60$ and

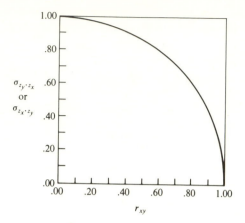

*Figure 6-4*  Relationship between extent of variation around regression line and coefficient of correlation.

we use Equation 6-21. Then $\sigma_{z_y \cdot z_x}$ is 0.80. The standard error of estimate is interpreted similarly to the standard deviation. In the present case, due to less than perfect prediction ($r < 1.00$), we predict that given any $z_x$, the predicted $z_y$ will fall within $\pm 1$ standard deviation. Thus if for a given $z_x$, Equation 6-9 would yield a predicted $z_y$ (for example, 2), that would indicate, assuming a normal distribution, that there would be a 2 to 1 chance (68%) that the predicted score would be between 1.2 and 2.8 (that is, $2 \pm .8$). (These estimates of the chances or probabilities are obtained from Appendix A. In column *b* we see that a standard score of $-1.00$ surpasses 15.9% of the cases, whereas a standard score of $+1.00$ surpasses 84.1% of the cases. Thus the percentage of cases between $-1.00$ and $+1.00$ is 84.1 minus 15.9 or 68.2%.)

### Interpreting Standard Error of Estimate

In linear correlation we make predictions of scores on one variable from scores on the other by means of the regression line. This is true whether we deal only with those situations wherein the means of the columns and of the rows all fall precisely on the same straight lines that are the regression lines or whether the regression lines are taken as the best-fitting straight lines in a least-squares sense. The deviations from the regression line are our errors in prediction, and the standard deviation of these deviations—the standard error of estimate or prediction, $\sigma_{y \cdot x}$ and $\sigma_{x \cdot y}$—describes the extent of our errors in prediction. Now how shall we regard the standard error of estimate? The problems of interpretation revolve around homoscedasticity and normality of the distribution of the deviations from the regression line, as discussed in Chapter 5.

We might say that we shall consider linear correlation as referring only to that circumstance wherein homoscedasticity holds. That is, we shall compute the Pearsonian coefficient only when the standard deviations of the distributions of the scores in the various columns are all equal to each other and when the standard deviations of the scores in the various rows are equal to each other. As we have seen, under these circumstances the error of prediction is precisely the same for all values on the predictor variable. The error in predicting $y$ from low values of $x$ would be precisely the same as the error of predicting $y$ from high values of $x$. The difficulty with adopting homoscedasticity as a necessary condition is that it seldom if ever occurs. As a consequence, this condition would be too restrictive so that the Pearsonian coefficient would be of little value to us.

A second alternative is not to require homoscedasticity. In this case, as we saw, the standard error of estimate or prediction then gives us an average of the errors of prediction. However, with any average, important differences may be obscured, and it may well be that the bivariate distribution is fan-shaped, like a spindle or a dumbbell, so that at one level of scores on the predictor variable the error of prediction is considerably greater than it is at other levels.

As is the case with all standard deviations, the standard error of estimate or prediction is most interpretable when the distribution of scores from which it is calculated is a normal frequency distribution. If the distributions of scores in the columns and in the rows are normal, then we can set limits within which an individual's predicted score will fall with a given probability. For example, in a normal frequency distribution 68 percent of the cases fall between plus and minus one standard deviation of the mean. Therefore if on the basis of the regression equation, we predict an individual's score as 50, the standard error of estimate being 5, we can say that the chances are 68 in 100 that the individual's score will be between 45 and 55. Since there is error in our prediction (because $r_{xy} < 1.00$), then we are saying the predicted score can fall within a range. This range is less than the range for the total distribution that is our range for the predicted $y$ score when we do not use the $x$ information. Thus we have a safer "guess" when there *is* correlation than when there is not. Hence if the distributions of scores in the columns and in the rows are normal, the standard error of estimate has considerable meaning. If the scores in the total distributions of the two variables are normal, then with linear correlation the scores in the columns and in the rows will be normally distributed, and in addition the columns and rows will be homoscedastic. (In addition to

each of the values, *X* or *Y,* being normally distributed, we can talk
about joint distributions. Another assumption we make in correlational
analyses is that the *joint pair* of values, *X* and *Y,* is normally distributed.
The joint distribution of *X* and *Y* values is assumed to follow a *bivariate
normal distribution.*)

Therefore we might specify that the scores in the marginal distributions of the scatter diagram must form normal frequency distributions.
However, we know that distributions of scores are seldom if ever precisely normal. Only if we can justify transmuting the scores on our
variables to other values that are precisely normally distributed would
this stipulation not be too restrictive.

If we adopt the position that there is to be no restriction on the
shapes of the marginal distributions, and hence on the shapes of the
distributions of scores in the columns and rows, the Pearsonian coefficient can be widely applied. But as we have just noted, the standard
error of estimate then is difficult to interpret.

Finally, we might adopt what is termed *normal linear correlation* as a
model. In normal linear correlation the distributions of scores in the
two marginal distributions and the distributions of scores in each of the
columns and rows also are normal (as well as bivariate normal) and in
addition homoscedastic. Furthermore, in this model the means of the
columns and of the rows all fall precisely on the same straight lines. In
this model are included all the models we referred to in our earlier
discussions. As we have seen, the model is taken as a representation of
the facts. There is no implication that the characteristics of the model
exactly represent the characteristics of the facts, but only that the two
sets of characteristics are quite similar.

Suppose that with a particular bivariate distribution we find that the
marginal distributions of scores have shapes not too unlike a normal
frequency distribution. In addition suppose that the means of the columns and of the rows seem to fluctuate in a random fashion around the
regression lines and do not depart too much from them, the regression
lines being the best-fitting lines in a least-squares sense. Then in this
case the model of normal correlation would be a useful model. We can
attribute differences between our model and the actual facts to the
random effects of sampling, or we can say that the model is sufficiently
close to the facts to be considered an acceptable description of them.
Adopting the model, we can then calculate the Pearsonian coefficient
by means of Equation 5-23 or its equivalents, using it as a description of
the extent to which our two variables are related. We use Equation 6-9
and its equivalents as the regression equation and make predictions by
means of it, and we use Equation 6-19 and its equivalents as the standard error of estimate to describe the extent of error in making predictions from any value of our predictor variable. Whenever we use a

model, however, we should always bear in mind that the model is only a representation of the facts and not necessarily a precise description of them.

---

## Technical Section

### Least-Squares Regression Equation

We wish to develop the equation for the straight line from which the mean of the squares of the deviations is at a minimum.* As we have seen, there are two regression lines in a scatter diagram, one cutting through the columns and the other cutting through the rows. Let us first consider the best-fitting line cutting through the columns.

For convenience in derivation let us take the scores on both variables as deviation scores. We saw in Equation 6-5 that under these circumstances the intercept $a$ is zero and that the formula for a straight line is

$$\bar{y} = b_{y \cdot x} x_i$$

We are not now saying that the straight line necessarily passes through the means of the columns; so let us write the equation as

$$y' = b_{y \cdot x} x_i \qquad (6\text{-}23)$$

where $y'$ merely refers to that point in column $x_i$ through which the straight line passes.

The question now is: What is the straight line described by $b_{y \cdot x}$ from which the mean of the squared deviations is at a minimum? There are a variety of values we could take as a first estimate of $b_{y \cdot x}$, but let us take

$$b_{y \cdot x} = \frac{\Sigma xy}{n \sigma_x^2}$$

Again note that we are not saying that the line described by the foregoing value of $b_{y \cdot x}$ passes through the means of the columns. All we are saying is that it is a value we can calculate from the scores on the two variables, a value we can use as our first estimate of the slope of the best-fitting line in a least-squares sense.

---

* We shall employ a very roundabout procedure, using only simple algebra to develop the equation for the best-fitting straight line. By means of the calculus the same proof could be made in very few steps.

We use the symbol $y_i$ to represent the deviation of an individual's score from $\bar{y}_i$, the mean of his or her column. We also use the symbol $v$ to represent the deviation of an individual's score from the $y'$ of his or her column when the slope of the line, $b_{y \cdot x}$, is $\Sigma xy/n\sigma_x^2$. Then

$$v = y - y'$$

Substituting for $y'$ from Equation 6-23, we have

$$v = y - b_{y \cdot x} x_i \tag{6-24}$$

Squaring both sides of the equation gives

$$v^2 = y^2 - 2b_{y \cdot x} x_i y + b_{y \cdot x}^2 x_i^2$$

This is the square of the deviation score of any individual from $y'$ in the column in which his or her $x$ score falls when $b_{y \cdot x} = \Sigma xy/n\sigma_x^2$.

Now let us sum the squared deviations for all individuals in all columns:

$$\Sigma v^2 = \Sigma y^2 - 2b_{y \cdot x}\Sigma xy + b_{y \cdot x}^2 \Sigma x^2$$

Dividing both sides of the equation by $n$, the total number of cases, gives

$$\frac{\Sigma v^2}{n} = \frac{\Sigma y^2}{n} - 2b_{y \cdot x}\frac{\Sigma xy}{n} + b_{y \cdot x}^2 \frac{\Sigma x^2}{n}$$

Remembering we are taking $b_{y \cdot x}$ as $\Sigma xy/n\sigma_x^2$, then $\Sigma xy/n = b_{y \cdot x}\sigma_x^2$:

$$\frac{\Sigma v^2}{n} = \sigma_y^2 - 2b_{y \cdot x}b_{y \cdot x}\sigma_x^2 + b_{y \cdot x}^2 \sigma_x^2$$

$$= \sigma_y^2 - b_{y \cdot x}^2 \sigma_x^2 \tag{6-15}$$

This is the mean of the squares of the deviations from a line when its slope is taken as

$$b_{y \cdot x} = \frac{\Sigma xy}{n\sigma_x^2}$$

If we can show that the mean of the squares of the deviations from a straight line with any other slope (say $\Sigma xy/n\sigma_x^2 + A$ or, more simply, $b_{y \cdot x} + A$) is greater than this, we shall have proved that the regression line as given by Equation 6-1 and its equivalents is the straight line from which the squares of the deviations are at a minimum.

Let us symbolize a deviation from a line with a slope other than $b_{y \cdot x} = \Sigma xy/n\sigma_x^2$ as $d$. Then, parallel to Equation 6-24, we would write this deviation as

$$d = y - (b_{y \cdot x}x_i + A)$$
$$= y - b_{y \cdot x}x_i - A$$

Squaring both sides of the equation gives

$$d^2 = y^2 - 2b_{y \cdot x}x_iy + b_{y \cdot x}^2x_i^2 - 2Ay + 2Ab_{y \cdot x}x_i + A^2$$

This is the square of the deviation score of any individual from the $y'$ of the column in which his or her $x$ score falls when the slope of the line that describes $y'$ is some value other than $b_{y \cdot x}$, namely, $b_{y \cdot x} + A$. Summing the deviation scores for all individuals in all columns gives

$$\Sigma d^2 = \Sigma y^2 - 2b_{y \cdot x}\Sigma xy + b_{y \cdot x}^2\Sigma x^2 - 2A\Sigma y + 2Ab_{y \cdot x}\Sigma x + \Sigma A^2$$

Dividing both sides of the equation by $n$, the total number of cases, we get

$$\frac{\Sigma d^2}{n} = \frac{\Sigma y^2}{n} - 2b_{y \cdot x}\frac{\Sigma xy}{n} + b_{y \cdot x}^2\frac{\Sigma x^2}{n} - 2A\frac{\Sigma y}{n} + 2Ab_{y \cdot x}\frac{\Sigma x}{n} + \frac{\Sigma A^2}{n}$$

Since the mean of the deviation scores is zero, the terms involving $\Sigma x/n$ and $\Sigma y/n$ are zero and drop out. The sum of the constant $A^2$ divided by the number of cases is equal to the constant. That is, $\Sigma A^2/n = A^2$. Finally, we can substitute $b_{y \cdot x}\sigma_x^2$ for $\Sigma xy/n$. Hence

$$\frac{\Sigma d^2}{n} = \sigma_y^2 - 2b_{y \cdot x}b_{y \cdot x}\sigma_x^2 + b_{y \cdot x}^2\sigma_x^2 + A^2$$
$$= \sigma_y^2 - b_{y \cdot x}^2\sigma_x^2 + A^2 \qquad (6\text{-}25)$$

Let us now compare Equation 6-15 with Equation 6-25:

$$\frac{\Sigma v^2}{n} = \sigma_y^2 - b_{y \cdot x}^2\sigma_x^2$$

$$\frac{\Sigma d^2}{n} = \sigma_y^2 - b_{y \cdot x}^2\sigma_x^2 + A^2$$

It is clear from the above equations that $\Sigma v^2/n$ is smaller than $\Sigma d^2/n$. In other words, we have proved that the regression line as given by Equation 6-1 and its equivalents is that straight line that in a scatter diagram is the line of best fit in a least-squares sense. The same reasoning, of course, would hold for the line drawn through the rows.

### *Standard Error of Estimate*

Differences between predicted and actual $y$ scores are represented as

$$v = y - \bar{y}_i$$

Since we are dealing with deviation scores, the variance is

$$\frac{\Sigma v^2}{n} = \sigma_y^2 - b_{y \cdot x}^2 \sigma_x^2 \tag{6-15}$$

In Equation 5-13 we have

$$b_{y \cdot x} = \frac{\Sigma xy}{n \sigma_x^2}$$

Substituting for $b_{y \cdot x}$ from Equation 5-13 in Equation 5-15, we have

$$\frac{\Sigma v^2}{n} = \sigma_y^2 - \left(\frac{\Sigma xy}{n}\right)^2 \frac{\sigma_x^2}{\sigma_x^4}$$

From Equation 5-23 we know that $\Sigma xy/n = \sigma_x \sigma_y r_{xy}$. Hence

$$\begin{aligned} \frac{\Sigma v^2}{n} &= \sigma_y^2 - \frac{\sigma_x^2 \sigma_y^2 r_{xy}^2 \sigma_x^2}{\sigma_x^4} \\ &= \sigma_y^2 - \sigma_y^2 r_{xy}^2 \\ &= \sigma_y^2 (1 - r_{xy}^2) \end{aligned} \tag{6-17}$$

### *Summary*

Seldom, if ever, do the means of the columns and the means of the rows fall precisely on straight lines. However, they often appear to be random fluctuations from such lines. Therefore, normal linear correlation is commonly adopted as a model. In such a case the best-fitting straight line in a least-squares sense is taken to describe the relationship. The line itself is used to give estimates of the mean $Y$ values for specified $X$ values, whereas the regression coefficient is represented by the slope. In practical terms, we use the regression equation in industry or education to predict performance given information on a test. If there is no correlation between a test ($X$) and performance ($Y$), then the best estimate of one's performance is $\bar{Y}$. If there is some degree of correlation, then the best estimate of $Y$ is the average $Y$ value for the specific $X$. An estimate of the degree of error in predicting the $Y$ score is given by the standard error of estimate or prediction. This statistic is a summary statistic of the variation of the $Y$ or $X$ values from the line of best fit.

## Suggested Readings

Cohen, J., and P. Cohen. 1975. *Applied multiple regression/correlation analysis for the behavioral sciences*. Hillsdale, N.J.: Lawrence Erlbaum Associates. Chap. 2.

Hays, W. L. 1973. *Statistics for the social sciences*. 2nd ed. New York: Holt, Rinehart and Winston. Chaps. 15 and 16.

Kerlinger, F. N., and E. J. Pedhazur. 1973. *Multiple regression in behavioral research*. New York: Holt, Rinehart and Winston. Chap. 2.

McNemar, Q. 1969. *Psychological statistics*. 4th ed. New York: Wiley. Chaps. 9 and 11.

# 7

## *Combining Component Variables into a Composite*

Many of the scores that result from our operations of measurement are composites made up of the sum or average of the scores on a series of component variables. Perhaps the most familiar composite in psychological measurement is the score an individual is assigned on most achievement, aptitude, and ability tests. Ordinarily such tests are composed of a series of items each of which is scored 1 when the answer is correct and 0 when it is incorrect. An individual's score on the test is the sum of the scores earned on the individual items. The items, then, are the components forming the composite, which is the total test. Many tests are made of up several subtests, and the individual's score is the total of scores on all the component subtests. Here the subtests are the components, and the total test the composite. Similarly, in many rating procedures each person is rated on a series of different scales, and the final score is the sum or average of the ratings assigned on the various scales. The individual rating scales are the components, and the sum or average of the ratings on them is the composite variable.

There are many situations in which we wish to combine scores on two or more variables into a single composite score. An individual's scores on several tests might be combined in order to obtain a picture of the general level of his or her abilities or traits in a particular area. Sometimes by combining the scores earned by an individual on several applications of the same test, a more accurate or representative measure of the trait is obtained. In some instances we can obtain a better prediction of scores on one variable from a composite of scores on a series of predictor tests than we can from scores on any one of the predictor tests.

Let us consider some examples. A general measure of arithmetic ability would be given by the combination of scores on four tests, one of which is composed of addition items, a second of subtraction items, a third of multiplication items, and a fourth of division items. In a like manner an overall index of the job proficiency of salespersons could be obtained from a composite made up of their total volume of sales, the number of new accounts they develop, and the number of repeat sales they make to the same customers.

Sometimes several measurements are taken on an individual with the same measuring instrument to obtain a more accurate or representative description of this person. Thus when we measure reaction time, it is common practice to take a number of determinations of speed of response and to average them. Similarly, if we are measuring some trait such as sociability by the rating method, we may combine the ratings assigned by different raters to each person. By this means we hope to obtain a more reliable index of the trait than is provided by the ratings assigned by a single rater.

Many of the types of behavior we wish to predict, such as academic performance or occupational success, are quite complex. Therefore a single test that measures only a restricted scope of traits will not give good predictions by itself. Hence we are likely to use a composite of a number of tests each measuring somewhat different traits so as to obtain better predictions of the complex variable.

Composite variables, then, are so common in psychological measurement that we need to examine their nature and special characteristics. In this chapter we relate the mean and variance of composite scores to the means and variances of scores on the components that make them up. Since components often are expressed in different kinds of units, we consider the matter of making them comparable. We examine the correlation of composites with other single variables and with other composites, and we compare summed composite scores with average composite scores.

The overall objective of this chapter is to show how the characteristics of a composite (or total) score are influenced by the characteristics of the components that make it up. Once we know what these relationships are, we will have a better understanding of how to select components that will meet our measurement objective.

## Describing Composites

The type of composite with which we are concerned in this chapter is a simple additive composite, one in which the individual's score on all components are merely added together to obtain a total score. The formula for an individual's composite of raw scores is simply

$$X_c = X_1 + \cdots + X_k \qquad (7\text{-}1)$$

where $c$ refers to the composite score and $k$ is the number of variables (or items) entering into the composite. Suppose a composite is formed by four tests. An individual who earns scores of 11, 14, 21, and 12, respectively, on the component tests would have a composite score of 58. Although this method of a total, or composite, score is a rather simple one, it permits us to derive some important relationships between component scores and composites.

For a composite of deviation scores, Equation 7-1 becomes

$$x_c = x_1 + \cdots + x_k \qquad (7\text{-}2)$$

and for standard scores

$$z_c = z_1 + \cdots + z_k \qquad (7\text{-}3)$$

### Mean of Composite Scores

From Equation 7-1 the mean of composite scores can be written as

$$\bar{X}_c = \frac{\Sigma X_c}{n} = \frac{\Sigma(X_1 + \cdots + X_k)}{n}$$

Now we can take the summation sign inside the parentheses such that

$$\bar{X}_c = \frac{\Sigma X_1}{n} + \cdots + \frac{\Sigma X_k}{n}$$
$$= \bar{X}_1 + \cdots + \bar{X}_k \qquad (7\text{-}4)$$

Equation 7-4 shows that the mean of composite scores is equal simply to the sum of the means of the individual components. If the means of the three component variables that form a composite are 42, 78, and 31, then the mean of the composite scores is 151.

From Equation 7-4 it is apparent that if the scores on the component variables are in deviation- or standard-score form, the mean of the composite scores must necessarily be zero since the mean of each of the component variables is zero.

### Variance and Standard Deviation of Composite Scores

We would now like to show what the variance and standard deviation of a composite look like in terms of the properties of its components. Again, we ask you to try and work through this derivation, tedious though it might be. This particular line of reasoning is a basic building block for a number of other relationships, and a little extra work now will pay off later. Some of the other derivations in this book need not be looked at so carefully, but this one is fundamental.

Using Equation 7-2 as a basis, we can write the formula for the variance of composite scores as

$$\sigma_c^2 = \frac{\Sigma x_c^2}{n} = \frac{\Sigma(x_1 + \cdots + x_k)^2}{n} \tag{7-5}$$

The first step, as in so many situations like this, is to multiply out the numerator to get rid of the exponent. When we square the sum in the numerator, we multiply each term by itself and with every other term, as in Table 7-1. As can be seen in this table, when we square the sum, there are $k$ terms involving $x^2$, one for each of the 1 to $k$ component variables. In addition there are $k(k - 1)$ terms involving the product of the scores on two components. Each of the unique cross-product terms appears twice in the table, once above the diagonal running from $x_1^2$ to $x_k^2$ and once below it. Hence in the table there are $[k(k - 1)]/2$ terms of $2x_i x_{i'}$, where $i$ and $i'$ are any two components. Therefore we can write Equation 7-5 as

$$\sigma_c^2 = \frac{\Sigma(x_1^2 + \cdots + x_k^2 + 2x_1 x_2 + \cdots + 2x_{k-1}x_k)}{n}$$

$$= \frac{\Sigma x_1^2}{n} + \cdots + \frac{\Sigma x_k^2}{n} + 2\frac{\Sigma x_1 x_2}{n} + \cdots + 2\frac{\Sigma x_{k-1}x_k}{n}$$

Since $\Sigma x^2/n = \sigma_x^2$, and $\Sigma x_i x_{i'}/n\sigma_i\sigma_{i'} = r_{ii'}$, so that $\Sigma x_i x_{i'}/n = \sigma_i\sigma_{i'}r_{ii'}$,

$$\sigma_c^2 = \sigma_1^2 + \cdots + \sigma_k^2 + 2\sigma_1\sigma_2 r_{12} + \cdots + 2\sigma_{k-1}\sigma_k r_{(k-1)k} \tag{7-6}$$

The standard deviation of composite scores is

$$\sigma_c = \sqrt{\sigma_1^2 + \cdots + \sigma_k^2 + 2\sigma_1\sigma_2 r_{12} + \cdots + 2\sigma_{k-1}\sigma_k r_{(k-1)k}} \tag{7-7}$$

**Table 7-1**  Square of the sum $(x_1 + \cdots + x_k)$

|         | $x_1$        | $x_2$        | $\cdots$ | $x_{k-1}$     | $x_k$        |
|---------|--------------|--------------|----------|---------------|--------------|
| $x_1$   | $x_1^2$      | $x_1 x_2$    | $\cdots$ | $x_1 x_{k-1}$ | $x_1 x_k$    |
| $x_2$   | $x_1 x_2$    | $x_2^2$      | $\cdots$ | $x_2 x_{k-1}$ | $x_2 x_k$    |
| $\cdots$| $\cdots$     | $\cdots$     | $\cdots$ | $\cdots$      | $\cdots$     |
|         |              |              | $\cdots$ |               |              |
|         |              |              | $\cdots$ |               |              |
|         |              |              | $\cdots$ |               |              |
| $x_{k-1}$ | $x_1 x_{k-1}$ | $x_2 x_{k-1}$ | $\cdots$ | $x_{k-1}^2$   | $x_k x_{k-1}$ |
| $x_k$   | $x_1 x_k$    | $x_2 x_k$    | $\cdots$ | $x_k x_{k-1}$ | $x_k^2$      |

Note that *if* the components are independent of each other (that is, there is no relationship between the components and the $r_{ii'}$ all equal 0.00), then the variance of the composite is simply the sum of the component variances.

An example of the computation of the variance of composite scores from the variances, standard deviations, and intercorrelations among the component variables from Equation 7-6 is given in Table 7-2. The component variables in the illustrations given in Table 7-2 are multistep variables. The variance of total composite scores is precisely the same whether it is computed directly from the composite scores or from Equation 7-6 from the variances, standard deviations, and intercorrelations among the component items.

Equation 7-6 also can be expressed in terms of the mean of the variances and of the covariances. By the *covariance* is meant the product of the standard deviations and the coefficient of correlation between two variables, $\sigma_i \sigma_{i'} r_{ii'}$. From Equation 5-23, the formula for the Pearsonian correlation coefficient, we can write the covariance as

$$\sigma_i \sigma_{i'} r_{ii'} = \frac{\Sigma x_i x_{i'}}{n}$$

The mean of a set of values is their sum divided by the number of values. Therefore the sum of a set of values is equal to the number of values times their mean; that is, $\Sigma X = n\bar{X}$. If we look at Equation 7-6, we see that in the first part we have the sum of the variances, which are $k$ in number, and in the second part we have the covariances, which are $k(k-1)$ in number. We can therefore write Equation 7-6 as

$$\sigma_c^2 = k\bar{\sigma}_i^2 + k(k-1)\overline{\sigma_i \sigma_{i'} r_{ii'}} \tag{7-8}$$

*Table 7-2*  Computation of variance of composite scores from
intercorrelations among components and their standard deviations

| | Component | | | | | |
|---|---|---|---|---|---|---|
| | 1 | 2 | 3 | 4 | $\sigma$ | $\sigma^2$ |
| 1 | | .20 | .40 | .00 | 5 | 25 |
| 2 | | | .30 | .10 | 3 | 9 |
| 3 | | | | .50 | 6 | 36 |
| 4 | | | | | 4 | 16 |

$$\sigma_c^2 = 25 + 9 + 36 + 16 + 2(5)(3)(.20) + 2(5)(6)(.40) + 2(5)(4)(.00)$$
$$+ 2(3)(6)(.30) + 2(3)(4)(.10) + 2(6)(4)(.50)$$
$$= 153.2$$

where $\bar{\sigma}_i^2$ is the mean of the variances of the $k$ variables, $r_{ii'}$ is the
correlation between any pair of components, and $\overline{\sigma_i \sigma_{i'} r_{ii'}}$ is the mean of
the $k(k - 1)$ covariance terms. Equation 7-8 has very little utility as a
computational formula since seldom do we know the averages required
by it. However, as we shall see later, it is of considerable value in
helping to explain other formulas.

### Composites Formed of Components Expressed in Standard Scores

In some instances the components that enter into a composite are so
very nearly the same in character that the question of their comparability in measuring units does not arise. An example is the composite
formed by the sum of the ratings assigned by several raters to each
member of a group of individuals when all raters use the same rating
scale. But in other instances the components are quite different in
nature. As an overall index of aggressiveness in nursery school children, a composite might be formed of the number of times a child
strikes other children, the number of toys he or she destroys, and the
decibels of loudness of screams of rage. If we merely sum the raw
scores on the three variables for each child, we certainly have a very
strange composite.

In the case of ratings we might say that since all raters use the same
rating method, all the ratings are comparable. Hence a simple sum or
average of the components would be considered acceptable. However,
in the composite of aggressiveness, we are adding together such different things as the number of punches, toys, and decibels. This does not
seem quite right.

To deal with this problem, we must return to our earlier discussion of standardizing scores. In that discussion we considered various ways of rendering scores on different variables comparable. We saw that the use of standard scores, or of the several allied varieties of standardized scores, is a convenient way of accomplishing this. We express the scores on each variable in terms of the distribution of scores earned by the entire group. Scores on each variable, then, have the same meaning in terms of referencing the scores to those of the entire group. Thus by expressing each of the component variables in standard or standardized scores, the scores earned by each person on them can more reasonably be summed into a composite.

Let us now consider the standard deviation and variance of composite scores when the scores on each component variable are transformed into standard scores. If the scores are transformed in this manner, then all standard deviations are equal. That is, the standard deviation, $\sigma_i$, of each component is equal to 1.0. Likewise, the variance, $\sigma_i^2$, of each component is equal to 1.0, since 1 multiplied by 1 equals 1.

If scores on all components are expressed as standard scores, then the variance and standard deviation of the *composite* score are given by Equations 7-9 and 7-10. The terms corresponding to the variances and standard deviations of the component scores have dropped out, and it is much easier to see how the number of components and their intercorrelations influence the variability of the composite. The composite standard deviation $\sigma_{c_z}$ must carry the subscript $z$ to show that it is formed by adding standard scores.

$$\sigma_{c_z}^2 = k + k(k - 1)\bar{r}_{ii'} \qquad (7\text{-}9)$$

$$\sigma_{c_z} = \sqrt{k + k(k - 1)\bar{r}_{ii'}} \qquad (7\text{-}10)$$

### Standard Deviation of Composite Scores and Number of Components

Sometimes the measuring device we use does not give us a sufficient range of scores for our purposes, so to increase the range we may add more components. For example, suppose we have a test consisting of 20 items, and the range of individual differences is only 10 points. This may not give us enough differentiation among individuals, enough different classes of persons, so we may double the number of items, expecting thereby to increase the range of scores from 10 to 20 points.

If we propose to increase the number of components in a composite, presumably the added components will be similar to the original ones in having the same average variance and average intercorrelations. Grant-

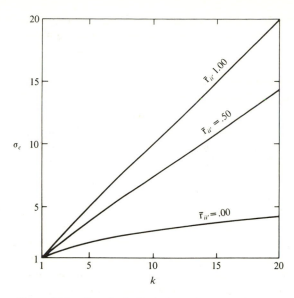

*Figure 7-1*  Standard deviation of composite scores ($\sigma_c$), in relation to number of components in composite ($k$), and average of their intercorrelations ($\bar{r}_{ii'}$).

ing this, we can turn to Equation 7-10 to discover what effect the addition of components has on the standard deviation of composite scores. This formula shows that the intercorrelation among the components is a critical factor. Equation 7-10 is plotted in Figure 7-1 for three values of $\bar{r}_{ii'}$, the average of the intercorrelations among the components. From this figure we can derive the following principles:

1. As the number of components in the composite increases, the standard deviation of composite scores increases.
2. The higher the level of the intercorrelations among the components, the greater the effect on the standard deviation of composite scores of increasing the number of components.

The intercorrelations among the components that form a composite seldom if ever will be of the order of 1.00. Indeed if the components were perfectly correlated with one another, one of them alone would be as good as any number of them; and by adding together a number of them, nothing new would be added in terms of traits measured. Therefore for all practical purposes we can say that if we increase the number of components by a given amount, the increase in the range of scores will be less than that amount and ordinarily will be substantially less.

## Correlation Between Scores on a Composite and Another Variable

In a variety of circumstances we are interested in the relationship between scores on a composite variable and those on another variable. The other variable could be some external variable that is independent of the composite, or it could be one of the components in the composite. For example, we might have several different measures of the academic success of students, such as grades earned in different courses, which we have pooled together to obtain an overall index of academic success. If we are interested in the relationship between academic success and some outside variable, say intelligence, then we should obtain the coefficient of correlation between the composite scores on academic success and the scores on an intelligence test. As another example, we might be interested in predicting scores on some variable, for instance, a measure of performance on a job. We might believe that a better prediction would be obtained from a composite of predictor tests than from any single test. A single test may measure only one aspect of the behavior we are trying to predict, whereas a combination of tests each measuring somewhat different traits may be expected to give better prediction. Again we should be concerned with the relationship between scores on a composite variable and scores on an outside variable. These kinds of examples and relationships will be discussed again in the chapters on validity and multiple regression.

We might also be interested in the correlation of the composite score with one of its own components. For example, we might have administered to a sample of employed people, a number of questionnaire items having to do with satisfaction with different aspects of work. If we sum the scores on all the items, we could perhaps think of the total score as a measure of overall job satisfaction. If we then compute the correlation between an individual item and the total score, what does the correlation tell us? It (the correlation coefficient) is an index of the degrees of correspondence between satisfaction with the specific aspect of the job measured by the item (for example, satisfaction with opportunities for promotion) and overall job satisfaction.

As you read this section, you should keep in mind that the objective is to show how the correlation between the composite and some other variable is influenced by the characteristics of the individual components making up the composite. If we know which characteristics make the correlation go up and which make it go down, we are in a better position to select the components we want.

### Correlation Between a Composite and an Outside Variable

Our aim here is to arrive at a formula that will specify how the correlation between a composite score and an external variable ($x_0$) is influenced by the characteristics of the components making up the composite. The characteristics we have in mind are the number of components and their covariances, or intercorrelations.

The full derivation of this formula is given in the Technical Section at the end of this chapter. Here are only the beginning and the end of the story. In this chapter we will use $c$ to denote a composite and $O$ to denote the external variable. We could just as easily use $X$ and $Y$ to denote $c$ and $O$, respectively, to represent a test composed of several subtests (components) and a criterion or variable in which we are interested in predicting. The notation adopted here more readily demonstrates the intent of this chapter, composites and their relationship to other variables.

The definitional formula for the correlation between a composite ($c$) and an external variable ($x_o$) in deviation-score form is as follows:

$$r_{x_oc} = \frac{\Sigma x_O x_c}{n\sigma_O \sigma_c}$$

where $x_c = (x_1 + x_2 + \cdots + x_k)$.

If we make the appropriate substitution for $x_c$, work through the algebra, and transform component scores to standard-score form at the crucial moment, we arrive at a formula that expresses this correlation in terms of component characteristics.

In raw-score form

$$r_{x_oc} = \frac{k\sigma_i\sigma_{Oi}}{\sqrt{k\bar{\sigma}_i^2 + k(k-1)\overline{\sigma_i\sigma_{i'}r_{ii'}}}} \tag{7-11}$$

or in standard-score form

$$r_{z_Oc_z} = \frac{k\bar{r}_{Oi}}{\sqrt{k + k(k-1)\bar{r}_{ii'}}} \tag{7-12}$$

If we use the appropriate algebraic steps to divide both the numerator and the denominator of Equation 7-12 by $k$, we can illustrate some interesting phenomena.

Under these circumstances

$$r_{z_O c_z} = \frac{\bar{r}_{oi}}{\sqrt{1/k + \left(\dfrac{k-1}{k}\right)\bar{r}_{ii'}}} \qquad (7\text{-}13)$$

If the composite is formed of a very, very large number of components, then $1/k$ very closely approximates zero and $(k - 1)/k$ very closely approximates 1.00. Then symbolizing composite scores as $c_{z_\infty}$ to indicate that the composite is formed of an infinitely large number of components, we can write Equation 7-13 as

$$r_{z_O c_{z_\infty}} = \frac{\bar{r}_{oi}}{\sqrt{\bar{r}_{ii'}}} \qquad (7\text{-}14)$$

The practicalities of most situations limit the length of the composites and the number of measurements we can use. Sometimes the amount of time available for measurement is the limiting factor. If we were measuring the school achievement of graduating high school seniors, we might like to have a test of several hundred items to give full coverage of all subjects, but in a one-hour examination perhaps all we can use is a test of 100 items. In other situations it is physically or administratively impossible to obtain all the measurements we wish. Thus when friendliness is measured by ratings, we might like to have the subjects rated by a very large number of acquaintances, but perhaps we can obtain only three such raters.

Equation 7-14 permits us to estimate the correlation between an outside variable and a composite variable when the composite is formed of an infinitely large number of components of the same nature, that is, components having the same average correlations as that of the components we actually use. For example, suppose we wish to predict college grades ($O$) from the high school achievement test. If $\bar{r}_{oi} = .50$ and $\bar{r}_{ii'} = .81$, Equation 7-13 tells us that a 100-item test ($k = 100$) with these characteristics predicts college grades with a correlation of .555, and Equation 7-14 tells us that even if we had an infinitely large number of such items, the correlation would be only .556. Hence it would not be worthwhile to increase the length of the test. Suppose we wish to examine the relationship between friendliness and scores on a "sociability" inventory and $\bar{r}_{oi} = .20$ and $\bar{r}_{ii'} = .25$. Equation 7-13 tells us that ratings with these characteristics made by three individuals ($k = 3$) are correlated with inventory scores only .284, and Equation 7-14 tells us that inventory scores would be correlated .40 with ratings if an infinitely large number of such raters could be used.

Equation 7-13 shows that the correlation between scores on a composite variable and an outside variable is a function of the number of component variables in the composite and of the magnitude of the intercorrelations among them, together with the magnitude of the correlations between the components and the outside variable. Entering the three illustrative values of .20, .50, and .80 for $\bar{r}_{ii'}$ and for $\bar{r}_{Oi}$ in Equation 7-13, together with a number of values of $k$, the formula is solved for $r_{x_Oc_z}$, and the values are plotted in Figure 7-2. From this figure the following principles can be derived:

1. The higher the correlations between the components and the outside variable, the higher the correlation between the composite and the outside variable.

2. The lower the intercorrelations among the components, the higher the correlation between the composite and the outside variable.

3. As the number of components in the composite increases (assuming the additional components are the same as the original components in terms of their average correlations with the other components and with the outside variable), the correlation between the composite and the outside variable increases.

We have seen that two general purposes for forming a composite are to obtain a better, more precise, or more representative measure of the variable in which we are interested and to obtain a better device for predicting another variable. These two purposes are likely to lead us to form composites made up of components that have quite different levels of intercorrelation.

If we form a composite in order to obtain a better, more precise, or more representative measure of the variable in which we are interested, it is probable that the component variables we select will tend to measure the same kinds of traits and hence have relatively high intercorrelations. For example, if we were making up a test of arithmetic ability, we would include items involving computations but not items involving memory span for numbers, knowledge of algebraic formulas, or interest in mathematics. The correlations among the scores people earned on computational items undoubtedly would be higher on the average than the correlations among the scores they earned on items involving memory span for numbers, knowledge of algebraic formulas, or interest in mathematics.

Similarly, if we were developing an index of the job proficiency of department heads in a business organization, such as the supervisors of persons in lower positions, we might include rating scales designed to measure the extent to which they communicate with their subordinates, clarify duties and standards of work, and administer discipline

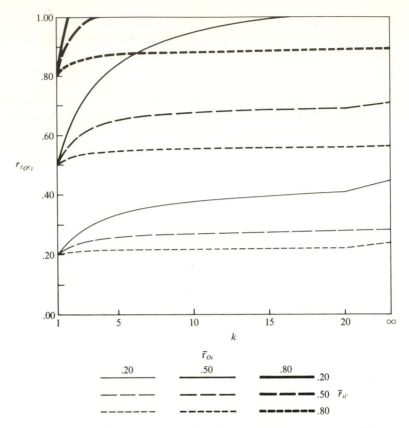

*Figure 7-2* Effects on correlation between scores on an outside variable and scores on a composite variable ($r_{z_O c_z}$) of number of components ($k$), intercorrelations among components ($\bar{r}_{ii'}$), and correlations between components and outside variable ($\bar{r}_{Oi}$).

fairly. However, we would not include rating scales intended to measure effectiveness in planning new activities, qualifications for promotion, and developing budgets, since these characteristics may have nothing to do with the trait of supervisory ability. Again it is likely that scores on these first three scales would be more closely correlated with one another than scores on all six scales, since the former pertain to one domain of behavior whereas the latter pertain to quite different aspects of behavior.

The point is that when we form a composite of this sort, the very process we use—the definition of the variable we follow in selecting components—will ordinarily result in the selection of component variables that on the average bear at least moderately substantial relationships to one another. Furthermore it is highly probable that the components in the composite will be more highly related to one another than to any outside variable; that is, ordinarily,

$$\bar{r}_{ii'} > \bar{r}_{oi}$$

Referring to Figure 7-2, we can see that while increasing the number of components does increase the correlation between composite scores and scores on the outside variable, the increase is not very great. Indeed, increasing the number of components by more than about five times produces little or no increase in the correlation.

On the other hand, when we develop a composite that we intend to use as a basis for predicting an outside variable, it is likely that the components we select to form the composite will have relatively low intercorrelations. When we seek to predict some variable from several other variables, we try to select predictor variables that measure different aspects of the outside variable.

For example, suppose we wish to develop a battery of tests to predict success in a mechanics training course. On the basis of our analysis of the content and nature of the course, we might decide that there are four general aspects that should be measured, namely, ability to learn, ability to understand written material, capacity to perceive the shapes and forms of objects, and manual dexterity. We might propose using an intelligence test to measure learning ability and a reading test to measure ability to understand written material. However, the intelligence test as well as the reading test involves reading and understanding what is read. Therefore we would probably not include the latter in our battery. Because performance on both tests depends heavily on verbal ability, it is not surprising to find that the scores are highly correlated. Consequently in our process of selecting tests, we should deliberately exclude a test whose scores are highly correlated with those of another test already included.

To measure the capacity to perceive the shapes and forms of objects, we might use a paper-and-pencil test wherein the individual makes judgments about the similarity and differences among two-dimensional geometric figures, or a performance test wherein spatial ability is measured by the speed and accuracy with which the individual places solid figures of different shapes in appropriately shaped holes in a board. It is likely that we would select the second type of test rather than the first because the first involves reading instructions printed on the test and we already have measured verbal ability. Scores on a paper-and-pencil spatial-ability test are more highly correlated with an intelligence test than are scores on a performance spatial-ability test. Hence again we deliberately select a component for the composite on the basis of the fact that its correlations with other components are low.

Manual dexterity ordinarily is measured by means of a test involving speed and accuracy of placing pegs in holes in a board. However, this ability is measured to a substantial degree by the test we selected to measure spatial ability, so we would not include a pegboard test. Again a variable that is correlated to a high degree with some other component in the composite is excluded.

Therefore when we form a composite with which we intend to predict some outside variable, we seek components that are relatively independent of one another. Naturally we also seek variables as components that also are highly correlated with the outside variable we wish to predict. The situation we try to achieve, then, is one wherein

$$\bar{r}_{ii'} < \bar{r}_{oi}$$

Specifically, the optimal cases illustrated in the Figure 7-2 are

| $\bar{r}_{ii'}$ | $\bar{r}_{oi}$ |
|---|---|
| .50 | .80 |
| .20 | .80 |
| .20 | .50 |

Referring to Figure 7-2, we can see that increasing the number of components substantially increases the correlation between composite scores and scores on the outside variable. However, with the types of tests ordinarily usable in a practical predictive situation—as in the example given above for the mechanics training course—it is not easy to find many tests that bear low correlations with other tests and at the same time are highly correlated with the outside variable, the one to be predicted. Indeed in most cases the fact will be that at the best $\bar{r}_{oi}$ is equal to, but not higher than, $\bar{r}_{ii'}$. The curves in Figure 7-2 then rise more rapidly as the number of components increases than is likely to be the case in practice.

### Correlation Between a Composite and One of Its Components

We have been considering the correlation between scores on a single variable and a composite variable when the single variable is outside of the composite. Sometimes we are interested in the correlation between scores on a single and a composite variable when the single variable is a member of the composite. We would like a formula for this correlation that shows how it was influenced by the characteristics of the components in the composite. Again the complete derivation is given in the

Technical Section at the end of this chapter. For now we will show only where it starts and where it ends.

In deviation-score form, the definitional formula for the correlation between a composite $(c)$ and a component within the composite $(x_1)$ is as follows:

$$r_{x_1 x_c} = \frac{\Sigma x_1 x_c}{n \sigma_1 \sigma_c}$$

where $x_c = (x_1 + x_2 + \cdots + x_k)$. If we make the appropriate substitution for $x_c$, work through the algebra, and transform component scores to standard-score form at the crucial time, the resulting explanatory formula for the correlation between a composite made up of a sum of standard scores and one of the components (in standard-score form) is as follows:

$$r_{z_1 c_z} = \frac{1 + (k - 1)\bar{r}_{1i}}{\sqrt{k + k(k - 1)\bar{r}_{ii'}}} \tag{7-15}$$

In Equation 7-15, $\bar{r}_{1i}$ is equal to the average correlation of the single component in question with each of the other components. Everything else is as before.

Let us consider for a moment the meaning of $\bar{r}_{ii'}$ in Equation 7-15. This term is the average of the coefficients of correlation among all the components in the composite. If this value is high, then we can say that the composite is homogeneous in the sense that the components tend to measure the same traits to a high degree; and if the value is low, then the composite is heterogeneous since the components measure few if any traits in common. Obviously $\bar{r}_{ii'}$ is equal to the average of the coefficients of each of the components with all others. That is,

$$\bar{r}_{ii'} = \frac{\bar{r}_{1i} + \bar{r}_{2i} + \cdots + \bar{r}_{ki}}{k} \tag{7-16}$$

The relationship between $\bar{r}_{1i}$ and $\bar{r}_{ii'}$ can be better seen if we think of all the intercorrelations among components in the form of a matrix. Suppose $k = 5$ and we intercorrelate all possible pairs of components. That means for each component we correlate scores on it with scores on each of the four remaining components. These 20 intercorrelations are shown in Figure 7-3. Note that the 10 correlations in the upper triangle are the same values as the 10 correlations in the lower triangle. The average of the values in the first row or first column (they are identical) is the value in the numerator of Equation 7-15. The overall average of all 20 intercorrelations, which is identical to the mean corre-

|        | $x_1$ | $x_2$ | $x_3$ | $x_4$ | $x_5$ |               |
|--------|-------|-------|-------|-------|-------|---------------|
| $x_1$  | —     | $r_{12}$ | $r_{13}$ | $r_{14}$ | $r_{15}$ | $\bar{r}_{1i}$ |
| $x_2$  | $r_{12}$ | —     | $r_{23}$ | $r_{24}$ | $r_{25}$ | $\bar{r}_{2i}$ |
| $x_3$  | $r_{13}$ | $r_{23}$ | —     | $r_{34}$ | $r_{35}$ | $\bar{r}_{3i}$ |
| $x_4$  | $r_{14}$ | $r_{24}$ | $r_{34}$ | —     | $r_{45}$ | $\bar{r}_{4i}$ |
| $x_5$  | $r_{15}$ | $r_{25}$ | $r_{35}$ | $r_{45}$ | —     | $\bar{r}_{5i}$ |
|        | $\bar{r}_{1i}$ | $\bar{r}_{2i}$ | $\bar{r}_{3i}$ | $\bar{r}_{4i}$ | $\bar{r}_{5i}$ | $\bar{r}_{ii'}$ |

*Figure 7-3*   Matrix of correlations among five components. On the margins are shown the averages of each row and each column. Overall average $\bar{r}_{ii'}$ is average of all 20 values in matrix.

lation of either the upper or the lower triangles, is the value in the denominator of Equation 7-15.

### *Developing Homogeneous Composites*

Equation 7-16 shows that if we wish to increase the *homogeneity of a composite,* we should eliminate those component variables that on the average have the lowest correlations with the other components. However, Equation 7-15 shows us that a coefficient of correlation between a component and the total composite is related to the average of the coefficients between the component and the other components. To show this effect, Equation 7-15 is plotted in Figure 7-4. From this figure we can derive the following principles:

1. The average of the coefficients of correlation between a component and the other components of a composite is directly proportional to the correlation between the component and the total composite.

2. The coefficient of correlation between a component and the total composite is higher than the average of the coefficients of

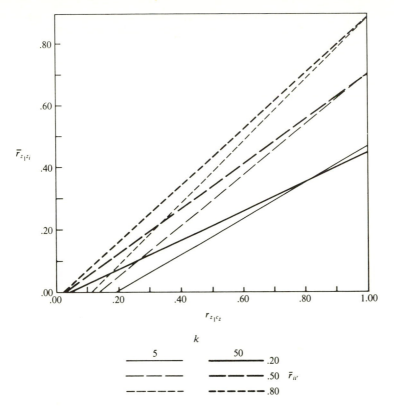

*Figure 7-4* Average of coefficients of correlation between one component of a composite and the other components ($r_{z_1 z_i}$) in relation to coefficient of correlation between that component and total composite scores ($r_{z_1 c_z}$), average of intercorrelations among components ($\bar{r}_{ii'}$), and number of components ($k$).

correlation between the component and the other components. (This is because the component itself is included in the total composite.) The higher the average correlation (homogeneity) among the components, the less this effect.

3. The number of components has relatively little effect on the proportional relationship between the correlation between a component and the total composite and the average of the correlations between the component and the other components.

An example of how eliminating the components that have the lowest correlation with the total composite scores results in increasing the homogeneity of the composite ($\bar{r}_{ii'}$) is shown in Table 7-3. Recall that

***Table 7-3***  Increasing homogeneity among component variables through elimination of components with lowest correlation with total composite scores

### Intercorrelations Among Components ($r_{ii'}$)

|    | 1 | 2 | 3 | 4 | 5 | 6 | 7 | 8 | 9 | 10 |
|----|---|----|----|----|----|----|----|----|----|----|
| 1  |   | .07 | .75 | .77 | .04 | .59 | .01 | .51 | .07 | .02 |
| 2  |   |   | .03 | .05 | .03 | .10 | .05 | .07 | .09 | .03 |
| 3  |   |   |   | .72 | .02 | .64 | .08 | .43 | .10 | .09 |
| 4  |   |   |   |   | .06 | .65 | .00 | .48 | .00 | .06 |
| 5  |   |   |   |   |   | .08 | .01 | .09 | .07 | .00 |
| 6  |   |   |   |   |   |   | .02 | .40 | .03 | .01 |
| 7  |   |   |   |   |   |   |   | .06 | .04 | .10 |
| 8  |   |   |   |   |   |   |   |   | .04 | .08 |
| 9  |   |   |   |   |   |   |   |   |   | .05 |
| 10 |   |   |   |   |   |   |   |   |   |   |

| Component | Composite Containing All Original Components | | Composite After Eliminating Components with Lowest $r_{1c}$ | |
|-----------|---------|-----------|---------|-----------|
|           | $r_{1c}$ | $\bar{r}_{1i}$ | $r_{1c}$ | $\bar{r}_{1i}$ |
| 1  | .76 | .31 | .88 | .66 |
| 2  | .30 | .06 |     |     |
| 3  | .77 | .32 | .86 | .64 |
| 4  | .75 | .31 | .88 | .66 |
| 5  | .28 | .04 |     |     |
| 6  | .70 | .28 | .80 | .57 |
| 7  | .27 | .04 |     |     |
| 8  | .63 | .24 | .69 | .46 |
| 9  | .30 | .05 |     |     |
| 10 | .29 | .05 |     |     |
|    | $\sigma_c = 5.03$ | | $\sigma_c = 4.10$ | |
|    | $\bar{r}_{ii'} = .17$ | | $\bar{r}_{ii'} = .59$ | |

under ordinary circumstances we do not know either the intercorrelations among the components or the average of the correlations between each component and the other components ($\bar{r}_{1i}$). These values are given in Table 7-3 to make the matter more comprehensible. In the example we see that components 2, 5, 7, 9, and 10 have the lowest correlations with the total composite score and therefore also the lowest average correlations with the other components. If we eliminate these components, not only do the remaining components have higher correlations with the new total composite scores and consequently higher average coefficients of correlation with the remaining components, but also the homogeneity of the composite is substantially increased. As would be expected, when the number of components is reduced, the standard deviation of composite scores is reduced, but not very much because the components selected for elimination have low intercorrelations. Frequently the process illustrated in Table 7-3 is repeated several times, eliminating in successive stages those components with the lowest correlations with the total composite until there remains a composite that is quite homogeneous. When the components are items in a test, this process is termed *item analysis against total test scores.*

The particular coefficient used for $r_{1c}$ depends on the nature of the data and on the shortcuts we take to reduce the labor of computation. If the components are the items of a test each of which is scored as "pass" or "fail," the biserial or the point biserial may be the most appropriate coefficient. If the components are continuous variables, we may wish to use the Pearsonian coefficient.

It should be recalled that our discussion of the process whereby the homogeneity of a composite can be increased was developed from Equation 7-15, which presupposes that all components are expressed in standard-score form. While it may be that in some cases the standard deviations of all components are equal, as when we deliberately equate the standard deviations of the scores in all components to make them comparable, in most instances they are not. For example, seldom if ever do we find all the items of a test having standard deviations of exactly the same value.

It can be demonstrated that as the components differ among themselves more and more in the magnitude of their standard deviations, the effect is to reduce the proportionality between $r_{1c}$ and $\bar{r}_{1i}$. That is, the relationship between these two values, while still positive, is not perfect. Therefore two components could have different values of $\bar{r}_{1i}$ and yet have the same value of $r_{1c}$.

However, in practice the differences in magnitude of the standard deviations of the components often are not great, and therefore the relationship between $r_{1c}$ and $\bar{r}_{1i}$ is quite high. Hence in many instances the values of $\sigma_i$ do not make a great deal of difference. Consequently the procedure illustrated in Table 7-3 will in most situations prove adequate in eliminating the less homogeneous components.

### Correlation Between Two Composites

We now turn to the relationship between scores on two composite variables. For example, we might be interested in the correlation between a test of creativity made up of several individual items and a test of intelligence made up of several individual items. As before, we want to see how this correlation is influenced by the properties of the individual items in the two tests. In general, let us term one composite $x$, saying that it contains $k$ components, and the other composite $y$, saying that it contains $m$ components. (Note that we are returning to the typical correlational notation.) What we need is a formula for the correlation between composite $x$ and composite $y$ that expresses the correlation in terms of the component properties making up the two composites. Again the complete derivation is given in the Technical Section at the end of this chapter. Only the start and the finish are shown below.

The deviation-score form of the definitional formula for the correlation between two composites is as follows:

$$r_{c_x c_y} = \frac{\Sigma c_x c_y}{n \sigma_{c_x} \sigma_{c_y}}$$

where $c_x = x_1 + x_2 + \cdots + x_k$ and $c_y = y_1 + y_2 + \cdots + y_m$. If we make the proper substitutions for $x_{c_x}$ and $x_{c_y}$, follow through the algebra, and transform component scores to standard-score form, we arrive at the following illustrative formula for the correlation between two composites.

$$r_{c_{z_x} c_{z_y}} = \frac{km\bar{r}_{xy}}{\sqrt{k + k(k-1)\bar{r}_{xx'}} \sqrt{m + m(m-1)\bar{r}_{yy'}}} \tag{7-17}$$

In this expression $\bar{r}_{xy}$ is the value obtained when we average all the unique correlations between pairs of components when one of the pair comes from component $x$ and one comes from component $y$. In our previous example of an intelligence test and a creativity test, each item in the intelligence test would be correlated with each item in the creativity test. The value for $\bar{r}_{xx'}$ is the average intercorrelation between pairs of components in the first composite, say the intelligence test. The value for $\bar{r}_{yy'}$ is the average intercorrelation between pairs of components in the second composite, say the creativity test.

If we divide both the numerator and the denominator of Equation

7-17 by $(km)$, we can again illustrate some basic truths. The correlation then has the form:

$$r_{z_{c_x}z_{c_y}} = \frac{\bar{r}_{x_k y_m}}{\sqrt{\frac{1}{k} + \frac{(k-1)}{k}\bar{r}_{xx'}} \sqrt{\frac{1}{m} + \frac{(m-1)}{m}\bar{r}_{yy'}}} \qquad (7\text{-}18)$$

If both composites are formed of a very large number of components, say that $k$ and $m$ are infinitely large numbers, then $1/k$ and $1/m$ very closely approximate zero and $(k-1)/k$ and $(m-1)/m$ very closely approximate 1.00. Symbolizing composite scores as $c_{z_x,\infty}$ and $c_{z_y,\infty}$ to indicate that the composites are formed of infinitely large numbers of components, we can write Equation 7-18 as

$$r_{c_{z_x,\infty}c_{z_y,\infty}} = \frac{\bar{r}}{\sqrt{\bar{r}_{xx'}}\sqrt{\bar{r}_{yy'}}} \qquad (7\text{-}19)$$

Entering illustrative values of .20, .50, and .80 for $\bar{r}_{xx'}$, $\bar{r}_{yy'}$, and $\bar{r}_{xy}$ in Equation 7-18, together with a number of different values of $k$ and $m$, and for simplicity letting $k = m$, the formula is solved for $r_{c_x c_y}$ and the values are plotted in Figure 7-5. From this figure the following principles concerning the correlation between scores on two composite variables can be derived:

1. The higher the correlations between the components of the two composites (the cross correlations), the higher the correlation between the two composites.

2. The lower the intercorrelations among the components (the less homogeneous the components), the higher the correlation between the two composites.

3. As the numbers of components in the two composites increase (assuming the additional components are the same as the original components in terms of their average intercorrelations and cross correlations), the correlation between the two composites increases. The lower the intercorrelations among the components that comprise the two composites, the greater this effect.

These principles are useful in a variety of ways for dealing with practical problems in psychological measurement. As we have seen, we frequently deal with composite variables and often are concerned with the relationship between such variables.

When we wish to increase the degree of relationship between two composites, we sometimes try to do so by increasing the number of

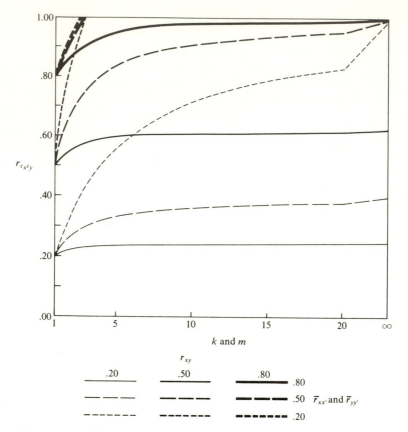

*Figure 7-5*  Effects on correlation between scores on two composite variables ($r_{c_x c_y}$) of number of components ($k$ and $m$, where $k = m$), intercorrelations among components ($\bar{r}_{xx'}$ and $\bar{r}_{yy'}$, where $\bar{r}_{xx'} = \bar{r}_{yy'}$), and cross correlations between components of two composites ($\bar{r}_{x_k y_m}$).

components in them and expect thereby to improve precision of measurement. As we can see from Figure 7-5, this increase in the correlation between two composites is greatest when the correlations among the components are low, that is, when the composite is a heterogeneous one. Yet frequently the composites we deal with are homogeneous, and therefore increasing the number of components has relatively little effect on the correlation between the two composites.

For example, the correlation between the ratings assigned by different raters to the same individual often is relatively low, perhaps .50 or less. Sometimes it is argued that this results from the fact that the trait being rated is so ambiguous that the different raters cannot agree on its meaning. As a remedy we may fractionate the trait into its different aspects and have each rater evaluate every individual on a number of subtraits. A composite in this case is the series of scales measuring these subtraits. The correlation between composites is the degree of relationship between the total rating assigned by two raters. The procedure of fractionation just described is not likely to improve the agreement between raters, inasmuch as raters commonly manifest the so-called halo error. That is, the ratings assigned by a rater on different scales usually are very highly correlated, perhaps .70 or above. Thus the composite that is formed of the ratings assigned by a rater on a number of scales is very likely to be homogeneous; and therefore such a fractionation will only slightly, if at all, improve the degree of agreement between two raters.

In some situations we need two or more forms of the same test. The forms must differ in the specific items they contain so that, having taken one form, an individual will not thereby obtain a relatively higher score on the second form because he or she remembers what was on the first. Furthermore the scores on both forms should be highly correlated so that we can be assured they measure the same abilities or traits. It may be that we want several forms of a test so that if something happens to disturb a testing situation when an individual is taking the test, we can give him another. Or we may wish to administer a test before and after some treatment—experimental, therapeutic, or otherwise—to observe any change that might have occurred as a result of the treatment.

When we make up a test or series of forms of a test, we begin by developing a series of items. We develop these items from the definition of the variable we propose to measure. When we assemble the items into different forms, we know from Equation 7-18 that those items that are likely to be highly correlated should be placed into different forms and that those items that are likely to be less correlated should be placed in the same form. For example, if we were developing two forms of a test designed to measure knowledge of American history and we had two questions concerning the Civil War and two questions concerning the foreign policy of the Wilson administration, we would place one of each type of question in one form of the test and the other in the second form. It seems likely that the correlations between scores on the two Civil War items and on the two Wilson administration items will be higher than the correlation between the scores on either one or the other of the Civil War items and either one or the other of the Wilson administration items.

---

## Technical Section

For the patient and stout-hearted reader this Technical Section gives a fuller account of how the illustrative formulas for the correlations of composites with other variables were developed. Careful study of these derivations should pay off in a greater understanding of the internal workings of composite scores. However, they are not a necessary prerequisite for reading the rest of the book.

### Correlation Between a Composite and an Outside Variable

The formula for the correlation between scores on a composite variable and scores on an outside variable can be derived from Equation 5-23 as follows. The composite variable $c$ is comprised of 1 to $k$ components, and the outside variable is symbolized as $O$:

$$r_{xoc} = r_{xo(x_1 + \cdots + x_k)} = \frac{\Sigma x_0(x_1 + \cdots + x_k)}{n\sigma_0\sigma_c}$$

$$= \frac{\Sigma(x_0 x_1 + \cdots + x_0 x_k)}{n\sigma_0\sigma_c}$$

$$= \frac{\Sigma x_0 x_1 + \cdots + \Sigma x_0 x_k}{n\sigma_0\sigma_c}$$

$$= \frac{\Sigma x_0 x_1/n + \cdots + \Sigma x_0 x_k/n}{\sigma_0\sigma_c}$$

Remembering that the sum of the cross products of deviation scores divided by the number of cases is equal to the product of the standard deviations of the two variables and the coefficient of correlation between them (their *covariance*), we have

$$r_{xoc} = \frac{\sigma_0\sigma_1 r_{01} + \cdots + \sigma_0\sigma_k r_{0k}}{\sigma_0\sigma_c}$$

$$= \frac{\sigma_0(\sigma_1 r_{01} + \cdots + \sigma_k r_{0k})}{\sigma_0\sigma_c}$$

$$= \frac{\sigma_1 r_{01} + \cdots + \sigma_k r_{0k}}{\sigma_c}$$

If all the component variables are expressed in standard-score form, then the values for the standard deviations in the numerator all become 1.00, and in the denominator we can substitute for the standard deviation of composite scores from Equation 7-10. This gives us

$$r_{z_0c_z} = r_{z_0(z_1 + \cdots + z_k)} = \frac{r_{01} + \cdots + r_{0k}}{\sqrt{k + k(k - 1)\bar{r}_{ii'}}}$$

where $\bar{r}_{ii'}$ represents the average of the coefficients of correlation among the component variables. In the numerator we have a set of values for which we can substitute their mean times the number of values:

$$r_{z_0 c_z} = \frac{k \bar{r}_{0i}}{\sqrt{k + k(k - 1)\bar{r}_{ii'}}}$$

where $\bar{r}_{0i}$ represents the average of the coefficients of correlation between the outside variable and all the component variables. If we divide the numerator and the denominator by $k$, we have

$$r_{z_0 c_z} = \frac{\bar{r}_{oi}}{(1/k) \sqrt{k + k(k - 1)\bar{r}_{ii'}}}$$

$$= \frac{\bar{r}_{oi}}{\sqrt{k/k^2 + \frac{[k(k - 1)]}{k^2} \bar{r}_{ii'}}}$$

$$= \frac{\bar{r}_{oi}}{\sqrt{1/k + \left(\frac{k - 1}{k}\right) \bar{r}_{ii'}}} \tag{7-13}$$

### Correlation Between a Composite and One of Its Components

The composite consists of 1 to $k$ components, and we wish to obtain the coefficient of correlation between scores on one of these components, say component 1, and the total composite of scores. This correlation is

$$r_{1c} = r_{x_1(x_1 + \cdots + x_k)} = \frac{\Sigma x_1(x_1 + \cdots + x_k)}{n \sigma_1 \sigma_c}$$

$$= \frac{\Sigma x_1/n + \Sigma x_1 x_2/n + \cdots + \Sigma x_1 x_k/n}{\sigma_1 \sigma_c}$$

$$= \frac{\sigma_1^2 + \sigma_1 \sigma_2 r_{12} + \cdots + \sigma_1 \sigma_k r_{1k}}{\sigma_1 \sigma_c}$$

In the numerator we have the sum of the covariances between 1 and each of the other $k - 1$ components. Remembering that the sum of a set of values is equal to their mean times the number of values, we can write

$$r_{1c} = \frac{\sigma_1^2 + (k - 1)\overline{\sigma_1 \sigma_i r_{1i}}}{\sigma_1 \sigma_c}$$

where $\sigma_1 \sigma_i r_{1i}$ represents the mean of the covariances of component 1 with all the other components.

If all the components are expressed in standard-score form, then the standard deviations in the numerator become 1.00 and we can substitute for the standard deviation of composite scores from Equation 7-9.

We then have

$$r_{z_1c_z} = \frac{1 + (k - 1)\bar{r}_{1i}}{\sqrt{k + k(k - 1)\bar{r}_{ii'}}} \tag{7-15}$$

### Correlation Between Two Composites

From Equation 5-23 we can write the coefficient of correlation between scores on two composites as

$$
\begin{aligned}
r_{c_x c_y} &= r_{(x_1 + \cdots + x_k)(y_1 + \cdots + y_m)} \\
&= \frac{\Sigma(x_1 + \cdots + x_k)(y_1 + \cdots + y_m)}{n\sigma_{c_x}\sigma_{c_y}} \\
&= \frac{\Sigma x_1 y_1 + \cdots + \Sigma x_1 y_m + \cdots + \Sigma x_k y_1 + \cdots + \Sigma x_k y_m}{n\sigma_{c_x}\sigma_{c_y}}
\end{aligned}
$$

Since each of the $k$ components of composite $x$ is paired with each of the $m$ components of composite $y$, the numerator of the above formula contains $km$ terms. Dividing the numerator and the denominator by $n$, the number of cases, we have

$$r_{c_x c_y} = \frac{\Sigma x_1 y_1/n + \cdots + \Sigma x_1 y_m/n + \cdots + \Sigma x_k y_1/n + \cdots + \Sigma x_k y_m/n}{\sigma_{c_x}\sigma_{c_y}}$$

$$= \frac{\sigma_{x_1}\sigma_{y_1}r_{x_1 y_1} + \cdots + \sigma_{x_1}\sigma_{y_m}\sigma_{x_1 y_m} + \cdots + \sigma_{x_k}\sigma_{y_1}r_{x_k y_1} + \cdots + \sigma_{x_k}\sigma_{y_m}r_{x_k y_m}}{\sigma_{c_x}\sigma_{c_y}}$$

An example of the computation of the coefficient of correlation between scores on two composite variables is given in Table 7-4. If all the component variables are expressed in standard-score form, the values for the standard deviations in the numerator become 1.00, and in the denominator we can substitute the standard deviation of composite scores. This gives us

$$r_{c_{z_x} c_{z_y}} = \frac{r_{x_1 y_1} + \cdots + r_{x_1 y_m} + \cdots + r_{x_k y_1} + \cdots + r_{x_k y_m}}{\sqrt{k + k(k - 1)\bar{r}_{xx'}}\sqrt{m + m(m - 1)\bar{r}_{yy'}}}$$

where $\bar{r}_{xx'}$ is the average of the intercorrelations among the $k$ components of composite $x$, and $\bar{r}_{yy'}$ is the average of the intercorrelations

**Table 7-4** Computation of coefficient of correlation between scores on two composites (from Equation 7-9, $\sigma_{c_i} = 9.24$; $\sigma_{c_j} = 13.30$)

| | Composite x | | | Composite y | | $\sigma$ |
|---|---|---|---|---|---|---|
| | $x_1$ | $x_2$ | $x_3$ | $y_1$ | $y_2$ | |
| $x_1$ | | .40 | .60 | .20 | .15 | 4 |
| $x_2$ | | | .50 | .15 | .10 | 2 |
| $x_3$ | | | | .00 | .30 | 5 |
| $y_1$ | | | | | .80 | 6 |
| $y_2$ | | | | | | 8 |

$$r_{c_x c_y} = \frac{(4)(6)(.20) + (4)(8)(.15) + (2)(6)(.15) + (2)(8)(.10) + (5)(6)(.00) + (5)(8)(.30)}{(9.24)(13.30)}$$

$$= \frac{25.00}{122.89}$$

$$= .20$$

among the $m$ components of composite $y$. Examination of Table 7-4 shows that there are $km$ terms in the numerator. We can express the terms in the numerator as means and write

$$r_{c_{z_x} c_{z_y}} = \frac{km\bar{r}_{xy}}{\sqrt{k + k(k - 1)\bar{r}_{xx'}} \ \sqrt{m + m(m - 1)\bar{r}_{yy'}}} \tag{7-17}$$

where $\bar{r}_{xy}$ represents the average of the coefficients of the correlation among the $k$ components of composite $x$ and among the $m$ components of composite $y$, that is, the average of the cross correlations. Dividing the numerator and the denominator by $km$, we have

$$r_{c_{z_x} c_{z_y}} = \frac{\bar{r}_{xy}}{\frac{1}{k}\sqrt{k + k(k - 1)\bar{r}_{xx'}} \ \frac{1}{m}\sqrt{m + m(m - 1)\bar{r}_{yy'}}}$$

$$= \frac{\bar{r}_{xy}}{\sqrt{\frac{k}{k^2} + \frac{k(k - 1)}{k^2}\bar{r}_{xx'}} \ \sqrt{\frac{m}{m^2} + \frac{m(m - 1)}{m^2}\bar{r}_{yy'}}}$$

$$= \frac{\bar{r}_{xy}}{\sqrt{\frac{1}{k} + \frac{k - 1}{k}\bar{r}_{xx'}} \ \sqrt{\frac{1}{m} + \frac{m - 1}{m}\bar{r}_{yy'}}} \tag{7-18}$$

## Summary

Many of the scores used in psychological measurement are composites made up of the sum of the scores on a series of component variables. The mean of composite scores is merely the sum of the means of the components, and the variance is the sum of the variances of the components plus the sum of their covariances, a covariance being the product of the standard deviations of the two variables and the coefficient of correlation between them.

In many instances the units in which the components are expressed are so different from component to component that it does not make sense to add them together in forming composite scores. Since in certain terms standard scores on different variables are comparable, scores on the components often are transformed into standard scores before adding them together to form composite scores. When composite scores are formed from components expressed as standard scores, the mean of the composite score is zero, and their variance is the number of components plus the sum of their intercorrelations.

The correlation between a composite and a variable outside of it is a function of the correlations between the components and the outside variable, the intercorrelations among the components, and the number of components. The higher the correlations between the components and the outside variable, the higher the correlation; and the larger the number of components, the lower the intercorrelations among the components.

One way to increase the homogeneity of a composite is to eliminate those components that have the lowest correlations with the other components. If there are many components, it is a long task to calculate all their intercorrelations. However, the magnitude of the correlation between a component and the total composite is a function of the magnitude of the correlations between that component and the other components. Therefore by eliminating those components that have the lowest correlations with the composite, the homogeneity of the composite can be increased.

The correlation between two composites is a function of the cross correlations between the components of the two composites, the intercorrelations among the components of each composite, and the number of components in each composite. The higher the cross correlations, the higher the correlation; and the larger the number of components, the lower the intercorrelations among the components.

## Suggested Reading

Lord, F. M., and M. R. Novick. 1968. *Statistical theories of mental test scores.* Reading, Mass.: Addison-Wesley. Chap. 4.

# 8

---

# *Reliability*
# *of Measurement*

The intent of psychological measurement is to give us quantitative descriptions of individuals in terms of the extent to which they manifest various psychological traits and abilities. However, it is a fact of life in the behavioral sciences that if we administer the same measuring device several times to the same individual, we usually find that he or she does not obtain exactly the same score on all applications. Sometimes the score changes in a systematic fashion, increasing or decreasing in magnitude or fluctuating regularly in a cyclical fashion. On other occasions the scores earned by an individual seem to fluctuate in a random and unsystematic fashion. For example, when we measure the height of a person several times with the same ruler, the first application of our operation might tell us that this person's height is 6.16 feet, and on subsequent times they might tell us the height is 6.23, 6.19, 6.25, or 6.20 feet. It becomes legitimate to ask: Does an individual have a height? If so, what is it? Similarly, when we administer the same psychological test to an individual on several different occasions, he or she might obtain scores of 83, 86, 85, 81, and 84.

When this state of randomlike, unsystematic fluctuation occurs, it means that we cannot depend too much on any single score earned by an individual since on another application of the same measuring device this individual might earn a different score. The differences in behavior from one time to the next are not due to systematic causes or trends, such as learning or growth, but are simply random fluctuations. It is from this common observation of unsystematic variation or fluctuation in the scores earned by an individual on repeated applications of the same measure that the problem termed the *reliability of measurement* arises. When an individual obtains different scores on subsequent administrations of the same test and the variation among these scores is unsystematic, we can say that the quantitative descriptions given by the test are not reliable. This variation is not the fault, or even under the control, of the individual. Rather it is a problem of the measurement device. Reliability of measurement, then, refers to the degree of self-consistency among the scores earned by an individual. It is our task in this chapter to consider the types of variation that may occur in the scores earned by an individual on a given test and to formalize the concept of the reliability of measurement. Only if we formalize it, can we deal with the reliability problem in any practical way.

The point is that we cannot measure behavior perfectly. There is error in our measurement devices as well as fluctuation in the behavior being observed (tested, scored, and so on). In this chapter we are concerned with the concepts involved and the procedures and statistics used to determine the reliability (or unreliability) of measurement.

The reader is forewarned that many people in psychometric theory regard the reliability problem as the fundamental problem in psychological measurement. It goes to the very heart of how we should think about descriptions of human psychological characteristics. Every individual past the age of three or four confronts the reliability problem every day when he or she makes decisions or takes actions on the basis of an assessment of another individual's appearance, behavior, skill, and the like.

Reliability is a problem because psychological characteristics can never be measured perfectly. If you think you are a perfect judge of character (that is, the operation of measurement, comprising your own judgment processes are really superduper), you are quite mistaken and you should get rid of such quaint notions. Since a certain amount of uncertainty is always with us, it would be wise to deal with it as intelligently as we can. That is what reliability theory is all about. It is meant to be an intelligent way to look at the uncertainty in measurement. Our first task is to come up with some concepts and procedures that will allow us to portray or describe in some useful fashion the degree of reliability that a measure possesses.

## Unsystematic Variation

If a measure yields scores for an individual that differ markedly from one occasion to another, they are of little value. Such a test does not give reliable or self-consistent scores, and therefore we can predict only with a low degree of accuracy the score an individual will obtain on any one administration of a test from any other administration of it. Unreliable scores are of little value when we wish to compare two or more individuals on the same measure, to assign individuals to groups or classes, to predict other types of behavior (for example, scholastic success or job performance), or to assess the effects of various factors (for example, a new teaching method) on an individual's performance. Let us consider examples of each of these so that we can see the importance of the reliability of measurement.

### Comparisons Among Individuals on Same Measure

Often we wish to know whether one person ranks higher than another in the trait or ability measured by a particular test. If we know that people vary in their scores from one administration of the test to another by as much as 10 points and that the difference between the scores of two persons is 30 points, we probably would be willing to conclude that the one person indeed scores higher than the other and the difference would hold even if we tested them on another occasion. The one who was superior on the first application of the test might earn a score as much as 10 points lower on the second test, and the one who was inferior on the first test might improve his or her score by as much as 10 points, but there would still be at least a 10-point difference between the two individuals. However, we would not be so willing to say that the one person scores higher than the other if we found that people vary as much as 20 points from one application of the test to another. In this case, if we tested both persons twice, the individual who earned the higher score on the first test might well earn the lower score on the second application. Thus the extent to which we are willing to trust the difference between the scores earned by two individuals as reflecting a real or stable difference between them is a function of the reliability of that test.

### Assigning Individuals to Groups

Suppose that students in a school are to be placed in reading sections on the basis of the scores they earned on a reading achievement test, with those earning scores of 60 and above being assigned to the advanced section, those with scores of 50 to 59 to the average section, and those with scores of 49 and below to the remedial section. Now further suppose that variation in scores of as much as 6 points occurs when an individual takes the test a number of times. A student who earns a score of 55 on the test will be assigned to the average section. However, if the student had taken the test on another occasion, he or she might have earned a score as high as 61 and have been assigned to the advanced section, or the individual might have earned a score as low as 49 and have been assigned to the remedial section. It is therefore obvious that the degree of the reliability of measurement of this test is insufficient to assign students to sections with very much certainty. On the other hand, if the variation among scores in subsequent administrations of the test is only 1 point, then a very large proportion of students can be assigned with a high degree of certainty. Assignment to differential levels in this fashion has become an important issue in many school districts and sometimes includes racial overtones. The reliability of the classifications that are made looms as an important problem.

### Reliability and Prediction

Scores on psychological measures often are used to predict other types of behavior. For example, scores on tests of academic aptitude commonly are used to predict success in college. If the particular test used in making predictions of this kind happens to be highly unreliable, then from the score earned by an individual on one occasion a high degree of scholastic success might be anticipated for him or her, but from the score he or she earned on another occasion just the opposite conclusion might be reached. It would, therefore, be difficult under such circumstances to make predictions with any satisfactory degree of certainty and thereby to counsel the individual wisely and help him or her to make sound educational and career decisions. Consequently we can see that accuracy of prediction from one variable to another is limited by the degree of reliability with which these variables are measured. In other words, if we cannot measure a particular behavior in a reliable way, then we should not expect to be able to use that behavior to predict other behaviors.

### Effects of Systematic Factors

Psychological measures are often used as dependent variables in experiments. That is, they serve as criteria with which to assess whether or not some independent factor, or experimental manipulation, had its intended effect. For example, what is the effect of a certain drug on an individual's state of depression, as measured by the depression subscale of a standardized personality test; or what is the effect of sensitivity training on racial attitudes, as measured by a specially constructed attitude scale; or what is the effect of specialized job training on job performance, as measured by a job-performance rating scale? Now suppose we look at the differences in scores between the pretest and the posttest, or between the experimental group and the control group, and ask whether the difference is due to the experimental manipulation (that is, systematic variation produced by the drug, the T-group, or the job training) or whether it is what we would expect to find if we just measured people a number of times (unsystematic variation). If we know the extent of this unsystematic (random) variation and find that it is greater than the amount of change in scores, then we would not be willing to say that the change in scores is the result of the factors in question. On the other hand, if the amount of unsystematic variation is less than the amount by which the individual's score changes, then we could conclude with considerable confidence that the change in scores is the result of the factors that have been introduced.

To be more specific, suppose when we administer a test a number of times to an individual under the same conditions, we find that his or her scores vary about 20 points. Thus on subsequent administrations of the same test a person might earn a score as low as 50 and as high as 70, and another person might earn a score as low as 80 and as high as 100. Now we administer the test to a person, submit the individual to some treatment—say some special method of educational instruction—and administer the test again. If after the treatment the individual's score increases by 15 points, we would be very hesitant to say that the increase is due to the treatment, because changes of this magnitude occur frequently just in the normal course of events when there are no special changes in conditions between testing periods. However, if the variation between subsequent applications of the test when there are no special conditions is only 5 points, then we would feel that the treatment was beneficial. Again, the purpose of determining reliability is to assess the extent of variation (systematic and unsystematic) that exists in our measurements.

## Sources of Systematic and Unsystematic Variation

As we have seen, there are two major types of variations in the scores earned by an individual over repeated testing. One type we termed *systematic variation,* and the other *unsystematic variation.* We must examine both types of variations so that we can differentiate unsystematic from systematic variations in order to develop further the concept of the reliability of measurement.

Suppose we examine the different scores obtained by an individual on successive applications of the same measure. It might be that a trend appears in the scores. Thus if we measure the height of an individual at different hours of the day, we are likely to find that from morning to evening the values become smaller and smaller. We might attribute this phenomenon to a gradual sagging of the backbone. Similarly, if we administer the same arithmetic test over and over to the same individual, his or her scores may gradually increase. This would suggest that the series of testing situations operate as practice periods and that the individual gradually is improving his or her skill in solving arithmetic problems. We could persuade the current men's Olympic gold medalist in the 1500-meter run to run successive 1500's as fast as he could, with only two minutes of rest between trials. His scores would change drastically, but systematically: Even winners get tired.

Sometimes, however, when we examine the various scores obtained by an individual on successive repetitions of a given measure, no trend of any kind can be discerned even though the scores differ on the different testing occasions. Rather the scores seem to vary in a random fashion. If we have an individual react as quickly as possible in a specific manner to each stimulus in a series of stimuli, we would find that some of the responses are more rapid than others. When we compare the times taken to respond to stimuli that occur early in the series with those that occur later, we may find that on the average they are the same. We might attribute variation in reaction-time scores to unsystematic moment-to-moment changes in the environmental conditions, the smoothness of the operation of the reaction-time apparatus, the individual's motivation, and his or her attention.

There are, then, two kinds of variations in scores. One is systematic, and the other unsystematic. Systematic variations are characterized by an orderly progression or pattern, with the scores obtained by an individual changing from one occasion to the next in some trend. Systematic changes appear as a regular increase or decrease in scores, or they may follow some cycle. It is usually not difficult to hypothesize or attribute a reason or factor for the changes. Unsystematic variation, on the other hand, is characterized by a complete absence of order. The scores of an individual fluctuate from one occasion to the next in a completely haphazard manner.

The two types of variations, of course, may occur simultaneously. Thus we may find that on the average the scores of an individual increase as he or she is repeatedly tested with the same instrument, and around this trend the scores appear to vary in a random fashion, sometimes being above the trend and sometimes below it.

While it is inappropriate here to discuss at length the philosophical problems of causation, it might still be valuable to talk a bit about the various sources of systematic and unsystematic variation. Just as the members of a particular population of objects can be classified in a variety of different ways, so can the phenomena with which we are here concerned, namely, factors that affect scores on psychological measures. We can classify people according to sex, age, or place of birth. Similarly, we can classify factors that affect scores as environmental or individual, genetic or acquired, unimportant or important, or—for our present purposes—factors having systematic or unsystematic effects. Classification of the factors according to whether their effects on test scores are systematic or unsystematic will help us to understand their mode of operation, to identify specific kinds of determiners, and above all to help us to formalize the concept of the reliability of measurement.

A *systematic factor* is one that produces systematic changes in scores. Learning, training, and growth produce regular and progressive increases in scores. Fatigue, forgetting, and senescence result in regular and progressive decreases in scores. When systematic factors are at work, then, scores show a regular disposition or arrangement—an order.

An *unsystematic factor* is one that produces unsystematic changes in scores. Moment-to-moment variations in attention result in random fluctuations in reaction time. The marks given to an elementary school student as he or she progresses through the various grades are sometimes higher and sometimes lower, depending on whether the teacher to whom the student happens to be assigned tends to be lenient or strict in evaluating students' performance. When unsystematic factors are at work, scores fluctuate in a random fashion and do not manifest any consistent pattern.

The factors that affect scores seem to be almost infinite in number and variety. An individual's performance is a function of the numerous qualities with which he or she was endowed at birth, elaborated on by the process of maturation and by numerous experiences, together with the many environmental influences operating at any given moment. The inferences we draw in attempting to explain variation in scores are a function of the knowledge we have about these factors. In some instances our inferences have quite substantial foundation because our knowledge is direct and extensive. Suppose we give an individual a test of knowledge of French vocabulary and find this person's score is zero. We then have the person take an elementary course in French and retest him or her. Now the score is higher. The person continues to take more and more courses in French, and after completion of each course we can administer the test. Undoubtedly we shall find a continuous increase in scores, and with a great deal of certainty we could attribute this increase in scores to the training to which the individual has been deliberately subjected. In other instances our knowledge may be indirect and not complete, so that we are less sure of our inferences. Finally, we may have such limited knowledge about conditions that our inferences are little more than guesses. For example, why do scores on measures of general intelligence change from time to time?

One moral of this story is that systematic variation in scores is variation for which we can postulate some reasonable explanation of the causal factors, while unsystematic is variation that cannot be readily explained.

## Defining Reliability of Measurement

Having examined the kinds of variations that occur in scores and the types of factors that cause them, we are now in a better, albeit still shaky, position to define the reliability of measurement. We do so in terms of the extent of unsystematic variation in scores. To specify our definitions further, we then present the concept of *parallel tests*. On the basis of our definition of reliability and of the concept of parallel tests, we are then able to indicate the ways in which reliability can be measured. We can then make some additional theoretical statements about reliability that in turn will enable us to give still more precise definitions of reliability.

### Measurement Operations

It will be recalled that the problems of the reliability of measurement arise from the unsystematic variation in scores earned by an individual when we obtain a number of measurements indicative of the degree to which he or she possesses or manifests a particular trait or quality. Recall also that the distinction between systematic and unsystematic factors is somewhat arbitrary and rests on whether the variation appears nonrandom and whether the factors causing it can be reasonably explained. However, once this distinction is made, the reliability of measurement pertains to the precision (that is, the lack of unsystematic variation) with which some trait is measured by means of specified operations; it is the extent to which our measurements do not reflect random fluctuations or unexplainable factors. It is important to note that our concern is not with one particular measurement instrument, but rather with the operations of measurement that stem from the definition of our variable. The theoretical and practical implications of this concern will be clearer later, when we discuss parallel tests and the estimation of the extent of the reliability of measurement; but for now consider the following example.

As we saw in Chapter 2, from the definition of a given variable a variety of different operations of measurement may follow. For example, if we define the ability to perform simple addition as the speed and accuracy with which numbers are added together, we can utilize a test comprised of a series of items such as $3 + 4 =$ ____, $9 + 2 =$ ____, and $1 + 7 =$ ____, as well as a series comprised of items such as $4 + 3 =$ ____, $2 + 9 =$ ____, and $7 + 1 =$ ____. Differences in scores between these two series for one individual, if obtained under constant conditions, would probably be labeled as unsystematic variation and taken as evidence of unreliability. However, what about the difference between a single-digit series and a two-digit series, such as $15 + 27 =$ ____? Whether or not we mean these two kinds of operations to be measures of the same variable depends on our definition. If our definition is meant to be all-inclusive, then differences in total scores, for one individual, between the following two measures of "addition" would be considered unsystematic variation.

| Test *A* | Test *B* |
|---|---|
| $3 + 4 =$ ____ | $11 + 17 =$ ____ |
| $9 + 2 =$ ____ | $24 + 97 =$ ____ |
| $1 + 7 =$ ____ | $53 + 12 =$ ____ |
| $3 + 8 =$ ____ | $69 + 96 =$ ____ |
| $4 + 5 =$ ____ | $10 + 29 =$ ____ |

However, we may not want our definition of the variable to allow both these tests to serve as measurement operations for the same thing. Adding two-digit numbers may represent a different ability from adding one-digit numbers, and which one we choose depends in part on our theory of "addition." As we have said before, it also depends on whether the empirical pattern of scores appears to be random or exhibits some orderly pattern. Similar examples could be dredged up for the measurement of particular personality characteristics, political attitudes, job performance, and the like. More about this later.

## A Beginning Definition

Keeping the above considerations in mind, let us offer a first definition of reliability: *The reliability of measurement (or the lack of it) is the extent of unsystematic variation in the quantitative description of some characteristic of an individual when the same individual is measured a number of times.* This definition makes the assumption that the repeated measurements of one individual were conducted in such a way that the differences in one individual's scores represent unsystematic variation, and not systematic variation that can be accounted for.

In the field of psychometric theory the name for sets of measurement operations that are designed to reflect unsystematic (and also thereby systematic) variation is *parallel tests*.

### Concept of Parallel Tests

There have been many definitions of parallel tests, some rational and some mathematical. We begin by giving a rational definition, and this ultimately will lead us to two different mathematical formulations or models of reliability.

We have defined the reliability of measurement as the extent of unsystematic variation in scores of an individual on some trait when that trait is measured a number of times. To ascertain the extent of this unsystematic variation, we need to obtain for an individual a series of scores by the application of a number of sets of operations all of which follow from the same definition of the variable. In conceptualizing these operations, we needn't stipulate that the same specific measuring device is always used. On the other hand, we needn't stipulate that it should not be. What we are concerned with is a series of operations of measurement, or tests, that measure the same traits to the same degree, that is, tests that evoke the same psychological processes. Measures of this kind are termed parallel tests. For now, they could be the same measure or they could be different measures. The only stipulation at this point is that they measure the same thing to the same degree.

In essence, what we are saying is that reliability can be defined as the extent of unsystematic variation of one individual's scores on a series of parallel tests, and that by parallel tests we mean sets of operations all of which follow from a particular definition of a trait. Suppose we have a series of tests, $k$ in number, and we have scores on all these $k$ tests for one or more individuals. If we were measuring with perfect reliability, then any given individual would obtain precisely the same score on all the $k$ parallel tests. In other words, there would be no variation at all in this person's scores over the $k$ tests. On the other hand, if we were measuring with less than perfect reliability, then his or her scores would be different on the different parallel tests, the variation among the scores being completely unsystematic, since we are obtaining different scores for an individual on tests measuring the same trait, ability, or whatever. The less the variation, the greater the reliability of measurement; and the greater the variation, the less the reliability of measurement. Consequently it is through the use of parallel tests that we are able to find out the degree to which a variable is being reliably measured.

While this definition of reliability may give an adequate general orientation to the problem, it is in fact too loose and too vague to be of any direct value, either as a basis for theoretical developments or as a guide to indicate practical ways for estimating the reliability of tests. We shall find it necessary to take some theoretical position before we can define the reliability of measurement with sufficient precision to be practically useful.

## Degree of Reliability of Measurement

We have just argued that the reliability of measurement refers to the extent of unsystematic variation in one individual's scores over a number of parallel tests. Our task now is to set up indices that give quantitative descriptions of the degree of such variation. Such indices will be useful for comparing different measures to determine which one gives the most precise or stable scores and also to determine whether the reliability of a given measure is "sufficient" for our purposes. The two most common indices are the *standard error of measurement* and the *reliability coefficient*. The standard error of measurement is an index of the extent to which an individual's scores vary over a number of parallel tests, and the reliability coefficient is an index of the extent to which scores on any one parallel test can predict scores on any other.

### Standard Error of Measurement

In Table 8-1 we have a representation of parallel tests. Here we have the scores of $n$ individuals on $k$ different parallel tests. In any given column we have the scores of the $n$ individuals on one parallel test, and in any given row we have the scores of any one individual over the $k$ parallel tests. We could compute the mean and standard deviation of the scores in any given column. These values are the mean and standard deviation of the scores on that one parallel test and are represented in the last two rows of Table 8-1.

In a similar fashion we could compute the mean and standard deviation of the scores in any given row. These values are the mean and the standard deviation of the scores of that individual. These means and standard deviations are represented in the last two columns in the table, labeled $\bar{X}_i$ and $S_i$. The symbol $S_i$ is used rather than $\sigma_i$ to distinguish it as being the standard deviation of one individual's scores over $k$ parallel tests. $S_i$ is termed the standard error of measurement. When this standard deviation is large, it means that an individual's scores differ considerably across repeated parallel measurements, and the reliability of measurement is poor. When this standard deviation is zero, it means that an individual obtains precisely the same score on all parallel tests, and the reliability of measurement for him or her is perfect.

*Table 8-1*   Raw scores on parallel tests

| Individual | Parallel Tests | | | | | $\bar{X}$ | $S$ |
|---|---|---|---|---|---|---|---|
| | 1 | 2 | $\cdots$ | $k-1$ | $k$ | | |
| $a$ | $X_{1_a}$ | $X_{2_a}$ | $\cdots$ | $X_{(k-1)_a}$ | $X_{k_a}$ | $\bar{X}_a$ | $S_a$ |
| $b$ | $X_{1_b}$ | $X_{2_b}$ | $\cdots$ | $X_{(k-1)_b}$ | $X_{k_b}$ | $\bar{X}_b$ | $S_b$ |
| . | . | . | | . | . | . | . |
| . | . | . | | . | . | . | . |
| . | . | . | | . | . | . | . |
| $n-1$ | $X_{1_{n-1}}$ | $X_{2_{n-1}}$ | $\cdots$ | $X_{(k-1)_{n-1}}$ | $X_{k_{n-1}}$ | $\bar{X}_{n-1}$ | $S_{n-1}$ |
| $n$ | $X_{1_n}$ | $X_{2_n}$ | $\cdots$ | $X_{(k-1)_n}$ | $X_{k_n}$ | $\bar{X}_n$ | $S_n$ |
| $\bar{X}$ | $\bar{X}_1$ | $\bar{X}_2$ | $\cdots$ | $\bar{X}_{k-1}$ | $\bar{X}_k$ | | |
| $\sigma_x$ | $\sigma_1$ | $\sigma_2$ | $\cdots$ | $\sigma_{k-1}$ | $\sigma_k$ | | |

### Reliability Coefficient

The reliability of measurement can also be thought of in terms of predictability, or the degree to which scores on one parallel test predict scores on another. When the variation in an individual's scores over parallel tests is great, this means that the prediction of his or her score on one parallel test from his or her score on another is poor. On the other hand, if there is no variation at all among an individual's scores, then it means that we could predict perfectly the individual's score on one parallel test from his or her score on another. Casting reliability in terms of the coefficient of correlation between parallel tests provides another way of describing the precision of measurement. After all, the basic meaning of a correlation coefficient is the extent to which individuals exhibit the same score from one set of measures to the next. The coefficient of correlation between parallel tests is termed the reliability coefficient. When the coefficient is low, it means that an individual's scores over $k$ parallel tests show a great deal of variation; and when it is high, it means that an individual's scores on the $k$ parallel tests are very nearly the same. The relationship between the reliability coefficient and the standard error of measurement, as well as their statistical procedures, will be discussed later in the chapter.

## Theoretical Models of Reliability of Measurement

We defined reliability of measurement as the extent of unsystematic variation in the scores of an individual on some trait when that trait was measured a number of times. Parallel tests we defined as sets of operations that follow directly from the definition of the trait. In other words, parallel tests are tests that measure the same traits to the same degree. With this definition of parallel tests we were then able to specify our definition of the reliability of measurement by saying that it is the extent of unsystematic variation of the scores of an individual over a number of parallel tests.

However, these definitions of the reliability of measurement and of parallel tests are still too vague to permit us to develop specific procedures for describing or estimating the precision with which a trait is measured. To be specific, our definition of reliability says we should determine either the standard deviation of one individual's scores across several parallel tests or the correlation between two parallel tests. But how will we know a parallel test when we see it? So far we have no clear guidelines. To set up guidelines for the identification of parallel measures in the real world, we are forced back on some kind of theory about the basic nature of the scores that reflect psychological characteristics. That is, we must adopt a theory or model that makes some simplifying assumptions about the nature of such scores before we can develop practical ways to recognize parallel tests and to estimate reliability. The necessity for simplifying assumptions is forced on us because we can never identify and explain *all* the factors that produce variation in scores. If we could, there would be no need for reliability theory.

In the history of psychological measurement from approximately 1900 to the present, there have been two major theoretical positions with regard to the reliability problem. To estimate reliability, an investigator really has to adopt one or the other. The first position is the so-called *theory of true and error scores,* or the *"classical"* *theory* of reliability. The second major position is the *theory of domain sampling,* or the *generalizability theory* as some of its later modifications have been labeled. Of course there have been a number of variations on these two basic themes down through the years, but differences between them and the two positions described here are not sufficient to warrant considering them in this book.

## Theory of True and Error Scores

One way of thinking about and describing unsystematic variation in scores is to conceive of the individual as possessing a certain amount of the trait being measured by a particular test and the score he or she actually earned on the test as being an imperfect function of this quantity. Performance on any given administration of a test does not reflect with complete accuracy the "true" or "real" amount of the trait the individual possesses because of the effects of unsystematic or chance factors. The score an individual actually obtains on a test is termed the *observed* or *fallible score,* and the amount of the trait being measured that he or she in fact possesses is termed the *true score.* The difference between the fallible and the true scores is termed the *error score.* The error score sometimes causes the fallible score to be too high and sometimes causes it to be too low. The fallible scores an individual obtains on a series of parallel tests, then, vary in a random fashion around his or her true score.

### Basic Concepts*

The relationship among fallible, true, and error scores can be symbolized by the following equation:

$$X_i - X_\infty = e_i \tag{8-1}$$

where $X_i$ is the fallible score earned on one administration of the test, $X_\infty$ the true score, and $e_i$ the error score on that particular administration of the test. The terms of this equation may also be arranged as follows:

$$X_i = X_\infty + e_i \tag{8-2}$$

Thus the observed score is equal to the true score plus an error score. Note that errors can be either plus or minus and therefore make the observed score higher or lower than the true score. If we administer several parallel tests of the same trait to the same individual, say $k$ of them, there will be an equation for each repetition:

$$
\begin{aligned}
X_1 &= X_\infty + e_1 \\
X_2 &= X_\infty + e_2 \\
&\cdots\cdots\cdots \\
X_k &= X_\infty + e_k
\end{aligned}
\tag{8-3}
$$

These equations show that the individual's true score (for example, true ability, true aptitude, true diagnosis) remains the same over the $k$

---

* Historically it can be said that Spearman and Yule were the originators of the theory of true and error scores. Other strong adherents to this point of view are Thurstone and Guilford. It has also been stressed by Gulliksen. The notion of domain sampling is newer and was originally developed by Tryon and also by Jackson and his colleagues at the University of London. Later developments were made by Cronbach and his associates. See the Suggested Readings at the end of this chapter.

parallel tests, but that his or her fallible score changes because the extent of error on the different applications of the test is different, the errors being sometimes positive and sometimes negative. This is merely symbolizing mathematically what we have already said about fallible, true, and error scores.

Equation 8-2 does not necessarily mean that scores on a measure are due only to a single factor within the individual. The fact that a single term $X_\infty$ has been used to describe the amount of the trait an individual possesses should not be taken to imply that individual differences in scores on a given test are determined by a single factor. The true score could be a summation of true scores on a number of different traits, and Equation 8-2 might be written as

$$X = X_{A\infty} + X_{B\infty} + \cdots + X_{N\infty} + e \qquad (8\text{-}4)$$

where $A$ to $N$ are the factors determining trait $X$. For example, we might think of the true score on a variable such as overall management ability as being comprised of a true score on the ability to supervise subordinates, the ability to solve production problems, the ability to communicate to higher management, and the like. The term $X_\infty$ therefore merely stands for the sum of all systematic factors that are operating. Furthermore, we should not take Equation 8-4 to imply that all factors have equal weight in determining the score of one individual on a test. More properly Equation 8-4 should be written as

$$X = W_A X_{A\infty} + W_B X_{B\infty} + \cdots + W_N X_{N\infty} + e \qquad (8\text{-}5)$$

where $W$ is the relative weight of the factor.

In our example of overall management ability, the ability to supervise subordinates may play a much more important role than any of the other factors.

### Fundamental Assumptions

In order to develop the concept of reliability on the basis of the theory of true and error scores, it is necessary to make three fundamental assumptions. One of these assumptions has to do with true scores, another with error scores, and the last with the way in which these two scores are combined.

*Assumption 1: The individual possesses stable characteristics or traits (that is, true scores) that persist through time.* For the concept of true and error scores to be meaningful, some assumption such as the foregoing must be made. If the individual's true scores changed continuously from moment to moment, there would be no stability whatsoever in his or her characteristics or traits. It is therefore necessary for the theory of true and error scores to consider the individual as possessing stable characteristics that are different from the error factors that produce differences in fallible scores on different parallel tests. These stable characteristics of the individual are his or her true scores on various tests. Within the theory of true and error scores, the characteristics represented by the true scores are irrelevant. They could be an ability, aptitude, interest, pathological disorder, and so on. The point is that for whatever characteristic we are interested in measuring, individuals must possess some stable amount. Again, however, the theory is neutral about the identity of the true score. This notion of true score must be qualified to some degree. Though we have indicated that a fallible score equals a true score plus an error score (Equation 8-2), we have been talking about systematic and unsystematic factors or sources of variation. Also we indicated that reliability is the extent of unsystematic variation or random error. There is another kind of error, *constant error,* which is systematic in that all individuals are affected in the same way by the same amount. Thus, if it were possible to actually break down a fallible score into components (this process will be discussed in subsequent sections), the true score would represent the true amount of the ability plus the possibility of a constant factor (such as "accidentally" adding 5 points to everyone's score). The error component, however, is unsystematic, unpredictable error.

*Assumption 2: Errors are completely random.* From the essential notion of the theory of true and error scores, it follows that variations in fallible scores on parallel tests are due entirely to unsystematic factors, the effects of which change from moment to moment. It must therefore be assumed that error scores are completely random and consequently are independent of all other characteristics. It follows then that the error scores on any one administration of a test are uncorrelated with scores on any other variable. Therefore

$$r_{e_1 e_2} = r_{x_x e_1} = \cdots = r_{x_x e_k}$$
$$= r_{y e_1} = \cdots = r_{y e_k} = .00 \qquad (8\text{-}6)$$

where there are 1 to $k$ parallel tests and $y$ is any variable other than these parallel tests. If error scores are a random variable, it also follows that there are just as many errors in the negative direction as in the positive direction, and further that they are distributed normally with a mean of zero.

*Assumption 3: Fallible scores are the result of the addition of true and error scores.* A review of Equations 8-1 to 8-5 shows that they are all based on this assumption of the additivity of true and error scores. Thus Equation 8-2 states that the fallible score is equal to the true score *plus* the error score. Equation 8-5 is a more complex statement, but even here we see a simple sum. It is apparent that a number of other states of affairs could be assumed. For example, fallible scores might be taken as the product or the quotient of true and error scores. The formulation given, however, appears to be the most reasonable. But most of all, it is comprehensible and concise. If we can explain phenomena on simple grounds and make satisfactory predictions with a simple formulation, there is no point in seeking a more complex formulation. Hence we use a simple sum in our basic equation, and in our more elaborate forms of Equation 8-2 we continue to use sums. Given the conceptualization of an observed score as being comprised of a true score and an error score and given these three assumptions, it is now possible to specify the real-world characteristics of parallel tests.

### Parallel Tests

It will be recalled that we defined parallel tests as tests measuring exactly the same thing. Therefore in terms of the concept of true and error scores, it follows that when an individual is measured by a series of parallel tests, his or her true scores on all of them are precisely the same. If the true score differed from one test to another, then by definition the tests would not be measuring the same trait. The fallible scores, of course, may vary from one parallel test to another since the error factors operating on the different occasions of testing may differ. This is the situation we represented earlier in Equation 8-3. In the concept of true and error scores the situation with respect to scores on parallel tests is that represented in Table 8-2. In the rows we have the scores of each person over the $k$ parallel tests, and in the columns the scores of the $n$ individuals on one parallel test.

Since different individuals possess different amounts of the trait being measured on any given parallel test, we find a variation among individuals in true scores. If there were no differences in true scores among people, everybody in the world would be alike and all of behavioral and biological science could close up shop and go home! However, if we consider not the differences in true scores across people down a column for one test, but the true scores across a row for one individual, we see that an individual has exactly the same true score on each test. In other words, the set of true scores on any one parallel test

Table 8-2 Scores on parallel tests in terms of theory of true and error scores

| Individual | Parallel Tests | | | | |
| --- | --- | --- | --- | --- | --- |
| | 1 | 2 | ⋯ | $k-1$ | $k$ |
| $a$ | $X_{1_a} = X_{\infty_a} + e_{1_a}$ | $X_{2_a} = X_{\infty_a} + e_{2_a}$ | ⋯ | $X_{k-1_a} = X_{\infty_a} + e_{(k-1)_a}$ | $X_{k_a} = X_{\infty_a} + e_{k_a}$ |
| $b$ | $X_{1_b} = X_{\infty_b} + e_{1_b}$ | $X_{2_b} = X_{\infty_b} + e_{2_b}$ | ⋯ | $X_{k-1_b} = X_{\infty_b} + e_{(k-1)_b}$ | $X_{k_b} = X_{\infty_b} + e_{k_b}$ |
| ⋮ | ⋮ | ⋮ | | ⋮ | ⋮ |
| $n-1$ | $X_{1_{n-1}} = X_{\infty_{n-1}} + e_{1_{n-1}}$ | $X_{2_{n-1}} = X_{\infty_{n-1}} + e_{2_{n-1}}$ | ⋯ | $X_{(k-1)_{n-1}} = X_{\infty_{n-1}} + e_{(k-1)_{n-1}}$ | $X_{k_{n-1}} = X_{\infty_{n-1}} + e_{k_{n-1}}$ |
| $n$ | $X_{1_n} = X_{\infty_n} + e_{1_n}$ | $X_{2_n} = X_{\infty_n} + e_{2_n}$ | ⋯ | $X_{(k-1)_n} = X_{\infty_n} + e_{(k-1)_n}$ | $X_{k_n} = X_{\infty_n} + e_{k_n}$ |

are precisely the same as the true scores for any other parallel test. Consequently, we can say that the means and standard deviations of true scores on all tests are exactly the same. That is, the mean and standard deviation of all the true scores in a column are equal to the mean and standard deviation of true scores in any other column, or

$$\bar{X}_{\infty_1} = \cdots = \bar{X}_{\infty_k} \qquad (8\text{-}7)$$

and

$$\sigma_{\infty_1} = \cdots = \sigma_{\infty_k} \qquad (8\text{-}8)$$

Since error scores are assumed to vary in a completely random fashion, the distribution of error scores for any one individual (the values in any row) necessarily is equal to the distribution of error scores for any other individual (the values in any other row). That is, when there are repeated parallel measurements, the distribution of error scores for individuals all have a mean of zero, are normally distributed, and have equal variances. Hence when the number of parallel tests, $k$, is very large, the standard deviation of the error scores of each person over the $k$ parallel tests necessarily is equal to the standard deviation of the error scores of every other person. That is,

$$S_a = \cdots = S_n \qquad (8\text{-}9)$$

Furthermore, since the error scores vary in a completely random fashion, when the number of individuals is very large, the distribution of error scores in any column necessarily is equal to the standard deviation of the error scores in any other column. Hence the standard deviations of error scores on all parallel tests necessarily are equal. That is,

$$\sigma_{e_1} = \cdots = \sigma_{e_k} \qquad (8\text{-}10)$$

Finally, since the error scores vary in a completely random fashion equally in the rows and columns of Table 8-2, the distributions of error scores in the rows necessarily are equal to the distributions of error scores in the columns. That is,

$$S_a = \cdots = S_n = \sigma_{e_1} = \cdots = \sigma_{e_k} \qquad (8\text{-}11)$$

In the concept of true and error scores, by definition errors are factors that sometimes cause the fallible scores to be higher than the true scores and sometimes cause them to be lower. This means, then, that the error scores are sometimes positive and sometimes negative; and because they vary in a random fashion they are positive as frequently as they are negative, and every positive error of a given amount is matched by a negative error of the same amount. Consequently, if there are repeated parallel measurements, the mean of error scores is zero. This would be true whether we consider the mean of the error scores in any row of Table 8-2 or the mean of the error scores in any column. Hence

$$\bar{e}_a = \cdots = \bar{e}_n = \bar{e}_1 \cdots = \bar{e}_k = 0 \qquad (8\text{-}12)$$

Although we cannot show the proofs here, any garden-variety mathematical statistician can prove that distributions of random variables would behave in the above manner, and he or she would use the principles of probability to do so.

*Mean of scores*   An individual's fallible score is a composite score, being the sum of his or her true and error scores. In Equation 7-4 we saw that the mean of composite scores is equal to the sum of the means of the components. Hence we can write

$$\bar{X}_1 = \bar{X}_\infty + \bar{e}_1$$
$$\vdots \qquad \vdots \qquad \vdots$$
$$\bar{X}_k = \bar{X}_\infty + \bar{e}_k$$

However, as we have just seen in Equation 8-12, the mean of the error scores on a test is zero. Hence in the above equations the terms $\bar{e}_1, \cdots, \bar{e}_k$ are all zero. Consequently in each of the foregoing equations the mean of the fallible scores equals the mean of the true scores so that

$$\bar{X}_1 = \cdots = \bar{X}_k = \bar{X}_\infty \qquad (8\text{-}13)$$

From Equation 8-13 we can say that the means of the fallible or observed scores on all parallel tests are equal to one another and are equal to the mean of the true scores. This is our first real-world criterion for recognizing parallel tests: They have equal means.

*Standard deviation of scores*   Again considering fallible scores as composite scores, we can think back to Chapter 7 and write the variance of fallible scores from Equation 7-6 in terms of the true-score and error-score components as

$$\sigma_x^2 = \sigma_{x_\infty}^2 + 2r_{x_\infty e}\sigma_{x_\infty}\sigma_e + \sigma_e^2$$

Now from our assumption that errors are random, we know that the correlation between true and error scores is .00. Therefore the entire second term in the above equation becomes zero and drops out. We can then write the variances of a series of parallel tests as

$$\sigma_{x_1}^2 = \sigma_{x_\infty}^2 + \sigma_{e_1}^2$$
$$\sigma_{x_2}^2 = \sigma_{x_\infty}^2 + \sigma_{e_2}^2$$
$$\cdot \qquad \cdot \qquad \cdot$$
$$\cdot \qquad \cdot \qquad \cdot$$
$$\cdot \qquad \cdot \qquad \cdot$$
$$\sigma_{x_k}^2 = \sigma_{x_\infty}^2 + \sigma_{e_k}^2$$

From Equation 8-10 we know that the variances or standard deviations of error scores for all parallel tests are equal to one another. Hence in each of the above equations we can write $\sigma_e^2$ for the variances of error scores. Therefore all the above equations are equal, and we can write them as

$$\sigma_{x_1}^2 = \cdots = \sigma_{x_k}^2 = \sigma_{x_\infty}^2 + \sigma_{x_e}^2 \qquad (8\text{-}14)$$

Equation 8-14 shows us that the variances or standard deviations of all parallel tests are equal to one another, and that is our second criterion for recognizing parallel tests in the real world: They have equal standard deviations.

*Correlations among parallel tests*    Our aim here is to show that the correlation between any pair of parallel tests is equal to the correlation between any other pair. Let us begin with any pair, say $x_1$ and $x_2$, and state the correlation between them (as we did so often in Chapter 7) in terms of the true- and error-score components. Thus

$$r_{x_1 x_2} = \frac{\Sigma x_1 x_2}{n\sigma_{x_1}\sigma_{x_2}} = \frac{\Sigma(x_\infty + e_1)(x_\infty + e_2)}{n\sigma_{x_1}\sigma_{x_2}}$$

If we multiply out the numerator and simplify the equation as much as possible, as was done many times in Chapter 7, a convenient thing happens. Most of the terms in the resulting equation involve a correlation between an error score and something else. Since error scores correlate zero with everything else, all such terms drop out and what's left is

$$r_{x_1 x_2} = \frac{\sigma_{x\infty}^2}{\sigma_{x_1}^2} \qquad \text{or} \qquad \frac{\sigma_{x\infty}^2}{\sigma_{x_2}^2} \qquad (8\text{-}15)$$

Since the variances of test 1 and test 2 are equal (they are parallel tests remember), it makes no difference which variance appears in the denominator.

In a similar fashion we can show that the coefficient of correlation between any pair of parallel tests other than $x_1$ and $x_2$ is equal to the ratio of the variance of true scores to the variance of fallible scores. Consequently we can write the general expression as follows:

$$r_{x_1 x_2} = \frac{\sigma_{x_\infty}^2}{\sigma_x^2} = r_{xx} \tag{8-16}$$

We conclude from Equation 8-16 that all parallel tests are correlated with one another to the same degree, and we can write the coefficient of correlation between parallel tests as $r_{xx}$. We now have our third real-world criterion for recognizing parallel tests: They have equal intercorrelations.

We should note here that demanding equal intercorrelations does not imply that these intercorrelations are high or low. However, by definition parallel tests with low intercorrelations are unreliable tests and may have little practical value.

Inasmuch as the coefficient of correlation between scores on parallel tests is the *reliability coefficient,* we can also see from Equation 8-16 that in terms of the concept of true and error scores the reliability coefficient is the ratio of the variance of true scores to the variance of fallible scores.

*Correlation between parallel and other tests*    Let us now think about the correlation between scores on any one parallel test, $x_i$, and scores on any other variable, $y$:

$$r_{x_i y} = \frac{\Sigma(x_\infty + e_i) y}{n \sigma_{x_i} \sigma_y}$$

If we gathered our patience one more time and worked this out, as is done in the Technical Section at the end of this chapter, we would see that the correlations between the variable $y$ and each one of the parallel tests are all equal to the same quantity and therefore all equal to one another. Thus we have arrived at our fourth and final real-world criterion for parallel tests: They have equal correlations with other variables. This is a quite reasonable conclusion in view of the fact that we have defined parallel tests to be measures that measure the same thing to the same degree and thus they should correlate similarly with some of these independent variables.

*Characteristics*   In summary the criteria we have developed for parallel tests under the "classical" theory of reliability are the following:

1. The mean of the scores is exactly the same for all parallel tests.
2. The standard deviation of the scores is exactly the same for all parallel tests.
3. The scores on all parallel tests are correlated with one another to exactly the same degree.
4. The scores on all parallel tests are correlated to exactly the same degree with the scores on any other variable.

It will be recalled that these characteristics were derived from the basic model of true and error scores, Equation 8-2, and from the three fundamental assumptions involved in this theory. If a set of tests satisfies these criteria, then they are parallel tests; and if it does not, they are not parallel tests.

## Indices of Reliability

The reliability of measurement, we said, refers to the extent of variation in an individual's scores over a series of parallel tests. We saw that the standard error of measurement and the reliability coefficient both give descriptions of the degree of reliability. Let us now examine the relationship between these two indices in terms of the concept of true and error scores. Suppose we take Equation 8-16 apart as follows:

$$r_{xx} = \frac{\sigma^2_{x_\infty}}{\sigma^2_x}$$

$$= \frac{\sigma^2_x - \sigma^2_e}{\sigma^2_x}$$

$$= \frac{\sigma^2_x}{\sigma^2_x} - \frac{\sigma^2_e}{\sigma^2_x}$$

$$r_{xx} = 1 - \frac{\sigma^2_e}{\sigma^2_x}$$

This latter formula is a conceptual definition of reliability, that is, the extent to which the measures are free from error variance.

$$\frac{\sigma^2_e}{\sigma^2_x} = 1 - r_{xx}$$

$$\sigma^2_e = \sigma^2_x(1 - r_{xx}) \tag{8-17}$$

$$\sigma_e = \sigma_x\sqrt{1 - r_{xx}} \tag{8-18}$$

This says that the standard deviation of the distribution of error scores on any one administration of a test (that is, within a column) is equal to the standard deviation of fallible scores on that administration times the square root of 1 minus the reliability coefficient. Again, this is a formula by which we can estimate the variability of the error-score components of the observed scores across people for one parallel test. All we need is the variance of the observed scores for any one parallel test and the correlation between observed scores on any two parallel tests. However, what we are really after is not the standard deviation of the error scores down a column but the standard deviation of the error scores across a row (that is, across tests for one person). As we have shown many times already, given the ingredients of the classical theory, the variability across parallel tests for one person is due to unsystematic (random) error and is an index of the degree of reliability we have. How then can we estimate the more relevant standard deviation?

The assumption of the model that error scores are random makes it all quite easy. In Equation 8-11 we showed that the standard deviation of error scores on any one administration of a test is equal to the standard deviation of the error scores of any one individual over $k$ parallel tests. That is, $\sigma_e = S$. Hence we can write Equation 8-18 as the standard error of measurement:

$$S = \sigma_x \sqrt{1 - r_{xx}} \qquad (8\text{-}19)$$

The variability of an individual's scores over a number of parallel tests then is *also* equal to the standard deviation of the fallible scores on any one administration times the square root of 1 minus the reliability coefficient. Again the most common label for this expression is the standard error of measurement.

As an example of how this index might be used, consider two parallel measures of so-called general intelligence expressed in IQ units. A typical observed-score standard deviation for a single such test is about 15 points. A typical correlation between two parallel forms is .91. Applying Equation 8-19 yields the following value for the standard error of measurement.

$$S = 15\sqrt{1 - .91} = 15\sqrt{.09}$$
$$= (15)(.30)$$
$$= 4.5 \text{ points}$$

Thus if we administer many such parallel tests of general intelligence to the same individual, we would expect the standard deviation of his or her scores to be 4.5 IQ points. Furthermore, if an individual obtains a score of 110 on a single administration and we assume a normal model, and then assert that his or her true score is between 105.5 and 114.5, we will be correct 68 percent of the time. This probability statement is appropriate when one individual is measured many times and when many individuals are measured on one occasion.

Notice one very important point that is implicit in the above discussion. By virtue of the way it is conceived, the theory of true and error scores implies that the standard error of measurement is the same value for every individual. It does not allow the possibility that on particular traits some individuals may exhibit more measurement error than others. As a behavioral scientist you may or may not wish to believe that this is correct. Recent empirical research has suggested that individuals do in fact differ "reliably" in their self-consistency.

Both the reliability coefficient as indicated by Equation 8-16 and the standard error of measurement as indicated by Equation 8-19 are indices of the extent of systematic or unsystematic variance. Examination of Equation 8-19 illustrates some notions about measurement. If reliability is perfect, $r_{xx} = 1.00$, then $S = 0.00$. That is, an observed or fallible score equals the true score. If, however, there is no correlation, then $S = \sigma_x$. This indicates that a person's true score can fall within the range of the distribution of observed scores; or more simply since we cannot measure the characteristic reliably, one individual's score, on retesting, can be like any other individual's in that distribution.

### Estimating True from Fallible Scores

More for historical reasons than anything else, suppose we ask whether or not we can determine the degree of association (that is, correlation) between true scores and observed scores. If we adopt the theory of true and error scores as our model of a score, the answer is yes, and quite easily at that. In the usual fashion we could look at the correlation in question,

$$r_{xx_\infty} = \frac{\Sigma x x_\infty}{n \sigma_x \sigma_\infty} = \frac{\Sigma (x_\infty + e) x_\infty}{n \sigma_x \sigma_\infty}$$

work through some relatively obvious algebraic steps, and arrive at the answer that this correlation is simply equal to the square root of the reliability coefficient:

$$r_{xx_\infty} = \sqrt{r_{xx}} \qquad (8\text{-}20)$$

Traditionally this value is termed the *index of reliability*. It is the coefficient of correlation between fallible and true scores and indicates how good fallible scores are as measures of true scores. It is apparent that when the reliability of a test is low, fallible scores are poor indices of true scores; and when reliability is high, true scores can be very accurately predicted from fallible scores.

It should be pointed out that though the reliability coefficient, Equation 8-16, and the index of reliability, Equation 8-20, are related to each other, the former is the one of practical interest. In Chapter 9 we present the empirical methods for estimating the reliability of measures. The reliability that we will be assessing is the reliability coefficient; it is the reliability that should be reported in manuals and that should serve as one very important aspect to be considered in evaluating our tests. In contrast, the index of reliability is another way of interpreting reliability, since it is derived from the reliability coefficient. However, the index cannot be *directly* determined.

## Eclectic Model of True Scores and Parallel Tests

Based on its simplifying assumptions, the theory of true and error scores can provide criteria for the identification of parallel measures and for the specification for how the standard error of measurement can be computed. However, the notion that a fallible score is composed of the sum of a fixed true score and a random error score is not really necessary to arrive at much the same end point. The same representation for the means and variances of parallel tests and the means and variances of true scores can be obtained by beginning with a definition of a true score as the average of the scores of a large number of parallel tests; that is,

$$X_\infty = \frac{X_1 + X_2 + \cdots + X_k}{k}$$

The principal difference between starting with this less stringent set of initial assumptions and beginning with the initial assumptions of the theory of true and error scores is in the way the standard error of measurement is interpreted. For the theory of true and error scores the standard error of measurement is viewed as being the same for everybody. The less stringent eclectic point of view leads to the specification of the standard error of measurement as an average across individuals. That is, some individuals may exhibit a larger standard error of measurement than others. Whether this is a more reasonable point of view is a matter for empirical research. In any event, the computation is exactly the same regardless of the starting point; only the interpretation differs.

## *Domain Sampling Model*

Since approximately 1904 the theory of true and error scores has been the dominant model of reliability and measurement error in psychometric theory and practice. Serious competition did not arise until the mid-1950s in the form of *domain sampling theory* (Tryon, 1957). The struggle between these two models—if indeed there is one—has not yet been resolved, and all the practical implications of their differences have not really been clearly worked out as yet. We will necessarily have to talk about some rather subtle and abstract issues. What follows is an attempt to keep things as down-to-earth as possible and still not lose the flavor of the argument.

In general, domain sampling's principal reason for being is that it tries to reflect more realistically the kinds of variables and measures with which psychologists deal, while the classical theory of true and error scores seems more appropriate for the physical sciences, where there indeed may be a true score that remains constant over a long period of time. Tryon and others objected to the true-versus-error-score dichotomy and to the overall simplistic rigidity of the classical theory. What they felt was needed was a model that reflected the complexity and dynamics of psychological variables, and the domain-sampling model is intended to fill such a need. The model is also more in keeping with the obvious fact in psychological measurement that the majority of measuring instruments in use are made up of a series of components or items rather than a single component or operation.

Whether in the end choosing between the two models makes any practical difference for practical people trying to measure psychological variables is a relevant but separate issue. We attempt to speak to it in the next chapter. For the present we would like to look at the model itself in terms of what it says about the nature of psychological variables and the errors with which they are measured.

The model of domain sampling conceives of a trait as being a group of behaviors all of which have some property in common. This group of behaviors constitutes a domain of behavior and differs from other groups of behaviors or domains, which have other properties in common. To measure the trait in question, we provide a series of items or situations each of which elicits one or another of the behaviors in the domain. Some domains of behavior may be quite general, whereas others may be quite specific. Thus the domain ''aggression'' includes a wide variety of behaviors—from murderous acts and injury to others, through hitting and cursing, to malicious gossip and hostile glances. On the other hand, the domain ''simple addition'' involves only the addition of pairs of single-digit numbers. Some domains completely include other domains, whereas in other instances there is only partial overlap.

The domain "social interaction" completely includes the domain "aggression" since all aggression involves the interaction among people, whereas the domain "verbal fluency" would only partly overlap the domain "aggression" to include acts of cursing and malicious gossip but not murderous acts, hitting, angry glances, and the like.

### Statistical Description of a Domain

In principle at least, it would be possible to develop a component measure for every component behavior in the domain and to obtain scores for a large number of people on each component. If we obtained such data, it would then be possible to compute a number of descriptive statistics that would characterize some of the domain's properties. Such a description would involve statements about the distributional characteristics of the components (that is, mean and variance of the scores on each), the relationships among the components, and the relationships between the components and other variables. The components of any domain vary among themselves in these characteristics. They differ among themselves in their means, standard deviations, and covariances. To provide an overall statistical description of the components, we could describe their average characteristics. In describing a particular domain, then, we would give the following values:

$$\bar{X}_i = \text{average of means of scores on components}$$

$$\bar{\sigma}^2_{x_i} = \text{average of variances of scores on components}$$

$$\overline{\sigma_{x_i}\sigma_{x_{i'}}r_{x_i x_{i'}}} = \text{average of covariances among components}$$

$$\overline{\sigma_{x_i}\sigma_y r_{x_i y}} = \text{average of covariances between components and any}$$
$$\text{other variable, } y, \text{ outside the domain}$$

One reason for pointing to these properties now is to sensitize you to certain psycometric features of domains that will play a very important role in our subsequent conceptualizations of reliability. The variances of components and the covariances among them are probably the two most important, and we can already see that a domain with very high covariation among components is a different state of affairs than a domain with very low covariation among components. The former implies a much more homogeneous entity that might be much easier to define and measure than a domain comprised of very heterogeneous components. For example, compare in your mind's eye a domain labeled "spelling ability" and one labeled "managerial job performance."

Obviously, since testing time is limited and there are limitations on our ability to think up ways to measure all the behaviors in a domain, a particular instrument most likely cannot measure the complete domain but can only strive to tap what we hope is a good sample. For example, suppose we wish to measure the variable "interest in active occupations," which we define as "preference for occupations that involve moving about from one place to another." We can conceive of many items in which people are asked whether they would like or dislike such occupations as bus driver, traveling sales representative, airline pilot, patrol officer, and solicitor. From the many possible items, we choose for our test only a certain number, say 50. Consequently our test is comprised of a sample of 50 items from the total domain of items.

As another example, consider the measurement of reaction time to a light. We can conceive of a large number of presentations of the light to subjects, and these many presentations constitute the domain of reaction time to this particular light. However, because of the limitations of the experimental period, when we actually measure reaction time, we might present the light only 25 times. Hence we have taken a sample of responses from the many possible numbers of responses that constitute the domain.

It is not completely out of line to draw an analogy between the model of domain sampling and the principles of statistical estimation and inference as practiced by the statistician. That is, statisticians talk about populations and samples, and they use data obtained on samples to estimate the characteristics of the population. The population is the complete group in which they are interested. A sample is the subgroup of the total that it is actually possible to observe.

Likewise, from a particular domain (or population of components), we could draw a sample of some given size. In our test of "interest in active occupations" we could have 10 items, 38, 50, 164, or any other number. Similarly, in our reaction-time test we could take 3 reactions, or 17, 25, 45, or whatever we wish. If our domain is infinitely large, we could draw an infinite number of such samples.

Let us say that we draw $k$ samples from our domain, each sample being composed of $m$ items or situations. We then have 1 to $k$ samples each composed of $i$ to $m$ components. Such scores can be represented as follows:

$$X_1 = X_{1_i} + \cdots + X_{1_m}$$
$$\cdot$$
$$\cdot \qquad\qquad\qquad\qquad (8\text{-}21)$$
$$\cdot$$
$$X_k = X_{k_i} + \cdots + X_{k_m}$$

In deviation-score form we write these equations as

$$x_1 = x_{1_i} + \cdots + x_{1_m}$$

.

.

.

$$x_k = x_{k_i} + \cdots + x_{k_m}$$

If the sample we draw from the domain is representative, then its statistical characteristics are the same as those of the total domain. Now suppose every one of the $k$ samples we draw is *perfectly* representative of the total domain in terms of the averages of the means, variances, and covariances of the component items or situations. Then the following four conditions would hold:

1. The averages of the means of the scores on the components are the same for all samples and are equal to the average of the means of the scores on the components in the total domain.

2. The averages of the variances of the scores on the components are the same for all samples and are equal to the average of the variances of the scores on the components in the total domain.

3. The averages of the covariances among the components in all samples are equal to the average of the covariances between the components in the domain.

4. The averages of the covariances between the components and any other variable are the same in all samples and are equal to the average of the covariances among the components and any other variable in the total domain.

### Domain as Hypothetical Universe

The above discussion poses an important question: Should a specific domain of behavior, or more specifically the universe of components or items that measure it, be thought of as a real population that could be enumerated if we worked hard enough at it? Or should we conceptualize a domain strictly in hypothetical terms and give it the status of an intellectual construct? The theory of domain sampling says that the latter choice (that is, a hypothetical universe) is more theoretically and practically useful in the end.

One line of support for this choice goes as follows. For the sake of argument, first suppose that we conceive of a domain as a group of actual behaviors. We could begin by defining our variable, following the rationale we outlined in Chapter 2, and end up with a comprehensive verbal statement of the nature and characteristics of the trait we propose to measure. Taking this verbal statement as a set of specifications or a blueprint, we could then develop operations for measuring the trait.

Let us return to our example of the measurement of the trait "interest in active occupations." It might be that we develop some 1,000 items from the definition, but the practicalities of testing being what they are, we can only utilize an inventory consisting of 50 items. As a solution we could randomly draw 50 items from the total pool of 1,000 items.

Now we might say that these 1,000 items constitute our domain and that all the items are equally good because they all stem from the definition of our variable. Therefore the choice of any particular 50 items should be determined purely on a chance basis, with the likelihood of any given item's being chosen being precisely the same as that of any other item. In a similar fashion we could pick out other samples of 50 items, taking them as being parallel to our first since all samples are chosen in a purely random fashion. The reliability of measurement could be viewed as the variation in one individual's scores over these various parallel (that is, random) samples of components or by the intercorrelations among them.

If we adopt this point of view, then it is necessary to deal with the problem of the extent to which each of the samples is representative of the total domain. But this implies two propositions: first that we can precisely describe the totality of the domain, and second that all items or situations are equally good for measuring the variable.

But which items constitute our domain? The 50 we finally selected? The 1,000 that formed our original pool of items? Certainly if we had given more time and effort to the matter, we might have developed not just 1,000 items, but 10,000 or 100,000 or 1,000,000. Indeed, in many instances we could conceive of there being a limitless number of possible items that could be developed from the definition of our trait.

It may appear that there are some domains for which a finite and specific number of possible items can readily be identified. Suppose we wish to measure the trait "simple addition," which we define as "the addition together of pairs of single-digit numbers." Since there are 10 single-digit numbers ranging from 0 to 9, if they are taken two at a time, there are only 100 possible items. We might therefore take the position that these 100 items constitute the total domain. However, there is nothing in our definition that stipulates that items cannot be repeated, so that again we have a limitless number of possible items in our domain. Perhaps we should discard the notion of a finite population.

Furthermore, sampling randomly from a real finite population presupposes that we consider all the available items as being equally good "representatives" of the domain. In practice it is very unlikely that we would consider all the items we can think of as being equally good. Consider again our example of the inventory for measuring "interest in active occupations." Reasonable people would probably not consider all the items in the pool of 1,000 to be equally good as measures of "active occupations." For example, we might discard the item "patrol officer" because while patrol officers do move about, they do not do so to any great extent. The item "solicitor" might be discarded because it has certain immoral implications. So on one basis or another we probably could find 50 items that we believe to be better than the remaining 950, and as a consequence the basis of our choice of items would not be random but systematic.

In drawing items or situations from an actual or a potential pool, the decision of whether to include a given item or situation is not always easy. Of the items we might actually develop from the definition of our variable, it is obvious that some will be more representative of the domain as we have defined it than are others, but in many instances there will be doubt as to the degree to which they reflect the domain and whether they belong in the domain or not. Specific empirical techniques for deciding which components belong in a domain and the degree to which they reflect its central property are discussed in the chapters on test construction and scaling. For now let us accept the notion that by one means or another we do ultimately select operations of measurement that sample something, and the method of selection ordinarily is not based on chance. Further, the items or situations selected are those that best reflect our ideas about the nature of the domain, or variable, we wish to study.

Now here comes the crucial point. The *best* definition we can get of the domain or variable is given by the specific sample of items or situations that we *finally* select, by whatever means we do it. This is, of course, an operational definition of our trait. Consequently, it makes more sense to think of the universe (that is, the domain) not as a collection of actual items or situations, but as a hypothetical universe or population of behavior that has the same characteristics as those in our actual sample or test.

Please recognize that what we have done is reversed the conventional relationship between population and sample. Instead of specifying a population of some set of entities and then drawing a sample randomly from it, we have said we have a sample in hand that in turn *implies* a population (that is, a universe or domain) having the same characteristics as the sample. That is, there is a *hypothetical* universe of content from which our sample could have been randomly drawn. Going back to our statistician analogy for a moment, we should point out that the function of a sample is to provide data to make estimates about the characteristics of the population. That is, given a certain risk, the statistician wants to generalize from the sample to the population. Whether the population is observable or not is not the crucial issue. The important point is to correctly reflect the kinds of generalizations that can be made.

What follows is a bad example, but we will use it anyway. Suppose we do an experiment on college sophomores, and we do not select randomly from any place in particular. We can still think of the students in the experiment as a random sample from some population (although it may not conform to any currently enumerated one), and it is that population to which we must generalize the results of the experiment if we want to keep our scientific hands completely clean. The definition of this population might be something like "Midwestern state university sophomores who volunteer for experiments advertised on bulletin boards." It is *not* the population of the United States, or the population between the ages of 18 and 21, or some other such population. Again, so long as we are careful to specify the kind of generalization we are making, it does not matter whether the universe is hypothetical or real.

Saying that a domain is a hypothetical universe of behaviors from which our sample of components, or items, was randomly selected is similar in form to the above example. However, the sample of college sophomores used in the experiment is probably not the kind of sample the experimenter really would have wanted if he or she had been free to exercise a choice. It doesn't generalize back to a population that's as broad as some others he or she might think of. Unfortunately, the experimenter's locked in. In our case, the sample of components we develop for our measure generalizes back to a hypothetical population that is indeed the most interesting one we can think of. After all, we selected the *best* sample we could to measure the variable that interests us. Thus the converse of the conventional wisdom regarding populations and samples is precisely the way we *should* proceed.

The above constitutes a basic proposition of the concept of domain sampling. The domain is characterized by a hypothetical set of items or situations that on the average have the same means, variances, and covariances as those of our test.

### Defining a Domain

There is nothing contained in the concept of domain sampling that restricts us to the process of first defining a domain in verbal terms, then developing a series of items from that definition, and finally selecting those items that in our opinion best satisfy the definition. Indeed, in practice we often develop a measuring instrument in quite different ways. These other procedures yield collections of items or situations all of which are said to measure the same characteristics, as indicated by the fact that they are related to some other measure or measures of that characteristic.

Suppose, for example, we wish to measure leadership. We could define leadership as "the formal role in a group wherein the individual supervises and directs the behavior of other members of that group." Pursuant to this definition we could obtain two groups of individuals: those who have achieved the formal role of leader and those who have not. Thus we might obtain a group of 100 high school students who have been elected president of their class or club, captain of their team, or the like. Paired with them we could have another 100 students equal in age and in group or team membership, but none of whom have achieved the role of formal leader.

Now we administer a series of items to all students. For example, we might have them describe themselves on an adjective checklist, each student checking those adjectives that he or she believes describe him or her. We use an adjective checklist rather than some other type of device because we believe that "self-perception" is more likely to be related to leadership behavior. However, we do not know or have any ideas about what particular self-perceptions will be related to leader- ship behavior, so for each adjective or item we observe the difference in responses of the two groups of students. We could set some particu- lar difference as being significant and use in our final adjective check- list only those items that meet the criterion of significance. If there are more "significant" items than we need, we utilize those for which the differences in the responses of the two groups of students are the greatest since they are most closely related to the property we wish to measure.

Our domain then is comprised of a series of adjectives all of which have in common the property of differentiating those individuals who have manifested leadership from those who have not. In the develop- ment of our original pool of items, there need have been no selection on the basis of any definition of leadership. Perhaps all we did was to take a random sample of adjectives that describe personal characteristics in the hope that some of them would be useful for our particular purposes.

In this same manner we might develop an inventory designed to measure "interests of students in the physical sciences." We begin by collecting a series of items asking for expressions of interest in all sorts of occupations, hobbies, and school subjects. As we develop our items, we merely select those that have to do with activities people like or dislike. We then administer our interest items to a group of college students majoring in the physical sciences and to others majoring in other subjects. By comparing the responses of the two groups to each of the questions, we select as representative of our final domain of "interests of students in the physical sciences" those items on which the differences between the responses of the two groups meet some criterion of significance.

Both in the adjective checklist and in the interest inventory the items or situations themselves are not necessarily developed or selected on the basis of some definition of the specific domain or variable we are interested in measuring. Rather they may be chosen on some other grounds, that is, from a more general domain, such as personally descriptive adjectives in the one case and activities in the other. The final selection of items for the domain, however, is based on the degree to which the items have the common property of being related to some other measure of the trait in which we are interested.

A test developed in this way can be treated as a sample from a domain in just the same way as a test wherein the items are developed from a verbal definition of a trait. As a matter of fact, when we develop a series of items from a verbal definition of a trait, we often do not entirely trust our subjective judgment of whether a given item really follows from the definition or not. Therefore we sometimes eliminate items that are not related to some other independent measure of the same trait or that are related to it to a low degree. In other cases we may not trust our own judgment concerning a single item, but we do trust our collective judgment concerning the large bulk of items. In this case we may compute the score for each person on the total of all items in the available pool and eliminate those items that are unrelated or related only to a low degree to total scores.

We look at these alternative methods for selecting the "best" sample of components in much greater detail in later chapters of this book.

### Parallel Tests in Domain Sampling

Clearly implicit in the theory of true and error scores is the notion that it is possible to develop a set of actual tests that precisely meet the criteria of parallelism. Indeed, a set of actual parallel tests is necessary to estimate reliability, and an infinite number of actual parallel tests would be necessary to obtain a precise statement of the degree of reliability.

In the concept of domain sampling, parallel tests—or parallel samples if you will—are viewed as being hypothetical measures, and actual tests that meet certain criteria of parallelism are not necessary for estimating the degree of the reliability of measurement. It is not denied that tests that meet the criteria of parallelism in terms of having precisely equal means, standard deviations, and intercorrelations, as well as the same patterns of correlations with other tests, can exist. This is a matter left open for empirical investigation, but for the domain model it has no bearing on either the theory of reliability or the estimation of the degree of reliability.

If a behavioral scientist schooled in the theory of true and error scores were in fact to construct three 45-item measures of say interpersonal dominance, and handed the tests to a colleague who adhered to domain theory, something like the following might happen. The domain theorist would look at the tests and argue that not all the components within each of the three tests were equally good measures of interpersonal dominance. That is, within each of the tests, some of the components were better than others. Since our objective as either researchers or practitioners (says the domain theorist) is to construct the best measure we can of interpersonal dominance, why not take the 15 best items from each of the three parallel tests and put them together in a new 45-item test that is that much better than any of the other three? What we want to know is the reliability of the best sample, not the reliability of parallel tests that are not as good as the best measure of the variable we can get.

Once the best sample is in hand, the theory of domain sampling has no difficulty conceptualizing a number of *hypothetical* samples that are parallel to it. Further, as we shall see, the theory has no difficulty in conceptualizing the correlation between the actual scores on the best sample that is in hand and scores on a hypothetical parallel. Similarly, it is reasonable to think of the distribution of one individual's scores across many parallel samples, one of which is real and the rest hypothetical. In fact, we are about to show how the correlation between the real sample and a hypothetical sample and the standard deviation of an individual's score across a real sample plus many hypothetical ones can be estimated.

In our mathematical formulations of the concept of domain sampling, we have denoted parallel samples drawn from a domain as 1 to $m$, each sample containing $k$ items, situations, or the like. Any one sample can be our actual test or measuring instrument, and the remainder are intellectual constructs. For convenience let us designate sample 1 as the actual test and samples 2 to $m$ as the parallel constructs.

*Means and variances of parallel samples*   If we consider the means of our one real sample and of as many hypothetical samples as we might care to visualize, it is true virtually by definition that the means of the scores on all these samples are equal to one another. The domain-sampling model has already stipulated that we should think of the hypothetical samples as measuring the same thing to the same degree as the real samples. Therefore the means of the parallel samples are the same.

A similar argument can be made for the variances and standard deviations of parallel samples. By virtue of the way the theory is constituted, they are also equal across samples.

The fact that these means and variances are the same for parallel samples is not an earthshaking revelation. It was defined to be that way. The really important part is what develops next. Take heed.

*Correlations among parallel samples* Each of the parallel-test samples (both real and not real) is a composite of components that have been sampled randomly from the hypothetical universe of components. As we did so often, it is no trick to write down the expression for the correlation between two composites. In this case, one of the composites might be our real sample (composite I) and the other a hypothetical parallel (composite II) and each of them contains $k$ components. (The following was also developed in the Technical Section at the end of Chapter 7.)

The definitional formula for the correlation between these two composites is the ratio of their covariance to the product of their standard deviation (as it is for all definitional formulas for the correlation coefficient).

$$r_{x_I x_{II}} = \frac{\frac{1}{N} \Sigma x_I x_{II}}{\sigma_{x_I} \sigma_{x_{II}}}$$

If we substitute the component scores for the total scores on each sample, the correlation becomes:

$$r_{x_I x_{II}} = \frac{\frac{1}{N} \Sigma (x_{I_1} + x_{I_2} + \cdots x_{I_k})(x_{II_1} + x_{II_2} + \cdots x_{II_k})}{\sigma_{x_I} \sigma_{x_{II}}}$$

Multiplying out the numerator, bringing the summation sign inside the parentheses, and dividing each term by $N$ yields $k \times k$ covariance terms in the numerator. That is, there are terms corresponding to every possible pair when one of the pair comes from composite I (the real sample) and the other of the pair comes from composite II (the hypothetical sample).

Just to show how the elements get turned into covariances, let's consider two more steps.

$$r_{x_I x_{II}} = \frac{\frac{1}{N} \Sigma x_{I_1} x_{II_1} + \frac{1}{N} \Sigma x_{I_1} x_{II_2} + \cdots \frac{1}{N} \Sigma x_{I_k} x_{II_k}}{\sigma_{x_I} \sigma_{x_{II}}}$$

and

$$\frac{1}{N} \Sigma x_{I_1} x_{II_1} = \sigma_{I_1} \sigma_{II_1} r_{I_1 II_1}$$

Therefore

$$r_{x_I x_{II}} = \frac{\sigma_{I_1} \sigma_{II_1} r_{I_1 II_1} + \sigma_{I_1} \sigma_{II_2} r_{I_1 II_2} + \cdots \sigma_{I_k} \sigma_{II_k} r_{I_k II_k}}{\sigma_{x_I} \sigma_{x_{II}}}$$

It would take forever to write down all the $k \times k$ terms in the numerator if $k$ were very large. To aid in visualizing the situation, Figure 8-1 is provided. The covariance terms appearing in the above numerator can be found in either quadrant $B$ or quadrant $C$ of the figure.

We can make things much simpler in appearance by substituting $k^2$ (the number of terms) times the average cross covariance in quadrant $B$ or $C$ for the sum of the cross covariances in the previous equations. The correlation between the two samples then becomes

$$r_{x_I x_{II}} = \frac{k^2 \overline{\sigma_{x_{I_i}} \sigma_{x_{II_i}} r}_{x_{I_i} x_{II_i}}}{\sigma_{x_I} \sigma_{x_{II}}}$$

The next step is the really crucial one for the domain-sampling model. Since the two measures are random samples from the same universe, covariances between components within a particular sample should differ from covariances between components coming from different samples only because of sampling error; and on the average they should be the same. That is, because of the way we set up our hypothetical sampling procedure, a specific component has an equal probability of ending up in the hypothetical sample as in the real sample. Thus the average within composite covariance in quadrants $A$ and $D$ in the matrix should be the same as the average between composite covariance in quadrants $B$ and $C$. Further, as we argued above, there is no reason to expect any difference between the standard deviations of any two sample scores. Therefore the correlation can be rewritten as

$$r_{x_I x_{II}} = \frac{k^2 \overline{\sigma_{x_i} \sigma_{x_{i'}} r}_{x_i x_{i'}}}{\sigma_x^2}$$

where $x_i$ and $x_{i'}$ refer to pairs of variables *within* a particular sample and *not* to a pair of variables where one of the pair comes from one sample of components and the other of the pair comes from a second sample.

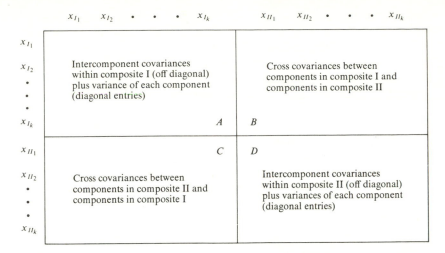

*Figure 8-1*   Covariance terms when a matrix of covariances is created among all items in composite I and composite II.

The important point is that we now have the estimate for the correlation between any two samples expressed in terms of the data *from just one administration of just one sample.*

You should be dancing in the streets at this point. We now have a theory of reliability that says we should go construct a measuring instrument of the best components we can find and then permits us to compute the correlation between that measure and a parallel one using only the data we actually have in hand.

### True Scores in Domain Sampling

In the concept of domain sampling a true score is defined as the sum, or more conveniently as the average, of an individual's scores on an infinitely large number of representative samples or parallel tests. If the number of parallel samples is increased without limit, then they will completely include all the components in the domain, and consequently the true score is the domain score.

### Correlation of True and Fallible Scores

We just defined an individual's true score as the total score on all the components in the domain. Suppose we wished to know the correlation of these true scores with scores on the sample of components we have in hand, which are the observed or fallible scores. Certainly we can measure a large number of people on the sample, but since the universe is hypothetical, we cannot actually obtain the true scores. As luck would have it, we don't need the true scores.

Suppose we pose the above problem as the determination of the correlation between scores on the observed sample and the average scores on an infinitely large number of hypothetical parallel samples. This latter quantity is the true score. If we start from this formulation and work through the mathematics, we will discover that the correlation between true and fallible scores is equal to the square root of the domain model's reliability coefficient.

$$r_{x\infty} = \sqrt{r_{xx}} = \sqrt{\frac{k^2 \overline{\sigma_{x_i} \sigma_{x_{i'}} r_{x_i x_{i'}}}}{\sigma_x^2}}$$

Again note that this correlation can be obtained from the data of just one administration of our sample of components to just one sample of people at just one point in time—which, as we shall see in the next chapter, is both a strength and a weakness. Note also that this correlation is identical in form to the reliability index derived from the classical theory. The difference lies in the interpretation of what parallel measures are used to compute $r_{xx}$.

### Measurement Error and Domain Sampling

Let us now consider the standard error of measurement in terms of the concept of domain sampling. The variance of any one individual's scores, say individual $a$ over $k$ parallel tests, the square of the standard error of measurement, is

$$S_a^2 = \sigma_{x_a - \bar{x}_a}^2 = \frac{\Sigma(x_a - \bar{x}_a)^2}{k}$$

Based on our previous arguments, we can substitute $x_\infty$ for the average of the individual's scores on $k$ parallel tests, which gives

$$S_a^2 = \frac{\Sigma(x_a - x_\infty)^2}{k} \tag{8-22}$$

In the concept of domain sampling, ordinarily no position is taken on whether the standard error of measurement is the same for all individuals or whether it varies in magnitude from person to person. Therefore to obtain a description of the variation in individual's scores over parallel tests, we would probably wish to calculate the average standard error. We would determine the standard error of each person from Equation 8-22 and then average the standard errors for all persons. We can write for the concept of domain sampling the formula for the average of the standard errors as

$$\bar{S}^2 = \sigma_x^2(1 - r_{xx}) \qquad (8\text{-}23)$$

## *Points of View on Reliability of Measurement*

Even though true scores are defined differently for each of the two concepts of the reliability of measurement that we have discussed and though the developments we made in each are different, we nevertheless arrived at exactly the same conclusions about the characteristics of parallel tests and of true scores. In both approaches parallel tests are seen as tests with the same means, standard deviations, and intercorrelations. True scores are seen as having the same means as fallible scores and having standard deviations equal to the standard deviation of fallible scores times the square root of 1 minus the reliability coefficient.

We might therefore question whether it is worthwhile considering different theoretical approaches to the reliability of measurement. If they all lead to the same conclusions, why bother about the fact that they have quite different bases? However, as we shall see in the following chapter, the differences among them in terms of their basic conceptualizations are of great importance when we come to empirically estimate the reliability of a test. The various ways for estimating the reliability of measurement will be seen to differ in appropriateness, depending on which point of view we adopt with respect to reliability. Therefore a given estimate of the reliability of a test may be viewed as being too high, exactly right, or too low, depending on whether we hold to the theory of true and error scores or the theory of domain sampling.

---

## *Technical Section*

In the main body of this chapter we omitted some of the algebraic manipulations that permitted certain principles and formulas to be derived from the theory of true and error scores. We present them here.

### Correlation Between Parallel Tests

From the theory of true and error scores, we can break down an observed score into its true-score and error-score components and write the correlation between two parallel tests as

$$r_{x_1 x_2} = \frac{\Sigma(x_\infty + e_1)(x_\infty + e_2)}{n\sigma_{x_1}\sigma_{x_2}}$$

The expression can then be worked through as follows.

Since we know that the standard deviations of all parallel tests are equal, we can write $\sigma_x^2$ for $\sigma_{x_1}\sigma_{x_2}$:

$$
\begin{aligned}
r_{x_1 x_2} &= \frac{\Sigma(x_\infty + e_1)(x_\infty + e_2)}{n\sigma_x^2} \\
&= \frac{\Sigma(x_\infty^2 + x_\infty e_1 + x_\infty e_2 + e_1 e_2)}{n\sigma_x^2} \\
&= \frac{\Sigma x_\infty^2/n + \Sigma x_\infty e_1/n + \Sigma x_\infty e_2/n + \Sigma e_1 e_2/n}{\sigma_x^2}
\end{aligned}
$$

Since the sum of the cross products of deviation scores divided by the number of cases is equal to the coefficient of correlation between the two variables times their standard deviations, we can write the last three terms in the numerator in this manner:

$$r_{x_1 x_2} = \frac{\sigma_{x_\infty}^2 + r_{x_\infty e_1}\sigma_{x_\infty}\sigma_{e_1} + r_{x_\infty e_2}\sigma_{x_\infty}\sigma_{e_2} + r_{e_1 e_2}\sigma_{e_1}\sigma_{e_2}}{\sigma_x^2}$$

From Equation 8-6 we know that the correlation between error scores and other variables is .00. Therefore the last three terms in the numerator become zero and drop out. Hence

$$r_{x_1 x_2} = \frac{\sigma_{x_\infty}^2}{\sigma_x^2}$$

In a similar fashion we can show that the coefficient of correlation between any pair of parallel tests other than $x_1$ and $x_2$ is equal to the ratio of the variance of true scores to the variance of fallible scores. Consequently we can write the general expression as

$$r_{x_1 x_2} = \frac{\sigma_{x_\infty}^2}{\sigma_x^2} = r_{xx} \tag{8-16}$$

### Correlation Between Parallel Tests and Another Variable

To examine the correlations between scores on any parallel test, say $x_i$, and some other variable, $y$, we could do the following:

$$r_{x_i y} = \frac{\Sigma(x_\infty + e_i)y}{n\sigma_{x_i}\sigma_y}$$

$$= \frac{\Sigma x_\infty y/n + \Sigma e_i y/n}{\sigma_{x_i}\sigma_y}$$

Since the sum of cross products of deviation scores divided by the number of cases is equal to the correlation coefficient times the two standard deviations,

$$r_{x_i} = \frac{r_{x_\infty y}\sigma_{x_\infty}\sigma_y + r_{e_i y}\sigma_{e_i}\sigma_y}{\sigma_{x_i}\sigma_y}$$

From Equation 8-6 we know that the correlation between error scores and scores on any other variable is .00. Therefore the entire second term in the numerator becomes zero and drops out. Hence

$$r_{x_i y} = \frac{r_{x_\infty y}\sigma_{x_\infty}\sigma_y}{\sigma_{x_i}\sigma_y}$$

$$= \frac{r_{x_\infty y}\sigma_{x_\infty}}{\sigma_{x_i}}$$

$$= r_{x_\infty y}\frac{\sigma_{x_\infty}}{\sigma_{x_i}}$$

From Equation 8-16 we know that the ratio of the variance of true scores to the variance of fallible scores is equal to the reliability coefficient. Hence

$$r_{x_i y} = r_{x_\infty y}\sqrt{r_{xx}}$$

By a similar derivation we can show that the above equation holds for any parallel test other than $x_i$. Consequently

$$r_{x_i y} = \cdots = r_{x_k y} = r_{x_\infty y}\sqrt{r_{xx}}$$

Hence we can conclude that all parallel tests correlate to the same degree with any other variable.

### Correlation Between True and Observed Scores

We have seen that under the classical theory

$$r_{xx} = \frac{\sigma_\infty^2}{\sigma_x^2}$$

Keeping this in mind, let us see what happens to the correlation between true scores and fallible scores.

$$
\begin{aligned}
r_{xx_\infty} &= \frac{\Sigma(x_\infty + e)x_\infty}{n\sigma_x\sigma_{x_\infty}} \\
&= \frac{\Sigma(x_\infty^2 + x_\infty e)}{n\sigma_x\sigma_{x_\infty}} \\
&= \frac{\Sigma x_\infty^2 + \Sigma x_\infty e}{n\sigma_x\sigma_{x_\infty}} \\
&= \frac{\Sigma x_\infty^2/n + \Sigma x_\infty e/n}{\sigma_x\sigma_{x_\infty}} \\
&= \frac{\sigma_{x_\infty}^2 + \sigma_{x_\infty}\sigma_e r_{x_\infty e}}{\sigma_x\sigma_{x_\infty}}
\end{aligned}
$$

From the second assumption in the theory of true and error scores as given in Equation 8-6, we know that the correlation between error scores and scores on any other variable is .00. Therefore the second term in the numerator of the above equation becomes zero and drops out.

$$
\begin{aligned}
r_{xx_\infty} &= \frac{\sigma_{x_\infty}^2}{\sigma_x\sigma_{x_\infty}} \\
&= \frac{\sigma_{x_\infty}}{\sigma_x}
\end{aligned}
$$

Substituting from the above, we have

$$r_{xx_\infty} = \sqrt{r_{xx}} \qquad (8\text{-}20)$$

Traditionally this value is termed the *index of reliability*. It is the coefficient of correlation between fallible and true scores and indicates how good fallible scores are as measures of true scores.

## Summary

When a test is administered a number of times to an individual, ordinarily he or she does not obtain the same score each time. Sometimes the scores vary systematically, showing an upward or a downward trend or cyclical variations, that we attribute to the effects of systematic factors. In addition, there are random variations in scores that we attribute to the effects of unsystematic factors. This unsystematic variation among measurements within an individual on the same trait is termed the reliability of measurement.

The reliability of measurement can be taken to be the variation in an individual's scores over a series of parallel tests. Parallel tests are tests that measure the same trait to the same degree. Two indices of reliability are the standard error of measurement, which is the standard deviation of an individual's scores over many parallel tests, and the reliability coefficient, which is the correlation between two parallel tests. When measurements are highly reliable, the standard error is small and the reliability coefficient is high; and when measurements are unreliable, the standard error is large and the reliability coefficient is low. Another index, the index of reliability, indicates the relationship between the fallible scores and the true scores. These three reliability indices have analogous conceptual definitions for the notion of validity.

The reliability of measurement has been conceptualized in a variety of ways in the attempt to specify its definition, to understand its effects, and to measure its extent. These different views are reasonably well represented by two theoretical models: the theory of true and error scores, which is the classical psychometric theory, and the theory of domain sampling.

According to the theory of true and error scores, the score an individual earns on a test (the fallible score) is a composite of the amount of the trait he or she actually possesses (the true score) and an error of measurement. This theory assumes that individuals possess stable characteristics or traits that persist over time, that errors are completely random and therefore uncorrelated with any other variable, and that fallible scores are the result of the addition of true and error scores.

From these assumptions it follows mathematically that tests that are parallel to one another have the same mean and standard deviation, correlate with each other to exactly the same degree, and correlate to the same degree with any other variable. It also follows that the standard error of measurement is the same for all individuals, and the reliability coefficient is the ratio of the variance of true scores to the variance of fallible scores. If the assumptions are granted, it is possible to develop formulas for estimating true from fallible scores (the index of reliability) and for determining the variance of true scores.

The second theory, domain sampling, conceives of a trait as being a domain of behaviors all of which have some property in common. This domain is infinitely large, so that in measuring the trait we can draw only a sample from the domain. The score on the sample is the individual's fallible score, and his or her score on the entire domain is the true score. Both fallible and true scores are therefore taken to be composites. Parallel tests are regarded as being samples from the domain that are representative of it. That is, the averages of the means and standard deviations of the components, the averages of the covariances among the components, and the averages of the covariances between the components and any other variable outside the domain are taken to be the same for all parallel tests and for the entire domain.

From these notions it follows mathematically, using formulas for composites and taking the number of components to be infinitely large, that parallel tests have the same means and standard deviations, correlate with one another to the same degree, and correlate to the same degree with any other variable. Formulas can be derived for estimating true from fallible scores. Though arrived at from an entirely different theoretical position, these formulas are exactly the same as those given by the classical theory. Again the reliability coefficient can be shown to be the ratio of the variance of true scores to the variance of fallible scores, but it does not follow that for all individuals the standard error of measurement has the same value.

---

## Suggested Readings

Cronbach, L. J., G. C. Gleser, H. Nanda, and N. Rajaratnam. 1972. *The dependability of behavioral measurements: Theory of generalizability for scores and profiles*. New York: Wiley.

Guilford, J. P. 1954. *Psychometric methods*. 2nd ed. New York: McGraw-Hill. Chap. 13.

Gulliksen, H. 1950. *Theory of mental tests*. New York: Wiley. Chaps. 2, 3, 4, 5, and 14.

Jackson, R. W. B. 1939. Reliability of mental tests. *British Journal of Psychology,* 29:267–287.

Lord, F. M., and M. R. Novick. 1968. *Statistical theories of mental test scores*. Reading, Mass.: Addison-Wesley. Chap. 2.

Lumsden, J. 1976. Test theory. In M. R. Rosenzweig and L. W. Porter (Eds.), *Annual Review of Psychology,* 27:251–280. Palo Alto, Ca.: Annual Reviews.

Novick, M. R. 1966. The axioms and principal results of classical test theory. *Journal of Mathematical Psychology,* 3:1–18.

Spearman, C. 1904. The proof and measurement of the association between two things. *American Journal of Psychology,* 15:72–101.

Spearman, C. 1910. Correlation calculated from faulty data. *British Journal of Psychology,* 3:271–295.

Stanley, J. C. 1971. Reliability. In R. L. Thorndike (Ed.), *Educational measurement.* Washington, D.C.: American Council on Education. Pp. 356–442.

Thurstone, L. L. 1931. *The reliability and validity of tests.* Ann Arbor, Mich.: Edwards Bros.

Tryon, R. C. 1957. Reliability and behavior domain validity: Reformulation and historical critique. *Psychological Bulletin,* 54:229–249.

# 9

## *Estimating Reliability of Measurement*

Having some notion of what is meant by the reliability of measurement and having examined the two major theoretical approaches to the problem, we are now in a position to examine its implications in more detail. The last part of this chapter is concerned with specific methods for estimating the reliability coefficient, but before we can consider those, we must examine several topics that are necessary preliminaries. The first of these is the effect on the reliability coefficient of increasing the length of a measure. The second is the role played by the actual range of true scores in whatever sample of people we have. Third, we want to look at how the reliability of a measure affects its correlation with other measures.

## *Number of Measurements*

We have seen that when an individual's scores on a series of parallel tests manifest considerable unsystematic variation (that is, the scores are unreliable), the score on any one test has limited value. When this situation occurs, there are several courses of action we can take. One option is to forget about trying to measure this particular variable. A second option is to make a drastic change in the type of measurement operation. A third alternative is to give several parallel tests to each person and use the total or average score as the individual's observed or fallible score.

The justification for choosing this third alternative is as follows. Up to now we have been thinking of an individual's observed or fallible score as a score on *one* parallel measure. We have also shown that the average score on an infinitely large number of parallel measures is equal to the individual's true score. The classical theory says this is because the error scores cancel each other out, and the domain model says it's because we eventually measure an individual on every behavior in the domain. Well, we obviously can't get the average scores on an infinite number of parallel measures, but how about averaging across three or four? This should cut the proportion of error variability down somewhat, perhaps enough to make measurement worthwhile. For the moment let's ignore the problem of the domain theorist, who may have difficulty getting more measures because he or she originally went after the best sample of components that could be gotten.

To look at it another way, suppose we originally could obtain the scores for one individual on 100 parallel tests, and the variability in his or her scores across these tests was considerable. Now suppose we formed 50 composites of two parallel tests each and compared the variability across the 50 scores comprised of the *average of two tests* with the variability across the original 100. For the reasons cited above, it should be less. The variability (that is, the unsystematic variation) should be even less if we looked at the variances of 25 scores each based on the average of four tests. It would be still less if we formed 10 composites of ten tests each. In other words, as we increase the number of measurements that enter into the determination of a score, there should be an increase in the reliability of measurement. Or more simply the more questions we ask to determine something about a situation, the more reliable will be our interpretation of that situation. Suppose we try to arrive at a technique for predicting what this increase in reliability will be.

### Influence on Reliability Coefficient

The reliability coefficient is the correlation between parallel tests. If we wish to ascertain the reliability of a composite of parallel tests, we need to have at least two composites formed of the same number of components. The correlation between any two such parallel composites is the reliability of the total or average score on however many individual parallel tests were combined to form the composites. Since we are after the correlation between two sets of composite scores, it does not matter whether we deal with the total or the average score of the components within a composite.

In Chapter 7 we saw that the standard-score form of the correlation between two composites (Equation 7-17) in terms of their component characteristics is as follows:

$$r_{c_1 c_2} = \frac{k \cdot k\bar{r}_{ij}}{\sqrt{k + k(k-1)\bar{r}_{ii'}}\sqrt{k + k(k-1)\bar{r}_{jj'}}}$$

where component $i$ comes from composite 1, component $j$ comes from composite 2, and each composite has $k$ components.

The fact that all the components in composite 1 and composite 2 are parallel measures makes for two very convenient features. First the variances of parallel tests are all equal, so it doesn't make any difference if the component scores are in standard-score form or not. All the variances and standard deviations that would be in the above equation if it were in raw-score form would cancel out anyway. Second all the intercorrelations among parallel tests are equal, and this one correlation is the reliability coefficient. Therefore the above correlation may be rewritten as

$$r_{cc'} = \frac{k^2 r_{xx}}{k + k(k-1)r_{xx}}$$

If we divide both numerator and denominator by $k$, we get

$$r_{cc'} = \frac{k r_{xx}}{1 + (k-1)r_{xx}} \tag{9-1}$$

The same correlation would be obtained no matter what pair of composites were chosen so long as they were each composed of $k$ parallel tests.

Equation 9-1 is a very famous one in psychometrics and is called the *Spearman–Brown formula* after the two men who first developed it. It indicates what the reliability of a lengthened test would be if the length were increased $k$ times (for example, doubled, tripled, quadrupled). Keep firmly in mind that the accuracy of the formula is dependent on the assumption that the components added to a measure are strictly parallel to those already there.

If each parallel composite contains only one parallel test, then Equation 9-1 resolves to the coefficient of correlation between two single parallel tests.

$$r_{cc'} = \frac{1 r_{xx}}{1 + 0 r_{xx}} = \frac{r_{xx}}{1} = r_{xx}$$

Now suppose we again divide the numerator and denominator of Equation 9-1 by $k$, which yields

$$r_{cc'} = \frac{r_{xx}}{\frac{1}{k} \frac{(k-1)}{k} (r_{xx})}$$

When each composite contains an infinitely large number of parallel tests, $1/k$ very closely approximates zero and $(k-1)/k$ very closely approximates 1. Therefore in this case the Spearman–Brown formula resolves to

$$r_{cc'} = \frac{r_{xx}}{0 + 1r_{xx}} = \frac{r_{xx}}{r_{xx}} = 1.00$$

Hence if the average scores are based on composites of an *infinitely* large number of parallel tests, the reliability coefficient of these scores is unity, and we measure with perfect reliability. This conclusion is quite consistent with both major theories of reliability.

Let us now examine more closely the relationship between the magnitude of the reliability coefficient and the number of measurements. In Figure 9-1 the relationship for three values of the reliability coefficient of single parallel tests, $r_{xx}$, is plotted. It can be seen in this figure that as the number of measurements increases, the reliability coefficient increases, the increase being greater in those cases where the reliability of the single parallel tests is initially low. Furthermore, it can be seen that in general the greatest increase in reliability occurs with the first increase in the additional measurements entering into the composite of scores.

Suppose we have a test that has a reliability coefficient of .70. If we increase the length of the test five times, we find that the reliability coefficient of the lengthened test, from Equation 9-1, is .92. Thus, for example, if we find that the reliability of the ratings assigned by single raters is .70, the average of the ratings assigned by five parallel raters is .92, a significant increase in reliability. This presumes, of course, that the standard deviations of the ratings assigned by the different raters are precisely the same, and the intercorrelations among the ratings assigned by the different raters are also equal. If this is not precisely the case, then Equation 9-1 provides only an estimate of the reliability resulting from an increased number of measurements.

The Spearman–Brown formula can also be used to estimate the effects on reliability of reducing the number of measurements. Suppose a test composed of 100 items has a reliability coefficient of .80. If this test takes too long to administer, we might wish to shorten it and use only 50 items. We should then want to estimate the reliability coefficient of a

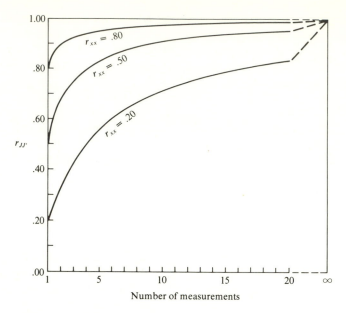

*Figure 9-1*    Relationship between reliability coefficient and number of measurements.

test one-half as long as the original test. In this case $k$ in Equation 9-1 is .5 and $k - 1$ is $-.5$. Applying Equation 9-1 would show us that a test half as long as the original test would have a reliability coefficient of .67. We presume, of course, that the standard deviations of, and intercorrelations among, the eliminated items are equal in magnitude to the standard deviations of, and intercorrelations among, the items that are retained.

### Standard Error of Measurement

Let us now ask what effect an increase in the number of measurements has on the standard error of measurement. That is, how does the variation among the scores of an individual over a series of single parallel tests compare with the variation among his or her scores over parallel composites?

On the basis of the theory of true and error scores, we developed the variance of an individual's scores over parallel tests in Equation 8-17 as

$$S^2 = \sigma_x^2(1 - r_{xx})$$

We saw that if we accept the assumptions on which the theory of true and error scores is based, this equation holds for all individuals. With the theory of domain sampling, we related in Equation 8-23 the average of the variances of all individuals' scores over parallel tests to the reliability coefficient as

$$\bar{S}^2 = \sigma_x^2(1 - r_{xx})$$

Let us generalize the above two equations, taking each parallel test to be a composite of $k$ component parallel tests. We should then write them as

$$\bar{S}_c^2 \text{ or } S_c^2 = \sigma_c^2(1 - r_{cc})$$

If we work through the right-hand side of this expression by writing it in terms of component characteristics and then simplifying the equation, we get the following results:

$$\bar{S}_c^2 \text{ or } S_c^2 = \frac{\sigma_x^2}{k}(1 - r_{xx}) \tag{9-2}$$

Equation 9-2 shows us the effects on the standard error of measurement of increasing the number of measurements. This equation is plotted as Figure 9-2. It can be seen in this figure that as the number of measurements entering into the average composite scores increases, the variation of an individual's scores on parallel composites decreases. It is apparent that such average composite scores give a much more consistent description of the individual than do scores on a single test.

By way of example, suppose the reliability of ratings assigned by a single rater is .70 and the standard deviation of the ratings assigned by any individual rater is 10; then the standard error of measurement is 5.5 (Equation 8-18). However, if we take as the individual's ratings the average of the ratings assigned by a group of five parallel raters, the standard deviation of the average composite ratings assigned the individual by a number of parallel raters (each group containing five raters), as calculated from Equation 9-2, would be only equal to 6, or the standard error of measurement is 2.4. This is consistent with our previously demonstrated point that as reliability increases, the standard error of measurement decreases. Equation 9-2, which was developed by Spearman–Brown type considerations is in fact analogous to the standard error of measurement.

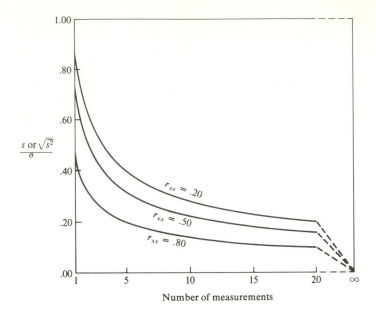

*Figure 9-2*   Relationship between standard error of
measurement and number of measurements.

### Seeking Desired Degree of Reliability

Sometimes we wish to achieve a particular degree of reliability of measurement, but the reliability of the only test available is insufficiently high. How much should we lengthen the test? Remember that there is always a cost involved when the number of measurements is increased, in terms of the time, effort, or money involved in developing parallel tests and in the increased testing itself. Hence we should prefer to increase the number of measurements by the least amount required, and we need a method to estimate the number of measurements it will take.

These formulas are obtained by solving Equations 9-1 and 9-2 for $k$. Equation 9-1 then becomes

$$k = \frac{r_{cc}(1 - r_{xx})}{r_{xx}(1 - r_{cc})} \tag{9-3}$$

where $r_{xx}$ is the reliability coefficient of single parallel tests and $r_{cc}$ is the reliability coefficient of the magnitude desired.

Equation 9-2 becomes

$$k = \frac{\sigma_x^2}{S_c^2} (1 - r_{xx}^2) \tag{9-4}$$

where $S_c^2$ is the square of the standard error of measurement desired. For example, suppose that the reliability coefficient of ratings assigned by a single rater is .50, and we wish to have ratings with a reliability coefficient of .90. Equation 9-3 tells us we need to employ nine such raters. Suppose we wish to have ratings that would vary for an individual only one-tenth as much as the variation among individuals. Equation 9-4 tells us we need five such raters. Before we use either Equation 9-3 or Equation 9-4 to determine the number of measurements needed to achieve a given degree of reliability, we should recall the conditions stipulated in their development. It is very unlikely that these conditions will hold exactly, and therefore these formulas should be taken as giving only estimates.

## Effects of Range of Individual Differences

Occasionally we wish to determine the reliability of a test for a particular group, but do not have available the entire range of individuals. Thus suppose we have a test that was administered to determine norms, and the mean and the standard deviation of the scores were found to be 100 and 16, respectively. Further suppose we want to determine the reliability of this test by measuring people several times. If we could obtain only a selected group for which the mean is 120 and the standard deviation is 9, then obviously the "reliability" group is more restricted in terms of range of scores than is the "norm" group. Sometimes we have the reverse problem. We know the reliability of a test when administered to a more heterogeneous group, but we wish to know whether it would yield sufficiently reliable scores when used with a group that is more homogeneous.

In any event, we can calculate the reliability for one group if we know the reliability for the other group and the variances of the observed scores for both groups. The appropriate formula, given that the bivariate distributions for both groups are homoscedastic, is presented without derivation below in Equation 9-5: $r'_{xx}$ is the reliability coefficient for the individuals whose range of scores is $\sigma'_x$ rather than $\sigma_x$; or in this case, $r'_{xx}$ is the estimated reliability for the "norm" group.

$$r'_{xx} = 1 - \left[ \left( \frac{\sigma_x}{\sigma'_x} \right)^2 (1 - r_{xx}) \right] \tag{9-5}$$

The relationship between reliability and the range of scores is shown graphically in Figure 9-3. The figure shows that as the range of talent is reduced, the magnitude of the reliability coefficient is correspondingly reduced. For example, suppose with a particular group of individuals we find that a test has a reliability coefficient ($r_{xx}$) of .70. Now suppose

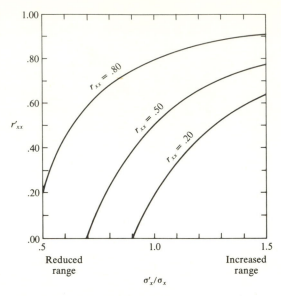

*Figure 9-3* Relationship between range of
scores and reliability coefficient.

we apply this test to another group, which has a smaller range of talent. Let us say that the standard deviation of the scores of the second group is only three-fourths the size of the standard deviation of the scores of the original group; that is, $\sigma_x/\sigma'_x = 4/3$. The reliability coefficient computed from the group with the smaller standard deviation would be only about .47. If the standard deviation of the group with the restricted range of scores is only 60 percent of the size of the standard deviation of the original group, the reliability coefficient would fall to about .16. Figure 9-3 shows that a small reduction in the range of scores has only a slight effect on the reliability coefficient, but when the reduction is greater than about 10 percent or more, the reduction in the magnitude of the reliability coefficient is quite significant. Furthermore, reduction in the range of scores is far more serious with tests that initially have lower reliability coefficients than with those that have higher coefficients.

## Correlation Between Two Variables: Correcting for Attenuation

The degree to which variables are related is a matter of prime importance in many psychological problems, both practical and theoretical.

The higher the relationship between two variables, the more accurately can scores on the one be predicted from scores on the other, and the greater the extent to which individual differences in both variables are determined by the same factors.

Suppose, for example, we wish to predict performance as an airplane mechanic from scores on a mechanical aptitude test. If we find that the coefficient of correlation between the two variables is only .10, we conclude that success in this type of job cannot be predicted by this particular test with sufficient accuracy to be useful. However, if for some reason performance ratings and test scores were in error and with the reduction of these errors the correlation were found to be .60, we would arrive at the opposite conclusion.

To take another example, suppose we are interested in the extent to which acute anxiety is an inherited characteristic and we develop a paper-and-pencil measure of this kind of anxiety. To control for environmental effects, we search the world for sets of identical twins who were separated at birth and reared apart. After giving the inventory to all of them, we pair up the twins for the purpose of computing the correlation across blood relatives. If we find that the correlation is only .20, we might conclude that genetic factors are not very important determinants. However, suppose the real problem were unsystematic error (that is, unreliability) in the anxiety measure, and if this unreliability could be eliminated, the correlation across identical twins reared apart would be .80. The behavior geneticist would draw far different conclusions in this case about the role of genetic factors in determining acute anxiety.

By these examples we have tried to show that the unreliability with which a variable is measured might mask its real relationship with other variables. Although it's a dangerous question in some respects, we might legitimately ask what the correlation between two variables might be if one or both of their reliabilities could be improved. If we push this question to the greatest extreme, we would ask what the correlation would be between two variables if one or both of their reliabilities were perfect. Let's see what happens when we do that.

There is only one kind of score for which reliability is perfect, and that is the true score. The classical theory of true and error scores says that true scores can be achieved by taking the average score on an infinite number of parallel tests. Domain-sampling theory says that the true score is the score on all the components in the domain or universe that can be achieved by averaging over an infinite number of random samples of components from the domain. In effect, what both these models argue is that to measure a variable with perfect reliability, we should allow the measure to grow to an infinite length.

Suppose we again consider the correlation between two composites (see the Technical Section at the end of Chapter 7). One of the composites has $k$ components, and one has $m$ components. The two composites do not necessarily measure the same variable (for example, one might purport to measure intelligence, and the other creativity), but the components within each composite constitute parallel tests. As we did in Chapter 7, we can again represent the correlation between these two composites as shown below. Again, no variances or standard deviations appear because they cancel out when the components are strictly parallel.

$$r_{c_x c_y} = \frac{km\ \bar{r}_{x_i y_j}}{\sqrt{k + k(k-1)\bar{r}_{x_i x_{i'}}}\ \sqrt{m + m(m-1)\bar{r}_{y_j y_{j'}}}}$$

Now since the components within $C_1$ and $C_2$ are parallel tests, this formula has several other convenient features:

1. The intercorrelations among components in composite 1 are all equal and therefore

$$\bar{r}_{x_i x_{i'}} = r_{xx} \text{ (the reliability for one component)}$$

2. The intercorrelations among components in composite 2 are all equal and therefore

$$\bar{r}_{y_j y_{j'}} = r_{yy} \text{ (the reliability for one component)}$$

3. The intercorrelations across components from the two composites are equal and therefore

$$\bar{r}_{x_i y_j} = r_{xy}$$

If we make these substitutions in the formula and further if we also divide the numerator and denominator by $1/km$, we get the following:

$$r_{c_x c_y} = \frac{r_{xy}}{\sqrt{\dfrac{1}{k} + \dfrac{k-1}{k}\bar{r}_{xx}}\ \sqrt{\dfrac{1}{m} + \dfrac{m-1}{m}\bar{r}_{yy}}}$$

We said previously that perfect reliability could be achieved by letting a measure become infinitely large. Look what happens to the above formula when $k$ and $m$ become infinitely large.

Since true scores are the average of the scores on an infinitely large number of tests, $1/k$ and $1/m$ closely approximate 0, and $(k-1)/k$ and

$(m - 1)/m$ closely approximate 1. The value $r_{c_1 c_2}$ then would be written as $r_{x_\infty y_\infty}$. Hence

$$r_{x_\infty y_\infty} = \frac{r_{xy}}{\sqrt{r_{xx} r_{yy}}} \tag{9-6}$$

Equation 9-6 is also a very famous one and is known as the *correction for attenuation*. It corrects for the degree to which the correlation between two variables is attenuated by their unreliability. It indicates the degree of relationship that is possible if we were able to measure each of our variables in a perfectly reliable fashion.

Suppose we find the coefficient of correlation between the scores on two tests to be .28. From the magnitude of this coefficient we might be led to say that the two traits measured by these tests are related to a rather low degree. But if we knew that the reliability coefficients of the two tests were .30 and .40, respectively, by applying the formula for the correction for attenuation (Equation 9-6), we would estimate that, had we measured the two traits with perfect reliability, the coefficient of correlation between their scores would have been

$$r_{x_\infty y_\infty} = \frac{.28}{\sqrt{(.30)(.40)}} = \frac{.28}{\sqrt{.12}} = \frac{.28}{.35} = .80$$

Now we would conclude that the two traits are quite substantially related. However, keep in mind that this is a hypothetical correlation obtained by hypothesizing perfect reliability. What it suggests is that work devoted to increasing the original low reliabilities might have substantial payoff.

Because its application ordinarily increases the magnitude of relationships, and in some cases quite substantially, the correction for attenuation is most attractive. However, it is important to note that the usefulness of the formula—and indeed of any formulas involving reliability coefficients—is a function of the adequacy with which the reliability coefficients are determined. The formula for the correction for attenuation is quite sensitive to variations in the magnitudes of the reliability coefficients. If our determination of the degree of the reliability of measurement is incorrect, even though the error be relatively small, our estimates of relationships between perfectly reliable scores may be substantially in error. For example, suppose our estimates of the reliability coefficients of the two tests considered in the previous paragraph were not .30 and .40, but were just slightly higher, being .40 and .50, respectively. By applying Equation 9-6, we would find our estimate of the correlation between perfectly reliable scores to be

$$r_{x_\infty y_\infty} = \frac{.28}{\sqrt{(.40)(.50)}} = \frac{.28}{\sqrt{.20}} = \frac{.28}{.45} = .62$$

This value is considerably lower than our previous estimate of .80, and by using it we would probably conclude that the two traits are only moderately related.

Suppose our estimates of the reliability coefficients were in the other direction, and the coefficients, instead of being .30 and .40, were .20 and .30. When Equation 9-6 is applied, we find our estimate of the coefficient of correlation between perfectly reliable scores to have the absurd value of 1.17:

$$r_{x_\infty y_\infty} = \frac{.28}{\sqrt{(.20)(.30)}} = \frac{.28}{\sqrt{.06}} = \frac{.28}{.24} = 1.17$$

This result could occur if an inappropriate method of assessing reliability were used or if different samples were used to estimate the intercorrelation and the reliabilities. Again we see the need to apply the formula for the correction for attenuation with caution. The appropriateness of different methods of assessing reliability is discussed in subsequent sections of this chapter.

Let us now examine the limiting effects of reliability on the correlation between tests. The highest possible correlation between two tests, of course, is represented by a coefficient of correlation of 1.00. Suppose that this is in fact the degree of relationship between two tests when both are measured with perfect reliability (that is, $r_{x_\infty y_\infty} = 1.00$). We then derive from Equation 9-6

$$r_{xy} = \sqrt{r_{xx}r_{yy}} \tag{9-7}$$

Values computed from Equation 9-7 are given in Table 9-1. This table shows that when the reliability of two tests is low, the highest possible coefficient of correlation between their scores is also low. On the other hand, when reliability is high, the highest possible coefficient of correlation between their scores is also high. From the table it can also be seen that the coefficient of correlation between scores on one test and those on another can be higher than the reliability coefficient of the first test, provided the reliability of the second test is higher. Remember that the values in Table 9-1 are upper limits. Thus the correlation between two measures both of which have reliability coefficients of .80 might in fact be .00, but it could be no higher than .80.

## Sources of Unsystematic Variation

Before we talk about some specific methods for estimating reliability in a real-life situation, we would like to discuss briefly some major sources

*Table 9-1*  Maximum value of coefficient of correlation between two
variables in relation to their reliability coefficients

| $r_{xx}$ | $r_{yy}$ | | | | | | | | | | |
|------|------|------|------|------|------|------|------|------|------|------|------|
|  | .00 | .10 | .20 | .30 | .40 | .50 | .60 | .70 | .80 | .90 | 1.00 |
| .00 | .00 | .00 | .00 | .00 | .00 | .00 | .00 | .00 | .00 | .00 | .00 |
| .10 | .00 | .10 | .14 | .17 | .20 | .22 | .24 | .26 | .28 | .30 | .32 |
| .20 | .00 | .14 | .20 | .24 | .28 | .32 | .35 | .37 | .40 | .42 | .45 |
| .30 | .00 | .17 | .24 | .30 | .35 | .39 | .42 | .46 | .49 | .52 | .55 |
| .40 | .00 | .20 | .28 | .35 | .40 | .45 | .49 | .53 | .57 | .60 | .63 |
| .50 | .00 | .22 | .32 | .39 | .45 | .50 | .55 | .59 | .63 | .67 | .71 |
| .60 | .00 | .24 | .35 | .42 | .49 | .55 | .60 | .65 | .69 | .73 | .77 |
| .70 | .00 | .26 | .37 | .46 | .53 | .59 | .65 | .70 | .75 | .79 | .84 |
| .80 | .00 | .28 | .40 | .49 | .57 | .63 | .69 | .75 | .80 | .85 | .89 |
| .90 | .00 | .30 | .42 | .52 | .60 | .67 | .73 | .79 | .85 | .90 | .95 |
| 1.00 | .00 | .32 | .45 | .55 | .63 | .71 | .77 | .84 | .89 | .95 | 1.00 |

of the unsystematic errors that produce unreliability. The primary reason for doing this here is that different methods of estimating reliability
will take certain of these sources into account, but not others. It makes
interpreting a reliability coefficient that much more difficult, but that's
the way the true score crumbles.*

### Errors Associated with Specific Situation

At any one time and place we might measure a group of individuals
with, for example, a test of knowledge of music. Various musical selec-
tions are played on a stereo system in a large room, and the group is
asked to identify them. Because of the nature of the room and the
placement of the speakers, some people can hear better than others,
but the sound quality is not a linear function of distance from the
speakers. That is, the room has "dead" spots and "live" spots, there is
the stereophonic effect to contend with, and so on. These randomlike
situational effects may produce randomlike alterations in individual
scores, and this will serve to increase the kind of variability in scores
across people that would be labeled "error variance." Similar things
could happen in almost any specific group testing situation. The important thing to note is that the individual differences observed among

---

* This is a naked attempt at kidding around before the crunch comes.

people on any one occasion will be in part due to these situational differences rather than be actual true score differences.

### Errors Associated with Different Occasions

If we are considering the variation in one person's score across parallel measures and the different measures are obtained at different points in time, a myriad of factors can influence scores between administrations. In general, they can be broken down into *situation-centered sources* and *person-centered sources*.

If the situational conditions under which the data are obtained are not precisely the same from time to time, then factors that produce error variation across people at any one time can rearrange themselves and produce error variation in one individual's scores across several times. Since a particular situation can never be exactly reproduced on successive occasions, a certain amount of such variation will result from measuring individuals on different occasions. We can reduce this variation by striving to make the situation as nearly similar as possible, but that raises a question: To what degree do we want our measure to show reliability *in spite of* these kinds of situational changes? Perhaps we indeed want our reliability coefficient to reveal how impervious our measure is to this source of unreliability. In that case we would not want to simulate conditions to such a degree that they constitute sterilized situations that could never be reproduced in anything but a highly controlled research environment. For example, the employment office is not the psychological laboratory, and the question of which place we actually want to use our measure is an important consideration.

Even if the situational conditions were perfectly the same from time to time, the state of the individual might not be, and person-centered sources of error across occasions might operate. If we are attempting to measure something like chronic anxiety via a paper-and-pencil inventory, most likely there are a number of things occurring within the individual that influence responses to the questionnaire and that are not a reflection of what we have defined as chronic anxiety. Stomach aches, anticipation of an evening's pleasure, the interpretation of a particular question, current feelings about what is a socially desirable questionnaire response, and the like are internal factors that might influence the score one way on one occasion and another way on a second occasion. In general, but not always, we might expect these sources of error variation to play a bigger and bigger role as the time between measurements becomes greater and greater.

One confusing factor with regard to internal sources of variation across time is that an individual's true score itself may also change. Fatigue, learning, maturation, and the like are constructs that attempt to explain why a true score might lawfully change. Previously we said that such changes are systematic variation and argued that they should not be counted as unreliability. Therefore the reliability coefficient should reflect how haphazard changes within the individual influence test scores, but not changes in the true score. The question of whether a true score could be expected to change across occasions is a very "iffy" one, and it's going to cause us trouble. However, avoiding the issue will do no good.

### Errors Associated with Different Test Contents

We have already argued in this chapter that one reason for low reliability is a "short" measure—one that does not sample very much of the substantive behaviors making up the complete variable or domain of interest. Regardless of which theory of reliability is adopted, the rationale for the greater reliability of longer measures is that the larger the sample, the higher the probability that the content of the test in hand will match the content of the complete domain. Thus there are errors of measurement associated with differences between test content and universe content, and the shorter our test, the greater the probability that there will be a divergence. Please take note that measurement errors arising from this difference are precisely what a reliability coefficient should reflect.

There is another kind of content difference besides the sample-versus-universe difference (if we state the problem in domain-theory terms) or the difference between scores on one parallel test and the average of an infinite number of parallel tests (if we state the problem in classical-theory terms). This second kind of content difference results from the fact that two measures that were thought to be parallel may indeed not be. To take a simpleminded example, two parallel measures of arithmetic ability may include both addition and multiplication items. However, one test may be slightly overbalanced with multiplication items as compared to the other. A third test might be underbalanced. Thus scores across these measures would vary because they are not precisely measuring the same thing to the same degree. The true scores are measuring slightly different things. Now it is this kind of variation due to content differences that we do *not* want to influence our estimate of reliability. The entire thrust of reliability theory says that to estimate the reliability with which we are measuring something, we should set up situations such that the reliability coefficient is computed between two measures that measure the same thing to the same degree.

That is, two measures for which the composition and the magnitude of the true scores are the same.

### *Errors Associated with Subjective Scoring Systems*

Not all psychological measures are paper-and-pencil tests or question-naires that can be scored by counting responses. Frequently the quantitative description of an individual's responses, in terms of some defined continuum, is made by another individual functioning as a scorer or rater. Assigning scores to essay achievement examinations is one example. Using a rating scale to rate an individual's job performance is another. Asking a clinician to judge the degree of neurosis exhibited by a patient in an interview is yet another. Rating a friend on the degree of his or her kindness or warmth is perhaps closer to home. The list could go on and on, but the point is that subjective scoring systems are quite prevalent, both in scientific investigation and in everyday life. Each of us makes many decisions each day on the basis of these kinds of scores.

Subjective scoring presents special problems for the estimation of reliability and constitutes another source of error variation in one individual's scores across repeated measures. If different raters or scorers are assigned (perhaps at random) to an individual on different occasions, then differences in standards *between* raters are a source of error. Even if the same rater is used on different occasions, we must still worry about internal changes of the *rater* across situations. Perhaps his or her standards are more stringent on some occasions than others. We are faced with the question of whether we want score changes produced by differences across and/or within raters to count as unreliability or to be excluded from our estimate. In effect, if subjective ratings are made of essay examination responses, then the unreliability of the rater is being piled on top of the unreliability of the student's response.

### *Perseveration*

As physicists are confronted with matter and antimatter, so the psychologist is confronted with measurement errors and antimeasurement errors. For example, suppose we administer parallel tests of complex mathematic aptitude to an individual on two occasions. Further suppose that some of the same questions are contained in both parallel tests. Regardless of whether he or she was acting in a correct or incorrect fashion, the individual may give the same answer to a question, or use the same strategy for answering questions, on the second test merely because that's the way he or she did it on the first test. The experimentalist calls this phenomenon *perseveration,* and the result is that scores appear to be more stable than they should, given the actual amount of true-score variation being measured. That is, the persevera- tion errors are erroneously counted as legitimate components of the true score and contribute to stable-appearing differences *between* people. It would be nice if the reliability coefficient we compute would not count them as reliable variance.

## Empirical Methods for Estimating Reliability of Tests

There are four basic methods that are customarily used for estimating the reliability of a measure. These consist of estimating reliability from: (1) the coefficient of correlation between scores on repetitions of the same test, (2) the coefficient of correlation between scores on parallel forms of a test, (3) the coefficient of correlation between scores on comparable halves of the test, and (4) the intercorrelations among all the components of a test. Let us now describe and evaluate each of these methods as well as some of the spin-offs from the basic methods. At the end of this discussion it is our intent that you will come to the conclusion that there is no such thing as *the* reliability of a measure. Each measure will be seen to have several reliabilities depending on the kind of trait we think we have and the purposes for which we want to use the scores.

### Repetitions of Same Test

This first method for estimating the reliability of measurement is called the *test–retest method.* A given measure is administered two or more times to the same group of individuals, and the intercorrelations among the scores on the various administrations are taken as the reliability coefficient. With tests of aptitude, personality, and achievement, the test ordinarily is administered only twice, so that only one estimate of the reliability coefficient is obtained. If the test is administered several times, the usual practice is to take the average of the intercorrelations among the scores obtained on the various occasions as the estimate of the reliability coefficient.

There are two main advantages with the test–retest method. Some other methods for estimating reliability require that more than one form of the test be available, but with the test–retest method nothing in addition to the test itself is required. A second advantage is that when this method is used, the particular sample of items or stimulus situations is held constant. The individuals are tested with precisely the same instrument. Superficially at least, it would seem that this tends to minimize the opportunity for actual measurement of traits other than those designed to be measured by the test.

The most serious disadvantages with the test–retest method lie in the variety of carry-over effects from one testing occasion to another that may either change the true scores or create perseveration effects. Sometimes there are practice effects, so that on subsequent occasions scores increase in a systematic fashion. The individual may learn the specific content of the test or develop improved approaches or attitudes toward the material so that his or her scores increase. In some instances these practice effects are different for different individuals. Of two people who obtain precisely the same score on the first occasion, one may discover certain general principles that help answer the questions in the test or may even rehash or rehearse the material during the interval between the first and the second test. Therefore on the second testing occasion the score of one individual may improve and that of the other remain the same. If the correlation between the scores on the two occasions is low, we do not know whether the test is unreliable or whether differential systematic factors have been at work. On the other hand, if the coefficient between scores on the two occasions is high, then it would seem that factors having differential effects are not very important, and the correlation we obtain might be considered to be something like a lower limit of the reliability coefficient. This would be true, of course, only if we could rule out on the retest the effects of remembering the responses made on the first test.

In other instances there might be a specific carry-over effect in terms of remembering on one testing occasion the responses given on an earlier one and merely repeating these responses. The first time an individual takes a vocabulary test, he or she might respond "true" to the item *"Castigate* means the same as *throw out,"* and the second time he or she remembers this and again answers "true." Similarly, in an attitude test, on the first testing occasion a person might answer "indifferent" to the question "Do you approve of labor unions?" and remembering this on a second occasion, again responds in the same fashion. Having assigned her subordinate Joe Smith the rating of "superior" in January, a factory supervisor does so again in June when called on to rate Joe in order to demonstrate that she is consistent in her appraisals. These specific carry-overs from one occasion to another may not be deliberate on the part of the individual; indeed the individual may be completely unaware of them. They are important because they introduce a false consistency in scores, a consistency that would not have occurred without them. Hence in some circumstances the test–retest method may give an overestimate of reliability.

Another carry-over problem with the test–retest method is the fact that taking a test may change the individual in some more or less permanent fashion. For example, if a test requires an individual to evaluate himself or herself, the very process of self-evaluation may cause him or her to change behavior. Changes of this sort might well be expected with certain kinds of personality measures. Therefore with some types of tests the test–retest method would have to be considered inapplicable.

One troublesome problem with the test–retest method has to do with the time interval between testing occasions. It is desirable to maximize the interval between testing occasions in order to minimize the effects of memory. But the longer the time interval between the two testing occasions, the greater the likelihood that the true score of the individual will change. Therefore the correlation between scores on two occasions reflects more than just the reliability of measurement. Furthermore, increasing the time interval between testing occasions increases the administrative problem of getting the same group of individuals together on the second occasion. Consequently we expect lower and lower estimates of reliability as the time interval between the testing occasions increases. Because it focuses so heavily on stability over time, the test–retest reliability coefficient is often called the *stability coefficient*.

In terms of the theory of true and error scores, the test–retest method would seem to have a certain appeal. Indeed, if we forget the practical disadvantages discussed above, it would seem to be the very best method because the individual can be measured a number of times with precisely the same instrument. Whether the test–retest method is appropriate from the point of view of domain sampling is equivocal. If the one test in hand is the best sample we can get, then the domain model is not violated. However, the domain-sampling reliability coefficient is the correlation between the best sample and a hypothetical parallel. Errors due to the passage of time can play no part and since the test–retest method will always allow at least some of these errors to operate, the method is not strictly compatible with domain theory.

### Parallel Forms of a Test

*Parallel forms* of a test are a series of two or more tests that have the same type of content, but not the same specific components. An item in one parallel form of an arithmetic test might be "27 + 84 = ____" and an item in another form might be "48 + 72 = ____." An item in one form of an inventory designed to measure emotional stability might be "Do you sleep well at night?" and an item in another form might be "Do you have bad dreams at night?" In the rating of preschool children, nursery school teachers of the same age and experience might be considered parallel raters. In the latter example, parallel raters are simply a special case of parallel forms.

Perhaps we should make a distinction between parallel forms of a test and parallel tests. Parallel forms are tests intended to be similar in content and nature and designed to measure the same traits. Parallel tests are tests that in fact meet certain statistical criteria. We considered these criteria in Chapter 8 when we discussed theoretical approaches to reliability. If a series of parallel forms of a test meet these criteria, they are also parallel tests.

Having available two or more parallel forms of a test, we take as an estimate of the reliability the intercorrelations among the scores on the parallel forms. If there are more than two forms available, the common practice is to take the average of the intercorrelations as the estimate of the reliability coefficient. Because the various forms of a test may not contain precisely the same material, the possibility, if not the probability, exists that the various forms do not measure precisely the same traits. Therefore the intercorrelations among the tests reflect not only the degree of the reliability of measurement but also the extent to which they measure different traits. Hence we might say that the method of determining reliability from the intercorrelations among parallel forms probably gives estimates that are too low.

Because the specific components of parallel forms are not the same, the carry-over effects from one test to another are minimized. In many instances there will be no specific carry-over effects at all, because there is no opportunity to utilize memory of specific responses made to an earlier form. However, there is still the possibility of general carry-over in terms of modes of responses, attitudes toward the material, and the like. In the case of ratings where different raters are taken as "parallel forms" and make their ratings independently, there nonetheless may be contamination of the judgment of one rater by that of another if the raters have had an earlier opportunity to discuss the individuals being evaluated. For example, it is quite natural for nursery school teachers to discuss the various characteristics of their charges, so if they are called on to rate the children, these conversations will certainly affect their ratings even though the ratings are done independently.

One prime difficulty with the use of parallel forms as a means for estimating reliability is the labor required to develop them. If we are dealing with an objective test of 100 items, 200 are required for two forms, 300 for three forms, and so on. In the construction of just one form of a test, a great deal of time and effort is required. Thus while it might be possible to develop two forms, three or more forms frequently are just out of the question. In obtaining ratings of workers, it usually is difficult enough to obtain ratings from two supervisors who are familiar with all members of a working group, and finding more than two is likely to be impossible. Because this particular coefficient relies so heavily on the degree to which the two forms are really equivalent or parallel, it is often called the *equivalent-forms coefficient*.

Ordinarily when the method of parallel forms is used to estimate the reliability of measurement, the various forms are administered on different occasions. Again we have the problem of the longer the time interval, the higher the probability that the true score might change *and* that more error factors will come into play.

In terms of the theory of true and error scores, the method of determining reliability from the correlation between parallel tests is quite satisfactory, provided, of course, that the parallel forms meet the statistical criteria of parallel tests. In terms of the concept of domain sampling, the method is not pertinent. As we argued in the previous chapter, the reliability coefficient according to the domain model is the correlation between the best sample of components we can get and the hypothetical parallel. Dividing our best components between two parallel forms is watering down our efforts and will underestimate reliability.

### Comparable Parts of a Test

In many instances individuals cannot be measured on more than one occasion, and furthermore on that occasion it is possible to administer the test only once. Under such circumstances we can obtain an estimate of the reliability of measurement if we consider the test not as a single test, but rather as the sum total of a number of parallel forms of a test.

Suppose, for example, we have an objective test comprised of 100 items all of which pertain to the same trait. Instead of saying that we have one test of 100 items, we might say that we have two tests each of 50 items or four tests each of 25 items. Having two or more parallel forms available, we can now proceed to estimate reliability by the method of the correlation between scores on parallel forms. Note that we do not have the reliability of a test of 100 items, but rather the reliability of a shorter test. If we have split the items in our test into two groups of 50 items each, we have the reliability of a 50-item test.

If, having split our test into shorter tests, we find the reliability of the shorter tests to be fully adequate, we can use the scores on either part. However, we may not feel that the shorter tests adequately sample the trait we wish to measure, and since we have the total test, we may as well use it and thereby gain in precision of measurement. We developed the Spearman–Brown formula as Equation 9-1, which relates the reliability of measurement to the number of measurements. We can apply this formula to the intercorrelations among the parts of the test and estimate the reliability of the total test. For this purpose $r_{cc'}$ refers to the reliability coefficient of the total test, and $r_{xx}$ to the reliability coefficient of the parts.

The common procedure is to divide a test into two parts and, from the correlation between the two parts, to estimate the reliability of a test twice as long—the total test—by means of the Spearman–Brown formula. For this *split-half method* of estimating reliability, the Spearman–Brown formula becomes

$$r_{11} = \frac{2r_{1/2\ 1/2}}{1 + r_{1/2\ 1/2}} \tag{9-8}$$

where $r_{11}$ refers to the reliability coefficient of the total test and $r_{1/2\ 1/2}$ to the reliability coefficient of half the test. Thus if the correlation between scores on two halves of a test were .50, the reliability coefficient of the total test would be estimated to be

$$r_{11} = \frac{2(.50)}{1 + .50} = \frac{1.00}{1.50} = .67$$

If the total test is divided into more than two parts, then the average of the intercorrelations among the parts is used as the estimate of the reliability coefficient of the parts and is used in Equation 9-1. In this case $k$ is the number of times that the total test is longer than the parts. If the total test has 100 items and we divide it into four parts of 25 items each, then $k$ is 4. Suppose in this case the average of the intercorrelations among the four parts is .40. Then from Equation 9-1 we estimate the reliability of the total test to be

$$r_{11} = \frac{4(.40)}{1 + (4 - 1)(.40)} = \frac{1.60}{2.20} = .76$$

It will be recalled that in the development of the Spearman–Brown formula, it was presumed that the tests are truly parallel tests having equal standard deviations and intercorrelations. Therefore, strictly speaking, the reliability of a test cannot be determined from comparable parts unless their standard deviations and intercorrelations are precisely the same. Since these conditions seldom if ever are satisfied in the real world of measurement, the reliability coefficient determined by this method can be considered only as an estimate. It appears likely that variations among the parts in terms of their standard deviations and intercorrelations will cause the obtained value of the reliability coefficient of the total test to be too low. However, please note that the two half scores are obtained at the same time, and measurement error resulting from testing on different occasions can play no part.

The problem arises as to how to divide a total test into parts. With a 100-item test we could take the first 50 items as one half and the last 50 as the other half, or we could take the odd-numbered items as one half and the even-numbered ones as the other half. The second procedure, the *odd–even method,* is the one generally used, since it controls for any systematic factors operating during the testing period that change the performance from early in the testing session to later in the session. An example of such a factor is fatigue. In order to maximize the probability that the two halves measure the same trait, sometimes the division is made on the basis of an analysis of the content of the items, making sure that both halves contain items of the same sort. So as to maximize the probability that the means and the standard deviations of the two halves are equal, the items are assigned to the two halves so that for every item of a given level of difficulty in one half, there is an item of similar difficulty in the other half. The important thing is to maximize the equality of the two halves so as to satisfy the requirements of the Spearman–Brown formula.

The prime advantage of the method of determining reliability from the intercorrelations among comparable parts of a test is its simplicity. A test need be given only once to a group of individuals. No repetition of the test or comparable forms is required. Obviously the method is not applicable to certain types of tests that are an integrated whole and cannot be divided into separate and equivalent parts, as is the case, for example, with speed tests. The score is the number of questions correctly answered in the time allowed. Since an individual's score is a function of the rapidity with which he or she works, dividing up the items into two parts, but having the individual take them not with independent timing but all within the same time limit, does not give two or more independent determinations. For example, if you think about it for a bit, you will see that if the split is made odd versus even and there is an even number of consecutive items completed, the correlation between the two halves will be 1.0.

Inasmuch as with the method of comparable parts of a test the individual is tested on only one occasion, the test–retest coefficient will not reflect measurement errors resulting from being tested on two occasions. Thus if you want to assess the resistance of the measure to those kinds of errors, you are out of luck.

If we adhere to the concept of true and error scores, the method of determining reliability from the intercorrelations between comparable halves appears to be quite appropriate. We have parallel forms and ascertain the degree of relationship among them. However, the method is inappropriate in terms of the concept of domain sampling for the same reasons that were discussed with regard to parallel forms.

### Intercorrelations Among Test Elements

The logical extreme of the method of determining the reliability of measurement from the intercorrelations among comparable parts of a test is the division of a test into its smallest parts. If we have a test comprised of 100 items, instead of dividing it into two parts of 50 items each or four parts of 25 items each, we could divide it into 100 parts of 1 item each. As before, we use the intercorrelations among the parts as the estimate of the reliability of the parts and estimate the reliability of the total test by means of the Spearman–Brown formula. The obvious advantage of this method lies in the fact that we avoid the troublesome problem of deciding how to divide the test into halves or quarters. As a simple example, if we have a test consisting of 4 items, we could form the following halves:

$$1 + 2 \text{ and } 3 + 4 \qquad 1 + 3 \text{ and } 2 + 4 \qquad 1 + 4 \text{ and } 2 + 3$$

As the number of items increases, the number of possible divisions of the items into halves increases astronomically. Hence it would be impossible to determine the average of the correlations among all possible halves. The method of estimating reliability from the intercorrelations among the elements of a test avoids this difficulty. Inasmuch as this method is merely a logical extension of the method of estimating reliability from the correlation between comparable parts, it too cannot be used with tests that are integrated wholes, such as speed tests.

The development of this method can proceed from one of two points of view, corresponding to the theory of true and error scores and the domain-sampling model. Suppose we take them in turn.

If we begin from the perspective of the classical theory, the implication is that we view each component of our measure as parallel to every other component. That is, if the measure is a 20-item test of "garden-variety anxiety," the implication is that each of the 20 items measures garden-variety anxiety to the same degree. If that is the case, then we can enter the correlation between any two components in the Spearman–Brown prophecy formula, where $k$ is equal to the number of components (for example, 20) in the test, and the result is the reliability of the total test.

$$r_{xx} = \frac{k r_{x_i x_{i'}}}{1 + (k - 1) r_{x_i x_{i'}}}$$

If the individual items or components are not strictly parallel to one another, then the formula does not hold because among other things the variances and covariances of the components are not equal and would not have canceled out of the formula.

Another form of the above equation can be obtained if we substitute the equivalent variance components for correlations. It's a long, round-about task and we will not go through it here, but the result is another expression that can be used to compute the reliability of the full-length test from the characteristics of parallel items or components. This second expression, which is directly derivable from the first, is

$$r_{xx} = \frac{k}{k-1} \left(1 - \frac{k\sigma_{x_i}^2}{\sigma_x^2}\right) \tag{9-9}$$

The number of components is still $k$, but the correlations have been replaced by variances where $\sigma_{x_i}^2$ is the variance of any one of the parallel items and $\sigma_x^2$ is the variance of the total score.

Now seldom if ever do the components of a measure, such as the items in an objective test, have equal variances and intercorrelations; therefore they are not parallel tests. As a consequence, Equation 9-9 is of little value for any practical purposes. As an approximation, sometimes the average of the variances of the elements, $\bar{\sigma}_{x_i}^2$, is used in place of $\sigma_{x_i}^2$. If this average value is used in Equation 9-9, it is

$$r_{xx} = \frac{k}{k-1} \left(1 - \frac{\overline{k\sigma_{x_i}^2}}{\sigma_x^2}\right)$$

Since the number of cases times the mean of a variable is equal to the sum of that variable, we can write the formula as

$$r_{xx} = \frac{k}{k-1} \left(1 - \frac{\Sigma\sigma_{x_i}^2}{\sigma_x^2}\right) \tag{9-10}$$

If the elements of the test are dichotomous variables, as is usually the case with the items in an aptitude test scored as "correct" or "incorrect," the formula is written as

$$r_{xx} = \frac{k}{k-1} \left(1 - \frac{\Sigma pq}{\sigma_x^2}\right) \tag{9-11}$$

where $pq$ refers to the variances of the items (see Chapter 3) and $\sigma_x^2$ to the variance of total scores. These last two equations are also quite famous and are called the *Kuder–Richardson Formula 20* (K–R 20) and *Kuder–Richardson Formula 21* (K–R 21), respectively.

The Kuder–Richardson formulas were developed with discrete or dichotomously scored components in mind. A generalized expression, appropriate for continuous part scores and any desired division of the total score into separately scored part scores is *Cronbach's coefficient alpha* shown below:

$$
\begin{aligned}
r_{xx} &= \frac{k}{k-1} \left( \frac{V_x - \Sigma V_i}{V_x} \right) \\
&= \frac{k}{k-1} \left( \frac{\Sigma\Sigma CV_{ii'}}{V_x} \right)
\end{aligned}
$$

where $\Sigma\Sigma CV_{ii'}$ = sum of the "interpart" covariances and $V_x$ = variance of the total score, or in its more familiar form:

$$
r_{xx} = \frac{k}{k-1} \left( 1 - \frac{\Sigma V_i}{V_x} \right)
$$

Again the denominator is the variance of the total score, $\Sigma V_i$ is the sum of the part variances, and $k$ equals the number of parts.

One can see from the above expressions that the magnitude of coefficient alpha is a function of the ratio of the sum of the interitem, or interpart, covariances to the variance of the total score. The sum of the covariances in turn is largely a function of the intercorrelations among the parts.

From the perspective of the theory of true and error scores, the appropriateness of the Kuder–Richardson formulas is dependent on the condition that each component constitutes a parallel measure. Domain theory makes no such assumption and develops this reliability coefficient in a different way. In the preceding chapter we saw that reliability under the domain model is indexed by the correlation between the best sample of components we have and a hypothetical parallel. To compute the correlation, we need only the data from one sample and the general form of the coefficient was shown to be

$$
r_{xx} = \frac{k^2 \overline{\sigma_{x_i} \sigma_{x_{i'}} r_{x_i x_{i'}}}}{\sigma_x^2}
$$

Again this simply came from the correlation between two composites, given that the probabilities a component would end up in one or the other are the same. As you might have already suspected, it is not very difficult to transform the above form of the domain-sampling reliability coefficient into a form exactly the same as the Kuder–Richardson. Simply by changing the denominator from $\sigma_x^2$ to its equivalent in terms of component variances and covariances and going through a few algebraic steps, we arrive at

$$r_{xx} = \frac{k}{k-1}\left(1 - \frac{\Sigma\sigma_{x_i}^2}{\sigma_x^2}\right)$$

Again we need only the data from one sample of components to compute this coefficient, and it corresponds precisely to the reliability coefficient as it is characterized by domain theory. What it says is that if we could actually administer another measure, strictly parallel to our best sample, at exactly the same time, the correlation between them would be equal to the above. Under these conditions there would be no carry-over effects and no measurement errors arising from the passage of time.

Suppose we have each child in a class rated on the same scale of sociability by the same five teachers. For each child then we have the ratings by each of the five teachers (the elements) and the sum of the ratings by all teachers (total scores). Let us further suppose that the variances of the ratings of the five teachers are 2, 3, 3, 4, and 6, respectively ($\Sigma\sigma_{x_i}^2 = 18$), and the variance ($\sigma_x^2$) of total ratings is 45. Then by Equation 9-10 we estimate the reliability coefficient of total ratings to be

$$r_{xx} = \frac{5}{5-1}\left(1 - \frac{18}{45}\right) = \frac{5}{4}(1 - .40) = (1.25)\,(.60) = .75$$

Suppose we have an objective test with 50 dichotomously scored items, the sum of the variances of the items being 7.00 and the variance of the total scores being 49.00. Then by Equation 9-10 the reliability coefficient of the test is

$$r_{xx} = \frac{50}{50-1}\left(1 - \frac{7}{49}\right) = \frac{50}{49}(1 - .14) = (1.02)\,(.84) = .86$$

On the basis of the theory of domain sampling, K–R 20 involves no presumptions at all concerning the nature of the elements of which a test is composed. Furthermore, it is not an approximation of the reliability coefficient; rather it is the only correct way for determining it.

There are other formulas in the psychometric literature that are algebraically equivalent to the Kuder–Richardson. Their virtue lies in their specific conveniences for easier computation, given different kinds of data. As a group, the Kuder–Richardson formulas and their numerous equivalents are called *internal-consistency estimates* of reliability. The estimates are a function of the number of components and their interrelationships. The greater the number of components and the higher the covariation among components, the higher the estimates.

To the extent that the components are not homogeneous and do not have high covariances, the internal-consistency estimate will be lowered. This situation arises when the domain or universe from which the components are sampled represents more than one characteristic or factor of behavior.

Many pages ago we argued that there was no restriction in either the classical theory or in the domain theory that the true score could only refer to one homogeneous characteristic of people. The true score may indeed be comprised of components that tap somewhat different factors of human behavior. For example, the true score for a variable such as "academic achievement" includes many such components. Achievement in chemistry, achievement in psychology, achievement in English, and so on are probably related to some degree but also have their own distinctive features. Components intended to measure achievement in chemistry probably intercorrelate more highly with one another, on the average, than they intercorrelate with the components intended to measure achievement in English. In this intercorrelational sense, the behaviors signifying achievement in chemistry can be distinguished, as a group, from the behaviors signifying achievement in some other subject matter.

To the extent that a true score or a domain (universe) score represents more than one factor of behavior, the correlation between our best sample of components and its hypothetical parallel, which is sampled *randomly* from the same hypothetical universe, will be *lower* than the corrected split-half estimate. This assumes that the two halves are not obtained by a random division, but through very careful matching of factors such that each factor is represented to exactly the same degree in each half. Thus if we think of the reliability coefficient as the correlation between two measures obtained at exactly the same time, the internal-consistency estimate will be a lower-bound estimate to the extent that the total domain of behavior represents more than one factor.

As it turns out, the Kuder–Richardson estimate or any of its equivalents is equal to the *average* of all possible corrected split-half reliability coefficients. That is, suppose we divided a test into as many unique halves as possible and got the average correlation between each pair of halves. If there are very many items in a test, there is a very large number of different ways to split it in half.

Now suppose our domain is comprised of two factors, achievement in psychology and achievement in mathematics, and our test has 100 items, 50 pertaining to psychology and 50 to mathematics. The split that would produce the lowest corrected split-half coefficient would be all 50 psychology items in one half and all 50 mathematics items in the other half. The *highest* correlation would be produced by putting 25 of each in each half; and further to consider the two very best psychology items and to put one in each half, and so on. Again the Kuder–Richardson is the average of the highest and the lowest corrected split half and everything in between.

## Choosing a Reliability Coefficient

We have now examined four basic alternative methods for computing the *reliability coefficient*. In any given measurement situation, which one should we choose? Which one is best? The answer is, of course, "It depends." Suppose we discuss in turn the major considerations on which the choice depends.

### Model Adopted

We have talked a lot about which coefficients are viewed as legitimate by each of the two major reliability models. The test–retest method does not violate the spirit of either model, but it presents certain practical difficulties with regard to carry-over effects and the like. The equivalent-forms coefficient and the corrected split-half coefficient are clearly compatible with the classical theory, but they cannot determine the correlation of the "best" sample with its parallel and thus are looked on with disfavor by the domain model. An internal-consistency estimate via the Kuder–Richardson or one of its equivalents is precisely the estimate called for by domain theory, but is looked on rather equivocally by the classical theory because of the assumptions that must be made.

### Dynamic Versus Static Traits

We have already seen that the question of whether the true score changes over time looms as an important one in the estimation of reliability. For example, consider a variable such as "garden-variety anxiety," that is, the kind of anxiety that results from life's frequent ups and downs that all of us experience week in and week out. Most likely, the true score on this variable changes a good deal across time for a specific individual as the result of many things that might happen. Doing poorly (or well) on a midquarter exam, being called a lousy (good) lover, and so on are things that could lead to changes in the true score. For such a *dynamic* trait it would be inappropriate to use test–retest or equivalent forms separated by a time interval to determine reliability. These coefficients would be low, but the cause would not be the presence of error variation but changes in the true score. At any one time our garden-variety anxiety could be reliably measured, and if an individual gets a high score at any one time, it really means his or her true score is high at this time, although at another time his or her true score might be low. Thus for dynamic traits the appropriate method for estimating reliability is corrected split half or internal consistency; whereas the reliability of static traits can be assessed by any of the methods.

How do we know if the characteristics being measured by our operations are dynamic or static? We can give a better answer after we discuss construct validity in the next chapter, but for now we could compute both the split-half and the equivalent-forms coefficient or both the internal-consistency estimate and the test–retest method. If the estimates based on data from one administration are consistently high and the estimates based on two administrations are consistently low, there is a strong likelihood that the trait is dynamic.

### Unifactor Versus Multifactor Variables

As we noted in a previous section of this chapter, if a test contains components that tap more than one factor, it is possible to split the test into halves such that the corrected split-half reliability coefficient is higher than the internal-consistency reliability coefficient. Under these conditions the split-half coefficient would be a more accurate estimate of what the correlation would be if we could give the same measure again at exactly the same time but with no carry-over effects. Thus if our measure is a multifactor one and we wish to estimate reliability on the basis of one administration, the split half may be the more appropriate estimate. This assumes that we indeed know how to split the components such that the two halves precisely match each other in content.

### Purpose for Which Scores Are Used

The point we wish to make here is that conditions under which scores on a measure are going to be used to make decisions about individuals should be similar to the conditions under which reliability is estimated. If a test is going to be used to predict what the general level of someone's behavior (for example, job performance) is going to be over some fairly long period, then the test must demonstrate reliability across time and an internal-consistency or split-half estimate is not sufficient. If a test is to be used to predict an individual's reaction to a drug or to some other treatment given at the same time, then an estimate based on one administration rather than two is called for. If the data for decisionmaking is to be gathered in a noisy, crowded room, then reliability should be determined under the same conditions.

We could list many examples, but the moral is clear: The method used to estimate reliability should be in line with the way in which the scores are to be used.

## Improving Reliability of Measurement

It is apparent that the lack of reliability of measurement is an undesirable state of affairs. A test that gives a useful quantitative description is one that yields scores characteristic of an individual. Therefore in the actual use of a measure, we wish to minimize the effects of unsystematic factors. Let us then consider ways for decreasing the effects of unsystematic factors and thereby increasing the reliability of measurement. Note that we are now talking about the conditions under which we are actually going to use the measure to make decisions about people.

### Increasing Number of Measurements

We have seen that as the number of measurements increases, the reliability of measurement also increases. That is, if instead of using the scores on a single test, we take the sum or average of the scores on two, three, or more parallel forms of the test, we increase reliability. We can accomplish this by increasing the number of items in an objective test, being sure that the new items have the same characteristics as the original items. If we are dealing with ratings, we can increase the reliability by increasing the number of raters, being sure that the new raters have the same characteristics as the original raters.

### Good "Housekeeping" Procedures

Another way of reducing the effects of unsystematic factors is by exercising good experimental controls when we obtain our measurements. Such controls can be effected in a variety of ways. For example, with speed tests we can utilize exact timing devices that automatically signal starting and stopping time rather than depend on a fallible human reading a watch. We can take steps to ensure that the lighting is the same throughout the testing room and for all occasions when the tests are being administered. We can train raters so that they all interpret the traits being rated in the same way and so that their personal biases are minimized. We can reduce variation among scores by the use of clear and consistent instructions. In other words, by means of a variety of housekeeping measures, we can "clean up" our testing situation and thereby reduce the effects of unsystematic factors. This is not to imply that we can completely eliminate them; rather we seek to minimize their effects.

### Choosing Better Items

This method of improving reliability should be obvious, but it is true that if we define our variable poorly and do not select very good components, the resulting scores will probably not be very reliable. After all, the aim of psychological measurement is to reflect in some sense the way human beings are actually structured. If our theory is bad and the operations of measurement do not map that structure, then we are being poor scientists and we deserve low reliability.

---

## Summary

It follows mathematically from both theories about the reliability of measurement—the theory of true and error scores and the theory of domain sampling—that as the number of measurements entering into a score increases, so does the reliability of measurement. The formula that relates number of measurements and reliability is termed the Spearman–Brown formula. This formula assumes that the added measures are parallel to the original measures, having the same standard deviations and intercorrelations.

If we are willing to assume that the correlation between true and fallible scores is homoscedastic, then it is possible to develop a formula that shows the effects of reducing or increasing the range of fallible scores on the reliability coefficient. Reducing the range reduces the magnitude of the reliability coefficient, and increasing the range increases it.

The correlation between two variables is influenced by the reliability with which they are measured. As their reliability decreases, so does the correlation between their fallible scores. The formula that relates the correlation between two variables and the reliability with which they are measured, the correction for attenuation, follows mathematically from both theories about reliability. This formula also shows the limiting effects of reliability on correlation. The lower the reliability, the lower the maximum possible correlation between fallible scores.

The four common ways for estimating reliability of measurement are from the coefficient of correlation between scores on repetitions of the same test, from the coefficient of correlation between scores on parallel forms of a test, from the coefficient of correlation between scores on comparable parts of a test, and from the intercorrelations among the elements of a test.

Both the test–retest method and the parallel-forms method require more than one test administration. Carry-over effects from one test administration to another are likely to distort the estimate of reliability given by the test–retest method. The method of parallel tests involves a good deal of labor in the development of the required forms. When a test is an integrated whole, its reliability cannot be estimated from the correlation between comparable parts of it nor from the intercorrelations among its elements. If we hold to the theory of true and error scores, then all methods for estimating reliability are appropriate, though the estimate obtained from the intercorrelations among the elements of the test is likely to be the poorest. But if we hold to the theory of domain sampling, then the estimation of reliability from the intercorrelations among the elements is the only appropriate method.

Choosing the appropriate method for estimating reliability depends on the theory of reliability we adopt, the nature of the trait we are measuring, and the way in which we are going to use our measure to make decisions.

Reliability can be improved by increasing the number of measurements and through good "housekeeping" procedures. The simultaneous testing of all individuals will minimize the variation in their scores over parallel tests and at the same time control the effects of unsystematic factors.

## Suggested Readings

Cronbach, L. J. 1951. Coefficient alpha and the internal structure of tests. *Psychometrika,* 16:297–334.

Cronbach, L. J., P. Schonemann, and D. McKie. 1965. Alpha coefficients for stratified parallel tests. *Educational and Psychological Measurement,* 25:291–312.

Cureton, E. E. 1958. The definition and estimation of test reliability. *Educational and Psychological Measurement,* 18:715–738.

Guion, R. M. 1965. *Personnel testing.* New York: McGraw-Hill. Pp. 34–38.

Gulliksen, H. 1950. *Theory of mental tests.* New York: Wiley. Chaps. 6, 7, 8, 10, and 15.

Kuder, G. F., and M. W. Richardson. 1937. The theory of the estimation of test reliability. *Psychometrika,* 2:151–160.

Linn, R. L. 1968. Range restriction problems in the use of self-selection groups for test validation. *Psychological Bulletin,* 69:69–73.

Novick, M. R., and C. Lewis. 1967. Coefficient alpha and the reliability of composite measurements. *Psychometrika,* 32:1–13.

Rulon, P. J. 1939. A simplified procedure for determining the reliability of a test by split-halves. *Harvard Educational Review,* 9:99–103.

# 10

## *Validity of Measurement*

To set about measuring a psychological characteristic of individuals, we first define it and then develop operations designed to yield quantitative descriptions of the extent to which individuals possess or manifest it. Since the definition is only a blueprint, which may or may not be exactly followed in developing the operations of measurement, we may well wonder about the degree to which the properties measured by a set of operations *in fact* correspond to the characteristic as defined. Thus before a set of operations is accepted, it may be necessary to obtain some indications that it measures what is intended.

Also we are often interested in predicting or forecasting behavior. For example, in connection with counseling high school students, we may wish to predict from their scholastic aptitude test score the level of academic success they are likely to attain if they go to college. Similarly, in appraising applicants for a sales job, we might wish to forecast their probable success from the scores they earn on a test of sociability. In these circumstances we have some clearly specified type of behavior or characteristic, such as college grades earned or dollar value of merchandise sold, measured by one set of operations, and we are concerned about the accuracy with which we can predict it from the traits measured by another set of operations.

It is from these and similar situations that the problem termed *validity of measurement* arises. In general it is apparent that validity pertains to the nature of the variable being measured by a set of operations. But it will also be apparent that there is not a high degree of agreement on what constitutes the problem of validity. Consequently there also is no consensus on what constitutes proper *validation* (that is, the procedure by means of which the validity of tests or other operations of measurement is determined).

## Defining Validity and Validation

As is the case with the reliability of measurement, the term validity of measurement means different things to different people. While it is possible to formulate different definitions of reliability in reasonably precise ways, this is not always the case with the validity of measurement.

Recall the variety of purposes, both theoretical and practical, for which individuals are measured. Each of these many purposes has led to somewhat different notions about what the validity of measurement is and to the development of different procedures for determining validity. Keeping these ambiguities in mind, we would like to present the following framework for thinking about validity problems. It is meant to be reasonably orthodox.

Historically the most common definition of validity is that it refers to the extent to which a test or a set of operations measures what it is supposed to measure. A more recent, and perhaps better, definition is the "official" one given in the American Psychological Association, American Educational Research Association, National Council on Standards for Educational and Psychological Tests (1974): "[V]alidity refers to the appropriateness of inferences from test scores or other forms of assessment" (p. 25). Loosely paraphrased, this means: Given a set of specific questions we want a psychological measure to help answer, how useful or appropriate (that is, valid) are the answers (that is, the information) provided by the test scores? One advantage of this definition is that it ties the degree of validity of a measure directly to the extent to which it is appropriate for answering specific questions. For example, how valid is a measure for predicting (that is, inferring) future job success? How valid is a measure for assessing an individual's degree of dominance? How valid is a measure for assessing how much an individual has learned in a course? There are literally dozens of such questions that can be asked, and the methods used to validate the appropriateness of a measure for answering them would most likely also differ. It follows from this definition that it is difficult to talk about different "types" of validation or validity evidence. The nature of validity varies to greater or lesser degree as a function of the specific question being considered. Nevertheless talking about types of validity is what people in the field have traditionally done and we will follow suit.

Prior to 1954 (seems like a long time ago) the concept of validity was in considerable disarray. There were almost as many definitions and varieties of validity as there were people interested in psychometric theory. Something had to be done. Naturally a committee was formed (in this case by the American Psychological Association) to look into the matter, and in 1954 the APA's *Technical Recommendations for Psychological Tests and Diagnostic Techniques* were published. This document has gone through two major revisions (APA, 1966; APA, AERA, NCME, 1974) and work is beginning on a third (as of this writing).

Since the *Recommendations* reflect the consensus of a great many of the people who work in this field, we would like to briefly discuss the major types of validity and/or validation as they are portrayed in this document. However, the reader should keep in mind that, as we argued above, any such classification of validity types is potentially misleading. The nature of validity, and the data it demands for its substantiation, may vary with the nature of the specific questions being asked. Thinking of validity in terms of "types" may mislead an investigator as to how he or she should try to establish the validity of a measure. Nevertheless discussing validity types does help get the conversation started.

## Criterion-Related Validity

In many instances the hypotheses to be tested or the questions to be asked about the validity of a test or other measure concern how well the scores on the test correspond to, are related to, or predict scores on another variable called a *criterion*. The criterion is the individual characteristic (variable) of real interest. In such instances, the test is of interest only insofar as it is related to the criterion, and can appropriately be used as a substitute for it. In general, we will refer to this substitute variable as the *predictor,* although sometimes the word is a bit of a misnomer. If it were always possible to obtain criterion scores, there would be no need for the predictor measure and no need for criterion-related validities. However, it is unfortunately the case that criterion scores are not always obtainable or available. They may already have occurred in the past and thus are no longer available, they may not occur until sometime in the future, or they may simply be too expensive or too dangerous to obtain for each person under consideration.

In U.S. society some examples of criteria that have been deemed important enough to worry about in terms of how strongly they are related to other, more readily available measures are the following. Certainly one of the most important is job performance. How well will someone do if he or she is hired? How well will *you* do if you take a particular job? Notice the distinction here between the importance of job performance from the perspective of the organization doing the hiring and the perspective of the individual seeking the job. Performance may be defined and measured differently by each. The organization may be interested in how much you contribute to its profits. You may be interested in whether you will be able to use your skills in such a way that you will feel a strong sense of accomplishment. It follows that different kinds of information may be used to predict each of these two kinds of performance criteria and that their validities would be determined differently. Whether or not a criterion is an appropriate one is first and foremost a value judgment. To be sure, we may worry about the reliability of the criterion measure (for example, the stability of performance ratings over time), but the determination of its actual content is a value judgment, and it should be confronted as such.

In education the analogy to job performance is school or university achievement. When someone enters a college or university, how well will he or she do on various measures of scholastic achievement (for example, grade-point average)?

For both employers and schools a criterion of great importance is how long the individual will stay in the organization or whether he or she will finish the prescribed curriculum. Thus tenure, turnover, and finish/not finish are all examples of criterion measures that reflect individual tendencies to stay in the organization.

The above are all examples of criteria that will occur sometime in the future and thus are currently unavailable. But suppose a decision must be made about the individual *now*. Thus comes the question: Are there economical measures that are available now and that can be used as a substitute?

An example of a currently available criterion that may simply be too expensive to obtain is a full assessment of the degree to which an individual exhibits some form of mental illness. A complete clinical and psychiatric workup is expensive and may take several days. If the task is to screen a large number of people for such symptoms, a cheaper substitute may have to be found. The question then arises as to how strongly the cheaper substitute (for example, a paper-and-pencil personality inventory) is related to the results of the full examination, which is the variable of real interest (that is, the criterion).

Another reason for the unavailability of the criterion is that it may reflect events that occurred in the past and cannot be currently assessed. For example, physicians may attempt to infer whether or not an individual has had a heart attack on the basis of an electrocardiogram (EKG) record. The EKG (the predictor) is of no real interest in and of itself. It is only of interest in terms of how well it allows the physician to infer whether a particular individual did or did not have a heart attack. To cite another example, it is the task of the jury in criminal cases to infer whether or not an individual committed a crime in the past (the criterion) from the current presentation of the evidence in the courtroom (the predictor).

The criterion-related validity of a test is described in an objective and quantitative fashion by the degree of relationship between predictor scores and criterion scores. Thus the Pearsonian correlation coefficient or its variants, such as the point biserial, biserial, phi, or tetrachoric coefficient, are commonly used to describe the degree of predictive validity. When these coefficients are used to indicate the degree of relationship between predictor and criterion scores, they are termed *validity coefficients*.

It is obvious that the relationship between two variables can be indicated by means other than the coefficient of correlation. A scatter diagram or bivariate distribution graphically depicts the relationship between two variables. The difference between the means of the $Y$ (criterion) scores of those individuals earning high and low $X$ (predictor) scores also tells us something about the relationship between the two variables. But the coefficient of correlation, the validity coefficient, is most commonly used because it seemingly gives the most precise description of the degree of relationship in a simple and convenient manner. We will come back to this seductive simplicity later.

Again the moral of this entire story is that the criterion is the variable of real interest, and its importance stems from the value judgments of some significant segment of society (for example, the Congress, your boss). The appropriateness with which other variables can be used as a substitute for the criterion speaks to the criterion-related validities of these other variables.

Before discussing different varieties of criterion-related validities, one further point should be made. A particular variable may serve as a criterion on one occasion and as a predictor on another. That is, what's a criterion today might not be tomorrow. For example, a relevant validity problem might be to predict subsequent college grade-point average (GPA) from a scholastic aptitude test taken while an individual is a high school senior. The criterion is college GPA. Four years later an employer may try to predict future performance on job $X$ from college GPA. Now performance on job $X$ is the criterion, and GPA is the substitute variable (predictor). Still later the employer may want to predict future performance on job $Y$ from an assessment of current performance on job $X$. Now performance on job $Y$ is the criterion, and performance on job $X$ is the predictor. In sum, which variable is labeled as the criterion is a function of the specific intent of the decisionmaker at a specific time.

### Predictive Validity

Predictive validity describes the accuracy with which we can estimate the extent to which some individual characteristic will be manifested in the future from the extent to which the individual currently manifests or possesses some other property. For example, when a high school student is counseled, it is helpful to be able to predict what his or her performance in college is likely to be. Consequently we would be interested in knowing the degree of validity of high school grades for predicting college grades. When applicants for a job are considered, it is helpful to estimate which applicants are most likely to perform well later on. Therefore we would like to know the validity with which scores on a test or other measure administered at the time of hiring predict later performance on the job.

*Evidence for predictive validity*   It is one thing to define predictive validity as the degree to which a current measure (the predictor) is related to (correlated with) the variable of real interest (the criterion), which is not observed until sometime in the future. Collecting the appropriate data so as to compute the required correlation, now termed a *predictive validity coefficient,* is another matter. Spouting definitions is easy; collecting good data is difficult.

Simply put, a predictive validity study involves (1) obtaining an appropriate sample of people, (2) measuring them on the predictor, (3) waiting for the necessary weeks, months, or years to pass, (4) obtaining the criterion scores for the same sample of people, and (5) computing the correlation between the predictor score and the criterion score. The higher the correlation, the greater the predictive validity, *other things being equal.* We shall get to some of these "other things" in a moment.

An example of such a study would be (1) measuring a representative sample of job applicants on the predictor measure (for example, aptitude test or interviewer ratings), (2) hiring everyone, (3) allowing everybody to work on the job for a period that is long enough to go beyond the initial learning phase and thus allowing differences in job proficiency to emerge, (4) assessing job performance with a standardized criterion measure, and (5) computing the correlation between the predictor measure and the job-performance measure. From this point on, there is one important fact that should be remembered. Establishing any kind of criterion-related validity requires that *for at least one sam-*

*ple of people* both the predictor and the criterion score must be obtained, no matter how difficult or expensive it is. Within the limits of sampling error, we can then infer what the accuracy of the predictor will be in subsequent samples, and use it accordingly. But without data from at least one representative sample, we cannot generate any kind of criterion-related validity.

Obviously there are a number of factors that enhance or detract from the usefulness of a predictive validity study. One of the most important is the *attrition rate,* or the frequency with which people drop out of the validation sample between the time the predictor scores are obtained and the time the criterion scores are obtained. Besides simply decreasing the sample size, and thereby increasing the sampling error inherent in the estimate of the predictive validity coefficient, the attrition may be on a selective and not a random basis. That is, the people who quit the job, drop out of school, and so on, may not be at all representative of the original applicant pool, and thus the people who are left in the sample may not be representative either. As a result, the validity coefficient computed on the sample suffering from selective attrition may be much different from a coefficient computed on the entire population of interest.

Another potential difficulty with predictive validity studies is that it may be hard to wait too long. Many such studies have gone down the drain because the pressures (economic and/or political) to start using the predictor information before it's time are simply too great.

Finally, the nature of the predictive study tends to make it very expensive. Not all organizations are willing to stand the cost of such research.


## Concurrent Validity

Sometimes we are interested in the precision with which we can estimate the extent to which the individual *currently* possesses a given trait or behaves in a particular way (the criterion) from the extent to which he or she *currently* possesses some other trait or behaves in some other way (the predictor). We use scores on one variable, then, to estimate scores on another, both variables measuring *present* properties of the individual. It may be too difficult, expensive, or time-consuming to measure the criterion directly, and therefore we prefer to use some other way to obtain quantitative descriptions of that property. This type of validity is often called *concurrent validity*.

If we were interested in measuring proficiency in repairing automobiles, it would be necessary to measure the speed and accuracy with which the individual could rectify all the various automotive dysfunctions, from the fuel system to the differential. We would have to gather a large number of cars manifesting all the sundry mechanical disorders. Each person would be required to do all the repair tasks, and we would have to be sure that each person was presented with exactly the same series of problems. Since it probably would take a number of days to measure the speed and accuracy of a single individual's performance, it would be expensive to do it very often. Consequently, if we found that scores on a paper-and-pencil test of knowledge of automotive mechanics and repair were substantially related to performance scores, we could use them as substitutes for the cumbersome and costly performance measures.

In any event, the touchstone of concurrent validity is that both predictor and criterion are measured at about the same time.

*Substitute for predictive validity*    We noted previously that one drawback to determining predictive validity is that the people footing the bill may not have the patience to wait for the necessary time to pass. Then why not use a concurrent design to estimate validity? For example, if the problem is to estimate the predictive validity of a job-simulation test, why not give the test to a sample of people who are already on the job and measure their job performance at the same time? Such a study might take only a few weeks, while a predictive study might take several years. The analogy in an educational setting would be to give a scholastic aptitude test to a sample of students who had just finished one or more years of college and obtain their grade-point average at the same time. The correlation between these two sets of scores would then be the estimate of how well we could predict future college success when the scholastic aptitude test is given to high school students.

There is nothing inherently wrong in this procedure. The effects of attrition are about the same since the individuals who drop out of a predictive validity sample are the same people who aren't around any more when a concurrent study is conducted. The usual effect of attrition is to lower the validity coefficient. Why is that so? Because the people who drop out are usually from one extreme of the criterion distribution or the other (they are either underqualified or overqualified), and this reduces the variance, or range, of scores. We noted in an earlier chapter that reducing the variability of either $X$ or $Y$ reduces the correlation between them.

In certain circumstances, however, it can be dangerous to substitute a concurrent design for a predictive one. Sometimes the predictor might be influenced by, or reactive to, the subsequent experiences of the individual. For example, if success in medical school is to be predicted in part by the ratings made of the candidate by a selection committee after a face-to-face interview, then experience in medical school may change the individual's response to certain questions. Suppose the candidates were asked about what they thought being a physician would be like and suppose those who initially had realistic expectations do better in medical school. Actual experience in medical school may change the individual's response even though he or she strives mightily to recall what their thoughts were like at the time of application. Another example would be a job-sample test, or simulation, for which actual experience on the job would yield a higher score. Thus if the predictor is reactive to experience, one should substitute a concurrent design for a predictive one with extreme caution. Keep in mind that there are also many predictors that are not reactive to experience. Obviously, in the above example, undergraduate GPA would not be reactive to experience in medical school nor would scores on a general intelligence test. General intelligence is conceptualized as a relatively stable characteristic of people that does not change much over the adult years.

With the above complexities in mind, remember that while a concurrent design might sometimes reasonably be used as a substitute for a predictive design, the coefficient being *estimated* is still a predictive validity coefficient.

### Postdictive Validity

Finally, sometimes we are interested in the accuracy with which we can estimate the extent to which an individual possessed a given trait in the past; this is termed *postdictive validity*. In other words, we wish to estimate a criterion score that describes certain characteristics he or she manifested at an earlier time. Why not get these criterion scores directly? Because it may be too difficult, expensive, or time-consuming to do this, and furthermore such records may not be available for all individuals.

For example, suppose we wish to know whether an individual has ever been arrested for a traffic violation. We would have to make inquiries of the appropriate agencies in every state where the person in question has driven a car. This would be quite time-consuming and probably not very easy. A much simpler and quicker approach would be to ask the individual the question: "Have you ever been arrested for a traffic violation?" In response to this question we might expect some falsification and errors of memory, so that answers might not correspond exactly to past history. Nevertheless, if it were found that responses to the question were substantially related to past history, we might well be willing to substitute the question (predictor) for the more time-consuming direct approach (criterion).

### Summary Comment on Criterion-Related Validity

Keep firmly in mind that a given test may be used for more than one type of prediction. For example, an arithmetic test may have moderate validity in predicting success in clerical occupations, good validity in the diagnosis of failure in mathematics courses, and some but low validity in predicting whether or not the individual had formal schooling. Similarly, for any one given kind of prediction, a given test may have differing validity. A test of ability to visualize spatial relations may have low validity in predicting success in clerical occupations, moderate validity in predicting success in engineering school, and good validity in predicting success in a machinist's apprentice training course. One cannot separate questions about validity from a consideration of the specific purposes for which the predictor is to be used.

## Content Validity

The *content validity* of a set of measurement operations refers to the degree to which those operations measure the characteristics we wish to measure, as *judged* from the appropriateness of the *content* of those operations. We examine a test or other measuring instrument and then, on the basis of our experience or expertise, judge its validity. The question asked is: "To what extent do the operations measure what they are supposed to measure?" The answer is based on professional judgment.

When we recall the many different situations in which we obtain quantitative descriptions of individuals on one trait or another, it would appear that content validity is the type of validity with which we are most frequently concerned. Consider, for example, classroom examinations, thousands of which must be constructed and administered to students every week. They are taken to be valid measures of knowledge of school subjects because the questions they contain all pertain to the subject matter and are drawn from the class discussions, the lectures, and the textbooks. Similarly, in the laboratory we use a wide variety of devices to measure different motor, perceptual, and cognitive abilities. These devices are taken to be valid because the behavior they elicit seems so obviously to reflect the pertinent traits. What else could be measured by an aesthesiometer but touch sensitivity, by a stereoscope but binocular vision, by a maze but learning ability? Indeed a very large proportion of the measuring devices we use seem by their very nature to measure the intended traits.

*Determining Content Validity*

The nature of content validity and the processes involved in determining it will be clearer if we consider a few examples. We might conclude that a test of simple reaction time is highly valid as a measure of simple reaction time because from our analysis of the situation it is apparent that the individual is not required to make complex decisions, the intensity of the stimulus is considerably above threshold, and the response required is merely to depress a key with the forefinger. In similar fashion, on the basis of our examination of the questions comprising a test of knowledge of U.S. history, we might conclude that the test has only moderate content validity because even though all the questions in it require knowledge of U.S. history, none of them deal with the Civil War period. As another example, we might say that a rating scale designed to measure artistic creativity is a very poor measure of this characteristic because we find that the teachers using it base their ratings almost entirely on the children's ability to draw realistic pictures.

From a study of the content or nature of the operations, then, we arrive at a judgment of the extent to which those operations measure the characteristics we intend them to measure. There are, in fact, two judgments involved: the extent to which each element or item of the test pertains to the variable of interest as it is defined, and the extent to which the entire set of elements or items represents all aspects of the designated domain.

The grounds for judging the extent to which a test item measures the desired properties are not always entirely clear and could easily be incorrect. For example, consider the question: "Would you rather read a book or go to a movie with a friend?" This might be included as a question in an inventory designed to measure the trait of sociability because it involves the choice between a solitary and a social activity. However, it may be that people respond to it on the basis of their interest in literature rather than on their gregariousness. Or it may be that in answering the question, the individual tends to give the "sociable" response as a result of a need to conform and not as a result of a desire to be with others.

Nevertheless, in many instances the components of a test so manifestly reflect the trait that the test is intended to measure, and the situation in which the test is administered so clearly minimizes the effects of other factors, that the judgments about validity seem quite reasonable. For example, to correctly answer the following question in a vocabulary test, the individual must understand the meaning of the key word and of the alternative words.

> Which of the following words means the same as *garish*?
>     gaudy        tarnished        irregular        rude

Other types of knowledge would be of no value. Therefore while in some instances there may be good and sufficient reason to question the validity of a test as judged by the nature and content of the operations, in others the traits measured seem so obvious that they can be agreed upon by all or almost all judges.

As noted above, not only do we want to know whether each of the components of a test reflects the domain being measured, but also we want to know whether the components taken as a whole cover it in a representative fashion. Judgments of the validity of a test, then, must take into account the extent to which the elements or items that make it up cover all aspects and facets of the trait. For a test of arithmetic ability to be considered to have a high degree of content validity, it should contain questions involving not only addition, subtraction, and multiplication, but also division. A test of knowledge of English literature obviously would not be representative of the subject if it did not have questions dealing with Shakespeare. The content validity of a measure of proficiency in typing would be found wanting if individuals were evaluated only in terms of their speed, and accuracy of performance were ignored.

We should establish the content validity of a test, then, by showing that its elements or items are a representative sample of all aspects and facets of the trait as prescribed by the definition. It is therefore apparent that the adequacy with which we can judge the validity of a test from its content is a function of the adequacy of the definition of the trait. The less detailed and complete the definition, the less well can we judge how representative its components are of the entire trait. When we have a precise definition of a trait, we have a good idea of its limits and we have reasonable knowledge about the nature of its parts. Thus the trait of eye–hand coordination might be defined thus:

> Eye–hand coordination is the ability to make quick and accurate movements guided solely by information obtained through vision. This ability involves moving an object by means of the hand to a fixed target or maintaining an object on a moving target. Eye–hand coordination is not just simple speed or accuracy of response or visual acuity, but the combination of these two abilities in the performance of movements relative to a target.

We may not like this particular definition, believing that it covers too much or not enough; but it is reasonably specific, indicates what is included in the trait and what is not, and describes the various areas covered by it.

On the basis of this definition we should know that a valid test of eye–hand coordination must involve movements of the hand relative to both stationary and moving targets. A test involving just one or the other type of target would not be representative. Similarly, the quantitative description of the individual's performance, his or her score, must reflect both the speed and the accuracy of his or her movements. Furthermore, if the test provides clues to the location of the target through sense modalities other than vision, its validity is impaired.

Unfortunately, even in seemingly clear-cut cases it cannot always be held that equal representativeness of all parts of the domain is sufficient for content validity. Thus it might be argued that the events that took place in American history from 1776 to 1780 shaped the course of the United States far more than those that took place from 1800 to 1840. Hence to be valid, a test of knowledge of American history should have five times as many items dealing with the shorter early period than with the longer later period. In the same way, a mathematician might argue that since the process of division merely involves multiplication and subtraction in an arithmetic test, there should be far fewer division items than those of the other three types. Unless the definition of the trait specifies the relative importance of the various aspects of phases of a trait, subjective judgment is required to determine whether in a test designed to measure that trait they should be equally represented or should have different weights. Again subjective judgment is involved in all phases of content validity and is its paramount characteristic.

## Enhancing Content Validity

Depending on the circumstances and the characteristics to be measured there are a number of ways that expert judgments about content validity can be augmented. These are in no way a replacement for subjective judgments. They are merely some possible strategies for enhancing it.

*Item homogeneity*    One approach to enhancing subjective judgment and giving a more precise statement of the degree of validity is to view the relative homogeneity of the components of the test as an indication of content validity. The argument is that if the component parts of the test are intended to measure the same trait, their scores should be positively correlated; and the higher their intercorrelations, the more content-valid is the test. Following this notion, the total score over all the items, the pooled judgment as it were, is viewed as the best available measure of the characteristic that the test is designed to measure. The next step is to eliminate those items that are unrelated to the total test score or that have only a low relationship with it and to retain those items that have high correlations with the total score. To do this, an item analysis, such as that described in Chapters 7 and 13, is performed in which the correlations between scores on the items and total scores are computed.

By the above process a test can be developed that has greater homogeneity than the original test because the relationships among the items are higher. Thus in addition to the judgmental process by means of which the original test elements were selected or developed, we have added homogeneity as a basis for gauging validity. This is a somewhat different notion from the basic concept of content validity, and has theoretical implications akin to those of the concept of domain sampling described in Chapter 8. Content validity in and of itself depends on subjective judgment alone. Nevertheless, even if we consider the homogeneity of the elements of a test as an "aid" to judgment, it pertains only to that aspect of content validity that is concerned with the intentional sampling of homogeneous content elements. It does not deal with the problem of the extent to which the elements of a test cover all aspects and phases of the trait or characteristic. Indeed, by discarding those elements, we may eliminate an important aspect or phase of the variable. For example, suppose mechanical aptitude is defined as knowledge of mechanical principles, ability to perceive spatial relationships, and manual dexterity. It is likely that those test elements pertaining to the first two aspects of mechanical aptitude would be positively related to a substantial degree, while those pertaining to the last aspect would be unrelated to the other two. If on these grounds the manual-dexterity elements were eliminated, an important aspect of mechanical aptitude *as defined* would not be measured.

Discarding parts of a test to ensure that the remaining elements are homogeneous, then, may result in a new test of lower content validity—lower validity in the sense that it does not measure the trait as defined as well as did the original, heterogeneous test. What we have now is a test that measures only certain aspects of the trait. This new test may be more useful and perhaps will give us new and fruitful ideas about the nature of human abilities, but it does not measure the trait as it was originally defined.

The overall message here is that content validity can be enhanced by selecting homogeneous items only when the definition of the variable specifies that homogeneity is desirable.

*Parallel-panels method*    Another procedure that could enhance our confidence in judgments of content validity is for two or more panels of experts to go through the content-validity procedure independently and to compare the final product. That is, without knowledge of what the others were doing, each panel would study the definition of the domain, generate a pool of possible items, refine the item pool by judging the extent to which each item is representative of the domain of interest and the extent to which the item pool adequately samples all relevant parts of the domain.

If the measures produced by these independent panels of experts are similar in content, and in fact scores on the measures are highly correlated (as in parallel forms reliability), then the content validity of the measure is enhanced.

*Multiple judges*   It is perhaps too obvious to mention that confidence in content-validity assessments would be enhanced if multiple judges were used and all necessary areas of expertise were represented. That is, if the objective is to build a comprehensive graduate-level test of knowledge of chemistry, many varieties of chemists (for example, organic, physical) would have to be included in the expert panel. It would also be wise to include more than one chemist of each kind. Statistically speaking, the more experts there are, the more the various errors in judgment can be averaged out. Further, at some point it is wise to include a sample of potential users as judges. Often the test takers themselves can spot validation errors that the content experts miss.

### Cautions About Content Validity

It is perhaps the case that establishing content validity is especially difficult in those situations where it is needed most. A prime example is in the development of predictors for job performance. The desire to make accurate and fair employment-selection decisions is intense, and it results in considerable pressure to leave no stone unturned in the validation process. Unfortunately job performance is an exceedingly complex domain to sample for purposes of establishing the content validity of predictors, and it is difficult to represent tasks in the selection tests precisely as they occur on the job. The content fidelity of the predictor cannot be perfect even for tasks such as typing, since the office (performance) situation is not quite the same as the test situation. Thus one must use the content-validity strategy with caution. If there is not clear agreement among experts that a sample of measurement operations is content-valid, then additional strategies must be used. In general, these fall under the rubric of construct validity, and they are the topic of the next section.

Finally Guion (1978) has cogently pointed out that merely obtaining a sample of content that is judged to have high content validity is not the end of the battle. An individual's performance *on the test* must still be *scored* so as to yield some indication of whether the individual ranks high, low, or in between on the characteristic(s) measured by the test.

Do the individual differences that appear across scores on a content-valid work-sample test reflect the individual differences that appear across people who are actually performing on the job? The moral of this story is that we must worry about whether the content sample represents the population of content and whether the scoring system for individual proficiency on the sample is correspondent with what it takes to score high or low in the population of content. For example, adequate performance on a work-sample test for an auto mechanic may be assessed by one judge employed by the personnel department to test applicants. However, there are multiple judges on the job (including customers) and these on-the-job appraisal processes may not be the same as the scoring procedures used for applicants.

In summary it might be wise to follow Guion's (1978) lead and speak of content-oriented test development rather than content validity. It really makes no sense to introduce the expert judgments only for assessing the adequacy of the sample of test components after they have been selected. Such judgments should be an integral part of working out the definition of what's to be measured, generating the content sample, and developing the scoring system. Thus content validity really is a label for the complex process of test, or predictor, construction.

## Construct Validity

The term *construct validity* (Cronbach and Meehl, 1954) was invented to describe a validation process that was often used but that had never been identified with a label. Such a process takes place whenever the primary objective is to develop a measure of an individual characteristic for its own sake, and we want to know how well the test, or measurement operations, measure this characteristic. That is, the principal focus is not on the prediction of a criterion or on the one-to-one correspondence between the content of the test and a specific domain of knowledge or behavior, but on the ability of the test itself to measure the individual trait or characteristic of interest.

Most often such questions arise when someone thinks it is important to develop a measure of a psychological property of individuals for which, in fact, there is no existing, real-world measure (criterion). Mental abilities such as general intelligence, mechanical aptitude, and spatial relations; and personality characteristics such as sociability, dominance, the need for achievement, and introversion fall in this category. Since such things are hypothesized to exist, but have no direct real-world counterpart (That's why they are *hypothesized* to exist!), the variables in question are called *constructs,* and hence the term construct validity. Our interest is in developing a test that actually measures such things because having such a measure would be important in a broad range of practical and theoretical situations. For example, clinicians and counselors want to know something about their clients' personality characteristics so as to more intelligently explore how a client might react to a variety of future situations. Motivation researchers might need a good measure of need achievement because it is necessary before they can test their favorite theory in a controlled experiment (for example, people scoring high on the need for achievement will act one way; people low on the need for achievement will act another). Researchers interested in the question of genetic versus environmental control of general intelligence really need a good measure of intelligence before they can proceed. In sum, such characteristics are referred to as constructs since they are hypothesized to exist but there is no one criterion measure for them. Such constructs are all around us and are not limited to personality factors and mental abilities. For example, in athletics there is a construct called "endurance" that is frequently talked about. Trying to be more systematic Fleishman (1975) identified five underlying "strength" constructs (for example, static strength, dynamic strength) that he argued would explain performance on a wide range of specific motor tasks (pushups, the 100-meter dash, distance swimming, and the like). When leadership behavior is studied, constructs such as "consideration for subordinates" (giving praise, explaining reasons for action, asking opinions) and "initiating structure" (setting goals, keeping on schedule) are used, and searching questions are asked about how validly these constructs are measured by the questionnaires that were designed for them. In sum then construct validity asks the question: How well does a set of operations (that is, a test) measure an individual's standing on a construct?

We are not asking how valid the test is for predicting a particular criterion. When we concern ourselves with predictive validity, we are in effect saying that we have no real interest as such in the operations that form the predictor, but only in the criterion. Criterion scores are precisely what we want, but because of the force of circumstances we cannot obtain them directly. Therefore, we seek some other operations that we can use to obtain estimates of criterion scores. However, in general, this occurs only in those limited practical situations where we wish to forecast some future behavior such as success in school or on a job. More often our interests are broader. For theoretical purposes we are concerned with the relationships among psychological traits that are intellectual constructs and with the effects of various conditions on such traits. To be sure, we may be interested in the predictive value of the traits, asking such questions as the extent to which measures of intelligence forecast later success in school. However, in such instances of specific decisionmaking, our interest clearly shifts to a concern for the operations as predictors and not as a means for assessing an individual's standing on a construct.

In many instances, while predictive validity may seem to be the primary focus, in fact it is not. For example, if we wish to establish the validity of a test of scholastic aptitude, we might do it by ascertaining the correlation between test scores and grades earned in college. But what college, what major, and for what period of time? The power of a test to predict grades may appear to differ from one college to another, from one major to another within the same college, and from one time period to another. We might explain away these variations in relationship by saying that grades in some colleges are more reliable than in others and hence more predictable, that in some colleges grades are based less on academic achievement than on other factors, and that some college majors depend more heavily on cognitive ability factors than do other majors. We also might say that in the past almost any high school student was admitted to college, where as now there is a considerable restriction in the range of ability of those who are admitted; or that the high school preparation of students in the past was better or poorer than that at present. In other words, we are taking the point of view that our test measures a construct called scholastic aptitude, but that there is never a single satisfactory criterion available for the evaluation of its validity. To put it another way, we are saying that there is a trait of scholastic aptitude that is measured by our test, and we offer as evidence the fact that test scores are positively related to success in a variety of different academic situations. Because these correlations are not perfect, we conclude that academic success is determined by factors other than scholastic aptitude. Indeed we may be able to demonstrate this by showing that among individuals with the same scholastic aptitude, that is, with the same score on our test, those who are highly motivated earn higher grades than do those who are less motivated.

All of this is not to deny the legitimate role of criterion-related validity. Indeed there are many instances where it is of primary concern. Rather the point is that in many situations predictive validity alone cannot tell us what we want to know about a measure.

### Describing Construct Validity

The establishment of construct validity must begin with the theoretical definition for the construct. Most likely the construct is embedded in some theory about behavior, and the theory specifies in some fashion or other (1) the meaning of the construct, (2) how it is related to other constructs, and (3) how it is related to specific observable behaviors. For example, we might be interested in a construct called "garden-variety anxiety.'' Let's suppose that this type of anxiety is not the deep-seated psychopathological kind that characterizes people for long periods of time, leads to suicide, can be relieved only by powerful drugs, and so on. Neither is it the kind of momentary anxiety you feel as the result of being caught in a blizzard or spilling gravy on yourself in a restaurant. Rather it is the kind that you experience as the result of anticipating fairly major events in your life such as entrance exams for law school, the possibility of a divorce, or losing your job. Such anxiety would be expected to fluctuate over a period of months as major circumstances in your life change, and *some people would react more strongly to such changes than others*. This kind of anxiety is *not* related to general intelligence (says our theory), but is negatively related to self-esteem. Further there is a curvilinear (inverted U-shaped) relationship between garden-variety anxiety and performance on course examinations. That is, if you want to do well, it is best to have a moderate amount of such anxiety.

If we were really serious about investigating this construct, we would have to be much more thorough about defining it and mapping out its hypothesized relationships with specific behaviors and other constructs. The above brief discussion is meant to be illustrative only.

Once a definition of the construct is available, a set of measurement operations must be developed, using the methods that are discussed elsewhere in this book. For example, we might construct a paper-and-pencil test of garden-variety anxiety.

One major confusion regarding construct validity at this point concerns the breadth of its interpretation. In its widest sense one could think of construct validity as pertinent to any theory of behavior. That is, understanding the construct, or knowing the theory, permits a host of predictions about behavior when the construct is used as the independent variable. In this sense, construct validation is a *deductive* process, and construct validity is established to the extent that specific hypotheses deduced from the theory are substantiated in empirical studies. By contrast, an investigator could be concerned with giving substantive meaning to a particular set of measurement operations (for example, a specific paper-and-pencil inventory) for which he or she was not yet ready to predict empirical relationships. Thus the process becomes *inductive,* and what's being validated is not a theory about some characteristic of individual differences, but the content of a particular test. Consequently, construct validity would be established to the extent that a large number of relationships between the test and other variables was determined, and the pattern of relationships that was found clearly indicated the meaning of the test score.

The original APA Technical Recommendations made construct validity sound almost synonymous with the standard ingredients of deductive theory building, which detracted somewhat from its uniqueness in the validity taxonomy. The 1966 statement of test standards moved away from this position a bit, but remained committed to the deductive view. In our opinion, taking either extreme is not in the best interests of psychometric theory. Viewing construct validity as purely deductive theory building gives it no distinctive reason for being. Also the psychological study of individual differences is still at a primitive enough level that many promising avenues of research could be dried up prematurely if a deductive approach were required and the first few hypotheses based on the theory about the construct went down the drain. It would seem more productive for a validity model to give investigators some guidance for a certain amount of inductive "fishing" before moving to substantive hypothesis testing. At the other extreme, adopting a strictly inductive view throws away the power of hypothesis testing. If investigators never stick their necks out with regard to what they think their instruments are measuring, they will never establish surplus meaning or rule out competing explanations as to why a measure acts the way it does in the empirical world.

A second important distinction regarding construct validity is whether the theory being validated concerns the construct as it is represented by a specific set of measurement operations or whether it is independent of any specific measuring instrument. The latter option again makes construct validity synonymous with the validity of almost any psychological theory and detracts from its unique character. The power of the construct-validity notion is derived from its function as a means for assessing the validity of a specific measuring instrument intended to measure a human characteristic for which there is no naturally occurring criterion.

*Determining Construct Validity*

Again construct validity applies when the investigator wants a measure of a characteristic that is deemed important by somebody, but for which there is no already available indicator. The "thing" being validated is a set of measurement operations, and the process should include both an inductive and a deductive component. The following kinds of studies make useful contributions to construct validity:

1. The theory (definition) of the construct should say something about how the individual measurement operations (for example, the items in a test) should be interrelated. If the test is designed to measure only one factor, then the individual items should all intercorrelate positively. If, for example, our theory of garden-variety anxiety says that we have anxieties about

social situations and anxieties about achievement situations, then the intercorrelations should reveal two groups of items. The items referring to social situations should correlate highly among themselves and so should the items referring to achievement situations. However, the correlations between the two types of items should not be as high. In general, the clustering of the item intercorrelations should be consistent with the nature of the factors specified in the construct definition.

2. Given the definition of the construct, we might expect some reliability estimates to be high and some to be low. For garden-variety anxiety, the parallel-forms or test–retest method over a several-month period may yield rather low estimates, while the split-half estimate should be high.

3. The measure of the construct certainly can be correlated with many other measures. If the theory says that some of these measures reflect the same construct, then these correlations should be high, and vice versa.

4. Correlating the measure of the construct with other variables that might account for, or rule out, potential sources of bias or irrelevant variance in the instrument being validated is also useful. For garden-variety anxiety such sources of nonvalid variance might be associated with substantive content (say, verbal fluency) or methodological elements (item format, social desirability). For example, it would be good to know if responses to our paper-and-pencil anxiety measure were related to vocabulary proficiency. We wouldn't want that. Also, if responses to the anxiety test were too highly related to measures of social desirability, then we would try to modify the anxiety test to get rid of that extraneous source of individual differences.

5. A special kind of correlational evidence is provided by the *multitrait, multimethod matrix (MTMM)*. Such a matrix can be generated when we have at least two constructs being measured by at least two different methods (Campbell and Fiske, 1959). Consider the simple example of an MTMM matrix in Table 10-1, where there are two traits, *A* and *B* (for example, anxiety and sociability), and two methods (paper-and-pencil inventory and observer ratings of behavior).

It follows that if we understand what we are measuring, two different measures of the same thing should intercorrelate highly. Campbell and Fiske called this *convergent validity*. A more stringent consideration is to stipulate that if we under-

*Table 10-1*    Example of a multitrait, multimethod matrix (MTMM)

|  |  | Trait A | | Trait B | |
|  |  | Method 1 | Method 2 | Method 1 | Method 2 |
|---|---|---|---|---|---|
| Trait A | Method 1 | $r_{1A,1A}$ | $r_{1A,2A}$ | $r_{1A,1B}$ | $r_{1A,2B}$ |
|  | Method 2 |  | $r_{2A,2A}$ | $r_{2A,1B}$ | $r_{2A,2B}$ |
| Trait B | Method 1 |  |  | $r_{1B,1B}$ | $r_{1B,2B}$ |
|  | Method 2 |  |  |  | $r_{2B,2B}$ |

stand what we are doing, the correlation between two methods designed to measure the same trait (for example, $r_{1A,2A}$) should be substantially higher than the correlation between two traits when they are measured with the same method ($r_{1A,1B}$). This stipulation is called *divergent validity,* and it has humbled many an investigator. The correlation between two variables should not be a function of similarity in measurement method. It should be a function of similarity in substantive content.

We should note one important caution at this point. The MTMM strategy really assumes that the two methods have been constructed with equal skill. If one or the other is shortchanged (for example, if any old method of quick and dirty observation is compared with a carefully developed paper-and-pencil inventory), it most likely will be unreliable, therefore not correlate with anything, and neither convergent nor divergent validity will be observed. Proceed with caution here.

6. Valuable sources of information on construct validity are experimental studies using the measure being validated either as the dependent variable or as a cross-classification variable. For example, to investigate garden-variety anxiety, we could (if we were mean enough) divide a college class randomly into two groups at the beginning of the term. One group could be told that only 10 percent of the class will get an A and 50 percent will fail, while the second group could be told that no one will fail and at least 50 percent will get an A. The mean score on our anxiety test for these two groups *should* be different after this experimental treatment is imposed. In general, there should be any number of experiments for which we can predict changes on our construct measure *if* we understand it.

7. Content validity becomes a part of construct validity if and when we ask experts to judge the adequacy of the methods

used to sample item content from the universe of content, and the adequacy with which the measurement operations seem to reflect the theoretical definition of the construct.

8. A final line of evidence is derived from what we will call a *process analysis* of individuals responding to a construct measure. This would entail such things as the detailed questioning of subjects as to why they responded a certain way to a test item or the questioning of raters as to how and why they actually chose a particular rating for an individual. The subjects, or raters, should be using a process reasonably close to that which the researcher had in mind when he or she developed the instrument. Such process data is often an eye-opener.

Almost all of these different lines of evidence can be used in both an inductive and a deductive manner. At some point, however, things must get serious and the investigator must stick his or her neck out and *predict* how the instrument will work in empirical studies. Two principal characteristics make one type of hypothesis better than another. First, more construct validity can be attributed to the instrument to the extent that the hypotheses being tested are nonoverlapping. That is, much less is gained from confirming the same hypothesis ten times than from confirming ten hypotheses of very different kinds. If we are validating a measure of garden-variety anxiety, we could predict its correlation with grade-point average in ten different random samples from the same population, or we could make ten different predictions, such as the responsiveness of the anxiety scores to threats of low grades, the kinds of reliability that would be high and low, the correlation of the anxiety test with intelligence, and so on. Second, more construct validity is accumulated to the extent that hypotheses are more stringent and are easier to negate. For example, it is not very stringent—and we don't learn very much—if we support the hypothesis that under conditions $X$, $Y$, and $Z$, garden-variety anxiety correlates with job performance somewhere between $-.60$ and $+.60$. It would mean a great deal more to confirm a prediction that these two variables are correlated between $+.30$ and $+.40$.

If construct validity is viewed in the above fashion, it does have a unique place in psychometric theory. However, we should keep in mind that it does not come cheaply.

## Methodological and Statistical Problems in Criterion-Related Validity

There are a number of methodological and statistical problems that arise in connection with criterion-related validity. Because criterion-related validity plays a part in the determination of construct validity, these matters are also pertinent to it. In this section we discuss the prediction of criterion scores, reliability as it relates to validity, prediction when there are multiple criteria, and validity in relation to the range of individual differences.

### Estimating Criterion from Predictor Scores

In our discussion of correlation and regression in Chapters 5 and 6 we learned that if we know an individual's predictor score $X$, our best estimate of that individual's criterion score is the average of the criterion scores, $\bar{Y}_{i,}$ of all those individuals in the sample who have the same predictor score. If we take the relationship between predictor and criterion scores to be linear, then we can express the degree of relationship by means of the Pearsonian coefficient and, it will also be recalled from Chapters 5 and 6, we can then use the regression equation to give us a value we take as representative of the $Y$ scores of individuals all of whom earn the same $X$ score. That is, when we have a single predictor, we use the regression line (the straight line of best fit in a least-squares sense); and when we have several predictors, we use the regression plane (the plane of best fit in a least-squares sense) to make our prediction from $X$ to $Y$.

The accuracy with which these predictions are made is described by the standard error of estimate or prediction (Equation 6-19 when the predictor is a single variable and Equation 11-25—discussed in the next chapter—when it is a composite variable). The standard error of estimate is the standard deviation of the criterion scores of those individuals all of whom have the same predictor score. It should be recalled from our discussion in Chapters 5 and 6 that when the relationship is taken as being linear and is described by the Pearsonian coefficient, the deviations on which the standard error are based are deviations from the regression line and not from the means of the $Y$ scores in the columns, unless those means happen to fall on the regression line. The standard error of estimate or prediction, then, describes the accuracy with which individual predictions are made by the regression equation. It will be remembered that we must adopt either of two points of view about the standard error of estimate. If we are willing to presume the relationship is homoscedastic, then we can take the standard error as descriptive of the accuracy of predictions at all levels of predictor scores. If we are not willing to do this, we must take the standard error as a weighted average of the errors of prediction.

### Index of Forecasting Efficiency

Of some historical interest is another index of how well criterion scores can be estimated from predictor scores; it is called the *index of forecasting efficiency (E)*. Since the objective is to represent the proportional decrease in the standard deviation of the predicted scores when the new predictor is compared to no information (that is, predict the overall mean of $Y$ for everybody), the index is defined as

$$E = \frac{\sigma_y - \sigma_y\sqrt{1 - r_{xy}^2}}{\sigma_y}$$

$$= 1 - \sqrt{1 - r_{xy}^2} \tag{10-1}$$

The second term in the numerator of the first expression is obviously the standard error of estimate using the predictor.

### Effects of Reliability

Equation 9-6 shows how the reliability with which two variables are measured affects the correlation between them. This formula rearranged is

$$r_{xy} = r_{x_\infty y_\infty} \sqrt{r_{xx} r_{yy}}$$

That is, given $r_{x_\infty y_\infty}$ (the correlation between true predictor and true criterion scores), we find that as $r_{xx}$ (the reliability of the predictor) and $r_{yy}$ (the reliability of the criterion) change, so does the empirically determined validity coefficient, $r_{xy}$. We can see that as the reliability of either the predictor or the criterion becomes lower and lower, the validity becomes lower and lower. As we saw in Table 9-1, if either the predictor or the criterion is completely unreliable, then fallible scores on the two variables will be completely uncorrelated and the validity will be zero. Hence we can say that reliability limits validity and that for optimal prediction both the predictor and the criterion should be measured with as high reliability as possible, so that $r_{xy}$ approaches $r_{x_\infty y_\infty}$, the highest possible validity.

### Correcting for Attenuation

If the validity coefficient is limited by the lack of predictor and/or criterion reliability, it is said to be attenuated. As noted in Chapter 9, if we keep certain precautions in mind, we can forecast what validity would be if the predictor and/or the criterion were measured with perfect reliability. That is, we can correct for the attenuation.

From the discussion in Chapter 9 and by rearranging the above formula, we can see that if the reliability of the predictor $X$ were perfect, then the correlation between a predictor with perfect reliability and a fallible criterion would be

$$r_{x_\infty y} = \frac{r_{xy}}{\sqrt{r_{xx}}} \tag{10-2}$$

Similarly, if only the criterion were corrected for attenuation, then the forecast of the correlation between a fallible predictor and a criterion with perfect reliability would be

$$r_{xy_\infty} = \frac{r_{xy}}{\sqrt{r_{yy}}} \tag{10-3}$$

Finally, if both predictor and criterion were corrected for attenuation, then the correlation between a perfectly reliable predictor and a perfectly reliable criterion would be

$$r_{x_\infty y_\infty} = \frac{r_{xy}}{\sqrt{r_{xx} r_{yy}}} \tag{10-4}$$

Again, in line with the discussion in Chapter 8, the estimates of reliability that are used in these corrections must be appropriate ones. For example, if true scores change over time, then a test–retest or equivalent-forms coefficient would count such changes as error, or unreliability, and the reliability *estimate* would be artifically low. If the reliability estimate were artificially low then the corrections for attenuation given by the above formulas would be artificially high. The same reasoning would apply if an internal-consistency method (for example, coefficient alpha) were used to estimate the reliability of a multidimensional measure.

Given these cautions, it is often argued that when criterion-related validity is estimated, the correlation between a predictor and a criterion of perfect reliability should also be estimated; that is, the validity coefficient is corrected for attenuation in the criterion. For example, if the validity coefficient is .35 and the reliability of the criterion (for example, a measure of job performance) is .49, the "corrected" validity coefficient is .35 ÷ $\sqrt{.49}$ or .50. Which number is the better estimate of what the validity of the predictor will be with future samples of people from this same population? If the reliability coefficient of .49 is an appropriate one, and is therefore an indicator of the unsystematic random errors of measurement, then .50 is the better estimate of validity. After all, the individual's actual contributions to the organization are not limited by the errors inherent in the method used to measure the criterion. Defined as we are defining them, there is no measurement error in *actual* contributions.

However, if the reliability coefficient used to make the correction is not an appropriate one, in the context discussed above, all we can say is that the fallible-score coefficient is too conservative, but we don't know to what extent.

Finally, when considering criterion-related validity, it is generally not appropriate to correct for unreliability in the predictor. In applied psychology we must always deal with fallible predictor scores. That is, the decision must be made on the basis of the predictor data in hand, and it is the validity of the fallible predictor information that is at issue. For example, it matters not if near-perfect predictor reliability could be achieved by increasing the length of the test to 3,000 items. The "best" sample of 100 items may be all we can get, and it is the reliability of those 100 items with which we must live.

## Prediction with Multiple Criteria

We have been discussing predictive validity as if the criterion were always a single variable. However, as is the case with other measures of psychological characteristics, the criterion often is a composite variable. A criterion of leadership might be a series of rating scales designed to measure various facets of that domain. The criterion of success for a particular sales job might involve the total dollar volume of sales, the number of new accounts developed, and the number of repeat sales to the same customers. In cases such as these, when we have multiple criteria, we must somehow combine them in order to compute the coefficient of correlation between criterion and predictor scores so as to describe predictive validity.

In combining criteria, we can take all of them to be of equal importance or we can differentially weight them. Criteria can be taken to be of equal importance either in the sense that the units of measurement in which each is expressed are equivalent, so that they can be summed or averaged, or in the sense that they contribute equally to the variation in composite scores. If we wish to have the various component criteria contribute differently to the composite, they can be assigned differential nominal weights based on personal judgment about their relative importance, their reliability, or their correlation with a principal construct that underlies all the component criteria.

Finally, critical points may be set on each criterion and individuals placed into various classes, depending on the number or pattern of criterion cutoff points they exceed.

*Assuming that multiple criteria are equally important*    In many instances the scales on which the different criteria are expressed are assumed to be equivalent, and scores on all component criteria are assumed to be comparable and therefore simply summed or averaged. Thus when academic success in college is measured by grades received in different courses, all these grades are taken as being scores on comparable scales and are averaged to obtain a total criterion score. This is also likely to be done with ratings, where ratings on a series of scales designed to measure different facets of a trait are merely summed or averaged. In some cases it is possible to change the units in which the various scales are expressed to other units that are equivalent. For example, suppose the success of production employees is gauged both by the number of items of work they produce and by the number of accidents in which they are involved. If the value of an item of work is known, production can be expressed in terms of dollars. Similarly, if the cost of an accident is known, it too can be expressed in terms of dollars. The composite criterion score for an individual would then be the dollar value of production minus the dollar cost of accidents. The net value would be the individual's contribution to his or her job.

If we wish to consider the various criteria as being of equal importance in the sense that they contribute equally to the variation in composite scores, the common procedure is to transmute the scores on each of the component criteria to standard or standardized scores. However, as we saw in Chapter 7, this ignores the intercorrelations among the criteria, and these intercorrelations also contribute to the variation in total scores. Therefore transmuting scores on each component criterion to standard or standardized scores does not result in a situation wherein each contributes equally to the variation in composite scores, though this result may be approximated thereby. But as we saw in Chapter 4, the use of standard or standardized scores does in a sense make the units comparable.

*Differential weighting of component criteria*    When it is believed that the various component criteria should be differentially weighted, integer weights can be assigned and differentially weighted composite scores obtained. Ordinarily differential weights are applied to component criterion scores after the scales have been made comparable, by means of standard or standardized scores. Either we can use weights that in our personal judgment best describe the relative importance of the component criteria, or we can differentially weight them in terms of their reliability of their correlations with a construct that we assume under-lies all of them.

Perhaps the most common method of developing differential weights is through personal judgment. On the basis of our theoretical notions about the characteristic being measured, our analysis of the charac-teristic, our values, or similar considerations, we make decisions about the relative importance of the various component criteria. Thus, in gauging the performance of sales personnel, the management of the department store might believe that dollar volume of sales is twice as important as number of absences and four times as important as accu-racy in making change. Then the weights of 4, 2, and 1, respectively, would be assigned to the three component criteria.

Seldom does it make sense to weight the various component criteria in terms of their reliability. While it can be argued that the less reliable criteria should not be given as much weight as the more reliable ones, since scores on them are largely determined by unsystematic factors, there is no necessary relationship between reliability and importance. Indeed it may very well be that the least important criterion elements are the easiest to measure. The world does seem to work that way. That is, the things most worth having are the most difficult to get.

In general, the differential weighting of criterion components is, and should be, a value judgment that should be faced directly, and not swept under the rug.

*Critical cutoff points*    In some situations, where the criterion has many different facets each of which is measured by a different component criterion, it may seem that a simple or weighted summation of standard or standardized scores is not appropriate. For example, an airplane pilot whose takeoffs are smooth and whose cross-country flights are precise, but who is unable to land the aircraft without serious conse-quences, could not be considered a successful pilot. Similarly, a child who is well-mannered at home and in adult groups and whose behavior in the classroom is excellent, but who in play situations is forever hitting, biting, and kicking other children, cannot be considered to be making a satisfactory social adjustment. In these instances as in many others it appears that critical points can be set on the component crite-ria, below which any score automatically marks the individual as being low on the characteristic the total criterion is designed to measure. A low score on any one component is not taken as being compensated for by high scores on the others as is the case when we average the scores on the component criteria. On the other hand, an individual will be categorized as successful if his or her scores on all criteria fall above the critical points, even though they exceed them by very small amounts. Individuals, then, are placed in one or the other of two categories, those who are successful or high on the criterion and those who are unsuccessful or low on it. Consequently, we have a discontinuous dichotomous criterion, and validity coefficients are most appropriately expressed by the point biserial or phi coefficient.

The critical points might well be set at different points on the different component criteria, depending on what we consider critical performance on each to be. In this sense this multiple-cutoff procedure does provide a system of differential weights for the component criteria, but because each component is given a complete "veto" power, in another sense they are all equally important.

In our opinion, almost all jobs or educational programs are complex enough to yield multiple criteria of performance that are too distinct to be automatically combined (weighted or unweighted) into a single composite. That is, performance on one critical component is not highly correlated with performance on another. Adding them together hides too much information. However, it is also true that overall decisions such as pass/fail, hire/not hire, promote/not promote must be made about individuals based on all the evidence. In such instances we can only argue, as others have done, that the criterion and predictive validity information should not be combined until the very last minute, and then with the realization that the weight given to each item of information is a necessary value judgment.

### Range of Individual Differences

Sometimes we are unable to compute the validity coefficient on the entire range of scores for which the predictor *will actually be used*. The only data available are the predictor and criterion scores for a *restricted range* of individuals. As is the case with the reliability coefficient, or any correlation coefficient, the magnitude of the validity coefficient is affected by the range of individual differences. Consequently, a description of the validity of the predictor based on the scores of the restricted range might not be considered satisfactory, and would generally underestimate the actual validity.

There are two common situations where this circumstance occurs, one involving two variables and the other three variables. In the first situation a restriction of range results from a selection of individuals on the basis of their predictor scores, as would be the case if the predictor were already being used to select people above a certain cutoff score. That is, predictor $(X)$ and criterion $(Y)$ scores are available only for individuals whose predictor scores are above some critical point, and we must estimate the validity of the predictor from this restricted sample of scores alone. There is, then, a *direct* or *explicit* restriction of the range of individual differences on the basis of $X$ scores, and consequently the standard deviation of $X$ scores is reduced. Any effects of this restriction on the extent of variation in $Y$ scores are *indirect* or *incidental*.

In the second common situation the explicit selection is made on the basis of another variable, $Z$. Criterion ($Y$) and predictor ($X$) scores are available only for individuals whose $Z$ scores fall above a certain critical point, and we must estimate the validity of the predictor from their scores alone. There is, then, explicit restriction on the basis of $Z$ scores, and consequently the standard deviation of $Z$ scores is reduced. Any effects of this restriction on the extent of variation of $Y$ and $X$ scores are *incidental*.

As an example of the first situation, suppose a company uses scores on a clerical test to select office personnel. All those whose scores fall above a given critical point are offered employment, and all those whose scores fall below this point are rejected. As a consequence, test and criterion scores are available only for those persons whose test scores fall above the critical point. Therefore the coefficient of correlation between the test and the criterion of job success describes the accuracy of prediction only for this restricted range of persons and not for the entire range of applicants. Obviously it would be very helpful if we could estimate the validity of the test for the entire range of applicants from that of the restricted range of those who are selected since, in fact, selection of job applicants via the test is from the entire range.

As an example of the second situation, let us say that students have been admitted to college on the basis of their high school grades, with only those whose grades are above a given point being admitted. Suppose a scholastic aptitude test is being considered as a substitute admission procedure. To determine the validity of the test in predicting college grades, it might be administered to entering freshmen. However, these individuals have *already* been selected on the basis of their high school grades, which are most likely correlated with the scholastic aptitude test scores, and as a consequence the correlation between their test scores and college grades would describe the accuracy of prediction only for a restricted range and not for the entire range of applicants. Again it would be helpful if the validity of the test for the entire range could be estimated from its validity over the restricted range.

In the two foregoing examples we have illustrated the restriction of range by the selection of high-scoring individuals. In the following developments, however, no presumptions at all are made about the zone where the scores of the selected individuals fall, but only that their scores do not cover the entire range. It might be that only low-scoring individuals are selected or those in the middle of the distribution, so that individuals at both extremes are excluded.

Given certain assumptions, there are many formulas that can be developed to estimate the validity coefficient and/or the variance of the predictor and/or the criterion in the restricted or in the unrestricted group. Discussing all possible variations of this problem would take too much space, so we present only what seem to be the most common situations. In general, to obtain these estimates, the investigator must know both the restricted and the unrestricted variance for one of the variables (predictor or criterion) and their correlation either in the restricted sample or in the unrestricted sample.

*Restriction of range in two-variable situation*    Let us symbolize the characteristics of the distributions of predictor and criterion scores and their relationships for the restricted and for the unrestricted range as in Table 10-2. We are concerned with the effects of deliberate or explicit restriction of range of predictor scores on the validity coefficient. The ratio $\sigma'^2_x/\sigma^2_x$ describes the amount of explicit restriction on predictor scores, and the ratio $\sigma'^2_y/\sigma^2_y$ the resulting amount of incidental restriction of criterion scores. In each case the amount of restriction is expressed as the ratio of the variation in scores of the restricted group to the variation in scores of the unrestricted, or total, group.

To proceed further, it is necessary to make two assumptions. First we must assume that the slope of the best-fitting regression line through the $Y$ scores in the columns is the same both for the restricted and for the total range of $X$ scores. That is, we assume

$$b'_{y \cdot x} = b_{y \cdot x} \tag{10-5}$$

Second we must assume that the standard error of estimate, or the standard deviation of the $Y$ scores in the columns, is the same both for the restricted and for the total range of $X$ scores. That is, we assume

$$\sigma'_{y \cdot x} = \sigma_{y \cdot x} \tag{10-6}$$

What we are assuming is that the characteristics of that portion of the bivariate distribution, or scatter diagram, that we do have are the same as those of the total bivariate distribution. If the amount of restriction is small, so that $\sigma'_x$ is almost as large as $\sigma_x$ and the ratio $\sigma'_x/\sigma_x$ approaches 1, the chances are greater that the characteristics of the restricted bivariate distribution will be the same as those of the total distribution.

It is not necessary to assume that the relationship between test and criterion scores is linear in the sense that the means of the $Y$ scores in each column fall precisely on the same straight line and that all the

*Table 10-2*  Predictor and criterion scores for restricted and unrestricted range

|  | Unrestricted Range | Restricted Range |
|---|---|---|
| Standard deviation of predictor scores | $\sigma_x$ | $\sigma'_x$ |
| Standard deviation of criterion scores | $\sigma_y$ | $\sigma'_y$ |
| Validity coefficient | $r_{xy}$ | $r'_{xy}$ |
| Regression coefficient | $b_{y \cdot x}$ | $b'_{y \cdot x}$ |
| Standard error of estimate or prediction | $\sigma_{y \cdot x}$ | $\sigma'_{y \cdot x}$ |

standard deviations of the $Y$ scores in the columns are equal, so that homoscedasticity holds. In Chapter 5 we saw that the regression coefficient describes the slope of the straight line of best fit in a least-squares sense. All we need to assume is that the best-fitting straight line through that portion of the bivariate distribution we do have is also the best-fitting straight line through the remaining portion. Also in Chapter 5 we saw that $\sigma^2_{y \cdot x}$ can be thought of as the weighted mean of the variances of the $Y$ scores in the columns. Thus it is necessary for us to assume only that the weighted mean of the variances of the $Y$ scores in the columns of that portion of the bivariate distribution we do have is equal to the weighted mean of the variances of the $Y$ scores in the columns of the remaining portion.

From Chapter 5 we can write the regression coefficient as

$$b_{y \cdot x} = \frac{\Sigma xy}{n \sigma^2_x}$$

Since $r_{xy} = \Sigma xy / n \sigma_x \sigma_y$, we can write $r_{xy} \sigma_y = \Sigma xy / n \sigma_x$. Consequently

$$b_{y \cdot x} = r_{xy} \frac{\sigma_y}{\sigma_x}$$

and similarly

$$b'_{y \cdot x} = r'_{xy} \frac{\sigma'_y}{\sigma'_x}$$

Since, by assumption in Equation 10-5, $b'_{y \cdot x} = b_{y \cdot x}$,

$$r'_{xy} \frac{\sigma'_y}{\sigma'_x} = r_{xy} \frac{\sigma_y}{\sigma_x} \qquad (10\text{-}7)$$

Solving for $\sigma'_y$, we have

$$\sigma'_y = \frac{r_{xy}\sigma_y\sigma'_x}{r'_{xy}\sigma_x} \tag{10-8}$$

By assumption in Equation 10-6, $\sigma'_{y \cdot x} = \sigma_{y \cdot x}$; so substituting from Equation 6-19, the standard error of estimate, we have

$$\sigma'_y \sqrt{1 - r'^2_{xy}} = \sigma_y \sqrt{1 - r^2_{xy}} \tag{10-9}$$

Squaring Equation 10-9 and substituting for $\sigma'_y$ from Equation 10-8 gives

$$\frac{r^2_{xy}\sigma^2_y\sigma'^2_x}{r'^2_{xy}\sigma^2_x}(1 - r'^2_{xy}) = \sigma^2_y(1 - r^2_{xy})$$

Dividing both sides of the equation by $\sigma^2_y$ gives

$$\frac{r^2_{xy}\sigma'^2_x}{r'^2_{xy}\sigma^2_x}(1 - r'^2_{xy}) = 1 - r^2_{xy} \tag{10-10}$$

Multiplying both sides of the equation by $\sigma^2_x/r^2_{xy}\sigma'^2_x$ gives

$$\frac{\sigma^2_x}{r^2_{xy}\sigma'^2_x}\frac{r^2_{xy}\sigma'^2_x}{r'^2_{xy}\sigma^2_x}(1 - r'^2_{xy}) = \frac{\sigma^2_x}{r^2_{xy}\sigma'^2_x}(1 - r^2_{xy})$$

$$\frac{1 - r'^2_{xy}}{r'^2_{xy}} = \frac{\sigma^2_x(1 - r^2_{xy})}{r^2_{xy}\sigma'^2_x}$$

$$\frac{1}{r'^2_{xy}} - 1 = \frac{\sigma^2_x(1 - r^2_{xy})}{r^2_{xy}\sigma'^2_x}$$

$$\frac{1}{r'^2_{xy}} = 1 + \frac{\sigma^2_x(1 - r^2_{xy})}{r^2_{xy}\sigma'^2_x}$$

$$= \frac{r^2_{xy}\sigma'^2_x + \sigma^2_x(1 - r^2_{xy})}{r^2_{xy}\sigma'^2_x + \sigma^2_x}$$

Inverting gives

$$\frac{r'^2_{xy}}{1} = \frac{r^2_{xy}\sigma'^2_x}{r^2_{xy}\sigma'^2_x + \sigma^2_x(1 - r^2_{xy})}$$

Dividing the numerator and denominator of the fraction on the right-hand side of the equation by $\sigma^2_x$ and taking the square root of each side gives

$$r'_{xy} = \frac{r_{xy}(\sigma'_x/\sigma_x)}{\sqrt{1 - r^2_{xy} + r^2_{xy}(\sigma'^2_x/\sigma^2_x)}} \tag{10-11}$$

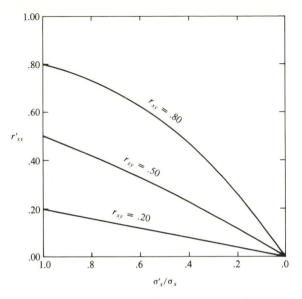

*Figure 10-1* Effects of deliberate or explicit restriction of range of predictor ($X$) scores on validity of predictor ($r'_{xy}$).

Equation 10-11 shows what the validity of a predictor, $r'_{xy}$, would be if we deliberately reduced the variation in $X$ scores from $\sigma_x$ to $\sigma'_x$. To show these effects, Equation 10-11 is plotted in Figure 10-1. In this figure we can see that as the variation in predictor scores is decreased, that is, as $\sigma'_x/\sigma_x$ becomes smaller, the validity of the test, $r'_{xy}$, also becomes smaller. It is therefore apparent that if a test is validated on a group whose predictor scores do not represent the total range, the validity coefficient will be underestimated.

Equation 10-11 shows that the validity coefficient will be reduced when the range of predictor scores is reduced. Ordinarily we have data on a group with a restricted range and we wish to estimate what the validity coefficient would be if we had the total range. That is, we want to estimate $r_{xy}$ rather than $r'_{xy}$. To obtain this value, we start with Equation 10-10, solving for $r_{xy}$. The solution is parallel to that for $r'_{xy}$, so we can write

$$r_{xy} = \frac{r'_{xy}\,(\sigma_x/\sigma'_x)}{\sqrt{1 - r'^2_{xy} + r'^2_{xy}(\sigma^2_x/\sigma'^2_x)}} \qquad (10\text{-}12)$$

Suppose that individuals are selected for an office job on the basis of their scores on a clerical aptitude test, the standard deviation of the scores of all the applicants being 10 and the standard deviation of those

selected being 5. For those persons who are hired, we find the coefficient of correlation between test and criterion scores to be .30. From
Equation 10-12 we can estimate the validity the test would have if all
persons had been hired and there were no restriction in range. Placing
the appropriate values in Equation 10-12, we have

$$r_{xy} = \frac{(.30)\,\frac{10}{5}}{\sqrt{1 - (.30)^2 + (.30)^2[(10)^2/(5)^2]}} = \frac{.60}{1.13} = .53$$

Clearly, the coefficient of .30 considerably underestimates the validity
of the test.

*Estimating validity from incidental selection*    It might also be the case
that we want to estimate what the validity coefficient would be for the
full range from knowledge of the correlation in the restricted sample
and the restricted and unrestricted variance in the variable subject to
*incidental selection*. That is, if the variance in the predictor ($X$) were
restricted directly by accepting only those people above a certain cutoff
score, but we were only able to obtain data for the criterion ($Y$), we
wish to estimate $r_{xy}$ given knowledge of $r'_{xy}$, $\sigma_y$, and $\sigma'_y$.

The appropriate solution may be obtained by beginning with Equation 10-9.

$$\sigma'_y \sqrt{1 - r'^2_{xy}} = \sigma_y \sqrt{1 - r^2_{xy}}$$

If we simply square both sides, divide by $\sigma^2_y$, and solve for $r_{xy}$, the
result is

$$r_{xy} = \sqrt{1 - (1 - r'^2_{xy})\frac{\sigma'^2_y}{\sigma^2_y}} \tag{10-13}$$

Most likely, a need for this formula would seldom arise in practice.
However, one should be extremely careful not to confuse calculating
$r_{xy}$ from knowledge of incidental restriction versus knowledge of direct
restriction. Equations 10-12 and 10-13 are not the same. Make sure you
match your situation with the appropriate formula.

Another note of caution: It could be the case that *direct* restriction
has taken place with regard to the criterion ($Y$), not the predictor ($X$).
For example, suppose a test is given to all applicants, but is not used in
selection. Subsequently 25 percent of the low performers on the criterion ($Y$) are explicitly asked to leave the organization. In this case the
direct restriction is on the criterion ($Y$), and the role of the predictor
and criterion in the previous formulas should be *reversed*.

We might also wish to know how the explicit selection on the predictor affects the *variation* in the criterion rather than the correlation between predictor and criterion. The extent of incidental variation in the criterion is indicated by $\sigma'_y/\sigma_y$. Dividing both sides of Equation 10-8 by $\sigma_y$ gives

$$\frac{\sigma'_y}{\sigma_y} = \frac{r_{xy}(\sigma'_x/\sigma_x)}{r'_{xy}} \tag{10-14}$$

Substituting for $r'_{xy}$ from Equation 10-11 and simplifying gives

$$\frac{\sigma'_y}{\sigma_y} = 1 - r^2_{xy} + r^2_{xy}\frac{\sigma'^2_x}{\sigma^2_x} \tag{10-15}$$

To show the incidental effects on the variation of criterion scores of the explicit restriction of range on the predictor scores, Equation 10-15 is plotted in Figure 10-2. In this figure we can see that the greater the deliberate restriction on the predictor, the greater the incidental restriction on the criterion.

If we wished to express the incidental restriction on $Y$ in terms of $r'_{xy}$, the correlation in the restricted sample, rather than $r_{xy}$, the correlation across the entire range, we should substitute for $r_{xy}$ from Equation 10-12 in Equation 10-13 and simplify. Then

$$\sigma_y = \sigma'_y \left(1 - r'^2_{xy} + r'^2_{xy}\frac{\sigma^2_x}{\sigma'^2_x}\right) \tag{10-16}$$

In the foregoing example of the selection of office personnel, let us say that the standard deviation of the criterion scores of those persons who were hired is 8. Variation in criterion scores has been subjected to incidental restriction. We estimate the standard deviation of criterion scores had all applicants been hired from the above formula as follows:

$$\sigma_y = 8 \left(1 - (.30)^2 + (.30)^2 \frac{(10)^2}{(5)^2}\right) = 8(1.27) = 10.16$$

*Restriction of range in three-variable situation*    Here we are concerned with the deliberate or explicit restriction of range of scores on one variable, $Z$, on the validity with which $X$ predicts $Y$. The ratio $\sigma'_z/\sigma_z$ describes the amount of explicit restriction of scores on variable $Z$, the ratio $\sigma'_x/\sigma_x$ describes the amount of incidental restriction of predictor scores, and the ratio $\sigma'_y/\sigma_y$ describes the amount of incidental restriction on criterion scores.

In addition to the two assumptions we have already made that

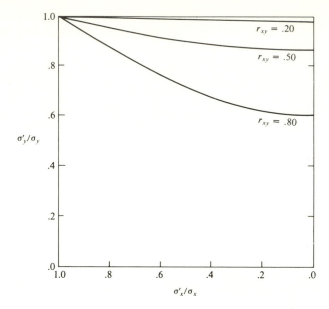

**Figure 10-2**   Incidental effects of deliberate or explicit restriction of range of predictor ($X$) scores on variation in criterion ($Y$) scores.

$b'_{y \cdot x} = b_{y \cdot x}$ and $\sigma'_{y \cdot x} = \sigma_{y \cdot x}$, we must assume that the two partial correlations are the same. That is, we assume

$$r'_{xy \cdot z} = r_{xy \cdot z} \tag{10-17}$$

We are here making the not unreasonable assumption that if we hold scores of variable $Z$ constant, the correlation between $X$ and $Y$ scores will be the same regardless of whether we have only a restricted range of $Z$ scores or the entire range. Since $Z$ is the variable on which there is a deliberate restriction of range, from Equation 10-7 we can write

$$r'_{zx} \frac{\sigma'_x}{\sigma'_z} = r_{zx} \frac{\sigma_x}{\sigma_z} \tag{10-18}$$

and

$$r'_{zy} \frac{\sigma'_y}{\sigma'_z} = r_{zy} \frac{\sigma_y}{\sigma_z} \tag{10-19}$$

Solving these two equations for $r'_{zx}$ and $r'_{zy}$, we have

$$r'_{zx} = r_{zx} \frac{\sigma_x \sigma'_z}{\sigma'_x \sigma_z} \tag{10-20}$$

and

$$r'_{zy} = r_{zy} \frac{\sigma_y \sigma'_z}{\sigma'_y \sigma_z} \tag{10-21}$$

Since $Z$ is the variable on which there is deliberate restriction of range, we can write

$$\sigma'_x \sqrt{1 - r'^2_{zx}} = \sigma_z \sqrt{1 - r^2_{zx}}$$

and

$$\sigma'_y \sqrt{1 - r'^2_{zy}} = \sigma_y \sqrt{1 - r^2_{zy}}$$

Dividing both sides of the first of these two equations by $\sigma'_x$ and both sides of the second equation by $\sigma'_y$ gives us

$$\sqrt{1 - r'^2_{zx}} = \frac{\sigma_x}{\sigma'_x} \sqrt{1 - r^2_{zx}} \tag{10-22}$$

and

$$\sqrt{1 - r'^2_{zy}} = \frac{\sigma_y}{\sigma'_y} \sqrt{1 - r^2_{zy}} \tag{10-23}$$

Since by assumption $r'_{xy \cdot z} = r_{xy \cdot z}$, we can write the equality of these two partial coefficients of correlation as

$$\frac{r'_{xy} - r'_{zx} r'_{zy}}{\sqrt{(1 - r'^2_{zx})(1 - r'^2_{zy})}} = \frac{r_{xy} - r_{zx} r_{zy}}{\sqrt{(1 - r^2_{zx})(1 - r^2_{zy})}}$$

In this equation we can substitute for $\sqrt{1 - r'^2_{zx}}$ from Equation 10-22 and for $\sqrt{1 - r'^2_{zy}}$ from Equation 10-23.

$$\frac{r'_{xy} - r'_{zx} r'_{zy}}{(\sigma_x/\sigma'_x) \sqrt{1 - r^2_{zx}} \, (\sigma_y/\sigma'_y) \sqrt{1 - r^2_{zy}}} = \frac{r_{xy} - r_{zx} r_{zy}}{\sqrt{(1 - r^2_{zx})(1 - r^2_{zy})}}$$

Multiplying both sides of the equation by $\sqrt{(1 - r^2_{zx})(1 - r^2_{zy})}$ gives

$$\frac{r'_{xy} - r'_{zx} r'_{zy}}{\sigma_x \sigma_y / \sigma'_x \sigma'_y} = r_{xy} - r_{zx} r_{zy}$$

$$r'_{xy} = (r_{xy} - r_{zx} r_{zy}) \frac{\sigma_x \sigma_y}{\sigma'_x \sigma'_y} + r'_{zx} r'_{zy}$$

Substituting for $r'_{zx}$ and $r'_{zy}$ from Equations 10-20 and 10-21 gives

$$r'_{xy} = (r_{xy} - r_{zx} r_{zy}) \frac{\sigma_x \sigma_y}{\sigma'_x \sigma'_y} + r_{zx} \frac{\sigma_x \sigma'_z}{\sigma'_x \sigma_z} r_{zy} \frac{\sigma_y \sigma'_z}{\sigma'_y \sigma_z}$$

$$= \frac{\sigma_x \sigma_y}{\sigma'_x \sigma'_y} \left( r_{xy} - r_{zx} r_{zy} + r_{zx} r_{zy} \frac{\sigma'^2_z}{\sigma^2_z} \right) \tag{10-24}$$

Recalling that the explicit restriction is on variable $Z$ and the incidental restriction is on both variables, $X$ and $Y$, from Equation 10-15 we can write

$$\frac{\sigma'_x}{\sigma_x} = \sqrt{1 - r^2_{zx} + r^2_{zx} \frac{\sigma'^2_z}{\sigma^2_z}}$$

and

$$\frac{\sigma'_y}{\sigma_y} = \sqrt{1 - r^2_{zy} + r^2_{zy} \frac{\sigma'^2_z}{\sigma^2_z}}$$

Therefore

$$\frac{\sigma_x \sigma_y}{\sigma'_x \sigma'_y} = \frac{1}{\sqrt{[1 - r^2_{zx} + r^2_{zx}(\sigma'^2_z/\sigma^2_z)][1 - r^2_{zy} + r^2_{zy}(\sigma'^2_z/\sigma^2_z)]}} \tag{10-25}$$

Substituting for $\sigma_x \sigma_y / \sigma'_x \sigma'_y$ from Equation 10-25 in Equation 10-24 gives

$$r'_{xy} = \frac{r_{xy} - r_{zx}r_{zy} + r_{zx}r_{zy}(\sigma'^2_z/\sigma^2_z)}{\sqrt{[1 - r^2_{zx} + r^2_{zx}(\sigma'^2_z/\sigma^2_z)][1 - r^2_{zy} + r^2_{zy}(\sigma'^2_z/\sigma^2_z)]}} \tag{10-26}$$

Equation 10-26 shows what the validity of a predictor, $r'_{xy}$, would be if we deliberately reduced the variation in scores on variable $Z$ from $\sigma_z$ to $\sigma'_z$. Although not really complicated, the above formulas are long and noxious-appearing, so it may (or may not) help matters to consult Figure 10-3. In this figure we can see that as the variation in $Z$ scores is reduced, that is, as $\sigma'_z/\sigma_z$ becomes smaller, the validity of the test, $r'_{xy}$, also becomes smaller. It will also be seen that the lower the correlation between the restricted variable ($Z$) and the predictor ($X$) and the criterion ($Y$), the less will be the effect of restriction of range on the validity coefficient. In some extreme cases where the correlation between the restricted variable and both the predictor and the criterion is higher than the correlation between the predictor and the criterion, restriction of range may even change a positive relationship to a negative one. It is therefore obvious that if a test is validated on a group whose scores are restricted on another variable, which is related to both the predictor and the criterion, the validity coefficient will be underestimated.

Equation 10-26 shows that the validity coefficient will be reduced as the variation in scores on variable $Z$ is reduced. Ordinarily we have data on a group with restricted range and wish to estimate what the validity coefficient would be if we had the total range. That is, we want to know $r_{xy}$ rather than $r'_{xy}$. To obtain this value, we start with Equations 10-18 and 10-19, solving for $r_{zx}$ and $r_{zy}$. The solution is parallel to that for $r'_{xy}$, so that, equivalent to Equation 10-26, we can write

$$r_{xy} = \frac{r'_{xy} - r'_{zx}r'_{zy} + r'_{zx}r'_{zy}(\sigma^2_z/\sigma'^2_z)}{\sqrt{[1 - r'^2_{zx} + r'^2_{zx}(\sigma^2_z/\sigma'^2_z)][1 - r'^2_{zy} + r'^2_{zy}(\sigma^2_z/\sigma'^2_z)]}} \tag{10-27}$$

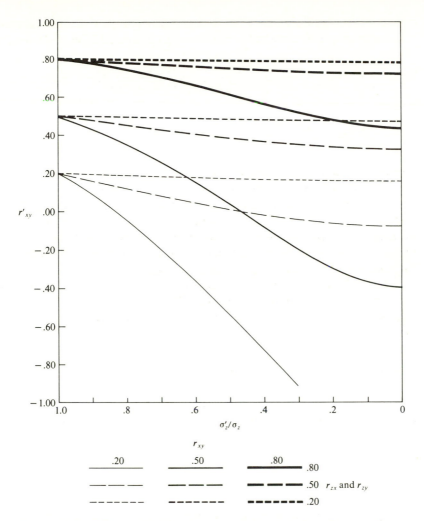

*Figure 10-3*    Effects of deliberate or explicit restriction of range of scores on variable $Z$ on validity coefficient ($r_{xy}$).

Suppose that students are admitted to college on the basis of their high school grade average, the standard deviation of the grade average of all applicants being .50 and that for those who are accepted being .25. Let us say that we wish to determine the validity of a scholastic aptitude test and administer it to entering freshmen, the high school graduates who have acceptable grades. Suppose we find with this selected group that the validity of high school grade average, $Z$, in predicting college grades is .30 ($r'_{zy}$), the validity of the scholastic aptitude test is .40 ($r'_{xy}$), and the correlation between high school grade average and scores on the scholastic aptitude test is .20 ($r'_{zx}$). We can estimate the validity for the entire range of applicants ($r_{xy}$) from Equation 10-27 as follows:

$$r_{xy} = \frac{.40 - (.20)(.30) + (.20)(.30)[(.50)^2/(.25)^2]}{\sqrt{\{1 - (.20)^2 + (.20)^2[(.50)^2/(.25)^2]\}\{1 - (.30)^2 + (.30)^2[(.50)^2/(.25)^2]\}}}$$

$$= \frac{.58}{\sqrt{1.42}} = .49$$

***Summary comment on restriction of range***    Our attempt to keep this story short was not very successful, and we apologize for that. Do not get too bogged down in the details of the formulas. The important things are to understand the assumptions on which they are based and to match the data you have with the parameters you want to estimate. Make sure the distinctions between direct and incidental selection and the variables involved in each are kept clear.

When used appropriately, the correction for reduction of range is a valuable aid in the interpretation of criterion-related validity. It can help give a fairer picture of what the actual validity of a predictor will be.

## Alternative Indices of Validity

During recent years considerable discussion has centered around the appropriate index for assessing criterion-related validity. As we have already noted, the conventional index is the Pearsonian correlation coefficient, which is imbedded in the so-called classical validity model in the form of the normal bivariate distribution. The model implies that (1) there is one normally distributed criterion or criterion composite, (2) there is one normally distributed predictor or predictor composite, (3) the relationship between them is linear and homoscedastic, and (4) the index of validity is some form of the product moment correlation coefficient.

Alternatives to the one predictor–one criterion configuration have been proposed, and these are discussed elsewhere in this book. What concerns us here is the role of the correlation coefficient itself.

As an index of the level of practical predictive accuracy, the product moment coefficient is not that easy to translate into meaningful terms. How useful is a value of .55? Most people have a feeling that .55 is reasonably good, but they would be hard-pressed to say why explicitly. Pointing to the relative magnitude of the standard error of estimate [$SE_{est} = \sigma_y \sqrt{1 - r^2_{xy}}$] is one kind of answer, but even here the meaning is not always perfectly clear.

## Decision Accuracy

Another alternative is to think of the prediction problem as a task in predicting *discrete* criterion outcomes. Almost all practical situations can be translated into the problem of predicting "criterion categories" of various kinds, the most frequent being success and failure. Once the problem is recast in these terms, it becomes meaningful to talk about validity, or accuracy, as the proportion of correct predictions.

If the variable to be predicted is a dichotomy, the bivariate distribution reduces to a fourfold table and four different outcomes are possible: (1) correctly predict the high-criterion category, (2) correctly predict the low-criterion category, (3) overpredict (false positive), and (4) underpredict (false negative). This simple arrangement is shown in Figure 10-4.

Certain things can be discerned from looking at the figure. In general, the relative proportion of correct predictions versus errors in prediction is a function of three principal factors. The first factor is the criterion "split" that defines the two criterion categories (for example, success/failure). Although this statement is offered without proof, it is true that (other things being equal) the greatest *gains* in accuracy from using new and more valid predictors occur when the split is 50–50. In general, this is because the variance of a dichotomous variable is equal to $P \times Q$, where $P$ and $Q$ are the two proportions, and the variance is at a maximum when $P = Q = .50$. As we have seen before, the greater the variance, the greater the potential relationship with the predictor. The proportion of people in the high-criterion group is often called the *base rate for success,* or simply the *base rate.*

The second factor is the *cutting score* on the predictor, or the predictor score above which we predict success and below which we predict failure. The cutting score is under the control of the decisionmaker, and one can see that as it is set higher or lower, the relative number of observations in the four cells will change accordingly. However, by changing the cutting score, and nothing else, we can reduce the frequency of one kind of error only at the expense of increasing the second kind.

Finally, the relative number of hits and misses is a function of the degree of association between the predictor and the criterion. The higher the correlation, the "narrower" the bivariate distribution; and the greater the percentage of cases in cells $A$ and $B$, the fewer the percentage of cases in cells $C$ and $D$.

One can also see from the figure that the two different kinds of errors are affected differentially by changes in the cutting score and in the base rate. For example, moving the cutting score to the right reduces the proportion of false positives at the expense of more false negatives.

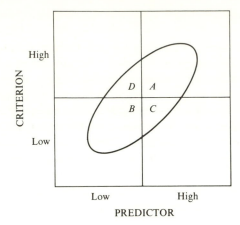

*Figure 10-4* Continuous bivariate distribution between predictor and criterion reduced to dichotomous prediction decision.

The Taylor–Russell tables (1939), shown in Appendix B, take advantage of this fact and portray the increase in the percentage of correct predictions over and above the base rate as the cutting score is raised, given a particular *selection ratio* (percentage hired) and correlation coefficient. The tables do this by assuming that both predictor and criterion are actually continuous and that their joint distribution is bivariate normal. Then the mathematical description of the bivariate distribution can be used to specify the areas (percentage of cases) above or below any particular cutting score or base rate. However, the tables deal with only one kind of error—false positives—and one kind of correct prediction—high hits. Thus, in the Taylor–Russell sense the increase in the percentage of correct predictions is

$$\% \text{ increase} = \frac{A}{A + C} - \frac{A + D}{A + B + C + D}$$

The latter quantity is simply the base rate. What is often forgotten is that this choice of an accuracy statistic is very much a value judgment by somebody. Traditionally, the false positive (cell *C* in Figure 10-4) may indeed have been the prediction mistake to avoid in personnel or educational selection. However, the weight of public policy is often in favor of minimizing the false negative (cell *D*), especially with regard to minority and disadvantaged groups. It seems safe to predict that our society will endure considerable conflict and soul-searching before the issue of who bears the implicit and explicit costs of both false positives and false negatives is decided. Nevertheless, it must be considered, and the issue is obscured by looking only at the correlation coefficient as an index of accuracy.

Relative to the base rate, maximum gain in decision accuracy from a specific validity coefficient is obtained when the base rate equals .50. Again this is nothing more than a restatement of the fact that for a dichotomous variable, the variance is at a maximum when $P = Q = .50$. As the base rate becomes more extreme in either direction, achieving large increases in the number of correct decisions becomes progressively more difficult (that is, it takes greater validity and/or smaller selection ratios). At some point, when the increase in correct decisions is compared to the cost of prediction, the prediction system may not seem worth it. If the proportion of people who fail is very small, it may make more sense to use the base rate and predict "success" for everyone. In a selection situation we might then select on the basis of first-come/first-served, random assignment, or some other strategy deemed as equitable by prevailing community standards. If the proportion of people who succeed is very small, the situation is a bit different. In a personnel selection situation nobody would be hired if we used the base rate to predict. It would make more sense to restructure the applicant pool to increase the relative number of talented people and thus make the base rate less extreme. To take an obvious but extreme example, we could accept as applicants only those individuals who have successfully performed the job in the past in some other organization (for example, university presidents).

As will be explained more fully in a moment, we can assert that if the predictor has greater than zero validity, there will almost always be *some* improvement in predictive accuracy in excess of the base rate, although it may not be great. The "almost" will be examined below. It is also true that under certain conditions the base rate can be beaten even when a predictor has *zero* validity (in the correlational sense), but let's ignore these unnamed conditions for the moment.

If, as in the Taylor–Russell tables, the primary concern is with the false positives, the base rate can be beaten by setting a higher and higher predictor cutting score. However, if the total number of errors $(C + D)$ is important, then the base rate can still be beaten if the cutting score is set at the point where the predictor distributions for the high- and low-criterion groups intersect as in Figure 10-5a. This rule holds even for peculiar distributions, as when there are two points of intersection (Figure 10-5b). In this instance, applicants would be accepted if they scored between the two cutting scores ($CS_1$ and $CS_2$) and rejected otherwise. The classic example concerns aptitude measures as a predictor and a criterion that individuals below $CS_1$ are not capable of meeting and people above $CS_2$ are too uninterested to meet. However, we should keep in mind that if the cutting scores are not set properly,

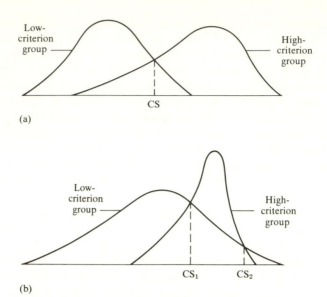

*Figure 10-5* Optimal cutting scores when objective is to minimize total number of prediction errors (that is, false positives + false negatives).

even a valid predictor can yield less accuracy than the base rate. For example, if the base rate is high (a large percentage of the unselected group would succeed) and the cutting score is set too high, a slightly higher percentage of high hits will be identified at the cost of many more false negatives.

Notice that focusing on the specific proportion of correct predictions in a particular situation, rather than the correlation coefficient, makes no assumptions about the form of the distribution and takes advantage of the nonlinear as well as linear components of association between the two variables. If the bivariate distribution is heteroscedastic, then predictions may be better at one end than the other (that is, successes or failures). As always, we are faced with the question of whether departures from the normal bivariate distribution are real or merely reflect sampling error. If we opt for the latter, then it might be more advantageous in the long run to "smooth out" the frequencies in the fourfold table by computing the product moment correlation and converting the coefficient to the corresponding proportions of hits and misses via the Taylor–Russell tables, if both predictor and criterion are dichotomous. However, even though the correlation coefficient may underestimate the degree of association in a truly curvilinear relationship, if the variables are continuous, the phi coefficient will overestimate the relative number of correct predictions when the variables are dichotomous and the splits depart very much from 50–50. Thus under these conditions entering a phi coefficient in the Taylor–Russell tables would be inappropriate.

At this point it might be informative to ask how the correlation coefficient is related to the proportion of correct predictions if the bivariate distribution is indeed linear and homoscedastic. Curtis and Alf (1969) have shown that the proportion of total correct predictions—that is, considering both kinds $(A + B)/(A + B + C + D)$—is a near-linear function of $r$, not $r^2$. Thus an increase in predictability from $r_{xy} = .20$ to $r_{xy} = .40$ is as valuable as an increase from .50 to .70, providing we accept the proportion of total correct predictions as the appropriate index. Further, Brogden (1946) has shown that the difference, or increase, in the criterion mean when the selected group is compared to the unselected group is also a linear function of $r_{xy}$.

A more elaborate set of tables for converting a correlation coefficient to frequencies of correct predictions has been provided by Tiffin and McCormick (1965). In the Tiffin and McCormick tables the predictor distribution (assumed to be normal) is divided into five equal portions (0–20th percentile, 20–40th percentile, and so on). For a specific criterion base rate and a specific value for the validity coefficient, the percentage of people *in each score range* on the predictor who fall in the high-criterion, or success, category is specified. The situation is as portrayed in Figure 10-6.

The tables presented by Tiffin and McCormick are called *expectancy tables* or *expectancy charts*. When the percentages of expected successes are obtained by using the areas specified by the normal bivariate distribution corresponding to a particular correlation, the table is called a *theoretical expectancy chart*. If the observed percentages obtained from a specific sample are entered in the table, then it is referred to as an *empirical expectancy chart*.

The correlation coefficient can be transformed to its equivalent increase in the criterion mean via the Naylor–Shine tables (Blum and Naylor, 1968). These are analogous to the Taylor–Russell tables, but the focus is on the increase in the mean criterion score, not the increase in the percentage of correct predictions. The existing criterion distribution in the organization is assumed to be unit normal, and the validity coefficient is taken as a concurrent validity coefficient computed on the existing organizational population that has been selected by whatever procedures were previously in use. Then for a particular selection ratio, the increase in the criterion mean (in standard-score units) that would be obtained by employing the new selection method can be read from the table. Keep in mind that using the Naylor–Shine tables, or for that matter the Taylor–Russell tables, to convert $r_{xy}$ to a more meaningful index is dependent on the degree of *linear association*.

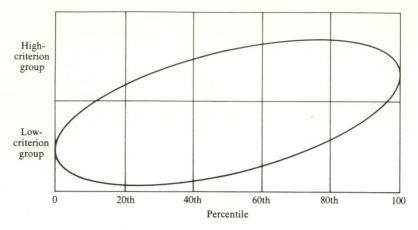

*Figure 10-6*  Normal bivariate distribution partitioned by dichotomous criterion and predictor distribution divided into quintiles.

### More Complex Situations

The above discussion of cutting scores and errors of prediction has been fairly simpleminded in terms of all the relevant parameters that might possibly be involved. Again the appropriate portrayal of the cutting score(s) and the resulting prediction errors is a plot of the predictor distributions for both criterion groups, as in Figure 10-5. Consider a list of all the parameters contained in this picture:

1. The difference between the means of the two distributions (validity).
2. The relative number of observations in the two distributions (base rate).
3. The cutting score(s).
4. The shape of each distribution.
5. The difference between the standard deviations of each distribution.

So far we have discussed some of the implications of differences in validity, base rate, and cutting score, as well as touching on the problem of the shape of the distribution. We have said nothing about what happens when the variability of the two distributions is different and have been implicitly assuming they are the same.

We observed previously that if the base rates depart very far from 50–50, relatively small changes in the cutting score can lead to relatively large changes in the number of prediction errors. The same danger arises when the standard deviations of the two distributions begin to depart from each other. When the base rate departs from 50–50 *and* the standard deviations depart from equality, things really begin to get complicated. For example, it is possible for no cutting scores to exist (as in Figure 10-7a). Here one distribution is completely contained in the other because the base rate for success is very high, meaning that not very many people "fail," and the standard deviation for the low-criterion group is relatively small. In this situation, *even though the mean predictor scores for the two groups differ,* any cutting score that is chosen will yield many more additional errors than additional correct predictions.

On the other side of the coin, it is also true that even though the predictor means for the two criterion groups may be identical (as in Figure 10-7b), and "validity" therefore is zero, the proper cutting scores may still be able to improve the accuracy of prediction over and above the base rate. The leverage for this seemingly incongruous result is provided by the difference in standard deviations. One can "fail" on this criterion by possessing too much or too little of the attribute measured by the predictor score (intelligence, interest in artistic/creative tasks, and so on). It is the people who possess a moderate amount that do best. Consequently, by setting two cutting scores and predicting success for those in the middle, the increase in correct predictions is greater than the increase in errors of prediction.

### From Accuracy to Utility

We have now moved from a notion of predictive validity in the form of a correlation coefficient to predictive accuracy in the form of the proportion of correct predictions in excess of the base rate. One could still wonder about how to interpret the value of a particular increase in predictive accuracy. Given a specific base rate, is the value of a 15 percent increase in predictive accuracy always the same?

In their now classic statements on this issue, Brogden (1949) and Cronbach and Gleser (1965) have reminded us that it is not. The *value* of an increase in predictive accuracy is dependent on the *costs* associated with obtaining it versus the *payoffs* or benefits obtained from each additional correct prediction. For example, in most situations the costs of increasing predictive accuracy for selecting people into managerial positions may be considerable, but they pale beside the payoff from making even one more correct selection decision. In short this argument moves us from a concern with predictive validity and predictive accuracy to a concern for predictive usefulness.

The Cronbach and Gleser presentation of these ideas has become a

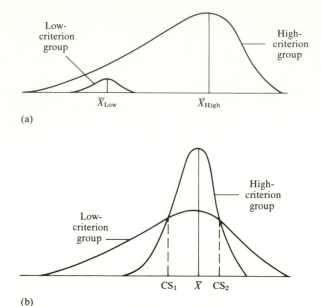

*Figure 10-7*  Effects of extreme differences in base rates and predictor variances on dichotomous prediction decisions. (a) Predict success for everyone. (b) Predict success for individuals between $CS_1$ and $CS_2$.

classic in spite of the fact that their prescriptions for how to judge utility make considerable demands on our measurement technology and may not always be possible to implement. Much of the value of these formulations lies instead in posing the very central issues that always must be considered in any prediction situation, however imperfectly, and they deserve at least a brief summary here.

The basic notions were first advanced by Brogden (1949) and went something like this. Suppose criterion scores ($Y$) are expressed in terms of the overall value or benefit they represent (for example, an individual performer's economic value, in dollar terms, to the organization). Further recall that the simple linear regression coefficient $b_{y \cdot x}$ discussed in Chapters 5 and 6 can be represented as

$$b_{yx} = r_{xy} \left( \frac{\sigma_y}{\sigma_x} \right)$$

As before, the simple linear regression equation then becomes

$$Y_i' = A_{y \cdot x} + r_{xy} \left( \frac{\sigma_y}{\sigma_x} \right) \cdot X_i$$

Now suppose we express the predictor $(X)$ in standard scores and the criterion $(Y)$ in deviation scores. The regression equation then becomes

$$Y_i' - \bar{Y} = r_{xy}(\sigma_y)(z_{x_i})$$

The constant $A$ disappears because we are subtracting the mean of the criterion scores from each individual score, and thus the intercept $(A)$ moves to zero on the $y$ axis. The standard deviation of the predictor score disappears because converting to standard scores makes $\sigma_x = 1.0$.

If the validity coefficient $r_{xy}$ is positive (hopefully), then $Y_i' - \bar{Y}$ is the *increase* in utility to be expected from using the predictor, as compared to random selection; that is, predicting $\bar{Y}$ for everybody. This quantity is usually referred to as $\Delta u_i$ (for the change in utility obtained by using the predictor).

To go just one step further, what we might like to have is the *average* gain in utility per person. One thing we could do is compute $\Delta u_i$ for each person and average them. However, if we are willing to assume that the predictor is normally distributed (still with mean zero and $\sigma_x = 1.0$), then the mean predictor score for those selected is $E(x')$, which is the height (or ordinate) of the normal curve at the point on the $x$ axis corresponding to the selection ratio. The equation for the average utility gain then becomes

$$\Delta u = r_{xy}\sigma_y E(x') \qquad (10\text{-}28)$$

It remained for Cronbach and Gleser (1965) to remind everyone that few things in life are free, and besides the benefits to be gained from using a particular predictor, there are also costs to be considered. Costs refer to such things as buying test booklets, training and/or paying additional interviewers, and the like. For some situations costs may be low (administering a 15-minute test), and in some cases they may be high (multiple interviews by a number of people flown to a central location).

Given the added component of cost, Cronbach and Gleser's basic definitional formula for the average gain in value associated with a predictor

$$\Delta u = r_{xy}\sigma_y E(x') - C_x \qquad (10\text{-}29)$$

where

$\Delta u$ = net gain in utility

$r_{xy}$ = validity coefficient obtained concurrently on *present* organizational population

$\sigma_y$ = standard deviation of payoff (criterion) distribution

$E(x')$ = ordinate of unit normal distribution at point on base line corresponding to cutting score (*selection ratio*) on predictor distribution

$C_x$ = cost of obtaining predictor information

To use this algorithm effectively, it should be computed for a variety of alternative predictors, including the one currently in use. If this could be done, the interaction of the validity and costs of prediction for different predictors would be made quite clear.

The problem, of course, is the metric for the payoff distribution. It must reflect the differential benefits of correct predictions associated with different jobs, different organizational needs, and so on. It seems obvious that the value for $\sigma_y$ would vary tremendously across situations. Also since the basic algorithm involves the correlation coefficient, another problem is the implication that payoff is linearly associated with the predictor continuum and that false positives and false negatives are given equal weight.

A number of interpretive principles flow from the utility-theory view, and Cronbach and Gleser worked out the mathematics for many of them. We summarize only a few of them here:

1. The predictor with the highest validity coefficient may not have the highest utility, compared to alternatives, if
   a. It is proportionately more costly than it is more valid.
   b. It predicts a criterion that is proportionately less important.

2. Even predictors with low validities may be very useful if $\sigma_y$ is large and the selection ratio is not too extreme.

3. If "adaptive treatments" are possible, then the gain in utility, given a particular gain in validity, is no longer a linear function, but becomes positively accelerated. For example, a validity increase of .40 to .60 is worth more and more to the extent that the sample can be partitioned, on the basis of the predictor score, and different training or different task assignments provided for the people in each category. For example, using a math aptitude test to select people for math instruction is more and more valuable to the extent that, high, low, and medium scorers can be given instruction appropriate for their level of readiness.

4. Relative to the choice among using two tests as a battery (that is, weighted sum), sequentially (for example, successive hurdles), or singly (just one of them), the model replies:
   a. As the selection ratio moves from .50 to the extremes, the strategy of choice goes from using both tests as a battery to using them sequentially, to using just one test. This pro-

gression is speeded up to the extent that the tests are inter-correlated and have different costs associated with them. Obviously, if the costs are quite different and the predictors are highly intercorrelated, it literally "pays" to use the cheapest one.

b. A similar progression of choices exists as the difference between the two validity coefficients becomes greater and greater—other things, such as intercorrelations and costs, being equal.

5. In sequential testing, the predictor given first is the one with the greatest difference between cost and benefit. This is in contrast to the more conventional wisdom, which says to use the most "valid" predictor first.

In sum, the Cronbach and Gleser treatment highlights a number of considerations that people interested in practical decisionmaking should keep in mind, although perfect answers to the questions posed by the model aren't always possible.

*Further Utility Considerations*

It may indeed be a difficult task to measure utility, but it is there nevertheless; and no matter what type of validity model is used, utilities play an important role even if unrecognized. For example, if we act as if the values of all kinds of errors are equal, we have made an implicit value judgment about utilities that may be so far from the "truth" (as judged by "reasonable" people) that the organization is seriously hurt because of it. If we ignore costs for the time being and again adopt a decisionmaking framework (for example, prediction of a dichotomous outcome), much ground can be regained if the *ratio* of the utilities for correct predictions of success and correct predictions of failure can be reasonably estimated.

Keep firmly in mind here that relative utilities and/or their ratios are value judgments by the management, stockholders, policymakers, citizens' groups, or whoever else has, or should have, a stake in the decision being made. Relative utilities result from whatever policymaking process is operating in a particular situation, and they should be argued about within this framework.

In some prediction situations the cutting scores may be a "given," as when the predictor is a single-test item that is scored right or wrong. For this situation there is a relatively simple method for trying out different utility ratios, such that the relative utility of using the predictor versus using the base rate can be determined.

Consider then the situation portrayed in Figure 10-8. The first matrix

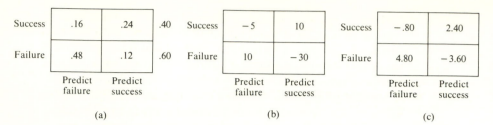

*Figure 10-8*  Relative utilities applied to dichotomous prediction decision with fixed cutting score (that is, proportion above CS = .36). (a) Proportion of total for each outcome state. (b) Relative utilities of each outcome. (c) Products of relative frequencies and relative utilities.

shows the proportions of people at each possible outcome. The second matrix shows a hypothetical set of relative utilities for each outcome. The third matrix contains the cross products for each cell.

The relative utility of using the predictor is the sum of the cell entries in matrix c, or +2.8. If we do not use the predictor, we can either predict success for everybody or predict failure for everybody. Our estimate of the base rate is that 40 percent of the population will succeed and 60 percent will fail. If we predict failure for everybody, the relative utility is (.60 × 10) + (.40 × −5) = 4.0. If we predict success for everybody, the relative utility is (.60 × −30) + (.40 × 10) = −14.0. Obviously predicting success for everybody is not the thing to do, and predicting failure for everybody is somewhat better than using the predictor. However, if the *costs* of not filling the job outweigh the *gain* in overall utility from hiring no one, the predictor should be used. The thing that produced this result is the relatively small utility assigned to someone who succeeds. However, if these relative utilities are deemed reasonable, the moral is that a rough but reasonable assignment of relative utilities can give a more detailed picture of what's going on in a selection situation than we have without an assignment of relative utilities.

### Summary Comment on Criterion-Related Indices

There is no easy "cookbook" one can follow to select the way in which criterion-related validity should be portrayed. If the linear and homoscedastic correlation model is deemed an appropriate representation of the form of the relationship between predictor and criterion, then the correlation coefficient is the place to start. It is an indication of the extent to which the variability in the criterion can be accounted for by the factors measured by the predictor. For certain conceptual questions (for example, "To what extent does garden-variety anxiety relate to number of days of illness per year?") that may be sufficient and appropriate.

However, criterion-related validities are usually obtained to aid us in making some kind of decision about individuals (hire/not hire, admit/not admit, treat/not treat) and therefore should be interpreted in a decisionmaking context. When this is done, we must face questions such as: How many predictor (decision) categories should there be? How many criterion (outcome) categories should there be? How should they be defined; that is, what are the base rate and cutting score(s)? When viewed this way, it is readily apparent that a given validity (correlation) coefficient may be more or less useful depending on the base rate and cutting score (selection ratio). For example, if the base rate is near 50–50 and the cutting score can be set fairly high, even very small validity coefficients can improve decisionmaking accuracy by a significant amount. In general the crucial consideration here is the precise specification of the decision for which the information is to be used.

After the nature of the decision under consideration has been specified, questions of costs and benefits *must* also be considered. Even if costs and benefits can't be measured precisely, "all available" information should be examined and the value judgments of the relevant people involved should be reviewed. To use a predictor wisely, we simply must find out as much as possible about the costs of prediction (both direct and indirect), the benefits to be gained from correct predictions, and the costs of making errors. If there are genuine conflicts over the magnitude of the consequences of various errors, these must be confronted directly. For example, is it worse to admit people who will fail than not to admit someone who would have succeeded? Psychometric theory cannot provide the answers. Society itself must do so.

## Equal Opportunity and Concepts of Validity and Fairness

There is one last complicating factor in the criterion-related validity picture that we must discuss. While it is not really a formal part of psychometric theory, it often becomes the paramount issue when validity models are used in applied settings, and it reflects one of the most fundamental social problems in U.S. society. We are speaking of equal educational and employment opportunity considerations as embodied in Title VII of the Civil Rights Act of 1964. Does a predictor discriminate against members of various minority groups in employment or educational selection? Can a predictor be valid and discriminatory (unfair) at the same time? If so, what can be done to insure that prediction decisions are both valid *and* fair?

These are important questions, and they are most often considered in the context of comparing the effects of prediction rules for women versus men or minority versus majority groups in educational or job selection. Unfortunately they are not precisely answerable, for reasons we will come to. Also they incorporate a number of important value judgments that cannot be made by appealing to psychometric theory or to some other algorithmic solution. Our brief discussion attempts only to highlight the major issues and to identify some of the more important value judgments.

The situation is further complicated because there are different definitions of discrimination, or fairness, among which it is not easy to choose. In general fairness refers to whether a difference in mean predictor scores between two groups represents a useful distinction for society, relative to a decision that must be made, or whether the difference represents a bias that is irrelevant to the objectives at hand (for example, selecting good people for law school).

### When Predictor *"Fairness"* Is a Problem

In general, in an applied prediction setting, the signal for when to worry about the fairness of a predictor is when there is *adverse impact*. Adverse impact occurs when, for the groups under consideration, the proportion of people selected from each group differs substantially from their relative proportion in the total available applicant population. For example, if a minority group constitutes 35 percent of the available applicants, but only 5 percent of those eventually selected, adverse impact has occurred. The question is then whether the adverse impact is in some sense "justifiable." If the situation involves using one predictor score to make selection decisions, adverse impact is mirrored by a difference in mean predictor scores for the two groups.

How should this difference be interpreted? Does it reflect a corresponding criterion difference? Does it reflect discriminatory practices that have nothing to do with criterion performance? Should different prediction rules be used for the two groups so as to remedy the adverse impact brought on by the group differences in predictor scores? As always, we cannot proceed very far in answering these questions unless we adopt some sort of model of the situation that permits a distinction between validity and fairness. Unfortunately, as you have probably also guessed, there are several models from which to choose. They differ in the assumptions they make and the conclusions (that is, remedies) they suggest. Most of the distinctions are a function of value judgments that someone must make, and not the result of formal measurement-theory considerations. For this reason the multiplicity of models is useful. That is, they force us to think through what is algebra and what are value judgments, and they help to spell out the specific value judgments that must be made.

### Alternative Models of Predictor Fairness

Currently there are a number of models of predictor fairness over which there is much argument, and a full treatment of their algebraic, legal, and national policy implications are far beyond the scope of this book. We can only outline what we think are the most important issues, with due apologies to those people who have contributed much more.

The basic situation considered by almost all models is when the people in each of two groups (male versus female or majority versus minority) are all measured on a predictor $X$ and a criterion $Y$. Thus the overall univariate distributions on $X$ and $Y$ can be separated into distributions on $X$ and on $Y$ for each subgroup, and the overall bivariate distribution can be separated into bivariate distributions for each subgroup. Consequently there are a mean and a variance for each group on $X$ and $Y$ and a regression line for each group. To simplify things, let us worry no further about differences in variances between the two groups or about whether the two regression lines have unequal slopes. The crucial features are the differences in means for $X$ and $Y$ and the differences in intercepts for the regression lines. Differences in means and intercepts allow for considerable variation in situations that might be observed. Consider the four variations shown in Figure 10-9.

In Figure 10-9a the two groups are on the same regression line (that is, they have the same intercept), and, relatively speaking, the difference between the predictor means is greater than the difference between the criterion means. For the situation Figure 10-9b there is no mean difference in criterion performance, but there is a large mean difference on the predictor. Many people would regard this as a case of pure discrimination. The two groups exhibit comparable criterion performance; but for any cutting score that is set, many more members of group II will be selected. In Figure 10-9c the situation is the converse; while there are no mean differences on the predictor, there is a large difference in mean performance on the criterion. Such a picture may result from discrimination or bias in the performance measure, as when members of a minority group are rated lower (or higher) simply because of their group membership. Although unusual, it is also possible for such a situation to exist in the real world. If groups I and II are female and male respectively, if the predictor is a test of general intelligence,

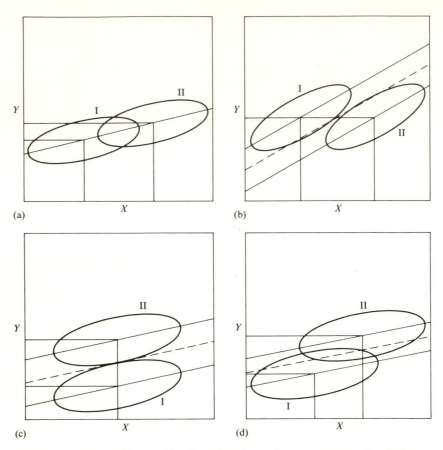

*Figure 10-9*    Four different bivariate situations when two groups (I and II) are measured on predictor (*X*) and criterion (*Y*).

and if the criterion requires *both* intellectual ability *and* physical strength, a picture such as Figure 10-9c could be obtained.

Given this basic portrayal of the validity-and-fairness picture, we can turn to some alternative models for identifying which is which. The thing to watch for is how the models treat the relative differences between the predictor and criterion means for the two groups. Are they "real" differences, or are they the result of discrimination? If it is the latter, what sort of remedy does the model suggest?

*Quota model*    The simplest formulation, and perhaps the easiest to deal with in a public-policy sense, is the *quota model*. From this point of view the difference, if any, in criterion means is ignored, and the difference between predictor means is regarded as bias. The remedy then is to select people in equal proportions by ranking the people within each group on the predictor and admitting the appropriate percentage of high scorers.

In many situations this might be quite justifiable. It may even be justifiable to go further and select a higher proportion of people from the minority group. The payoff, in terms of providing new role models, for example, may surpass the cost of any loss in validity.

One factor that complicates the quota model is that in real life the two groups of applicants are seldom sampled from comparable populations. That is, one group may be systematically more highly trained or experienced than the other, one group may be older, or in some sense or other one group may be a more highly select sample from its own reference population. Many such differences can result because the recruiting process for the two groups is very different. For example, if professional schools such as law and medicine were guilty in the past of discrimination against women, and admitted only a very few, then it is reasonable to assume that the female applicant pool was much more highly self-selected and therefore of higher average ability than was the male applicant pool. In general, even though the average predictor scores for the two groups may be equal in the general population, the recruitment process seldom draws comparable samples from the population and thus the predictor means may differ somewhat, not because of predictor bias but because of noncomparable recruitment.

One way to account for such nondiscriminatory group differences on the predictor is to examine group differences, if any, on the criterion, in light of the relationship between predictor and criterion (that is, validity). A number of models attempt to specify how these predictor and criterion differences should be interpreted, and it is to some of these that we now turn.

*Regression model*    Within the context of psychometric theory, perhaps the most popular model for conceptualizing predictor fairness is the *regression model* or *classical model* of predictor "bias." This model stipulates that no bias exists if the bivariate distributions for the two groups fall on a common regression line, as in Figure 10-9a. The test for fairness then is to compute the common regression equation for the two groups combined and to determine whether the criterion performance of the people in either group is systematically over- or underpredicted. For example, consider Figure 10-9d in which the dotted line represents the common regression line. For any given predictor score the performance of people in group I will be systematically overpredicted, and the performance of people in group II will be systematically underpredicted. Also, for any given cutting score on $X$, a greater proportion of group II will be selected.

The remedy suggested by the model is to generate a separate regression equation for each group. That is, the slope $b_{y \cdot x}$ and the intercept $A_{y \cdot x}$ are computed for each group, and each individual's predicted criterion score $Y'$ is computed using the regression line of the appropriate group. The people with the highest predicted criterion scores are then selected. That is, the cutting score is not on the predictor distribution, but on the combined distribution of predicted criterion scores. Such a model will maximize the performance of the selected group and for this reason should be valued by the organization doing the selecting.

The effect of the regression model's remedy on the relative proportions of people selected from the two groups depends on the nature of the situation. In Figure 10-9b using a common regression line would select a greater percentage of group II than group I. The regression model would select them in equal proportions. In Figure 10-9c a single cutting score based on a common regression line would select in equal proportions, but the regression model would take a much higher percentage of people from group II. These are the two extremes. For situations "in between," such as in Figure 10-9d, the relative proportions admitted using the common regression line versus using the regression model must be determined for each specific case.

Regardless of the relative proportion selected in a given situation, it is important to note that the regression model equates fairness to the individual with unbiased prediction. That is, if a prediction rule does not systematically over- or underpredict for individuals with a particular predictor score, it is said to be "fair." Thus the regression model uses the observed group differences in criterion scores to "interpret" group differences on the predictor via the least-squares rule. If, as in Figure 10-9b, there are no criterion differences, then all of the differences between groups on the predictor are interpreted as bias and it is remedied by using separate regression equations.

*Equal-risk model*    The *equal-risk model* of fairness attributed to Einhorn and Bass (1971) is built on a definition of selection fairness proposed by Guion (1966), which states that people with an equal probability of being successful on the job should have an equal probability of being hired. In essence what the equal-risk model does is to argue that selection is fair if the probability of failure (or success) *for those people selected* is the same for the two groups. To achieve this goal, the strategy is to set the cutting scores for the two groups on the predictor so as to equate the risk. The method begins by selecting a point on the criterion distribution as the minimal acceptable level of performance. Next it considers the people from both groups all of whom have the same predicted criterion score. *If* the standard error of estimate (that is, the variation within columns) is not the same for the two groups, then the risk (that is, the probability) of falling below the minimal acceptable level of performance is also not the same for the two groups. The level of risk (proportion of people in the column distribution falling below a certain point on $Y$) can be adjusted by selecting a different cutting score on $X$ and moving up or down to a different column. Specifying the complete procedure by which the cutting scores are set is a bit too long a story to be recounted here, but the outcome is to select individuals from the two groups who have an equal risk of failure or an equal probability of success.

Thus instead of selecting only people with the highest predicted criterion scores, as does the regression model, the equal-risk model equates the probability of making the success/fail prediction correctly for the two groups. If the regression lines for the two groups are parallel and the standard errors of measurement are equal for the two groups then the equal-risk model is equivalent to the regression model.

*Constant-ratio model*    An example of a different class of fairness models is the *constant-ratio model* originally proposed by Thorndike (1971). This model first partitions the bivariate distribution into the same quadrants, or cells, shown in Figure 10-4 and defines them in the same way. Fairness is then defined as a situation in which, for a particular group, the percentage of people that succeed on the criterion is the same as the percentage that pass the cutting score on the predictor. Thus if 50 percent of a minority group and 70 percent of a majority group succeed on a criterion, but 30 percent of the minority group and 80 percent of the majority group pass the original cutting score on the predictor, two new cutting scores must be set on the predictor such that 50 percent of the minority group and 70 percent of the majority group are selected.

Several things are noteworthy about this model. First it does not deal with continuous criterion scores, but only with the dichotomous success/fail outcome. However, for purposes of specifying which part of the predictor difference is due to discrimination and which is not, it transforms predictor and criterion scores to percentiles. Percentile differences between the criterion means of the two groups are assumed to represent real differences in criterion performance, not bias. Comparing the constant-ratio method to the regression model and the equal-risk model is difficult. They are all the same if the regression slopes and standard errors of measurement are equal and if the mean criterion score is the same for the two groups, as in Figure 10-9b. If the scores of the minority group are generally lower than the scores of the majority group, then the constant-ratio model will usually select a greater proportion of minority applicants than will the other models. In essence, this is because all people who exceed the criterion score that defines success are regarded as equally successful regardless of how high their criterion score actually is. So long as two individuals fall in the success category, the model does not distinguish between one who barely qualifies and one whose performance is two standard deviations higher. This gives the people in the lower distribution a greater chance of being selected than if the actual magnitude of the criterion scores were taken into account.

As regards criterion performance, the central issue here is: "How much is enough?" Can the organization sacrifice some of the top scorers for the sake of selecting a greater number of minority individuals? The answer to this question is the answer to the question of which model is the most appropriate in a given situation.

### Summary Comment on Validity and Fairness

With the exception of the quota model, all the fairness models just discussed interpret the mean difference in criterion scores between two groups as a real difference in performance. If there is racial or sex bias in the criterion, then the regression, equal-risk, and constant-ratio models must be further modified or discarded. At this point we can only say that one should worry about this issue and should try by every means possible to develop criterion measures that are free of such bias.

Assuming that criterion differences do, however, represent real performance differences, how then should we choose among the available models for promoting fairness? Ideally, two things are needed. First, we must have some notion of what the payoff (criterion) distribution, in Cronbach and Gleser terms, looks like. That is, what are higher and higher criterion scores worth to the organization? Does payoff become greater and greater, or do higher performance scores not produce much additional payoff once performance exceeds a certain critical point? Second, value judgments must be made as to the utility of correctly selecting additional members of minority groups, failing to select minority-group members who would have been successful, failing to select majority-group members who would be successful, and so on. Once these value judgments are made, it will be possible to choose among fairness models. We would then have some basis for trading off lower (or higher) average criterion scores for the increased (or decreased) participation of specific groups. These initial and fundamental questions are questions of value, and we all must face them.

---

## Summary

Perhaps the most fundamental distinction we can make within the entire topic of validity is that there are two principal themes. One theme concerns the validity of a predictor (or set of predictors) for making a specific prediction or decision. As we argued at some length in this chapter, the variable of principal interest here is the *criterion*. The predictor is of interest only insofar as it can be used as a substitute for the criterion. In this context we discussed a number of specific *criterion-related validity situations* (for example, predictive, concurrent, postdictive) and the identifying characteristics of each.

Keep in mind that while the objective of criterion-centered validity is to identify predictors that can be used in place of the criterion because the latter is too expensive or not available, at least one sample of individuals must be measured on both the predictor and the criterion. The indicator of validity is the degree of relationship between the predictor and criterion, and it is most often represented by the correlation coefficient. In this context a number of special issues surrounding criterion-related validity were discussed. Chief among them were the effects of unreliability and/or restriction of range on either the predictor or the criterion. There are "corrections" for the effects of unreliability and/or restriction of range that may be useful in some instances, but they must be used with extreme caution.

A major concern regarding criterion-related validity has to do with alternative ways to interpret or portray the usefulness of a particular magnitude of validity. The correlation coefficient is limited in this regard. In this chapter we discussed the rudiments of a *decisionmaking* and a *utility* approach to interpreting validity. The chief lesson to be learned is that the usefulness of a particular *validity coefficient* may vary considerably depending on a number of other characteristics of the situation (for example, base rate, selection ratio, values attached to different types of errors).

The second major theme in this chapter has to do with the validity of our understanding of what a particular set of operations measure. The focus here is not on the criterion, but on the meaning of the scores or the psychological variable of interest. *Content validity* and *construct validity* were discussed in this regard, and a variety of methods that can be used to establish such validities were considered. The touchstone of content validity is the judgment of experts regarding the degree to which the content of a measure constitutes a representative sample of the population of knowledges, skills, behaviors, or a variety of methods, some of which involve making predictions about how scores on the measure will be related to other observable events. The degree of construct validity is reflected by the degree of convergence of positive results from a series of relatively "demanding" empirical tests.

Finally we tried in this chapter to use what we have learned about the validity concept to illuminate some of the issues surrounding the problem of providing valid *and* nondiscriminatory prediction in the contexts of educational and employment selection. These issues are not easily resolved, and they incorporate both technical questions and value judgments. If only we can keep these two considerations distinct and not shy away from either, we will have achieved much.

## Suggested Readings

American Psychological Association. 1954. *Technical recommendations for psychological tests and diagnostic techniques.* Washington, D.C.: American Psychological Association.

American Psychological Association. 1966. *Standards for educational and psychological tests and manuals.* Washington, D.C.: American Psychological Association.

American Psychological Association, Division of Industrial–Organizational Psychology. 1980. *Principles for the validation and use of personnel selection procedures.* 2nd ed. Berkeley: American Psychological Association.

American Psychological Association, AERA, NCME. 1974. *Standards for educational and psychological tests.* Washington, D.C.: American Psychological Association.

Blum, M. L., and J. C. Naylor. 1968. *Industrial psychology: Its theoretical and social foundations.* Rev. ed. New York: Harper and Row.

Brogden, H. E. 1946. On the interpretation of the correlation coefficient as a measure of predictive efficiency. *Journal of Educational Psychology,* 37:65–76.

Brogden, H. E. When testing pays off. 1949. *Personnel Psychology,* 2:171–183.

Campbell, D. T., and D. W. Fiske. 1959. Convergent and discriminant validation by the multitrait–multimethod matrix. *Psychological Bulletin,* 56:81–105.

Cronbach, L. J., and G. Gleser. 1965. *Psychological tests and personnel decisions.* 2nd ed. Urbana: University of Illinois Press.

Cronbach, L. J., and P. E. Meehl. 1955. Construct validity in psychological tests. *Psychological Bulletin,* 52:281–302.

Curtis, E. W., and E. F. Alf. 1969. Validity, predictive efficiency, and practical significance of selection tests. *Journal of Applied Psychology,* 53:327–337.

Einhorn, H. J., and A. R. Bass. 1971. Methodological considerations relevant to discrimination in employment testing. *Psychological Bulletin,* 75:261–269.

Fleishman, E. A. 1975. Toward a taxonomy of human performance. *American Psychologist,* 30:1127–1149.

Guion, R. M. 1966. Employment tests and discriminatory hiring. *Industrial Relations,* 5:20–37.

Guion, R. M. 1978. Scoring of content domain samples. *Journal of Applied Psychology,* 63:499–506.

Taylor, H. C., and J. T. Russell. 1939. The relationship of validity coefficients to the practical validity of tests in selection: Discussion and tables. *Journal of Applied Psychology,* 23:565–578.

Thorndike, R. L. Concepts of culture fairness. 1971. *Journal of Educational Measurement,* 8:63–70.

Tiffin, J., and E. J. McCormick. 1965. *Industrial Psychology.* 5th ed. Englewood Cliffs, N.J.: Prentice-Hall.

Zedeck, S., and M. L. Tenopyr. Issues in selection, testing, and the law. In L. J. Hausman et al. (Eds.), *Equal rights and industrial relations.* Madison, Wis.: Industrial Relations Research Association, 1977. Pp. 167–195.

# 11

---

# *Multiple Regression and Differential Weighting*

In Chapters 5 and 6 we considered the relationship between two variables and the prediction of one variable from a second variable. That is, we considered simple correlation and regression. We examined the relationship between the two variables in terms of the proportion of accountable variation and the accuracy of prediction. Usually, with behavioral science data, a single variable predicts about 10–20 percent of the variance in another variable. Thus in many cases it is worthwhile to determine the proportion of accountable variation, or the accuracy of prediction of an outside variable or criterion, if we utilize two or more variables as predictors. The problem we are faced with is that we may want the two variables to carry equal weight or differential weights. The reason for the concern with weighting is that we can make the composite more predictive of the criterion variable or more precise, reliable, or meaningful. The basic question is whether we should simply add the composite or obtain optimal statistical weights. Should we use simple weights such as unit weights ($w = 1$), or equal weights, and then determine $R_{(w_1X_1+w_2X_2+\cdots+w_nX_n)\cdot Y}$, or should we obtain statistical weights (beta weights) that would maximize $R_{(b_1X_1+b_2X_2+\cdots+b_bX_n)\cdot Y}$? The answer to this question is a function of the amount of variance in the criterion variable that can be explained by the composite.

The attempt to use several variables to optimally predict a criterion involves multiple correlation and multiple regression. For example, success in college (as measured by grade-point average) is often predicted by a scholastic aptitude exam administered in the last year of high school. Suppose the relationship is $r = .30$. Thus the aptitude test accounts for 9 percent of the variance in grade-point average. We might want to see if the use of another predictor such as high school average, in conjunction with aptitude test scores would explain more than 9 percent of the college grade-point average. Multiple correlation and regression provides an index of the relationship between the criterion and the weighted composite. Since multiple regression is used, the weighted composite is based on a least-squares solution, and the weights of the variables are typically different. An alternative to multiple regression is to simply sum the two predictors, thereby *assuming* equal weights (as was essentially done in Chapter 7, on composites), or to develop some differential weighting scheme. In this chapter we examine differential weighting in terms of multiple regression weights and in terms of differential, general weighting.

## Multiple Correlation

Through the process termed *multiple correlation* we can obtain a set of optimal weights. When these optimal weights are multiplied by scores on the appropriate components to form a composite, the correlation between differentially weighted composite scores and scores on a criterion is at a maximum. The application of any other weights to the components would result in composite scores that bear a lower correlation with scores on the criterion.

Multiple correlation is similar to simple correlation, which we discussed in Chapter 5. Simple correlation tells us how well we can predict scores on one variable from scores on another, and multiple correlation tells how well we can predict scores on one variable from the optimally weighted composite of scores on several other variables. In simple correlation we deal with variation in one variable, holding constant variation in another; and in multiple correlation we are dealing with variation in one variable, simultaneously holding constant variation in a number of other variables. Just as we developed a regression equation for simple correlation, we shall develop a multiple regression equation; but the multiple regression equation is considerably more complicated than the regression equation in the case of the simple correlation between two variables. This multiple regression equation gives us the optimal pattern of weights we want. The multiple coefficient of correlation, symbolized as $R_{Y.12...k}$, where $Y$ is the criterion and 1 to $k$ the components forming the composite, gives us the magnitude of the correlation between the optimally weighted composite and the criterion.

## Multidimensional Scatter Diagram

When we are dealing with a correlation between two variables, the *scatter diagram* is represented on a flat surface or plane as a large square, and the columns and rows form a series of small squares or cells. The scatter diagram has two dimensions, $x_Y$ and $x_1$. We find the row representing a person's score on one variable and the column representing this person's score on the other and then plot his or her score in the cell at the intersection of the row and the column.

When we are dealing simultaneously with the relationships among a number of variables, our scatter diagram must have as many dimensions as there are variables. If there are $k$ variables, there are $k$ dimensions to our scatter diagram. If $k$ is 3, our scatter diagram takes the form of a cube with the three dimensions $x_Y$, $x_1$, and $x_2$. The cells now are little cubes in the big cube. A three-dimensional scatter diagram is shown in Figure 11-1. For each person there are three scores, $x_Y$, $x_1$, and $x_2$. When plotting an individual's scores, we find the row representing his or her score on one variable (for example, $x_1$) and the column representing his or her score on another variable (for example, $x_2$). If we look at Figure 11-1, we see that a "row" and a "column" are slices through the large cube. The intersection of these two slices or planes forms a vertical straight line. In Figure 11-1 the intersection is a "tower" of cells or small blocks. Now we locate in this tower the cell representing the individual's score on the last variable, $x_Y$. A tally in this cell represents the individual's scores on all three tests.

If we have more than three variables, we cannot, of course, represent the scatter diagram in this simple graphic fashion. We can, however, represent these variables mathematically. Indeed we have done this before. When we discussed composites, we presented various formulas in which a number of different variables or dimensions were represented. The regression equation as given in Equation 5-11 is a mathematical representation of the two dimensions in simple correlation. In deriving the multiple coefficient of correlation and formulas pertinent to it, we shall deal with the three-variable problem so that easy reference can be made to the scatter diagram in Figure 11-1; then we shall generalize these formulas to many dimensions. In subsequent notation we will represent the outside variable, or the criterion, or the dependent variable as $Y$; the other variables will be represented by $X$'s or the subscripts of the $X$'s (for example, 1, 2, . . . .).

## Correlation Between Two Variables with a Third Partialed-Out

As indicated above, a tally in one cell represents the individual's scores on all three tests. The underlying mathematical rationale of multiple

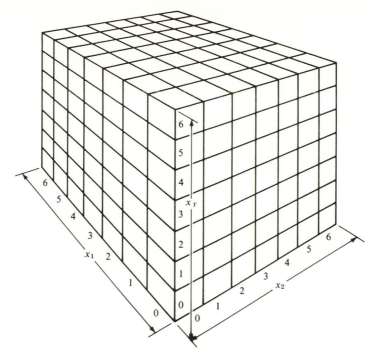

*Figure 11-1* Three-dimensional scatter diagram.

correlation, as we develop it, is a function of the relationship between the $Y$ and one predictor, with each of the other predictors held constant. That is, from simple correlation we know the relationship between $Y$ and $x_1$. If we add a second variable, $x_2$, what contribution does this make to criterion explanation? To determine the response, we can look at the relationships between $Y$ and $x_1$ with $x_2$ held constant and between $Y$ and $x_2$ with $x_1$ held constant. This rationale of holding one or more variables constant while examining the relationship between two other variables or, in other words, the process of partialing, is the essence of multiple regression.

To get a better picture of the process, suppose we take slices through the cube shown in Figure 11-2, say through variable 2. Then in any given slice all individuals have the same $x_2$ score. For these individuals $x_2$ is constant, but they still differ among themselves in variables $Y$ and 1. Each slice is a scatter diagram of the correlation between variables $Y$ and 1 when the effects of variable 2 have been held constant or partialed-out.

We could, of course, have taken slices through variable $x_1$. Then we would have had a series of scatter diagrams giving the relationship between $x_Y$ and $x_2$ with the effects of $x_1$ held constant. Indeed we could

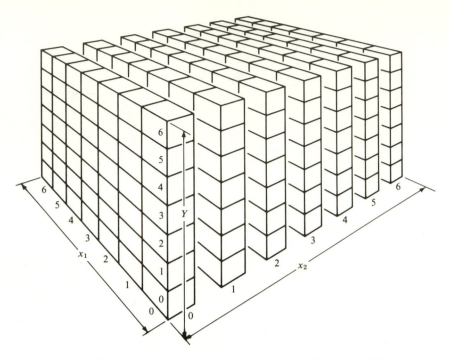

***Figure 11-2***  Slices through three-dimensional scatter diagram to illustrate correlation between variables $Y$ and $x_1$, with $x_2$ held constant.

have taken horizontal slices through variable $Y$, and then we would have had a series of scatter diagrams giving the relationship between $x_1$ and $x_2$ with the effects of $Y$ held constant.

### Multiple Correlation and Linearity of Relationships

In dealing with simple correlation, we saw that we could take linear relationships in either of two senses. First we could take linear relationships to refer only to those situations wherein the means of the scores in the columns and the means of the scores in the rows all fall precisely on straight lines. However, we saw this to be very restrictive since such a situation seldom if ever occurs. Therefore we saw the desirability of taking linear correlation as a model, using as regression lines not lines drawn through the means of the columns and rows but rather straight lines that are the best-fitting lines in a least-squares sense. We take linearity as our model and use the best-fitting straight line as the specific description of our model.

As we did with simple correlation, let us first take linear correlation to refer to the case where the means of the columns and rows fall precisely on straight lines. We have seen that slices through $x_2$ (Figure 11-2) give us a series of scatter diagrams representing the relationship between $x_1$ and $Y$. In each scatter diagram, of course, $x_2$ is constant. Now if there is no relationship at all between $x_1$ and $Y$, that is, if $r_{Y1} = .00$, then in each scatter diagram the means of the $Y$ scores in all the columns (towers) will be equal. Hence the regression line running through the means of the columns (towers) will be a straight line parallel to the base line $x_1$.

Now suppose that, in addition, $x_2$ and $Y$ are completely unrelated. Then in every slice through $x_1$—every slice being a scatter diagram of the relationship between $x_2$ and $Y$ with $x_1$ held constant—a similar state of affairs exists. That is, all the means of the $Y$ scores in the columns (towers) of $x_2$ are equal, and the regression line running through them is parallel to the base line $x_2$. Consequently, if both $x_1$ and $x_2$ are completely unrelated to $Y$, that is, $r_{Y1} = r_{Y2} = .00$, then the means in all the towers in Figure 11-1 are precisely equal to one another. This being the case, we could pass a plane through these points and all points would fall precisely on the plane.

Just as in simple correlation the regression line running through the means of the columns describes the relationship between one variable and another, so in multiple correlation where we are dealing with the relationship between two variables simultaneously ($x_1$ and $x_2$) and another variable ($Y$), the *plane* running through the means of the towers describes the relationship. This is shown graphically in Figure 11-3. In this figure the regression lines in all the slices through $x_1$ and through $x_2$ are shown, and the intersections of these lines are the means of the $Y$ scores in these columns.

Let us now consider the circumstance where $x_2$ and $Y$ are unrelated ($r_{Y2} = .00$), but $x_1$ and $Y$ are positively related. In every slice through $x_2$, which is a scatter diagram of the relationship between $x_1$ and $Y$, the means of the $Y$ scores in the columns (towers) fall on a straight line that runs diagonally across the slice. Recall, however, that since the relationship between $x_2$ and $Y$ is zero in every slice through $x_1$, which is a scatter diagram of the relationship between $x_2$ and $Y$, the means of the $Y$ scores in all the columns (towers) are equal and the line running through them is parallel to the base line $x_2$. However, these lines obviously are at different levels in the different slices through $x_1$, since $x_1$ and $Y$ are positively related. This is shown in Figure 11-4. Consequently a plane running through the means of the towers would be tilted.

If both $x_1$ and $x_2$ are positively related to $Y$, then the regression plane running through the means of the columns will be tilted in two dimen-

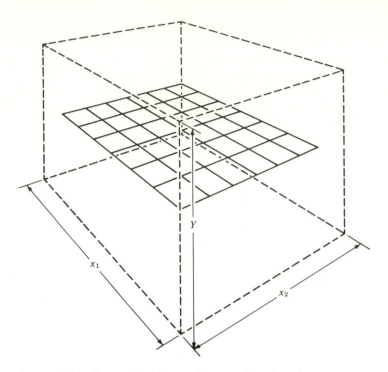

***Figure 11-3***   Regression lines and regression plane in
three-dimensional scatter diagram when $r_{Y1} = r_{Y2} = .00$.

sions, as is shown in Figure 11-5. In this case the correlation between
variables 1 and $Y$ is higher than the relationship between variables 2 and
$Y$; consequently the regression lines for $x_1$ and $Y$ are steeper than those
for $x_2$ and $Y$. The regression plane therefore tilts more in one direction
than in the other. If the relationship between either $x_1$ and $x_2$ with $Y$
were negative, then the tilt of the plane would be in the opposite direction.

Now if we take the regression lines in simple correlation not as
running through the means of the columns and rows but rather as the
best-fitting straight lines in a least-squares sense, then it follows that
the regression plane does not pass through the means of the towers, but
rather is the plane of best fit in a least-squares sense in the three-
dimensional scatter diagram. Thus the composite correlated with the
criterion is maximum. If we passed any other plane through the three-
dimensional scatter diagram, we would find that the sum or the mean of
the squares of the deviations of $Y$ from it would be greater. Of course in
this case a curved or irregular surface of some sort that does pass
precisely through the means of the towers would be the best-fitting

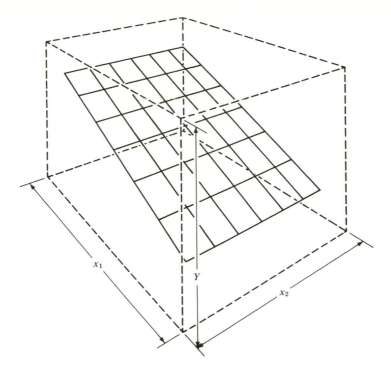

*Figure 11-4*   Regression lines and regression plane in three-dimensional scatter diagram when $r_{Y1}$ is positive and $r_{Y2} = .00$.

surface. But if we wish the simplicity and comprehensibility that go along with linearity, we must take a plane surface as our model, just as we take a straight line as our model in simple correlation.

### Variation in One Variable Holding Another Constant

Let us return to the two-variable problem and consider the relationship between $Y$ and $x_1$. Our scatter diagram is represented in two dimensions on a plane surface and is composed of rows and columns. Consider any given row described by $x_1$. All individuals in this row have the same $x_1$ score, but they differ in their scores on $Y$ (unless variables $Y$ and 1 are perfectly correlated). For individuals in this row the distribution of $Y$ scores describes the extent of variation in scores on test $Y$ when scores on test 1 are held constant.

Now we compute the mean of the $Y$ scores in this particular row. For each person who falls in this row let us subtract this mean $\bar{Y}_{x_1}$ from his

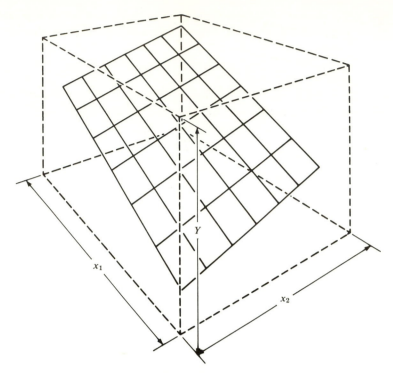

*Figure 11-5* Regression lines and regression plane in three-dimensional scatter diagram when both $r_{Y1}$ and $r_{Y2}$ are positive.

or her score $Y$. This gives us deviation scores in variable $Y$ with the effects of variable 1 held constant and therefore eliminated. We could go through this process for every row, obtaining deviation scores for each person on variable $Y$ with the effects of variable 1 held constant.

It will be recalled that we are dealing with linear correlation. Therefore the means of the rows all fall on the same straight line, or the regression line is taken as the estimates of the means. These means are described by the regression equation, which, from Equation 6-5, is

$$\bar{y}_{x_1} = b_{y \cdot 1} x_1 \tag{11-1}$$

where

$$b_{y \cdot 1} = r_{y1} \frac{\sigma_y}{\sigma_1} \tag{11-2}$$

We have shown in Equation 6-19 that the standard deviation of scores in one variable with the effects of a second one held constant is

$$\sigma_{y1} = \sigma_y \sqrt{1 - r_{y1}^2} \qquad (11\text{-}3)$$

This value is the standard deviation of the distribution of our errors of prediction, the standard error of estimate. It is also the partial standard deviation.

### Variation in One Variable Holding Several Others Constant

Let us now consider the effects on the variation in one variable $y$ when the variation in two other variables $x_1$ and $x_2$ is held constant simultaneously. We are now dealing with a given tower of cells in the large cube shown in Figure 11-1. All individuals who fall in any given tower have the same $x_1$ score *and* the same $x_2$ score and differ only in terms of their scores on $y$.

What is our regression equation, the equation for the prediction of variable $y$ from the combination of variables 1 and 2? Whereas with the two-variable problem the regression equation describes a line, now we wish a regression equation that describes a plane. We can write the equation we wish by analogy from Equation 11-1, the regression equation for the two-variable problem. If we look at Equation 11-1, we see that we have a value $b$, the regression coefficient, which is the slope of the regression line. In the three-variable problem, however, we are dealing with a plane with two slopes, one as the plane cuts through $x_1$ and the other as it cuts through $x_2$. But note in Equation 11-1 that $b$ involves partialing out only one variable. Now for each regression coefficient we must partial out two variables. Thus by analogy we can write

$$\bar{y}_{12} = b_{y\cdot(1\cdot2)}x_1 + b_{y\cdot(2\cdot1)}x_2 \qquad (11\text{-}4)$$

or, in more common nomenclature,

$$\bar{y}_{12} = b_{y1\cdot2}x_1 + b_{y2\cdot1}x_2 \qquad (11\text{-}5)$$

The regression coefficients in Equation 11-5 can be thought of as weights applied to $x_1$ and $x_2$ to give us our best estimate of $y$. That is, $\bar{y}$ is our estimate of the score in variable $y$ obtained by an individual when we know his or her scores in variables 1 and 2. The expression $b_{y1\cdot2}$ is the constant by which we multiply scores on variable 1, and $b_{y2\cdot1}$ is the constant by which we multiply scores on variable 2 in making a weighted composite score that gives us the best prediction of variable $y$.

By analogy with the one-variable case, we can write deviation scores in variable $y$ with the effects of both variables 1 and 2 held constant as

$$
\begin{aligned}
y_{12} &= y - \bar{y} \\
&= y - b_{y1 \cdot 2} x_1 - b_{y2 \cdot 1} x_2
\end{aligned}
\qquad (11\text{-}6)
$$

We also want to write the formula for the regression coefficients and for the standard error of prediction. Reference to Equations 11-2 and 11-3 shows that we shall have to deal with the correlation between two variables when the effects of a third are held constant.

### Partial Correlation

As we have seen, if we take a slice anywhere through the cube representing the three-dimensional scatter diagram, we have a scatter diagram of the relationship between scores on two variables with scores on a third held constant. For example, Figure 11-2 represents a series of scatter diagrams of the relationship between variables $Y$ and 1 with the effects of variable 2 held constant. We could compute the coefficient of correlation in each slice. We would like to have a single coefficient describing the relationships in all the slices, a summary value for the relationship between variables $Y$ and 1 with variable 2 held constant. Such a coefficient is termed the *coefficient of partial correlation* and is symbolized as $r_{Y1 \cdot 2}$. Conceptually it is similar to partial standard deviation, which is the weighted average of column (or row) standard deviations.

In the case we are considering here, we wish to obtain the coefficient of correlation between scores on variable $Y$ and variable 1 with the effects of variable 2 held constant. In other words, we wish to eliminate the effects of variable 2 from *both* variable $Y$ and variable 1. We can write this formula as

$$
\begin{aligned}
r_{y1 \cdot 2} &= r(y - b_{y \cdot 2} x_2)(x_1 - b_{1 \cdot 2} x_2) \\
&= \frac{\Sigma(y - b_{y \cdot 2} x_2)(x_1 - b_{1 \cdot 2} x_2)}{n \sigma_{y - b_{y \cdot 2} x_2} \sigma_{x_1} - b_{1 \cdot 2} x_2}
\end{aligned}
$$

The development of this formula, which is presented in the Technical Section at the end of this chapter, results in

$$
r_{y1 \cdot 2} = \frac{r_{y1} - r_{y2} r_{12}}{\sqrt{(1 - r_{y2}^2)(1 - r_{12}^2)}}
\qquad (11\text{-}7)
$$

*Table 11-1*  Computation of coefficient of partial correlation

| Intercorrelation Among Three Variables | | | |
|---|---|---|---|
| | Y | 1 | 2 |
| Y | | .50 | .30 |
| 1 | | | .40 |
| 2 | | | |

$$r_{Y1\cdot2} = \frac{r_{Y1} - r_{Y2}r_{12}}{\sqrt{(1 - r_{Y2}^2)(1 - r_{12}^2)}} = \frac{.50 - (.30)(.40)}{\sqrt{[1 - (.30)^2][1 - (.40)^2]}} = .4346$$

$$r_{Y2\cdot1} = \frac{r_{Y2} - r_{Y1}r_{12}}{\sqrt{(1 - r_{Y1}^2)(1 - r_{12}^2)}} = \frac{.30 - (.50)(.40)}{\sqrt{[1 - (.50)^2][1 - (.40)^2]}} = .1259$$

$$r_{12\cdot Y} = \frac{r_{12} - r_{Y1}r_{Y2}}{\sqrt{(1 - r_{Y1}^2)(1 - r_{Y2}^2)}} = \frac{.40 - (.50)(.30)}{\sqrt{[1 - (.50)^2][1 - (.30)^2]}} = .3026$$

This is the formula for partial correlation, the correlation between two variables when we wish to hold constant variation in a third variable. The general formula for partial correlation, the correlation between two variables when variation in a number of other variables is held constant, is

$$r_{y1\cdot23\ldots k} = \frac{r_{y1\cdot23\ldots(k-1)} - r_{yk\cdot23\ldots(k-1)}r_{1k\cdot23\ldots(k-1)}}{\sqrt{[1 - r_{yk\cdot23\ldots(k-1)}^2][1 - r_{1k\cdot23\ldots(k-1)}^2]}} \qquad (11\text{-}8)$$

The computation of the coefficient of partial correlation is illustrated in Table 11-1.

### Partial Standard Deviation

Recall from Chapter 6 that we were able to express the regression equation for two variables in terms of correlations and standard deviations (for example, Equation 6-11). The same can be done for multiple regression. Except now, as already indicated, the concept of partialing is important to the formularization. The above section presented the concept of partial correlation. Now we need to discuss the concept of partial standard deviations.

In Equation 11-3 we presented the formula for the variation in one variable when variation in another is eliminated. This is the *partial standard deviation*. As we gave it in Equation 11-3, it is the variation in variable $y$ when variation in variable 1 is held constant. Now we wish to hold variation in variable 2 constant in addition to holding constant variation in variable 1.

Let us inspect Equation 11-3. We can see that the value under the square-root sign is the important one. In the value $(1 - r_{y1}^2)$ we have held constant that part of the variation in variable $Y$ that can be ascribed to the same factors that produce variation in variable 1. Now in addition we wish to hold constant that part of the variation in variable $Y$ that can be ascribed to the factors that produce variation in variable 2. But if variables 1 and 2 are correlated and we hold variable 2 constant as it stands, we are partialing out some of the effects of variable 1 that we already dealt with in $(1 - r_{y1}^2)$. Therefore all we wish to partial out now from the variation in variable $Y$ is the variation in variable 2 that is not accounted for by variable 1. Hence by analogy with Equation 11-3, we write

$$\sigma_{y\cdot12} = \sigma_y\sqrt{(1 - r_{y1}^2)(1 - r_{y2\cdot1}^2)} \tag{11-9}$$

The general formula for the partial standard deviation is

$$\sigma_{y\cdot12\ldots k} = \sigma_y\sqrt{(1 - r_{y1}^2)(1 - r_{y2\cdot1}^2)(1 - r_{y3\cdot12}^2)\cdots(1 - r_{yk\cdot12\ldots(k-1)}^2)} \tag{11-10}$$

The computation of the partial standard deviation is illustrated in Table 11-2.

### Multiple Regression Equation

In Equation 11-5 we gave the multiple regression equation using the regression coefficient $b$. Knowing the formulas for the partial correlation and the partial standard deviation, we can by analogy with Equations 11-1 and 11-2 write the formulas for the multiple regression coefficients in terms of correlations and standard deviations as

$$b_{y1\cdot2} = r_{y1\cdot2}\,\frac{\sigma_{y\cdot2}}{\sigma_{1\cdot2}} \tag{11-11}$$

$$b_{y2\cdot1} = r_{y2\cdot1}\,\frac{\sigma_{y\cdot1}}{\sigma_{2\cdot1}} \tag{11-12}$$

The general formula is

$$b_{y1\cdot23\ldots k} = r_{y1\cdot23\ldots k}\,\frac{\sigma_{y\cdot23\ldots k}}{\sigma_{1\cdot23\ldots k}} \tag{11-13}$$

***Table 11-2***  Computation of partial standard deviation

| | | | |
|---|---|---|---|
| Intercorrelations Among and Standard Deviations of Three Variables | | | |

| | Y | 1 | 2 | $\sigma$ |
|---|---|---|---|---|
| Y | | .50 | .30 | 10 |
| 1 | | | .40 | 8 |
| 2 | | | | 12 |

$\sigma_{Y1\cdot2} = \sigma_Y \sqrt{(1 - r_{Y1}^2)(1 - r_{Y2\cdot1}^2)} = 10 \sqrt{[1 - (.50)^2][1 - (.1259)^2]} = 8.5910$

$\sigma_{1\cdot Y2} = \sigma_1 \sqrt{(1 - r_{Y1}^2)(1 - r_{12\cdot Y}^2)} = 8 \sqrt{[1 - (.50)^2][1 - (.3026)^2]} = 6.6032$

$\sigma_{2\cdot Y1} = \sigma_2 \sqrt{(1 - r_{Y2}^2)(1 - r_{12\cdot Y}^2)} = 12 \sqrt{[1 - (.30)^2][1 - (.3026)^2]} = 10.9106$

The coefficients of partial correlation were computed in Table 11-1.

---

The multiple regression equation in raw-score form is

$$\bar{Y}_i = b_{Y1\cdot23\ldots k}X_1 + \cdots + b_{Y\cdot12\ldots(k-1)}X_k + \bar{Y}$$
$$- b_{Y1\cdot23\ldots k}\bar{X}_1 - \cdots - b_{Yk\cdot12\ldots(k-1)}\bar{X}_k \quad (11\text{-}14)$$

When the component variables are given in standard-score form, the regression coefficients are indicated by the symbol $\beta$ (beta). The multiple regression equation in standard-score form is

$$\bar{z}_y = \beta_{y1\cdot23\ldots k}z_1 + \cdots + \beta_{yk\cdot12\ldots(k-1)}z_k \quad (11\text{-}15)$$

The beta coefficients can be developed for the three-variable case as follows, parallel to Equations 11-11 and 11-12:

$$\beta_{y1\cdot2} = r_{y1\cdot2} \frac{\sigma_{y\cdot2}}{\sigma_{1\cdot2}}$$

Substituting for the coefficient of partial correlation from Equation 11-7 and for the partial standard deviations from Equation 11-3, we have

$$\beta_{y1\cdot2} = \frac{r_{y1} - r_{y2}r_{12}}{\sqrt{(1 - r_{y2}^2)(1 - r_{12}^2)}} \frac{\sigma_y\sqrt{1 - r_{y2}^2}}{\sigma_1\sqrt{1 - r_{12}^2}}$$

Since the scores are in standard-score form, all standard deviations have the value of 1. Hence

$$\beta_{y1\cdot2} = \frac{r_{y1} - r_{y2}r_{12}}{1 - r_{12}^2} \quad (11\text{-}16)$$

By a similar derivation we can show that the other beta coefficient is

$$\beta_{y2\cdot1} = \frac{r_{y2} - r_{y1}r_{12}}{1 - r_{12}^2} \tag{11-17}$$

From Equation 11-13 and parallel to the above two equations, we can write the general formula as

$$\beta_{y1\cdot23\ldots k} = r_{y1\cdot23\ldots k} \frac{\sigma_{y\cdot23\ldots k}}{\sigma_{1\cdot23\ldots k}}$$

$$= \frac{\beta_{y1\cdot3\ldots k} - \beta_{y2\cdot3\ldots k}\beta_{21\cdot3\ldots k}}{1 - \beta_{12\cdot3\ldots k}\beta_{21\cdot3\ldots k}} \tag{11-18}$$

The computations of the multiple regression coefficients and the multiple regression equations are illustrated in Table 11-3.

### Coefficient of Multiple Correlation

We are now in a position to consider the problem of the prediction of scores on one variable from the optimally weighted composite of scores on several others. The coefficient of correlation between scores on one variable and the optimally weighted composite of scores on several others is termed the *coefficient of multiple correlation*. To distinguish this coefficient from other coefficients of correlation, it is symbolized as $R_{Y\cdot12\ldots k}$, where variable $Y$ is the variable being predicted and variables 1 to $k$ are the predictor variables.

From the simple correlation between two variables (Equation 5-7), we know that

$$r_{Y1} = \sqrt{1 - \frac{\sigma_{Y\cdot1}^2}{\sigma_Y^2}}$$

when the bivariate distribution is linear.

By analogy we can write the coefficient of multiple correlation for the three-variable case as

$$R_{y\cdot12} = \sqrt{1 - \frac{\sigma_{y\cdot12}^2}{\sigma_y^2}} \tag{11-19}$$

The general formula would be

$$R_{y\cdot12\ldots k} = \sqrt{\frac{1 - \sigma_{y\cdot12\ldots k}^2}{\sigma_y^2}} \tag{11-20}$$

*Table 11-3*   Computation of multiple regression coefficients
and multiple regression equations

Intercorrelations Among and Means and Standard Deviations of Three Variables

|   | Y | 1 | 2 | $\bar{X}$ | $\sigma$ |
|---|---|---|---|---|---|
| Y |  | .50 | .30 | 50 | 10 |
| 1 |  |  | .40 | 40 | 8 |
| 2 |  |  |  | 70 | 12 |

$$b_{Y1\cdot2} = r_{Y1\cdot2} \frac{\sigma_{Y\cdot2}}{\sigma_{1\cdot2}} = .4346 \frac{(9.539)}{(7.332)} = .5654$$

$$\sigma_{Y\cdot2} = \sigma_Y \sqrt{1 - r_{Y2}^2} = 10 \sqrt{1 - (.30)^2} = 9.539$$

$$\sigma_{1\cdot2} = \sigma_1 \sqrt{1 - r_{12}^2} = 8 \sqrt{1 - (.40)^2} = 7.332$$

$$b_{Y2\cdot1} = r_{Y2\cdot1} \frac{\sigma_{Y\cdot1}}{\sigma_{2\cdot1}} = .1259 \frac{(8.660)}{(10.998)} = 0.991$$

$$\sigma_{Y\cdot1} = \sigma_Y \sqrt{1 - r_{Y1}^2} = 10 \sqrt{1 - (.50)^2} = 8.660$$

$$\sigma_{2\cdot1} = \sigma_2 \sqrt{1 - r_{21}^2} = 12 \sqrt{1 - (.40)^2} = 10.998$$

$$\bar{Y}_i = b_{Y1\cdot2}X_1 + b_{Y2\cdot1}X_2 + \bar{Y} - b_{Y1\cdot2}\bar{X}_1 - b_{Y2\cdot1}\bar{X}_2$$

$$= .5654X_1 + .0991X_2 + 50 - (.5654)(40) - (.0991)(70)$$

$$\beta_{Y1\cdot2} = \frac{r_{Y1} - r_{Y2}r_{12}}{1 - r_{12}^2} = \frac{.50 - (.30)(.40)}{1 - (.40)^2} = .4524$$

$$\beta_{Y2\cdot1} = \frac{r_{Y2} - r_{Y1}r_{12}}{1 - r_{12}^2} = \frac{.30 - (.50)(.40)}{1 - (.40)^2} = .1190$$

$$\bar{Z}_Y = \beta_{Y1\cdot2}Z_1 + \beta_{Y2\cdot1}Z_2 = .4524Z_1 + .1190Z_2$$

The coefficients of partial correlation were computed in Table 11-1.

The computational formula, which is developed in the Technical
Section at the end of this chapter, is

$$R_{y\cdot12}^2 = \frac{r_{y1}^2 + r_{y2}^2 - 2r_{y1}r_{y2}r_{12}}{1 - r_{12}^2} \tag{11-21}$$

$$R_{y\cdot12} = \sqrt{\frac{r_{y1}^2 + r_{y2}^2 - 2r_{y1}r_{y2}r_{12}}{1 - r_{12}^2}} \tag{11-22}$$

The sign of $R$ is always positive since the sign of the regression weights
always work out in such fashion to produce a $+R$. This occurs even if
there is a negative correlation between $Y$ and $X_1$, $Y$ and $X_2$, and so on.

Equation 11-22 is a computational formula for the coefficient of multiple correlation involving three variables. For the general case, the
formula is

$$R_{y\cdot12\ldots k} = \sqrt{\beta_{y1\cdot23\ldots k}r_{y1} + \cdots + \beta_{yk\cdot12\ldots(k-1)}r_{yk}} \tag{11-23}$$

An important distinction should be made at this point. We developed the formula (Equation 11-16) for beta weights from the formula for partial correlation (Equation 11-7). As already indicated, partial correlation indicates the relationship between two variables ($Y$ and 1) when the effect of a third variable (2) is eliminated from *both* $Y$ and 1. However, the beta weights take into account the relationship between two variables with the effect of the third variable eliminated from only *one* variable. The reason for this is that we are interested in knowing the relationship between $Y$ and one variable of the components when the effects of the other components are eliminated from the first one. If each of the beta weights takes into account the relationship between $Y$ and one variable with the effects of the other variable eliminated from the first component, then in essence the beta-weight terms in Equation 11-23 are each providing somewhat of an indication of the independent contribution of the components to the accountable variation of the outside variable.

In fact, we can get a direct estimate of the relationship between two variables with the effect of a third variable eliminated from only *one* variable by using the following formula, which is referred to as a *semipartial* or *part correlation:*

$$r_{y(1 \cdot 2)} = \frac{r_{y1} - r_{y2} r_{12}}{\sqrt{1 - r_{12}^2}} \tag{11-24}$$

This is the relationship between variables $Y$ and 1 with the effects of variable 2 eliminated from variable 1. Note that it differs from the formula for partial correlation (Equation 11-7) by having one less term in the denominator. In any event, we can see that the coefficient of multiple correlation is the square root of the sum of the products of the regression coefficients and coefficients of correlation for each component and the criterion. It is an *index* of the linear relationship between an optimally weighted composite and a criterion. The expression $R_{Y \cdot 12}^2$ is interpreted as the *percentage* of variance that is common to $Y$ and the weighted composite.

The computation of the coefficient of multiple correlation is illustrated in Table 11-4.

***Standard error of prediction***    Equation 11-3 relates the standard error of prediction and the coefficient of correlation as follows:

$$\sigma_{y \cdot 1} = \sigma_y \sqrt{1 - r_{y1}^2}$$

We can see that the coefficient of correlation is directly related to the extent of error in prediction as measured by $\sigma_{y \cdot 1}$. When the coefficient of correlation is high, the error of prediction is small; and when the

*Table 11-4*   Computation of coefficient of multiple correlation

| | Intercorrelations Among Three Variables | | |
|---|---|---|---|
| | $Y$ | 1 | 2 |
| $Y$ | | .50 | .30 |
| 1 | | | .40 |
| 2 | | | |

$$R_{Y \cdot 12} = \sqrt{1 - \frac{\sigma^2_{Y \cdot 12}}{\sigma^2_Y}} = \sqrt{1 - \frac{(8.5910)^2}{10}} = .5118$$

$$R_{Y \cdot 12} = \sqrt{\frac{r^2_{Y1} + r^2_{Y2} - 2r_{Y1}r_{Y2}r_{12}}{1 - r^2_{12}}}$$

$$= \sqrt{\frac{(.50)^2 + (.30)^2 - 2(.50)(.30)(.40)}{1 - (.40)^2}} = .5118$$

$$R_{Y \cdot 12} = \sqrt{\beta_{Y1 \cdot 2}r_{Y1} + \beta_{Y2 \cdot 1}r_{Y2}} = \sqrt{(.4524)(.50) + (.1190)(.30)} = .5118$$

The partial standard deviation was computed in Table 11-2, and the multiple regression coefficient in Table 11-3.

coefficient is low, the error is large. When we are dealing with two variables, the distribution of scores in any column (or row, as the case may be) is the distribution of our errors. The combined distribution of errors in all columns is measured by $\sigma_{y \cdot 1}$.

We can write the relationship between the standard error of prediction and the coefficient of multiple correlation just as we did above for simple correlation:

$$\sigma_{y \cdot 12 \ldots k} = \sigma_y \sqrt{1 - R^2_{y \cdot 12 \ldots k}} \qquad (11\text{-}25)$$

The partial standard deviation describes our errors of predicting variable $Y$ from the weighted composite of the other variables. If we refer to Figure 11-1, we can see that the distribution of scores in the towers is the distribution of our errors of prediction. The combined distribution of errors in all towers is the partial standard deviation. Therefore the coefficient of multiple correlation relates to the accuracy of the prediction of scores on one variable from the optimally weighted combination of scores on several other variables. When the multiple correlation is high, the error of prediction is small; and when the coefficient is low, the error is large.

## Conditions Yielding Highest Multiple Correlations

As can be readily ascertained from the various formulas presented for multiple correlation, the magnitude of the coefficient of multiple corre-

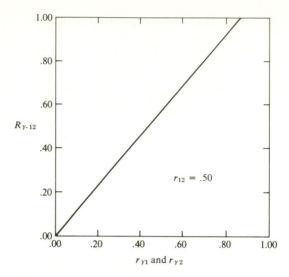

*Figure 11-6*   Effects on multiple correlation of magnitude of correlation between predictor variables and predicted variable.

lation is a function of the intercorrelations that enter into it. If we know the conditions that yield high and low multiple correlations, then by judicious elimination of variables that do not add significantly to the multiple, we can reduce the number of variables with which we are concerned. The important conditions can be illustrated simply with the three-variable problem.

### Correlation Between Predicted and Predictor Variables

Let us take a simple case where $r_{12}$ is equal to .50 and $r_{Y1} = r_{Y2}$. We shall vary the latter values and ascertain the effects on the multiple correlation. Figure 11-6 shows the relationship between the magnitude of the correlation between the predicted and predictor variables and the coefficient of multiple correlation. It can be seen in this figure that as the magnitude of the correlation between the predicted and predictor variables increases, $R$ increases. It is therefore apparent that, other things being equal, the multiple correlation increases as the coefficient of correlation between the predictor and predicted variables increases. Whenever a choice can be made, then, we should include variables that correlate high with the variable being predicted and eliminate those that have a low correlation.

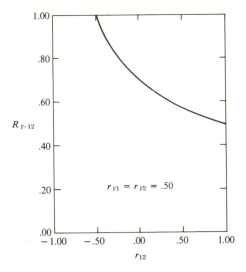

*Figure 11-7* Effects on multiple correlation of magnitude of correlation among predictors.

### Intercorrelations Among Predictor Variables

Let us now examine a case where both $r_{Y1}$ and $r_{Y2}$ are .50, and we vary the magnitude of $r_{12}$. The effects of varying the magnitude of the intercorrelation between the two predictors on the coefficient of multiple correlation are shown in Figure 11-7. It can be observed in this figure that when the correlation between the predictors is very high, their joint prediction is little better than the prediction given by either the one or the other alone. As the correlation between the predictors falls in magnitude, their joint prediction increases and becomes quite significant when the correlation between them is high and negative. It is therefore apparent that, other things being equal, the multiple correlation increases as the coefficients of correlation among the predictors decrease or become negative. Whenever a choice can be made, then, we should include variables whose intercorrelations are low or negative.

The effect of the intercorrelations among the predictor variables also can be illustrated by Venn diagrams. Figure 11-8 shows that high intercorrelation among predictors (1 and 2) leads to little increased explanation of or overlap with $Y$. The additional amount of explanation of $Y$ is represented by the crosshatched pattern. Individually the two predictors explain a good amount of $Y$, but they are explaining a good deal of similar variance (shaded area). In contrast, Figure 11-9 shows that low intercorrelation (for example, $r_{12}$ = .00) will result in more combined

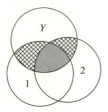

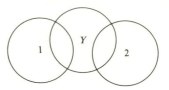

**Figure 11-8**
Venn diagram:
High intercorrela-
tion among pre-
dictors (1 and 2).

**Figure 11-9**   Venn diagram:
Uncorrelated predictors.

explained variance of $Y$ or, in other words, a higher $R$ than either $r_{Y1}$ or $r_{Y2}$ explains alone.

### Suppressor Variables

Occasionally a variable that is uncorrelated with the variable to be predicted nonetheless contributes to the multiple correlation. Let us consider a case where $r_{Y1} = .50$ and $r_{Y2} = .00$, varying $r_{12}$ and observing the effects on the coefficient of multiple correlation. The relationship is shown in Figure 11-10. In this figure we can see that when a variable is unrelated to the variable to be predicted, the net effect is to increase the multiple correlation. Such a variable is termed a *suppressor variable* since in effect it partials out or suppresses that part of the other predictor variable that is unrelated to the variable to be predicted.

Figure 11-11 illustrates the suppressor effect. Since predictor 2 is explaining some of the variability in predictor 1 (crosshatched), the proportion of variance in $Y$ explained by predictor 1 is greater. That is, the shaded portion represents a greater area of the $Y$ space and the remaining space of predictor 1 not explained by predictor 2 than it represents the whole spaces of $Y$ and 1.

Suppressor variables are rarely encountered in psychological measurement, but they are sometimes found. For example, scores on paper-and-pencil tests of mechanical aptitude and intelligence tests usually are substantially related. In part this is because both tests involve verbal abilities. Mechanical aptitude tests usually show some relationship to measures of practical mechanical performance, but intelligence tests do not. In such a circumstance a combination of the mechanical aptitude test and the intelligence test gives a better prediction of practical mechanical performance than the mechanical aptitude

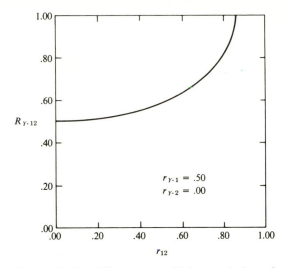

*Figure 11-10* Effects on multiple correlation of correlation between predictor variables when one of them is uncorrelated with predicted variable.

test alone, because the intelligence test acts as a suppressor variable, partialing out from the mechanical aptitude test the verbal abilities that are unimportant in mechanical performance. In effect the suppressor variable negates the differences in job performance due to differences in test scores.

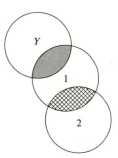

*Figure 11-11* Venn diagram: Suppressor effect when two predictors are correlated, but predictor 2 is uncorrelated with criterion (*Y*).

In a job interview situation an applicant may be rated in terms of the adequacy of his or her previous experience and overall goodness as a person. Ratings on these two scales are likely to be highly correlated as a result of the interviewer's general impression, sometimes called the *halo effect.* Sometimes it is found that the ratings of previous experience are predictive of later success on the job, but ratings of overall goodness have little predictive value. The two ratings together, then, would give better predictions than experience ratings alone, because the ratings of overall goodness would operate as a suppressor variable, partialing out from the experience ratings the effects of the interviewer's general impression.

## Contribution of Components

The question of the importance of the components with respect to their contribution to explaining the variance of the outside variable or criterion is often raised. That is, which of the variables in a test battery is contributing most to explaining the variance in the criterion? This question has, in one case, a simple answer and, in a second case, an ambiguous if not meaningless answer.

In the simple case, we will assume that the intercorrelation between the predictors or components is zero. Thus, Equation 11-21

$$R_{Y \cdot 12}^2 = \frac{r_{Y1}^2 + r_{Y2}^2 - 2r_{Y1}r_{Y2}r_{12}}{1 - r_{12}^2}$$

reduces to $R_{Y \cdot 12}^2 = r_{Y1}^2 + r_{Y2}^2$. Thus the square of the multiple correlation coefficient is the sum of the proportions of variance in the criterion variable accounted for by the predictor variables. In other words, when the predictor variables are not correlated, the proportion of variance attributable to a predictor variable is the squared simple correlation between it and the criterion variable.

Suppose we have the following relations: $r_{Y1} = .4$, $r_{Y2} = .3$, and $r_{12} = .00$. Then $R_{Y \cdot 12}^2 = .25$ and $R_{Y \cdot 12} = .5$. In this case we would conclude that variable 1 was the most "important."

Another measure of "importance" of variables when the components are not correlated is the beta coefficient. From Equation 11-16

$$\beta_{Y1 \cdot 2} = \frac{r_{Y1} - r_{Y2}r_{12}}{1 - r_{12}^2}$$

we can see that when $r_{12} = 0.00$, $\beta_{Y1 \cdot 2} = r_{Y1}$. Thus each beta coefficient is equal to the simple correlations between the criterion variable and the variable with which it is associated. The square of the $\beta$ coefficients equals the square of the simple correlation, and as we saw above, this represents the amount of variance contributed by that variable.

Research in psychology and education, however, rarely involves a situation in which the predictor variables are independent of each other. In this case, it is virtually impossible to determine the exact contribution of accounted variance by each of the predictor variables. Thus if again we have $r_{Y1} = .4$ and $r_{Y2} = .3$, but $r_{12} = .3$, the $R_{Y·12}$ is .45 and $R^2_{Y·12} = .20$. Variable 1 by itself explains 16 percent of the criterion variance, variable 2 by itself explains 9 percent of the criterion variance, yet together they explain 20 percent of the criterion variance. Because of the predictor intercorrelation, it is difficult to determine the exact contribution of variable 1 (or 2) to explaining the breakdown of the 20 percent accountable variance.

There are estimates, however, of the importance of variables. First we can ignore the intercorrelations and simply conclude that the variable with the highest squared simple correlation with the criterion is the most important. It is the only estimate of importance that is uninfluenced by the other components in the regression equation.

A second estimate of "importance" is the squared partial correlation (Equation 11-7). This value indicates the amount of variance in the criterion variable attributed by one predictor variable when the other variables are held constant. Suppose the difference (in a two-predictor case) between $r_{Y1}$ and $r_{Y1·2}$, where both are high values, is small. Then we can conclude that variable 1 is contributing to the variance in the criterion.

A third way of estimating the importance of a variable is to determine whether there is a difference between the squared multiple $R$ when the variable is in the analysis and when it is omitted. Thus to determine the "importance" of variable 2, we would look at $R^2_{Y·12}$ minus $R^2_{Y·1}$. This "difference index" is heavily influenced by the intercorrelation between variables 1 and 2. In effect, though, the difference is simply a squared semipartial correlation, $r^2_{Y(2·1)}$. If this is a high and significant value, then variable 2 is contributing. In sum, the indices tell the "usefulness" of including a variable in a test battery.

## Nonlinear Models for Predictions from Weighted Composites

The correlational and regression models discussed in this book have mostly been based on linear functions. Most of the formulas and equations discussed have assumed linear relationships between the composite and the outside variable. The reason for assuming this relationship is that linear prediction functions often turn out to do as well as non-linear prediction functions. They do as well in the sense that they explain as much variance as do nonlinear functions. The point of this section, though, is to *acquaint* you with the logic behind *nonlinear regression or prediction functions and models*.

The linear model, in the simple case where we have one $X$ and one $Y$, assumes that equal differences in $X$ are associated with equal differences in $Y$. That is, the amount of change in $Y$ when we go from 4 to 6 on $X$ is the same as when we go from 10 to 12 on $X$. The same holds in the multiple-variable case where equal changes in the composite result in equal changes in the criterion.

In nonlinear models, either we have the case where equal differences in $X$ are associated with different amounts of change in $Y$ (see Figure 5-1c) or we have a reversal of trend in the relationship. This latter case is illustrated where increases in $X$ are associated with increases in $Y$ up to a certain point and then the increases in $X$ are associated with decreases in $Y$—a U-shaped relationship (see Figure 5-1d).

The choice between a linear or a nonlinear model is one of explanatory power. Linear models are the simplest descriptions of data; nonlinear or higher-order models may explain more of the relationships between data. Since one purpose of data analysis is to achieve some simplicity or parsimony in explaining and predicting behavior, the choice between the two models becomes one of attempting to determine the relatively simplest equation necessary to adequately describe a set of data.

Thus, the first question we are concerned with is: How do we know if a nonlinear relationship is more appropriate than a linear relationship? There are several ways to answer this question. First we can look at the scatter diagram (see Figure 5-1). This is relatively simple for the two-variable case, but more difficult for the multiple-variable case. Nonlinear prediction functions can involve quadratic, tertiary, etc. terms. One way to determine a possibly appropriate equation is to examine the scatter diagram. Eyeball analysis would indicate whether the shape was of the form of a parabola, hyperbola, logarithm, exponent, and so on. The appropriate equation would then be applied to the data. Second we can compare the linear correlation coefficient to that of the general formula for correlation, etc. In the multiple-variable case, we would use Equation 5-7, except that we would substitute the square of the partial multiple standard deviation (Equation 11-10) for the two-variable partial variance. That is, multivariate eta would be represented as

$$\eta_{Y \cdot 12} = \sqrt{1 - \frac{\sigma_{Y \cdot 12}^2}{\sigma_Y^2}} \qquad (11\text{-}26)$$

If $\eta_{Y \cdot 12}$ is substantially greater than $R_{Y \cdot 12}$, then we could apply a non-linear equation to better represent the relationship.

The procedure for analyzing nonlinear functions is to use linear methods. That is, the linear function in raw-score form adapted from Equation 11-14,

$$\bar{Y}_i = \bar{Y} + b_1 X_1 + b_2 X_2$$

can be generalized to include quadratic terms that would be represented as

$$\bar{Y}_i = \bar{Y} + b_1 X_1 + b_2 X_2 + b_3 X_1^2 + b_4 X_2^2 + b_5 X_1 X_2 \qquad (11\text{-}27)$$

Equation 11-27 is linear in the $b$ coefficients and thus can be solved by linear regression procedures. Note that there are five regression coefficients that must be solved, yet only two tests or $X$'s. To handle this situation, suppose the following results were obtained for some subjects:

| Subject | Test 1 $(X_1)$ | Test 2 $(X_2)$ |
|---------|---------|---------|
| Tom | 4 | 9 |
| Dick | 3 | 7 |
| Harriet | 8 | 2 |

To solve the above nonlinear equation, we merely treat the squares and cross-product terms as additional variables. That is, the five data points for each subject would be as follows:

| Subject | $X_1$ | $X_2$ | $X_1^2$ | $X_2^2$ | $X_1 X_2$ |
|---------|-------|-------|---------|---------|-----------|
| Tom | 4 | 9 | $(4)^2 = 16$ | $(9)^2 = 81$ | $(4)(9) = 36$ |
| Dick | 3 | 7 | $(3)^2 = 9$ | $(7)^2 = 49$ | $(3)(7) = 21$ |
| Harriet | 8 | 2 | $(8)^2 = 64$ | $(2)^2 = 4$ | $(8)(2) = 16$ |

The linear procedure discussed earlier in this chapter (Equations 11-14 and 11-23) is now used to obtain the multiple correlation coefficient and multiple regression equation. The interpretation of the nonlinear $R^2$ is equivalent to that of $R^2$; that is, the proportion of accountable variation.

## Moderated Regression

A special case of nonlinear prediction has been referred to as *moderated regression*. The essential notion underlying moderated regression is that it is possible to improve prediction (that is, increase $R^2$) by taking into account certain characteristics that would distinguish one subgroup from another in the total sample. Moderated regression is concerned with the particular way these characteristics influence multiple correlation and the accompanying regression equation. These characteristics of subgroups that influence the coefficient and equation are referred to as *moderator variables*. For example, it is possible that the relation between grades in college and aptitude would be improved if we considered only those students who have a high need for achievement as opposed to those who have a low need for achievement. In this case, need for achievement is moderating or influencing the relationship between the predictor and the criterion. Need for achievement is thus a moderator variable.

Essentially the moderator variable is interacting with the predictor. There have been several suggested approaches for conceptualizing this relationship. One is the moderated regression equation proposed by Saunders (1956). The form of the equation is

$$\bar{Y}_i = \bar{Y} + b_1 X_1 + b_2 Z + b_3 X_1 Z \qquad (11\text{-}28)$$

where $Y$ is college grades (the criterion), $X_1$ is the aptitude predictor, and $Z$ is the need-achievement moderator. The use of the cross-product term, $X_1 Z$, distinguishes this equation from the general linear Equation 11-14 and indicates that we are involved with a multivariate, nonlinear regression equation.

The utility of the moderated regression equation is determined by comparing its multiple correlation coefficient to the multiple correlation coefficient associated with the equation that would simply have two predictors, $X_1$ and $Z$, and *no* cross-product term. If the former $R$ is higher than the latter $R$, then a moderator variable is in fact operating. That is, the linear multiple correlation for a group may be .30. If we use the moderated regression equation, the multiple correlation coefficient may be increased to .40.

Note that the use of a moderator variable can be looked on as a third way of improving prediction. The first two ways were previously mentioned in our discussion of linear multiple regression and the effects of the relationship among predictors and criterion on multiple correlation. First we indicated that correlation can be improved if predictors are chosen whose intercorrelations are low or negative. Second we indicated that a suppressor variable or a variable that is highly correlated with the predictor, but not with the criterion, can improve correlation. Now the third way is to use moderator variables. Generally moderators have been found to be linearly uncorrelated with both the predictor and the criterion; yet $R$ is improved. This occurs because of the nonlinear, interactive effects of the predictor and the moderator.

A slight departure is necessary at this point. As we add variables in our multiple regression model or as we begin using higher-order nonlinear equations, we are bound to improve the amount of accountable variation. Recall that $r_{Y1}$ is a simple explanation of the state of affairs. If we add $X_2$ or use an equation with a squared value, we can do no worse than $r_{Y1}$. What we are doing is using more complex explanations to fit a recognized complex situation.

If the moderated regression model proposed by Saunders (1956) is adopted, the result is one regression equation for the whole sample. There are other approaches, though, for dealing with moderators and improving prediction. Recall that the general definition of a moderator variable is that it differentiates one subgroup from another. More specifically, it identifies a subgroup for whom a regression equation is appropriate. This specific definition is reflected in *subgroup analysis*. This involves separating a sample on the basis of a moderator into two subgroups; for example, high need achievers and low need achievers. The linear regression equation and correlation coefficient between the predictor and the criterion for each subgroup is then computed. Differential regression equations would indicate the operation of a moderator effect. For example, suppose the correlation between the criterion and the predictor for the total sample is .30, and at the same time we obtain the equation representing this relationship. If we subgroup on the basis of a moderator, the correlations for the two subgroups may be .45 and .05, respectively, *and* the intercepts and regression coefficients for the respective equations may differ. Results such as these would indicate that we could predict better for a subgroup than for a total group.

Ghiselli (1956) has proposed another method for moderator variables, which is concerned with differential predictability. Ghiselli's procedure identifies the degree to which persons in a sample deviate from a regression line, and thus identifies those for whom the predictor is relatively appropriate and inappropriate. The technique involves obtaining absolute difference scores, $|D|$, between each person's standardized predictor $(z_p)$ and standardized criterion $(z_c)$ scores. That is, for each person, we compute

$$|D_i| = z_c - z_p \qquad (11\text{-}29)$$

The magnitude of $|D|$ serves as an index of predictability; the smaller the $|D|$, the better the relation between criterion and predictor and the closer the person lies to the regression line. If the $|D|$ is zero, then the person's standardized test score equals his or her standardized criterion score; in a scatter diagram this person's pair of scores would fall directly on the regression line.

Correlates of the $|D|$ scores for the group are subsequently identified and used as *predictors of predictability* or moderators; for example, need for achievement may correlate with the $|D|$ scores. A high positive correlation indicates that the validity of the predictor should be higher for those scoring low on the predictor of predictability. That is, in this positive relationship, low $|D|$ scores are of those who are predictable and also have low scores on the predictor of predictability, or those who have low need for achievement. The total group is then divided into low and high scorers on the predictor of predictability, need for achievement, and the relationships between the predictor and the criterion for each subgroup are examined to test for the expected results. For example, we may find that the correlation between the test and the criterion for the predictable group, those with low need achievement, is .40; whereas the correlation between the test and the criterion for those high in need achievement is .05. If we get this differential predictability, that is, better prediction for one subgroup, then in the future we would administer the predictor of predictability to a whole group, and subsequently administer the predictor *only* to the low scorers. It is this latter subgroup for whom the predictor is most appropriate.

### Actuarial Pattern Analysis

Actuarial pattern analysis or configural scoring is concerned with the relationship between a *response pattern* to individual item or test components and an outside variable or a criterion. These terms have been used to apply to nonlinear combinations of test or item scores. Specifically, *pattern analysis* concerns the pattern of continuous predictors, whereas *configural scoring* concerns the pattern of categorical or discrete item scores. Regardless of the term, which we will use interchangeably, the logic is the same.

Two persons can have the same total score on a test. Suppose this score is 40. The way the total was obtained can obviously be a function of many response patterns. That is, one person could have correctly responded to the first 40 items on a 100-item test. Another person could have responded correctly to items 1, 3, 9, 11, 26, 48, 57, and so forth, resulting in a total correct score of 40. The purpose of pattern analysis is to predict a criterion score from the individual's answer pattern.

Lubin and Osburn (1957) have demonstrated that an analytical procedure appropriate for the above situation is simply a least-squares solution of a nonlinear polynomial function. Their solution pertains to the case where we have $n$ dichotomous items (the response to each item is "right" or "wrong"). Thus it is possible to have $2^n$ answer patterns. If we have 10 items, then it is possible to have $2^{10}$ or 1,024 different response patterns. That is, three persons could have an answer pattern such as:

| | Items | | | | | | | | | | | Criterion |
|---|---|---|---|---|---|---|---|---|---|---|---|---|
| | 1 | 2 | 3 | 4 | 5 | 6 | 7 | 8 | 9 | 10 | Total | Score |
| Tom | R | W | R | W | R | W | R | W | R | W | 5 | 10 |
| Dick | W | R | W | R | W | R | W | R | W | R | 5 | 12 |
| Harriet | R | W | R | W | R | W | R | W | R | W | 5 | 8 |

where R, or right, is scored as 1 and W, or wrong, is scored as 0. For each different answer pattern, a mean outside criterion score can be obtained; there are $2^n$ possible criterion scores. Every individual with the same answer pattern receives the same criterion score, which is the mean criterion score for that answer pattern. Thus the configural score for Tom and Harriet is 9; that is, $(8 + 10)/2 = 9$. These scores are referred to as configural scores. The distribution of configural scores is a configural scale. The prediction of the obtained criterion score, obtained through a least-squares solution, is best achieved by use of an individual's configural score.

Note here again that two individuals with the same total score on a test could have different configural scores because of different response patterns. This is shown in the above results where Tom, Dick, and Harriet obtained a total score of 5 "right." If two persons have the same answer pattern, their configural score is obtained by averaging their criterion score.

Lubin and Osburn (1957) have proved the theorem that the configural scale is a polynomial, nonlinear function of the item scores. The prediction of a criterion score is obtained through

$$Y = \bar{Y} + b_1X_1 + b_2X_2 + \cdots + b_nX_n + b_{12}X_1X_2 + b_{13}X_1X_3 \\ + \cdots + b_{123}X_1X_2X_3 \quad (11\text{-}30)$$

where $Y$ is the predicted criterion score, $X_n$ are the item scores (1 or 0), and the $b$'s are the regression coefficients. The number of terms would be $2^n$. Again the coefficients are determined by a linear solution of an equation with cross-product terms.

The essence of pattern analysis is that it identifies those individuals who have similar answer patterns rather than similar total scores. The best prediction of a criterion is the pattern rather than the total score. Rather than using raw total scores or subtotal scores as predictors of a criterion, we use the configural scores.

The above example presented by Lubin and Osburn may be seen as a special case of the situation where either continuous item scores or continuous test scores are the $X_n$. In any event, the solution is a least-squares one for a nonlinear combination of test or item scores.

Another approach to actuarial pattern analysis was suggested by

Lykken (1956). The procedure involves plotting profiles of individuals as points in a test space. That is, suppose we have two tests, $X_1$ and $X_2$, which can be two scores from, for example, the California Psychological Inventory, and we are interested in predicting the criterion of success as a police officer. The scores are transformed into standardized scores and divided at the median. The test space for $X_1$ and $X_2$ can be represented as shown in Figure 11-12. There are four quadrants. The best estimate for the criterion for any profile in the quadrant is the mean criterion value found for that quadrant. If the function of the relationship was $Y = X_1X_2$, then the means of quadrants $A$ and $C$ would be about equal, and the means of quadrants $B$ and $D$ would be about equal. In addition, the means for the former set of two quadrants would differ from the means for the latter set of quadrants. The psychological interpretation of these data is that police officers who are either high on both factors or low on both factors are different (more successful) than those who are high on one and low on the other. This relationship is nonlinear. If the relationship were linear, then the order of cell criterion means would be $A > B = C > D$. In essence an examination of the patterns of cell means points out the linearity or nonlinearity of the relationships. The data can be analyzed, though, without the need for specifying the linearity or nonlinearity of the relationship.

A similar cellular approach, suggested by Lykken and Rose (1963), is simple from a conceptual and computational point of view. In essence, the method consists of constructing an actuarial table. One begins by partitioning each of the $X$ predictors into $k$ intervals, thus yielding a predictor space of $k^X$ cells or regions. Then the criterion mean and variance of each cell is computed. The result is that the mean of the $i$th cell ($\bar{Y}_i$) is the best estimate of $Y$ for future cases whose $X_i$ pattern places them in that cell. For example, suppose we had two tests, $X_1$ (or aggressiveness) and $X_2$ (or sales aptitude), and we were interested in predicting a continuous criterion, $Y$, such as yearly sales. Suppose further that we divide each of the predictors into $k = 3$ intervals such that each interval contains one-third of the sample. The results of the partitioning is $3^2$ or 9 cells such as in Figure 11-13. The average yearly sales, $\bar{Y}$, is then computed for each cell, and this average is the predicted score for those having the $X_1$ and $X_2$ pattern. That is, an individual whose $X_1$ is in the second interval and whose $X_2$ is in the third interval will have a criterion of $\bar{Y}_{23}$.

The above example assumed a continuous criterion. If the criterion were categorical, then frequencies of the modal category in each cell would be determined. Again suppose we have the two predictors of the above example, $X_1$ and $X_2$, but the criterion is simply "high yearly sales" (HYS) and "low yearly sales" (LYS). Next we partition each predictor into three intervals and then indicate the frequencies of

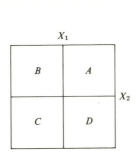

Figure 11-12   Quadrants for profile analysis.

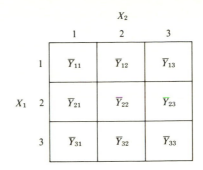

*Figure 11-13*   Cellular approach for analyzing patterns; continuous predictors.

HYS and LYS in each cell. The result may be as shown in Figure 11-14. Examination of the 3 × 3 cell layout indicates that there is a greater frequency of HYS's in all cells except for 3,1. Therefore, the best prediction will be that individuals falling into all the *other* cells will have high yearly sales and those whose predictor pattern is such as to place them in the third interval of $X_1$ and the first interval of $X_2$ will have low sales. Calculation of the number of HYS's in cell 3,1 and the number of LYS's in the remaining cells (15 HYS in 3,1 and 25 LYS in the eight remaining cells) yields a total of 40 misclassified. The number of hits, 414, divided by the total in the sample, 454, yields a hit rate of 91.2 percent. Note that the determination of hit rate does not involve a check on how accurately a subsequent sample is predicted. Such a determination, referred to as cross-validation, is necessary; this topic is discussed in Chapter 13.

   In any event, the above examples employing cells are simple from a computational point of view and avoid problems of linearity and heteroscedasticity. The latter, categorical criterion example can be solved, however, through a regression procedure, known as discriminant function analysis (briefly discussed in the next section).

   In a summary of pattern analysis, Gaier and Lee (1953) have indicated that configural scoring or pattern analysis may yield better discriminations or predictions than those obtained by the usual linear, additive, technique that ignores interitem relationships. The essence of the procedures is the *joint* presence of traits as indicated by scores on items or tests, or the interaction of tests. When these interactions are analyzed in a nonlinear relationship, it is possible that a nonlinear function will explain more of the variance in a criterion than does a linear function.

$X_2$

|  | 1 | 2 | 3 |
|---|---|---|---|
| 1 | 42 HYS<br>4 LYS | 49 HYS<br>5 LYS | 51 HYS<br>0 LYS |
| $X_1$  2 | 47 HYS<br>1 LYS | 49 HYS<br>0 LYS | 44 HYS<br>5 LYS |
| 3 | 15 HYS<br>42 LYS | 48 HYS<br>2 LYS | 42 HYS<br>8 LYS |

*Figure 11-14*   Cellular approach for analyzing patterns; frequency data.

One final note on pattern analysis is that it can be very impractical. Given that the equations deal with many terms to represent the interactions, analysis of items numbering as large as 10 would require more than 1,000 subjects in order to solve the equation unambiguously and to have confidence in the results. The problem is one of stability of the regression weights of the many terms in the equation; it is a problem of cross-validation to which we will return in Chapter 13.

## Discriminant Function Analysis

Discriminant function analysis is algebraically similar to regression analysis. In multiple regression, we are concerned with the composite of predictors that yields the best explanation of variance in the *continuous,* univariate *criterion.* In *discriminant function analysis,* we are interested in a composite of variables that has maximum potential for distinguishing between members of groups, where *group membership is the criterion.* Through discriminant analysis it is possible to determine the likelihood of someone being a member of one of the criterion groups given that person's composite of predictor scores. The criterion in this case is categorical, dichotomous, or discrete. For example, we may have two groups defined, a priori, as interested in medicine and interested in sports. The purpose of discriminant function analysis is to distinguish one group from another on the basis of their score profiles established from several cognitive tests.

Figure 11-15 illustrates the representation of discriminant analysis. $S$ is a person in the sports group, and $M$ is a person in the medicine group; $X_1$ and $X_2$ are the cognitive test data available on all subjects. The profile

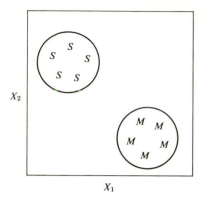

**Figure 11-15** Discriminant function analysis.

point is represented by an $M$ or an $S$. Results indicate that the medicine group tends to be high on $X_1$, and the sports group tends to be high on $X_2$.

To derive the same conclusion as the pictorial representation yields, a discriminant function analysis is done. Algebraically, discriminant function analysis is equivalent to regression analysis except that the criterion is dichotomous rather than continuous. Also again the purpose of the latter is to explain variation of "success" within a group rather than to explain variation between groups, which is basically an attempt to predict the likelihood of group membership.

The discriminant analysis produces a function ($Y$) that is a weighted composite of the two tests, such as

$$Y = a_1X_1 + a_2X_2 \tag{11-31}$$

where $a$ = discriminant weights. A useful discriminant function would be one in which the mean $Y$ for the sports group would be different from the mean $Y$ for the medicine group. In other words, the composite of the tests yields a score, $Y$, which distinguishes the two groups. Thus $Y$ can be used to predict group membership.

If there are more than two a priori groups, then the solution is multiple discriminant function analysis. This topic will not be discussed in this book. The only point to be made is that the principles are the same. That is, a composite of test scores, a profile is used to distinguish among the $G$ (which is greater than two) groups. The purpose is to maximize the differences among groups or to weight tests or predictors to maximally distinguish between established groups.

## Differential Weighting of Components

To this point, the chapter has focused on conditions for which we want to obtain a statistically optimal set of weights for forming a composite. There are situations where we want to assign weights that are not based on an optimization strategy, but rather are based on a theory, practice, experience, or the like. We may feel that some of the components should carry greater weight than others in the composite. Differential weighting on a relatively subjective basis may result in a composite being more precise, meaningful, or reliable.

There are several situations and means for assigning weights. Suppose we wish to have factory workers rated in terms of job performance. We could obtain ratings of their performance from their supervisors, the department heads, and the factory general manager. In forming a composite of the three ratings assigned to each worker, we might wish to assign greatest weight to the supervisor's ratings and least weight to the ratings by the factory general manager, since the supervisors are most intimately acquainted with the performance of the workers and the factory general manager is the least acquainted. In this case we are assigning weights based on our *judgment* of who is the best rater.

We might measure the sociability of nursery school children by counting the number of times in a 3-hour play period each child approaches, helps, comforts, or smiles at other children. We might find that the measurements of approaches and helpings are highly reliable, whereas those of comfortings and smilings are of low reliability. In making a composite measure of sociability, we might prefer to give greater weight to the first two components and less weight to the last two. In these examples we see that we might be able to achieve a composite of greater accuracy in prediction or reliability if we differentially weighted the components—weighting on the basis of *reliability*.

The job proficiency of salespeople can be measured by their total volume of sales, the number of new accounts they develop, and the number of repeat sales they make to the same customers. The economics of a particular situation might suggest that total volume of sales is most important and the number of repeat sales least important. We would then wish to give greatest weight to the first index and least to the third—weighting on the basis of *importance*.

Suppose we are measuring achievement in a course in psychological measurement. We may have questions concerning the application of principles, matters of fact, and the derivation of formulas. Because we believe that the objective of the course is to provide the students with principles they can apply and that derivations merely give them the logic underlying formulas, we may wish to weight the first type of question most and the last type least. By differentially weighting the components that form a composite, then, we may feel that we have a composite that is more *meaningful* in the sense that it more accurately reflects the definition of the trait we wish to measure.

If we are using tests of mechanical aptitude and intelligence to select students for a shop course, we may wish to give greater weight to the former than to the latter. The amount of abstract material to be learned in such a course is relatively small and has little influence on the grades the students earn in the course. On the other hand, if we were using these two tests to select students for an engineering college, we might wish to weight the tests in just the reverse fashion, giving greater weight to the intelligence test because in engineering college the student does have to learn a great deal of abstract material. By differentially weighting the two tests in one way for the shop course and in another way for the engineering college, we hope to obtain better predictions of grades in both.

In the foregoing examples we have indicated cases where we desire to differentially weight the components that form a composite. We can weight components based on judgment, reliability, importance, and meaningfulness. But sometimes we may wish to have all the components carry *equal weight*. If we were measuring knowledge of American literature, we might wish to have questions concerning novels, plays, essays, and poetry carry equal weight in determining total scores. Consequently it is also important in some cases to know that the components forming a composite are equally weighted. In all of these cases concerning weights, the researcher, practitioner, or the like has the option of determining the weights that the components will carry. We could opt for maximizing the correlation (multiple regression), or we could emphasize subjective weights.

In the remainder of this chapter we consider the nature of weights and their effects on composite scores. We examine the effects on the composite mean and the standard deviation and on the order of individuals in composite scores. We are now interested in the general problem of differential weighting and not the specific case of optimizing weights, or multiple regression.

## Process of Differential Weighting

Let us now examine the nature of weights and see how we go about applying relatively differential weights to the components in obtaining a total weighted composite score.

When we differentially weight component scores, we multiply each score by its appropriate weight, all scores in a given component being multiplied by the same value, and then we sum the products to obtain the composite score. Weights are symbolized by *W*, with the subscripts referring to the particular weight assigned to each component. Thus the scores of each of the *a* to *n* individuals on component 1 are multiplied by $W_1$, and each of their scores on component *k* is multiplied by $W_k$. After each component score of an individual is multiplied by its appropriate weight, the products are summed to form the total weighted composite score $X_c$.

The general formula representing the differential weighting of raw component scores in a composite is

$$X_{c_W} = W_1 X_1 + \ldots + W_k X_k \qquad (11\text{-}32)$$

Different sets of weights applied to the component scores of a given composite might not only give distributions of scores that differ in shape but also order the individuals in a different manner. To illustrate this, let us take a case where we have three component variables forming a composite. The raw scores for five individuals on each of the components are listed in Table 11-5, and in this table the scores have been treated with two different sets of weights. The weights in the first set are 1, 2, and 3, respectively, for the three components; and the weights in the second set are 7, 2, and 5, respectively. Figure 11-16 gives the distributions of composite scores when the two different sets of weights are applied to the component scores. We can see from this example that not only are the relative differences among individuals different, thereby giving distributions of scores of different shapes, but also the order of individuals is different. Notice that persons *b* and *c* have equal total scores when the components have equal weights ($W = 1$), but the first set of differential weights results in *b* having a lower composite than *c*, whereas the second set of differential weights results in *b* having a higher composite than *c*.

### Weights as Relative Values

In terms of their effects on the relative differences among individuals, the shape of the distribution of composite scores, and the order of individuals in composite scores, it is not the absolute magnitude of the weights that is important; rather it is their magnitudes relative to one another. It makes no difference, either in terms of the relative positions of individuals in composite scores or in terms of the shape of the distribution of composite scores, whether we multiply or divide all the weights by any given number.

To illustrate this, let us take the same case we have just considered of a composite made up of three components. Let us assign them the

*Table 11-5*  Effects of two different sets of differential weights on composite scores

| Person | Raw Component Scores | | | | Scores When: $W_1 = 1, W_2 = 2, W_3 = 3$ | | | | Scores When: $W_1 = 7, W_2 = 2, W_3 = 5$ | | | |
|---|---|---|---|---|---|---|---|---|---|---|---|---|
| | $X_1$ | $X_2$ | $X_3$ | $X_c$ | $X_1$ | $X_2$ | $X_3$ | $X_c$ | $X_1$ | $X_2$ | $X_3$ | $X_c$ |
| a | 4 | 3 | 2 | 9 | 4 | 6 | 6 | 16 | 28 | 6 | 10 | 44 |
| b | 11 | 5 | 1 | 17 | 11 | 10 | 3 | 24 | 77 | 10 | 5 | 92 |
| c | 6 | 7 | 4 | 17 | 6 | 14 | 12 | 32 | 42 | 14 | 20 | 76 |
| d | 7 | 10 | 3 | 20 | 7 | 20 | 9 | 36 | 49 | 20 | 15 | 84 |
| e | 9 | 8 | 6 | 23 | 9 | 16 | 18 | 43 | 63 | 16 | 30 | 109 |

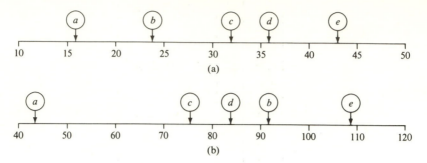

**Figure 11-16** Effects of two different sets of differential weights on scores. Scores when (a) $W_1 = 1$, $W_2 = 2$, $W_3 = 3$; and (b) $W_1 = 7$, $W_2 = 2$, and $W_3 = 5$.

weights of 1, 2, and 3, respectively. We could divide the weights, say, by their average, 2, which gives us the values 0.5, 1.0, and 1.5; or we could multiply them, say, by 2, which gives us the values 2, 4, and 6. Let us now apply all three sets of weights to the scores of the five individuals. The computations are given in Table 11-6, and the distribution of composite scores is shown in Figure 11-17. This figure clearly shows that if we maintain the same relative values among the weights, even though we use different absolute values for them, the relative differences among individuals in composite scores are exactly maintained.

### Nominal and Effective Weights

We can differentiate two different kinds of weights: the *nominal weights,* which are those we deliberately assign to components; and the *effective weights,* which are those the components actually carry in the composite. The effective weights are determined by the variance of the components. The greater the variance of a variable, the more discriminations we can make. For example, if a variable has a variance of 2, we conclude that members of that data pool are relatively alike. This is in contrast to the situation where we have a variable with a variance of 10. In the latter situation we conclude that people differ greatly. Consider the example where final grades in a course are determined by adding two test grades together to form a total score for each student. On the first test, the variance is large; for example, $\sigma^2 = 25$. Thus students are pretty well spread along the distribution. On the second test the $\sigma^2$ is small; for example, $\sigma^2 = 4$. If we add the two grades together, the addition of the second grade to the first will change the order of the

Table 11-6  Effects of various sets of differential weights on composite scores when weights maintain same relative values to each other

| Person | Raw Component Scores | | | Scores When: $W_1 = 1, W_2 = 2, W_3 = 3$ | | | | Scores When: $W_1 = 0.5, W_2 = 1, W_3 = 1.5$ | | | | Scores When: $W_1 = 2, W_2 = 4, W_3 = 6$ | | | |
|---|---|---|---|---|---|---|---|---|---|---|---|---|---|---|---|
| | $X_1$ | $X_2$ | $X_3$ | $X_1$ | $X_2$ | $X_3$ | $X_c$ | $X_1$ | $X_2$ | $X_3$ | $X_c$ | $X_1$ | $X_2$ | $X_3$ | $X_c$ |
| a | 4 | 3 | 2 | 4 | 6 | 6 | 16 | 2.0 | 3 | 3.0 | 8.0 | 8 | 12 | 12 | 32 |
| b | 11 | 5 | 1 | 11 | 10 | 3 | 24 | 5.5 | 5 | 1.5 | 12.0 | 22 | 20 | 6 | 48 |
| c | 6 | 7 | 4 | 6 | 14 | 12 | 32 | 3.0 | 7 | 6.0 | 16.0 | 12 | 28 | 24 | 64 |
| d | 7 | 10 | 3 | 7 | 20 | 9 | 36 | 3.5 | 10 | 4.5 | 18.0 | 14 | 40 | 18 | 72 |
| e | 9 | 8 | 6 | 9 | 16 | 18 | 43 | 4.5 | 8 | 9.0 | 21.5 | 18 | 32 | 36 | 86 |

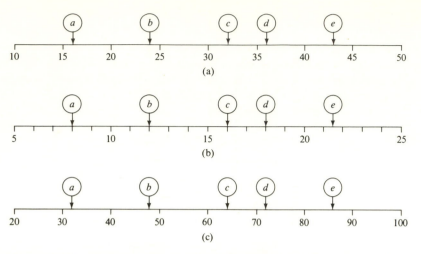

*Figure 11-17*    Effects of various sets of differential weights on composite scores when weights maintain same relative values to each other. Scores when (a) $W_1 = 1$, $W_2 = 2$, $W_3 = 3$; (b) $W_1 = 0.5$, $W_2 = 1.0$, $W_3 = 1.5$; and (c) $W_1 = 2$, $W_2 = 4$, $W_3 = 6$.

students in the distribution very slightly. Since the students did about the same on the second test, the final grade will be based mainly on performance on the first test.

The nominal and effective weights may or may not be the same. Suppose the nominal weights assigned to three component variables that form a composite are 5, 3, and 1, respectively. We then multiply the scores on the first component by 5; the scores on the second by 3, and the scores on the third by 1. If, unknown to us, the three components already carry weights (relative variances) of 1, 4, and 7, respectively, then after applying our nominal weights, the total effective weights carried by the components are 5 ($1 \times 5$) for the first component, 12 ($3 \times 4$) for the second, and 7 ($7 \times 1$) for the third. Clearly, this is a different pattern of weights than we had in mind. In order for the effective weights to correspond to the nominal weights, we have to be sure that the components carry equal weight to begin with.

As we shall see, in many situations it is doubtful whether we can actually determine the effective weights. As a consequence, when we assign nominal weights, we cannot be sure that the weights the components actually carry in the composite are in fact those we wish them to carry. This is also a troublesome problem when we do not assign differential weights but expect all the components to carry equal weight.

## Contribution of Components to Composite Scores

Let us now attempt to determine the relative contribution of the components to total composite scores when we simply sum them together. It will be recalled that we are concerned with a simple additive composite where

$$X_c = X_1 + \ldots + X_k$$

### Contribution to Mean

In Equation 7-4 we showed that the mean of composite scores is simply the sum of the means of the components. This formula is

$$\bar{X}_c = \bar{X}_1 + \ldots + \bar{X}_k$$

It is clear from this formula that the mean of composite scores is solely and entirely a function of the means of the components, and each component contributes to the mean in direct proportion to its magnitude.

In a simple summed composite, then, the effective weight of a component in determining the mean of composite scores is the magnitude of the mean of that component. If we wish to have all components carry equal effective weights in the composite, we simply divide the scores in each composite by its mean. All scores in component 1 are divided by $\bar{X}_1$, and all scores in component $k$ are divided by $\bar{X}_k$. If now we assign nominal weights, we can be sure that they are also the effective weights.

### Contribution to Variance

In Equation 7-6 we saw that the variance of composite scores is

$$\sigma_c^2 = \sigma_1^2 + \cdots + \sigma_k^2 + 2\sigma_1\sigma_2 r_{12} + \cdots + 2\sigma_{k-1}\sigma_k r_{(k-1)k} \quad (11\text{-}33)$$

This formula shows that the variance of composite scores is determined by the variances of the components and their covariances.

As in the case of the mean of composite scores, we would like to know the contribution of each component to the composite variance. Let us begin by taking a special case, one where all the components are independent, that is, where the intercorrelations among the components are all zero. If we look at Equation 11-33, we see that there is a whole series of covariance terms. Since we are taking all the coefficients of correlation to be zero, all these terms drop out. We are therefore left with the following:

$$\sigma_c^2 = \sigma_1^2 + \ldots + \sigma_k^2 \qquad (11\text{-}34)$$

From this formula it is clear that when we are dealing with a composite of uncorrelated components, each component contributes to the variance of the composite in direct proportion to its own variance. That is, the component on which people differ most will be the component that is the biggest determinant of difference on this composite. To equalize the contribution of all components, we simply divide the scores in each component by its variance in the same fashion as we divided them by their means in order to equalize the contributions of the means.

However, it is very unlikely that all the components in a composite of psychological variables will ever be completely uncorrelated. For all practical purposes we can say that this situation will never occur, though it may be closely approximated. Therefore the case of independent components is only of theoretical interest.

### Transmuting to Standard-Score Form

In dealing with composite scores, it is common practice to transmute the scores on the components to standard-score form in the belief that this procedure equalizes the weights carried by the components. Let us examine this proposition.

It will be recalled that we found the contribution of each component to the mean of composite scores to be directly proportional to the magnitude of its mean. Expressing Equation 7-4, the formula for the mean of composite scores, in standard-score form, we have

$$\bar{X}_{c_z} = \bar{z}_1 + \cdots + \bar{z}_k \qquad (11\text{-}35)$$

Since the mean of standard scores is zero, when all components are expressed in standard-score form, they contribute equally to the mean of composite scores, which in this case also would be zero.

However, the situation is quite different with the variance of composite scores. The formula, adapted from Equation 7-8, for the variance of composite scores when the scores on each of the components is expressed in standard-score form is

$$\sigma_c^2 = k + 2r_{12} + \cdots + 2r_{(k-1)k} \qquad (11\text{-}36)$$

This formula shows us that transmuting component scores to standard-score form does not eliminate the troublesome correlation terms. As we have indicated, it is these terms that prevent us from separating out the contributions of the individual components. As pointed out in Chapter 7, what is accomplished by transmuting component scores to standard-score form is to render their scores comparable in terms of the performance of some specified norming group.

## Effects of Differential Weighting

Let us now see what effects the assignment of differential nominal weights have on the mean and standard deviation of composite scores and on the order of composite scores. If we do not assign differential weights to the components, we are in effect assigning them each the nominal weight of 1. In examining the effects of differential weighting, then, we compare composite scores differentially weighted, the average of the weights being 1, with composite scores when all the components are assigned the same weight of 1.

### Effects on Mean

The mean of composite scores when the components are differentially weighted can be written from Equation 11-32 as

$$\bar{X}_{c_W} = \frac{\Sigma(W_1X_1 + \cdots + W_kX_k)}{n}$$
$$= W_1\bar{X}_1 + \cdots + W_k\bar{X}_k \qquad (11\text{-}37)$$

Equation 11-37 shows us that the mean of composite scores when the components are differentially weighted is simply equal to the sum of the means of the components, each multiplied by its weight. Therefore it is apparent that the components that are assigned higher weights contribute proportionally more to the composite mean than do the components assigned lower weights.

### Effects on Standard Deviation

When the components are differentially weighted, the variance of the composite scores can be written from Equation 11-33 as

$$\sigma^2_{c_W} = W_1^2\sigma_1^2 + \cdots + W_k^2\sigma_k^2 + 2W_1W_2\sigma_1\sigma_2r_{12} + \cdots$$
$$+ 2W_{k-1}W_k\sigma_{k-1}\sigma_kr_{(k-1)k} \quad (11\text{-}38)$$

The standard deviation is $\sqrt{\sigma^2_{c_W}}$.

It is a little difficult to see in Equation 11-38 the various factors that affect the magnitude of the composite variance when the components are differentially weighted. Therefore let us carry Equation 11-38 a bit further, and for simplicity let us consider that all the components are given in standard scores, which have the value of 1, and all the intercorrelations among the components are equal in magnitude so that

$$r_{12} = \cdots = r_{(k-1)k} = r$$

Then we can write Equation 11-38 as

$$\sigma^2_{c_W} = W_1^2 + \cdots + W_k^2 + 2W_1W_2r + \cdots + 2W_{k-1}W_kr$$
$$= \Sigma W^2 + rW_1(W_2 + \cdots + W_k) + \cdots + rW_k(W_1 + \cdots + W_{k-1})$$

Based on the formulas for variances (Equation 3-7) and means (Equation 3-1),

$$\sigma^2_{c_W} = k[\sigma^2_W(1 - r) + r\bar{W}^2(k - 1) + \bar{W}^2] \tag{11-39}$$

$$\sigma_{c_W} = \sqrt{k[\sigma^2_W(1 - r) + r\bar{W}^2(k - 1) + \bar{W}^2]} \tag{11-40}$$

This development is presented in the Technical Section at the end of the chapter.

Let us look at the term $\sigma_W$ in Equations 11-39 and 11-40. This is the standard deviation of the weights and is an index of the extent to which the weights differ among themselves in magnitude. If the weights differ greatly, then $\sigma_W$ is large; and if they are very similar, then $\sigma_W$ is small. In fact, if they are all of exactly the same magnitude, that is, if the components are all assigned the same weight (for example, the weight of 1), then $\sigma_W$ is zero and Equation 11-39 resolves to Equation 7-6, the variance of a simple composite.

To show the effects of differentially weighting the components on the standard deviation of composite scores, Equation 11-40 is plotted as Figure 11-18. Ordinarily the standard deviation of a set of values, all values being positive, is smaller in magnitude than the mean of those values. That is, usually $\sigma_x < \bar{X}$. When the standard deviation is equal to the mean, we nave an extreme condition of variation. Therefore when $\sigma_W/\bar{W} = 1$, we have about as much variation among weights as we are ever likely to encounter. To facilitate comparisons, in Figure 11-18 the standard deviation of differentially weighted composite scores is plotted against the relative variation of weights. From this figure we can derive the following principles:

1. The larger the variation among the nominal weights, the larger the standard deviation of composite scores; but even when the

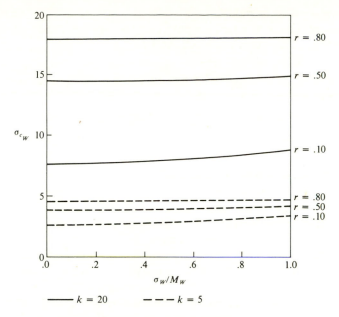

*Figure 11-18* Effects on standard deviation of composite scores ($\sigma_{c_w}$) of relative variation among weights assigned to components ($\sigma_w / M_w$), number of components ($k$), and level of intercorrelations among components ($r$).

variation among the weights is very large, the standard deviation of composite scores is not greatly increased.

2. The lower the intercorrelations among the scores of the components, the more pronounced the effect of differentially weighting the components.

### Effects on Order of Individuals

Let us now examine the effects of differential weighting of components on the order of individuals in composite scores. If differentially weighting the components does not greatly change the order of individuals in composite scores over that given by composite scores based on components with equal nominal weights, then there is little point in assigning such weights. We are therefore interested in the correlation between differentially and equally weighted composite scores. It will be understood, of course, that we are speaking of nominal rather than effective weights. Consequently, when we speak of equally weighted components, we merely mean that they all carry the same nominal weight of 1. The correlation we wish to examine is the one between composites based on equal weights and composites based on differential weights. This correlation is found by

$$r_{c_wc} = r_{(W_1x_1+\cdots+W_kx_k)(x_1+\cdots+x_k)}$$

$$r_{c_wc} = \frac{\begin{aligned}W_1\sigma_1^2 + \cdots + W_k\sigma_k^2 + (W_1\sigma_1\sigma_2r_{12} + \cdots \\ + W_1\sigma_1\sigma_kr_{1k}) + \cdots + (W_k\sigma_k\sigma_1r_{k1} + \cdots \\ + W_k\sigma_k\sigma_{k-1}r_{k(k-1)})\end{aligned}}{\sigma_{c_w}\sigma_c} \quad (11\text{-}41)$$

This correlation is developed in the Technical Section at the end of the chapter. A high correlation would indicate that differential weighting was not yielding a different ordering of individuals than was equal weighting. (For the denominator Equation 11-38 is used for computing $\sigma_{c_w}$ and Equation 7-7 for computing $\sigma_c$.)

Note that in each set of parentheses in the numerator of Equation 11-41 there are $k - 1$ terms. The terms within a set of parentheses are all the covariance terms for a given component with all the other components, each covariance being multiplied by the weight of that component. As we did for convenience in deriving the standard deviation of differentially weighted composite scores, for simplicity let us again take all the intercorrelations among the components as being equal and the scores on all the components as being given in standard-score form. Then we can write Equation 11-41 as

$$r_{c_wc} = \frac{\begin{aligned}W_1 + \cdots + W_k + (W_1r + \cdots + W_1r) \\ + \cdots + (W_kr + \cdots + W_kr)\end{aligned}}{\sigma_{c_w}\sigma_c}$$

$$r_{c_wc} = \frac{\Sigma W[1 + r(k - 1)]}{\sigma_{c_w}\sigma_c}$$

Further elaboration of this equation results in

$$r_{c_wc} = \sqrt{\frac{1 + (k - 1)r}{(\sigma_w/\bar{W})^2(1 - r) + 1 + (k - 1)r}} \quad (11\text{-}42)$$

Equation 11-42 is plotted in Figure 11-19. From this figure we derive the following principles:

1. The greater the relative variation among the nominal weights, the more the order of individuals in composite scores is changed.

2. The lower the intercorrelations among the components, the greater the effects of differential weighting on the order of individuals in composite scores.

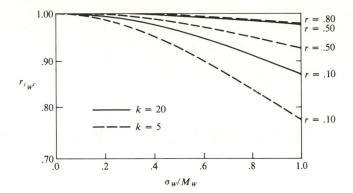

**Figure 11-19**   Effects of relative variation of weights ($\sigma_W/M_W$), level of correlations among components ($r$), and number of components ($k$) on correlation between composite scores when components are differentially weighted and when they are equally weighted ($r_{cwc}$).

3. The fewer the number of components, the greater the effects of differential weighting on the order of individuals in composite scores.

## Differentially Weighted Composite Scores and an Outside Variable

In Chapter 7 we saw that the correlation between scores on a composite and scores on an outside variable is a function of the magnitude of the correlations between the components and the outside variable and the magnitude of the intercorrelations among the components (Figure 7-2). Let us now examine the correlation between scores on a differentially weighted composite and scores on a criterion. We shall see that with a differentially weighted composite the pattern of weights assigned the components is also a factor in the relationship between composite scores and scores on a criterion.

### Coefficient of Correlation

The correlation between differentially weighted composite scores and scores on a criterion is

$$r_{Yc_W} = r_{Y(W_1 x_1 + \cdots + W_k x_k)}$$
$$= \frac{W_1 \sigma_1 r_{Y1} + \cdots + W_k \sigma_k r_{Yk}}{\sigma_{c_W}} \tag{11-43}$$

The development of Equation 11-43 follows the statistical logic employed for the development of the correlation between a differentially weighted composite and an equally weighted composite.

If scores on all components are given as standard scores, then Equation 11-43 resolves to

$$
\begin{aligned}
r_{Yc_{z,W}} &= r_{Y(W_1 z_1 + \cdots + W_k z_k)} \\
&= \frac{W_1 r_{Y1} + \cdots + W_k r_{Yk}}{\sqrt{W_1^2 + \cdots + W_k^2 + 2W_1 W_2 r_{12} + \cdots + 2W_{k-1} W_k r_{(k-1)k}}}
\end{aligned}
\tag{11-44}
$$

### Pattern of Weights

By the term *pattern of weights* we refer to the relative magnitude of the nominal weights assigned to the components of a composite variable. For example, if we have a composite formed of four components, the weights assigned them might be 1, $-0.5$, 3, and 15, respectively, or 2, 7, $-11$, and $-3$. Different patterns of weights assigned to the components would result in different orderings of individuals in terms of total weighted composite scores, and consequently the magnitude of the correlation between composite scores and scores on an outside variable might be expected to vary with the different patterns of weights.

By way of illustration, four examples are given in Figure 11-20. Each of these composites consists of two components, and in each case there is a different pattern of correlations among the two components and the outside variable. In these examples the weight assigned to the first component is 1, and the weight assigned to the second component has been varied from $-2$ to $+2$, thus providing widely varying patterns of differential weights. Applying Equation 11-43 in each case, we can see in Figure 11-20 that the magnitude of the correlation between a differentially weighted composite and an outside variable does in fact vary considerably with the pattern of weights assigned to the components.

In addition, we can see in Figure 11-20 that there is in every case an optimal pattern of weights, optimal in the sense that the particular pattern of weights results in the highest possible correlation between differentially weighted composite scores and scores on the outside variable. If we are interested in predicting scores on an outside variable from scores on a composite, the optimal pattern of weights is determined by multiple regression.

We could, of course, use Equation 11-43 or 11-44, inserting our standard deviations and intercorrelations, as well as a number of different combinations of weights, and discovering the optimal weights by trial and error. However, as compared to multiple correlation, this is an

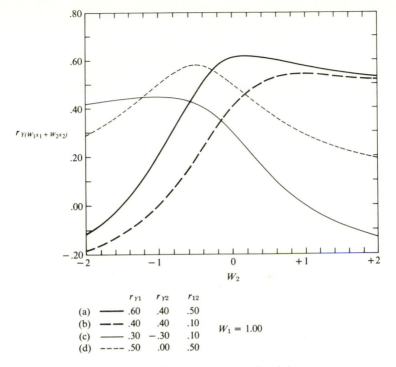

$r_{Y(W_1x_1 + W_2x_2)}$

|     |       | $r_{Y1}$ | $r_{Y2}$ | $r_{12}$ |
|-----|-------|------|------|------|
| (a) | ——    | .60  | .40  | .50  |
| (b) | — — — | .40  | .40  | .10  |
| (c) | ———   | .30  | −.30 | .10  |
| (d) | - - - -| .50  | .00  | .50  |

$W_1 = 1.00$

*Figure 11-20*  Effects of different patterns of weights on correlation between composite variable and criterion.

inefficient process and a laborious one, especially when there are many variables involved.

## Comparing Regression Coefficients with Other Weights

The best prediction of an individual's score in variable *Y* is, of course, the mean of the *Y* scores in the tower in which he or she falls. This mean is given or estimated by the multiple regression equation. Therefore it follows that if we were dealing with linear correlation, in a differentially weighted composite, use of any values other than the regression coefficients would not give us the best prediction of an individual's score, since the value we obtained would not be the mean of the tower described by a particular $x_1$ score and a particular $x_2$ score.

Let us examine the validity of the proposition that the regression coefficients are the best weights in the formation of a differentially weighted composite for use in predicting scores on an outside variable. Figure 11-21 gives three illustrative cases involving the correlations

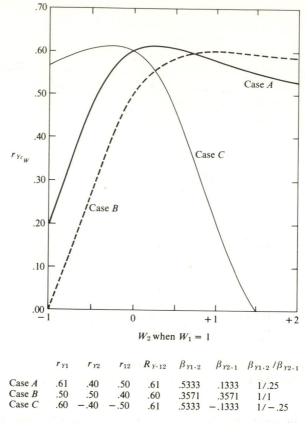

| | $r_{Y1}$ | $r_{Y2}$ | $r_{12}$ | $R_{Y \cdot 12}$ | $\beta_{Y1 \cdot 2}$ | $\beta_{Y2 \cdot 1}$ | $\beta_{Y1 \cdot 2}/\beta_{Y2 \cdot 1}$ |
|---|---|---|---|---|---|---|---|
| Case *A* | .61 | .40 | .50 | .61 | .5333 | .1333 | 1/.25 |
| Case *B* | .50 | .50 | .40 | .60 | .3571 | .3571 | 1/1 |
| Case *C* | .60 | −.40 | −.50 | .61 | .5333 | −.1333 | 1/−.25 |

*Figure 11-21*    Effects of various differential weights assigned components of a composite on correlation between composite and a criterion.

among three variables. The figure gives for each case the coefficients of multiple correlation computed from Equation 11-22 and the two beta coefficients computed from Equations 11-16 and 11-17.

Now let us assign various combinations of weights to variables 1 and 2 in each of the three cases and compute the coefficients of correlation between the weighted composite of 1 and 2 and $Y$ by means of Equation 11-43, the coefficient of correlation between a weighted composite and a criterion. To simplify the task, the weight of 1 is always assigned to variable 1, and the weight assigned to variable 2 is varied. Thus when we wish variable 2 to carry half the weight of variable 1, the weights of variable 1 and 2 are 1 and 0.5, respectively. When we wish to assign half again as much weight to variable 2 as that assigned to variable 1, the weights of variables 1 and 2 are 1 and 1.5, respectively. In addition, we can assign both positive and negative weights to variable 2.

The coefficients of correlation between the various weighted composites and the outside variable are shown in Figure 11-21. In each of the three cases we can see that there is an optimal combination of weights that gives the highest correlation between the composite and the outside variable. Reading from the graphs, we can see that for case $A$ the optimal weights for variables 1 and 2 are 1 and 0.25, respectively, which yield a correlation between composite scores of .61; for case C the optimal weights are 1 and $-0.25$. In every case the optimal weights correspond precisely with the ratio of the beta coefficients, and the maximal coefficient of correlation between the weighted composite and the outside variable corresponds precisely with the coefficient of multiple correlation. Therefore the beta coefficients are the best weights. That is, when they are used as weights for the predictor variables, the highest possible coefficient of correlation is obtained between the composite and the outside variable. Any other pattern of weights applied to the components necessarily results in lower correlations.

## Multiple Cutoffs

In a practical sense, the value of multiple correlation and differential weighting is that several tests can be combined and be used to predict performance on a criterion. One aspect of this combinatorial process is that performance on one component, predictor, or subtest can compensate for performance on another subtest. Suppose that the desired level of performance on the criterion $Y$ is 10 and we have two subtests ($X_1$ and $X_2$) each of which has a weight of 1. Thus in an employment situation where a predicted score of 10 indicates "hire" and scores below 10 indicate "not hire," there would be several combinations of the two subtests to produce a composite of 10. Just to name a few: $10 + 0, 9 + 1, 5 + 5, 4 + 6$. The first combination permits a high performance on $X_1$ to compensate for an extremely poor performance (and possibly deficiency) on $X_2$.

There are situations, however, where compensation is not desirable. It is doubtful that we would want to hire an applicant for the position of airplane pilot who was blind though the person was "best" on a test of aeronautical principles and "best" in coordination and dexterity. The applicant preferred is one who possesses *at least* certain minimum skills on all valid and necessary abilities. Adopting this strategy leads us to

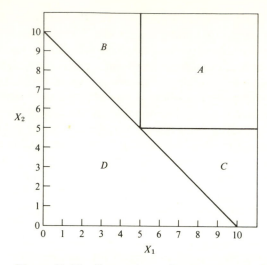

*Figure 11-22*   Comparison of results of
compensatory and multiple-cutoff models.

utilize a *multiple-cutoff procedure* for making predictions from various
subtests or composites.

The multiple-cutoff procedure involves setting a minimum acceptable level on each subtest that is related to the criterion. If the tests are
given in standard scores, we could prescribe that individuals who are at
least one standard deviation above the mean on $X_1$ are hired, provided
that they are also at least half a standard deviation above the mean on
$X_2$. The different cutoffs can be a function of the importance and individual validities of the respective tests.

Decisions with respect to who is hired will differ depending on
whether the compensatory multiple-regression model or the multiple-
cutoff model is used. These differences are illustrated in Figure 11-22.
Suppose we adopt the multiple-regression model, where again the desired score on the criterion is 10, and we have $X_1$ and $X_2$, each with unit
weights. All those subjects whose two scores, in some combination,
total 10 and thus fall above the oblique line will be hired. In contrast,
suppose that the multiple-cutoff model is adopted, in which a minimum
score of 5 on each test is required. Those persons whose scores place
them in the upper square (*A*) of the figure would be hired. Note that
only those persons falling in area *A* would be hired by *both* models, and
only those falling in area *D* would be rejected by *both* models, whereas
those falling in area *B* or *C* would be hired by one model and not the
other.

## Technical Section

### Formula for Partial Correlation

We wish to develop the formula for partial correlation, the correlation between two variables when we hold constant variation in a third variable. Given the following

$$\bar{y}_{x_1} = b_{y\cdot1}x_1 \tag{11-1}$$

$$b_{y\cdot1} = r_{y1}\frac{\sigma_y}{\sigma_1} \tag{11-2}$$

we can write the formula for partial correlation as

$$r_{y1\cdot2} = r_{(y-b_{y\cdot2}x_2)(x_1-b_{1\cdot2}x_2)}$$
$$= \frac{\Sigma(y - b_{y\cdot2}x_2)(x_1 - b_{1\cdot2}x_2)}{n\sigma_{y-b_{y\cdot2}x_2}\sigma_{x_1-b_{1\cdot2}x_2}}$$

Let us first consider the numerator divided by $n$:

$$\frac{\Sigma(y - b_{y\cdot2})(x_1 - b_{1\cdot2}x_2)}{n}$$

$$= \frac{\Sigma(yx_1 - b_{1\cdot2}yx_2 - b_{y\cdot2}x_1x_2 + b_{y\cdot2}b_{1\cdot2}x_2^2)}{n}$$

$$= \frac{\Sigma yx_1}{n} - b_{1\cdot2}\frac{\Sigma yx_2}{n} - b_{y\cdot2}\frac{\Sigma x_1x_2}{n} + b_{y\cdot2}b_{1\cdot2}\frac{\Sigma x_2^2}{n}$$

$$= \sigma_y\sigma_1 r_{y1} - b_{1\cdot2}\sigma_y\sigma_2 r_{y2} + b_{y\cdot2}\sigma_1\sigma_2 r_{12} + b_{y\cdot2}b_{1\cdot2}\sigma_2^2$$

From Equation 11-2 we can substitute for the regression coefficients $b$ their equivalents in terms of coefficients of correlation and standard deviations:

$$\frac{\Sigma(y - b_{y\cdot2})(x_1 - b_{1\cdot2}x_2)}{n}$$

$$= \sigma_y\sigma_1 r_{y1} - r_{12}\frac{\sigma_1}{\sigma_2}\sigma_y\sigma_2 r_{y2} - r_{y2}\frac{\sigma_y}{\sigma_2}\sigma_1\sigma_2 r_{12} + r_{y2}\frac{\sigma_y}{\sigma_2}r_{12}\frac{\sigma_1}{\sigma_2}\sigma_2^2$$

$$= \sigma_y\sigma_1 r_{y1} - \sigma_y\sigma_1 r_{y2}r_{12} - \sigma_y\sigma_1 r_{y2}r_{y1} + \sigma_y\sigma_1 r_{y2}r_{12}$$

$$= \sigma_y\sigma_1(r_{y1} - r_{y2}r_{12} - r_{y2}r_{12} + r_{y2}r_{12})$$

$$= \sigma_y\sigma_1(r_{y1} - r_{y2}r_{12})$$

Now we can turn to the denominator and derive the first standard deviation:

$$\sigma^2_{y-b_{y\cdot2}x_2} = \frac{\Sigma(y - b_{y\cdot2}x_2)^2}{n}$$

$$= \frac{\Sigma(y^2 - 2b_{y\cdot2}yx_2 + b^2_{y\cdot2}x^2_2)}{n}$$

$$= \frac{\Sigma y^2}{n} - 2b_{y\cdot2}\frac{\Sigma yx_2}{n} + b^2_{y\cdot2}\frac{\Sigma x^2_2}{n}$$

Substituting from Equation 11-2 the equivalents of the $b$ terms, we have

$$\sigma^2_{y-b_{y\cdot2}x_2} = \sigma^2_y - 2r_{y2}\frac{\sigma_y}{\sigma_2}\sigma_y\sigma_2 r_{y2} + r^2_{y2}\frac{\sigma^2_y}{\sigma^2_2}\sigma^2_2$$

$$= \sigma^2_y - 2r^2_{y2}\sigma^2_y + r^2_{y2}\sigma^2_y$$

$$= \sigma^2_y - r^2_{y2}\sigma^2_y$$

$$= \sigma^2_y(1 - r^2_{y2})$$

$$\sigma_{y-b_{y\cdot2}x_2} = \sigma_y\sqrt{1 - r^2_{y2}}$$

By analogy, the other standard deviation in the denominator is

$$\sigma_{x_1-b_{1\cdot2}x_2} = \sigma_1\sqrt{1 - r^2_{12}}$$

Putting together the numerator and the denominator, we have

$$r_{y1\cdot2} = \frac{\sigma_y\sigma_1(r_{y1} - r_{y2}r_{12})}{\sigma_y\sqrt{1 - r^2_{y2}}\,\sigma_1\sqrt{1 - r^2_{12}}}$$

$$= \frac{r_{y1} - r_{y2}r_{12}}{\sqrt{(1 - r^2_{y2})(1 - r^2_{12})}} \tag{11-7}$$

*Formula for Coefficient of Multiple Correlation*

The coefficient of multiple correlation for the three-variable case is

$$R_{y\cdot12} = \sqrt{1 - \frac{\sigma^2_{y\cdot12}}{\sigma^2_y}} \tag{11-19}$$

Squaring both sides of the equation results in

$$R^2_{y\cdot12} = 1 - \frac{\sigma^2_{y\cdot12}}{\sigma^2_y}$$

Substituting for $\sigma^2_{y\cdot 12}$ from Equation 11-9, we have

$$R^2_{y\cdot 12} = 1 - \frac{\sigma^2_y(1 - r^2_{y1})(1 - r^2_{y2\cdot 1})}{\sigma^2_Y}$$
$$= 1 - 1(1 - r^2_{y1})(1 - r^2_{y2\cdot 1})$$

Substituting for $r_{y2\cdot 1}$ from Equation 11-7 gives

$$R^2_{y\cdot 12} = 1 - (1 - r^2_{y1}) \left\{ 1 - \left[ \frac{r_{y2} - r_{y1}r_{12}}{\sqrt{(1 - r^2_{y1})(1 - r^2_{12})}} \right]^2 \right\}$$

$$= 1 - (1 - r^2_{y1}) \left[ 1 - \frac{r^2_{y2} - 2r_{y1}r_{y2}r_{12} + r^2_{y1}r^2_{12}}{(1 - r^2_{y1})(1 - r^2_{12})} \right]$$

$$= 1 - (1 - r^2_{y1}) \left[ \frac{(1 - r^2_{y1})(1 - r^2_{12})}{(1 - r^2_{y1})(1 - r^2_{12})} \right.$$
$$\left. - \frac{r^2_{y2} - 2r_{y1}r_{y2}r_{12} + r^2_{y1}r^2_{12}}{(1 - r^2_{y1})(1 - r^2_{12})} \right]$$

$$= 1 - \frac{(1 - r^2_{y1})(1 - r^2_{12})}{(1 - r^2_{y1})(1 - r^2_{12})} + \frac{(1 - r^2_{y1})(r^2_{y2} - 2r_{y1}r_{y2}r_{12} + r^2_{y1}r^2_{12})}{(1 - r^2_{y1})(1 - r^2_{12})}$$

$$= \frac{1 - r^2_{12}}{1 - r^2_{12}} - \frac{(1 - r^2_{y1})(1 - r^2_{12})}{1 - r^2_{12}} + \frac{(r^2_{y2} - 2r_{y1}r_{y2}r_{12} + r^2_{y1}r^2_{12})}{1 - r^2_{12}}$$

$$= \frac{(1 - r^2_{12}) - (1 - r^2_{y1})(1 - r^2_{12}) + (r^2_{y2} - 2r_{y1}r_{y2}r_{12} + r^2_{y1}r^2_{12})}{1 - r^2_{12}}$$

$$= \frac{1 - r^2_{12} - (1 - r^2_{12} - r^2_{y1} + r^2_{y1}r^2_{12}) + r^2_{y2} - 2r_{y1}r_{y2}r_{12} + r^2_{y1}r^2_{12}}{1 - r^2_{12}}$$

$$= \frac{1 - r^2_{12} - 1 + r^2_{12} + r^2_{y1} - r^2_{y1}r^2_{12} + r^2_{y2} - 2r_{y1}r_{y2}r_{12} + r^2_{y1}r^2_{12}}{1 - r^2_{12}}$$

$$R^2_{y\cdot 12} = \frac{r^2_{y1} + r^2_{y2} - 2r_{y1}r_{y2}r_{12}}{1 - r^2_{12}} \tag{11-21}$$

$$R_{y\cdot 12} = \sqrt{\frac{r^2_{y1} + r^2_{y2} - 2r_{y1}r_{y2}r_{12}}{1 - r^2_{12}}} \tag{11-22}$$

Equation (11-22) is a computational formula for the coefficient of multiple correlation involving three variables.

### Effects of Differential Weighting on Standard Deviation

$$\sigma^2_{c_W} = W^2_1\sigma^2_1 + \cdots + W^2_k\sigma^2_k + 2W_1W_2\sigma_1\sigma_2r_{12} + \cdots + 2W_{k-1}W_k\sigma_{k-1}\sigma_kr_{(k-1)k} \tag{11-38}$$

If we have standard scores and all intercorrelations are equal, then

$$\sigma^2_{c_W} = W^2_1 + \cdots + W^2_k + 2W_1W_2r + \cdots + 2W_{k-1}W_kr$$
$$= \Sigma W^2 + rW_1(W_2 + \cdots + W_k) + \cdots + rW_k(W_1 + \cdots + W_k - 1)$$

From Equation 3-7 we know that the variance of a set of values is equal to the mean of the squares of those values minus the square of their mean. Hence

$$\sigma_W^2 = \frac{\Sigma W^2}{k} - \bar{W}^2$$

and consequently

$$k\sigma_W^2 + k\bar{W}^2 = \Sigma W^2$$

Therefore

$$\sigma_{c_W}^2 = k\sigma_W^2 + k\bar{W}^2 + rW_1(\Sigma W - W_1) + \cdots + rW_k(\Sigma W - W_k)$$
$$= k\sigma_W^2 = k\bar{W}^2 + rW_1\Sigma W - rW_1^2 + \cdots + rW_k\Sigma W - rW_k^2$$

Rearranging terms gives

$$\sigma_{c_W}^2 = k\sigma_W^2 + k\bar{W}^2 + rW_1\Sigma W + \cdots + rW_k\Sigma W - rW_1^2 - \cdots - rW_k^2$$
$$= k\sigma_W^2 + k\bar{W}^2 + r\Sigma W(W_1 + \cdots + W_k) - r\Sigma W^2$$

Again substituting for $\Sigma W^2$ as we did above we get

$$\sigma_{c_W}^2 = k\sigma_W^2 + k\bar{W}^2 + r\Sigma W\Sigma W - kr\sigma_W^2 - kr\bar{W}^2$$

Recall that the mean of a set of values is equal to their sum divided by their number. Hence

$$\bar{W} = \frac{\Sigma W}{k}$$

and consequently

$$k\bar{W} = \Sigma W$$

Therefore

$$\sigma_{c_W}^2 = k\sigma_W^2 + k\bar{W}^2 + k^2r\bar{W}^2 - kr\sigma_W^2 - kr\bar{W}^2$$

$$= k(\sigma_W^2 + \bar{W}^2 + kr\bar{W}^2 - r\sigma_W^2 - r\bar{W}^2)$$

$$\sigma_{c_W}^2 = k[\sigma_W^2(1 - r) + r\bar{W}^2(k - 1) + \bar{W}^2] \qquad (11\text{-}39)$$

$$\sigma_{c_W} = \sqrt{k[\sigma_W^2(1 - r) + r\bar{W}^2(k - 1) + \bar{W}^2]} \qquad (11\text{-}40)$$

### Correlation Between Differentially and Equally Weighted Composites

$$r_{c_w c} = r_{(W_1 x_1 + \cdots + W_k x_k)(x_1 + \cdots + x_k)}$$

$$= \frac{(W_1 x_1 + \cdots + W_k x_k)(x_1 + \cdots + x_k)}{n \sigma_{c_w} \sigma_c}$$

$$= \frac{\Sigma(W_1 x_1^2 + W_1 x_1 x_2 + \cdots + W_1 x_1 x_k + \cdots + W_k x_k x_1 + \cdots + W_k x_k x_{k-1} + W_k x_k^2)}{n \sigma_{c_w} \sigma_c}$$

$$= \frac{W_1 \dfrac{\Sigma x_1^2}{n} + W_1 \dfrac{\Sigma x_1 x_2}{n} + \cdots + W_1 \dfrac{\Sigma x_1 x_k}{n} + \cdots + W_k \dfrac{\Sigma x_k x_1}{n} + \cdots + W_k \dfrac{\Sigma x_k x_{k-1}}{n} + W_k \dfrac{\Sigma x_k^2}{n}}{\sigma_{c_w} \sigma_c}$$

$$= \frac{W_1 \sigma_1^2 + W_1 \sigma_1 \sigma_2 r_{12} + \cdots + W_1 \sigma_1 \sigma_k r_{1k} + \cdots + W_k \sigma_k \sigma_1 r_{k1} + \cdots + W_k \sigma_k \sigma_{k-1} r_{k(k-1)} + W_k \sigma_k^2}{\sigma_{c_w} \sigma_c}$$

Rearranging terms gives

$$r_{c_w c} = \frac{W_1 \sigma_1^2 + \cdots + W_k \sigma_k^2 + (W_1 \sigma_1 \sigma_2 r_{12} + \cdots + W_1 \sigma_1 \sigma_k r_{1k}) + \cdots + (W_k \sigma_k \sigma_1 r_{k1} + \cdots + W_k \sigma_k \sigma_{k-1} r_{k(k-1)})}{\sigma_{c_w} \sigma_c} \quad (11\text{-}41)$$

## Summary

The correlation between a differentially weighted composite and a criterion varies with the pattern of weights—the relative magnitudes of the nominal weights assigned to the components of the composite. For any given composite there is an optimal pattern of weights. This pattern is optimal in the sense that when the weights are applied to the components, the highest possible correlation between the composite and the outside variable results.

The optimal weights are given by the multiple regression equation, and the coefficient of correlation between the optimally weighted composite and the criterion is termed the coefficient of multiple correlation. This coefficient is derived from partial correlation—the correlation between two variables when scores on other variables are held constant. It is parallel to the simple Pearsonian correlation coefficient between two variables and is interpreted in the same way with respect to linearity and homoscedasticity.

The higher the correlations between the components and the criterion and the lower the intercorrelations among the components, the higher the coefficient of multiple correlation. In addition, a component that correlates low with the criterion, but is highly correlated with the other components adds to the multiple correlation. Variables of this sort are termed suppressors, since they suppress or hold constant that part of other components that is unrelated to the criterion.

Rather than emphasizing linear multiple regression, we can also adopt nonlinear regression models such as moderated regression or pattern analysis. The focus in these models is on the interactive effects of the predictor. The former approach emphasizes the influence of a third variable, a moderator, on the relationship between tests and a criterion. The latter approach focuses on the relationship of response patterns with the criterion. In this case we are particularly interested in the pattern of scores regardless of the linearity of the relationship. Often we simply look at particular response patterns and the associated criterion scores for groups having this pattern. Such attention is also applied in discriminant function analysis, which though conceptually equivalent to multiple regression analysis, emphasizes prediction of group membership.

If we want to weight according to experience, theory, or practice, we can adopt general weighting schemes. When scores on the components forming a composite are *deliberately* weighted differentially, each score is multiplied by its appropriate weight. It is not the absolute magnitude of the weights that is important; rather it is their relative magnitudes. Weights deliberately assigned to components are termed nominal, and the weights components actually carry in the composite are termed effective.

The mean of composite scores is solely and entirely a function of the means of the components. When the intercorrelations among the components differ from zero, the contribution of the components to the standard deviation of composite scores cannot be determined.

When components are deliberately weighted differentially, those components that are assigned higher weights contribute more to the composite mean than do those that are assigned lower weights. The greater the variation among the nominal weights, the larger the standard deviation of composite scores, and this effect is more pronounced the lower are the intercorrelations among the components. When differential weights are applied to components, the greater the relative variation among the weights, the lower the intercorrelations among the components, and the smaller the number of components, the more changed is the order of individuals in composite scores.

Most of the chapter focused on one form of weighting or another. Any weighting system is compensatory; that is, effective performance on one variable or test can compensate for deficiency on another test in the composite. An alternative to compensatory weighting is a multiple-cutoff procedure, which requires that some *minimal* amount of proficiency be possessed for *all* components or tests in the composite.

## Suggested Readings

Cohen, J. 1968. Multiple regression as a general data analytic system. *Psychological Bulletin*, 70:426–443.

Cohen, J., and P. Cohen. 1975. *Applied multiple regression/correlation analysis for the behavioral sciences*. Hillsdale, N.J.: Lawrence Erlbaum Associates. Chaps. 3 and 4.

Conger, A. J. 1974. A revised definition for suppressor variables: A guide to their identification and interpretation. *Educational and Psychological Measurement*, 34:35–46.

Darlington, R. B. 1968. Multiple regression in psychological research and practice. *Psychological Bulletin*, 69:161–182.

Gaier, E. L., and M. C. Lee. 1953. Pattern analysis: The configural approach to predictive measurement. *Psychological Bulletin*, 50:140–148.

Ghiselli, E. E. 1956. Differentiation of individuals in terms of their predictability. *Journal of Applied Psychology*, 40:374–377.

Ghiselli, E. E. 1960a. The prediction of predictability. *Educational and Psychological Measurement*, 20:3–8.

Ghiselli, E. E. 1960b. Differentiation of tests in terms of the accuracy with which they predict for a given individual. *Educational and Psychological Measurement*, 20:675–684.

Gordon, R. A. 1968. Issues in multiple regression. *American Journal of Sociology*. 73:592–616.

Horst, P. 1954. Pattern analysis and configural scoring. *Journal of Clinical Psychology*, 10:3–11.

Kerlinger, F. N., and E. J. Pedhazur. 1973. *Multiple regression in behavioral research*. New York: Holt, Rinehart and Winston. Chaps. 3, 4, 5, and 12.

Lubin, A. 1957. Some formulae for use with suppressor variables. *Educational and Psychological Measurement*, 17:286–296.

Lubin, A., and H. G. Osburn. 1957. A theory of pattern analysis for the prediction of a quantitative criterion. *Psychometrika*, 22:63–73.

Lykken, D. T. 1956. A method of actuarial pattern analysis. *Psychological Bulletin*, 53:102–107.

Lykken, D. T., and R. Rose. 1963. Psychological prediction from actuarial tables. *Journal of Clinical Psychology*, 19:139–151.

Meehl, P. E. 1950. Configural scoring. *Journal of Consulting Psychology,* 14:165–171.

Saunders, D. R. 1956. Moderator variables in prediction. *Educational and Psychological Measurement,* 16:209–222.

Tatsuoka, M. M. 1970. *Discriminant analysis: The study of group differences.* Champaign, Ill.: Institute for Personality and Ability Testing.

Weiss, D. J. 1976. Multivariate procedures. In M. D. Dunnette (Ed.), *Handbook of industrial and organizational psychology.* Chicago, Rand McNally. Pp. 327–362.

Wherry, R. J., and R. H. Gaylord. 1946. Test selection with integral score weights. *Psychometrika,* 11:173–183.

Zedeck, S. 1971. Problems with the use of "moderator" variables. *Psychological Bulletin,* 76:295–310.

# 12

## Basic Concepts in Psychological Scaling

To this point we have been concerned with the ways, problems, and considerations of analyzing quantitative, numerical data; that is, after a test has been taken, a questionnaire responded to, an interview scored, or any other means by which data can be collected, we have computed means and standard deviations, determined reliability and validity, examined relationships, and possibly made predictions. We are now concerned with procedures for inferring numerical values from the kinds and types of responses analyzed. How do we get the numbers that are to be subsequently analyzed? What do the numbers represent?

*Scaling* is the process by which we record and measure variables. Recall that measurement involves the assignment of numbers or values according to rules. Scaling procedures provide a variety of such rules. These procedures are the operations needed to construct the measurement devices that behavioral scientists use for research, theory development, and practice. Scaling is an attempt to quantify individuals' responses to stimuli. Thus the major goal of scaling is to study the relationship between overt responses and objectively definable stimuli. As will be seen, scaling is achieved by applying equations or formulas to obtained data. Not only are the formulas used for scaling stimuli, but they represent theories of behavior such as choice behavior when the task is to indicate preference among stimuli. Thus another purpose of scaling is for psychological modeling. In brief, scaling involves the application of a specific model (equation) to the analysis of data in order to arrive at numbers to attach to the stimuli. The result of any scaling model is a continuum on which persons or objects (stimuli) are located. For example, a scale for an attribute or a stimulus such as compulsiveness can be developed such that subjects' responses to the scale permit us to indicate that subject *A* is higher in the attribute than subject *B,* but lower than subject *C.*

Finally keep in mind that a test has been broadly defined as any device that is used to provide descriptions of persons and their attributes, either for prediction or for assessment purposes. Thus another purpose for discussing scaling, and the problems associated with it, is to further enhance the emphasis that we have placed on making our variables of interest more quantifiable. This is true whether we are in education, industry, or community-health settings. Increasing quantification leads to standardization, precision, and consensus in measurement, assessment, and prediction.

There are several issues and considerations to be examined in a discussion of scaling and its procedures. In this chapter, as we briefly describe several scaling procedures, we will do so in terms of three considerations. First, what are the differences when the attempt is to *scale persons as opposed to an attempt to scale stimuli?* Stimuli are the "things" researchers usually present to a subject for the purpose of eliciting some response. That is, we can present such stimuli as a list of personality adjectives, a series of arithmetical operations, or statements about abortion. A list of people to be evaluated, such as in performance evaluation systems, is also considered a stimulus. Responses and data gathered about the stimuli permit us to form a scale that indicates differences between the adjectives, or between the arithmetical operations, and so on. Scaling persons is more obvious and simpler, and it permits us to identify differences between persons. Is Harry a better employee than Jane? Is Mary more aggressive than Bill? If we are scaling persons as opposed to stimuli, adjectives, or items, then we may need different scaling procedures.

Scaling stimuli is usually preliminary to eventually scaling people. We must be certain of the adequacy of the attribute or stimulus before we can measure people. That is, if we are concerned with whether Jane is more aggressive than Mary, then the items measuring various levels of aggressiveness to which Jane and Mary will respond should in fact be representative and appropriate measures of aggressiveness.

At this point we also make an important distinction. Scaling stimuli involves the use of experts or judges. Scaling persons involves the use of subjects, usually randomly sampled from an available, larger pool of subjects. That is, if we want to develop a scale composed of items measuring attitudes toward abortion, the people providing the responses needed for development are treated as if they were experts or judges; they indicate the degree of positiveness or negativeness of each potential item. Typically the average value of each statement is the scale value. In this case the respondents, the judges, are part of the measurement process. In contrast, when we scale people, we have a group of subjects; we are interested in the differences in this group on some attribute. In this case the statements or stimuli are combined (summed) to yield a score for each subject in the sample.

The issue of whether we are interested in scaling persons or stimuli leads us to our second consideration. That is, what kind of *response* is required of the respondent? Respondents can be required to make absolute evaluative assessments or categorical judgments about things or other subjects. Alternatively, respondents can be asked to make comparative evaluations between subjects or stimuli.

The kind of response a subject provides leads to the third consideration in this chapter. When a subject responds, the response can usually be on an ordinal scale or on an interval scale. The question, though, is whether the *resulting* scale is ordinal, interval, or perhaps ratio. Thus the third consideration in our discussion of scaling procedures is whether a resulting scale is formed through *direct estimation* (that is, interval responses leading to a scale that identifies differences between subjects or stimuli on an interval scale); or we can have *indirect estimation* (that is, ordinal responses that are transformed for the purpose of allowing differences to be discussed on an interval-scale basis).

## Scaling Persons and Stimuli

There are usually two main reasons for employing scaling procedures. One reason is to *scale persons:* that is, we are interested in the assessment of differences between persons. Is the difference between the views of Tom and Dick the same as the difference between the views of Harry and Dick? When the notion is to scale persons, all subjects in a sample would respond to the same set of stimuli (questions), and any obtained differences in obtained scale scores reflect real differences among the respondents. It is assumed that the stimuli are interpreted identically by all respondents. In brief, stimuli are held constant while persons vary.

The methods, statistics, and issues raised in the previous chapters are highly pertinent for the study of these individual differences. The area of psychological measurement concerned with individual differences is referred to as *psychometrics*. Most of the previous chapters have been concerned with this area.

A second reason for using scaling procedures is to *scale stimuli*. The concern here is with the assignment of numerical values to different stimuli based on the responses of one or more subjects. Is the degree to which the Calder is more artistic than the Picasso the same as the degree to which the Picasso is more artistic than the Peter Max? The value assigned to each stimulus reflects the magnitude of that stimulus on the psychological characteristic studied, in this case, the artistic merit of a work of art. Thus, in this situation, stimuli vary and persons are constant.

The purpose of scaling stimuli is to determine *perceived characteristics* of the stimuli. For example, we might be concerned with the perceived loudness of tones, the perceived favorability of statements about issues, the perceived preferences for stimuli, and the like. The stimuli-scale values developed for the constant group of subjects represents the "average" person of that group. Comparison studies can then be undertaken. If we scale preferences for brands of color-television sets (stimulus) on one type of group of subjects, we could then compare scale values with those of another group of subjects who differ on some attribute. This attribute could be young/old, poor/rich, college-educated/high-school-educated. In sum, the basic concern is the relationship between different scalings of the stimuli. For example, if the Zenith color-television set is rated 1 by the old, is it also rated 1 by the young?

The area of psychological measurement related to scaling stimuli is *psychophysics*. An example encountered in this area is the examination of the relationship between the physical weight of a stimulus and the psychological impact of the stimulus on the subject's perception. That is, suppose we asked you to compare an object weighing 10 pounds with an object weighing 30 pounds. It is obvious that you would perceive the second object to be heavier. However, suppose you were holding a 30-pound weight and we began adding weights in your hand in increments of half a pound. When will you notice or perceive a difference in weight? In the physical world, 30 pounds is not as heavy as 30.5 pounds; but from a psychological view, do you perceive a difference? One of the reasons for scaling would be to determine when enough half-pound weights have been added to produce a noticeable difference in perception.

## Responses Required by Scaling Procedures

Different responses may be required when we are scaling persons as opposed to scaling stimuli. Likewise, different responses may be required by different scaling procedures for both stimuli and persons.

In scaling stimuli, such as in the example of the weights in the preceding section, the subject is asked for a *judgment* that can be compared to a known standard. The subject's responses can, in essence, be verified by relating the perceived weight to the real physical weight. The subject is responding to the stimulus with respect to a designated attribute. We can compare the scale of judgments to the scale of physical magnitude.

We also can ask the subject for a *subjective evaluation.* In this case we are interested in the subject's opinion (interest, attitude, preference, personal reaction) concerning stimuli or persons. With this type of response, we have no real way of verifying. Obviously the subject's bias, as well as the relative position of the stimulus among other stimuli, interact to affect the response. For example, your attitude about abortion, as well as the intended reflected position of the statement, would influence your response to a question on abortion. Our main interest is in the consistency or reliability of such responses. However, we do strive to relate these subjective evaluations to external behaviors.

There is yet another way in which responses differ. A response can be *comparative* in that one stimulus or subject is compared to another. For example, high salary (stimulus) may be *preferred more than* job security (stimulus) when the subject is seeking employment. Or the superior indicates that John is a *better* employee than Pete. The response can also be *categorical,* such that the subject places the stimulus or person into one of two or more categories on a given dimension. That is, the subject endorses or agrees with a statement. For example, a response could be "moderately agree" when the possible responses range from "strongly agree" to "strongly disagree." Or the subject could indicate that the painting (stimulus) is "fair" with respect to its beauty (dimension) when the range of possible responses is from "ugly" to "beautiful." Or, yet, the subject is indicated to be an "average" employee on an organizational-ability dimension.

## Direct or Indirect Estimate of Scale Values

Another way in which the response is important for a discussion of scaling is with respect to the instructions given to the respondent and the form of the scale provided on which the subject is to respond. Keep in mind that we are interested in being able to scale stimuli or persons. We have an option of nominal, ordinal, interval, or ratio scales. However, in the development of these scales, the respondent may be provided with an ordinal scale on which to provide the response. If we want an ordinal scale of the stimuli or persons, then the instructions and procedures are such that provide a *direct estimate* of ordinal-scale values. A simple example of a direct estimate for an ordinal scale is to request the subjects to *rank order* the stimuli. On the other hand, we may want to scale stimuli or persons on an interval scale in such a way that the responses called for are *indirect estimates* that must be transformed to form a scale with interval-scale properties. In this case, subjects' responses are analyzed to yield a scale value rather than assumed to *be* the scale value. In essence, the basic distinction between direct and indirect scales is that in the former we assume that persons can produce desired scales directly, whereas in the latter the data must be transformed. We begin with indirect estimate methods.

*Indirect estimate methods* result in interval or ratio scales of attributes, stimuli, people, and the like, even though the developmental data are based on ordinal responses. The immediate question with regard to indirect estimate methods is why they are necessary. The answer is that ordinal responses are simpler to provide and less time-consuming, whereas interval scales are more susceptible to mathematical manipulation (refer to Chapter 2). An ordinal response is one that, for example, requires the respondents to rank order a group of scientists in terms of creativity. However, the resulting ordinal scale or ranking is deficient in several respects. First there is no real, meaningful measure of central tendency for this group. What is the average level of creativity of this group of scientists? Second there is no real measure of variability within the group. Especially if we did not permit ties in the rankings provided by each respondent, we have no way of determining how similar or dissimilar the members of the group are in creativity. In essence we are limited in the value of the information obtained from such scales.

In contrast, interval scales, as previously indicated, provide information about the distances between subjects in the sample. It is possible to determine an average level of the attribute studied and the deviation from this average for each member of the group. Interval as well as ratio scales are open to many forms of mathematical treatment, from the fundamental operations of addition, subtraction, multiplication, and division, to the methods of calculus. But again the ordinal response is the easiest to obtain from a respondent.

The basic model for achieving the desired scales comes from the work of Thurstone (1927a, 1927b). The model assumes as a given that a stimulus ($S$) elicits a response, reaction, or opinion ($R$) on a psychological continuum. That is, a subject can judge or evaluate ($R$) stimuli ($S$) on some psychological continuum. The problem in scaling is to place stimuli on the psychological scale of the attribute of interest.

Each stimulus in a set will elicit a response. Since we are dealing with psychological phenomena, with judgments, with perceptions, the *same* stimulus will elicit *different* responses. That is, at one time, you might indicate that you have a "very strong" preference ($R$) for the stimulus

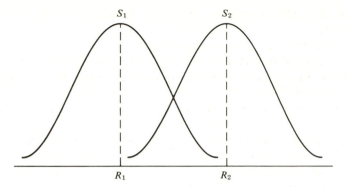

*Figure 12-1* Frequency distribution on a psychological continuum of responses associated with two stimuli.

$(S)$, while the next day you might indicate only a "strong" preference $(R)$ for the same stimulus $(S)$. If we present each stimulus a number of times, each time asking for a response or reaction, we can form a frequency distribution on the psychological continuum. The variations from occasion to occasion are treated as random error, and the responses are assumed to be normally distributed. Figure 12-1 is an example of a frequency distribution on a psychological continuum of responses associated with two stimuli, $S_1$ and $S_2$. $R_1$ and $R_2$, respectively, represent the modal responses to the two stimuli, $S_1$ and $S_2$. The responses can either be the *same* subject's responses to the stimuli on a number of different occasions, or they may be the responses of *many* subjects, each responding only once to the set of stimuli. In the former case, the $R_1$ is the average of the subject's responses to $S_1$. In the latter case, the $R_1$ is the average of the *group* of subjects to $S_1$.

An important aspect of indirect estimate methods and the requisite data is the variation in the responses: variation from subject to subject for each stimulus or within subject from occasion to occasion for each stimulus. As a simplified example of this variation, consider a study whose purpose is to scale the preferences for universities. If we repeatedly presented a list of universities to a subject for reactions on a scale ranging from 1 (excellent) to 7 (poor), the modal value of $S_1$ (perhaps, University of California at Berkeley, UCB) would be 3 ($\bar{R}_1$) and that of $S_2$ (University of Minnesota, UM) would be 5 ($\bar{R}_2$). Recall that a frequency distribution shows all the responses. In this case, for each stimulus we are assuming that there will be a range of different reactions or responses. That is, from occasion to occasion, the subject might assign values of 2, 3, or 4 to UCB and 3, 4, or 5 to UM. These variations are again due to random error and not to true changes in the *perceptions* of the universities or to actual changes in the universities over time.

The assumption, which we have made on many occasions in this book, is that the frequency distribution is normally distributed. Thus the modal value is also the mean or median. Since there are different reactions on different occasions, we obtain response standard deviations. Thus, for each stimulus, we obtain a mean and a standard deviation.

Note that the stimuli values are not directly obtainable from the observer. We do not ask for *one* response and assume it to be the *typical* reaction. Recall that there is error in measurement, and by repeating the task we obtain a representative value (mean) of the reaction to a stimulus. Models have been postulated that can be used to relate judgments of relations among stimuli to scale values and standard deviations of the stimuli on a psychological scale of interest, such as preference for universities. The scaling problem is to determine the differences between $R_1$ and $R_2$ and between other $R$ values for the stimuli being evaluated on the psychological scale.

## Indirect Estimate Methods

We will now discuss two specific indirect estimate models: first the law of comparative judgment, and then the law of categorical judgment.

### Law of Comparative Judgment

The *law of comparative judgment* is used when the task of the respondent is to directly compare each stimulus in a set with others in the set. For example, the task could be to scale preferences for universities and to determine whether UCB ($S_1$) is more desirable than UM ($S_2$), $S_3$, $S_4$, and so on. There would be a sample of universities on the list, and in essence each university is compared with every other one. This task requires, basically, ordinal judgments. One procedure for obtaining ordinal responses is known as the method of *paired comparisons*. If we compared 10 universities, then we would make $N(N - 1)/2$ (where $N$ is the number of stimuli) or 45 comparisons.

For illustrative purposes, let us now consider only the comparison of $S_1$ and $S_2$. If this comparison were made on many occasions, then we could determine the *proportion of times* UCB was preferred over UM. Or we could have many subjects do the paired comparisons and determine the proportion of subjects who prefer $S_1$ over $S_2$.

Either way, the essential datum is the proportion of times or subjects

$S_1$ is preferred over $S_2$, $S_3$, and so on. Stopping our analyses at this point results in the direct estimate of an ordinal scale. From this information, however, we hope to provide scale values to the universities that will have the properties of an interval scale. Such a scale is more meaningful than an ordinal scale, especially in its role as another variable (such as a dependent variable) in studies examining postulated relationships among a host of variables.

To obtain interval-scale values, we utilize the Table of Areas under the Normal Curve (see Appendix). We do this because of the assumptions that

1. Responses to $S_1$ and $S_2$ are normally distributed.
2. The mean of the distribution of the differences (which is normally distributed) between responses ($\bar{R}_d$) is the best estimate of the interval separating the two stimuli, or $\bar{R}_d = \bar{R}_1 - \bar{R}_2$.
3. The standard deviation of the difference is

$$\sigma_{\bar{R}_1 - \bar{R}_2} = \sqrt{\sigma_1^2 + \sigma_2^2 - 2r_{12}\sigma_1\sigma_2} \qquad (12\text{-}1)$$

where $r_{12}$ is the correlation between values of responses to stimuli.

The above assumptions are consistent with the assumptions that we made in the previous chapters on measurement theory and psychometrics. That is, true scores, error scores, and distributions are normally distributed. $\bar{R}_1$ and $\bar{R}_2$ are the best estimates of scale positions for those stimuli. Finally, the third assumption is a simple statement of the standard deviation of a composite *difference* score (in contrast to Equation 7-6, which is the standard deviation of a composite formed by *summing* two scores).

To return to our example, if $S_1$ is judged greater than $S_2$ 85 percent of the time, then the Table of Areas under the Normal Curve would indicate the $z$ value of 1.04. That is, 1.04 is one estimate of the difference from $S_1$ to $S_2$. Or the zero point on the scale of response differences is 1.04 standard deviations below the mean. The closer the stimuli are to each other (proportion of preference close to 50 percent), the closer the zero point of the scale is to $\bar{R}_d$. Figure 12-2 illustrates this point. The shaded portion represents the proportion of times $S_1$ is preferred over $S_2$ (85 percent); the unshaded portion represents the proportion of times $S_2$ is preferred over $S_1$. The mean of this distribution is equal to the difference in scale values of the two stimuli ($\bar{R}_d$).

The above $z$ value of 1.04 takes into account only the comparison of $S_1$ with $S_2$. However, suppose $S_1$ were also compared to $S_3$, $S_4$, ..., $S_{10}$; likewise, that $S_2$ were compared to $S_3$, $S_4$, ..., $S_{10}$. We can use this information to get a more accurate estimate of $R_2 - R_1$. That is, the difference between ($R_2 - R_3$) and ($R_1 - R_3$) also reflects $R_2 - R_1$; $R_2 -$

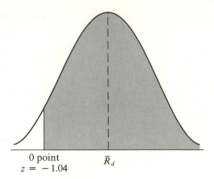

*Figure 12-2*    Distribution of response differences. Shaded portion
is percentage of times $S_1$ was preferred over $S_2$.

$R_1 = (R_2 - R_3) - (R_1 - R_3)$. Likewise, $R_2 - R_1 = (R_2 - R_{10}) - (R_1 - R_{10})$. Essentially, to get an accurate estimate of the difference between stimuli, for example, between $S_1$ and $S_2$, we want to include as much information as possible that we have on $S_1$ and $S_2$. Thus we include data for all comparisons involving $S_1$ and all comparisons involving $S_2$. However, since the standard deviations of response differences might be different for different pairs of stimuli, we express the interval separating two stimuli, $\bar{R}_d$, as a function of the normal deviation associated with the proportion and the standard deviation of the difference (Equation 12-1) or

$$\bar{R}_1 - \bar{R}_2 = \bar{R}_d = z\sigma_{\bar{R}_1 - \bar{R}_2} \tag{12-2}$$

$$\bar{R}_d = z\sqrt{\sigma_1^2 + \sigma_2^2 - 2r_{12}\sigma_1\sigma_2} \tag{12-3}$$

Again in the above equation $z$ is the value obtained from the Table of Areas under the Normal Curve. Equation 12-3 is the *complete form of the law of comparative judgment.* As will be shown shortly, we determine an $\bar{R}_d$ for each pair of stimuli, thereby providing scale values for each stimulus. All we need to know to determine the $\bar{R}_d$ values is the proportion of times each stimulus is judged to be "greater" ("better," "more desirable") than another stimulus, the standard deviations of the stimuli, and the correlation between the two stimuli.

As indicated, Equation 12-3 is the complete form of the law of comparative judgment. It is known as case I. Rarely is all this information known, and thus certain additional assumptions are made. One assumption is that the correlation between responses are independent and hence $r_{12}$ is zero. This is known as case III. Applying this assumption leads to the removal of the correlation part of Equation 12-3, and the law now becomes

$$\bar{R}_d = z \sqrt{\sigma_1^2 + \sigma_2^2} \qquad (12\text{-}4)$$

A second assumption is that the standard deviations of the responses are all equal. This is case V. The law is now represented as

$$\bar{R}_d = z\sigma \sqrt{2} \qquad (12\text{-}5)$$

Nunnally (1978) has reduced $\bar{R}_d$ to simply $z$ on the basis that $\sigma \sqrt{2}$ is a constant for all pairs of stimuli and thus its omission would result in the same proportional ordering of scale values as if it were applied. Thus

$$\bar{R}_d = z \qquad (12\text{-}6)$$

This is probably the most frequent use of the law. In essence, case V states that the difference between two stimuli, or the interval separating two stimuli, can be represented by the normal deviate value associated with the proportion that one stimulus is preferred over another (that is, the $z$ value associated with $R_d$, which is $R_1 - R_2$).

To complete Thurstone's cases, case II uses the general equation, Equation 12-3, but a group of observers are involved, each observer making only one judgment for each pair of stimuli. Case IV assumes that the standard deviations are approximately equal and must be estimated. This is not as simple computationally as is case V.

Essentially, the five cases presented are models to which we referred in the introduction of this chapter. Recall that we indicated that scaling is the application of specific models or equations to the analysis of data in order to arrive at numbers for stimuli. The five cases are models differing in assumptions. The purpose of the assumptions is to simplify computation and analysis without affecting the meaningfulness of the raw data while at the same time permitting the outcomes (resulting interval scales) to be used in additional ways, such as in the determination of relationships among variables.

*Paired-comparisons method*  Almost any method requiring ordinal responses can be used with the law of comparative judgment. To illustrate the procedure, we use the *method of paired comparisons,* and return to our example of preferences for universities, where we will now consider how scale values are obtained for all stimuli according to case V assumptions. This is basically achieved by determining the proportion of times each stimulus is preferred over each of the others. For illustrative purposes, we will assume that 100 subjects did a paired

***Table 12-1***   Proportion of subjects who preferred each university $(k)$ in comparison to each of the other universities $(j)$

|  |  | University $(k)$ | | | | |
|---|---|---|---|---|---|---|
|  |  | A | B | C | D | E |
| University $(j)$ | A | .50 | .79 | .16 | .48 | .67 |
|  | B | .21 | .50 | .03 | .21 | .25 |
|  | C | .84 | .97 | .50 | .76 | .81 |
|  | D | .52 | .79 | .24 | .50 | .68 |
|  | E | .33 | .75 | .19 | .32 | .50 |

comparison of five universities. Thus each subject had to do 10 comparisons. The data can easily be put into the form of a matrix such as in Table 12-1. *A–E* represent the five universities. The body of the table contains the obtained proportions or the percentage of subjects who preferred the column university $(k)$ over the row university $(j)$. For example, as shown in Table 12-1, 79 percent of the subjects preferred *B* over *A*, 21 percent preferred *D* over *B*, and so on. The sums of the two proportions $(p)$ pertaining to, for example, *A* preferred over *B* and *B* preferred over *A* must be equal to 1.00: $P_{BC} + P_{CB} = 1.00$, $P_{DC} + P_{CD} = 1.00$, and so forth. The diagonal can be left blank, or an alternative is to insert the proportion .50.

The next step is to convert each proportion to a *z* score obtained by examining the Table of Areas under the Normal Curve (Appendix A). The normal deviate is used as the *z* score with all proportions over .50 yielding positive *z* values and all proportions under .50 yielding negative *z* values. These *z* values can be put into a table similar to Table 12-1, and is illustrated in Table 12-2. Instead of proportions, we have normal deviate values. Applying case V implies that each of the normal deviates can be considered an interval between the two stimuli involved. That is, each *z* value in Table 12-2 is an estimate of a scale value for one equation of the law. We have as many equations as we have number of stimuli. We have *A* versus *B*, versus *C*, versus *D*, and versus *E*. Thus to obtain final scale values for each of the stimuli, we average the *columns* of the normal deviate matrix. That is, we average the results of the five equations. The results are shown in Table 12-2. The average of the *A* column is − .04; of the *B* column, it is .83; and so on. These average values can be taken as the scale values for the stimuli. Or we can remove negative values by adding the positive value of the lowest value in the row of averages. In the present example, we add .89 (the positive value of university *C*, which is the lowest value in the row) to each of the other values in the row. The results of this step are shown

***Table 12-2*** Normal deviate values for proportions found in Table 12-1

|  |  | University ($k$) | | | | | |
|---|---|---|---|---|---|---|---|
|  |  | A | B | C | D | E |  |
| University ($j$) | A | 0.00 | .81 | −.99 | −.05 | .44 |  |
|  | B | −.81 | 0.00 | −1.88 | −.81 | −.67 |  |
|  | C | .99 | 1.88 | 0.00 | .71 | .88 |  |
|  | D | .05 | .81 | −.71 | 0.00 | .47 |  |
|  | E | −.44 | .67 | −.88 | −.47 | 0.00 |  |
|  |  |  |  |  |  |  | Sum |
| Sum |  | −.21 | 4.17 | −4.46 | −.62 | 1.12 | 0.00 |
| Average |  | −.04 | .83 | −.89 | −.12 | .22 | 0.00 |
| Final scale value |  | .85 | 1.72 | .00 | .77 | 1.11 | 4.45 |

in the final row of Table 12-2. Rearranging these values from lowest to highest indicates that preferences for universities increased from *C* (least preferred) to *D* to *A* to *E* to *B* (most preferred).

There are several checks that can be made on the calculations. The sum of the sums and of the averages should be zero. Also the sum of the final scale values should be *n* (the number of stimuli) times the value added to each average; in this case, .89 × 5 = 4.45.

Various other analytical procedures for determining scale values are fully discussed by Torgerson (1958). The results of the present paired-comparisons procedure is an interval scale reflecting differences in preference for universities. The interpretation is that university *C* is obviously the least preferred university (scale value of 0.00), and university *B* (scale value of 1.72) is the most preferred. The final scale is an interval scale of preferences for universities. Now these differences can be examined in their relationship to other characteristics or dimensions. For example, how do preferences relate to size of university, location, reputation, and the like? In any event, we have quantified preferential data that were ordinal, but result in an interval scale.

The law of comparative judgment can be applied to any procedure or body of data in which the responses are ordinal but convertible to percentages. Thus, procedures such as rank ordering stimuli and paired comparisons are accommodated and transformed into interval scales. However, an equally frequent task in the behavioral sciences is to assess stimuli in terms of some attribute, with the assessment being such that it is a response on some continuum. Essentially the respondent places the stimulus into a category or point on a continuum, but there is no assumption about the equality of differences between categories or points on the continuum. For example, often we are asked to indicate the degree to which we disagree or agree with a statement where the scale is

strongly disagree      disagree      uncertain      agree      strongly agree

In this case, we may have no basis for assuming anything about the difference between "agree" categories. To transform such a scale into an interval scale requires the application of another law, the law of categorical judgment.


## Law of Categorical Judgment

The *law of categorical judgment* applies to the situation where the task is to place several stimuli into one of several categories that differ quantitatively along a defined continuum. For example, the task of a person could be to evaluate each of 100 attitude statements on the basis of political ideology. The instructions would be to place each statement into one of five categories that could be

| extremely liberal | moderately liberal | middle-of-the-road | moderately conservative | extremely conservative |

There is *no* assumption of equality of category intervals. In fact, since the real values of the categories are unknown prior to scaling, we assume that there are boundaries or upper and lower limits for each category. That is, the placement of an item into the "middle-of-the-road" category is a point within the range of categories from above "moderately liberal" to below "moderately conservative." Due to various random fluctuations, responses for a stimulus are not fixed at a single point on the continuum, but rather the responses reflect a normal distribution of positions on the continuum. The purpose of applying the law of categorical judgment, its equations, and assumptions is to obtain interval-scale values of the items that reflect real differences among the items on a political liberal/conservative scale. The scaling problem is to estimate the values of the categories on the continuum, and from these reference values to derive interval-scale values for the items.

Again no assumption is made about the psychological equality of category intervals. It is assumed, however, that the categories are in some psychologically meaningful rank order. For convenience' sake, we could substitute the numbers 1 through 5 for the category titles of "extremely liberal" through "extremely conservative." As long as the categories are meaningfully ordered, titles are not important for these statistical analyses.

The basis for the law of categorical judgment is similar to that of the law of comparative judgment. One contrast between the laws is comparative versus categorical or absolute judgments. Comparative judgments become prohibitive when the number of stimuli or subjects evaluated, $N$, becomes too large. If 50 stimuli are to be compared, there could be 1,225 paired comparisons. It may be easier for the judge to provide 50 absolute judgments. In any event, though the two laws and accompanying procedures are applicable for similar situations, not only are they different in analytical procedure, but they vary in the task required of the respondent.

The law of categorical judgment assumes that the psychological dimensions being examined can be ordered into categories. It is further assumed that due to error and other factors, category boundaries are not fixed. That is, the same item can, on repeated occasions, be placed into different categories, or subjects will vary in the placement of items into categories. Finally, the subject judges a given stimulus (item) to be below a given category boundary whenever the value of the stimulus on the continuum is less than that of the category boundary. This latter assumption means that placement of an item into the "moderately liberal" category is really placing the item below the upper boundary of the "moderately liberal" category. These assumptions recognize the fact that boundaries between adjacent categories behave like stimuli. That is, there is a modal value and variation for the category. The task of scaling categorical judgments, as opposed to the previous task of comparative judgments, is to determine both stimulus (item) values and category values. Thus we now have to pay attention not only to the items but also to statistical characteristics of the categories.

The results of the above assumptions lead to a *complete form of the law of categorical judgment,* which is

$$C_g - R_j = z_{jg} \sqrt{\sigma_j^2 + \sigma_g^2 - 2r_{jg}\sigma_j\sigma_g} \qquad (12\text{-}7)$$

where $C_g$ represents the mean location of the $g$th category, $R_j$ is the scale value of the $j$th item, and the other notations are similar to those in the law of comparative judgment.

Again, as in the law of comparative judgment, there are simplifying assumptions in the law of categorical judgment, which lead to different cases (see Torgerson, 1958). The most often used equation is

$$C_g - R_j = z_{jg}\sigma_j \qquad (12\text{-}8)$$

**Table 12-3**    Proportion of judges who sorted each item into a category (Note that category numbers 1 through 5 represent category labels ranging from "extremely liberal" to "extremely conservative" in the text.)

|            | Category |      |      |      |      |
|------------|----------|------|------|------|------|
| Statement  | 1        | 2    | 3    | 4    | 5    |
| 1          | .04      | .16  | .20  | .25  | .35  |
| 2          | .10      | .20  | .30  | .35  | .05  |
| 3          | .20      | .25  | .40  | .10  | .05  |
| 4          | .30      | .40  | .20  | .06  | .04  |
| 5          | .45      | .35  | .15  | .03  | .02  |

Equation 12-8 is used to determine the average scale value of the item by taking into account the average value of the category.

*Successive-intervals method*    To illustrate the law of categorical judgment, we will use an example applying the *method of successive intervals*. Basically, the person is required to sort a series of stimuli (for example, statements or items) into categories that have been ordered, such as the five liberal/conservative categories previously mentioned. The exact procedure calls for many subjects to do this sorting. (However, the Thurstone models assume that the frequency distributions generated by one person making repeated sorts are the same as the frequency distributions generated by a number of people making one sort.) Thus the basic datum is the proportion of judges who sort a statement into a category. Table 12-3 contains the proportion of judges who sorted each of five statements into one of five categories. As seen in Table 12-3, subjects placed item 1 into the "extremely liberal" category (category 1 in the table) 4 percent of the time; likewise subjects placed item 3 into the "moderately conservative" category (category 4 in the table) 10 percent of the time. Next we are concerned with cumulative proportions; that is, the proportion of judges who sorted the item into a *given category or lower*. Thus cumulative proportions for the statements are shown in Table 12-4. The circled proportion indicates that 95 percent of the judges sorted statement 2 into category 4 or lower. For each of the cumulative proportions, we then obtain the normal deviates, found in the Table of the Areas under the Normal Curve. (The upper category, 5, always has a cumulative proportion equal to 1.00 and thus is not used for further analyses.) The normal deviates are shown in Table 12-5.

The data in Table 12-5 are used to obtain the information necessary to

*Table 12-4*  Cumulative proportions

| Statement | Category | | | | |
|-----------|------|------|------|------|------|
|           | 1    | 2    | 3    | 4    | 5    |
| 1         | .04  | .20  | .40  | .65  | 1.00 |
| 2         | .10  | .30  | .60  | .95  | 1.00 |
| 3         | .20  | .45  | .85  | .95  | 1.00 |
| 4         | .30  | .70  | .90  | .96  | 1.00 |
| 5         | .45  | .80  | .95  | .98  | 1.00 |

solve Equation 12-8. These data are used to find the true boundary positions of the categories as well as the true item values. First we determine the category boundaries. This is done by calculating the average value of each column in Table 12-5. Thus for boundary 1 the value is $-.90$; values for the remaining boundaries appear in the bottom row of Table 12-5. The reason for this averaging process is that we have as many scales as there are items, each with its own unit and origin. By averaging within the columns, we obtain a single set of values for the boundaries, each value corresponding to the width of the interval for adjacent categories. The next step is to calculate the average of the category boundaries, which in this case is .34.

To determine the values of the stimuli, we first average the $z$ values in each row of Table 12-5. For item 1 this value is $-.61$. We then apply Equation 12-8, which results in the value of .95 ($.34 - (-.61) = .95$). This calculation is repeated for the remaining four items. (The average of these stimulus values will be 0.00.) These values are interval values for the stimuli. Again they have been determined by taking into account the variance in category assignment as well as the variance in category boundaries. Persons in whose attitude we are interested are given the scale, and their score is the mean or median of the endorsed scale values.

The above scaling procedures have been mainly concerned with scaling stimuli. For many situations, however, we could substitute persons for stimuli and then obtain scale values for those persons. For example, we could obtain paired-comparison data for the purpose of assessing employees or students. A supervisor can be asked to rank order his or her 10 staff members in terms of overall effectiveness. Or he or she can do a paired comparison. In either case, the data can be transformed into interval scales whereby we can interpret the differences between the staff members. Likewise the supervisor can be asked to evaluate each of the 10 staff members on scales ranging from "ineffective"

**Table 12-5**   Normal deviates for cumulative proportions

| Statement | Category Boundary | | | | Row Sum | Row Av- erage | Scale Value |
|---|---|---|---|---|---|---|---|
| | 1 | 2 | 3 | 4 | | | |
| 1 | −1.75 | −.84 | −.25 | .39 | −2.45 | −.61 | .95 |
| 2 | −1.28 | −.52 | .25 | 1.65 | .10 | .03 | .31 |
| 3 | −.84 | −.13 | 1.04 | 1.65 | 1.72 | .43 | −.09 |
| 4 | −.52 | .52 | 1.28 | 1.75 | 3.03 | .76 | −.42 |
| 5 | −.13 | .84 | 1.66 | 2.05 | 4.42 | 1.11 | −.77 |
| Column sum | −4.52 | −.13 | 3.98 | 7.49 | 6.82 | | |
| Category boundary | −.90 | −.03 | .80 | 1.50 | | .34 | |

through "effective" with any number of categories between these extremes. Here again interval differences can be determined. In all of these cases, we are able to speak in terms of differences within the samples; these differences can be an end in and of themselves, or they can be correlated with other measures of performance, satisfaction, ability test results, and the like.

## Direct Estimate Methods

Direct estimates of ordinal or interval scale values are obtained by requiring the subject to respond with or generate the scale desired. No analytical technique is needed to transform the response from one type of scale to another; rather the desired scale is obtained directly from the subject who responded according to specified operations that lead to the scale.

### Rank-Order Method

The simplest example of a direct-estimate procedure is that of *rank order*. Suppose we have 10 students in a class. The instructions for the teacher are to rank order the students from "best" to "poorest" with respect to overall performance. The required response of the teacher is ordinal, and the result of the ranking is an ordinal scale. If we had 2 teachers who were familiar with each of the students, the responses received by each student would be averaged and then converted to ranks. (In addition we could get a measure of interrater reliability.) Thus in this procedure we go from ordinal responses to an ordinal scale.

To fully demonstrate the rank-order procedure, let us be more ambitious and assume that we have 10 professors who have the task of selecting a dean of a college, a position for which there are 8 candidates. The decision has been made that the candidate viewed as "best" by these professors will be chosen and that "best" will be defined as that candidate who has the highest overall ranking. Thus each professor independently ranks the candidate from "best" to "worst." (No ties are permitted.) The data are presented in Table 12-6. Candidate A was ranked first by professors 1, 3, 8, and 10; candidate A was ranked second by professors 2, 6, and 9; and so on. The average rank for each candidate is shown in the next to last column; these averages are then ranked to obtain the rank values for each candidate (shown in the last column of Table 12-1). The decision is to award the dean's position to candidate A.

Note that to find the difference between two stimuli, for example, between candidates A and B, we simply take the difference between their average rankings or converted ranks. This is equivalent to the indirect-estimate procedures, which obtain differences between stimuli by also taking the difference between averages ($\bar{R}_d = \bar{R}_1 - \bar{R}_2$).

## Equal-Appearing-Intervals Method

An example of requiring interval responses for forming an interval scale is the *method of equal-appearing intervals* (Thurstone, 1929). This procedure is widely used by researchers in the field of attitude theory and change. In this method the respondent is told to sort stimuli, such as statements about capital punishment, into a number of categories. The key aspect of this procedure is that the instructions to the persons involved in the development of the interval scale, who are referred to as judges, state that the intervals between categories should be assumed to be equal. That is, if we are to sort 100 statements into 10 categories, ranging from positive to negative, then we *assume* that the intervals between the adjacent categories are equal.

Let us develop the method of equal-appearing intervals. The first step is to collect as many potential statements (items) as possible pertaining to the dimension of interest—in this case, attitude toward capital punishment. The items should cover the range of the dimensions, from those very positive to those very negative.

The second step is to have known experts or judges evaluate these

Table 12-6  Data for rank-order procedure as direct estimate of an ordinal scale

| Candidate | Professor | | | | | | | | | | $\bar{X}$ | Converted Rank |
|---|---|---|---|---|---|---|---|---|---|---|---|---|
| | 1 | 2 | 3 | 4 | 5 | 6 | 7 | 8 | 9 | 10 | | |
| A | 1 | 2 | 1 | 4 | 3 | 2 | 3 | 1 | 2 | 1 | 2.0 | 1 |
| B | 4 | 3 | 2 | 1 | 2 | 3 | 2 | 2 | 3 | 3 | 2.5 | 2 |
| C | 5 | 4 | 4 | 3 | 5 | 1 | 1 | 3 | 1 | 2 | 2.9 | 3 |
| D | 3 | 1 | 3 | 5 | 1 | 5 | 5 | 4 | 5 | 4 | 3.6 | 4 |
| E | 2 | 5 | 8 | 2 | 4 | 4 | 4 | 5 | 4 | 6 | 4.4 | 5 |
| F | 6 | 8 | 7 | 6 | 7 | 6 | 6 | 6 | 7 | 5 | 6.4 | 6 |
| G | 8 | 6 | 6 | 7 | 8 | 7 | 7 | 7 | 6 | 8 | 7.0 | 7 |
| H | 7 | 7 | 5 | 8 | 6 | 8 | 8 | 8 | 8 | 7 | 7.2 | 8 |

statements to determine the degree of favorability toward the attitude. Judges might be lawyers, humanitarians, law enforcement officers or even "real" judges. Usually each judge is requested to sort each statement into one of 11 categories that range from "extremely favorable" to "extremely unfavorable." Judges are told to disregard their own attitudes and biases, but instead to sort on the basis of the statement's favorability toward the issue. Also, again, judges are told that the subjective distance between the 11 categories is equal. After all the judges have completed the sorting process, the mean and standard deviation for each item is determined.

Suppose we have 50 judges evaluate 50 potential items to reflect attitude toward capital punishment. The data can be represented by the layout in Table 12-7. For example, 35 judges placed item 1 into category 1, 10 placed item 1 into category 2, and 5 placed the item into category 3. Thus the mean and standard deviation for item 1 are 1.40 and 0.67, respectively. The standard deviation reflects *ambiguity*. If there is a large standard deviation, then it indicates that the group of judges disagreed in the favorableness of the statement. Small standard deviations reflect agreement among the judges. Thus items with large standard deviations are eliminated from the item pool. For example, items 48, 49, and 50 each have the same mean value 5.00. However, the smaller standard deviation (0.64) for item 48 indicates that more judges were in agreement as to its value than they were for items 49 and 50.

Items are chosen for the final scale based on the mean values. In the above case, item 48 would be chosen to represent the approximate midpoint of the favorable/unfavorable continuum, whereas items 49 and 50 would not be chosen. Usually 20 to 30 statements are chosen such that the statements cover the range of the dimension (favorable to unfavorable). The assumption is that the differences between items on the final scale fulfill the properties of an interval scale. This assumption of the final scale's property is based on the essential assumption of the procedure, that is, that the judge who does the sorting of statements does so in intervals that are psychologically equal.

The final scale is composed of the series of statements (without item values). Keep in mind that there is a difference between those who served as judges in the development of the scales and those who are subsequently to be judged. The latter is our population of interest, the ones whose attitudes in which we are interested.

Instructions to those whose attitudes we are measuring vary. Either the respondent is told to indicate all those items with which he or she agrees or to select a certain number that best represents his or her attitude. In any event a respondent's score is determined by averaging the scale values of those items agreed with. If the scale is properly constructed, it is expected that the items chosen would be similar in

**Table 12-7**  Data for equal-appearing intervals method as direct estimate of an interval scale

| Item | Category | | | | | | | | | | | $\bar{X}$ | SD |
| | 1 | 2 | 3 | 4 | 5 | 6 | 7 | 8 | 9 | 10 | 11 | | |
|---|---|---|---|---|---|---|---|---|---|---|---|---|---|
| 1 | 35 | 10 | 5 | 0 | 0 | 0 | 0 | 0 | 0 | 0 | 0 | 1.40 | 0.67 |
| 2 | 15 | 15 | 12 | 4 | 4 | 0 | 0 | 0 | 0 | 0 | 0 | 2.34 | 1.22 |
| 3 | 8 | 8 | 8 | 8 | 7 | 7 | 4 | 0 | 0 | 0 | 0 | 3.70 | 1.91 |
| . . . | . . . | . . . | . . . | . . . | . . . | . . . | . . . | . . . | . . . | . . . | . . . | . . . | . . . |
| 48 | 0 | 0 | 0 | 10 | 30 | 10 | 0 | 0 | 0 | 0 | 0 | 5.00 | 0.64 |
| 49 | 0 | 0 | 5 | 5 | 30 | 5 | 5 | 0 | 0 | 0 | 0 | 5.00 | 1.01 |
| 50 | 0 | 3 | 4 | 3 | 30 | 3 | 4 | 3 | 0 | 0 | 0 | 5.00 | 1.37 |

value. Keep in mind that reliability and validity analyses of this scale will determine its appropriateness and usefulness.

There are also methods for the direct development of ratio scales. However, these are rarely encountered in educational and psychological measurement and are not discussed in this book. Interested readers should consult Torgerson (1958) or Nunnally (1978) for ratio scales and other scaling issues.

*Likert Scales*

A frequently used scale that we will now discuss is developed by Likert's method (1932). This method is derived from categorical scaling procedures similar to the one identified above. Likert scaled five response categories—"strongly approve," "approve," "undecided," "disapprove," and "strongly disapprove." Attitude statements were evaluated on the basis of responses to the categories; that is, he used the obtained scale values as weights for the responses. However, he found that the simple weights of 1 through 5 correlated very highly with the obtained scale weights. Thus, today, a response format with five categories is referred to as a *Likert scale* and is used to obtain "summated ratings." That is, scores are obtained by adding the appropriate value for the responses to all items.

The purpose of Likert's method is to scale subjects. Items are selected for the purpose of yielding as much individual differences as possible. Subjects receive scores.

In general the procedure is as follows. If we were trying to assess the attitude toward an issue, items would be collected and presented to respondents. The respondent examines each item and indicates his agreement or disagreement with the statement on a five-point scale. The five points are usually labeled

strongly disagree    disagree    undecided    agree    strongly agree

These categories are assigned the values 1 through 5; thus again there is no direct category scaling as there is when the law of categorical judgment is applied.

It is now an a priori decision to use the 1–5 values with the direction of weighting determined from knowledge of the item content. The respondent's score is determined by summing the values over all items. A response of "strongly agree" to items presumed to be positive toward the issue receives the same value as does a "strongly disagree" response to an item whose presumed connotation is negative. The fact that "agree" or "disagree" types of responses are used means that usually moderately favorable and moderately unfavorable statements are selected. Extreme statements are thus not necessary.

As previously indicated, Likert identified response category values that subsequently correlated with 1 through 5 values. Since Likert's research, most researchers have maintained the five response category scoring of 1 through 5, though the response category labels have not necessarily been "strongly approve" through "strongly disapprove." In our example, we used "agreement;" others have used five response categories of "frequency," "intensity," or "difficulty," and the like. The equal-interval properties have been assumed when in fact the assumption may have been false. Thus respondents to summated-rating scales may have treated the response choices as equal intervals, but this may have been misleading. Fortunately, we have recently seen a renewal of efforts to scale response categories. Bass, Cascio, and O'Connor (1974) have scaled expressions of "frequency," and Spector (1976) has scaled expressions of "agreement," "evaluation," and "frequency." Of particular interest with regard to Spector's research results is the finding that a majority of existing attitude scales *do* use categories of approximately equal intervals.

A final point about Likert scales. Once the scales are constructed, item reliability should be assessed. Of special importance is item analysis. The items on the final scale should have high item–total correlations, which would indicate that the items are measuring the same dimension. This is especially important since items are chosen on an a priori, subjective basis. This issue is discussed in the next chapter.

### Guttman Scalogram Analysis

The scaling procedures we have discussed to this point—successive intervals, equal-appearing intervals, summated ratings—have focused on the assignment of values to stimuli and/or categories. It has been an assumption that the items in fact measure the attribute they are intended to measure; it may be that the items are measuring more than one dimension, and thus the average score or total score may not be too psychologically meaningful. There is, however, a scaling procedure available whose purpose is to determine whether the characteristics being studied involve only a single dimension. This is *Guttman scalogram analysis* (1947). Scalogram analysis is more concerned with testing the notion of the existence of a single dimension (unidimensionality) than with scale development. It is an analytical technique for determining whether an existing set of items meets the requirements of a particular scale.

Guttman's procedure relies heavily on the homogeneity of items. In this procedure, items are chosen on an a priori basis to reflect the attitude at issue. Items are selected in terms of increasing extremeness with regard to the attitude. That is, the first few items should be agreed with by most people, the next few items also should be selected by those who have moderate attitudes toward the issue, and the final items should also be selected by those with extreme feelings toward the issue. If the scale is operating correctly, then a respondent who endorses an extreme item (or favorable position) should have responded positively to all less extreme items and responded negatively (or not endorsed) all more extreme items.

For example, consider the following three statements that might be used to measure the attitude toward off-track betting:

1. Off-track betting might be financially beneficial to the state.

2. It would be beneficial for the state to adopt off-track betting.

3. Off-track betting would be the best thing for the state.

If you agreed with item 3, then you should agree with items 2 and 1. If you disagreed with item 3, but agreed with item 2, you should have agreed with item 1. In other words, since the items are in ascending order of positive reaction to the attitude, the respondent's behavior is reproducible.

Though the items are initially chosen on an a priori basis, retention in the final scale is based on their ordinal properties. That is, data would indicate that the above 3 items indicate *increasing* favorableness toward off-track betting. Thus items are scaled. These data are found by examining the pattern of responses of the subjects. The *ideal* result is for the pattern of responses to a series of items (say, 5) to model the following triangular pattern:

| Stimulus Item | Subject | | | | |
|---|---|---|---|---|---|
| | *A* | *B* | *C* | *D* | *E* |
| 5 | X | | | | |
| 4 | X | X | | | |
| 3 | X | X | X | | |
| 2 | X | X | X | X | |
| 1 | X | X | X | X | X |
| Total score | 5 | 4 | 3 | 2 | 1 |

That is, if subject *A* endorsed item 5, then he or she also endorsed the four other items. Item 5 would be the item most positive toward the dimension of interest. Subject *C*, whose total score is 3, does not endorse the most positive items, but does endorse the moderate ones (1 through 3). We can say as a result of these data that subject *A* is more favorable toward the dimension than is subject *C*. The essence of a Guttman scale is to come close to this triangular pattern. In this way, a given obtained score always has the same meaning.

If there are reversals, such as agreeing with item 2 but not with item 1, then the homogeneity of the scale is in doubt. The amount of reversals or error is used to compute the *index of reproducibility* and is equal to

$$1 - \frac{\text{total errors}}{\text{total responses}} \times 100 \qquad (12\text{-}9)$$

The data for the totals are obtained by examining the number of reversals for all items for all respondents. Usually an index of less than 85 implies that more work is needed in the formation of the unidimensional scale.

One way in which scalogram analysis has been applied is as follows: Ten subjects respond to each of three statements; for example, the above three statements dealing with off-track betting. Subjects respond by indicating "agree" (*a*) or "disagree" (*d*) to each item. The items are then ordered in terms of their frequencies of endorsement, and subjects are ordered in terms of their total scores (sum of items endorsed). For example, the responses of the ten subjects can be represented as shown in Table 12-8. Item 1 is agreed to by seven of the ten respondents (70 percent); item 2 is agreed to by six of the ten respondents (60 percent); and item 3 is agreed to by five (50 percent). Thus one way to interpret these preliminary results is that item 1 represents a more "pervasive" attitude and item 3 a more "extreme" attitude; if you endorsed item 3, you should have endorsed items 1 and 2. However, the above pattern is not perfect, for there are reversals. Subject *E* agreed with 2 items, but they were items 1 and 3, rather than 1 and 2; likewise subject *F* agreed with 2 items, but they were items 2 and 3. To determine the reproducibility of the scale for these ten subjects, the number of changes necessary to produce a scale pattern for each subject (row) is assessed, and these changes are considered to be the number of errors. For the above data there are two errors (subjects *E* and *F*). Applying Equation 12-8 yields

$$1 - \frac{2}{30(\text{i.e., } 10 \times 3)} = .93$$

or a reproducibility coefficient of .93. If the coefficient were low (that is, less than 85), we would conclude that the items of interest did not form

*Table 12-8* Data for Guttman scalogram analysis

| | Item | | | | | | |
|---|---|---|---|---|---|---|---|
| | 1 | | 2 | | 3 | | |
| Subject | *a* | *d* | *a* | *d* | *a* | *d* | Score |
| *A* | X | | X | | X | | 3 |
| *B* | X | | X | | X | | 3 |
| *C* | X | | X | | X | | 3 |
| *D* | X | | X | | | X | 2 |
| *E* | X | | | X | X | | 2 |
| *F* | | X | X | | X | | 2 |
| *G* | X | | X | | | X | 2 |
| *H* | X | | | X | | X | 1 |
| *I* | | X | | X | | X | 0 |
| *J* | | X | | X | | X | 0 |

a unidimensional scale and that some items would need to be eliminated or changed.

## Multidimensional Scaling

The procedures described in this chapter are used for studying psychological phenomena where it is generally assumed that there is one dimension underlying the phenomenon (or we can use the Guttman procedure to develop a unidimensional scale). That is, the phenomenon is assumed to be unidimensional, and the responses are a result of that single dimension. The comparative evaluations or categorical judgments are based on a single dimension. If, however, there is more than one dimension underlying the object being measured, and this is not taken into account, then we have problems in interpretation. Essentially the meaningfulness of the score is minimized. Two subjects could have the same score, yet we may have assessed different aspects of the object. For example, we often ask workers to indicate how satisfied they are with their jobs. We administer a questionnaire of satisfaction items and sum the scores. Two workers with the same score can be satisfied with different aspects of their jobs. The assumption of unidimensionality for our dimension as measured by the questionnaire would lead to erroneous conclusions. One worker could be satisfied with the work itself and with salary; the second worker could be satisfied with supervision and opportunity for promotion. The point is that "satisfaction with work" is composed of different dimensions, and this must be recognized and ascertained. Multidimensional scaling procedures would identify these dimensions.

In true *unidimensional scaling* the stimuli differ on one variable; the investigator controls or eliminates other factors that could influence judgments. If we are concerned with judging the beauty of paintings, we could present all the stimuli in color, all 8 × 10's, no mention of artist, and so on. In addition, instructions to the respondents would specifically state that beauty is being measured and all other variables should be ignored.

*Multidimensional scaling,* on the other hand, is more involved from the standpoint of statistics and assumptions. In multidimensional scaling, the number of dimensions differentiating the stimuli is usually unknown. The complex psychological phenomenon studied is usually represented by geometrical space. Individual stimuli are represented by points in that space. The more similar the stimuli, the closer the points. The objective of multidimensional scaling is to first determine the number of dimensions. The second step is to obtain scale values for the stimuli on a selected set of dimensions. The procedures for these two steps are presented elsewhere (Nunnally, 1978; Torgerson, 1958). The instructions usually require responses in terms of similarities or dissimilarities among stimuli.

Whether data are collected by multidimensional or unidimensional scales, there are two points to be emphasized. First, many models in this chapter have involved many assumptions. A test of these assumptions is replication and duplication. If similar results are obtained on repeated use of the scales and if several scales for the same objectives yield similar results, then the assumptions are tenable.

The second point is that all data points involve a true component and an error component. The error component is essential. Reduction in the amount of error will yield more appropriate data and provide more weight to *scores* than can presently be given.

## Summary

Scaling is the process by which we record and measure attributes. Scaling procedures apply specific models of behavior and provide the rules for assigning numbers or values. In determining which scaling procedure to apply to our problem of interest, three issues must be considered. First, are we scaling persons or scaling stimuli? That is, are we interested in identifying differences between persons on an attribute or in identifying differences among statements reflecting an attribute?

Second, what kind of response is required of the respondent? Judgments are potentially verifiable, usually by relating the judgments to a physical scale. Subjective evaluations are opinions, interests, preferences, reactions, and the like. Subjective evaluations are usually compared to external behavior since they are difficult to verify; a primary interest is to determine their reliability, and subsequently their relation to other attributes.

A distinction is also made between comparative responses and categorical or absolute responses. The former concerns a direct comparison between the stimuli, such as "I like A more than B." The latter type of response involves an absolute judgment of A and an absolute judgment of B.

A third consideration pertains to the type of scale desired. Usually the respondent provides information on an ordinal scale. If we want an ordinal scale for the attribute, then we use a direct-estimate procedure such as rank order and equal-appearing intervals. If we want an interval scale, then the ordinal data must be transformed. In these cases we can use Thurstone's models of comparative or categorical judgment. By applying certain equations, given certain assumptions, we can transform these ordinal data into an interval scale.

Likert scales are also used for scaling purposes. These scales have not been based so much on scaling properties, as on test-construction principles (which are discussed in the next chapter). The typical end result of a Likert scale is a "summated rating."

Guttman scalogram analysis is used to develop unidimensional scales. This procedure is based on the homogeneity of item content. If certain conditions are satisfied, persons can be scaled in such a way that their pattern of responses are reproducible simply by knowledge of the total score.

The procedures described in this chapter are basically used for studying unidimensional psychological phenomena. Keep in mind that there are multidimensional scaling procedures, but these are beyond the scope of this chapter.

---

## Suggested Readings

Bass, B. M., W. F. Cascio, and E. J. O'Connor. 1974. Magnitude estimations of expressions of frequency and amount. *Journal of Applied Psychology,* 59:313–320.

Edwards, A. L. 1957. *Techniques of attitude scale construction.* New York: Appleton-Century-Crofts.

Guttman, L. 1947. The Cornell technique for scale and intensity analysis. *Educational and Psychological Measurement,* 7:247–249.

Likert, R. 1932. A technique for the measurement of attitude scales. *Archives of Psychology,* Whole No. 140.

Maranell, G. M. 1974. *Scaling: A source-book for behavioral scientists.* Chicago: Aldine.

Nunnally, J. C. 1978. *Psychometric theory.* 2nd ed. New York: McGraw-Hill. Chap. 2.

Spector, P. E. 1976. Choosing response categories for summated rating scales. *Journal of Applied Psychology,* 61:374–375.

Thurstone, L. L. 1927a. A law of comparative judgment. *Psychological Review,* 34:273–286.

Thurstone, L. L. 1927b. Psychophysical analysis. *American Journal of Psychology,* 38:368–389.

Thurstone, L. L. 1929. Theory of attitude measurement. *Psychological Bulletin,* 36:222–241.

Torgerson, W. S. 1958. *Theory and methods of scaling.* New York, Wiley.

# 13

## *Basic Concepts in Test Construction*

The scaling procedures discussed in the preceding chapter gave us the rules for forming scales for measuring psychological attributes. More specifically, we examined the means by which numerical values can be applied to items, statements, adjectives, and the like. In other words, we have to this point developed items. In addition, in previous chapters, we have seen that the reliability and the validity of tests are essentially functions of the characteristics of the items. Recall that the qualitative and quantitative characteristics of the composite test depend on the quantitative and qualitative characteristics of the components (the items). The composite test scores have few statistical properties that cannot be derived from analysis of single items or the relationship between items.

Thus, given that we have already discussed reliability, validity, and composites, and that we have seen how values are assigned to items, it is the purpose of this chapter to discuss the relationship between item properties and the objectives of tests as one goes about constructing a test. In other words, this chapter is concerned with the basic concepts in test construction and item analysis. The basic presentation is from a conceptual point of view, since the necessary statistics underlying the analyses have been developed in previous chapters (to which the reader will be referred).

Item analysis has several purposes. As already indicated, item properties affect the reliability and the validity of the composite test. Since item properties are assessed on data collected in a pretest or pilot study, it is possible to construct tests with certain reliability and validity. The final form of the test can be improved through the selection, replacement, or revision of items.

Item analysis permits us to shorten a test while at the same time increasing the test's validity and reliability. Although we previously indicated that longer tests are more reliable and valid, and demonstrated the point with the Spearman–Brown formula, selective elimination of noncontributing items (removing items that are equivalent to those that remain) can increase the validity and reliability of item properties. In addition, knowledge of item properties permits us to develop new but parallel forms.

Prior to a discussion of item properties as they affect a test and its objectives, it is necessary to detour for a while and concern ourselves with a basic concept—a test. Throughout this book we have mentioned the word "test," defined it in general terms, used it casually, and generally assumed that the reader is aware of what we mean. However, it seems appropriate in a chapter on test construction to elaborate and at the same time summarize what is meant by the notion of a test. In addition, we shall focus on the objectives of tests, and then proceed to the main concerns of this chapter—item analysis, item properties, and test construction.

## Defining a Test

As behavioral scientists, our primary interest is in behavior. The observation of behavior is a *test*. Since we are scientists, we want to exercise some standardization and control over our observation of behavior. One way to do this is to specify the situations and conditions in which behavior is to occur and then to elicit behavior of the kind in which we are interested.

By specifying the situations and conditions for an individual, we are essentially providing a task on which the individual is to perform. The task can be repeated for that individual, or several similar tasks can be provided to that individual, or the same task(s) can be provided to several individuals for the purpose of comparing persons. The interpretation of some responses to a task is obvious. Other responses to a task need to be interpreted on the basis of inference with respect to the "type" of behavior it represents.

In any event, we have treated a task given to an individual for the purpose of obtaining information on that individual's behavior as an *item.* Providing a series of tasks on which the individual is to perform is a *test.* With this definition in mind, let us briefly mention several types of tests.

### Types of Tests

*Achievement*    Such tests contain items, questions, tasks, and the like, that attempt to determine what an individual knows or can do. Usually these tests measure the skill and knowledge that a person has acquired in a subject matter. These tests attempt to elicit the best performance from the respondent. Perhaps the clearest example of a test is a work sample. This test requires the individual to perform a task directly, such as a typing test.

Examples of achievement tests are those commonly used in industrial settings for the purpose of hiring those who have requisite skills. There are many standardized tests (see Buros, 1978) for measuring skills such as typing, stenography, bookkeeping, and so on, that are used by industry to choose those who have minimal proficiency levels or to predict trainability.

In educational settings, there exist standardized tests, such as those developed by the American College Testing Program, which measure achievement in school subjects (English, mathematics, social studies, and natural sciences). The items on these tests, like all achievement tests, are verifiable; that is, they have correct answers and are used to determine how much a student has learned.

*Aptitude*    Such tests contain tasks similar to those on achievement tests, but are administered for the purpose of inferring how well a person *will do* in some future situation. The above-mentioned American College Testing Program becomes an aptitude test if it is used to predict how well students will do in similar courses in college. Perhaps a more familiar aptitude test is the Scholastic Aptitude Test, which provides verbal and mathematical aptitude scores. Essentially this test assesses an individual's reading comprehension and mathematical reasoning ability and is used to predict success in college.

For selection in industry, a common aptitude battery is the Differential Aptitude Tests, which measure verbal reasoning, numerical ability, abstract reasoning, spatial relations ability, mechanical reasoning, and clerical speed and accuracy.

Examples of items measuring the above abilities are similar to the following (regardless of whether they are found in achievement or aptitude tests):

a. *Verbal reasoning*. Verbal analogies in which the first and fourth missing words must be filled in. For example:

_____ is to chair as sleep is to _____.
(1) table–tired   (2) climb–down   (3) sit–bed   (4) walk–run

(The correct answer is alternative 3.)

b. *Numerical ability*. Often involves simple addition, subtraction, multiplication, and division problems, or algebraic manipulations. The respondent is required to do as many as possible within a specified time period. Or the following type of question may be asked:

If John bought a 7 and ¾ kilogram turkey at 27 cents a kilogram, how much did the turkey cost? ____

c. *Abstract reasoning*. An abstract problem is presented that the respondent must complete. For example, the respondent must provide the fifth box in the following link:

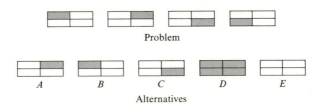

Problem

Alternatives

(The correct answer is alternative *B*.)

d. *Spatial relations ability*. The purpose is to identify one's ability for completing objects through visualization; that is, how objects will look if parts are moved about, transformed, or reassembled. For example, which of the figures can be made from the following pattern?

(The correct answer is alternative D.)

e. *Mechanical reasoning*. Respondents are required to solve mechanical problems. For example, which end, *A* or *B*, is supporting the greater weight? (If equal, the respondent is to mark a *C* on the answer sheet.)

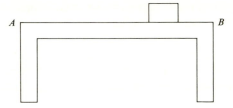

(The correct answer is alternative *B*.)

f. *Clerical speed and accuracy*. Measures speed of responses to simple perceptual tasks. For example, two long columns of numbers are presented to a respondent whose task is to identify as many incorrect pairs of sets of numbers in a specified period of time. The following is a portion of two sets:

|   |         |         |
|---|---------|---------|
| A | 1798426 | 1798426 |
| B | 4692152 | 4682152 |
| C | 9324721 | 9324721 |
| D | 8421682 | 8421682 |
| E | 7249156 | 7246156 |

(The incorrect pairs of sets are *B* and *E*.)

*Personality*    Such tests are concerned with affective or nonintellectual aspects of behavior. These tests attempt to elicit the typical response for that individual to a task.

Personality tests take several forms. They can require informational or factual responses from the subject that are interpreted by the examiner. For example, the question can be: Do you have nightmares? Or the respondent can be called upon to recall incidents that are also interpreted by the examiner. A second form of personality test is the open-ended type, requiring the subject to complete sentences, tell a story about a picture that is shown, and so on. A third type is the projective kind, such as the popular Rorschach inkblot test, in which the item or stimulus has little clear structure, yet the respondent is to describe it in terms of real structure. Other forms include adjective checklists, in which the respondent checks adjectives or phrases that are descriptive of him- or herself. There are other forms that are used to assess the personality of the respondent, but these will not be described here. The main purpose is to point out that tasks can be constructed so as to permit the inference of the affective or nonintellectual behavior likely to be exhibited by the respondent.

The above three general types of tests encompass the kinds of tests with which we are generally familiar. In summary, tests usually administered by educational psychologists, such as classroom exams, diagnostic exams for assessing deficiencies or particular strengths, and scholastic aptitude tests fall under the first two categories. Projective tests, administered by clinicians, are forms of personality assessment. Vocational interest tests administered by counselors and industrial psychologists are also forms of personality tests, in that they attempt to determine the typical behavior of someone in a given type of situation. Interviews can be administered either for the purpose of assessing what someone knows or for the purpose of determining personality characteristics. The same is true for motivational tests. Even biographical information blanks provide information from which inferences about behavior can be drawn. (Keep in mind that all of these inferences should be validated; see Chapter 10).

Perhaps the most general way to define a "test" is to state that it is any device or task that is presented to the individual for the purpose of permitting one to predict or diagnose or assess someone's behavior. Keep in mind, though, that we are interested in behavior. There are an infinite number of tasks or items that could be presented to a person for the purpose of measuring a particular characteristic or behavior. Thus tests only *sample* behavior. An achievement test on the subject of the American Revolution does not contain every possible question that could be asked to determine whether students have learned their history. Likewise, a personality test for the purpose of assessing emotional stability does not contain all possible tasks for assessing this characteristic. Rather tests provide a small sample of tasks from the larger domain. Because we are sampling behavior, it is particularly important that we consider the validity and reliability of our tests, which in turn means that we must consider item properties.

### Item Format

The purpose of presenting an item or task is to elicit information. However, there are many formats in which the item can be presented, and thus the amount and kind of information obtained will vary. In achievement tests some item formats emphasize the recall of information or require the construction of a response, as opposed to the recognition or identification of a correct response. Examples of the former type of item are essays or short-answer definitions such as: "Compare and contrast the different measures of central tendency." Or "Define homoscedasticity." An example of the latter type of item format is the typical multiple-choice question or matching of statements in one list with statements in another list. The common ingredient of both of these types of items is that they are considered to be *objective items*.

In contrast, we can have open-ended, *subjective items*. In these cases, there is no right or correct answer. The essential point to be made is that if we are going to use results (test scores) for a decision, then the items ought to be in a form such that they are quantifiable and able to be validated. This holds for objective as well as subjective items. Most of the following discussion with respect to item properties holds for all kinds of items. We will, however, discuss most of the issues in terms of multiple-choice items.

Since we are emphasizing multiple-choice items, several points should be considered in item writing. Consideration of these points, as well as others provided in the numerous test-construction manuals, should result in the subsequent test scores, obtained by administering the items, being more accurate of the respondent's true behavior, ability, and so on. Wood (1961) has discussed item writing in detail; some of the considerations are:

1. Be sure the item deals with a central thought.
2. Ensure clarity of expression and precise language.
3. Strive for brevity of expression, that is, economy in use of language.
4. Avoid dangling constructions and awkward word arrangements.
5. Avoid irrelevant facts in the statement of the problem or the alternatives.
6. Include as much as possible in the problem that is common to the alternatives.
7. Present items in positive form; avoid double negatives—that is, avoid asking for that which is *not* a characteristic of something.
8. Use plausible alternatives.
9. Make all alternatives parallel in grammar, structure, length, and so on.
10. Avoid synonymous alternatives that are incorrect.
11. Randomize the position of the best answer among the alternatives.

As you can see, the above considerations in item writing are mainly a matter of common sense. And applying common sense facilitates the statistical analyses necessary for evaluating tests.

## Test Objectives

Though we have occasionally specifically stated, or more frequently alluded to, the objectives of tests throughout the book, it is helpful to review and summarize at this point. A consideration of objectives is essential since the kinds of item analyses we perform and the item properties we desire are both a function of and affect the objectives of the test. Since we will be discussing item properties and item analyses in the next section, we need to briefly summarize the objectives of tests, or the purposes for which tests are used.

As mentioned in the previous sections, a test is a standardized device that measures a sample of behavior and that is used for decisionmaking purposes. Essentially all decisions involve predictions, and therefore the objective of a test is to predict behavior. We will, however, view prediction in two ways: (1) as a diagnostic, assessment, or classification prediction; and (2) as a temporal prediction. The reason for this distinction will become obvious, hopefully, after we elaborate on these two objectives.

### Diagnosis, Assessment, or Classification Prediction

A test is a standardized measure of a sample of behavior. If we can diagnose a patient's present emotional stability, assess someone's present knowledge of calculus, or classify another person as presently high in need achievement, then we have observed and recorded behavior on topics of our interest. The fact that we have assessed persons on the dimensions suggests a course of action. For example, a diagnosis of emotional disturbance will call for a certain treatment. Assessing a student as having a great deal of calculus knowledge may call for advising that person to pursue a degree in mathematics or physics. Finding an employee who is extremely high in need achievement may suggest means for reinforcement by the supervisor. In essence we are interested in obtaining descriptions of individuals' *present* behaviors. We are interested in their "state" at the time of measurement. The fact that we take a course of action, however, implies some prediction. The diagnosis tells us that the person is liable to exhibit certain behavior and that certain treatment is necessary. A person diagnosed with a certain emotional problem may receive psychoanalysis, behavior therapy, or the like. It is implied that the problem can be helped by one or more of the therapies. The essence of this objective is on the degree to which we reliably measured the behavior. We want to have a reliable, valid description of the respondents.

### Temporal Prediction

In *temporal prediction* we are interested in the direct prediction of *future* behavior from performance on a present or past task. That is, an employment test will be used to select some people for a job and to reject others. The emphasis is on those selected. Usually we are no longer in a position to measure or assess those rejected. The essence of temporal prediction is on the utility of the selection system.

The above distinction may be rather fine, but if we emphasize diagnosis, we may want to emphasize reliability or the internal consistency of our measurement device. Such an emphasis may hinder the predictive validity of the device. We will examine item characteristics and properties in light of this distinction.

## Item Properties

We indicated that the objectives of tests influence the kinds of item properties for which we strive in developing tests. Topics discussed in other chapters, such as reliability (Chapters 8 and 9), validity (Chapter 10), and weighting components of tests (Chapters 7 and 11), also have a relationship to desired item properties. As will be shown, if our goal is to have an internally consistent test that will be used to diagnose a specific characteristic of an individual, then the item properties may be different from those achieved in a test that is concerned with the stability of a characteristic on which we wish to select people. In this section we look at several item properties and relate them to reliability, validity, weighting, and/or test objective. First, we consider item selection considerations such as difficulty level.

### Difficulty

*Item difficulty* is based on the proportion, $p$, of persons who pass or correctly answer the item. The *greater* the value of $p$, the *easier* the item. Thus in the developmental stages of test construction, we administer a large number of items to a large number of people. For example, suppose we want to develop an achievement test of ability in calculus. We can administer a large number of items to a randomly sampled large number of students and then determine the proportion of students who passed each item.

A primary reason for assessing difficulty levels of items is to permit us to construct a test in a specific way with specific characteristics. One usually acceptable way to construct a test is to place items that are relatively easy at the beginning of the test. This is a good practice that tends to reduce a test taker's anxiety and should be followed for most achievement (or aptitude) tests.

Item-difficulty information facilitates the choice of items for the final form. Those items passed by everyone ($p = 1.00$) or failed by everyone ($p = 0.00$) obviously are worthless, since the items do not affect the variability of the composite scores. It is similar to adding a constant to each person's score, and as you recall, adding a constant has no effect on variance and thus has no effect on the reliability or validity of tests. Thus $p$ values affect the characteristics of the test-score distribution, its shape and variance.

A problem in test construction is to determine the optimum level of item difficulty. The solution is based on the amount of discrimination that the item yields. If an item-difficulty level is $p = 1.00$, all persons responding answer the item correctly and thus the item does not distinguish among those persons. If $p = 0.00$, then the item does not discriminate between any test takers. However, the closer the difficulty level approaches $p = 0.50$, the more discriminations that are possible. For example, if an item had $p = .50$ and there were 100 persons involved, then 50 percent pass and 50 percent failed. This means that *each* of the 50 persons who passed is distinguished from *each* of the 50 persons who failed; in other words, $50 \times 50 = 2,500$ discriminations. If $p = .75$, then 75 persons passed and 25 failed. Thus each of the 75 persons who passed is distinguishable from each of the 25 who failed, or $75 \times 25 = 1,875$ discriminations. If $p = .30$, then each of the 30 who passed is distinguished from each of the 70 who failed, or $30 \times 70 = 2,100$ discriminations. In essence, the more the $p$ value departs from 0.50, the more the distribution becomes skewed. Thus, when each item has a difficulty level of $p = .50$, maximum differentiation or variability would result, and consequently has the potential for high reliability and validity.

However, often it is difficult to have each item in a test obtain a $p$ of .50. And as already noted, we often want the initial items in a test to be relatively easy (for example, $p > .70$). Thus the solution is to construct a test whose *average* item difficulty is .50. Some items will have high $p$ values, others will have low $p$ values, and still others will have moderate $p$ values.

Difficulty level of a test is, however, influenced by the extent of intercorrelations among items. If items are highly intercorrelated (that is, homogeneous), then the result is a dichotomization of the total group into those who pass and those who fail, or in other words, a bimodal distribution. If $p = .50$ for each item and the items are perfectly correlated to each other (average intercorrelation, $\bar{r} = 1.00$), then the *same*

50 people pass all of the items and the *same* 50 people fail all of the items. (The desired degree of intercorrelation will be discussed in subsequent sections.) Thus, as Ebel (1972) has demonstrated, it is best to choose items whose average difficulty level is $p = .50$, and these items should deviate only slightly from this level. This yields the maximum variance among test scores. Obtaining maximum differentiation among the sample is desired when we use tests to assess achievement, proficiency, or mastery of subject matter and the results will be used in correlational studies for predictive purposes.

There are instances, however, when we are not really interested in obtaining maximum differentiation among our test-takers, but are more interested in having only a certain portion of the test takers achieve a certain level. For example, if we are hiring applicants for a position in an organization, and we only have 30 vacancies, then the selection ratio (number of applicants hired given the number of applicants) should reflect this fact. If 100 applicants are available, the selection ratio is .30. Thus, if we construct a test whose items have an average difficulty level of .30, we increase our chances of screening in 30 applicants who are suitable for the position.

Likewise, if we are only interested in diagnosis for the purpose of classification, then we may not be too concerned with achieving maximum differentiation. Rather we are interested in broad classification, in identifying a few "classes" of respondents. In this situation we might choose a difficulty level other than .50 to achieve our purposes.

In this section on item difficulty, we have indicated that a $p$ value of .50 for each item or the average of the items is typically desired. One further consideration, however, may be the target population, the group for whom the test will be used. Suppose we have a test of arithmetical ability and, for practical reasons, we want to use this test for junior high schools (seventh-, eighth-, and ninth-graders). It may not be advisable to construct a test with each item or the average of the items having a $p$ value of .50 for the group as a whole (which means essentially eighth-graders). Rather one-third of the items should have an average $p$ value determined on seventh-graders, one-third an average $p$ value of .50 for eighth-graders, and one-third an average $p$ value of .50 for ninth-graders.

## Homogeneity

We briefly alluded in the above section to the homogeneity of a set of items, or the intercorrelations among items, termed *item homogeneity*. It is a desirable goal to have the items measuring a particular, specific characteristic correlate with each other. In fact, only if they do correlate with each other can we be confident that we are measuring the characteristic we intended to measure. That is, if the average intercorrelation of the items is high, then we are measuring the same characteristic with the items; the test is internally consistent. (We discussed this notion in a more statistical sense in Chapter 7, where we were concerned with components and composites.) The value of high intercorrelations, besides validity for the characteristic, is that the internal-consistency reliability of the source resulting from item responses is maximized. (In Chapter 9 we discussed and demonstrated the effect of item intercorrelations on reliability.)

To determine the degree of homogeneity or internal consistency in the test, we can examine item intercorrelations (Equation 7-16) or correlations between item score and total test score (Equation 7-15). We have already shown (in Chapter 7) that we can develop a homogeneous test by selecting those items that have the highest correlations with the other items.

To briefly repeat the discussion in Chapter 7, items can be chosen on the basis of correlation between item score and total score. Essentially, a biserial correlation between "pass" and "fail" on each item and total test score can be computed. This analysis indicates whether the item and total scores are assessing the behavior in the same way. In other words, item–total correlations indicate the amount of homogeneity or internal consistency within the test. In general, items should be answered correctly by those obtaining high total scores. Conversely, if most low total scores are answering an item correctly (in the same behavioral way), then the item and the test are *not* measuring the same behavior. The property of internal consistency is especially important for tests used for assessment. We want to be certain that the behavior being sampled is reliable and meaningful. However, as shown in the next section, a single test with high internal consistency usually does not have a high relationship to an external criterion, which is the goal of tests as temporal predictors. Thus, for some investigations, we are faced with the dilemma of whether to select items based on their empirical relationship to an external criterion or on the basis of their internal consistency, or homogeneity. The next section offers a solution to this dilemma in terms of the relation of item validity to test validity.

### Validity

*Test validity* is an indication of the relationship between total test scores and scores on an outside variable, an external criterion. For example, the relationship between an aptitude test and future job performance indicates test validity. Likewise, items have validities; that is, the relationship between scores on each of the items and some external criterion represents *item validity*. Though most test constructors are interested in test validity, they should also be interested in item validity. The reason for this is that test validity is a function of item validity. The following equation represents the relationship

$$r_{XY} = \frac{\overline{r_{iY}\sigma_i}}{\overline{r_{iX}\sigma_i}} \tag{13-1}$$

where $X$ is the total test score, $Y$ is the external criterion score, and $i$ is the item score. The numerator of Equation 13-1 is an expression of item validity, whereas the denominator is an expression of item reliability. Thus test validity is a function of the ratio of the average validity index to the average reliability index, where the averages are determined across all items in the test.

Let us pursue further Equation 13-1 and its implications. Essentially, this equation is similar to Equation 7-12,

$$r_{z_0z_c} = \frac{k\overline{r}_{0i}}{\sqrt{k + k(k - 1)\overline{r}_{ii'}}}$$

which we developed to show that the relationship between a composite (in the present case, the test score) and an outside variable (in the present case, the criterion score) is a function of the relationship between the components and the composite relative to the intercorrelation of the items. The numerators in Equations 13-1 and 7-12 are conceptually identical, and the denominators are conceptually equivalent. The latter is true since the average correlations of items with one another (Equation 7-16) are highly related to the correlations of items with total scores (Equation 7-15).

Given the above similarities, the discussion associated with the composites in Chapter 7 is appropriate for our present purposes. That is, to achieve maximum test validity, all other things being equal, Equation 13-1 suggests that we should choose items that have a high relationship to the criterion, yet have small relationships to total test scores. This statement is essentially a repetition of principles 1 and 2 on page 165 in Chapter 7. However, to maximize test reliability, which as we have indicated limits validity, we want our items to have high intercorrelations. Thus we have a dilemma, but one that we discussed in Chapter 7. That is, if our objective is to form a test in order to have a precise, representative, and reliable measure of the characteristic in which we are interested, then we should select items that have relatively high intercorrelations. This will lead to a "purer" measure of the characteristic.

If, on the other hand, our objective is to develop a test to predict an external criterion, then we should follow Equation 13-1 and develop a *battery* of tests that have low intercorrelations. That is, a composite test made up of several tests, each of which is reliable but also independent of the others. This procedure makes good sense since most criterion measures are complex and several different, "pure" tests are needed to predict this complex behavior. For example, the occupation of fire fighter is multifaceted in that it requires several abilities, such as mechanical skill, communications skill, and interpersonal relations ability. Tests for each of these abilities should have items that are correlated to other items within the test, but each test should be relatively independent of the other tests. This will result in maximum test validity for the battery. In sum, we attempt to develop several internally consistent tests to predict a complex criterion.

To return to item validity, there is another way to assess this property and that is to obtain an index of the degree to which items can distinguish between external criterion groups. Suppose we want to develop a test of sales aptitude to predict success in sales. What is the percentage of scorers passing the item in extreme, contrasting criterion groups? Assume that the criterion is a multistep, continuous variable (such as amount of sales in dollars), and the criterion is divided into extremely high scorers (high dollar sales) and extremely low scorers (low dollar sales). Items on the test passed by a significantly greater number in one group than the other group are more effective.

A common procedure for forming the extreme groups is to take the upper and lower 27 percent of scorers. That is, if we had 1,000 test takers on whom to compute item-analysis statistics, our extreme groups would be composed of the 270 high scorers and the 270 low scorers. The reason for choosing 27 percent rather than some other arbitrary percentage is to maximize the difference in ability between the two groups while at the same time having large sample sizes in our extreme groups. The confidence (determined statistically) that the upper group is superior to the lower group is greatest when 27 percent of the total is used as a basis for forming extreme groups (Kelley, 1939).

Once members of extreme groups are identified, discrimination indices are computed (Engelhart, 1965). The simplest *discrimination index,* $D$, is the difference between the number of correct responses for the high ($H$) and the low ($L$) groups. That is, if $80\,H$ scorers answered the item correctly, while $10\,L$ scorers answered it correctly, the $D = H - L = 70$. If on the other hand, $20\,H$ scorers answered the item correctly, while $40\,L$ scorers did likewise, then $D$ is $-20$. The purpose of item analysis, when discrimination indices are used, is to select positive and high $D$ value items for inclusion in the final form of the test. Note that this last statement stressed the use of *positive D* values. This is particularly appropriate when we are developing achievement or aptitude tests and the two groups of scorers are distinguished by the *amount* of knowledge they possess. However, high *negative D* values can be useful if we are constructing tests to measure interest or personality. In these cases, we are interested in differences between *types* of groups. Any high *D* value will be useful. This use of positive and negative values relates to a discussion to which we will shortly come: the identification of the criterion groups.

The number of scorers passing an item in the *H* and the *L* groups can also be expressed as a proportion. Then *D* becomes the difference between the two proportions and is thus independent of the sample sizes. *D* thus ranges between $-1.00$ and $+1.00$.

*D* has value in that it is related to two other item-analysis concepts already discussed: difficulty and differentiation. Findley (1956) has shown that *D* is proportional to the difference between the correct and the incorrect differentiations of items. That is, the higher the *D*, the more differentiations among test scorers will there be. In essence, *D* tells us how well we can distinguish among our test takers.

*D* is also related to item difficulty, and in general is biased in favor of moderate difficulty levels. If the difficulty level (*p*) is 1.00 (all scorers passed the item), then *D* is 0.00. If the difficulty level approaches .50, the *opportunity* for *D* to approach 1.00 is maximized. If $p = .50$, then it is *possible* for *all* the *H* scorers to pass the item and *all* the *L* scorers to fail it, yielding a *D* of $+1.00$.

Obviously a crucial concern in the above discrimination is our ability to form or identify external criterion groups. There must be a meaningful differentiation between the high and the low groups (high and low scorers). This is not too difficult if the objective of our test is to predict future performance on a meaningful external criterion. The external criterion is a measure of that future performance.

An alternative procedure to determine item discrimination involves a criterion group and a control group. For example, we can determine whether items distinguish between hospitalized, emotionally disturbed individuals (criterion group) and nonhospitalized, normal individuals (control group). The essence, though, is on the item's ability to distinguish and not on its content. It is not of major importance what the items state, only that they discriminate (fairly). This procedure is referred to as *empirical keying,* a topic to which we will return shortly.

On the other hand, if we are interested in assessment, there may not be an external criterion. Thus we may opt to use the total score on our test of interest as the criterion and determine the upper and lower 27 percent of scorers. The discrimination index is determined now just as it was when there was an external criterion. This index tells us which items are essentially related to the total score. It is another form of internal consistency.

The above discussion on validity and the previous discussions on internal consistency and homogeneity are the central issues of different points of view toward the development of tests. The issue, typically referred to as *empirical keying* versus *homogeneous scaling* is summarized below. In addition, to illustrate the differences, we will refer to several standardized tests developed by one or the other of these approaches.

### Empirical Keying Versus Homogeneous Scaling

If we are to choose items that correlate highly with total test scores, then we are in fact choosing items that have high intercorrelations. The result of this approach to item selection based on internal consistency is referred to as *homogeneous scaling*. This approach is most useful for tests whose purpose is assessment, in the sense of obtaining descriptive information. This approach typically results in tests based on theoretical grounds as opposed to purely statistical considerations. Essentially, psychological theory suggests the items to be constructed and evaluated for the assessment of the characteristic of interest. If results indicate that items are highly correlated, then the items are measuring the same characteristics, and the subsequent interpretation is that the theoretical characteristic is confirmed. Typically there is no external criterion against which the items are correlated. Thus the empirical validity of the test is determined after the scale has been developed.

The Kuder Preference Record—Vocational, Form C, was essentially developed on the basis of homogeneity of items. This is an interest inventory on which responses (likes and dislikes of activities) are used to place a respondent into vocational interest categories. Scores on items are counted in whatever key to which they correlate. Thus, correlation between item score and total score or item intercorrelations determined that sets of items were representative of certain vocational categories.

In contrast, choice of items based on item validity is referred to as *empirical keying*. Items are selected because they have high correlations with the external criterion and at the same time low intercorrelations. Thus both item validity and internal consistency are considered. The final choice of items is based on the empirical results and *not* on any underlying theory. There is no necessary underlying psychological characteristic that is measured by a test developed by empirical keying. This approach is most useful for temporal predictions, when we are interested in predicting performance on an external criterion.

An example of empirical keying, also in the field of interest inventories, is Strong's Vocational Interest Blank (now called the Strong–Campbell Interest Inventory). The basic empirical procedure used by

Strong is one we previously mentioned, using a criterion group and a control group. The respondent indicates his or her like or dislike of numerous activities or topics. The item score placing the individual into a particular occupational category is based on the developmental data indicating that the item score distinguished between satisfied members of that occupation (external criterion) and people in general (control group). Items on which the two groups differ are those that survived analysis to compose the final form of the inventory. In this case, correlation with external data determined the final test.

Is there a reason for attempting to maximize both internal consistency and validity with an external criterion? Again, the answer depends on the nature or complexity of the criterion. Internally consistent, homogeneous tests are "pure." All the items measure the same trait, ability, construct, and so on. Test validity will be maximized if the criterion is also "pure" or, in other words, if it is simply measuring a single construct. Most criteria are, however, complex and this would account for low *validity* coefficients when homogeneous scaling is the basis for item selection. The solution is to construct several subtests, each internally consistent, but when combined in a composite, the tests correlate with the complex criterion. The various factors underlying the criterion would then be explained by the various components of the heterogeneous total test. This latter solution may result in a prohibitively long test battery. Then the choice of empirical keying or homogeneity becomes one of purpose. Empirical keying results in obtaining a correspondence of our measures to behavior. We are not so interested in the content of the item as we are in its ability to discriminate. In addition, empirical keying frees us from dependence on a particular theory. We are simply relying on empirical evidence of the item's utility.

If the plan is to develop an empirically keyed test, then two issues must be considered. First, since the item is retained on the final form based on data, should we use the data to provide differential weights? Second, since an item is retained because of its correlation with an external criterion or because of its validity, is it necessary to now validate the test as a whole? These issues, weighting and the cross-validation of the final test, will now be discussed.

## Weighting Items

To this point, we have ignored the specific problem of the weights, if any, that should be assigned to individual items of a test. (The general problem of weights is discussed in Chapter 11.) If we agree that the purpose of item analysis is to develop a test with maximum reliability and validity, then we could argue that differential weights that achieve this goal be assigned to items. That is, rather than directly adding the number of correct responses to yield a total score, we might give 3 points to item 1, 2 points to item 2, and so on. (This example is purely arbitrary in the way weights are assigned and is not recommended.)

It has been suggested that we can increase the reliability of a test by weighting higher those items that contribute most to the reliability of a test. Those items with higher item–total correlations would be weighted more. If we had 20 items, each with an item–total correlation of .40 and another set of 20 items with an item–total correlation of .20, then each item in the first set would receive 2 points and each item in the second set would receive 1 point. In other words, we are valuing more those items that contribute most to reliability. Also, rather than having a test with a maximum possible score of 40 (equal, unit weights of the items), the weighted-item test has a maximum possible score of 60.

Likewise, we can weight items according to their validity, their correlation between item and external criterion. Those items that have the highest correlations (the highest $D$ values) would be weighted more.

Yet another alternative is that of equal, unit weights. Essentially this means no weighting of items, and total scores are obtained by simply adding the number of correct responses. This is the simplest procedure and, as the evidence indicates, the only procedure that is really necessary. It would be advantageous to use differential weights if it made a difference. However, empirical evidence indicates that reliability and validity usually are not increased when nominal differential weights are used. This conclusion is not surprising, especially if we reconsider the three principles derived from the development of Equation 11-42. To paraphrase the three principles: We indicated that nominal weighting has its greatest effect on the ordering of individuals in composite scores when there is considerable variation in the weights, when there is little intercorrelation among the components, and when there is a small number of components. Typically none of these three conditions exist once a test has been developed and the test constructor is faced with the decision to weight or not to weight. This is so because the typical *developed test* has a relatively large number of items (more than 15), has been developed with consideration for internal consistency (high item intercorrelations), and if the weighting is to be done on the basis of item reliability or item validity, the variation among weights will be minor. Thus empirical evidence indicates that the correlation between weighted and unit-weighted test scores is usually near perfect. In other words, the rank order of persons in a distribution of weighted scorers is almost identical to the rank order of the distribution of unweighted scorers. Consequently, it is recommended that items be unweighted. Reliability and validity can be more significantly improved by attending to appropriate test-development procedures than by using a weighting scheme.

One form of weighting that may be useful is to *correct for guessing* that occurs on objective tests. The purpose of correcting-for-guessing formulas is to provide a better estimate of an individual's "true" score; it is the score obtained without guessing, the score that reflects what the individual really knows. When an individual responds to an item, there is the potential that he or she does not know the answer and thus his or her response is a completely random guess. Or, especially in multiple-choice tests, the individual may have partial information about a topic, permitting him or her to quickly eliminate some alternatives and to guess from the remaining alternatives. Guessing in either of these situations results in a score—the number correct—which is higher than the score desired—the number of items which are really known. This problem occurs in all tests, whether the true–false type or the multiple-choice type, in which there are four or five alternatives from which to choose for each item.

Correcting-for-guessing formulas are available to permit the assessment of what the individual really knows. We present one formula that assumes that the individual answers correctly all of the items he or she knows and randomly guesses on the remaining items. This is a simplistic model that does not take into account partial information or misinformation that individuals have and use to eliminate certain alternatives. Complex formulas for these latter situations exist, but they will not be discussed here.

In a true–false type of test, there are essentially two alternatives, and thus an individual has a 50–50 chance of being correct by guessing alone. Assuming all incorrect responses were random guesses, then the corrected score for true–false types of tests is the number of items right ($R$) minus the number of items wrong ($W$), or corrected score $= R - W$. On a 50-item test, in which the student gets 28 right and 22 wrong, the student's corrected score is 6. In essence, this formula treats a wrong response as a wrong guess or an unlucky guess. The number of lucky guesses is assumed to be a function of the number of wrong guesses. In other words, since the student made so many incorrect responses, the formula assumes a considerable amount of lucky guessing and thus this student is penalized severely in that the obtained score (rights only) was 28, but the corrected score is 6. Contrast this to the student whose obtained score was 38. The corrected score is 26. The second obtained score was 10 points more than the first student's score, but the corrected score for guessing was 6 for the first student versus 26 for the second student. Essentially the formula assumes that those who correctly answer many questions have little need for guessing, whereas those with low scores guess more.

The rationale for multiple-choice types of tests is similar to the above. The number of lucky guesses is estimated as a fraction of the number of wrong guesses. If there are $A$ alternatives to each item, the chance score for a correct guess is $1/A$ and for an unlucky guess is $(A - 1)/A$. Thus the formula most often used is

$$\text{corrected score} = R - (W/(A - 1)) \qquad (13\text{-}2)$$

where $W/(A - 1)$ represents the number of items in the $R$ score that were lucky guesses. This number is subtracted from the obtained "right score" to provide an indication of what the individual really knows. Suppose that we construct a 50-item multiple-choice test, each item having four possible alternatives. If someone obtained a score of 38 on this test and answered all remaining 12 items incorrectly, the corrected score would be 34. It is estimated that the person "really" knows the answers to 34 items.

Again, Equation 13-2 is appropriate only when certain assumptions are met. Basically the assumptions are that if an individual does not know an answer, each of the alternatives is equally plausible and that no partial information is being used to eliminate, for example, two of the alternatives as definitely incorrect and leaving the remaining two from which to guess. In this case (partial information) the odds on getting the item correct are ½ instead of ¼.

Also the equation assumes that the amount of guessing is proportional to the number of wrong answers. Two persons with the same number of correct responses will have different corrected scores if the number of incorrect responses differ. This occurs only if a different number of items is attempted, a situation avoided if the instructions and time permit the respondent to attempt all items.

It is also assumed that those who "really" know the most (guess least) have the least to gain from guessing. A person who knows all the items will get a perfect score. A person who does not "really" know the answers to any of the questions will not get a score of zero, but will score $1/A$ times the number of items by chance alone. In a 60-item test, where the person is *always* guessing among the four possible alternatives and does not "really" know the answers, the result will be an obtained score of 15 (or $1/A$) and a corrected score of 0 (where $W/A - 1$ is 45/3 or 15). We expect someone who does not know the information asked for on a test to score 15 by chance alone, solely by guessing, but the corrected score is 0.

Likewise, it can be demonstrated that the variability of incorrect guesses is greatest for those who "really" know the least. In essence, what we are again saying is that persons with relatively low "true" ability benefit most from guessing. The performance over time for people with relatively low ability is least consistent. One day they can guess incorrectly on the items, and the next day guess correctly.

In summary, with the random guessing model each person has an obtained score ($R$), and of the items guessed, $1/A$ were by chance answered correctly. Of the remaining items that were guessed, $(A - 1)/A$, these were wrong guesses. Thus, $W/(A - 1)$ is the number of items in the $R$ group that were lucky guesses.

Since correcting for guessing can be perceived as a form of weighting, we can ask a question similar to the one we asked in the section on item weighting: Does it make a difference? The answer depends on two considerations, instructions and validity. If the instructions for the test indicate that *all* items should be responded to, then logically and statistically correcting for guessing is not meaningful. Logically we are telling the test taker to answer all items whether he knows the correct response or not. Statistically, if subjects respond to all items, then the corrected score would be perfectly positively correlated with the obtained score (a perfect negative correlation between $W$ and $R$). Thus corrected scores will not correlate differently with external criteria than do uncorrected scores.

If, however, we provide instructions that there is a penalty for guessing and that test takers should not guess wildly, then the question boils down to the effect on validity of guessing. Lord (1963) has demonstrated that some gain in validity can be obtained by using corrected-scoring formulas. Lord (1964) has also concluded that formula scoring is important when there is variability among the test takers in their tendency to guess, when $A < 5$, and when the test is positively skewed (that is, the test is hard).

## Cross-Validation

Whether items are chosen on the basis of empirical keying or whether they are corrected or weighted, the obtained results should, unless additional data are collected, be viewed as specific to the sample used for the statistical analyses. This is necessary because the obtained results have likely capitalized on chance factors operating in that group and therefore are applicable only to the sample measured.

What we do, then, is to determine the amount of capitalization by developing the item or test statistics on one sample and applying the resulting key or equation to a new sample (holdout group). For example, if we select items for a test and develop a scoring key by choosing items that distinguish between good and poor performers on a criterion, it is illogical to then correlate item scores with criterion scores *for that sample* to determine the validity of the test. The validity should be near perfect. We should, instead, apply the key to another sample in the same population, the holdout group, to determine if the criterion score predicted by the key matches the actual obtained score of the holdout group members. We do this, for example, by obtaining test scores and criterion scores for a group of subjects. This group is randomly divided into two groups, experimental and holdout. The scoring key is developed on the experimental group. The scoring key is then used to predict the criterion score of holdout group members. But we know their criterion scores. Thus we can check to see how well the predicted and actual criterion scores correlate.

Usually there will be shrinkage or lower correlations in the holdout group than in the original sample. This is because we are using a scoring key that took advantage of errors that were in the direction of validity in the original group, but probably not in the direction of validity in the cross-validation group. However, if there is not too much error in the original group, then there should not be very much shrinkage in the holdout group, and the scoring key is said to have been cross-validated.

The necessity for *cross-validation* of the results of an item analysis was effectively demonstrated by Cureton (1950) and by Locke (1961). Cureton administered to 29 students a test for which he wanted to develop a key. The criterion to be predicted by the new test was grade-point average. The experimental form of the test contained 85 items to which there were unequivocal plus or minus reactions. Cureton developed a scoring key for 24 items based on, essentially, the discrimination of the grade-point criterion by the item. He then scored the test for the same 29 students and correlated the scores with the criterion, resulting in a correlation of .82. Thus the group on whom the key was developed also served as the group on whom Cureton established validity. This is an incorrect procedure, and one of its problems is illustrated by Cureton's results. He found that the new test had an internal-consistency reliability of −.06; that is, validity exceeded the square root of the reliability coefficient of the predictor, a situation that we have indicated cannot occur (see Chapter 9). The real absurdity of the situation is demonstrated by an examination of the items of the new test. The items were 85 numbered tags, plus on one side and minus on the other, that were simply tossed on the table 29 times, once for each student in the "sample." When, for that "sample" of 29 people, the correlations of each of the 85 items and the criterion (grade-point average) were computed, 24 of the items had substantial correlation with the criterion *by chance*. Obviously, when the 24 "valid" items were scored in the holdout group, the total score on these 24 items no longer correlated with the criterion.

Locke (1961) presented a similarly developed test, whose items were personality adjectives and statements pertaining to characteristics, habits, and preferences. The criterion was the number of letters in the last name. His results also indicated the necessity of cross-validating the results of an item analysis. Though he found a validity of .97 for the test's prediction of letters in the last name for the original group, as well as a reliability coefficient of .67, he cross-validated on an independent sample and the resulting validity was −.08.

Cross-validation is also essential for checking on the weights derived in a multiple-regression analysis. The regression weights are appropriate for the group on whom they are developed. Whether they are effective in predicting the criterion in another sample from the same population is determined by cross-validation. This necessity was cited by Guion (1965), who reported a study in which the multiple correlation was .92 on the original sample but −.21 in a cross-validated sample. Cross-validation is necessary before any test is used for decisionmaking purposes. It is essential in situations where there are many items to be selected, but the sample size is small—for in such a situation the opportunity for capitalization on chance is maximized. The major problem with the holdout cross-validation procedure, however, is in determining sample size. Ideally we would like a large sample on which to compute our statistics. A sufficient size is rarely achieved. Cross-validation with a holdout group complicates this matter because it reduces the available size of the group on whom the equations are developed. Rather than using a total group for whom to develop equations that would maximize our statistical confidence, we reduce the sample size by forming a holdout group. We are thus in the paradox of reducing confidence in order to obtain unbiased estimates of our results. Unfortunately there is no suitable alternative. However, estimates of shrinkage can be obtained analytically (Cattin, 1980).

## A Further Look at Item Analysis

To this point we have examined the item properties of difficulty, discrimination, and homogeneity, and we have discussed the concern for cross-validation and alternatives for keying and weighting. All of this has been presented in terms of conventional testing and test theory. That is, the same test is administered to the group of individuals in whose ability, trait, or characteristic we are interested. Scores on this test are typically a function of the number correct or based on agreement with a key. There is, however, an alternative means by which to measure individuals, and that is to administer a "unique" set of items to a subject depending on his or her ability level. Generally this is done by adapting item difficulty to the ability level of each individual based on information obtained from each individual's responses to previous items on the test. Such procedures, or strategies, have been referred to as *adaptive testing, tailored testing, sequential testing, branched testing,* or *response-contingent measurement.* These strategies, as well as others we have not mentioned, involve the notion of adapting or individualizing the test (items) to a given individual based on responses that individual has made to test items already presented.

### Tailored Testing

*Tailored testing,* as we will call it, can be illustrated by considering one of the simpler strategies. Since we want to adapt the test to the individual's ability level, the first question to be answered is: What is the individual's ability level? This question can be answered in several ways. We can *estimate* the individual's level based on existing information, that is, on behaviors demonstrated in situations related to the ability of interest, or we can give a "quick test" for it. The latter alternative is the one we will pursue.

We can administer to an individual a short test of, for example, 10 items with variance among the item difficulty levels. Based on the score on this quick test, the individual is branched to one of a number of tests, each of which has a different level of difficulty and is designed to differentiate among the abilities of individuals within a narrower range of ability than does the quick test. In the 10-item quick test, suppose we have an individual who scores 3 correct. This is a relatively low score and reflects low ability. This individual will then be given a test appropriate for his or her ability, a test of, for example, 25 items with a difficulty level of about .80 (that is, 80 percent of a pretest group answered these items correctly). Such a test would be given to all individuals who are initially estimated to have low ability. Likewise, if someone scored 5 correct on the quick test, we would administer a 25-item test whose difficulty level would be about .60; those who score 8 on the quick test would then receive a 25-item test whose difficulty level would be about .30.

Since not all individuals take the same tests, the conventional scoring of number correct is inappropriate. Several methods have been developed and used. Perhaps the simplest is to determine the average difficulty of all the items answered correctly by the subject.

There is an obvious question related to the above strategy. What is the purpose and/or advantage of this strategy. Essentially the purpose is to have more precise measurement among those who have similar abilities. Rather than employing a test with a large number of items, each varying in difficulty, and whose purpose is to seek out the ability level, we can adapt a test such that we obtain maximum information and measurement per item. The advantages follow from the purpose. First, rather than administer a test of 85 items (three tests of 25 items plus the 10-item quick test), we have used only 35 items per subject. Thus we have a savings in time. Second we may minimize frustration and maximize test-taking motivation. The subject is not responding to too difficult or too easy items for his ability. Third there is some evidence that such tests, compared to conventional tests, lead to increased reliability and validity.

There are some disadvantages of the above strategy. First there will be errors in the initial estimate of the individual's ability, especially for those who are near the cutting score that determines which measurement set should be administered after the quick test. Second it may still be possible to vary the number of items to be administered to the person rather than requiring the full 25-item set. There has been some research to indicate that people vary in the number of items they require to achieve a desired degree of accuracy.

Several solutions have been offered to the above limitations, and we will present one as a further illustration of tailored testing. The procedure is a pyramidal model that involves multiple stages or a series of branching decisions. These decisions as to what item to present next are made after the person responds to each item.

In one type of pyramidal model, there are several stages, for example seven, with the number of items for each stage corresponding to the number of the stage. Figure 13-1 is an illustration of this model. At stage I there is 1 item (difficulty level of .50); at stage II there are 2 items (difficulty levels of about .58 and .42); at stage VI there are 6 items (difficulty levels ranging from .25 to .75); and so on. Within each stage, the average difficulty level is .50. (Recall that the *higher* the difficulty value, the easier the item.)

Rules are established on an a priori basis as to the branching that will occur after a response. For example, all subjects take the item of stage I. For a particular subject who responds correctly, he or she will take the item (3) at stage II that has a difficulty level of .42 (slightly more difficult than item 1). If he or she gets this item correct, he or she will go to stage III and respond to an item (6) with a difficulty level of .35. Suppose the subject correctly answers the items in stages I and II, but incorrectly responds to the item in stage III. This subject will then be presented with an item in stage IV that is slightly less difficult than the item in stage III (for example, item 7, 8, or 9).

There are several scoring procedures for the above model. Perhaps the simplest is to use as the score the difficulty value of the most

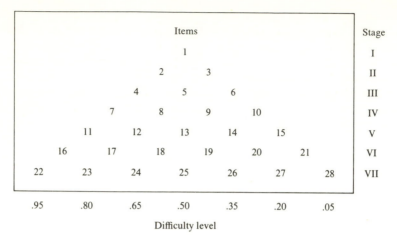

*Figure 13-1*  Pyramidal tailored-testing scheme.

difficult item answered correctly. Regardless of the scoring system adopted, the essential point is that the items administered are a function of responses to prior terms.

In summary, the major advantage of tailored testing is that ability estimates derived from the use of such testing strategies have equal precision of measurement throughout the range of measured ability. In conventional testing, it has been found that the most precise measurement occurs for those who have average ability. As one goes above or below average ability, the precision of measurement decreases. The problem is alleviated in tailored testing since the precision of measurement is equivalent for all ability levels.

The essential item characteristics used in tailored testing are the indices of item difficulty and item discrimination, as well as the assessment of the probability of chance success on the item as a result of random guessing. These characteristics can be assessed by the procedures discussed in this chapter.

Most of the tailored-testing strategies have emphasized item difficulty. We have previously indicated that this index is the proportion of the group, on whom we are pretesting the item, that answers the item correctly. This is conventional, classical test theory. Some of the tailored-testing strategies have focused on item difficulty from another point of view, often called *modern test theory*.

## Modern Test Theory

The purpose of tailored testing is to estimate the degree or quantity of a trait or ability that an individual possesses based on his or her responses to a series of ability or trait test items. That is, we are trying to identify and define underlying, latent traits of people based on observable data, that is, on responses to questions. *Modern test theory* is concerned with the relationship of the individual's item response to the underlying or latent psychological trait.

Latent-trait theories propose that one's test performance can be explained by the traits or abilities characterizing the individual; estimates of the ability are used to explain the test results. However, these abilities are not directly measurable. Various mathematical models are used to describe the relationship between the observed test performance and the unmeasurable latent traits.

There are two main features in general latent-trait models. First we assume that the trait or ability is unidimensional and that the items are homogeneous in that they are measuring a single trait or ability. Second we are interested in the mathematical function that relates the probability of success on an item to the ability measured. This mathematical function is described by an *item-characteristic curve*.

The item-characteristic curve indicates the probability of a correct response to an item as a function of the trait being measured. The mathematical representation of this curve is similar to that of a regression equation in that it has a slope or intercept to represent the fact that items vary in their difficulty and discriminating power. Several item-characteristic curves are shown in Figure 13-2. The abscissa of each of the item-characteristic curves in Figure 13-2 represents the continuum of the ability of interest. It is assumed that measurement of this ability represents the "true" component; that is, the ability is perfectly reliably measured. However, as previously pointed out, we cannot directly measure the "true" component, but rather we estimate it from fallible scores. The ordinate represents the probability of passing an item; Figure 13-2a represents an item that is likely to be answered correctly only by those with low ability. In contrast, Figure 13-2b represents an item that most probably will receive correct responses from those who have a greater amount of the ability. Figure 13-2c shows an item that most likely will be correctly answered by those who have a moderate amount of the ability.

The slopes and intercepts of the curves in Figure 13-2 indicate the degree to which the item discriminates along the continuum of the ability. The steeper the slope, the sharper the discrimination between various levels of the ability. For example, Figure 13-2b shows that the probability of a correct response gradually increases as ability increases. Now look at Figure 13-3. This item-characteristic curve shows that the item discriminates (intercepts) at one point on the ability continuum. That is, for all those below that point, the probability of a correct response is zero; whereas for all those at or above the point, the probability is one.

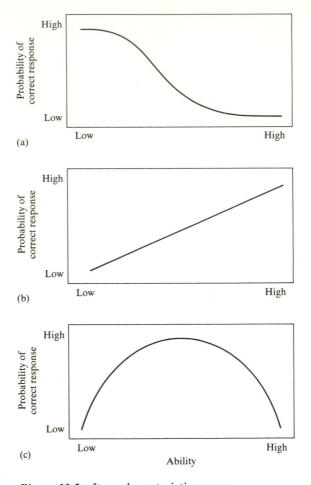

*Figure 13-2*   Item-characteristic curves.

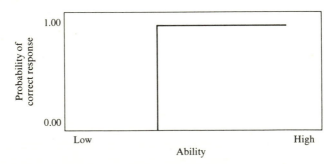

*Figure 13-3*   Item-characteristic curve that sharply discriminates ability.

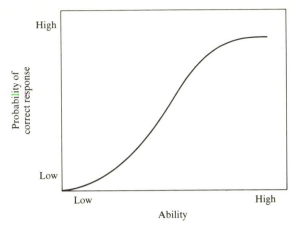

*Figure 13-4*   Normal-ogive curve.

A common latent-trait model is the normal-ogive model. This model has an item-characteristic curve like the one represented in Figure 13-4. This curve is smooth, increases as the amount of the ability increases, and has a horizontal asymptote for very high values of the ability. The steepest point on the curve is the point at which the item discriminates most effectively.

Item-characteristic curves are important because they enable us to quantify an important characteristic of individual test items and they permit us to predict how a test taker will respond to any chosen item. The curve specifies how the observed responses of a group of subjects depends on the latent trait. The curve is an important concept for making inferences in the reverse direction; that is, for making inferences about unobservable latent traits from the observed item responses. A summary of various models of curves can be found in Hambleton and Cook (1977).

One of the advantages of a latent-trait model is that it permits the comparison of individuals who have responded to different subsets of test items. Since latent-trait models take into account item difficulty and item discrimination, we can compare two individuals who responded to two different subsets of items, each with its own difficulty level. Classical theory would favor the student who took the easier test; modern theory compares on the basis of underlying ability. This advantage is, in essence, the basis of tailored testing, where we saw that subjects respond to different items as a function of ability level and item difficulty. If we want to measure accurately through a wide range of ability, then we match the difficulty level of the items to the ability level of the individual; as we presented earlier, this is tailored testing.

The notion of inferences about latent traits on the basis of observable responses is the focus of a type of analysis called *latent structure analy-*

*sis* (Lazarsfeld, 1954, 1959, 1966). Latent structure analysis (LSA) is concerned with the relation of item responses to latent traits, and thus uses the concept of item-characteristic curves (referred to as *trace lines* by Lazarsfeld).

The purpose of LSA is to provide a precise meaning of the measurements typically made in the behavioral and social sciences. LSA is a means by which the underlying concept of our measurements, the latent traits, are made more explicit. According to the rationale of LSA, for each item there are different probabilities of correct responses depending on the amount of the trait possessed by the respondent. That is, if we assume that there are different degrees of the trait, or different latent-trait classes, then there are different probabilities of correct responses depending on the class to which one belongs. The key problem for LSA is to solve for the frequency or number of people in the sample who are in each class and the probability of a correct response for each of these classes. The solutions to this problem will not be offered here. It is sufficient to merely indicate that there are equations formed on the basis of observed responses to items and patterns of items, as well as the testing of a priori models of traits, that lead to the assessment of the necessary parameters and, subsequently, to the ability to discuss items in terms of traits. (Details of LSA, including discussion of equations and model fitting, can be found in any of the Lazarsfeld readings at the end of this chapter.)

LSA is in some ways a different way of looking at data yet is somewhat similar to pattern analysis (see Chapter 11). There are also some obvious contrasts to conventional test theory. For example, in conventional test theory, all people who give correct responses to the same number of items receive the same score. Thus the score is the number of items correct. In LSA the score is a position on the latent continuum and is a function of the pattern of responses. (Pattern analysis is concerned with the pattern of responses in relation to an observed criterion score; LSA is concerned with the relation of a pattern of responses to an underlying trait.) The important aspect for us is that, as in tailored testing, responses to individual items become the focus of study rather than whole tests. Information obtained from LSA studies facilitates our understanding of traits and contributes to the development of tailored testing.

---

## Summary

The general notion of test construction is discussed in terms of item properties and their effect on the general objectives of tests. A test is defined as a device or a series of tasks presented to an individual for the purpose of obtaining, observing, and recording information about the person's behavior. The purpose of a test is (1) to diagnose, assess, or classify individuals, and (2) to make predictions about future behavior. These two purposes can create a dilemma in that for the former we want an internally consistent, highly reliable test of items whose inter-correlations are high. For predicting an external criterion, we want a test with items whose intercorrelations are low, but with high item–criterion correlation. It is difficult to fulfill both goals simultaneously.

In item analysis we are concerned with item difficulty. If the average item difficulty level is .50, then there will be maximum differentiation among the test takers. Varying the difficulty level is appropriate depending on the purpose of the test. Item validity is maximized when there is low item intercorrelation and high item–criterion correlation. This is obtained by empirical keying. Item reliability is achieved by obtaining high item intercorrelations; this results in a homogeneous scale. Choosing several internally consistent, but independent tests, and forming a battery are one way to maximize prediction.

Weighting and correction for guessing are also discussed. Differential weighting of items seems unnecessary. Guessing formulas can result in increased validity. Finally the importance of cross-validation of scoring keys cannot be overemphasized. A check on the possibility of bias, contamination, or chance in our results is essential prior to any use of a test.

Two additional topics discussed are tailored testing and latent structure analysis. These "modern" approaches emphasize adapting tests to the ability of the individual taking the test. The essential parameter of these procedures is the item-characteristic curve.

---

## Suggested Readings

Buros, O. K. (Ed.) 1978. *The eighth mental measurements yearbook.* Highland Park, N.J.: Gryphon Press.

Cattin, P. 1980. Estimation of the predictive power of a regression model. *Journal of Applied Psychology,* 65:407–414.

Ebel, R. L. 1972. *Essentials of educational measurement.* Englewood Cliffs, N.J.: Prentice-Hall.

Engelhart, M. D. 1965. A comparison of several item discrimination indices. *Journal of Educational Measurement,* 2:69–76.

Findley, W. G. 1956. Rationale for the evaluation of item discrimination statistics. *Educational and Psychological Measurement,* 16:175–180.

Guion, R. M. 1965. *Personnel testing.* New York: McGraw-Hill.

Gulliksen, H. 1949. Item selection to maximize test validity. *Proceedings of the 1948 Invitational Conference on Testing Problems—"Validity, Norms, and the Verbal Factor."* Princeton, N.J.: Educational Testing Service. Pp. 13–17.

Hambleton, R. K., and L. L. Cook. 1977. Latent trait models and their use in the analysis of educational test data. *Journal of Educational Measurement,* 14:75–96.

Herzberg, P. A. 1969. The parameters of cross-validation. *Psychometrika,* 34 (Monogr. Suppl. 16).

Kelley, T. L. 1939. The selection of upper and lower groups for the validation of test items. *Journal of Educational Psychology,* 30:17–24.

Lazarsfeld, P. F. 1954. A conceptual introduction to latent structure analysis. In P. F. Lazarsfeld (Ed.), *Mathematical thinking in the social sciences.* New York: Free Press. Pp. 349–387.

Lazarsfeld, P. F. 1959. Latent structure analysis. In S. Koch (Ed.), *Psychology: A study of a science.* Vol. 3: *Formulations of the person and the social context.* New York: McGraw-Hill. Pp. 476–543.

Lazarsfeld, P. F. 1966. Latent structure analysis and test theory. In P. F. Lazarsfeld and N. W. Henry (Eds.), *Readings in mathematical social sciences.* Cambridge, Mass.: M.I.T. Press. Pp. 78–88.

Lazarsfeld, P. F., and N. W. Henry. 1968. *Latent structure analysis.* Boston: Houghton Mifflin.

Locke, E. A. 1961. What's in a name? *American Psychologist,* 16:607.

Lord, F. M. 1963. Formula scoring and validity. *Educational and Psychological Measurement,* 23:663–672.

Lord, F. M. 1964. The effect of random guessing on test validity. *Educational and Psychological Measurement* 24:745–747.

Lord, F. M. 1966. The relation of test score to the trait underlying the test. In P. F. Lazarsfeld and N. W. Henry (Eds.), *Readings in mathematical social sciences.* Cambridge, Mass.: M.I.T. Press. Pp. 21–53.

Lord, F. M. 1970. Some test theory for tailored testing. In W. H. Holtzman (Ed.), *Computer-assisted instruction, testing, and guidance.* New York: Harper & Row. Pp. 139–183.

Lord, F. M., and M. R. Novick. 1968. *Statistical theories of mental test scores.* Reading, Mass.: Addison-Wesley. Chaps. 16–20.

Urry, V. W. 1977. Tailored testing: A successful application of latent trait theory. *Journal of Educational Measurement,* 14:181–196.

Weiss, D. J. 1973. *The stratified adaptive computerized ability test.* Research Report 73-3, Psychometric Methods Program, Department of Psychology, University of Minnesota, September.

Weiss, D. J. 1974. *Strategies of adaptive ability measurement.* Research Report 74-75, Psychometric Methods Program, Department of Psychology, University of Minnesota, December.

Weiss, D. J., and N. E. Betz. 1973. *Ability measurement: Conventional or adaptive?* Research Report 73-1, Psychometric Methods Program, Department of Psychology, University of Minnesota, February.

Wood, D. A. 1961. *Test construction: Development and interpretation of achievement tests.* Columbus, Ohio: Charles E. Merrill.

# *Appendix A*

## *Standard and Standardized-Score Equivalents of Percentile Ranks in a Normal Distribution*

The four columns represent:

a    Percent of cases earning lower scores.

b    Standard scores (z scores).

c    Standardized scores with a mean of 50 and a standard deviation of 10 (T scores).

d    Standardized scores with a mean of 100 and a standard deviation of 20.

The following examples will illustrate how this appendix can be used. Suppose we have a distribution of raw scores (on a variable or test) that is normally distributed. As we discussed in Chapter 4, we can transform these raw scores to other values that are also normally distributed. Column $a$ in the appendix is the percentile rank. Column $b$ shows the $z$-score equivalent of the percentile rank. That is, if we transform a person's raw score to a $z$ score and find the value to be 2.05, then a check of columns $a$ and $b$ indicates that such a score surpasses 98.0 percent of those scores in the distribution. If we had transformed this person's raw score to a $T$ score and found the value to be 71, then a check of column $c$ indicates that this $T$ score is equivalent to a $z$ score 2.05 (column $b$) and surpasses 98.0 percent of the cases (column $a$). Likewise column $d$ shows the values of raw-score equivalents when the distribution has a mean of 100 and a standard deviation of 20.

The appendix can also be used to answer a frequently asked question: What percentage of the distribution falls between two raw scores? For example, suppose we want to know the percentage of people who fall between the raw scores of 20 and 45 on a test. We convert to $z$ scores and find that the two raw scores are $-1.00$ and $1.50$ in $z$ scores, respectively. Now we can use the appendix to answer our question. By checking column $b$, we can find that a $z$ score of $-1.00$ is equivalent to a percentile rank (column $a$) of 15.9 or that 15.9 percent are surpassed by that score. A $z$ score of 1.50 has a percentile rank of 93.3 percent. Thus the percentage of cases *between* the two scores is 93.3 minus 15.9 or 77.4 percent of the cases. We would have arrived at the same result had the transformation of the raw scores been to other distributions, such as those in columns $c$ and $d$.

| a | b | c | d | a | b | c | d |
|------|------|----|-----|------|------|----|-----|
| 99.9 | 3.09 | 81 | 162 | 95.0 | 1.64 | 66 | 133 |
| 99.8 | 2.88 | 79 | 158 | 94.9 | 1.64 | 66 | 133 |
| 99.7 | 2.75 | 78 | 155 | 94.8 | 1.63 | 66 | 133 |
| 99.6 | 2.65 | 77 | 153 | 94.7 | 1.62 | 66 | 132 |
| 99.5 | 2.58 | 76 | 152 | 94.6 | 1.61 | 66 | 132 |
| 99.4 | 2.51 | 75 | 150 | 94.5 | 1.60 | 66 | 132 |
| 99.3 | 2.46 | 75 | 149 | 94.4 | 1.59 | 66 | 132 |
| 99.2 | 2.41 | 74 | 148 | 94.3 | 1.58 | 66 | 132 |
| 99.1 | 2.37 | 74 | 147 | 94.2 | 1.57 | 66 | 131 |
| 99.0 | 2.33 | 73 | 147 | 94.1 | 1.56 | 66 | 131 |
| 98.9 | 2.29 | 73 | 146 | 94.0 | 1.55 | 66 | 131 |
| 98.8 | 2.26 | 73 | 145 | 93.9 | 1.55 | 66 | 131 |
| 98.7 | 2.22 | 72 | 145 | 93.8 | 1.54 | 65 | 131 |
| 98.6 | 2.20 | 72 | 144 | 93.7 | 1.53 | 65 | 131 |
| 98.5 | 2.17 | 72 | 143 | 93.6 | 1.52 | 65 | 130 |
| 98.4 | 2.14 | 71 | 143 | 93.5 | 1.51 | 65 | 130 |
| 98.3 | 2.12 | 71 | 142 | 93.4 | 1.50 | 65 | 130 |
| 98.2 | 2.10 | 71 | 142 | 93.3 | 1.50 | 65 | 130 |
| 98.1 | 2.07 | 71 | 141 | 93.2 | 1.49 | 65 | 130 |
| 98.0 | 2.05 | 71 | 141 | 93.1 | 1.48 | 65 | 130 |
| 97.9 | 2.03 | 70 | 141 | 93.0 | 1.48 | 65 | 130 |
| 97.8 | 2.01 | 70 | 140 | 92.9 | 1.47 | 65 | 129 |
| 97.7 | 2.00 | 70 | 140 | 92.8 | 1.46 | 65 | 129 |
| 97.6 | 1.98 | 70 | 140 | 92.7 | 1.45 | 65 | 129 |
| 97.5 | 1.96 | 70 | 139 | 92.6 | 1.45 | 65 | 129 |
| 97.4 | 1.94 | 69 | 139 | 92.5 | 1.44 | 64 | 129 |
| 97.3 | 1.93 | 69 | 139 | 92.4 | 1.43 | 64 | 129 |
| 97.2 | 1.91 | 69 | 138 | 92.3 | 1.43 | 64 | 129 |
| 97.1 | 1.90 | 69 | 138 | 92.2 | 1.42 | 64 | 128 |
| 97.0 | 1.88 | 69 | 138 | 92.1 | 1.41 | 64 | 128 |
| 96.9 | 1.87 | 69 | 137 | 92.0 | 1.41 | 64 | 128 |
| 96.8 | 1.85 | 69 | 137 | 91.9 | 1.40 | 64 | 128 |
| 96.7 | 1.84 | 68 | 137 | 91.8 | 1.39 | 64 | 128 |
| 96.6 | 1.83 | 68 | 137 | 91.7 | 1.38 | 64 | 128 |
| 96.5 | 1.81 | 68 | 136 | 91.6 | 1.38 | 64 | 128 |
| 96.4 | 1.80 | 68 | 136 | 91.5 | 1.37 | 64 | 127 |
| 96.3 | 1.79 | 68 | 136 | 91.4 | 1.37 | 64 | 127 |
| 96.2 | 1.77 | 68 | 135 | 91.3 | 1.36 | 64 | 127 |
| 96.1 | 1.76 | 68 | 135 | 91.2 | 1.35 | 64 | 127 |
| 96.0 | 1.75 | 68 | 135 | 91.1 | 1.35 | 64 | 127 |
| 95.9 | 1.74 | 67 | 135 | 91.0 | 1.34 | 63 | 127 |
| 95.8 | 1.73 | 67 | 135 | 90.9 | 1.33 | 63 | 127 |
| 95.7 | 1.72 | 67 | 134 | 90.8 | 1.33 | 63 | 127 |
| 95.6 | 1.71 | 67 | 134 | 90.7 | 1.32 | 63 | 126 |
| 95.5 | 1.70 | 67 | 134 | 90.6 | 1.32 | 63 | 126 |
| 95.4 | 1.68 | 67 | 134 | 90.5 | 1.31 | 63 | 126 |
| 95.3 | 1.67 | 67 | 133 | 90.4 | 1.30 | 63 | 126 |
| 95.2 | 1.66 | 67 | 133 | 90.3 | 1.30 | 63 | 126 |
| 95.1 | 1.65 | 67 | 133 | 90.2 | 1.29 | 63 | 126 |

| a | b | c | d | a | b | c | d |
|------|------|----|-----|------|------|----|-----|
| 90.1 | 1.29 | 63 | 126 | 85.2 | 1.05 | 61 | 121 |
| 90.0 | 1.28 | 63 | 126 | 85.1 | 1.04 | 60 | 121 |
| 89.9 | 1.28 | 63 | 126 | 85.0 | 1.04 | 60 | 121 |
| 89.8 | 1.27 | 63 | 125 | 84.9 | 1.03 | 60 | 121 |
| 89.7 | 1.26 | 63 | 125 | 84.8 | 1.03 | 60 | 121 |
| 89.6 | 1.26 | 63 | 125 | 84.7 | 1.02 | 60 | 120 |
| 89.5 | 1.25 | 63 | 125 | 84.6 | 1.02 | 60 | 120 |
| 89.4 | 1.25 | 63 | 125 | 84.5 | 1.01 | 60 | 120 |
| 89.3 | 1.24 | 62 | 125 | 84.4 | 1.01 | 60 | 120 |
| 89.2 | 1.23 | 62 | 125 | 84.3 | 1.00 | 60 | 120 |
| 89.1 | 1.23 | 62 | 125 | 84.2 | 1.00 | 60 | 120 |
| 89.0 | 1.22 | 62 | 124 | 84.1 | 1.00 | 60 | 120 |
| 88.9 | 1.22 | 62 | 124 | 84.0 | 0.99 | 60 | 120 |
| 88.8 | 1.22 | 62 | 124 | 83.9 | 0.99 | 60 | 120 |
| 88.7 | 1.21 | 62 | 124 | 83.8 | 0.99 | 60 | 120 |
| 88.6 | 1.21 | 62 | 124 | 83.7 | 0.98 | 60 | 120 |
| 88.5 | 1.20 | 62 | 124 | 83.6 | 0.98 | 60 | 120 |
| 88.4 | 1.20 | 62 | 124 | 83.5 | 0.97 | 60 | 119 |
| 88.3 | 1.19 | 62 | 124 | 83.4 | 0.97 | 60 | 119 |
| 88.2 | 1.19 | 62 | 124 | 83.3 | 0.97 | 60 | 119 |
| 88.1 | 1.18 | 62 | 124 | 83.2 | 0.96 | 60 | 119 |
| 88.0 | 1.18 | 62 | 124 | 83.1 | 0.96 | 60 | 119 |
| 87.9 | 1.17 | 62 | 123 | 83.0 | 0.95 | 60 | 119 |
| 87.8 | 1.17 | 62 | 123 | 82.9 | 0.95 | 60 | 119 |
| 87.7 | 1.16 | 62 | 123 | 82.8 | 0.95 | 60 | 119 |
| 87.6 | 1.16 | 62 | 123 | 82.7 | 0.94 | 59 | 119 |
| 87.5 | 1.15 | 62 | 123 | 82.6 | 0.94 | 59 | 119 |
| 87.4 | 1.15 | 62 | 123 | 82.5 | 0.93 | 59 | 119 |
| 87.3 | 1.14 | 61 | 123 | 82.4 | 0.93 | 59 | 119 |
| 87.2 | 1.14 | 61 | 123 | 82.3 | 0.93 | 59 | 119 |
| 87.1 | 1.13 | 61 | 123 | 82.2 | 0.92 | 59 | 118 |
| 87.0 | 1.13 | 61 | 123 | 82.1 | 0.92 | 59 | 118 |
| 86.9 | 1.12 | 61 | 122 | 82.0 | 0.91 | 59 | 118 |
| 86.8 | 1.12 | 61 | 122 | 81.9 | 0.91 | 59 | 118 |
| 86.7 | 1.11 | 61 | 122 | 81.8 | 0.91 | 59 | 118 |
| 86.6 | 1.11 | 61 | 122 | 81.7 | 0.90 | 59 | 118 |
| 86.5 | 1.10 | 61 | 122 | 81.6 | 0.90 | 59 | 118 |
| 86.4 | 1.10 | 61 | 122 | 81.5 | 0.90 | 59 | 118 |
| 86.3 | 1.09 | 61 | 122 | 81.4 | 0.89 | 59 | 118 |
| 86.2 | 1.09 | 61 | 122 | 81.3 | 0.89 | 59 | 118 |
| 86.1 | 1.08 | 61 | 122 | 81.2 | 0.89 | 59 | 118 |
| 86.0 | 1.08 | 61 | 122 | 81.1 | 0.88 | 59 | 118 |
| 85.9 | 1.08 | 61 | 122 | 81.0 | 0.88 | 59 | 118 |
| 85.8 | 1.07 | 61 | 121 | 80.9 | 0.87 | 59 | 117 |
| 85.7 | 1.07 | 61 | 121 | 80.8 | 0.87 | 59 | 117 |
| 85.6 | 1.06 | 61 | 121 | 80.7 | 0.87 | 59 | 117 |
| 85.5 | 1.06 | 61 | 121 | 80.6 | 0.86 | 59 | 117 |
| 85.4 | 1.05 | 61 | 121 | 80.5 | 0.86 | 59 | 117 |
| 85.3 | 1.05 | 61 | 121 | 80.4 | 0.86 | 59 | 117 |

| a | b | c | d | a | b | c | d |
|---|---|---|---|---|---|---|---|
| 80.3 | 0.85 | 59 | 117 | 75.4 | 0.69 | 57 | 114 |
| 80.2 | 0.85 | 59 | 117 | 75.3 | 0.68 | 57 | 114 |
| 80.1 | 0.84 | 58 | 117 | 75.2 | 0.68 | 57 | 114 |
| 80.0 | 0.84 | 58 | 117 | 75.1 | 0.68 | 57 | 114 |
| 79.9 | 0.84 | 58 | 117 | 75.0 | 0.67 | 57 | 113 |
| 79.8 | 0.83 | 58 | 117 | 74.9 | 0.67 | 57 | 113 |
| 79.7 | 0.83 | 58 | 117 | 74.8 | 0.67 | 57 | 113 |
| 79.6 | 0.83 | 58 | 117 | 74.7 | 0.66 | 57 | 113 |
| 79.5 | 0.82 | 58 | 116 | 74.6 | 0.66 | 57 | 113 |
| 79.4 | 0.82 | 58 | 116 | 74.5 | 0.66 | 57 | 113 |
| 79.3 | 0.82 | 58 | 116 | 74.4 | 0.66 | 57 | 113 |
| 79.2 | 0.81 | 58 | 116 | 74.3 | 0.65 | 57 | 113 |
| 79.1 | 0.81 | 58 | 116 | 74.2 | 0.65 | 57 | 113 |
| 79.0 | 0.80 | 58 | 116 | 74.1 | 0.65 | 57 | 113 |
| 78.9 | 0.80 | 58 | 116 | 74.0 | 0.64 | 56 | 113 |
| 78.8 | 0.80 | 58 | 116 | 73.9 | 0.64 | 56 | 113 |
| 78.7 | 0.79 | 58 | 116 | 73.8 | 0.64 | 56 | 113 |
| 78.6 | 0.79 | 58 | 116 | 73.7 | 0.63 | 56 | 113 |
| 78.5 | 0.79 | 58 | 116 | 73.6 | 0.63 | 56 | 113 |
| 78.4 | 0.78 | 58 | 116 | 73.5 | 0.63 | 56 | 113 |
| 78.3 | 0.78 | 58 | 116 | 73.4 | 0.62 | 56 | 113 |
| 78.2 | 0.78 | 58 | 116 | 73.3 | 0.62 | 56 | 112 |
| 78.1 | 0.77 | 58 | 115 | 73.2 | 0.62 | 56 | 112 |
| 78.0 | 0.77 | 58 | 115 | 73.1 | 0.61 | 56 | 112 |
| 77.9 | 0.77 | 58 | 115 | 73.0 | 0.61 | 56 | 112 |
| 77.8 | 0.77 | 58 | 115 | 72.9 | 0.61 | 56 | 112 |
| 77.7 | 0.76 | 58 | 115 | 72.8 | 0.61 | 56 | 112 |
| 77.6 | 0.76 | 58 | 115 | 72.7 | 0.60 | 56 | 112 |
| 77.5 | 0.76 | 58 | 115 | 72.6 | 0.60 | 56 | 112 |
| 77.4 | 0.75 | 58 | 115 | 72.5 | 0.60 | 56 | 112 |
| 77.3 | 0.75 | 58 | 115 | 72.4 | 0.59 | 56 | 112 |
| 77.2 | 0.75 | 58 | 115 | 72.3 | 0.59 | 56 | 112 |
| 77.1 | 0.74 | 57 | 115 | 72.2 | 0.59 | 56 | 112 |
| 77.0 | 0.74 | 57 | 115 | 72.1 | 0.59 | 56 | 112 |
| 76.9 | 0.74 | 57 | 115 | 72.0 | 0.58 | 56 | 112 |
| 76.8 | 0.73 | 57 | 115 | 71.9 | 0.58 | 56 | 112 |
| 76.7 | 0.73 | 57 | 115 | 71.8 | 0.58 | 56 | 112 |
| 76.6 | 0.73 | 57 | 115 | 71.7 | 0.57 | 56 | 111 |
| 76.5 | 0.72 | 57 | 114 | 71.6 | 0.57 | 56 | 111 |
| 76.4 | 0.72 | 57 | 114 | 71.5 | 0.57 | 56 | 111 |
| 76.3 | 0.72 | 57 | 114 | 71.4 | 0.56 | 56 | 111 |
| 76.2 | 0.71 | 57 | 114 | 71.3 | 0.56 | 56 | 111 |
| 76.1 | 0.71 | 57 | 114 | 71.2 | 0.56 | 56 | 111 |
| 76.0 | 0.71 | 57 | 114 | 71.1 | 0.55 | 56 | 111 |
| 75.9 | 0.70 | 57 | 114 | 71.0 | 0.55 | 56 | 111 |
| 75.8 | 0.70 | 57 | 114 | 70.9 | 0.55 | 56 | 111 |
| 75.7 | 0.70 | 57 | 114 | 70.8 | 0.55 | 56 | 111 |
| 75.6 | 0.69 | 57 | 114 | 70.7 | 0.54 | 55 | 111 |
| 75.5 | 0.69 | 57 | 114 | 70.6 | 0.54 | 55 | 111 |

| a | b | c | d | a | b | c | d |
|------|------|----|-----|------|------|----|-----|
| 70.5 | 0.54 | 55 | 111 | 65.6 | 0.40 | 54 | 108 |
| 70.4 | 0.54 | 55 | 111 | 65.5 | 0.40 | 54 | 108 |
| 70.3 | 0.53 | 55 | 111 | 65.4 | 0.40 | 54 | 108 |
| 70.2 | 0.53 | 55 | 111 | 65.3 | 0.39 | 54 | 108 |
| 70.1 | 0.53 | 55 | 111 | 65.2 | 0.39 | 54 | 108 |
| 70.0 | 0.52 | 55 | 110 | 65.1 | 0.39 | 54 | 108 |
| 69.9 | 0.52 | 55 | 110 | 65.0 | 0.39 | 54 | 108 |
| 69.8 | 0.52 | 55 | 110 | 64.9 | 0.38 | 54 | 108 |
| 69.7 | 0.52 | 55 | 110 | 64.8 | 0.38 | 54 | 108 |
| 69.6 | 0.51 | 55 | 110 | 64.7 | 0.38 | 54 | 108 |
| 69.5 | 0.51 | 55 | 110 | 64.6 | 0.37 | 54 | 107 |
| 69.4 | 0.51 | 55 | 110 | 64.5 | 0.37 | 54 | 107 |
| 69.3 | 0.50 | 55 | 110 | 64.4 | 0.37 | 54 | 107 |
| 69.2 | 0.50 | 55 | 110 | 64.3 | 0.37 | 54 | 107 |
| 69.1 | 0.50 | 55 | 110 | 64.2 | 0.36 | 54 | 107 |
| 69.0 | 0.49 | 55 | 110 | 64.1 | 0.36 | 54 | 107 |
| 68.9 | 0.49 | 55 | 110 | 64.0 | 0.36 | 54 | 107 |
| 68.8 | 0.49 | 55 | 110 | 63.9 | 0.36 | 54 | 107 |
| 68.7 | 0.49 | 55 | 110 | 63.8 | 0.35 | 54 | 107 |
| 68.6 | 0.48 | 55 | 110 | 63.7 | 0.35 | 54 | 107 |
| 68.5 | 0.48 | 55 | 110 | 63.6 | 0.35 | 54 | 107 |
| 68.4 | 0.48 | 55 | 110 | 63.5 | 0.35 | 54 | 107 |
| 68.3 | 0.48 | 55 | 110 | 63.4 | 0.34 | 53 | 107 |
| 68.2 | 0.47 | 55 | 109 | 63.3 | 0.34 | 53 | 107 |
| 68.1 | 0.47 | 55 | 109 | 63.2 | 0.34 | 53 | 107 |
| 68.0 | 0.47 | 55 | 109 | 63.1 | 0.33 | 53 | 107 |
| 67.9 | 0.47 | 55 | 109 | 63.0 | 0.33 | 53 | 107 |
| 67.8 | 0.46 | 55 | 109 | 62.9 | 0.33 | 53 | 107 |
| 67.7 | 0.46 | 55 | 109 | 62.8 | 0.33 | 53 | 107 |
| 67.6 | 0.46 | 55 | 109 | 62.7 | 0.32 | 53 | 106 |
| 67.5 | 0.45 | 55 | 109 | 62.6 | 0.32 | 53 | 106 |
| 67.4 | 0.45 | 55 | 109 | 62.5 | 0.32 | 53 | 106 |
| 67.3 | 0.45 | 55 | 109 | 62.4 | 0.32 | 53 | 106 |
| 67.2 | 0.44 | 54 | 109 | 62.3 | 0.31 | 53 | 106 |
| 67.1 | 0.44 | 54 | 109 | 62.2 | 0.31 | 53 | 106 |
| 67.0 | 0.44 | 54 | 109 | 62.1 | 0.31 | 53 | 106 |
| 66.9 | 0.44 | 54 | 109 | 62.0 | 0.31 | 53 | 106 |
| 66.8 | 0.43 | 54 | 109 | 61.9 | 0.30 | 53 | 106 |
| 66.7 | 0.43 | 54 | 109 | 61.8 | 0.30 | 53 | 106 |
| 66.6 | 0.43 | 54 | 109 | 61.7 | 0.30 | 53 | 106 |
| 66.5 | 0.43 | 54 | 109 | 61.6 | 0.29 | 53 | 106 |
| 66.4 | 0.42 | 54 | 108 | 61.5 | 0.29 | 53 | 106 |
| 66.3 | 0.42 | 54 | 108 | 61.4 | 0.29 | 53 | 106 |
| 66.2 | 0.42 | 54 | 108 | 61.3 | 0.29 | 53 | 106 |
| 66.1 | 0.41 | 54 | 108 | 61.2 | 0.28 | 53 | 106 |
| 66.0 | 0.41 | 54 | 108 | 61.1 | 0.28 | 53 | 106 |
| 65.9 | 0.41 | 54 | 108 | 61.0 | 0.28 | 53 | 106 |
| 65.8 | 0.41 | 54 | 108 | 60.9 | 0.28 | 53 | 106 |
| 65.7 | 0.40 | 54 | 108 | 60.8 | 0.27 | 53 | 105 |

| a | b | c | d | a | b | c | d |
|------|------|----|-----|------|------|----|-----|
| 60.7 | 0.27 | 53 | 105 | 55.8 | 0.14 | 51 | 103 |
| 60.6 | 0.27 | 53 | 105 | 55.7 | 0.14 | 51 | 103 |
| 60.5 | 0.27 | 53 | 105 | 55.6 | 0.14 | 51 | 103 |
| 60.4 | 0.26 | 53 | 105 | 55.5 | 0.14 | 51 | 103 |
| 60.3 | 0.26 | 53 | 105 | 55.4 | 0.13 | 51 | 103 |
| 60.2 | 0.26 | 53 | 105 | 55.3 | 0.13 | 51 | 103 |
| 60.1 | 0.25 | 53 | 105 | 55.2 | 0.13 | 51 | 103 |
| 60.0 | 0.25 | 53 | 105 | 55.1 | 0.13 | 51 | 103 |
| 59.9 | 0.25 | 53 | 105 | 55.0 | 0.12 | 51 | 103 |
| 59.8 | 0.25 | 53 | 105 | 54.9 | 0.12 | 51 | 102 |
| 59.7 | 0.24 | 52 | 105 | 54.8 | 0.12 | 51 | 102 |
| 59.6 | 0.24 | 52 | 105 | 54.7 | 0.12 | 51 | 102 |
| 59.5 | 0.24 | 52 | 105 | 54.6 | 0.11 | 51 | 102 |
| 59.4 | 0.24 | 52 | 105 | 54.5 | 0.11 | 51 | 102 |
| 59.3 | 0.23 | 52 | 105 | 54.4 | 0.11 | 51 | 102 |
| 59.2 | 0.23 | 52 | 105 | 54.3 | 0.11 | 51 | 102 |
| 59.1 | 0.23 | 52 | 105 | 54.2 | 0.10 | 51 | 102 |
| 59.0 | 0.23 | 52 | 105 | 54.1 | 0.10 | 51 | 102 |
| 58.9 | 0.22 | 52 | 104 | 54.0 | 0.10 | 51 | 102 |
| 58.8 | 0.22 | 52 | 104 | 53.9 | 0.10 | 51 | 102 |
| 58.7 | 0.22 | 52 | 104 | 53.8 | 0.09 | 51 | 102 |
| 58.6 | 0.22 | 52 | 104 | 53.7 | 0.09 | 51 | 102 |
| 58.5 | 0.21 | 52 | 104 | 53.6 | 0.09 | 51 | 102 |
| 58.4 | 0.21 | 52 | 104 | 53.5 | 0.09 | 51 | 102 |
| 58.3 | 0.21 | 52 | 104 | 53.4 | 0.08 | 51 | 102 |
| 58.2 | 0.21 | 52 | 104 | 53.3 | 0.08 | 51 | 102 |
| 58.1 | 0.20 | 52 | 104 | 53.2 | 0.08 | 51 | 102 |
| 58.0 | 0.20 | 52 | 104 | 53.1 | 0.08 | 51 | 102 |
| 57.9 | 0.20 | 52 | 104 | 53.0 | 0.07 | 51 | 102 |
| 57.8 | 0.20 | 52 | 104 | 52.9 | 0.07 | 51 | 101 |
| 57.7 | 0.19 | 52 | 104 | 52.8 | 0.07 | 51 | 101 |
| 57.6 | 0.19 | 52 | 104 | 52.7 | 0.07 | 51 | 101 |
| 57.5 | 0.19 | 52 | 104 | 52.6 | 0.06 | 51 | 101 |
| 57.4 | 0.19 | 52 | 104 | 52.5 | 0.06 | 51 | 101 |
| 57.3 | 0.18 | 52 | 104 | 52.4 | 0.06 | 51 | 101 |
| 57.2 | 0.18 | 52 | 104 | 52.3 | 0.06 | 51 | 101 |
| 57.1 | 0.18 | 52 | 104 | 52.2 | 0.05 | 51 | 101 |
| 57.0 | 0.18 | 52 | 104 | 52.1 | 0.05 | 51 | 101 |
| 56.9 | 0.17 | 52 | 103 | 52.0 | 0.05 | 51 | 101 |
| 56.8 | 0.17 | 52 | 103 | 51.9 | 0.05 | 51 | 101 |
| 56.7 | 0.17 | 52 | 103 | 51.8 | 0.04 | 50 | 101 |
| 56.6 | 0.16 | 52 | 103 | 51.7 | 0.04 | 50 | 101 |
| 56.5 | 0.16 | 52 | 103 | 51.6 | 0.04 | 50 | 101 |
| 56.4 | 0.16 | 52 | 103 | 51.5 | 0.04 | 50 | 101 |
| 56.3 | 0.16 | 52 | 103 | 51.4 | 0.04 | 50 | 101 |
| 56.2 | 0.15 | 52 | 103 | 51.3 | 0.03 | 50 | 101 |
| 56.1 | 0.15 | 52 | 103 | 51.2 | 0.03 | 50 | 101 |
| 56.0 | 0.15 | 52 | 103 | 51.1 | 0.03 | 50 | 101 |
| 55.9 | 0.15 | 52 | 103 | 51.0 | 0.03 | 50 | 101 |

| a | b | c | d | a | b | c | d |
|------|-------|----|-----|------|--------|----|----|
| 50.9 | 0.02 | 50 | 100 | 46.0 | −0.10 | 49 | 98 |
| 50.8 | 0.02 | 50 | 100 | 45.9 | −0.10 | 49 | 98 |
| 50.7 | 0.02 | 50 | 100 | 45.8 | −0.10 | 49 | 98 |
| 50.6 | 0.01 | 50 | 100 | 45.7 | −0.11 | 49 | 98 |
| 50.5 | 0.01 | 50 | 100 | 45.6 | −0.11 | 49 | 98 |
| 50.4 | 0.01 | 50 | 100 | 45.5 | −0.11 | 49 | 98 |
| 50.3 | 0.01 | 50 | 100 | 45.4 | −0.11 | 49 | 98 |
| 50.2 | 0.00 | 50 | 100 | 45.3 | −0.12 | 49 | 98 |
| 50.1 | 0.00 | 50 | 100 | 45.2 | −0.12 | 49 | 98 |
| 50.0 | 0.00 | 50 | 100 | 45.1 | −0.12 | 49 | 98 |
| 49.9 | 0.00 | 50 | 100 | 45.0 | −0.12 | 49 | 98 |
| 49.8 | 0.00 | 50 | 100 | 44.9 | −0.13 | 49 | 97 |
| 49.7 | −0.01 | 50 | 100 | 44.8 | −0.13 | 49 | 97 |
| 49.6 | −0.01 | 50 | 100 | 44.7 | −0.13 | 49 | 97 |
| 49.5 | −0.01 | 50 | 100 | 44.6 | −0.13 | 49 | 97 |
| 49.4 | −0.01 | 50 | 100 | 44.5 | −0.14 | 49 | 97 |
| 49.3 | −0.02 | 50 | 100 | 44.4 | −0.14 | 49 | 97 |
| 49.2 | −0.02 | 50 | 100 | 44.3 | −0.14 | 49 | 97 |
| 49.1 | −0.02 | 50 | 100 | 44.2 | −0.14 | 49 | 97 |
| 49.0 | −0.03 | 50 | 99 | 44.1 | −0.15 | 48 | 97 |
| 48.9 | −0.03 | 50 | 99 | 44.0 | −0.15 | 48 | 97 |
| 48.8 | −0.03 | 50 | 99 | 43.9 | −0.15 | 48 | 97 |
| 48.7 | −0.03 | 50 | 99 | 43.8 | −0.15 | 48 | 97 |
| 48.6 | −0.04 | 50 | 99 | 43.7 | −0.16 | 48 | 97 |
| 48.5 | −0.04 | 50 | 99 | 43.6 | −0.16 | 48 | 97 |
| 48.4 | −0.04 | 50 | 99 | 43.5 | −0.16 | 48 | 97 |
| 48.3 | −0.04 | 50 | 99 | 43.4 | −0.16 | 48 | 97 |
| 48.2 | −0.04 | 50 | 99 | 43.3 | −0.17 | 48 | 97 |
| 48.1 | −0.05 | 49 | 99 | 43.2 | −0.17 | 48 | 97 |
| 48.0 | −0.05 | 49 | 99 | 43.1 | −0.17 | 48 | 97 |
| 47.9 | −0.05 | 49 | 99 | 43.0 | −0.18 | 48 | 96 |
| 47.8 | −0.05 | 49 | 99 | 42.9 | −0.18 | 48 | 96 |
| 47.7 | −0.06 | 49 | 99 | 42.8 | −0.18 | 48 | 96 |
| 47.6 | −0.06 | 49 | 99 | 42.7 | −0.18 | 48 | 96 |
| 47.5 | −0.06 | 49 | 99 | 42.6 | −0.19 | 48 | 96 |
| 47.4 | −0.06 | 49 | 99 | 42.5 | −0.19 | 48 | 96 |
| 47.3 | −0.07 | 49 | 99 | 42.4 | −0.19 | 48 | 96 |
| 47.2 | −0.07 | 49 | 99 | 42.3 | −0.19 | 48 | 96 |
| 47.1 | −0.07 | 49 | 99 | 42.2 | −0.20 | 48 | 96 |
| 47.0 | −0.07 | 49 | 99 | 42.1 | −0.20 | 48 | 96 |
| 46.9 | −0.08 | 49 | 98 | 42.0 | −0.20 | 48 | 96 |
| 46.8 | −0.08 | 49 | 98 | 41.9 | −0.20 | 48 | 96 |
| 46.7 | −0.08 | 49 | 98 | 41.8 | −0.21 | 48 | 96 |
| 46.6 | −0.08 | 49 | 98 | 41.7 | −0.21 | 48 | 96 |
| 46.5 | −0.09 | 49 | 98 | 41.6 | −0.21 | 48 | 96 |
| 46.4 | −0.09 | 49 | 98 | 41.5 | −0.21 | 48 | 96 |
| 46.3 | −0.09 | 49 | 98 | 41.4 | −0.22 | 48 | 96 |
| 46.2 | −0.09 | 49 | 98 | 41.3 | −0.22 | 48 | 96 |
| 46.1 | −0.10 | 49 | 98 | 41.2 | −0.22 | 48 | 96 |

| a | b | c | d | a | b | c | d |
|---|---|---|---|---|---|---|---|
| 41.1 | −0.22 | 48 | 96 | 36.2 | −0.35 | 46 | 93 |
| 41.0 | −0.23 | 48 | 95 | 36.1 | −0.36 | 46 | 93 |
| 40.9 | −0.23 | 48 | 95 | 36.0 | −0.36 | 46 | 93 |
| 40.8 | −0.23 | 48 | 95 | 35.9 | −0.36 | 46 | 93 |
| 40.7 | −0.23 | 48 | 95 | 35.8 | −0.36 | 46 | 93 |
| 40.6 | −0.24 | 48 | 95 | 35.7 | −0.37 | 46 | 93 |
| 40.5 | −0.24 | 48 | 95 | 35.6 | −0.37 | 46 | 93 |
| 40.4 | −0.24 | 48 | 95 | 35.5 | −0.37 | 46 | 93 |
| 40.3 | −0.24 | 48 | 95 | 35.4 | −0.37 | 46 | 93 |
| 40.2 | −0.25 | 47 | 95 | 35.3 | −0.38 | 46 | 92 |
| 40.1 | −0.25 | 47 | 95 | 35.2 | −0.38 | 46 | 92 |
| 40.0 | −0.25 | 47 | 95 | 35.1 | −0.38 | 46 | 92 |
| 39.9 | −0.25 | 47 | 95 | 35.0 | −0.39 | 46 | 92 |
| 39.8 | −0.26 | 47 | 95 | 34.9 | −0.39 | 46 | 92 |
| 39.7 | −0.26 | 47 | 95 | 34.8 | −0.39 | 46 | 92 |
| 39.6 | −0.26 | 47 | 95 | 34.7 | −0.39 | 46 | 92 |
| 39.5 | −0.27 | 47 | 95 | 34.6 | −0.40 | 46 | 92 |
| 39.4 | −0.27 | 47 | 95 | 34.5 | −0.40 | 46 | 92 |
| 39.3 | −0.27 | 47 | 95 | 34.4 | −0.40 | 46 | 92 |
| 39.2 | −0.27 | 47 | 95 | 34.3 | −0.40 | 46 | 92 |
| 39.1 | −0.28 | 47 | 94 | 34.2 | −0.41 | 46 | 92 |
| 39.0 | −0.28 | 47 | 94 | 34.1 | −0.41 | 46 | 92 |
| 38.9 | −0.28 | 47 | 94 | 34.0 | −0.41 | 46 | 92 |
| 38.8 | −0.28 | 47 | 94 | 33.9 | −0.41 | 46 | 92 |
| 38.7 | −0.29 | 47 | 94 | 33.8 | −0.42 | 46 | 92 |
| 38.6 | −0.29 | 47 | 94 | 33.7 | −0.42 | 46 | 92 |
| 38.5 | −0.29 | 47 | 94 | 33.6 | −0.42 | 46 | 92 |
| 38.4 | −0.29 | 47 | 94 | 33.5 | −0.43 | 46 | 91 |
| 38.3 | −0.30 | 47 | 94 | 33.4 | −0.43 | 46 | 91 |
| 38.2 | −0.30 | 47 | 94 | 33.3 | −0.43 | 46 | 91 |
| 38.1 | −0.30 | 47 | 94 | 33.2 | −0.43 | 46 | 91 |
| 38.0 | −0.31 | 47 | 94 | 33.1 | −0.44 | 46 | 91 |
| 37.9 | −0.31 | 47 | 94 | 33.0 | −0.44 | 46 | 91 |
| 37.8 | −0.31 | 47 | 94 | 32.9 | −0.44 | 46 | 91 |
| 37.7 | −0.31 | 47 | 94 | 32.8 | −0.44 | 46 | 91 |
| 37.6 | −0.32 | 47 | 94 | 32.7 | −0.45 | 45 | 91 |
| 37.5 | −0.32 | 47 | 94 | 32.6 | −0.45 | 45 | 91 |
| 37.4 | −0.32 | 47 | 94 | 32.5 | −0.45 | 45 | 91 |
| 37.3 | −0.32 | 47 | 94 | 32.4 | −0.46 | 45 | 91 |
| 37.2 | −0.33 | 47 | 93 | 32.3 | −0.46 | 45 | 91 |
| 37.1 | −0.33 | 47 | 93 | 32.2 | −0.46 | 45 | 91 |
| 37.0 | −0.33 | 47 | 93 | 32.1 | −0.47 | 45 | 91 |
| 36.9 | −0.33 | 47 | 93 | 32.0 | −0.47 | 45 | 91 |
| 36.8 | −0.34 | 47 | 93 | 31.9 | −0.47 | 45 | 91 |
| 36.7 | −0.34 | 47 | 93 | 31.8 | −0.47 | 45 | 91 |
| 36.6 | −0.34 | 47 | 93 | 31.7 | −0.48 | 45 | 90 |
| 36.5 | −0.35 | 46 | 93 | 31.6 | −0.48 | 45 | 90 |
| 36.4 | −0.35 | 46 | 93 | 31.5 | −0.48 | 45 | 90 |
| 36.3 | −0.35 | 46 | 93 | 31.4 | −0.48 | 45 | 90 |

| a | b | c | d | a | b | c | d |
|------|-------|----|----|------|-------|----|----|
| 31.3 | −0.49 | 45 | 90 | 26.4 | −0.63 | 44 | 87 |
| 31.2 | −0.49 | 45 | 90 | 26.3 | −0.63 | 44 | 87 |
| 31.1 | −0.49 | 45 | 90 | 26.2 | −0.64 | 44 | 87 |
| 31.0 | −0.49 | 45 | 90 | 26.1 | −0.64 | 44 | 87 |
| 30.9 | −0.50 | 45 | 90 | 26.0 | −0.64 | 44 | 87 |
| 30.8 | −0.50 | 45 | 90 | 25.9 | −0.65 | 43 | 87 |
| 30.7 | −0.50 | 45 | 90 | 25.8 | −0.65 | 43 | 87 |
| 30.6 | −0.51 | 45 | 90 | 25.7 | −0.65 | 43 | 87 |
| 30.5 | −0.51 | 45 | 90 | 25.6 | −0.66 | 43 | 87 |
| 30.4 | −0.51 | 45 | 90 | 25.5 | −0.66 | 43 | 87 |
| 30.3 | −0.52 | 45 | 90 | 25.4 | −0.66 | 43 | 87 |
| 30.2 | −0.52 | 45 | 90 | 25.3 | −0.66 | 43 | 87 |
| 30.1 | −0.52 | 45 | 90 | 25.2 | −0.67 | 43 | 87 |
| 30.0 | −0.52 | 45 | 90 | 25.1 | −0.67 | 43 | 87 |
| 29.9 | −0.53 | 45 | 89 | 25.0 | −0.67 | 43 | 87 |
| 29.8 | −0.53 | 45 | 89 | 24.9 | −0.68 | 43 | 86 |
| 29.7 | −0.53 | 45 | 89 | 24.8 | −0.68 | 43 | 86 |
| 29.6 | −0.54 | 45 | 89 | 24.7 | −0.68 | 43 | 86 |
| 29.5 | −0.54 | 45 | 89 | 24.6 | −0.69 | 43 | 86 |
| 29.4 | −0.54 | 45 | 89 | 24.5 | −0.69 | 43 | 86 |
| 29.3 | −0.54 | 45 | 89 | 24.4 | −0.69 | 43 | 86 |
| 29.2 | −0.55 | 44 | 89 | 24.3 | −0.70 | 43 | 86 |
| 29.1 | −0.55 | 44 | 89 | 24.2 | −0.70 | 43 | 86 |
| 29.0 | −0.55 | 44 | 89 | 24.1 | −0.70 | 43 | 86 |
| 28.9 | −0.55 | 44 | 89 | 24.0 | −0.71 | 43 | 86 |
| 28.8 | −0.56 | 44 | 89 | 23.9 | −0.71 | 43 | 86 |
| 28.7 | −0.56 | 44 | 89 | 23.8 | −0.71 | 43 | 86 |
| 28.6 | −0.56 | 44 | 89 | 23.7 | −0.72 | 43 | 86 |
| 28.5 | −0.57 | 44 | 89 | 23.6 | −0.72 | 43 | 86 |
| 28.4 | −0.57 | 44 | 89 | 23.5 | −0.72 | 43 | 86 |
| 28.3 | −0.57 | 44 | 89 | 23.4 | −0.73 | 43 | 85 |
| 28.2 | −0.58 | 44 | 88 | 23.3 | −0.73 | 43 | 85 |
| 28.1 | −0.58 | 44 | 88 | 23.2 | −0.73 | 43 | 85 |
| 28.0 | −0.58 | 44 | 88 | 23.1 | −0.74 | 43 | 85 |
| 27.9 | −0.59 | 44 | 88 | 23.0 | −0.74 | 43 | 85 |
| 27.8 | −0.59 | 44 | 88 | 22.9 | −0.74 | 43 | 85 |
| 27.7 | −0.59 | 44 | 88 | 22.8 | −0.75 | 42 | 85 |
| 27.6 | −0.59 | 44 | 88 | 22.7 | −0.75 | 42 | 85 |
| 27.5 | −0.60 | 44 | 88 | 22.6 | −0.75 | 42 | 85 |
| 27.4 | −0.60 | 44 | 88 | 22.5 | −0.76 | 42 | 85 |
| 27.3 | −0.60 | 44 | 88 | 22.4 | −0.76 | 42 | 85 |
| 27.2 | −0.61 | 44 | 88 | 22.3 | −0.76 | 42 | 85 |
| 27.1 | −0.61 | 44 | 88 | 22.2 | −0.77 | 42 | 85 |
| 27.0 | −0.61 | 44 | 88 | 22.1 | −0.77 | 42 | 85 |
| 26.9 | −0.61 | 44 | 88 | 22.0 | −0.77 | 42 | 85 |
| 26.8 | −0.62 | 44 | 88 | 21.9 | −0.77 | 42 | 85 |
| 26.7 | −0.62 | 44 | 88 | 21.8 | −0.78 | 42 | 84 |
| 26.6 | −0.62 | 44 | 88 | 21.7 | −0.78 | 42 | 84 |
| 26.5 | −0.63 | 44 | 87 | 21.6 | −0.78 | 42 | 84 |

| a | b | c | d | a | b | c | d |
|---|---|---|---|---|---|---|---|
| 21.5 | −0.79 | 42 | 84 | 16.6 | −0.97 | 40 | 81 |
| 21.4 | −0.79 | 42 | 84 | 16.5 | −0.97 | 40 | 81 |
| 21.3 | −0.79 | 42 | 84 | 16.4 | −0.98 | 40 | 80 |
| 21.2 | −0.80 | 42 | 84 | 16.3 | −0.98 | 40 | 80 |
| 21.1 | −0.80 | 42 | 84 | 16.2 | −0.99 | 40 | 80 |
| 21.0 | −0.80 | 42 | 84 | 16.1 | −0.99 | 40 | 80 |
| 20.9 | −0.81 | 42 | 84 | 16.0 | −0.99 | 40 | 80 |
| 20.8 | −0.81 | 42 | 84 | 15.9 | −1.00 | 40 | 80 |
| 20.7 | −0.82 | 42 | 84 | 15.8 | −1.00 | 40 | 80 |
| 20.6 | −0.82 | 42 | 84 | 15.7 | −1.00 | 40 | 80 |
| 20.5 | −0.82 | 42 | 84 | 15.6 | −1.01 | 40 | 80 |
| 20.4 | −0.83 | 42 | 83 | 15.5 | −1.01 | 40 | 80 |
| 20.3 | −0.83 | 42 | 83 | 15.4 | −1.02 | 40 | 80 |
| 20.2 | −0.83 | 42 | 83 | 15.3 | −1.02 | 40 | 80 |
| 20.1 | −0.84 | 42 | 83 | 15.2 | −1.03 | 40 | 79 |
| 20.0 | −0.84 | 42 | 83 | 15.1 | −1.03 | 40 | 79 |
| 19.9 | −0.84 | 42 | 83 | 15.0 | −1.04 | 40 | 79 |
| 19.8 | −0.85 | 41 | 83 | 14.9 | −1.04 | 40 | 79 |
| 19.7 | −0.85 | 41 | 83 | 14.8 | −1.05 | 39 | 79 |
| 19.6 | −0.86 | 41 | 83 | 14.7 | −1.05 | 39 | 79 |
| 19.5 | −0.86 | 41 | 83 | 14.6 | −1.05 | 39 | 79 |
| 19.4 | −0.86 | 41 | 83 | 14.5 | −1.06 | 39 | 79 |
| 19.3 | −0.87 | 41 | 83 | 14.4 | −1.06 | 39 | 79 |
| 19.2 | −0.87 | 41 | 83 | 14.3 | −1.07 | 39 | 79 |
| 19.1 | −0.87 | 41 | 83 | 14.2 | −1.07 | 39 | 78 |
| 19.0 | −0.88 | 41 | 82 | 14.1 | −1.08 | 39 | 78 |
| 18.9 | −0.88 | 41 | 82 | 14.0 | −1.08 | 39 | 78 |
| 18.8 | −0.89 | 41 | 82 | 13.9 | −1.08 | 39 | 78 |
| 18.7 | −0.89 | 41 | 82 | 13.8 | −1.09 | 39 | 78 |
| 18.6 | −0.89 | 41 | 82 | 13.7 | −1.09 | 39 | 78 |
| 18.5 | −0.90 | 41 | 82 | 13.6 | −1.10 | 39 | 78 |
| 18.4 | −0.90 | 41 | 82 | 13.5 | −1.10 | 39 | 78 |
| 18.3 | −0.90 | 41 | 82 | 13.4 | −1.11 | 39 | 78 |
| 18.2 | −0.91 | 41 | 82 | 13.3 | −1.11 | 39 | 78 |
| 18.1 | −0.91 | 41 | 82 | 13.2 | −1.12 | 39 | 78 |
| 18.0 | −0.91 | 41 | 82 | 13.1 | −1.12 | 39 | 78 |
| 17.9 | −0.92 | 41 | 82 | 13.0 | −1.13 | 39 | 77 |
| 17.8 | −0.92 | 41 | 82 | 12.9 | −1.13 | 39 | 77 |
| 17.7 | −0.93 | 41 | 81 | 12.8 | −1.14 | 39 | 77 |
| 17.6 | −0.93 | 41 | 81 | 12.7 | −1.14 | 39 | 77 |
| 17.5 | −0.93 | 41 | 81 | 12.6 | −1.15 | 38 | 77 |
| 17.4 | −0.94 | 41 | 81 | 12.5 | −1.15 | 38 | 77 |
| 17.3 | −0.94 | 41 | 81 | 12.4 | −1.16 | 38 | 77 |
| 17.2 | −0.95 | 40 | 81 | 12.3 | −1.16 | 38 | 77 |
| 17.1 | −0.95 | 40 | 81 | 12.2 | −1.17 | 38 | 77 |
| 17.0 | −0.95 | 40 | 81 | 12.1 | −1.17 | 38 | 77 |
| 16.9 | −0.96 | 40 | 81 | 12.0 | −1.18 | 38 | 76 |
| 16.8 | −0.96 | 40 | 81 | 11.9 | −1.18 | 38 | 76 |
| 16.7 | −0.97 | 40 | 81 | 11.8 | −1.19 | 38 | 76 |

| a | b | c | d | a | b | c | d |
|------|--------|----|----|------|--------|----|----|
| 11.7 | −1.19 | 38 | 76 | 6.8 | −1.49 | 35 | 70 |
| 11.6 | −1.20 | 38 | 76 | 6.7 | −1.50 | 35 | 70 |
| 11.5 | −1.20 | 38 | 76 | 6.6 | −1.50 | 35 | 70 |
| 11.4 | −1.21 | 38 | 76 | 6.5 | −1.51 | 35 | 70 |
| 11.3 | −1.21 | 38 | 76 | 6.4 | −1.52 | 35 | 70 |
| 11.2 | −1.22 | 38 | 76 | 6.3 | −1.53 | 35 | 69 |
| 11.1 | −1.22 | 38 | 76 | 6.2 | −1.54 | 35 | 69 |
| 11.0 | −1.22 | 38 | 76 | 6.1 | −1.55 | 34 | 69 |
| 10.9 | −1.23 | 38 | 75 | 6.0 | −1.55 | 34 | 69 |
| 10.8 | −1.23 | 38 | 75 | 5.9 | −1.56 | 34 | 69 |
| 10.7 | −1.24 | 38 | 75 | 5.8 | −1.57 | 34 | 69 |
| 10.6 | −1.25 | 37 | 75 | 5.7 | −1.58 | 34 | 68 |
| 10.5 | −1.25 | 37 | 75 | 5.6 | −1.59 | 34 | 68 |
| 10.4 | −1.26 | 37 | 75 | 5.5 | −1.60 | 34 | 68 |
| 10.3 | −1.26 | 37 | 75 | 5.4 | −1.61 | 34 | 68 |
| 10.2 | −1.27 | 37 | 75 | 5.3 | −1.62 | 34 | 68 |
| 10.1 | −1.28 | 37 | 74 | 5.2 | −1.63 | 34 | 67 |
| 10.0 | −1.28 | 37 | 74 | 5.1 | −1.64 | 34 | 67 |
| 9.9 | −1.29 | 37 | 74 | 5.0 | −1.64 | 34 | 67 |
| 9.8 | −1.29 | 37 | 74 | 4.9 | −1.65 | 33 | 67 |
| 9.7 | −1.30 | 37 | 74 | 4.8 | −1.66 | 33 | 67 |
| 9.6 | −1.30 | 37 | 74 | 4.7 | −1.67 | 33 | 67 |
| 9.5 | −1.31 | 37 | 74 | 4.6 | −1.68 | 33 | 66 |
| 9.4 | −1.32 | 37 | 74 | 4.5 | −1.70 | 33 | 66 |
| 9.3 | −1.32 | 37 | 74 | 4.4 | −1.71 | 33 | 66 |
| 9.2 | −1.33 | 37 | 73 | 4.3 | −1.72 | 33 | 66 |
| 9.1 | −1.33 | 37 | 73 | 4.2 | −1.73 | 33 | 65 |
| 9.0 | −1.34 | 37 | 73 | 4.1 | −1.74 | 33 | 65 |
| 8.9 | −1.35 | 36 | 73 | 4.0 | −1.75 | 32 | 65 |
| 8.8 | −1.35 | 36 | 73 | 3.9 | −1.76 | 32 | 65 |
| 8.7 | −1.36 | 36 | 73 | 3.8 | −1.77 | 32 | 65 |
| 8.6 | −1.37 | 36 | 73 | 3.7 | −1.79 | 32 | 64 |
| 8.5 | −1.37 | 36 | 73 | 3.6 | −1.80 | 32 | 64 |
| 8.4 | −1.38 | 36 | 72 | 3.5 | −1.81 | 32 | 64 |
| 8.3 | −1.38 | 36 | 72 | 3.4 | −1.83 | 32 | 63 |
| 8.2 | −1.39 | 36 | 72 | 3.3 | −1.84 | 32 | 63 |
| 8.1 | −1.40 | 36 | 72 | 3.2 | −1.85 | 31 | 63 |
| 8.0 | −1.41 | 36 | 72 | 3.1 | −1.87 | 31 | 63 |
| 7.9 | −1.41 | 36 | 72 | 3.0 | −1.88 | 31 | 62 |
| 7.8 | −1.42 | 36 | 72 | 2.9 | −1.90 | 31 | 62 |
| 7.7 | −1.43 | 36 | 71 | 2.8 | −1.91 | 31 | 62 |
| 7.6 | −1.43 | 36 | 71 | 2.7 | −1.93 | 31 | 61 |
| 7.5 | −1.44 | 36 | 71 | 2.6 | −1.94 | 31 | 61 |
| 7.4 | −1.45 | 35 | 71 | 2.5 | −1.96 | 30 | 61 |
| 7.3 | −1.45 | 35 | 71 | 2.4 | −1.98 | 30 | 60 |
| 7.2 | −1.46 | 35 | 71 | 2.3 | −2.00 | 30 | 60 |
| 7.1 | −1.47 | 35 | 71 | 2.2 | −2.01 | 30 | 60 |
| 7.0 | −1.48 | 35 | 70 | 2.1 | −2.03 | 30 | 59 |
| 6.9 | −1.48 | 35 | 70 | 2.0 | −2.05 | 29 | 59 |

| a | b | c | d | a | b | c | d |
|-----|-------|-----|-----|-----|-------|-----|-----|
| 1.9 | −2.07 | 29 | 59 | 0.9 | −2.37 | 26 | 53 |
| 1.8 | −2.10 | 29 | 58 | 0.8 | −2.41 | 26 | 52 |
| 1.7 | −2.12 | 29 | 58 | 0.7 | −2.46 | 25 | 51 |
| 1.6 | −2.14 | 29 | 57 | 0.6 | −2.51 | 25 | 50 |
| 1.5 | −2.17 | 28 | 57 | 0.5 | −2.58 | 24 | 48 |
| 1.4 | −2.20 | 28 | 56 | 0.4 | −2.65 | 23 | 47 |
| 1.3 | −2.22 | 28 | 55 | 0.3 | −2.75 | 22 | 45 |
| 1.2 | −2.26 | 27 | 55 | 0.2 | −2.88 | 21 | 42 |
| 1.1 | −2.29 | 27 | 54 | 0.1 | −3.09 | 19 | 38 |
| 1.0 | −2.33 | 27 | 53 | | | | |

# Appendix B

*Taylor–Russell Tables of Proportion Who Will Be Satisfactory Among Those Selected for Given Values of Proportion of Present Employees Considered Satisfactory and Predictor Validity (r)*

These tables show the increase in the percentage of correct predictions over and above the base rate (proportion considered satisfactory prior to the introduction of the predictor of interest) given a particular selection ratio (percentage hired) and validity coefficient. Each of the tables represents a different base rate. The following example will illustrate how this appendix can be used. Suppose our current base rate is 60 percent and we decide to implement a testing program to improve this proportion. We validate a test and obtain a validity coefficient of .30; we decide to hire 40 percent of the applicants (selection ratio = .40). Entering the 60 percent base rate table shows us that .71 or 71 percent of those hired will be satisfactory employees. In other words, we have a gain of 11 percent (.71 − .60) in satisfactory employees by utilizing the test. If we decide that we want to hire only 20 percent of the applicants (.20 selection ratio), then the gain in satisfactory employees with the same test ($r$ = .30) is 16 percent (.76 − .60). This latter example illustrates that shifting the cutoff score (that is, changing the percentage to be hired) affects the utility of the test.

Proportion of employees considered satisfactory = .05

| | Selection Ratio | | | | | | | | | | |
|---|---|---|---|---|---|---|---|---|---|---|---|
| r | .05 | .10 | .20 | .30 | .40 | .50 | .60 | .70 | .80 | .90 | .95 |
| .00 | .05 | .05 | .05 | .05 | .05 | .05 | .05 | .05 | .05 | .05 | .05 |
| .05 | .06 | .06 | .06 | .06 | .06 | .05 | .05 | .05 | .05 | .05 | .05 |
| .10 | .07 | .07 | .07 | .06 | .06 | .06 | .06 | .05 | .05 | .05 | .05 |
| .15 | .09 | .08 | .07 | .07 | .07 | .06 | .06 | .06 | .05 | .05 | .05 |
| .20 | .11 | .09 | .08 | .08 | .07 | .07 | .06 | .06 | .06 | .05 | .05 |
| .25 | .12 | .11 | .09 | .08 | .08 | .07 | .07 | .06 | .06 | .05 | .05 |
| .30 | .14 | .12 | .10 | .09 | .08 | .07 | .07 | .06 | .06 | .05 | .05 |
| .35 | .17 | .14 | .11 | .10 | .09 | .08 | .07 | .06 | .06 | .05 | .05 |
| .40 | .19 | .16 | .12 | .10 | .09 | .08 | .07 | .07 | .06 | .05 | .05 |
| .45 | .22 | .17 | .13 | .11 | .10 | .08 | .08 | .07 | .06 | .06 | .05 |
| .50 | .24 | .19 | .15 | .12 | .10 | .09 | .08 | .07 | .06 | .06 | .05 |
| .55 | .28 | .22 | .16 | .13 | .11 | .09 | .08 | .07 | .06 | .06 | .05 |
| .60 | .31 | .24 | .17 | .13 | .11 | .09 | .08 | .07 | .06 | .06 | .05 |
| .65 | .35 | .26 | .18 | .14 | .11 | .10 | .08 | .07 | .06 | .06 | .05 |
| .70 | .39 | .29 | .20 | .15 | .12 | .10 | .08 | .07 | .06 | .06 | .05 |
| .75 | .44 | .32 | .21 | .15 | .12 | .10 | .08 | .07 | .06 | .06 | .05 |
| .80 | .50 | .35 | .22 | .16 | .12 | .10 | .08 | .07 | .06 | .06 | .05 |
| .85 | .56 | .39 | .23 | .16 | .12 | .10 | .08 | .07 | .06 | .06 | .05 |
| .90 | .64 | .43 | .24 | .17 | .13 | .10 | .08 | .07 | .06 | .06 | .05 |
| .95 | .73 | .47 | .25 | .17 | .13 | .10 | .08 | .07 | .06 | .06 | .05 |
| 1.00 | 1.00 | .50 | .25 | .17 | .13 | .10 | .08 | .07 | .06 | .06 | .05 |

Proportion of employees considered satisfactory = .10

| | Selection Ratio | | | | | | | | | | |
|---|---|---|---|---|---|---|---|---|---|---|---|
| r | .05 | .10 | .20 | .30 | .40 | .50 | .60 | .70 | .80 | .90 | .95 |
| .00 | .10 | .10 | .10 | .10 | .10 | .10 | .10 | .10 | .10 | .10 | .10 |
| .05 | .12 | .12 | .11 | .11 | .11 | .11 | .11 | .10 | .10 | .10 | .10 |
| .10 | .14 | .13 | .13 | .12 | .12 | .11 | .11 | .11 | .11 | .10 | .10 |
| .15 | .16 | .15 | .14 | .13 | .13 | .12 | .12 | .11 | .11 | .10 | .10 |
| .20 | .19 | .17 | .15 | .14 | .14 | .13 | .12 | .12 | .11 | .11 | .10 |
| .25 | .22 | .19 | .17 | .16 | .14 | .13 | .13 | .12 | .11 | .11 | .10 |
| .30 | .25 | .22 | .19 | .17 | .15 | .14 | .13 | .12 | .12 | .11 | .10 |
| .35 | .28 | .24 | .20 | .18 | .16 | .15 | .14 | .13 | .12 | .11 | .10 |
| .40 | .31 | .27 | .22 | .19 | .17 | .16 | .14 | .13 | .12 | .11 | .10 |
| .45 | .35 | .29 | .24 | .20 | .18 | .16 | .15 | .13 | .12 | .11 | .10 |
| .50 | .39 | .32 | .26 | .22 | .19 | .17 | .15 | .13 | .12 | .11 | .11 |
| .55 | .43 | .36 | .28 | .23 | .20 | .17 | .15 | .14 | .12 | .11 | .11 |
| .60 | .48 | .39 | .30 | .25 | .21 | .18 | .16 | .14 | .12 | .11 | .11 |
| .65 | .53 | .43 | .32 | .26 | .22 | .18 | .16 | .14 | .12 | .11 | .11 |
| .70 | .58 | .47 | .35 | .27 | .22 | .19 | .16 | .14 | .12 | .11 | .11 |
| .75 | .64 | .51 | .37 | .29 | .23 | .19 | .16 | .14 | .12 | .11 | .11 |
| .80 | .71 | .56 | .40 | .30 | .24 | .20 | .17 | .14 | .12 | .11 | .11 |
| .85 | .78 | .62 | .43 | .31 | .25 | .20 | .17 | .14 | .12 | .11 | .11 |
| .90 | .86 | .69 | .46 | .33 | .25 | .20 | .17 | .14 | .12 | .11 | .11 |
| .95 | .95 | .78 | .49 | .33 | .25 | .20 | .17 | .14 | .12 | .11 | .11 |
| 1.00 | 1.00 | 1.00 | .50 | .33 | .25 | .20 | .17 | .14 | .13 | .11 | .11 |

Proportion of employees considered satisfactory = .20

| r | | | | | Selection Ratio | | | | | | |
|------|------|------|------|------|------|------|------|------|------|------|------|
| | .05 | .10 | .20 | .30 | .40 | .50 | .60 | .70 | .80 | .90 | .95 |
| .00 | .20 | .20 | .20 | .20 | .20 | .20 | .20 | .20 | .20 | .20 | .20 |
| .05 | .23 | .23 | .22 | .22 | .21 | .21 | .21 | .21 | .20 | .20 | .20 |
| .10 | .26 | .25 | .24 | .23 | .23 | .22 | .22 | .21 | .21 | .21 | .20 |
| .15 | .30 | .28 | .26 | .25 | .24 | .23 | .23 | .22 | .21 | .21 | .20 |
| .20 | .33 | .31 | .28 | .27 | .26 | .25 | .24 | .23 | .22 | .21 | .21 |
| .25 | .37 | .34 | .31 | .29 | .27 | .26 | .24 | .23 | .22 | .21 | .21 |
| .30 | .41 | .37 | .33 | .30 | .28 | .27 | .25 | .24 | .23 | .21 | .21 |
| .35 | .45 | .41 | .36 | .32 | .30 | .28 | .26 | .24 | .23 | .22 | .21 |
| .40 | .49 | .44 | .38 | .34 | .31 | .29 | .27 | .25 | .23 | .22 | .21 |
| .45 | .54 | .48 | .41 | .36 | .33 | .30 | .28 | .26 | .24 | .22 | .21 |
| .50 | .59 | .52 | .44 | .38 | .35 | .31 | .29 | .26 | .24 | .22 | .21 |
| .55 | .63 | .56 | .47 | .41 | .36 | .32 | .29 | .27 | .24 | .22 | .21 |
| .60 | .68 | .60 | .50 | .43 | .38 | .34 | .30 | .27 | .24 | .22 | .21 |
| .65 | .73 | .64 | .53 | .45 | .39 | .35 | .31 | .27 | .25 | .22 | .21 |
| .70 | .79 | .69 | .56 | .48 | .41 | .36 | .31 | .28 | .25 | .22 | .21 |
| .75 | .84 | .74 | .60 | .50 | .43 | .37 | .32 | .28 | .25 | .22 | .21 |
| .80 | .89 | .79 | .64 | .53 | .45 | .38 | .33 | .28 | .25 | .22 | .21 |
| .85 | .94 | .85 | .69 | .56 | .47 | .39 | .33 | .28 | .25 | .22 | .21 |
| .90 | 98 | .91 | 75 | .60 | .48 | .40 | .33 | .29 | .25 | .22 | .21 |
| .95 | 1.00 | .97 | .82 | .64 | .50 | .40 | .33 | .29 | .25 | .22 | .21 |
| 1.00 | 1.00 | 1.00 | 1.00 | .67 | .50 | .40 | .33 | .29 | .25 | .22 | .21 |

Proportion of employees considered satisfactory = .30

| r | | | | | Selection Ratio | | | | | | |
|------|------|------|------|------|------|------|------|------|------|------|------|
| | .05 | .10 | .20 | .30 | .40 | .50 | .60 | .70 | .80 | .90 | .95 |
| .00 | .30 | .30 | .30 | .30 | .30 | .30 | .30 | .30 | .30 | .30 | .30 |
| .05 | .34 | .33 | .33 | .32 | .32 | .31 | .31 | .31 | .31 | .30 | .30 |
| .10 | .38 | .36 | .35 | .34 | .33 | .33 | .32 | .32 | .31 | .31 | .30 |
| .15 | .42 | .40 | .38 | .36 | .35 | .34 | .33 | .33 | .32 | .31 | .31 |
| .20 | .46 | .43 | .40 | .38 | .37 | .36 | .34 | .33 | .32 | .31 | .31 |
| .25 | .50 | .47 | .43 | .41 | .39 | .37 | .36 | .34 | .33 | .32 | .31 |
| .30 | .54 | .50 | .46 | .43 | .40 | .38 | .37 | .35 | .33 | .32 | .31 |
| .35 | .58 | .54 | .49 | .45 | .42 | .40 | .38 | .36 | .34 | .32 | .31 |
| .40 | .63 | .58 | .51 | .47 | .44 | .41 | .39 | .37 | .34 | .32 | .31 |
| .45 | .67 | .61 | .55 | .50 | .46 | .43 | .40 | .37 | .35 | .32 | .31 |
| .50 | .72 | .65 | .58 | .52 | .48 | .44 | .41 | .38 | .35 | .33 | .31 |
| .55 | .76 | .69 | .61 | .55 | .50 | .46 | .42 | .39 | .36 | .33 | .31 |
| .60 | .81 | .74 | .64 | .58 | .52 | .47 | .43 | .40 | .36 | .33 | .31 |
| .65 | .85 | .78 | .68 | .60 | .54 | .49 | .44 | .40 | .37 | .33 | .32 |
| .70 | .89 | .82 | .72 | .63 | .57 | .51 | .46 | .41 | .37 | .33 | .32 |
| .75 | .93 | .86 | .76 | .67 | .59 | .52 | .47 | .42 | .37 | .33 | .32 |
| .80 | .96 | .90 | .80 | .70 | .62 | .54 | .48 | .42 | .37 | .33 | .32 |
| .85 | .99 | .94 | .85 | .74 | .65 | .56 | .49 | .43 | .37 | .33 | .32 |
| .90 | 1.00 | .98 | .90 | .79 | .68 | .58 | .49 | .43 | .37 | .33 | .32 |
| .95 | 1.00 | 1.00 | .96 | .85 | .72 | .60 | .50 | .43 | .37 | .33 | .32 |
| 1.00 | 1.00 | 1.00 | 1.00 | 1.00 | .75 | .60 | .50 | .43 | .38 | .33 | .32 |

Proportion of employees considered satisfactory = .40

| | Selection Ratio | | | | | | | | | | |
|------|------|------|------|------|------|------|------|------|------|------|------|
| r | .05 | .10 | .20 | .30 | .40 | .50 | .60 | .70 | .80 | .90 | .95 |
| .00 | .40 | .40 | .40 | .40 | .40 | .40 | .40 | .40 | .40 | .40 | .40 |
| .05 | .44 | .43 | .43 | .42 | .42 | .42 | .41 | .41 | .41 | .40 | .40 |
| .10 | .48 | .47 | .46 | .45 | .44 | .43 | .42 | .42 | .41 | .41 | .40 |
| .15 | .52 | .50 | .48 | .47 | .46 | .45 | .44 | .43 | .42 | .41 | .41 |
| .20 | .57 | .54 | .51 | .49 | .48 | .46 | .45 | .44 | .43 | .41 | .41 |
| .25 | .61 | .58 | .54 | .51 | .49 | .48 | .46 | .45 | .43 | .42 | .41 |
| .30 | .65 | .61 | .57 | .54 | .51 | .49 | .47 | .46 | .44 | .42 | .41 |
| .35 | .69 | .65 | .60 | .56 | .53 | .51 | .49 | .47 | .45 | .42 | .41 |
| .40 | .73 | .69 | .63 | .59 | .56 | .53 | .50 | .48 | .45 | .43 | .41 |
| .45 | .77 | .72 | .66 | .61 | .58 | .54 | .51 | .49 | .46 | .43 | .42 |
| .50 | .81 | .76 | .69 | .64 | .60 | .56 | .53 | .49 | .46 | .43 | .42 |
| .55 | .85 | .79 | .72 | .67 | .62 | .58 | .54 | .50 | .47 | .44 | .42 |
| .60 | .89 | .83 | .75 | .69 | .64 | .60 | .55 | .51 | .48 | .44 | .42 |
| .65 | .92 | .87 | .79 | .72 | .67 | .62 | .57 | .52 | .48 | .44 | .42 |
| .70 | .95 | .90 | .82 | .76 | .69 | .64 | .58 | .53 | .49 | .44 | .42 |
| .75 | .97 | .93 | .86 | .79 | .72 | .66 | .60 | .54 | .49 | .44 | .42 |
| .80 | .99 | .96 | .89 | .82 | .75 | .68 | .61 | .55 | .49 | .44 | .42 |
| .85 | 1.00 | .98 | .93 | .86 | .79 | .71 | .63 | .56 | .50 | .44 | .42 |
| .90 | 1.00 | 1.00 | .97 | .91 | .82 | .74 | .65 | .57 | .50 | .44 | .42 |
| .95 | 1.00 | 1.00 | .99 | .96 | .87 | .77 | .66 | .57 | .50 | .44 | .42 |
| 1.00 | 1.00 | 1.00 | 1.00 | 1.00 | 1.00 | .80 | .67 | .57 | .50 | .44 | .42 |

Proportion of employees considered satisfactory = .50

| | Selection Ratio | | | | | | | | | | |
|------|------|------|------|------|------|------|------|------|------|------|------|
| r | .05 | .10 | .20 | .30 | .40 | .50 | .60 | .70 | .80 | .90 | .95 |
| .00 | .50 | .50 | .50 | .50 | .50 | .50 | .50 | .50 | .50 | .50 | .50 |
| .05 | .54 | .54 | .53 | .52 | .52 | .52 | .51 | .51 | .51 | .50 | .50 |
| .10 | .58 | .57 | .56 | .55 | .54 | .53 | .53 | .52 | .51 | .51 | .50 |
| .15 | .63 | .61 | .58 | .57 | .56 | .55 | .54 | .53 | .52 | .51 | .51 |
| .20 | .67 | .64 | .61 | .59 | .58 | .56 | .55 | .54 | .53 | .52 | .51 |
| .25 | .70 | .67 | .64 | .62 | .60 | .58 | .56 | .55 | .54 | .52 | .51 |
| .30 | .74 | .71 | .67 | .64 | .62 | .60 | .58 | .56 | .54 | .52 | .51 |
| .35 | .78 | .74 | .70 | .66 | .64 | .61 | .59 | .57 | .55 | .53 | .51 |
| .40 | .82 | .78 | .73 | .69 | .66 | .63 | .61 | .58 | .56 | .53 | .52 |
| .45 | .85 | .81 | .75 | .71 | .68 | .65 | .62 | .59 | .56 | .53 | .52 |
| .50 | .88 | .84 | .78 | .74 | .70 | .67 | .63 | .60 | .57 | .54 | .52 |
| .55 | .91 | .87 | .81 | .76 | .72 | .69 | .65 | .61 | .58 | .54 | .52 |
| .60 | .94 | .90 | .84 | .79 | .75 | .70 | .66 | .62 | .59 | .54 | .52 |
| .65 | .96 | .92 | .87 | .82 | .77 | .73 | .68 | .64 | .59 | .55 | .52 |
| .70 | .98 | .95 | .90 | .85 | .80 | .75 | .70 | .65 | .60 | .55 | .53 |
| .75 | .99 | .97 | .92 | .87 | .82 | .77 | .72 | .66 | .61 | .55 | .53 |
| .80 | 1.00 | .99 | .95 | .90 | .85 | .80 | .73 | .67 | .61 | .55 | .53 |
| .85 | 1.00 | .99 | .97 | .94 | .88 | .82 | .76 | .69 | .62 | .55 | .53 |
| .90 | 1.00 | 1.00 | .99 | .97 | .92 | .86 | .78 | .70 | .62 | .56 | .53 |
| .95 | 1.00 | 1.00 | 1.00 | .99 | .96 | .90 | .81 | .71 | .63 | .56 | .53 |
| 1.00 | 1.00 | 1.00 | 1.00 | 1.00 | 1.00 | 1.00 | .83 | .71 | .63 | .56 | .53 |

Proportion of employees considered satisfactory = .60

| | | | | | Selection Ratio | | | | | | |
|---|---|---|---|---|---|---|---|---|---|---|---|
| r | .05 | .10 | .20 | .30 | .40 | .50 | .60 | .70 | .80 | .90 | .95 |
| .00 | .60 | .60 | .60 | .60 | .60 | .60 | .60 | .60 | .60 | .60 | .60 |
| .05 | .64 | .63 | .63 | .62 | .62 | .62 | .61 | .61 | .61 | .60 | .60 |
| .10 | .68 | .67 | .65 | .64 | .64 | .63 | .63 | .62 | .61 | .61 | .60 |
| .15 | .71 | .70 | .68 | .67 | .66 | .65 | .64 | .63 | .62 | .61 | .61 |
| .20 | .75 | .73 | .71 | .69 | .67 | .66 | .65 | .64 | .63 | .62 | .61 |
| .25 | .78 | .76 | .73 | .71 | .69 | .68 | .66 | .65 | .63 | .62 | .61 |
| .30 | .82 | .79 | .76 | .73 | .71 | .69 | .68 | .66 | .64 | .62 | .61 |
| .35 | .85 | .82 | .78 | .75 | .73 | .71 | .69 | .67 | .65 | .63 | .62 |
| .40 | .88 | .85 | .81 | .78 | .75 | .73 | .70 | .68 | .66 | .63 | .62 |
| .45 | .90 | .87 | .83 | .80 | .77 | .74 | .72 | .69 | .66 | .64 | .62 |
| .50 | .93 | .90 | .86 | .82 | .79 | .76 | .73 | .70 | .67 | .64 | .62 |
| .55 | .95 | .92 | .88 | .84 | .81 | .78 | .75 | .71 | .68 | .64 | .62 |
| .60 | .96 | .94 | .90 | .87 | .83 | .80 | .76 | .73 | .69 | .65 | .63 |
| .65 | .98 | .96 | .92 | .89 | .85 | .82 | .78 | .74 | .70 | .65 | .63 |
| .70 | .99 | .97 | .94 | .91 | .87 | .84 | .80 | .75 | .71 | .66 | .63 |
| .75 | .99 | .99 | .96 | .93 | .90 | .86 | .81 | .77 | .71 | .66 | .63 |
| .80 | 1.00 | .99 | .98 | .95 | .92 | .88 | .83 | .78 | .72 | .66 | .63 |
| .85 | 1.00 | 1.00 | .99 | .97 | .95 | .91 | .86 | .80 | .73 | .66 | .63 |
| .90 | 1.00 | 1.00 | 1.00 | .99 | .97 | .94 | .88 | .82 | .74 | .67 | .63 |
| .95 | 1.00 | 1.00 | 1.00 | 1.00 | .99 | .97 | .92 | .84 | .75 | .67 | .63 |
| 1.00 | 1.00 | 1.00 | 1.00 | 1.00 | 1.00 | 1.00 | 1.00 | .86 | .75 | .67 | .63 |

Proportion of employees considered satisfactory = .70

| | | | | | Selection Ratio | | | | | | |
|---|---|---|---|---|---|---|---|---|---|---|---|
| r | .05 | .10 | .20 | .30 | .40 | .50 | .60 | .70 | .80 | .90 | .95 |
| .00 | .70 | .70 | .70 | .70 | .70 | .70 | .70 | .70 | .70 | .70 | .70 |
| .05 | .73 | .73 | .72 | .72 | .72 | .71 | .71 | .71 | .71 | .70 | .70 |
| .10 | .77 | .76 | .75 | .74 | .73 | .73 | .72 | .72 | .71 | .71 | .70 |
| .15 | .80 | .79 | .77 | .76 | .75 | .74 | .73 | .73 | .72 | .71 | .71 |
| .20 | .83 | .81 | .79 | .78 | .77 | .76 | .75 | .74 | .73 | .71 | .71 |
| .25 | .86 | .84 | .81 | .80 | .78 | .77 | .76 | .75 | .73 | .72 | .71 |
| .30 | .88 | .86 | .84 | .82 | .80 | .78 | .77 | .75 | .74 | .72 | .71 |
| .35 | .91 | .89 | .86 | .83 | .82 | .80 | .78 | .76 | .75 | .73 | .71 |
| .40 | .93 | .91 | .88 | .85 | .83 | .81 | .79 | .77 | .75 | .73 | .72 |
| .45 | .94 | .93 | .90 | .87 | .85 | .83 | .81 | .78 | .76 | .73 | .72 |
| .50 | .96 | .94 | .91 | .89 | .87 | .84 | .82 | .80 | .77 | .74 | .72 |
| .55 | .97 | .96 | .93 | .91 | .88 | .86 | .83 | .81 | .78 | .74 | .72 |
| .60 | .98 | .97 | .95 | .92 | .90 | .87 | .85 | .82 | .79 | .75 | .73 |
| 65 | .99 | .98 | .96 | .94 | .92 | .89 | .86 | .83 | .80 | .75 | .73 |
| .70 | 1.00 | .99 | .97 | .96 | .93 | .91 | .88 | .84 | .80 | .76 | .73 |
| .75 | 1.00 | 1.00 | .98 | .97 | .95 | .92 | .89 | .86 | .81 | .76 | .73 |
| .80 | 1.00 | 1.00 | .99 | .98 | .97 | .94 | .91 | .87 | .82 | .77 | .73 |
| .85 | 1.00 | 1.00 | 1.00 | .99 | .98 | .96 | .93 | .89 | .84 | .77 | .74 |
| .90 | 1.00 | 1.00 | 1.00 | 1.00 | .99 | .98 | .95 | .91 | .85 | .78 | .74 |
| .95 | 1.00 | 1.00 | 1.00 | 1.00 | 1.00 | .99 | .98 | .94 | .86 | .78 | .74 |
| 1.00 | 1.00 | 1.00 | 1.00 | 1.00 | 1.00 | 1.00 | 1.00 | 1.00 | .88 | .78 | .74 |

Proportion of employees considered satisfactory = .80

| | Selection Ratio | | | | | | | | | | |
|---|---|---|---|---|---|---|---|---|---|---|---|
| r | .05 | .10 | .20 | .30 | .40 | .50 | .60 | .70 | .80 | .90 | .95 |
| .00 | .80 | .80 | .80 | .80 | .80 | .80 | .80 | .80 | .80 | .80 | .80 |
| .05 | .83 | .82 | .82 | .82 | .81 | .81 | .81 | .81 | .81 | .80 | .80 |
| .10 | .85 | .85 | .84 | .83 | .83 | .82 | .82 | .81 | .81 | .81 | .80 |
| .15 | .88 | .87 | .86 | .85 | .84 | .83 | .83 | .82 | .82 | .81 | .81 |
| .20 | .90 | .89 | .87 | .86 | .85 | .84 | .84 | .83 | .82 | .81 | .81 |
| .25 | .92 | .91 | .89 | .88 | .87 | .86 | .85 | .84 | .83 | .82 | .81 |
| .30 | .94 | .92 | .90 | .89 | .88 | .87 | .86 | .84 | .83 | .82 | .81 |
| .35 | .95 | .94 | .92 | .90 | .89 | .89 | .87 | .85 | .84 | .82 | .81 |
| .40 | .96 | .95 | .93 | .92 | .90 | .89 | .88 | .86 | .85 | .83 | .82 |
| .45 | .97 | .96 | .95 | .93 | .92 | .90 | .89 | .87 | .85 | .83 | .82 |
| .50 | .98 | .97 | .96 | .94 | .93 | .91 | .90 | .88 | .86 | .84 | .82 |
| .55 | .99 | .98 | .97 | .95 | .94 | .92 | .91 | .89 | .87 | .84 | .82 |
| .60 | .99 | .99 | .98 | .96 | .95 | .94 | .92 | .90 | .87 | .84 | .83 |
| 65 | 1.00 | .99 | .98 | .97 | .96 | .95 | .93 | .91 | .88 | .85 | .83 |
| .70 | 1.00 | 1.00 | .99 | .98 | .97 | .96 | .94 | .92 | .89 | .85 | .83 |
| .75 | 1.00 | 1.00 | 1.00 | .99 | .98 | .97 | .95 | .93 | .90 | .86 | .83 |
| .80 | 1.00 | 1.00 | 1.00 | 1.00 | .99 | .98 | .96 | .94 | .91 | .87 | .84 |
| .85 | 1.00 | 1.00 | 1.00 | 1.00 | 1.00 | .99 | .98 | .96 | .92 | .87 | .84 |
| .90 | 1.00 | 1.00 | 1.00 | 1.00 | 1.00 | 1.00 | .99 | .97 | .94 | .88 | .84 |
| .95 | 1.00 | 1.00 | 1.00 | 1.00 | 1.00 | 1.00 | 1.00 | .99 | .96 | .89 | .84 |
| 1.00 | 1.00 | 1.00 | 1.00 | 1.00 | 1.00 | 1.00 | 1.00 | 1.00 | 1.00 | .89 | .84 |

Proportion of employees considered satisfactory = .90

| | Selection Ratio | | | | | | | | | | |
|---|---|---|---|---|---|---|---|---|---|---|---|
| r | .05 | .10 | .20 | .30 | .40 | .50 | .60 | .70 | .80 | .90 | .95 |
| .00 | .90 | .90 | .90 | .90 | .90 | .90 | .90 | .90 | .90 | .90 | .90 |
| .05 | .92 | .91 | .91 | .91 | .91 | .91 | .91 | .90 | .90 | .90 | .90 |
| .10 | .93 | .93 | .92 | .92 | .92 | .91 | .91 | .91 | .91 | .90 | .90 |
| .15 | .95 | .94 | .93 | .93 | .92 | .92 | .92 | .91 | .91 | .91 | .90 |
| .20 | .96 | .95 | .94 | .94 | .93 | .93 | .92 | .92 | .91 | .91 | .90 |
| .25 | .97 | .96 | .95 | .95 | .94 | .93 | .93 | .92 | .92 | .91 | .91 |
| .30 | .98 | .97 | .96 | .95 | .95 | .94 | .94 | .93 | .92 | .91 | .91 |
| .35 | .98 | .98 | .97 | .96 | .95 | .95 | .94 | .93 | .93 | .92 | .91 |
| .40 | .99 | .98 | .98 | .97 | .96 | .95 | .95 | .94 | .93 | .92 | .91 |
| .45 | .99 | .99 | .98 | .98 | .97 | .96 | .95 | .94 | .93 | .92 | .91 |
| .50 | 1.00 | .99 | .99 | .98 | .97 | .97 | .96 | .95 | .94 | .92 | .92 |
| .55 | 1.00 | 1.00 | .99 | .99 | .98 | .97 | .97 | .96 | .94 | .93 | .92 |
| .60 | 1.00 | 1.00 | .99 | .99 | .99 | .98 | .97 | .96 | .95 | .93 | .92 |
| .65 | 1.00 | 1.00 | 1.00 | .99 | .99 | .98 | .98 | .97 | .96 | .94 | .92 |
| .70 | 1.00 | 1.00 | 1.00 | 1.00 | .99 | .99 | .98 | .97 | .96 | .94 | .93 |
| .75 | 1.00 | 1.00 | 1.00 | 1.00 | 1.00 | .99 | .99 | .98 | .97 | .95 | .93 |
| .80 | 1.00 | 1.00 | 1.00 | 1.00 | 1.00 | 1.00 | .99 | .99 | .97 | .95 | .93 |
| .85 | 1.00 | 1.00 | 1.00 | 1.00 | 1.00 | 1.00 | 1.00 | .99 | .98 | .96 | .94 |
| .90 | 1.00 | 1.00 | 1.00 | 1.00 | 1.00 | 1.00 | 1.00 | 1.00 | .99 | .97 | .94 |
| .95 | 1.00 | 1.00 | 1.00 | 1.00 | 1.00 | 1.00 | 1.00 | 1.00 | 1.00 | .98 | .94 |
| 1.00 | 1.00 | 1.00 | 1.00 | 1.00 | 1.00 | 1.00 | 1.00 | 1.00 | 1.00 | 1.00 | .95 |

# *Glossary*

*Achievement Test*   A test containing items, questions, and/or tasks that attempt to determine what an individual knows or can do. An achievement test is designed to elicit an individual's best performance in subject matter.

*Adverse Impact*   A determination stipulated in federal guidelines on employee selection. Occurs when the proportion of people selected differs for groups under consideration (for example, race or sex).

*Aptitude Test*   A test that is used to determine how well a person will do in some future situation.

*Arithmetic Mean*   See *Mean, Arithmetic*.

*Attenuation*   See *Correction for Attenuation*.

*Average*   A measure of central tendency. See *Mean, Arithmetic*.

*Base Rate*   Percentage of those scoring "high," "successful," or the like on the criterion.

*Biserial Coefficient*   A coefficient of correlation that describes the relationship between a dichotomized variable with an underlying continuum (for example, pass–fail a test) and a continuous variable (for example, grade-point average). The biserial coefficient is interpreted like all other coefficients of correlation. See Equation 5-30.

*Bivariate Distribution*   The joint frequency distribution of scores on two variables. Scatter diagrams are pictorial representations of bivariate distributions. See Figure 5-2.

*Central Tendency*   A measure of the "average" score of a distribution. Measures of central tendency include the *mean*, the *median*, the *mode*, and the *midpoint*.

*Classical Theory*    A theory of reliability alternatively labeled the theory of true and error scores. See *True and Error Score Theory*.

*Classification*    A qualitative description of a variable involving the use of categories representing types or kinds, and not frequency, amount, or degree.

*Coefficient of Multiple Correlation*    The coefficient of correlation between the optimally weighted composite of predictors and a criterion measure. See Equations 11-19, 11-20, 11-22, and 11-23.

*Coefficient of Partial Correlation*    A correlation coefficient that describes the relationship between two variables while variation in one or more other variables is held constant. See Equations 11-7 and 11-8.

*Composite*    A score made up of the sum or average of the scores on a series of component variables.

*Concurrent Validity*    The accuracy with which we can estimate the extent to which an individual currently behaves in some way or possesses some trait from the extent to which the individual currently behaves in some other way or possesses some other trait.

*Configural Scoring*    A procedure concerned with the relationship between a *response pattern* to individual items or test components and a criterion variable. Configural scoring is conceptually similar to actuarial pattern analysis, with the exception that pattern analysis is used when items are categorical or discrete.

*Constant*    A property in which individuals manifest the same amount or kind. For example, for a sample of females, the variable sex is a constant.

*Constant Error*    A systematic source of variation such that all individuals are affected in the same way by the same amount.

*Constant-Ratio Model*    A test-fairness model stipulating that fairness occurs when the percentage of people that succeed on the criterion is the same as the percentage that pass the cutting score on the predictor.

*Construct*    An intangible or nonconcrete characteristic or quality in which individuals differ.

*Construct Validity*    The degree to which a set of measurement operations measures hypothesized constructs.

*Content Validity*    The degree to which a set of measurement operations measures the characteristics we wish to measure, as *judged* from the appropriateness of the *content* of those operations.

*Continuous Scale*    A quantitative scale containing no categories, but rather a continuum that represents gradually increasing amounts of the characteristic being investigated.

*Convergent Validity*    One aspect of construct validity (the other aspect is *divergent validity*) as assessed by a multitrait multimethod matrix analysis. Concerned with the correlation between measures of the same construct or trait.

*Correction for Guessing*    A weighting formula that provides a better estimate of an individual's true score by subtracting that part of the observed score believed to be a function of guessing. See Equation 13-2.

*Correction for Attenuation*    A hypothetical coefficient that yields an estimate of the magnitude of correlation between two variables if both variables had perfect reliability. The correction for attenuation corrects for the degree to which the correlation is reduced by the unreliability of measurement contained in one or both of the variables. See Equation 9-6.

*Correlation Coefficient*  An index of the degree of association between two variables or the extent to which the order of individuals on one variable is similar to the order of individuals on a second variable. This quantitative description of the relationship between two variables indicates the accuracy with which scores on one variable can be predicted from scores on another as well as the extent to which individual differences on two variables can be attributed to the same determining factor. See Equations 5-21 and 5-23.

*Correlation, Index of*  A measure that takes into account the proportion of variance in one variable that is accounted for by variance in the second variable.

*Correlation Ratio*  A general index or coefficient of association (commonly referred to as eta) that reflects the relationship (linear and nonlinear) between two variables in terms of the variation in one variable accounted for by variation in a second variable. See Equations 5-7 and 5-8.

*Covariance*  The product of the standard deviations and the coefficients of correlation between two variables; that is, $\sigma_i \sigma_{i'} r_{ii'}$.

*Criterion-Related Validity*  The extent to which scores on a test correspond to, are related to, or predict scores on another variable, the criterion.

*Cronbach's Coefficient Alpha*  An estimate of test reliability based on item intercorrelations. See page 256.

*Cross-Validation*  A procedure that determines the amount of capitalization on chance that has affected either a homogeneous composite or an empirical key. Cross-validation determines to what degree the results are specific to the development sample.

*Deviation Score*  The difference between the raw score of an individual and the mean of the sample. See Equation 3-2.

*Dichotomous Variable*  A variable that is divided into two, and only two, distinct categories.

*Differential Weighting*  A procedure by which predictor variables are multiplied by assigned values. Variables that are assigned higher weights contribute more to the composite than those that are assigned lower weights. Weights can be derived theoretically, experientially, intuitively, or statistically, as in multiple regression.

*Direct Estimate*  A scaling procedure in which the type of response (for example, a ranking) leads to the same type of scaled values for the stimuli (for example, an ordinal scale).

*Discontinuous Scale*  A quantitative scale on which the categories are discrete and separate but ordered. With a discontinuous scale, individuals clearly fall into one of the distinct categories.

*Discriminant Function Analysis*  A technique directed at forming a composite (of variables) that has maximum potential for distinguishing between groups. Discriminant analysis is algebraically similar to multiple regression: in the former, group membership is the criterion; whereas in the latter, success within a group is the criterion. Prediction from discriminant-function analysis is in terms of likelihood of group membership and is based on the between-group variance explained by the composite of variables.

*Discrimination Index*  A quantitative description of the degree of difference between the number of correct responses for high-scoring and low-scoring criterion groups. The discrimination index tells us how well we can distinguish among the sample of test takers; it is another form of item validity.

*Divergent Validity*   One aspect of construct validity (the other aspect is *convergent validity*) as assessed by a multitrait multimethod matrix analysis. Reflected by higher correlation between two methods of measuring the same trait than between the correlations of two traits measured with the same method. That is, correlation should be a function of similarity in substantive content, not similarity in measurement method.

*Domain Sampling Theory*   A theory that challenges the theory of true and error scores by positing that the latter is more appropriate for the physical sciences while its assumptions are more consistent with the kinds of variables and measures used in psychology. Domain sampling conceives of a trait as being a group of behaviors all of which have some property in common; this property is an intellectual or hypothetical construct.

*Effective Weight*   The actual weight of a component, based on component variance, in a composite.

*Empirical Keying*   A technique whereby items are selected for inclusion on a test based on their validities in predicting an external criterion. Items incorporated into an empirical key have high correlations with the external criterion and low intercorrelations.

*Equal-Appearing Intervals*   A measurement technique, used extensively in attitude research, that is designed to create an interval scale on which the distance between every pair of successive scale points or items is the same.

*Equal-Risk Model*   A test-fairness model stipulating that fairness occurs when the probability of failure (or success) *for those people selected* is the same for the groups of interest (for example, males and females). To achieve this goal, the strategy is to set the test's cutting score for the two groups such as to equate the risk.

*Equivalent-Forms Coefficient*   A coefficient of reliability that reflects the consistency of measurement between two forms of a test believed to measure the same trait. The coefficient relies on the degree to which the two forms are really equivalent or parallel. The equivalent-forms coefficient of reliability is calculated by correlating the sample of individuals' scores on both forms of the test.

*Error Score*   The component of fallible or observed score that represents the unreliability of assessment. The error score is the difference between the fallible score and the true score.

*Eta Coefficient* ($\eta$)   See *Correlation Ratio.*

*Expectancy Charts* or *Tables*   A means by which validity coefficients are converted to information reflecting frequencies of a test's correct predictions.

*Fallible Score*   The observed score of an individual on a given test. The fallible score is a function of the actual amount of the trait possessed by the individual plus the error in the assessment of that trait.

*Forecasting Efficiency, Index of*   The proportional decrease in the standard deviation of predicted scores when the predictor is compared to *no* information. See Equation 10-1.

*Frequency Distribution*   A listing of obtained scores for a group of people and the number of people obtaining each score.

*Generalizability Theory*   See *Reliability of Measurement.*

*Guttman Scalogram Analysis*   A technique designed to develop scales for subjects and stimuli simultaneously. In scalogram analysis, items are ordered in terms of increasing extremeness with regard to the attitude. Knowing a subject's score allows us to reproduce his or her pattern of responses.

*Heteroscedasticity* A state of affairs, in a bivariate distribution, in which there are unequal column (or row) variances.

*Homogeneous Composite* A compilation of items, subtests, or scores with high intercorrelations. A homogeneous composite is formed by removing from the composite all components with low correlation with other components.

*Homogeneous Scaling* A technique by which the investigator chooses items that have high intercorrelations. The result of homogeneous scaling is the selection of items based on internal consistency.

*Homoscedasticity* A state of affairs, in a bivariate distribution, in which the standard deviations of the scores in all the columns are equal to one another, and the standard deviations of the scores in all the rows are also equal to one another.

*Index* See specific types.

*Indirect Estimate* A scaling procedure in which the type of response (for example, ordinal) is transformed, according to specified models, such that the stimuli are of a different scale type (for example, interval).

*Intercept* The point at which the regression line crosses the axis. The $Y$ intercept is the value of $Y$ on the scatter diagram at which $X = 0$. Similarly, the $X$ intercept is the value of $X$ when $Y = 0$. See Equations 6-7 and 6-8.

*Internal Consistency* Estimates of the reliability of measurement based on the interrelationship of test items or components. Internal-consistency measures indicate the degree of homogeneity of test items.

*Interval Scale* A continuous scale on which the distance between numbers is equal or otherwise known. With interval scales, meaning is given to the distance between points, and arithmetic operations are possible.

*Item Analysis* Statistical procedures used in test development to determine item homogeneity, item intercorrelation, item difficulty, and other item properties.

*Item-Characteristic Curve* A curve showing the probability of a correct response as a function of the trait being measured.

*Item Difficulty* A statistic that describes the proportion of persons in a sample who pass or correctly answer a test item. The larger the proportion, the easier the item.

*Item Homogeneity* The degree to which items are intercorrelated and thus measure the same trait.

*Item Validity* The relationship between a specific test item and an outside variable or criterion. In general, the greater the validity of the individual items, the greater the validity of the total test.

*Kuder–Richardson Formulas* Formulas that provide an index of the internal-consistency reliability of a measure. The index is a function of the number of components and their interrelationship. See Equations 9-10 and 9-11.

*Kurtosis* The property of a distribution of scores that reflects the degree to which individuals' scores pile up in one region of the scale. Distributions which contain a disproportionate number of scores in one narrow region have a positive index of kurtosis (leptokurtic). Distributions that have relatively even frequencies of scores across regions have a negative index of kurtosis (platykurtic). See Equation 3-10.

*Latent Structure Analysis (LSA)*    A procedure concerned with the relation of item responses to latent traits.

*Law of Categorical Judgment*    A law or model that applies to situations where the task is to place a stimulus into one of several categories that differ quantitatively along a defined continuum. The purpose of the application of the law of categorical judgment, its equations, and its assumptions is to obtain category values and item values on an interval scale that reflects real differences among the stimulus items. See Equation 12-8.

*Law of Comparative Judgment*    A scaling law or model for which the task of the respondent is to directly compare each stimulus in a set to the others. The data obtained (proportions) are transformed to an interval scale by application of the law's equation. See Equations 12-3, 12-4, 12-5, and 12-6.

*Least-Squares Solution*    The basis for determining the regression line. The best-fitting line is taken as that line from which the mean of the squared deviations is at a minimum. See the Technical Section on pages 149–152.

*Leptokurtic*    Referring to a distribution that has a heavy piling of scores in one region of the scale. A leptokurtic distribution is excessively peaked and has a positive index of kurtosis. See Equation 3-10.

*Likert Scales*    A method designed to scale subjects. For each of a number of items, the subject responds to one of several categories, the values of which are typically 1 through 5. A subject's score is summed over all items.

*Marginal Distributions*    The separate frequency distributions of the $X$ and $Y$ variables that are plotted in scatter diagrams.

*Mean, Arithmetic*    The average level of scores in a distribution. The mean ($\bar{X}$) is equal to the sum of all scores in the distribution divided by the number of scores in the distribution. See Equation 3-1.

*Measurement*    A quantitative description of individuals or objects on variables involving the use of numbers or values that can be manipulated to give further information about the variables. Measurement deals with the assignment of numbers according to specified rules.

*Measures of Central Tendency*    See *Central Tendency*.

*Median*    The score above and below which 50 percent of the scores in a distribution fall.

*Mode*    The most frequently occurring score of a distribution.

*Moderated Regression*    A regression equation that includes a cross-product term between a predictor and a moderator variable. Moderated regression is nonlinear regression examined for the purpose of achieving greater explanatory power of the criterion than is accomplished by linear regression. Typically the moderator variable is linearly uncorrelated with the predictor and the criterion. See Equation 11-28.

*Moderator Variable*    A variable that has been found to be linearly uncorrelated with both the predictor variable and the criterion variable, yet increases the multiple correlation beyond that obtained for only the predictor and criterion. Moderator variables increase prediction because of the nonlinear, interactive effects of the predictor and the moderator.

*Modern Test Theory*   The theory concerned with the relationship between an individual's responses to items and the underlying psychological trait.

*Multidimensional Scaling*   Scaling techniques that attempt to assess the number of dimensions underlying an attribute or issue. With multidimensional scaling the first test is to determine the number of dimensions and then to obtain scale values for the stimuli on selected dimensions represented.

*Multiple Correlation*   A coefficient of correlation between scores on one variable (criterion) and the optimally weighted composite of scores on several other variables (predictors). See Equations 11-19, 11-20, 11-22, and 11-23.

*Multiple Cutoffs*   A procedure for prediction that requires individuals to possess *at least* a minimum score on *all* predictor variables.

*Multiple Regression*   An extension of simple regression to include more than one predictor variable. Multiple-regression equations indicate the least-squares solution to the weighting of the variables for the purpose of optimally explaining or predicting the criterion variable. See Equations 11-5, 11-14, and 11-15.

*Multistep Scale*   See *Continuous Scale.*

*Multitrait, Multimethod Matrix (MTMM)*   A matrix for organizing correlational data such that construct validity can be assessed. Requires that at least two constructs be measured by at least two methods. Construct validity is based on the degree of convergent validity and divergent validity. See Table 10-1.

*Nominal Scale*   A scale that uses numbers to identify classes or individuals for purposes of distinguishing one from another. Since the numbers only represent classes or types, any mathematical manipulation is inappropriate.

*Nominal Weight*   The weight that is assigned (by theory, experience, intuition, and so on) to each component variable of a composite.

*Nonlinear Regression*   A situation when the variables being correlated do not have a straight, linear regression. Nonlinear regression exists, for example, when low and moderate scores on one variable are associated with low and high scores on a second variable, however high scores on the first variable are associated with low scores on the second.

*Norm*   The distribution of scores on a variable earned by a large sample of individuals who are similar in certain specified a priori dimensions. A norm established on a sample in the developmental stage is used to assess the performance of an individual from a new sample relative to individuals in the former sample who are assumed to be similar on stated dimensions.

*Normal Frequency Distribution*   A theoretical distribution of scores that is symmetrical and bell-shaped. A normal frequency distribution has a skewness of zero and a kurtosis of zero. Additionally in a normal distribution the mean is equal to the median and the mode. See Figure 3-5.

*Normalized Scores*   A procedure for transforming a sample of observed scores that do not approximate the normal distribution to values that are normally distributed.

*Observed Score*   See *Fallible Score.*

*Odd–Even Split*   One method for estimating the reliability of a test from a single administration. Reliability is determined by correlating scores on the odd-numbered items with scores on the even-numbered items and then correcting the coefficient by the Spearman–Brown formula (Equation 9-1) to yield a coefficient for a total test. See also *Split-Half.*

*Ordinal Scale*    A scale that orders individuals or groups in terms of frequency, amount, or degree to which they manifest the variable being investigated. With ordinal scales, we know only relative positions and nothing about the real differences between positions.

*Paired Comparisons*    A method by which stimuli are scaled according to subjects' responses that require comparison of each stimulus to every other stimulus. Determination of the individual's preference for one object over another across all possible pairs of stimulus objects provides data for either ordinal (direct estimate) or interval (indirect estimate) scales.

*Parallel Forms*    A series of two or more tests that have the same type of content, but not the same specific items or components. Parallel forms are tests intended to be similar in content and nature and designed to measure the same traits, but not subject to the rigorous statistical criteria for parallel tests.

*Parallel Tests*    Two or more tests that are designed to assess the same trait; sets of operations all of which follow from a particular definition of a trait. Additionally, tests are said to be parallel if they (1) have equal means, (2) have equal standard deviations, (3) have equal correlations with one another, and (4) correlate to an equivalent degree with the scores on any other variable.

*Part Correlation*    See *Semipartial Correlation*.

*Partial Standard Deviation*    A quantitative description of the extent of variation in one variable with the effects of a second variable held constant. The partial standard deviation is equal to the square root of the partial variance. See Equations 6-19, 11-3, and 11-10.

*Partial Variance*    A quantitative description of the extent of variation in one variable with the effects of a second variable held constant or eliminated. See Equation 5-1.

*Pattern Analysis*    A procedure concerned with the relationship between a response pattern to individual items or test components and a criterion variable. Essentially concerned with continuous prediction variables. See *Configural Scoring*.

*Pearsonian Correlation Coefficient*    A correlation coefficient, $r$, between two continuous variables that indicates the degree of association between the two variables or the degree to which the order of scores on one variable is similar to the order of scores on a second variable. The coefficient indicates both strength of association and direction. It is the most widely used correlation coefficient. See Equations 5-21, 5-22, 5-23, and 5-27.

*Percentile Rank*    A statement of the proportion of individuals that a particular individual exceeds in the characteristic or quality under investigation. The percentile rank of a score is the percentage of persons in the reference group who earn lower scores.

*Perseveration*    The tendency of individuals to give the same response to a question or to use the same strategy in answering a question on a second trial merely because it was the way they answered on the first trial.

*Personality Test*    A test designed to elicit an individual's typical response for affective or nonintellectual aspects of behavior.

*Phi Coefficient*    A coefficient of correlation used to describe the relationship between two discontinuous dichotomous variables (for example, sex and left- or right-handedness). The phi coefficient is interpreted like all other coefficients of correlation. See Equation 5-29.

*Platykurtic*   Referring to a distribution of scores that tends to have equal frequencies in each region of the scale. A platykurtic distribution of scores is one that is more or less flat and has a negative index of kurtosis. See Equation 3-10.

*Point Biserial Coefficient*   A coefficient of correlation used to describe the relationship between a discontinuous dichotomous variable (for example, sex) and a continuous variable (for example, grade-point average). The point biserial coefficient is interpreted like any other coefficient of correlation. See Equation 5-28.

*Point of Least Squares*   The mean of a distribution is referred to as the point of least squares since the sum of squares of the differences between the raw scores and the mean is smaller than the sum of the squares of the differences between the raw scores and any other point on the scale.

*Postdictive Validity*   The accuracy with which we can estimate the extent to which an individual possessed a given trait in the past.

*Predictive Validity*   The accuracy with which we can estimate the extent to which an individual will manifest a given trait in the future from the extent to which the individual currently manifests or possesses some other property.

*Predictor of Predictability*   A variable that identifies the degree to which persons in a sample deviate from a regression line representing a predictor–criterion relationship and thus identifies those for whom the predictor is relatively appropriate.

*Proportion of Accountable Variation*   An index or coefficient indicative of the degree of relationship between two variables. See Equations 5-5 and 5-6.

*Psychometrics*   The area of psychological measurement concerned with the assessment of individual differences.

*Psychophysics*   The area of psychological measurement concerned with the assessment of differences among stimulus objects.

*Qualitative Variable*   A variable on which individuals differ with regard to kind or type.

*Quantitative Variable*   A variable on which individuals differ with regard to frequency, degree, or amount.

*Quota Model*   A solution to test bias (where the difference between predictor means for groups of interest, such as males and females, is considered as bias) such that people are selected in equal proportions.

*Ranked Variable*   A quantitative variable providing a series of discrete and separate categories into which individuals or objects are successively ordered.

*Rank Order*   A measurement procedure that requires the respondent to indicate or order his or her preference for stimuli or subjects.

*Ratio Scale*   A continuous scale that has all the properties of an interval scale (equal distances between points, arithmetically manipulable) and also has a natural and meaningful zero point. With ratio scales the raw scores directly indicate the degree to which the variable is present.

*Raw Score*   The qualitative or quantitative description of observed individual differences on the variable being investigated.

*Regression Coefficient*   When the equation for a line is used to describe the linear relationship in a scatter diagram, the slope of that line, $b$, is termed the regression coefficient. The regression coefficient is a function of the degree of relationship between the two variables and the variance of each variable. See Equations 5-13 and 5-14.

*Regression Equation*   The equation used to describe the regression line of a bivariate distribution. The general form for the regression line of $X$ on $Y$ is $\bar{Y}_i = a_Y + b_{YX}X_i$, which is read: Predicted $Y$ is equal to the $Y$ intercept plus the product of a regression coefficient for $X$ and the observed $X$ score. Each bivariate distribution has two regression equations, one for the regression of $X$ on $Y$ and one for the regression of $Y$ on $X$. See Equations 5-9, 5-10, 6-1, 6-2, 6-5, 6-6, 6-9, 6-10, 6-11, 6-12, 6-13, and 6-14.

*Regression Line*   A line drawn through a scatter diagram to represent the trend of association between two variables. A regression line can be described by an equation consisting of two properties: the $X$ or $Y$ intercept and the slope of the line relative to either the $X$ or the $Y$ axis.

*Regression Model*   A test-bias model stipulating that *no* bias exists if the bivariate distributions for the groups of interest (for example, males and females) fall on a *common* regression line. The analysis focuses on whether the criterion performance of people in either group is systematically over- or underpredicted from a common regression line.

*Reliability, Index of*   The coefficient of correlation between fallible and true scores. The index of reliability indicates how good fallible scores are as a measure of true scores. See Equation 8-20.

*Reliability Coefficient*   The correlation between scores on parallel tests; an index of the extent to which scores on any one parallel test can predict scores on any other.

*Reliability of Measurement*   The degree of self-consistency among the scores earned by an individual. The extent of unsystematic variation in the quantitative description of an individual when that individual is measured a number of times.

*Reproducibility, Index of*   A statistical technique designed to assess the degree to which a scale possesses the properties of Guttman scalogram analysis. See Equation 12-9.

*Restriction of Range*   A condition that exists when the variability of the sample being tested is low. Restriction of range has the effect of limiting the magnitude of the correlation coefficient. Restriction of range is commonly incurred when test data are accumulated on a highly homogeneous sample.

*Robustness*   A property of a statistical test that refers to the test's ability to yield equivalent results regardless of whether or not the assumption of normality is violated.

*Scalar Variable*   A quantitative variable that provides a description of the frequency, degree, or amount of the characteristic being investigated.

*Scaling*   The process by which we record and measure variables according to rules. The goal of scaling is to study the relationship between overt responses and objectively definable stimuli, as well as to present a psychological model.

*Scatter Diagram*   A chart that represents the scores of a group of individuals on two variables simultaneously. Each point represents an individual's score on variable $X$ and on variable $Y$. Scatter diagrams are useful in examining the type of relationship (linear or nonlinear) that exists between the two variables.

*Selection Ratio*    Percentage of those scoring at or above the cutoff score on the predictor.

*Semipartial* or *Part Correlation*    The correlation between two variables with the effect of a third variable eliminated from only one variable. See Equation 11-24.

*Skewness*    The property of a distribution of scores that reflects the degree to which individuals disproportionately fall either at the low end (positively skewed) or at the high end (negatively skewed) of the scale. See Equation 3-9.

*Slope*    The slope of the regression line represents the unit change in one variable associated with the unit change in the second variable. It is an index of the trend of association between two variables. See *Regression Coefficient*.

*Spearman–Brown Prophecy Formula*    An indication of what the reliability of a test would be if the number of items or components of the test were increased or decreased. The formula is a function of the amount of increase or decrease in items and the original reliability of the measure. See Equation 9-1.

*Split-Half*    A method for estimating the reliability of a test from a single administration. The split-half reliability coefficient is obtained by dividing the test into two equivalent parts and correlating the two scores across the sample. Since the measure represents the reliability of the test based on only half of the items, the Spearman–Brown formula (Equation 9-1) is then applied to assess the reliability of the total test.

*Stability Coefficient*    A coefficient of reliability that reflects the consistency of measurement over time. The stability coefficient is assessed by a test–retest method. Subjects are measured on the same test at two different points in time, and these measures are then correlated.

*Standard Deviation*    A measure of the degree to which scores are distributed about the mean. The standard deviation is an index that specifies the amount of spread in the distribution of scores. See Equation 3-5.

*Standard Error of Estimate* or *Prediction*    A statistic used to describe the extent of error in predicting scores on one variable from scores on another. The standard error of estimate is a description of the extent to which individuals tend to cluster along the regression line. See Equations 6-19, 6-20, 6-21, 6-22, and 11-25.

*Standard Error of Measurement*    An index of the extent to which an individual's scores vary over a number of parallel tests. See Equation 8-19.

*Standard Error of Prediction*    See *Standard Error of Estimate*.

*Standardized Score* (*T Score*)    A form of standard score where the mean and the standard deviation are set at computationally convenient values. Essentially what is being done is multiplying the standard score times the desired standard deviation and adding the desired value of the mean as a constant to each score. See Equation 4-4.

*Standard Score* (*z Score*)    A mathematical transformation of raw scores taking into account the mean and the standard deviation of the total distribution for the purpose of referencing an individual's score to the total distribution of scores. The distribution of standard scores has a mean of 0 and a standard deviation of 1. See Equation 4-1.

*Subgroup Analysis*  A procedure that separates a sample, on the basis of a moderator, into two subgroups. The linear-regression equation and correlation coefficient between one or more predictors and the criterion is then computed for each group. In effect the "moderator" variable is influencing the relationship between the predictor(s) and the criterion.

*Successive Intervals*  A method of scaling stimuli in which the individual is required to sort a series of stimuli into categories that have been ordered. The method of successive intervals requires individuals to repeat this sorting procedure several times, thus yielding the proportion of times a given stimulus is placed in a specific category. This method results in an interval scale for the stimuli responded to.

*Suppressor Variable*  A variable in a multiple-regression equation that has no relationship with the criterion and still increases the multiple correlation. The suppressor variable partials out or suppresses that part of the variability in the other predictor variable that is unrelated to the criterion.

*Systematic Variation*  The fluctuation of scores, from time 1 to time 2, that is characterized by an orderly progression or pattern in some recognizable trend.

*Tailored Testing*  Involves the notion of adapting or individualizing test items to a given individual based on responses that individual has made to prior test items. Also referred to as *sequential testing, adaptive testing, branched testing,* and *response-contingent testing.*

*Temporal Prediction*  An attempt to predict future behavior from performance on a present or past task.

*Test*  Any device that is used to provide descriptions of persons and their attributes either for prediction or for assessment purposes. A test is the observation and recording of behavior under specified situations or conditions.

*Tetrachoric Coefficient*  A coefficient of correlation used to describe the relationship between two dichotomized variables each with underlying continuums (for example, pass–fail in a test and graduate–not graduate from school). The tetrachoric coefficient is interpreted in the same way as all other coefficients of correlation. See Table 5-1.

*Trait Name*  A concise label that represents the definition of a variable without specifying all details and facets of that variable.

*Transformed Score*  An arithmetic manipulation of the raw score that makes the numerical values more convenient or that provides more meaningful quantitative descriptions of the individuals. A $z$ score is an example of a transformed score.

*Trend of a Line*  See *Regression Line.*

*True- and Error-Score Theory*  A theory that states that the performance of an individual on a given administration of a test, observed or fallible score, is a function of the amount of the trait actually possessed by the individual (true score) plus the inaccuracy associated with the measurement (error score).

*True Score*  The amount of the trait being measured that the individual in fact possesses.

*T Score*  See *Standardized Score.*

*Unidimensional Scaling*  A scale developed under the assumption that there is one dimension underlying the phenomenon being investigated and that differences in responses are a result of this single dimension. In unidimensional scaling the stimuli differ on one and only one variable and the investigator controls other factors that could influence judgment.

*Unsystematic Variation*  The fluctuation of scores for individuals, from time 1 to time 2, in a completely haphazard or random manner.

*Validity*  The extent to which a test or a set of operations measure what it is supposed to measure; the appropriateness of inferences from test scores or other forms of assessment.

*Variable*  A property in which individuals differ either in quantity or quality among themselves.

*Variance*  A measure of the degree to which scores are distributed about the mean. The variance is an index that specifies the amount of spread in the distribution of scores. The variance is equal to the mean of the squared deviation scores or the square of the standard deviation. See Equation 3-6.

*z Score*  See *Standard Score.*

# *Index of Names*

# Index of Topics